THE MODERN AGE

IDEAS IN WESTERN CIVILIZATION

SELECTED READINGS

ARTHUR HABERMAN

Associate Professor of
History and Humanities
York University

gage EDUCATIONAL PUBLISHING COMPANY
A DIVISION OF CANADA PUBLISHING CORPORATION
TORONTO ONTARIO CANADA

Arthur Haberman is Associate Professor of History and Humanities in the Faculty of Arts, and Master of Founders College at York University. He completed his B.A. at the City College of New York and received his M.A. and Ph.D. from New York University. Professor Haberman has served as Associate Dean of the Faculty of Education at York and has extensive experience working with teachers and students in secondary schools. He has also worked on History and Social Studies curricula with the Ministry of Education of the Province of Ontario and with the National Faculty of Humanities, Arts and Science in the United States. Professor Haberman is the author of *The Making of the Modern Age: Europe and the West Since the Enlightenment*.

Cover and book design by Susan Hedley

Cover photograph from "L'Avenue de L'Opera" by C. Pissaro, collection of Musée Saint-Denis, Reims

Study material by Jim Christopher, Leaside High School, East York Board of Education

Written, Printed, and Bound in Canada

 2 3 4 5   JD   91 90 89

ISBN 0–7715–8345–1

Canadian Cataloguing in Publication Data

Main entry under title:

The Modern age : ideas in Western civilization

Companion volume to: Haberman, Arthur, 1938– The making of the modern age.
ISBN 0-7715-8344-3

1. Civilization, Modern – 18th century.
2. Civilization, Modern – 19th century.
3. Civilization, Modern – 20th century.
I. Haberman, Arthur, 1938–   .

D355.M63 1987   909.8   C87-093924-6

To Karen

Burke. Ed. Thomas H.D. Mahoney. Copyright © 1955, 1985 Macmillan Publishing Company.

McGraw-Hill Book Company for excerpts from *Understanding Media* by Marshall McLuhan. Copyright © 1964 by Marshall McLuhan.

The Museum of Modern Art for The Statement by Willem de Kooning, "What Abstract Arts Means to Me," from the *Bulletin*, New York, Vol. XVIII, No. 3 (Spring 1951). All rights reserved by The Museum of Modern Art.

NAL Penguin Inc. for excerpts from "A Doll House" from *Henrik Ibsen: Four Major Plays*. Tr. Rolfe Fjelde. Copyright © 1965 by Rolfe Fjelde; from "The Cherry Orchard" by Anton Chekhov, from *Chekhov: The Major Plays*. Tr. Ann Dunnigan. Copyright © 1964 Ann Dunnigan.

Navajivan Trust, India, for excerpts from *Readings from Gandhi* by Mohandas Gandhi, Publ. Lokmilap Trust, India.

W.W. Norton & Company, Inc. for "In 1940" from *Poems*, Anna Akhmatova. Selected and Tr. Lyn Coffin. Copyright © 1983 Lyn Coffin; for excerpts from: *The Lenin Anthology*. Selected, Ed., and Intro. Robert C. Tucker. Copyright © 1975 W.W. Norton & Company, Inc.; *Civilization and Its Discontents* by Sigmund Freud. Ed. James Strachey. Copyright © 1961 James Strachey; *On Liberty*, by John Stuart Mill. A Norton Critical Edition. Ed. David Spitz. Copyright © 1975 W.W. Norton & Company, Inc.; *An Essay on the Principle of Population* (1798) by Thomas Robert Malthus. Ed. Philip Appleman. Copyright © 1976 W.W. Norton & Company, Inc.; *A Vindication of the Rights of Woman* by Mary Wollstonecraft, A Norton Critical Edition. Ed. Carol H. Poston. Copyright © 1975 W.W. Norton & Company Inc.; *The Marx-Engels Reader*, 2nd ed., Robert C. Tucker, Ed. Copyright © 1978, 1972 W.W. Norton & Company, Inc.; *Gulliver's Travels* by Jonathan Swift, A Norton Critical Edition. Ed. Robert A. Greenberg. Copyright © 1970, 1961 W.W. Norton & Company Inc.; *The Feminine Mystique* by Betty Friedan. Copyright © 1983, 1974, 1973, 1963 Betty Friedan; *The Revolt of the Masses* by José Ortega y Gasset. Copyright 1932 W.W. Norton & Company, Inc. (Allen & Unwin Ltd.—UK). Copyright renewed 1960 by Teresa Carey; *A General Introduction to Psycho-Analysis* by Sigmund Freud. Tr. Joan Riviere. Copyright renewed 1973 Joan Riviere. Copyright 1920 Edward L. Bernays (Chatto & Windus/Hogarth Press—UK).

Open Court Publishing Company, LaSalle, Illinois, for excerpts from *Albert Einstein: Philosopher Scientist*. Ed. Paul Arthur Schilpp (Tudor Publ. 1951).

Orbis Books for excerpts from *The Power of the Poor in History* by Gustavo Gutierrez. Copyright © 1983 Orbis Books

Oxford University Press (UK), for excerpts from: *Documents of the Christian Church*. Ed. Henry Bettenson. Copyright © 1963 Oxford University Press; *War and Peace* by Leo Tolstoy. Tr. Louise and Aylmer Maude (1933).

Penguin Books Ltd, (UK), for excerpts from: *Germinal* by Émile Zola. Tr. Leonard Tancock (Penguin Classics, 1954). Copyright © Leonard Tancock, 1954; *Baudelaire: Selected Poems*. Tr. and Intro. Joanna Richardson. Copyright © 1975 Joanne Richardson; *Notes From Underground/The Double* by Fyodor Dostoyevsky. Tr. Jessie Coulson (Penguin Classics. 1972). Copyright © 1972 Jessie Coulson; *Old Goriot* by Honoré de Balzac. Tr. Marian Ayton Crawford (Penguin Classics, 1951). Copyright © 1951 Marian Ayton Crawford; *Fathers and Sons* by Ivan Turgenev. Tr. Rosemary Edmonds (Penguin Classics, 1965). Copyright © 1965 Rosemary Edmonds; *Discourse On Method and the Meditations* by René Descartes. Tr. F.E. Sutcliffe (Penguin Classics, 1968). Copyright © 1968 F.E. Sutcliffe.

Phaidon Press Ltd. for excerpts from: *What is the Third Estate?* by Emmanuel-Joseph Sieyès. Copyright © 1963 Phaidon Press Ltd.; *Memoirs of the Life of John Constable* by Charles Robert Leslie. Copyright © 1980 Phaidon Press; *Winckelmann: Writings On Art* by Johann Joachim Winckelmann. Ed. David Irwin. Copyright © 1972 Phaidon Press; "What is Romanticism?" from *Art In Paris 1845-1862* by Jonathan Mayne. Copyright © 1965 Phaidon Press.

Philosophical Library Inc. for excerpts from *Existentialism and Human Emotions* by Jean-Paul Sartre. Tr. Philip Mairet. Copyright © 1957, renewed © 1985 by Philosophical Library—US (Methuen—UK).

Pierre Cailler Editions for excerpts from *Realism and Tradition In Art 1848-1900* by Gustave Courbet. Ed. Linda Nochlin. Copyright © 1950 Editions Pierre Cailler.

Prentice-Hall, Inc. for excerpts from *Frederick the Great* (Great Lives Observed) Ed. Louis L. Snyder. Copyright © 1971 Prentice-Hall, Inc. (USA).

Random House, Inc. Alfred A. Knopf, Inc. for "Spain 1937" from *The English Auden: Poems, Essays & Dramatic Writings, 1927-1939*, by W.H. Auden. Ed. Edward Mendelson. Copyright 1940, renewed © 1968 W.H. Auden (Faber and Faber Limited—UK); "The Myth

of Sisyphus" from *The Myth of Sisyphus*, by Albert Camus. Tr. Justin O'Brien. Copyright © 1955 Alfred A. Knopf, Inc.; for excerpts from: *Madame Bovary*, by Gustave Flaubert. Tr. Francis Steegmuller. Copyright © 1957 Francis Steegmuller; "Mario and the Magician" from *Death in Venice and Seven Other Stories* by Thomas Mann. Tr. H.T. Lowe-Porter. Copyright 1931, renewed © 1959 Alfred A. Knopf, Inc.; *Democracy In America, Volumes I and II*, by Alexis de Tocqueville. Tr. Henry Reeve, revised by Francis Bowen and Ed. Phillips Bradley. Copyright 1945 and renewed © 1973 Alfred A. Knopf, Inc.; *Resistance, Rebellion, and Death* by Albert Camus. Tr. and intro. by Justin O'Brien. Copyright © 1960 Alfred A. Knopf, Inc.; *The Second Sex* by Simone de Beauvoir. Tr. and Ed. H.M. Parshley. Copyright 1952 Alfred A. Knopf, Inc.; "Jacques-Louis David—To the Revolutionary Convention," from *Artists On Art: From the XIV to the XX Century*. Ed. Robert Goldwater and Marco Treves. Copyright Pantheon Books—USA (John Murray—UK); "The Life of Galileo" from *Collected Plays-Volume 5* by Bertolt Brecht. Trs. Wolfgang Sauerlander and Ralph Manheim. Ed. Ralph Manheim and John Willett. Copyright © 1972 Stefan S. Brecht. Pantheon Books—USA (Methuen London—UK); *Candide* by François Marie Arouet. Tr. Richard Aldington. Random House, Inc. (1956), *The Wealth of Nations: Inquiry Into the Nature and Causes of the Wealth of Nations* by Adam Smith. Random House, Inc. (1937, 1965); *Gulliver's Travels and Other Writings* by Jonathan Swift. Random House, Inc. (1958).

Regnery Gateway, Inc. for excerpts from: *The God That Failed* by Arthur Koestler et al. Copyright © 1983 Regnery Books; *Beyond Good and Evil* by Friedrich Nietzsche. Copyright © 1955 Henry Regnery Company; *The Origin and Development of Psychoanalysis* by Sigmund Freud. Copyright © 1965 Henry Regnery Company.

SMC Press Ltd. Publishers for excerpts from *Letters From Prison* by Dietrich Bonhoeffer, Enlarged Edition. Copyright © 1971 SCM Press—UK (Macmillan Publishing Company—USA).

Charles Scribner's Sons for excerpts from *I and Thou* by Martin Buber. Tr. Walter Kaufmann. Copyright © 1970 Charles Scribner's Sons (T & T Clark—UK).

Simon & Schuster, Inc. for excerpts from: *The Social Contract and Discourse on the Origin of Inequality* by Jean-Jacques Rousseau. Ed. Lester G. Crocker. Copyright © 1967 Washington Square Press Inc. (a division of Simon & Schuster, Inc.); *The Basic Writings of Bertrand Russell*. Ed. Robert. E. Egner and Lester E. Denonn. Copyright © 1961 Simon and Schuster (Allan & Unwin—UK).

Gunther Stuhlmann, for excerpts from *Jackson Pollock: Energy Made Visible*, by B.H. Friedman. Copyright © 1972 B.H. Friedman. All rights reserved. Reprinted by permission of the Author's Representative, Gunther Stuhlmann.

Union of American Hebrew Congregations, for excerpts from *Out of the Whirlwind: A Reader of Holocaust Literature*. Ed. Albert H. Friedlander. Copyright © 1968 Union of American Hebrew Congregations.

University of California Press, for excerpts from *Sir Isaac Newton's Mathematical Principles of Natural Philosophy and His System of the World, Book III: The System of the World*. Tr. Andrew Motte, rev. by Floriann Cajori. Copyright © 1934, 1962 The Regents of the University of California.

The University of Chicago Press, for excerpts from: *A Soviet Heretic* by Yevgeny Zamyatin. Tr. Mirra Ginsburg. Copyright © 1970 University of Chicago Press; *On Social Evolution: Selected Writings*, "Progress: Its Law and Cause" by Herbert Spencer. Ed. J.D.Y. Peel. Copyright © 1972 The University of Chicago Press.

The University of Michigan Press for excerpts from *Manifestos of Surrealism* by André Breton. Copyright © 1969 The University of Michigan.

A.P. Watt Ltd. for "The Second Coming" from *The Collected Poems of W.B. Yeats*. By permission of A.P. Watt Ltd. on behalf of Michael B. Yeats and Macmillan London Ltd.—UK (Macmillan Publishing Company—USA).

Weidenfeld (Publishers) Limited (UK) for excerpts from *Sketch for a Historical Picture of the Progress of the Human Mind* by Antoine-Nicolas de Condorcet. Tr. Jean Barraclough. Copyright © 1955 George Weidenfeld & Nicolson Ltd.

Yale University Press for excerpts from: *From the Classicists to the Impressionists: Art and Architecture in the Nineteenth Century*, "The Painting of the Sabines" by Jacques-Louis David. Ed. Elizabeth Gilmore Holt. Copyright © 1966, 1986 by Elizabeth Gilmore Holt; *The Courage To Be* by Paul Tillich. Copyright © 1952 Yale University Press.

Every reasonable effort has been made to trace ownership of copyright material. Information will be welcomed which will enable the publisher to rectify any reference or credit in future printings.

CONTENTS

3 ROMANTICISM, NATIONALISM & INDUSTRIALISM, 1815-1848

7 CONTEMPORARY ISSUES & IDEAS: THE WEST SINCE 1945

PREFACE

Interest in modern Western civilization has greatly increased in the last several decades; students all over North America now take courses in intellectual history when studying their society and culture. This book attempts to collect the most important and representative sources in Western civilization, from the Enlightenment to the contemporary period. It proceeds chronologically in seven sections, though, within these sections, sources are grouped thematically rather than by dates of publication.

In any work of this sort there are essential individuals and readings that must be included – those judged to have had so great an impact on the West that they have forever changed the dialogue about the nature of humanity. I have included all those readings I believe to be part of this recognized canon – for example, Descartes, Locke, Rousseau, Marx, Darwin, and Freud. However, I have attempted to go beyond the more obvious sources, to also incorporate many other works that have shaped our thinking about the important issues: the nature of humanity; the relationship between the individual and society; the relationship between humanity and nature; the quest for personal, social, and communal values; the role of the creative artist in society; attitudes towards good and evil, and towards beauty and truth. Crucial subjects also receiving attention include the status and image of women in Western culture and society, human rights, and the role of science and art in relation to society.

This collection attempts to give full consideration to the twentieth century, now nearly over. It focusses on a number of themes that have been important in our time. Hence, the last section, on the contemporary world, is organized by topics, and the readings reflect important thinking on such matters as existentialism, human rights, nuclear warfare, feminism, colonialism and decolonization, the Holocaust, and contemporary theology. The whole work, however, is implicitly organized around those themes and issues which seem to me crucial to the intellectual history of the West in the modern age.

The major limitation facing the editor of such a volume is space. Every reader will realize that this book of readings could be much longer without losing quality. Still, it had to be put in a single volume, and that forced certain choices. I have endeavoured to present selections that represent the original works fairly. Often, the selections are those parts of the original that had the most impact on other thinkers and on the general public. Length was dictated by fairness to an idea and to the reader – to give the reader as full a sense as possible of the style and dimension of the original source. Naturally, reading an excerpt is not a substitute for reading an entire work by any of the authors included.

Those using the book as part of a course should realize that they, too, may need to choose from among the many selections. There are many ways to use this book to learn about modern Western civilization, while still maintaining the integrity of the historical development and touching all the essential themes. I have included enough material to keep any individual engaged far beyond the limits of a single educational experience. I hope those who read and use the book will enjoy it. There is, I know, much that is pleasurable and provocative in it.

I should like to acknowledge those individuals who contributed to the making of this book. Professor Sydney Eisen of York University was, as always, wise with his counsel and generous with his time. He brought to bear his deep experience in teaching Western civilization to questions about the style and organization of the work, as well as to individual selections. Professor William Whitla of York University also discussed a number of the selections with me and gave advice about the printing style. From Gage Educational Publishing Company, Graham Draper and Anne Marie Moro provided organization and sound editorial advice, and Donna Boyce, Susan Green, Todd Mercer, and Carol Waldock contributed to the style and clarity of the work. My wife and children cheerfully put up with my many questions and preoccupations, and their excellent suggestions and cautions helped to shape the content and tone of the work.

1

THE ENLIGHTENMENT: THE MODERN AGE TO 1789

During the Enlightenment many thinkers in the West were optimistic about the ability of human beings to understand the world and to change it for good. Scientists believed they had a far greater understanding of the heavens and the earth than ever before, and philosophers developed major new concepts about the relationship between human beings and society. Tolerance, optimism, and progress, with a critical attitude of reform, were the keynotes of the day.

The methods and substance of modern science were developed at that time. Bacon stressed induction and empiricism, and Descartes emphasized deduction and mathematical logic. Both helped to build a system of knowledge which was verifiable and in which modern scientists had confidence. Sometimes, science came into conflict with the old authority, as in the case of Galileo. Other important mathematicians and scientists, including Pascal and Newton, reflected on the relationship of the new science to prevailing religious beliefs and concepts of the deity.

Social and political philosophers made important statements during the Enlightenment. Hobbes, Locke, and Rousseau thought deeply about the nature of humanity, community, and the function and purpose of the state. In their works they discussed sovereignty, contract, and rights—all concepts which helped humanity in the modern period to mediate between individual will and collective responsibility. In economics, Adam Smith used ideas of modern science to discuss wealth, its creation, and individual rights. Social reformers such as Swift and Voltaire attempted to change institutions for the better in light of the new values of the times. The enlightened despot Frederick II sought to redefine the modern state.

In the visual arts, the dominant idea was classicism, the notion that art was to be modelled after that of classical Greece and Rome, ought to depict classical subjects, and should be orderly and symmetrical. Artists attempted to realize and transcend the ancients, in an effort to make the modern period one of enlightenment and progress.

Beginning with developments in modern science, the Enlightenment came to mean a concern with the present, a critical posture toward the state and other institutions, a belief in rights and reform, and a willingness to experiment with new ideas. Many believed that by the last half of the eighteenth century the moderns had indeed progressed beyond the ancients.

FRANCIS BACON

Francis Bacon (1561-1626) was among the most important contributors to the development of the scientific method and rational thought. A politician and lawyer as well as a philosopher, Bacon took all knowledge as his province. In *Novum Organum* (1620), he attempted to develop a new method of philosophical and scientific inquiry that was certain and secure. Bacon's empiricism, an insistence on basing all thought on data derived from experience, became one of the marks of modern intellectual life.

 Bacon's *Novum Organum*, never completed, consisted of a series of aphorisms, brief statements about science and knowledge.

> Man, being the servant and interpreter of Nature, can do and understand so much and so much only as he has observed in fact or in thought of the course of nature. Beyond this he neither knows anything nor can do anything.

> Neither the naked hand nor the understanding left to itself can effect much. It is by instruments and helps that the work is done, which are as much wanted for the understanding as for the hand. And as the instruments of the hand either give motion or guide it, so the instruments of the mind supply either suggestions for the understanding or cautions.

> Human knowledge and human power meet in one; for where the cause is not known the effect cannot be produced. Nature to be commanded must be obeyed; and that which in contemplation is as the cause is in operation as the rule. . . .

> The cause and root of nearly all evils in the sciences is this—that while we falsely admire and extol the powers of the human mind we neglect to seek for its true helps.

> The subtlety of nature is greater many times over than the subtlety of the senses and understanding; so that all those specious meditations, speculations, and glosses in which men indulge are quite from the purpose, only there is no one by to observe it.

> As the sciences which we now have do not help us in finding out new works, so neither does the logic which we now have help us in finding out new sciences.

> The logic now in use serves rather to fix and give stability to the errors which have their foundation in commonly received notions than to help the search after truth. So it does more harm than good.

> The syllogism is not applied to the first principles of sciences, and is applied in vain to intermediate axioms, being no match for the subtlety of nature. It commands assent therefore to the proposition, but does not take hold of the thing.

> The syllogism consists of propositions, propositions consist of words, words are symbols of notions. Therefore if the notions themselves (which is the root of the matter) are confused and overhastily abstracted from the facts, there

Source: Francis Bacon, *The New Organon and Related Writings*, edited by Fulton Anderson (Indianapolis: Bobbs-Merrill Company, Inc., 1960), pp. 39, 40-41, 42-43, 47-49, 87-91.

can be no firmness in the superstructure. Our only hope therefore lies in a true induction. . . .

The discoveries which have hitherto been made in the sciences are such as lie close to vulgar notions, scarcely beneath the surface. In order to penetrate into the inner and further recesses of nature, it is necessary that both notions and axioms be derived from things by a more sure and guarded way, and that a method of intellectual operation be introduced altogether better and more certain.

There are and can be only two ways of searching into and discovering truth. The one flies from the senses and particulars to the most general axioms, and from these principles, the truth of which it takes for settled and immovable, proceeds to judgment and to the discovery of middle axioms. And this way is now in fashion. The other derives axioms from the senses and particulars, rising by a gradual and unbroken ascent, so that it arrives at the most general axioms last of all. This is the true way, but as yet untried.

The understanding left to itself takes the same course (namely, the former) which it takes in accordance with logical order. For the mind longs to spring up to positions of higher generality, that it may find rest there, and so after a little while wearies of experiment. But this evil is increased by logic, because of the order and solemnity of its disputations.

The understanding left to itself, in a sober, patient, and grave mind, especially if it be not hindered by received doctrines, tries a little that other way, which is the right one, but with little progress, since the understanding, unless directed and assisted, is a thing unequal, and quite unfit to contend with the obscurity of things.

Both ways set out from the senses and particulars, and rest in the highest generalities; but the difference between them is infinite. For the one just glances at experiment and particulars in passing, the other dwells duly and orderly among them. . . .

 Bacon challenged old ''Idols,'' which he believed inhibited the development of knowledge.

The idols and false notions which are now in possession of the human understanding, and have taken deep root therein, not only so beset men's minds that truth can hardly find entrance, but even after entrance is obtained, they will again in the very instauration of the sciences meet and trouble us, unless men being forewarned of the danger fortify themselves as far as may be against their assaults.

There are four classes of Idols which beset men's minds. To these for distinction's sake I have assigned names, calling the first class *Idols of the Tribe;* the second, *Idols of the Cave;* the third, *Idols of the Market Place;* the fourth, *Idols of the Theater.*

The formation of ideas and axioms by true induction is no doubt the proper remedy to be applied for the keeping off and clearing away of idols. To point them out, however, is of great use; for the doctrine of Idols is to the interpretation of nature what the doctrine of the refutation of sophisms is to common logic.

The Idols of the Tribe have their foundation in human nature itself, and in the tribe or race of men. For it is a false assertion that the sense of man is the measure of things. On the contrary, all perceptions as well of the sense as of the mind are according to the measure of the individual and not according to the measure of the universe. And the human understanding is like a false mirror, which, receiving rays irregularly, distorts and discolors the nature of things by mingling its own nature with it.

The Idols of the Cave are the idols of the individual man. For everyone (besides the errors common to human nature in general) has a cave or den of his own, which refracts and discolors the light of nature, owing either to his own proper and peculiar nature; or to his education and conversation with others; or to the reading of books, and the authority of those whom he esteems and admires; or to the differences of impressions, accordingly as they take place in a mind preoccupied and predisposed or in a mind indifferent and settled; or the like. So that the spirit of man (according as it is meted out to different individuals) is in fact a thing variable and full of perturbation, and governed as it were by chance. Whence it was well observed by Heraclitus that men look for sciences in their own lesser worlds, and not in the greater or common world.

There are also Idols formed by the intercourse and association of men with each other, which I call Idols of the Market Place, on account of the commerce and consort of men there. For it is by discourse that men associate, and words are imposed according to the apprehension of the vulgar. And therefore the ill and unfit choice of words wonderfully obstructs the understanding. Nor do the definitions or explanations wherewith in some things learned men are wont to guard and defend themselves, by any means set the matter right. But words plainly force and overrule the understanding, and throw all into confusion, and lead men away into numberless empty controversies and idle fancies.

Lastly, there are Idols which have immigrated into men's minds from the various dogmas of philosophies, and also from wrong laws of demonstration. These I call Idols of the Theater, because in my judgment all the received systems are but so many stage plays, representing worlds of their own creation after an unreal and scenic fashion. Nor is it only of the systems now in vogue, or only of the ancient sects and philosophies, that I speak; for many more plays of the same kind may yet be composed and in like artificial manner set forth; seeing that errors the most widely different have nevertheless causes for the most part alike. Neither again do I mean this only of entire systems, but also of many principles and axioms in science, which by tradition, credulity, and negligence have come to be received. . . .

Included among the obstacles to scientific inquiry were superstition, religion, and despair.

Neither is it to be forgotten that in every age natural philosophy has had a troublesome and hard to deal with adversary—namely, superstition, and the blind and immoderate zeal of religion. For we see among the Greeks that those who first proposed to men's then uninitiated ears the natural causes for thunder and for stores were thereupon found guilty of impiety. Nor was much more forbearance shown by some of the ancient fathers of the Christian church to those who on most convincing grounds (such as no one in his senses would now think of contradicting) maintained that the earth was round, and of consequence asserted the existence of the antipodes.

Moreover, as things now are, to discourse of nature is made harder and more perilous by the summaries and systems of the schoolmen who, having reduced theology into regular order as well as they were able, and fashioned it into the shape of an art, ended in incorporating the contentious and thorny philosophy of Aristotle, more than was fit, with the body of religion.

To the same result, though in a different way, tend the speculations of those who have taken upon them to deduce the truth of the Christian religion from the principles of philosophers, and to confirm it by their authority, pompously solemnizing this union of the sense and faith as a lawful marriage, and entertaining men's minds with a pleasing variety of matter, but all the while disparaging things divine by mingling them with things human. Now in such mixtures of theology with philosophy only the received doctrines of philosophy are included; while new ones, albeit changes for the better, are all but expelled and exterminated.

Lastly, you will find that by the simpleness of certain divines, access to any philosophy, however pure, is well-nigh closed. Some are weakly afraid lest a deeper search into nature should transgress the permitted limits of sober-mindedness, wrongfully wresting and transferring what is said in Holy Writ against those who pry into sacred mysteries, to the hidden things of nature, which are barred by no prohibition. Others with more subtlety surmise and reflect that if second causes are unknown everything can more readily be referred to the divine hand and rod, a point in which they think religion greatly concerned—which is in fact nothing else but to seek to gratify God with a lie. Others fear from past example that movements and changes in philosophy will end in assaults on religion. And others again appear apprehensive that in the investigation of nature something may be found to subvert or at least shake the authority of religion, especially with the unlearned. But these two last fears seem to me to savor utterly of carnal wisdom; as if men in the recesses and secret thought of their hearts doubted and distrusted the strength of religion and the empire of faith over the sense, and therefore feared that the investigation of truth in nature might be dangerous to them. But if the matter be truly considered, natural philosophy is, after the word of God, at once the surest medicine against superstition and the most approved nourishment for faith, and therefore she is rightly given to religion as her most faithful handmaid, since the one displays the will of God, the other his power. For he did not err who said, ''Ye err in that ye know not the Scriptures and the power of God," thus coupling and blending in an indissoluble bond information concerning his will and meditation concerning his power. Meanwhile it is not surprising if the growth of natural philosophy is checked when religion, the thing which has most power over men's minds, has by the simpleness and incautious zeal of certain persons been drawn to take part against her.

Again, in the customs and institutions of schools, academies, colleges, and similar bodies destined for the abode of learned men and the cultivation of learning, everything is found adverse to the progress of science. For the lectures and exercises there are so ordered that to think or speculate on anything out of the common way can hardly occur to any man. And if one or two have the boldness to use any liberty of judgment, they must undertake the task all by themselves; they can have no advantage from the company of others. And if they can endure this also, they will find their industry and largeness of mind no slight hindrance to their fortune. For the studies of men in these places are confined and as it were imprisoned in the writings of certain authors, from whom if any man dissent he is straightway arraigned as a turbulent person and an innovator. But surely there is a great distinction between matters of state and the arts; for the danger from new motion and from new light is not the same. In matters of state a change even for the better is distrusted, because it unsettles what is established; these things resting on authority, consent, fame and opinion, not on demonstration. But arts and sciences should be like mines, where the noise of new works and further advances is heard on every side. But though the matter be so according to right reason, it is not so acted on in practice; and the points above mentioned in the administration and government of learning put a severe restraint upon the advancement of the sciences.

Nay, even if that jealousy were to cease, still it is enough to check the growth of science that efforts and labors in this field go unrewarded. For it does not rest with the same persons to cultivate sciences and to reward them. The growth of them comes from great wits; the prizes and rewards of them are in the hands of the people, or of great persons, who are but in very few cases even moderately learned. Moreover, this kind of progress is not only unrewarded with prizes and substantial benefits; it has not even the advantage of popular applause. For it is a greater matter than the generality of men can take in, and is apt to be overwhelmed and extinguished by the gales of popular opinions. And it is nothing strange if a thing not held in honor does not prosper.

But by far the greatest obstacle to the progress of science and to the undertaking of new tasks and provinces therein is found in this—that men despair and think things impossible. For wise and serious men are wont in these matters to be altogether distrustful, considering with themselves the obscurity of nature, the shortness of life, the deceitfulness of the senses, the weakness of the judgment, the difficulty of experiment, and the like; and so supposing that in the revolution of time and of the ages of the world the sciences have their ebbs and flows; that at one season they grow and flourish, at another wither and decay, yet in such sort that when they have reached a certain point and condition they can advance no further. If therefore anyone believes or promises more, they think this comes of an ungoverned and unripened mind, and that such attempts have prosperous beginnings, become difficult as they go on, and end in confusion. Now since there are thoughts which naturally present themselves to men grave and of great judgment, we must take good heed that we be not led away by our love for a most fair and excellent object to relax or diminish the severity of our judgment. We must observe diligently what encouragement dawns upon us and from what quarter, and, putting aside the lighter breezes of hope, we must thoroughly sift and examine those which promise greater steadiness and constancy. Nay, and we must take state prudence too into our counsels, whose rule is to distrust, and to take the less favorable view of human affairs. I am now therefore to speak touching hope, especially as I am not a dealer in promises, and wish neither to force nor to ensnare men's judgments, but to lead them by the hand with their good will. And though the strongest means of inspiring hope will be to bring men to particulars, especially to particulars digested and arranged in my Tables of Discovery (the subject partly of the second, but much more of the fourth part of my Instauration), since this is not merely the promise of the thing but the thing itself; nevertheless, that everything may be done with gentleness, I will proceed with my plan of preparing men's minds, of which preparation to give hope is no unimportant part. For without it the rest tends rather to make men sad (by giving them a worse and meaner opinion of things as they are than they now have, and making them more fully to feel and know the unhappiness of their own condition) than to induce any alacrity or to whet their industry in making trial. And therefore it is fit that I publish and set forth those conjectures of mine which make hope in this matter reasonable, just as Columbus did, before that wonderful voyage of his across the Atlantic, when he gave the reasons for his conviction that new lands and continents might be discovered besides those which were known before; which reasons, though rejected at first, were afterwards made good by experience, and were the causes and beginnings of great events. . . .

1. In your own words, explain Bacon's belief that true discovery depends on a combination of both thought and experimentation.
2. Outline the criticisms that Bacon levelled at the "logic now in use."
3. Compare the two methods of "searching into and discovering truth." In what ways were Bacon's conclusions an outgrowth of his earlier aphorisms?
4. Bacon believed that through "induction" individuals may escape the "idols" which "beset" their minds. Identify and explain each of Bacon's four "idols." In what way might inductive reasoning help a person to escape their influence?
5. Account for Bacon's belief that despair was a major obstacle to discovery, and outline his plan for conquering that emotion.

▪ ▪ ▪

RENÉ DESCARTES

The *Discourse on Method* (1637) of René Descartes (1596-1650) has had enormous influence on the development of rationalism, deduction, and modern science. Descartes was a mathematician, and he stressed the importance of using the mathematical method as the means of obtaining knowledge that was precise and verifiable. Emphasizing the centrality of the mind in defining human nature, Descartes' work lent authority to those who were investigating nature as an orderly system which could be understood by human beings.

The *Discourse on Method* was a kind of intellectual autobiography, in which Descartes told the reader how he arrived at his methodology. He discussed his early education and why he determined to seek a new method of obtaining knowledge.

> ... When I was younger, I had studied a little logic in philosophy, and geometrical analysis and algebra in mathematics, three arts or sciences which would appear apt to contribute something towards my plan. But on examining them, I saw that, regarding logic, its syllogisms and most of its other precepts serve more to explain to others what one already knows, or even, like the art of Lully, to speak without judgement of those things one does not know, than to learn anything new. And although logic indeed contains many very true and sound precepts, there are, at the same time, so many others mixed up with them, which are either harmful or superfluous, that it is almost as difficult to separate them as to extract a Diana or a Minerva from a block of unprepared marble. Then, as for the geometrical analysis of the ancients and the algebra of the moderns, besides the fact that they extend only to very abstract matters which seem to be of no practical use, the former is always so tied to the inspection of figures that it cannot exercise the understanding without greatly tiring the imagination, while, in the latter, one is so subjected to certain rules and numbers that it has become a confused and obscure art which oppresses the mind instead of being a science which cultivates it. This was why I thought I must seek some other method which, while continuing the advantages of these three, was free from their defects. And as a multiplicity of laws often furnishes excuses for vice, so that a State is much better ordered when, having only very few laws, they are very strictly observed, so, instead of this great number of precepts of which logic is composed, I believed I would have sufficient in the four following rules, so long as I took a firm and constant resolve never once to fail to observe them.
>
> The first was never to accept anything as true that I did not know to be evidently so: that is to say, carefully to avoid precipitancy and prejudice, and to include in my judgements nothing more than what presented itself so clearly and so distinctly to my mind that I might have no occasion to place it in doubt.

Source: René Descartes, *Discourse on Method and the Meditations*, Translated by F.E. Sutcliffe (Harmondsworth: Penguin Books, 1968), pp. 40-43, 53-57.

The second, to divide each of the difficulties that I was examining into as many parts as might be possible and necessary in order best to solve it.

The third, to conduct my thoughts in an orderly way, beginning with the simplest objects and the easiest to know, in order to climb gradually, as by degrees, as far as the knowledge of the most complex, and even supposing some order among those objects which do not precede each other naturally.

And the last, everywhere to make such complete enumerations and such general reviews that I would be sure to have omitted nothing.

These long chains of reasoning, quite simple and easy, which geometers are accustomed to using to teach their most difficult demonstrations, had given me cause to imagine that everything which can be encompassed by man's knowledge is linked in the same way, and that, provided only that one abstains from accepting any for true which is not true, and that one always keeps the right order for one thing to be deduced from that which precedes it, there can be nothing so distant that one does not reach it eventually, or so hidden that one cannot discover it. And I was in no great difficulty in seeking which to begin with because I knew already that it was with the simplest and easiest to know; and considering that, among all those who have already sought truth in the sciences, only the mathematicians have been able to arrive at any proofs, that is to say, certain and evident reasons, I had no doubt that it was by the same things which they had examined that I should begin, although I did not expect any other usefulness from this than to ac-custom my mind to nourish itself on truths and not to be content with false reasons. . . .

And, indeed, I dare say that the exact observation of these few precepts that I had chosen gave me such ease in unravelling all the questions covered by these two sciences in the two or three months which I spent on examining them, having begun by the simplest and most general, and each truth that I found being a rule which served afterwards to find others, not only did I resolve several questions which I had earlier judged to be very difficult, but it also seemed to me, towards the end, that I could determine, even in those of the solution of which I was ignorant, by what means and how far it would be possible to resolve them. In this I shall not perhaps appear to you to be too vain, if you consider that, as there is only one truth of each thing, whoever finds it knows as much about the thing as there is to be known, and that, for example, a child who has been taught arithmetic, having added up ac-cording to the rules, can be sure that he has found out, as far as the sum he was examining is concerned, all that the human mind is capable of finding out. For, after all, the method which teaches one to follow the true order and to enumerate exactly all the factors required for the solution of a problem, contains everything which gives certainty to the rules of arithmetic.

But what satisfied me the most about this method was that, through it, I was assured of using my reason in everything, if not perfectly, at least to the best of my ability. Moreover, I felt that, in practising it, my mind was accus-toming itself little by little to conceive its objects more clearly and distinctly, and not having subjected it to any particular matter, I promised myself that I would apply it just as usefully to the difficulties of the other sciences as I had to those of algebra. . . .

The mind-body distinction was an important one for Descartes. In the work he arrived at his famous definition of his own being: "I think, therefore I am."

I do not know if I ought to tell you about the first meditations I pursued there, for they are so abstract and unusual that they will probably not be to the taste of everyone; and yet, so that one may judge if the foundations I have laid are firm enough, I find myself to some extent forced to speak of them. I had long ago noticed that, in matters relating to conduct, one needs sometimes to follow, just as if they are absolutely indubitable, opinions one knows to be very unsure, as has been said above; but as I wanted to concentrate solely on the search for truth, I thought I ought to do just the opposite, and reject as being absolutely false everything in which I could suppose the slightest reason for doubt, in order to see if there did not remain after that anything in my belief which was entirely indubitable. So, because our senses sometimes play us false, I decided to suppose that there was nothing at all which was such as they cause us to imagine it; and because there are men who make mistakes in reasoning, even with the simplest geometrical matters, and make paralogisms, judging that I was as liable to error as anyone else, I rejected as being false all the reasonings I had hitherto accepted as proofs. And finally, considering that all the same thoughts that we had when we are awake can also come to us when we are asleep, without any one of them then being true, I resolved to pretend that nothing which had ever entered my mind was any more true than the illusions of my dreams. But immediately afterwards I became aware that, while I decided thus to think that everything was false, it followed necessarily that I who thought thus must be something; and observing that this truth: *I think, therefore I am*, was so certain and so evident that all the most extravagant suppositions of the sceptics were not capable of shaking it, I judged that I could accept it without scruple as the first principle of the philosophy I was seeking.

Then, examining attentively what I was, and seeing that I could pretend that I had no body and that there was no world or place that I was in, but that I could not, for all that, pretend that I did not exist, and that, on the contrary, from the very fact that I thought of doubting the truth of other things, it followed very evidently and very certainly that I existed; while, on the other hand, if I had only ceased to think, although all the rest of what I had ever imagined had been true, I would have had no reason to believe that I existed; I thereby concluded that I was a substance, of which the whole essence or nature consists in thinking, and which, in order to exist, needs no place and depends on no material thing; so that this 'I', that is to say, the mind, by which I am what I am, is entirely distinct from the body, and even that it is easier to know than the body, and moreover, that even if the body were not, it would not cease to be all that it is.

After this, I considered in general what is needed for a proposition to be true and certain; for, since I had just found one which I knew to be so, I thought that I ought also to know what this certainty consisted of. And having noticed that there is nothing at all in this, *I think, therefore I am*, which assures me that I am speaking the truth, except that I see very clearly that in order to think one must exist, I judged that I could take it to be a general rule that the things we conceive very clearly and very distinctly are all true, but that there is nevertheless some difficulty in being able to recognize for certain which are the things we see distinctly.

 God was conceived by Descartes as a "perfect Being," though he used concepts of nature and mathematics to discuss his idea of a deity.

Following this, reflecting on the fact that I had doubts, and that consequently my being was not completely perfect, for I saw clearly that it was a greater perfection to know than to doubt, I decided to inquire whence I had learned to think of some thing more perfect than myself; and I clearly recognized that this must have been from some nature which was in fact more perfect. As for the notions I had of several other things outside myself, such as the sky, the earth, light, heat and a thousand others, I had not the same concern to know their source, because, seeing nothing in them which seemed to make them superior to myself, I could believe that, if they were true, they were dependencies of my nature, in as much as it had some perfection; and, if they were not, that I held them from nothing, that is to say that they were in me because of an imperfection of my nature. But I could not make the same judgement concerning the idea of a being more perfect than myself; for to hold it from nothing was something manifestly impossible; and because it is no less contradictory that the more perfect should proceed from and depend on the less perfect, than it is that something should emerge out of nothing, I could not hold it from myself; with the result that it remained that it must have been put into me by a being whose nature was truly more perfect than mine and which even had in itself all the perfections of which I could have any idea, that is to say, in a single word, which was God. To which I added that, since I knew some perfections that I did not have, I was not the only being which existed (I shall freely use here, with your permission, the terms of the School) but that there must of necessity be another more perfect, upon whom I depended, and from whom I had acquired all I had; for, if I had been alone and independent of all other, so as to have had from myself this small portion of perfection that I had by participation in the perfection of God, I could have given myself, by the same reason, all the remainder of perfection that I knew myself to lack, and thus to be myself infinite, eternal, immutable, omniscient, all-powerful, and finally to have all the perfections that I could observe to be in God. For, consequentially upon the reasonings by which I had proved the existence of God, in order to understand the nature of God as far as my own nature was capable of doing, I had only to consider, concerning all the things of which I found in myself some idea, whether it was a perfection or not to have them; and I was assured that none of those which indicated some imperfection was in him, but that all the others were. So I saw that doubt, inconstancy, sadness and similar things could not be in him, seeing that I myself would have been very pleased to be free from them. Then, further, I had ideas of many sensible and bodily things; for even supposing that I was dreaming, and that everything I saw or imagined was false, I could not, nevertheless, deny that the ideas were really in my thoughts. But, because I had already recognized in myself very clearly that intelligent nature is distinct from the corporeal, considering that all composition is evidence of dependency, and that dependency is manifestly a defect, I thence judged that it could not be a perfection in God to be composed of these two natures, and that, consequently, he was not so composed; but that, if there were any bodies in the world or any intelligences or other natures which were not wholly perfect, their existence must depend on his power, in such a way that they could not subsist without him for a single instant.

I set out after that to seek other truths; and turning to the object of the geometers, which I conceived as a continuous body or a space extended indefinitely in length, width and height or depth, divisible into various parts, which could have various figures and sizes and be moved or transposed in all sorts of ways—for the geometers take all that to be in the object of their study—I went through some of their simplest proofs. And having observed that the great certainty that everyone attributes to them is based only on the fact that they are clearly conceived according to the rule I spoke of earlier, I noticed also that they had nothing at all in them which might assure me of the existence of their object. Thus, for example, I very well perceived that, supposing a triangle to be given, its three angles must be equal to two right angles, but I saw nothing, for all that, which assured me that any such triangle existed in the world; whereas, reverting to the examination of the idea I had of a perfect Being, I found that existence was comprised in the idea in the same way that the equality of the three angles of a triangle to two right angles is comprised in the idea of a triangle or, as in the idea of a sphere, the fact that all its parts are equidistant from its centre, or even more obviously so; and that consequently it is at least as certain that God, who is this perfect Being, is, or exists, as any geometric demonstration can be. . . .

1. Outline Descartes' reasons for rejecting the existing methods of logic, geometrical analysis, and algebra that he had inherited, as means of investigating problems.
2. List and explain, in your own words, Descartes' four rules of problem solving.
3. Discuss the method used by Descartes to eliminate all certainties, except for his own existence.
4. Explain the logical argument that Descartes used to defend his assertion "I think, therefore I am."
5. Outline Descartes' application of his first principle to a proof of the existence of God.

▪ ▪ ▪

GALILEO GALILEI

Galileo Galilei (1564-1642) was an Italian scientist whose works in astronomy and physics did much to set the basis for modern science. Through his use of the telescope Galileo discovered many things about the heavens, and he also made important contributions to the development of laws for bodies in motion. Galileo came into conflict with authorities of the Roman Catholic Church, as the Church denounced the new scientific system being worked out by him and others as an error.

In 1615 Galileo, who came from Florence in the province of Tuscany, wrote a defence of his work to Christina, the Grand Duchess of the province. The *Letter to the Grand Duchess Christina* opened with the problem of scientific truth and the challenge of theologians.

Some years ago, as Your Serene Highness well knows, I discovered in the heavens many things that had not been seen before our own age. The novelty of these things, as well as some consequences which followed from them in contradiction to the physical notions commonly held among academic philosophers, stirred up against me no small number of professors—as if I had placed these things in the sky with my own hands in order to upset nature and overturn the sciences. They seemed to forget that the increase of known truths stimulates the investigation, establishment, and growth of the arts; not their diminution or destruction.

Showing a greater fondness for their own opinions than for truth, they sought to deny and disprove the new things which, if they had cared to look for themselves, their own senses would have demonstrated to them. To this end they hurled various charges and published numerous writings filled with vain arguments, and they made the grave mistake of sprinkling these with passages taken from places in the Bible which they had failed to understand properly, and which were ill suited to their purposes.

These men would perhaps not have fallen into such error had they but paid attention to a most useful doctrine of St. Augustine's, relative to our making positive statements about things which are obscure and hard to understand by means of reason alone. Speaking of a certain physical conclusion about the heavenly bodies, he wrote: "Now keeping always our respect for moderation in grave piety, we ought not to believe anything inadvisedly on a dubious point, lest in favor to our error we conceive a prejudice against something that truth hereafter may reveal to be not contrary in any way to the sacred books of either the Old or the New Testament."

Well, the passage of time has revealed to everyone the truths that I previously set forth; and, together with the truth of the facts, there has come to light the great difference in attitude between those who simply and dispassionately refused to admit the discoveries to be true, and those who combined with their incredulity some reckless passion of their own. Men who were well grounded in astronomical and physical science were persuaded as soon as they received my first message. There were others who denied them or remained in doubt only because of their novel and unexpected character, and because they had not yet had the opportunity to see for themselves. These men have by degrees come to be satisfied. But some, besides allegiance to their original error, possess I know not what fanciful interest in remaining hostile not so much toward the things in question as toward their discoverer. No longer being able to deny them, these men now take refuge in obstinate silence, but being more than ever exasperated by that which has pacified and

Source: *Discoveries and Opinions of Galileo*, translated by Stillman Drake (Garden City, New York: Doubleday and Company, Inc., 1957), pp. 175-77, 182-84, 193-97.

quieted other men, they divert their thoughts to other fancies and seek new ways to damage me.

I should pay no more attention to them than to those who previously contradicted me—at whom I always laugh, being assured of the eventual outcome—were it not that in their new calumnies and persecutions I perceive that they do not stop at proving themselves more learned than I am (a claim which I scarcely contest), but go so far as to cast against me imputations of crimes which must be, and are, more abhorrent to me than death itself. I cannot remain satisfied merely to know that the injustice of this is recognized by those who are acquainted with these men and with me, as perhaps it is not known to others.

Persisting in their original resolve to destroy me and everything mine by any means they can think of, these men are aware of my views in astronomy and philosophy. They know that as to the arrangement of the parts of the universe, I hold the sun to be situated motionless in the center of the revolution of the celestial orbs while the earth rotates on its axis and revolves about the sun. They know also that I support this position not only by refuting the arguments of Ptolemy and Aristotle, but by producing many counter-arguments; in particular, some which relate to physical effects whose causes can perhaps be assigned in no other way. In addition there are astronomical arguments derived from many things in my new celestial discoveries that plainly confute the Ptolemaic system while admirably agreeing with and con-firming the contrary hypothesis. Possibly because they are disturbed by the known truth of other propositions of mine which differ from those commonly held, and therefore mistrusting their defense so long as they confine them-selves to the field of philosophy, these men have resolved to fabricate a shield for their fallacies out of the mantle of pretended religion and the authority of the Bible. These they apply, with little judgment, to the refutation of arguments that they do not understand and have not even listened to. . . .

 B Galileo defended the new method of scientific inquiry.

. . . I think that in discussions of physical problems we ought to begin not from the authority of scriptural passages, but from sense-experiences and necessary demonstrations; for the holy Bible and the phenomena of nature proceed alike from the divine Word, the former as the dictate of the Holy Ghost and the latter as the observant executrix of God's commands. It is necessary for the Bible, in order to be accommodated to the understanding of every man, to speak many things which appear to differ from the absolute truth so far as the bare meaning of the words is concerned. But Nature, on the other hand, is inexorable and immutable; she never transgresses the laws imposed upon her, or cares a whit whether her abstruse reasons and methods of operation are understandable to men. For that reason it appears that noth-ing physical which sense-experience sets before our eyes, or which necessary demonstrations prove to us, ought to be called in question (much less con-demned) upon the testimony of biblical passages which may have some dif-ferent meaning beneath their words. For the Bible is not chained in every expression to conditions as strict as those which govern all physical effects;

nor is God any less excellently revealed in Nature's actions than in the sacred statements of the Bible. . . .

From this I do not mean to infer that we need not have an extraordinary esteem for the passages of holy Scripture. On the contrary, having arrived at any certainties in physics, we ought to utilize these as the most appropriate aids in the true exposition of the Bible and in the investigation of those meanings which are necessarily contained therein, for these must be concordant with demonstrated truths. I should judge that the authority of the Bible was designed to persuade men of those articles and propositions which, surpassing all human reasoning, could not be made credible by science, or by any other means than through the very mouth of the Holy Spirit.

Yet even in those propositions which are not matters of faith, this authority ought to be preferred over that of all human writings which are supported only by bare assertions or probable arguments, and not set forth in a demonstrative way. This I hold to be necessary and proper to the same extent that divine wisdom surpasses all human judgment and conjecture.

But I do not feel obliged to believe that that same God who has endowed us with senses, reason, and intellect has intended to forgo their use and by some other means to give us knowledge which we can attain by them. He would not require us to deny sense and reason in physical matters which are set before our eyes and minds by direct experience or necessary demonstrations. This must be especially true in those sciences of which but the faintest trace (and that consisting of conclusions) is to be found in the Bible. . . .

C Disturbed by the limitations of contemporary theology, Galileo tried to find room for his new ideas.

Let us grant then that theology is conversant with the loftiest divine contemplation, and occupies the regal throne among sciences by dignity. But acquiring the highest authority in this way, if she does not descend to the lower and humbler speculations of the subordinate sciences and has no regard for them because they are not concerned with blessedness, then her professors should not arrogate to themselves the authority to decide on controversies in professions which they have neither studied nor practiced. Why, this would be as if an absolute despot, being neither a physician nor an architect but knowing himself free to command, should undertake to administer medicines and erect buildings according to his whim—at grave peril of his poor patients' lives, and the speedy collapse of his edifices.

Again, to command that the very professors of astronomy themselves see to the refutation of their own observations and proofs as mere fallacies and sophisms is to enjoin something that lies beyond any possibility of accomplishment. For this would amount to commanding that they must not see what they see and must not understand what they know, and that in searching they must find the opposite of what they actually encounter. Before this could be done they would have to be taught how to make one mental faculty command another, and the inferior powers the superior, so that the imagination and the will might be forced to believe the opposite of what the intellect understands. I am referring at all times to merely physical propositions, and not to supernatural things which are matters of faith.

I entreat those wise and prudent Fathers to consider with great care the difference that exists between doctrines subject to proof and those subject to opinion. . . .

From the above words I conceive that I may deduce this doctrine: That in the books of the sages of this world there are contained some physical truths which are soundly demonstrated, and others that are merely stated; as to the former, it is the office of wise divines to show that they do not contradict the holy Scriptures. And as to the propositions which are stated but not rigorously demonstrated, anything contrary to the Bible involved by them must be held undoubtedly false and should be proved so by every possible means. . . .

If in order to banish the opinion in question from the world it were sufficient to stop the mouth of a single man—as perhaps those men persuade themselves who, measuring the minds of others by their own, think it impossible that this doctrine should be able to continue to find adherents—then that would be very easily done. But things stand otherwise. To carry out such a decision it would be necessary not only to prohibit the book of Copernicus and the writings of other authors who follow the same opinion, but to ban the whole science of astronomy. Furthermore, it would be necessary to forbid men to look at the heavens, in order that they might not see Mars and Venus sometimes quite near the earth and sometimes very distant, the variation being so great that Venus is forty times and Mars sixty times as large at one time as another. And it would be necessary to prevent Venus being seen round at one time and forked at another, with very thin horns; as well as many other sensory observations which can never be reconciled with the Ptolemaic system in any way, but are very strong arguments for the Copernican. And to ban Copernicus now that his doctrine is daily reinforced by many new observations and by the learned applying themselves to the reading of his book, after this opinion has been allowed and tolerated for those many years during which it was less followed and less confirmed, would seem in my judgment to be a contravention of truth, and an attempt to hide and supress her the more as she revealed herself the more clearly and plainly. Not to abolish and censure his whole book, but only to condemn as erroneous this particular proposition, would (if I am not mistaken) be a still greater detriment to the minds of men, since it would afford them occasion to see a proposition proved that it was heresy to believe. And to prohibit the whole science would be but to censure a hundred passages of holy Scripture which teach us that the glory and greatness of Almighty God are marvelously discerned in all his works and divinely read in the open book of heaven. For let no one believe that reading the lofty concepts written in that book leads to nothing further than the mere seeing of the splendor of the sun and the stars and their rising and setting, which is as far as the eyes of brutes and of the vulgar can penetrate. Within its pages are couched mysteries so profound and concepts so sublime that the vigils, labors, and studies of hundreds upon hundreds of the most acute minds have still not pierced them, even after continual investigations for thousands of years. The eyes of an idiot perceive little by beholding the external appearance of a human body, as compared with the wonderful contrivances which a careful and practiced anatomist or philosopher discovers in that same body when he seeks out the use of all those muscles, tendons, nerves, and bones; or when examining the functions of the heart and the other principal organs, he seeks the seat of the vital faculties, notes and observes the admirable structure of the sense organs, and (without ever ceasing in his amazement and delight) contemplates the receptacles of the imagination, the memory, and the understanding. Likewise, that which presents itself to mere sight is as nothing in comparison with the high marvels that the ingenuity of learned men discovers in the heavens by long and accurate observation. And that concludes what I have to say on this matter. . . .

1. Galileo, in the opening passage of his letter to the Grand Duchess Christina, identified the varied responses to his initial discoveries.
    a) Categorize the three types of persons he describes.
    b) Based on Galileo's attitudes and character, as revealed in this excerpt, explain why the astronomer would have had such great difficulty in dealing with the religious establishment.
2. What arguments did Galileo present to show the futility of trying to suppress the truth?

■ ■ ■

SIR ISAAC NEWTON

Sir Isaac Newton (1642-1727) was the most important scientist of the modern period, the person who synthesized the laws of terrestrial and celestial mechanics into a single unified system in *The Mathematical Principles of Natural Philosophy* (1687). Newton was the thinker who was seen to have given final proof of an orderly universe governed by laws that were unchangeable. This mechanical model came to be accepted as the basis of the new scientific method.

 In the preface to his work, Newton discussed the relationship between mathematics and science. Mechanics, the branch of physics concerned with motion and its causes, was a central focus of his concern.

> Since the ancients . . . esteemed the science of mechanics of greatest importance in the investigation of natural things, and the moderns, rejecting substantial forms and occult qualities, have endeavored to subject the phenomena of nature to the laws of mathematics, I have in this treatise cultivated mathematics as far as it relates to philosophy. The ancients considered mechanics in a twofold respect; as rational, which proceeds accurately by demonstration, and practical. To practical mechanics all the manual arts belong, from which mechanics took its name. But as artificers do not work with perfect accuracy, it comes to pass that mechanics is so distinguished from geometry that what is perfectly accurate is called geometrical; what is less so, is called mechanical.

Source: *Sir Isaac Newton's Mathematical Principles of Natural Philosophy and his System of the World,* translated by Andrew Motte, revised by Florian Cajori (Berkeley: University of California Press, 1966), Volume I, pp. xvii-xviii, 6-7, Volume II, pp. 544-46.

However, the errors are not in the art, but in the artificers. He that works with less accuracy is an imperfect mechanic; and if any could work with perfect accuracy, he would be the most perfect mechanic of all, for the description of right lines and circles, upon which geometry is founded, belongs to mechanics. . . . But I consider philosophy rather than arts and write not concerning manual but natural powers, and consider chiefly those things which relate to gravity, levity, elastic force, the resistance of fluids, and the like forces, whether attractive or impulsive; and therefore I offer this work as the mathematical principles of philosophy, for the whole burden of philosophy seems to consider in this—from the phenomena of motions to investigate the forces of nature, and then from these forces to demonstrate the other phenomena; and to this end the general propositions in the first and second Books are directed. In the third Book I give an example of this in the explication of the System of the World; for by the propositions mathematically demonstrated in the former Books, in the third I derive from the celestial phenomena the forces of gravity with which bodies tend to the sun and the several planets. Then from these forces, by other propositions which are also mathematical, I deduce the motions of the planets, the comets, the moon, and the sea. I wish we could derive the rest of the phenomena of Nature by the same kind of reasoning from mechanical principles, for I am induced by many reasons to suspect that they may all depend upon certain forces by which the particles of bodies, by some causes hitherto unknown, are either mutually impelled toward one another, and cohere in regular figures, or are repelled and recede from one another. These forces being unknown, philosophers have hitherto attempted the search of Nature in vain; but I hope the principles here laid down will afford some light either to this or some truer method of philosophy. . . .

 Time and space were major concepts for Newton.

Hitherto I have laid down the definitions of such words as are less known, and explained the sense in which I would have them to be understood in the following discourse. I do not define time, space, place, and motion, as being well known to all. Only I must observe, that the common people conceive those quantities under no other notions but from the relation they bear to sensible objects. And thence arise certain prejudices, for the removing of which it will be convenient to distinguish them into absolute and relative, true and apparent, mathematical and common.

I. Absolute, true, and mathematical time, of itself, and from its own nature, flows equably without relation to anything external and by another name is called duration: relative, apparent, and common time, is some sensible and external (whether accurate or unequable) measure of duration by the means of motion, which is commonly used instead of true time; such as an hour, a day, a month, a year.

II. Absolute space, in its own nature, without relation to anything external, remains always similar and immovable. Relative space is some movable dimension or measure of the absolute spaces; which our senses determine by its position to bodies; and which is commonly taken for immovable space;

such is the dimension of a subterraneous, an aerial, or celestial space, deter-mined by its position in respect of the earth. Absolute and relative space are the same in figure and magnitude; but they do not remain always numerically the same. For if the earth, for instance, moves, a space of our air, which relatively and in respect of the earth remains always the same, will at one time be one part of the absolute space into which the air passes; at another time it will be another part of the same, and so, absolutely understood, it will be continually changed.

III. Place is a part of space which a body takes up, and is according to the space, either absolute or relative. I say, a part of space; not the situation, nor the external surface of the body. . . .

IV. Absolute motion is the translation of a body from one absolute place into another; and relative motion, the translation from one relative place into another. Thus in a ship under sail, the relative place of a body is that part of the ship which the body possesses; or that part of the cavity which the body fills; and which therefore moves together with the ship: and relative rest is the continuance of the body in the same part of the ship, or of its cavity. But real, absolute rest, is the continuance of the body in the same part of that immovable space, in which the ship itself, its cavity, and all that it contains, is moved. Wherefore, if the earth is really at rest, the body, which relatively rests in the ship, will really and absolutely move with the same velocity which the ship has on the earth. But if the earth also moves, the true and absolute motion of the body will arise, partly from the true motion of the earth, in immovable space, partly from the relative motion of the ship on the earth; and if the body moves also relatively in the ship, its true motion will arise, partly from the true motion of the earth, in immovable space, and partly from the relative motions as well of the ship on the earth, as of the body in the ship; and from these relative motions will arise the relative motion of the body on the earth. . . .

Newton also reflected on the broader implications of the new science.

. . . This most beautiful system of the sun, planets, and comets, could only proceed from the counsel and dominion of an intelligent and powerful Being. And if the fixed stars are the centres of other like systems, these, being formed by the like wise counsel, must be all subject to the dominion of One; especially since the light of the fixed stars is of the same nature with the light of the sun, and from every system light passes into all the other systems: and lest the systems of the fixed stars should, by their gravity, fall on each other, he hath placed those systems at immense distances from one another.

The Being governs all things, not as the soul of the world, but as Lord over all; and on account of his dominion he is wont to be called *Lord God* . . . or *Universal Ruler*; for *God* is a relative word, and has a respect to servants; and *Deity* is the dominion of God not over his own body, as those imagine who fancy God to be the soul of the world, but over servants. The Supreme God is a Being eternal, infinite, absolutely perfect; but a being, however perfect, without dominion, cannot be said to be Lord God; for we say, my God, your God, the God of *Israel*, the God of Gods, and Lord of Lords; but we do not say, my Eternal, your Eternal, the Eternal of *Israel*, the Eternal of Gods; we do not say, my Infinite, or my Perfect: these are titles which have no respect to servants. The word God usually signifies *Lord*; but every lord is not a God. It is the dominion of a spiritual being which constitutes a God: a true, supreme, or imaginary dominion makes a true, supreme, or imaginary God. And from his true dominion it follows that the true God is a living, intelligent, and powerful Being; and, from his other perfections, that he is supreme, or most perfect. He is eternal and infinite, omnipotent and omniscient; that is, his duration reaches from eternity to eternity; his presence from infinity to infinity; he governs all things, and knows all things that are or can be done. He is not eternity and infinity, but eternal and infinite; he is not duration or space, but he endures and is present. He endures forever, and is everywhere present; and, by existing always and everywhere, he constitutes duration and space. . . . God is the same God, always and everywhere. He is omnipresent not *virtually* only, but also *substantially*; for virtue cannot subsist without substance. In him are all things contained and moved; yet neither affects the other: God suffers nothing from the motion of bodies; bodies find no resistance from the omnipresence of God. It is allowed by all that the Supreme God exists necessarily, and by the same necessity he exists *always* and *everywhere*. Whence also he is all similar, all eye, all ear, all brain, all arm, all power to perceive, to understand, and to act; but in a manner not at all human, in a manner not at all corporeal, in a manner utterly unknown to us. As a blind man has no idea of colors, so have we no idea of the manner by which the all-wise God perceives and understands all things. He is utterly void of all body and bodily figure, and can therefore neither be seen, nor heard, nor touched; nor ought he to be worshiped under the representation of any corporeal thing. We have ideas of his attributes, but what the real substance of anything is we know not. In bodies, we see only their figures and colors, we hear only the sounds, we touch only their outward surfaces, we smell only the smells, and taste the savors; but their inward substances are not to be known either by our senses, or by any reflex act of our minds: much less, then, have we any idea of the substance of God. We know him only by his most wise and excellent contrivances of things, and final causes; we admire him for his perfections; but we reverence and adore him on account of his dominion: for we adore him as his servants; and a god without dominion, providence, and final causes, is nothing else but Fate and Nature. Blind metaphysical necessity, which is certainly the same always and everywhere, could produce no variety of things. All that diversity of natural things which we find suited to different times and places could arise from nothing but the ideas and will be a Being necessarily existing. But, by way of allegory, God is said to see, to speak, to laugh, to love, to hate, to desire, to give, to receive, to rejoice, to be angry, to fight, to frame, to work, to build; for all our notions of God are taken from the ways of mankind by a certain similitude, which, though not perfect, has some likeness, however. And thus much concerning God; to discourse of whom from the appearances of things, does certainly belong to Natural Philosophy. . . .

1. How did Newton describe the science of mechanics?
2. In what way did mechanics differ from mathematics?
3. Explain Newton's proposal to apply the "philosophy of mathematics" to natural phenomena.

4. Contrast Newton's idea of "absolute" and "relative" with regard to time, space, place, and motion. Once you have explained his examples in your own words, define, in general terms, the difference between the concepts of "absolute" and "relative."
5. Describe Newton's vision of the nature of God. How does this view relate to the scientist's conception of the natural universe? Compare this with Descartes' point of view.

▪ ▪ ▪

BLAISE PASCAL

Blaise Pascal (1623-62) was both a mathematician and a philosopher of religion. Pascal developed the modern theory of probability, invented a calculating machine, and did work in physics on atmospheric pressure. However, he was also deeply concerned with the question of religious faith, and he was associated with the Jansenist movement in France, a form of Catholicism which stressed great spiritual devotion and personal holiness. In his reflections on religious belief Pascal came to the conclusion that reason was inadequate to fully comprehend the nature of human beings or their purpose. His *Thoughts*, published posthumously, remain an important document on the nature of belief, faith, reason, and human nature.

 Pascal speculated on human nature:

> . . . Naturally we think ourselves more capable of reaching the center of things than of embracing their circumference. The visible expanse of the universe is visibly beyond our grasp. But since we surpass in size small things, we believe ourselves more capable of mastering them; and yet it requires no less capacity to reach the infinitely small than to reach the infinitely great. In either case it takes an infinite intelligence, and it seems to me that anyone who could have understood the ultimate principles of things could just as well succeed in knowing the infinite. One depends on the other, and one leads to the other. These extremities are contiguous and join one another by virtue of being so far apart, and meet in God and in God alone.
>
> Let us then recognize our scope. We are something, and we are not everything. What being we have prevents our having knowledge of first principles, which are born out of nothingness; and its pettiness hides from us a view of the infinite.
>
> Our intelligence occupies in the order of intelligible things the same rank as our body in the vastness of nature.
>
> Limited in all respects, this state which occupies a mid-position between two extremes prevails in all our faculties. . . .
>
> That is our true state. That is what makes is incapable of knowing with certainty, or of remaining absolutely ignorant. We float over a vast middle area, always uncertain and drifting, driven from one end toward the other.

Source: Blaise Pascal, *Selections from the Thoughts*, translated and edited by Arthur H. Beattie (Arlington Heights, Illinois: Harlan Davidson, Inc., 1965), pp. 6-7, 8, 9, 10, 87-91, 96-97.

Whenever we hope to moor ourselves and tie up to some point, it stirs and leaves us; and if we follow it, it escapes our grasp, eludes us, and flees in eternal flight. Nothing stops for us. That is our natural state, though utterly contrary to our inclination. We ardently desire to find a firm foundation, and at last a constant base upon which to erect a tower rising to infinity. But all our foundation cracks, and the earth opens to its very depths. . . .

Thus all things being caused and causing, aided and aiding, mediate or immediate, and all supporting one another by a natural and imperceptible bond which links the most distant and the most different, I maintain that it is impossible to know the parts without knowing the whole, just as it is impossible to know the whole without knowing the parts one by one.

The eternity of things in itself or in God must likewise astonish our brief duration. The fixed and constant immobility of nature in comparison with the continual change which takes place in us must produce the same effect.

And what completes our incapacity to know things is that they are simple, whereas we are compounded of two natures, opposite and differing in kind: body and soul. For it is impossible that the reasoning part in us should be anything but spiritual; and even though one might claim that we are simply corporeal, that would exclude us much more from the knowledge of things, there being nothing so inconceivable as to declare that matter knows itself. It is impossible for us to know how it might know itself. . . .

When I consider the short span of my life, absorbed in the eternity which precedes and the eternity which follows it, the little space that I fill, and even the space I see, swallowed up in the infinite immensity of the spaces which I know not and which know not me, I am frightened and astonished to see myself here rather than there, for there is no reason why here rather than there, why now rather than then. Why put me here? By whose order and act were this time and place destined for me? "As the remembrance of a guest of one day that passeth by." [The Wisdom of Solomon V, 15] . . .

 Pascal's "wager" dealt with deciding how to act when knowledge about the existence of God was not certain.

Let us speak now according to natural understanding.

If there is a God, he is infinitely incomprehensible since, having neither parts nor limits, he is totally unlike us. We are thus incapable of knowing either what he is, or if he is. That being so, who will dare to undertake to solve this question? Not we, who are of a totally different nature.

Who then will blame Christians for not being able to give a reasonable account of their belief, since they profess a religion for which this is impossible? They declare, in presenting it to the world, that it is a foolish thing; and then you complain that they do not prove it! If they proved it, they would not keep their word; it is by lacking proofs that they are being logically consistent. "Agreed; but even though that excuses those who offer it as such, and frees them from blame for presenting it without reasonable proofs, that does not excuse those who accept it."

Let us examine that point, and let us say, "Either God is, or he is not." But which side shall we favor? Reason can in no way settle the choice; there is an infinite chaos which separates us. A game is being played, at the extremity of that infinite distance in which either heads or tails will come up. Which will you bet on? By reason, you cannot choose one or the other; by reason, you can defend neither.

Now do not accuse of error those who have made a choice, for you know nothing about it. "No; but I do blame them for making, not that choice, but any choice at all; for, even though he who chooses heads and he who chooses tails are equally wrong, they are both in error. The proper thing is not to bet at all."

That is all very well; but you must bet. There is no alternative; you are involved. Which will you take, then? Come now. Since you must make a choice, let us see which interests you less. You have two things to lose—the true and the good; and two things to stake—your reason and your will, your knowledge and your bliss; and your nature has two things to avoid—error and misery. Your reason is no more offended by choosing one rather than the other, since you must necessarily make a choice. That is one point settled. But your happiness? Let us weigh what may be gained or lost by wagering that God does exist. Let us evaluate these two cases: if you win, you win everything; if you lose, you lose nothing. Wager then without hesitation that he exists.

"All right, then. Yes, I must wager. But perhaps I am wagering too much."

Let us see. Since the odds of winning or losing are even, if you had only to win two lives for one, you could still win. But if there were three to win, you would have to bet (since you face the necessity of so doing), and you would be rash, when you are forced to wager, not to risk your life in order to win three, in a game in which there is an even chance of winning or losing. But an eternity of life and happiness is at stake. And that being so, even though there might be an infinite number of chances, only one of which would be for you, you would still be right in risking one to win two; and you will act unreasonably, since you are obliged to play, to refuse to risk one life against three in a game in which out of an infinite number of chances there is one for you, if there were an infinity of infinitely happy life to be won. But there *is* here an infinity of infinitely happy life to win, a chance of gain against a finite number of chances of loss, and what you are staking is finite. That removes any reason for hesitation. Wherever the infinite is involved, and there is not an infinite number of chances of loss against the chance of gain, there is no room to hesitate, you must give all. And thus when you are forced to gamble, you must abandon reason if you wish to cling to your worldly life rather than to risk it for the infinite gain which is just as likely to occur as the loss of your nothingness.

For it does no good to say that it is uncertain whether you will win; and it is certain that you run a risk; and the infinite distance which exists between the certitude about what you are risking, and the uncertainty about what you may win, balances evenly the finite good that you are certainly risking, against the infinite gain which remains uncertain. This is not so. Indeed, any gambler ventures with certainty in the uncertain hope of winning; and yet he risks the finite with certainty in the uncertain hope of winning the finite, without transgressing against reason. There is not an infinity of distance between this certitude about what one is risking and the uncertainty of what one may win; that is false. There is, in truth, infinity between the certainty of winning and the certainty of losing. But the uncertainty of winning is in proportion to the certainty of what you are risking, according to the proportion of the chances of winning or losing. And thence it comes that, if there are as many chances on one side as on the other, the odds are even; and then the certainty of what you are staking is equal to the uncertainty of the gain, far indeed from its being infinitely distant. And thus our proposition is infinitely favorable, when you are risking the finite in a game in which there are equal chances of winning or losing, and with infinity to be won. That is perfectly capable of demonstration; and if men are capable of recognizing any truth, this is one.

"I confess it, I admit it. But once more, is there no way of knowing what cards are being dealt?"

Yes. The Scriptures, and the rest, etc.

"Yes, but my hands are tied and my mouth closed. I am being forced to wager, and I am not free; there is no escape for me. And I happen to be so constituted that I cannot believe. What then can you expect me to do?"

That is true. But learn at least that your incapacity to believe, since reason inclines you toward belief and since nonetheless you cannot believe, comes from your passions. Work, then, not to convince yourself by multiplying proofs of God's existence, but by diminishing your passions. You wish to advance toward faith, and you are ignorant of the road; you wish to recover from your lack of faith, and you seek remedies for it. Learn from people who have been bound like you, and who now stake everything they possess; they are persons who know that road which you would like to follow, and who are cured of an ill you wish to be cured of. Follow the way by which they began; it is by doing everything as if they believed, by taking holy water, by having masses said, etc. Naturally doing those very things will make you believe and will weaken your resistance.

"But that is what I fear."

And why? What have you to lose? . . .

But, in order to show you that that leads to faith, it is certain that that reduces the passions, which are your great obstacles.

End of this discourse—Now what harm will come to you by making this decision? You will be faithful, honest, humble, grateful, kind, a sincere and true friend. In truth, you will not be amid contaminated pleasures, adulated by men, and enjoying physical delights; but will you not have others? I tell you that you will gain by it in this life and that, at each step you take along this road, you will see much certitude of gain, and you will recognize so well the emptiness of what you are risking that you will realize ultimately that you have wagered on something certain and infinite, for which you have given nothing.

"Oh! What you say pleases me, delights me, etc."

If what I say pleases you and seems to you convincing, know that it is said by a man who fell on his knees before and afterwards in order to pray to that Being who is infinite and without parts, to whom he submits all his being, that he might accept submission also of your being, for your own good and for his glory, and that thus strength might be granted to weakness.

According to the principle of probabilities, you must take the trouble to seek the truth; for if you die without worshiping the True Cause, you are doomed.

"But," you say, "if he had wanted me to worship him, he would have left me signs of his will."

And so indeed he has done; but you neglect them. Just look for them; that is worth the trouble. . . .

Truth, for Pascal, had two sources:

. . . The heart has its reasons, which the reason does not know; . . .

We know the truth, not only through reason, but also through the heart; it is in this latter fashion that we know first principles, and it is in vain that reason, which has nothing to do with them, seeks to attack them. Skeptics, who devote all their attention to destroying them, work at it in vain. We know that we are not dreaming; however powerless we may be to prove it by reason, that incapacity reveals only the weakness of our reason, but not the uncertainty of all our knowledge, as the skeptics claim. For the knowledge of first principles, such as the existence of space, time, movement, numbers, is as firm as any knowledge our reasonings give us. And it is on this knowledge of the heart and of instinct that the reason must depend, and it builds on it all its arguments. The heart feels that there are three dimensions in space, and that numbers are infinite; and the reason demonstrates subsequently that there are no two squared numbers of which one is double the other. Principles are felt, propositions are concluded, and all with certitude though by different channels. And it is as useless and as ridiculous for reason to ask of the heart proofs of its first principles before being willing to accept them as it would be ridiculous for the heart to ask of reason an intuition of all the propositions it proves before consenting to admit them. . . .

And that is why those to whom God has given religion through the heart's feeling are very happy and quite legitimately convinced. But those who do not have it, we can only give it to them by reasoning until such time as God may grant it to them by the heart's feeling, otherwise faith is merely human and useless for salvation. . . .

1. What limitations did Pascal identify in the abilities of humanity to understand the universe?
2. How did he compare one's desire for a "firm foundation" with one's actual fate?
3. What was Pascal's perception of humanity's place in the universe?
4. Pascal's discourse on "The Wager" places the reader in an interesting position. Consider the following:
   a) What did Pascal say are the odds of winning or losing?
   b) What is a person being asked to risk?
   c) If one were to bet against the existence of God, and to lead one's life accordingly, what could one lose?
   d) If one were to bet on the existence of God, and to lead one's life accordingly, what could one win?
   e) Why then did Pascal say there is really no choice at all?

■ ■ ■

THOMAS HOBBES

Thomas Hobbes (1588-1679) wrote his *Leviathan* (1651) while England was in the midst of its civil wars. He was a rationalist and attempted to use the new methods of scientific inquiry in his work on politics, power, and human nature. Hobbes believed human beings were organisms in motion and that they needed to be restrained by authority from pursuing selfish ends. He rejected arguments which placed secular power under theological authority. His rationalism had great influence on subsequent writing about the state and political authority.

 Early in the work Hobbes speculated on human nature.

What is here meant by manners. BY MANNERS I mean not here decency of behavior as how one should salute another, or how a man should wash his mouth or pick his teeth before company, and such other points of the *small morals*—but those qualities of mankind that concern their living together in peace and unity. To which end we are to consider that the felicity of this life consists not in the repose of a mind satisfied. For there is no such *finis ultimus*, utmost aim, nor *summum bonum*, greatest good, as is spoken of in the books of the old moral philosophers. Nor can a man any more live whose desires are at an end than he whose senses and imaginations are at a stand. Felicity is a continual progress of the desire from one object to another, the attaining of the former being still but the way to the latter. The cause whereof is that the object of man's desire is not to enjoy once only and for one instant of time, but to assure forever the way of his future desire. And therefore the voluntary actions and inclinations of all men tend, not only to the procuring, but also to the assuring of a contented life; and differ only in the way, which arises partly from the diversity of passions in divers men, and partly from the difference of the knowledge or opinion each one has of the causes which produce the effect desired. So that, in the first place,

A restless desire of power in all men. I put for a general inclination of all mankind a perpetual and restless desire of power after power that ceases only in death. And the cause of this is not always that a man hopes for a more intensive delight than he has already attained to, or that he cannot be content with a moderate power, but because he cannot assure the power and means to live well which he has present without the acquisition of more. And from hence it is that kings, whose power is greatest, turn their endeavors to the assuring it at home by laws or abroad by wars; and when that is done, there succeeds a new desire—in some, of fame from new conquest; in others, of ease and sensual pleasure; in others, of admiration or being flattered for excellence in some art or other ability of the mind. . . .

Source: Thomas Hobbes, *Leviathan*, edited by Herbert Schneider (Indianapolis: The Bobbs-Merrill Company, 1958), pp. 86-87, 106-107, 108-109, 139, 142-43.

B The need for an authority to keep the peace was one of Hobbes' key ideas.

Again, men have no pleasure, but on the contrary a great deal of grief, in keeping company where there is no power able to overawe them all. For every man looks that his companion should value him at the same rate he sets upon himself; and upon all signs of contempt or undervaluing naturally endeavors, as far as he dares (which among them that have no common power to keep them in quiet is far enough to make them destroy each other), to extort a greater value from his contemners by damage and from others by the example.

So that in the nature of man we find three principal causes of quarrel: first, competition; secondly, diffidence; thirdly, glory.

The first makes men invade for gain, the second for safety, and the third for reputation. The first use violence to make themselves masters of other men's persons, wives, children, and cattle; the second, to defend them; the third, for trifles, as a word, a smile, a different opinion, and any other sign of undervalue, either direct in their persons or by reflection in their kindred, their friends, their nation, their profession, or their name.

Out of civil states, there is always war of every one against every one. Hereby it is manifest that, during the time men live without a common power to keep them all in awe, they are in that condition which is called war, and such a war as is of every man against every man. For WAR consists not in battle only, or the act of fighting, but in a tract of time wherein the will to contend by battle is sufficiently known; and therefore the notion of *time* is to be considered in the nature of war as it is in the nature of weather. For as the nature of foul weather lies not in a shower or two of rain but in an inclination thereto of many days together, so the nature of war consists not in actual fighting but in the known disposition thereto during all the time there is no assurance to the contrary. All other time is PEACE.

The incommodities of such a war. Whatsoever, therefore, is consequent to a time of war where every man is enemy to every man, the same is consequent to the time wherein men live without other security than what their own strength and their own invention shall furnish them withal. In such condition there is no place for industry, because the fruit thereof is uncertain: and consequently no culture of the earth; no navigation nor use of the commodities that may be imported by sea; no commodious building; no instruments of moving and removing such things as require much force; no knowledge of the face of the earth; no account of time; no arts; no letters; no society; and, which is worst of all, continual fear and danger of violent death; and the life of man solitary, poor, nasty, brutish, and short. . . .

In such a war nothing is unjust. To this war of every man against every man, this also is consequent: that nothing can be unjust. The notions of right and wrong, justice and injustice, have there no place. Where there is no common power, there is no law; where no law, no injustice. Force and fraud are in war the two cardinal virtues. Justice and injustice are none of the faculties neither of the body nor mind. If they were, they might be in a man that were alone in the world, as well as his senses and passions. They are qualities that relate to men in society, not in solitude. It is consequent also to the same condition that there be no propriety, no dominion, no *mine* and *thine* distinct; but only that to be every man's that he can get, and for so long as he can keep it. And thus much for the ill condition which man by mere nature is actually placed in, though with a possibility to come out of it consisting partly in the passions, partly in his reason.

The passions that incline men to peace. The passions that incline men to peace are fear of death, desire of such things as are necessary to commodious living, and a hope by their industry to obtain them. And reason suggests convenient articles of peace, upon which men may be drawn to agreement. These articles are they which otherwise are called the Laws of Nature, whereof I shall speak more particularly in the two following chapters.

◆ ⟨C⟩ Authority was given power in order for a commonwealth to exist and prosper. Rights were derived by the people from the sovereign.

The end of commonwealth, particular security. The final cause, end, or design of men, who naturally love liberty and dominion over others, in the introduction of that restraint upon themselves in which we see them live in commonwealths is the foresight of their own preservation, and of a more contented life thereby—that is to say, of getting themselves out from that miserable condition of war which is necessarily consequent, as has been shown to the natural passions of men when there is no visible power to keep them in awe and tie them by fear of punishment to the performance of their covenants and observation of those laws of nature set down in the fourteenth and fifteenth chapters.

Which is not to be had from the law of nature. For the laws of nature—as *justice, equity, modesty, mercy*, and, in sum, *doing to others as we would be done to*—of themselves, without the terror of some power to cause them to be observed, are contrary to our natural passions, that carry us to partiality, pride, revenge, and the like. And covenants without the sword are but words, and of no strength to secure a man at all. Therefore, notwithstanding the laws of nature (which everyone has then kept when he has the will to keep them, when he can do it safely), if there be no power erected, or not great enough for our security, every man will—and may lawfully—rely on his own strength and art for caution against all other men. . . .

The generation of a commonwealth. The only way to erect such a common power as may be able to defend them from the invasion of foreigners and the injuries of one another, and thereby to secure them in such sort as that by their own industry and by the fruits of the earth they may nourish themselves and live contentedly, is to confer all their power and strength upon one man, or upon one assembly of men that may reduce all their wills, by plurality of voices, unto one will; which is as much as to say, to appoint one man or assembly of men to bear their person, and everyone to own and acknowledge himself to be author of whatsoever he that so bears their person shall act or cause to be acted in those things which concern the common peace and safety, and therein to submit their wills every one to his will, and their judgments to his judgment. This is more than consent or concord; it is a real unity of them all in one and the same person, made by covenant of every man with every man, in such manner as if every man should say to every man, *I authorize and give up my right of governing myself to this man, or to this assembly of men, on this condition, that you give up your right to him and authorize all his actions in like manner.* This done, the multitude so united in one person is called a COMMONWEALTH, in Latin CIVITAS. This is the generation of that great LEVIATHAN (or rather, to speak more reverently, of that *mortal god*) to which we owe, under the *immortal God*, our peace and defense. For by this authority, given him by every particular man in the commonwealth, he has the use of so much power and strength conferred on him that, by terror thereof, he is enabled to form the wills of them all to peace at home and mutual aid against their enemies abroad. And in him consists the essence of the commonwealth, which to define it, is

The definition of a commonwealth. *one person, of whose acts a great multitude, by mutual covenants one with another, have made themselves every one the author, to the end he may use the strength and means of them all as he shall think expedient for their peace and common defense.*

Sovereign and subject, what. And he that carries this person is called SOVEREIGN and said to have *sovereign power*; and everyone besides, his SUBJECT.

The attaining to this sovereign power is by two ways. One, by natural force, as when a man makes his children to submit themselves and their children to his government, as being able to destroy them if they refuse, or by war subdues his enemies to his will, giving them their lives on that condition. The other is when men agree among themselves to submit to some man or assembly of men voluntarily, on confidence to be protected by him against all others. This latter may be called a political commonwealth, or commonwealth by *institution*, and the former a commonwealth by *acquisition*. . . .

1. In what way did Hobbes use the term "manners"?
2. What did Hobbes feel is the inherent nature of humanity, what he called the usual inclination of all people?
3. How did he explain the general inclination of humanity to gain more and more power?
4. According to Hobbes, what aspects of the nature of people lead them into a state of war?
5. Account for Hobbes' contention that without a "common power to keep them all in awe," humanity is incapable of productive achievement.
6. Expand on Hobbes' view of life in a state of war.
7. "The only way in which mankind may be safe from one another is to surrender their power to a central authority or commonwealth." Account for this statement in terms of Hobbes' views on the nature of man and the role of government.

▪ ▪ ▪

JOHN LOCKE

The political philosopher who placed rights at the center was John Locke (1632-1704), whose *Two Treatises of Government* (1690) challenged authority as it had been formulated by Hobbes. Locke was writing at the time of the debate and events which led to the Glorious Revolution of 1688, and he wished to find the proper limits of authority. He believed in a contract between the people and the government which was bilateral, and in a human nature which was characterized by tolerance and reason. Locke's ideas about natural rights and social contract had wide influence in constitutional thought and helped to form the basis of modern liberalism.

A Locke, like Hobbes, discussed the human condition in a "state of nature," a time when there was no government.

To understand Political Power right, and derive it from its Original, we must consider what State all Men are naturally in, and that is, a *State of perfect Freedom* to order their Actions, and dispose of their Possessions, and Persons as they think fit, within the bounds of the Law of Nature, without asking leave, or depending upon the Will of any other Man.

A *State* also of *Equality*, wherein all the Power and Jurisdiction is reciprocal, no one having more than another: there being nothing more evident, than that Creatures of the same species and rank promiscuously born to all the same advantages of Nature, and the use of the same faculties, should also be equal one amongst another without Subordination or Subjection, unless the Lord and Master of them all, should by any manifest Declaration of his Will set one above another, and confer on him by an evident and clear appointment on undoubted Right to Dominion and Sovereignty. . . .

But though this be a *State of Liberty*, yet it is *not* a *State of Licence*, though Man in that State have an uncontroleable Liberty, to dispose of his Person or Possessions, yet he has not Liberty to destroy himself, or so much as any Creature in his Possession, but where some nobler use, than its bare Preservation calls for it. The *State of Nature* has a Law of Nature to govern it, which obliges every one; And Reason, which is that Law, teaches all Mankind, who will but consult it, that being all equal and independent, no one ought to harm another in his Life, Health, Liberty, or Possessions. For Men being all the Workmanship of one Omnipotent, and infinitely wise Maker; All the Servants of one Sovereign Master, sent into the world by his order and about his business, they are his Property, whose Workmanship they are, made to last during his, nor one anothers Pleasure. And being furnished with like Faculties, sharing all in one Community of Nature, there cannot be supposed any such *Subordination* among us, that may Authorize us to destroy one another, as if we were made for one anothers uses, as the inferior ranks of Creatures are for ours. Every one as he is *bound to preserve himself*, and not

Source: John Locke, *Two Treatises of Government* (New York: New American Library, 1960), pp. 309, 311-12, 374-77, 446, 448, 460-61.

to quit his Station wilfully; so by the like reason when his own Preservation comes not in competition, ought he, as much as he can, *to preserve the rest of Mankind*, and may not unless it be to do Justice on an Offender, take away, or impair the life, or what tends to the Preservation of the Life, Liberty, Health, Limb or Goods of another.

And that all Men may be restrained from invading others Rights, and from doing hurt to one another, and the Law of Nature be observed, which willeth the Peace and *Preservation of all Mankind*, the *Execution* of the Law of Nature is in that State, put into every Mans hands, whereby every one has a right to punish the transgressors of that Law to such a Degree, as may hinder its Violation. For the *Law of Nature* would, as all other Laws that concern Men in this World, be in vain, if there were no body that in the State of Nature, had a *Power to Execute* that Law, and thereby preserve the innocent and restrain offenders, and if any one in the State of Nature may punish another, for any evil he has done, every one may do so. For in that *State of perfect Equality*, where naturally there is no superiority or jurisdiction of one, over another, what any may do in Prosecution of that Law, every one must needs have a Right to do. . . .

 B Individuals form a community, according to Locke, for their mutual benefit.

Men being, as has been said, by Nature, all free, equal and independent, no one can be put out of this Estate, and subjected to the Political Power of another, without his own *Consent*. The only way whereby any one devests himself of his Natural Liberty, and *puts on the bonds of Civil Society* is by agreeing with other Men to joyn and unite into a Community, for their comfortable, safe, and peaceable living one amongst another, in a secure Enjoyment of their Properties, and a greater Security against any that are not of it. This any number of Men may do, because it injures not the Freedom of the rest; they are left as they were in the Liberty of the State of Nature. When any number of Men have so *consented to make one Community* or Government, they are thereby presently incorporated, and make *one Body Politick*, wherein the *Majority* have a Right to act and conclude the rest.

For when any number of Men have, by the consent of every individual, made a *Community*, they have thereby made that *Community* one Body, with a Power to Act as one Body, which is only by the will and determination of the *majority*. For that which acts any Community, being only the consent of the individuals of it, and it being necessary to that which is one body to move one way; it is necesssary the Body should move that way whither the greater force carries it, which is the *consent of the majority*: or else it is impossible it should act or continue one Body, *one Community*, which the consent of every individual that united into it, agreed that it should; and so every one is bound by that consent to be concluded by the *majority*. And therefore we see that in Assemblies impowered to act by positive Laws where no number is set by that positive Law which impowers them, the *act of the Majority* passes for the act of the whole, and of course determines, as having by the Law of Nature and Reason, the power of the whole.

And thus every Man, by consenting with others to make one Body Politick under one Government, puts himself under an Obligation to every one of that Society, to submit to the determination of the *majority*, and to be concluded by it; or else this *original Compact*, whereby he with others incorporates into *one Society*, would signifie nothing, and be no Compact, if he be left free, and under no other ties, than he was in before in the State of Nature. For what appearance would there be of any Compact? What new Engagement if he were no farther tied by any Decrees of the Society, than he himself thought fit, and did actually consent to? This would be still as great a liberty, as he himself had before his Compact, or any one else in the State of Nature hath, who may submit himself and consent to any acts of it if he thinks fit.

For if *the consent of the majority* shall not in reason, be received, *as the act of the whole*, and conclude every individual; nothing but the consent of every individual can make any thing to be the act of the whole: But such a consent is next impossible ever to be had, if we consider the Infirmities of Health, and Avocations of Business, which in a number, though much less than that of a Common-wealth, will necessarily keep many away from the publick Assembly. To which if we add the variety of Opinions, and contrariety of Interests, which unavoidably happen in all Collections of Men, the coming into Society upon such terms, would be only like *Cato's* coming into the Theatre, only to go out again. Such a Constitution as this would make the mighty *Leviathan* of a shorter duration, than the feeblest Creatures; and not let it outlast the day it was born in: which cannot be suppos'd till we can think, that Rational Creatures should desire and constitute Societies only to be dissolved. For where the *majority* cannot conclude the rest, there they cannot act as one Body, and consequently will be immediately dissolved again.

Whosoever therefore out of a state of Nature unite into a *Community*, must be understood to give up all the power, necessary to the ends for which they unite into Society, to the *majority* of the Community, unless they expressly agreed in any number greater than the majority. And this is done by barely agreeing to *unite into one Political Society*, which is *all the Compact that* is, or needs be, between the Individuals, that enter into, or make up a *Common-wealth*. And thus that, which begins and actually *constitutes any Political Society*, is nothing but the consent of any number of Freemen capable of a majority to unite and incorporate into such a Society. And this is that, and that only, which did, or could give *beginning* to any *lawful Government* in the World. . . .

◁C▷ The people have a contract with a sovereign. If the sovereign breaks the arrangement, the right of resistance may be used.

As Usurpation is the exercise of Power, which another hath a Right to; so *Tyranny* is *the exercise of Power beyond Right*, which no Body can have a Right to. And this is making use of the Power any one has in his hands; not for the good of those, who are under it, but for his own private separate Advantage. When the Governour, however intituled, makes not the Law, but his Will, the Rule; and his Commands and Actions are not directed to the preservation of the Properties of his People, but the satisfaction of his own Ambition, Revenge, Covetousness, or any other irregular Passion. . . .

Where-ever Law ends Tyranny begins, if the Law be transgressed to another's harm. And whosoever in Authority exceeds the Power given him by the Law, and makes use of the Force he has under his Command, to compass that upon the Subject, which the Law allows not, ceases in that to be a Magistrate, and acting without Authority, may be opposed, as any other Man, who by force invades the Right of another. . . .

The Reason why Men enter into Society, is the preservation of their Property; and the end why they chuse and authorize a Legislative, is, that there may be Laws made, and Rules set as Guards and Fences to the Properties of all the Members of the Society, to limit the Power, and moderate the Dominion of every Part and Member of the Society. For since it can never be supposed to be the Will of the Society, that the Legislative should have a Power to destroy that, which every one designs to secure, by entering into Society, and for which the People submitted themselves to the Legislators of their own making; whenever the *Legislators endeavour to take away, and destroy the Property of the People*, or to reduce them to Slavery under Arbitrary Power, they put themselves into a state of War with the People, who are thereupon absolved from any farther Obedience, and are left to the common Refuge, which God hath provided for all Men, against Force and Violence. Whensoever therefore the *Legislative* shall transgress this fundamental Rule of Society; and either by Ambition, Fear, Folly or Corruption, *endeavour to grasp* themselves, *or put into the hands of any other an Absolute Power* over the Lives, Liberties, and Estates of the People; By this breach of Trust they *forfeit the Power*, the People had put into their hands, for quite contrary ends, and it devolves to the People, who have a Right to resume their original Liberty, and, by the Establishment of a new Legislative (such as they shall think fit) provide for their own Safety and Security, which is the end for which they are in Society. . . .

1. Describe Locke's position on the rights of man in the state of nature.
2. Compare Locke's view of the law of nature with that of Hobbes.
3. Outline Locke's opinion as to why an individual would voluntarily surrender some of his rights to the community.
4. Explain Locke's defence of majority rule.
5. "Whenever the Legislators endeavour to take away and destroy the Property of the people, or to reduce them to Slavery under Arbitrary Power, they put themselves into a state of war with the People, who are thereupon absolved from any further obedience." Using Locke's arguments, in your own words, defend this "right of revolution" against a government. Do you agree with Locke?

▪ ▪ ▪

JEAN-JACQUES ROUSSEAU

Jean-Jacques Rousseau (1712-78), one of the most controversial figures of the Enlightenment, challenged many of the assumptions of the mainstream of eighteenth century thought. He believed human beings were good in a state of nature, and that in civilization there is the basis of corruption. Yet, we cannot return to an ideal primitive moment and therefore must build a just community in which the individual will and the needs of the community are reconciled. Rousseau put emphasis on the importance of sentiment as well as on reason, and stressed emotional and intuitive elements in assessing human nature. Rousseau's *Social Contract* (1762) recognized many of the difficulties in thinking about freedom and authority, as he tried to reconcile the need for individual expression with the well-being of community life.

 Rousseau opened his work with a critique of society and a discussion of its foundations.

> Man was born free, and everywhere he is in chains. Many a one believes himself the master of others, and yet he is a greater slave than they. How has this change come about? I do not know. What can render it legitimate? I believe that I can settle this question.
>
> If I considered only force and the results that proceed from it, I should say that so long as a people is compelled to obey and does obey, it does well; but that, so soon as it can shake off the yoke and does shake it off, it does better; for, if men recover their freedom by virtue of the same right by which it was taken away, either they are justified in resuming it, or there was no justification for depriving them of it. But the social order is a sacred right which serves as a foundation for all others. This right, however, does not come from nature. It is therefore based on conventions. The question is to know what these conventions are. Before coming to that, I must establish what I have just laid down.

 Freedom for Rousseau was one of the conditions of our being human.

> The earliest of all societies, and the only natural one, is the family; yet children remain attached to their father only so long as they have need of him for their own preservation. As soon as this need ceases, the natural bond is dissolved. The children being freed from the obedience which they owed to their father, and the father from the cares which he owed to his children, become equally independent. If they remain united, it is no longer naturally but voluntarily; and the family itself is kept together only by convention.
>
> This common liberty is a consequence of man's nature. His first law is to attend to his own preservation, his first cares are those which he owes to himself; and as soon as he comes to years of discretion, being sole judge of the means adapted for his own preservation, he becomes his own master. . . .
>
> The strongest man is never strong enough to be always master, unless he transforms his power into right, and obedience into duty. Hence the right of the strongest—a right apparently assumed in irony, and really established in principle. But will this phrase never be explained to us? Force is a physical power; I do not see what morality can result from its effects. To yield to force is an act of necessity, not of will; it is at most an act of prudence. . . .
>
> Let us agree, then, that might does not make right, and that we are bound to obey none but lawful authorities. . . .

Source: Jean-Jacques Rousseau, *The Social Contract [and] Discourse on the Origin of Inequality* edited by Lester G. Crocker (New York: Washington Square Press, 1967), pp. 7-8, 10, 11-13, 17-22.

Since no man has any natural authority over his fellow men, and since force is not the source of right, conventions remain as the basis of all lawful authority among men.

If an individual, says Grotius, can alienate his liberty and become the slave of a master, why should not a whole people be able to alienate theirs, and become subject to a king? In this there are many equivocal terms requiring explanation; but let us confine ourselves to the word *alienate*. To alienate is to give or sell. Now, a man who becomes another's slave does not give himself; he sells himself at the very least for his subsistence. But why does a nation sell itself? So far from a king supplying his subjects with their subsistence, he draws his from them; and, according to Rabelais, a king does not live on a little. Do subjects, then, give up their persons on condition that their property also shall be taken? I do not see what is left for them to keep.

It will be said that the despot secures to his subjects civil peace. Be it so; but what do they gain by that, if the wars which his ambition brings upon them, together with his insatiable greed and the vexations of his administration, harass them more than their own dissensions would? What do they gain by it if this tranquillity is itself one of their miseries? Men live tranquilly also in dungeons; is that enough to make them contented there? The Greeks confined in the cave of the Cyclops lived peacefully until their turn came to be devoured.

To say that a man gives himself for nothing is to say what is absurd and inconceivable; such an act is illegitimate and invalid, for the simple reason that he who performs it is not in his right mind. To say the same thing of a whole nation is to suppose a nation of fools; and madness does not confer rights.

Even if each person could alienate himself, he could not alienate his children; they are born free men; their liberty belongs to them, and no one has a right to dispose of it except themselves. Before they have come to years of discretion, the father can, in their name, stipulate conditions for their preservation and welfare, but not surrender them irrevocably and unconditionally; for such a gift is contrary to the ends of nature, and exceeds the rights of paternity. In order, then, that an arbitrary government might be legitimate, it would be necessary that the people in each generation should have the option of accepting or rejecting it; but in that case such a government would no longer be arbitrary.

To renounce one's liberty is to renounce one's quality as a man, the rights and also the duties of humanity. For him who renounces everything there is no possible compensation. Such a renunciation is incompatible with man's nature, for to take away all freedom from his will is to take away all morality from his actions. In short, a convention which stipulates absolute authority on the one side and unlimited obedience on the other is vain and contradictory. Is it not clear that we are under no obligations whatsoever towards a man from whom we have a right to demand everything? And does not this single condition, without equivalent, without exchange, involve the nullity of the act? For what right would my slave have against me, since all that he has belongs to me? His rights being mine, this right of me against myself is a meaningless phrase. . . .

The state has its origins in the social contract.

I assume that men have reached a point at which the obstacles that endanger their preservation in the state of nature overcome by their resistance the forces which each individual can exert with a view to maintaining himself in that state. Then this primitive condition can no longer subsist, and the human race would perish unless it changed its mode of existence.

Now, as men cannot create any new forces, but only combine and direct those that exist, they have no other means of self-preservation than to form by aggregation a sum of forces which may overcome the resistance, to put them in action by a single motive power, and to make them work in concert.

This sum of forces can be produced only by the combination of many; but the strength and freedom of each man being the chief instruments of his preservation, how can he pledge them without injuring himself, and without neglecting the cares which he owes to himself? This difficulty, applied to my subject, may be expressed in these terms:—

"To find a form of association which may defend and protect with the whole force of the community the person and property of every associate, and by means of which each, coalescing with all, may nevertheless obey only himself, and remain as free as before." Such is the fundamental problem of which the social contract furnishes the solution.

The clauses of this contract are so determined by the nature of the act that the slightest modification would render them vain and ineffectual; so that, although they have never perhaps been formally enunciated, they are everywhere the same, everywhere tacitly admitted and recognized, until, the social pact being violated, each man regains his original rights and recovers his natural liberty, while losing the conventional liberty for which he renounced it.

These clauses, rightly understood, are reducible to one only, viz., the total alienation to the whole community of each associate with all his rights; for, in the first place, since each gives himself up entirely, the conditions are equal for all; and, the conditions being equal for all, no one has any interest in making them burdensome to others.

Further, the alienation being made without reserve, the union is as perfect as it can be, and an individual associate can no longer claim anything; for, if any rights were left to individuals, since there would be no common superior who could judge between them and the public, each, being on some point his own judge, would soon claim to be so on all; the state of nature would still subsist, and the association would necessarily become tyrannical or useless.

In short, each giving himself to all, gives himself to nobody; and as there is not one associate over whom we do not acquire the same rights which we concede to him over ourselves, we gain the equivalent of all that we lose, and more power to preserve what we have.

If, then, we set aside what is not of the essence of the social contract, we shall find that it is reducible to the following terms: "Each of us puts in common his person and his whole power under the supreme direction of the general will; and in return we receive every member as an indivisible part of the whole."

Forthwith, instead of the individual personalities of all the contracting parties, this act of association produces a moral and collective body, which is composed of as many members as the assembly has voices, and which receives from this same act its unity, its common self (*moi*), its life, and its will. This public person, which is thus formed by the union of all the individual members, formerly took the name of *city*, and now takes that of *republic* or *body politic*, which is called by its members *State* when it is passive, *sovereign* when it is active, *power* when it is compared to similar bodies. With regard to the associates, they take collectively the name of *people*, and are called individually *citizens*, as participating in the sovereign power, and *subjects*, as subjected to the laws of the State. But these terms are often confused and are mistaken one for another; it is sufficient to know how to distinguish them when they are used with complete precision.

D The nature of sovereign authority was one of Rousseau's most controversial sections, one debated ever since by all social and political philosophers in an attempt to grasp and solve the problems raised when considering differences between individual desires and community needs.

We see from this formula that the act of association contains a reciprocal engagement between the public and individuals, and that every individual, contracting so to speak with himself, is engaged in a double relation, viz., as a member of the sovereign towards individuals, and as a member of the State towards the sovereign. But we cannot apply here the maxim of civil law that no one is bound by engagements made with himself; for there is a great difference between being bound to oneself and to a whole of which one forms part.

We must further observe that the public resolution which can bind all subjects to the sovereign in consequence of the two different relations under which each of them is regarded cannot, for a contrary reason, bind the sovereign to itself; and that accordingly it is contrary to the nature of the body politic for the sovereign to impose on itself a law which it cannot transgress. As it can only be considered under one and the same relation, it is in the position of an individual contracting with himself; whence we see that there is not, nor can be, any kind of fundamental law binding upon the body of the people, not even the social contract. This does not imply that such a body cannot perfectly well enter into engagements with others in what does not derogate from this contract; for, with regard to foreigners, it becomes a simple being, an individual.

But the body politic or sovereign, deriving its existence only from the sanctity of the contract, can never bind itself, even to others, in anything that derogates from the original act, such as alienation of some portion of itself, or submission to another sovereign. To violate the act by which it exists would be to annihilate itself; and what is nothing produces nothing.

So soon as the multitude is thus united in one body, it is impossible to injure one of the members without attacking the body, still less to injure the body without the members feeling the effects. Thus duty and interest alike oblige the two contracting parties to give mutual assistance; and the men themselves should seek to combine in this twofold relationship all the advantages which are attendant on it.

Now, the sovereign, being formed only of the individuals that compose it, neither has nor can have any interest contrary to theirs; consequently the sovereign power needs no guarantee towards its subjects, because it is impossible that the body should wish to injure all its members; and we shall see hereafter that it can injure no one as an individual. The sovereign, for the simple reason that it is so, is always everything that it ought to be.

But this is not the case as regards the relation of subjects to the sovereign, which, notwithstanding the common interest, would have no security for the performance of their engagements unless it found means to ensure their fidelity.

Indeed, every individual may, as a man, have a particular will contrary to, or divergent from, the general will which he has as a citizen; his private interest may prompt him quite differently from the common interest; his absolute and naturally independent existence may make him regard what he owes to the common cause as a gratuitous contribution, the loss of which will be less harmful to others than the payment of it will be burdensome to him; and, regarding the moral person that constitutes the State as an imaginary being because it is not a man, he would be willing to enjoy the rights of a citizen without being willing to fulfil the duties of a subject. The progress of such injustice would bring about the ruin of the body politic.

In order, then, that the social pact may not be a vain formulary, it tacitly includes this engagement, which can alone give force to the others—that whoever refuses to obey the general will shall be constrained to do so by the whole body; which means nothing else than that he shall be forced to be free; for such is the condition which, uniting every citizen to his native land, guarantees him from all personal dependence, a condition that ensures the control and working of the political machine, and alone renders legitimate civil engagements, which, without it, would be absurd and tyrannical, and subject to the most enormous abuses.

1. "Man was born free, and everywhere he is in chains." Comment on the effectiveness of such a statement as a call to revolution.
2. Explain the way in which Rousseau's description of the family applies to political and social organizations.
3. Rousseau stated that "might does not make right." Explain this statement with reference to the difference between the use of force and the use of moral authority.
4. How did Rousseau refute the claim that individuals or nations willingly give their liberty to another individual?
5. Based on his opening assertion that "man is born free," how did Rousseau argue against the ideas of heredity, authority, and obedience?

• • •

JONATHAN SWIFT

Jonathan Swift's work raised satire to the level of high social criticism. Angry at some of the complacency of his time, Swift (1667-1745) attacked the smugness of the English aristocracy and the uncaring and selfish attitude he believed was held by most human beings. An Anglican minister who spent most of his life in Ireland, his works challenged established customs and institutions. Swift angrily criticized the role of England in Irish society and politics.

A Swift's *A Modest Proposal* (1729) attacked English policies and absentee English landlords in an effort to bring attention to the poverty and suffering in Ireland. The narrator, an Englishman blind to his own responsibility, position, and moral attitude, suggests that one way of solving the problems of Ireland is to sell the children of the poor as food for those who are wealthy.

> It is a melancholy Object to those, who walk through this great Town, or travel in the Country; when they see the *Streets,* the *Roads,* and *Cabbin-doors* crowded with *Beggars* of the Female Sex, followed by three, four, or six Children, *all in Rags,* and importuning every Passenger for an Alms. These *Mothers,* instead of being able to work for their honest Livelyhood, are forced to employ all their Time in stroling to beg Sustenance for their *helpless Infants;* who, as they grow up, either turn *Thieves* for want of Work; or leave their *dear Native Country, to fight for the Pretender in* Spain, or sell themselves to the *Barbadoes.*
>
> I THINK it is agreed by all Parties, that this prodigious Number of Children in the Arms, or on the Backs, or at the *Heels* of their *Mothers,* and frequently of their *Fathers,* is *in the present deplorable State of the Kingdom,* a very great additional Grievance; and therefore, whoever could find out a fair, cheap, and easy Method of making these Children sound and useful Members of the Commonwealth, would deserve so well of the Publick, as to have his Statue set up for a Preserver of the Nation. . . .
>
> I AM assured by our Merchants, that a Boy or a Girl before twelve Years old, is no saleable Commodity; and even when they come to this Age, they will not yield above Three Pounds, or Three Pounds and half a Crown at most, on the Exchange; which cannot turn to Account either to the Parents or the Kingdom; the Charge of Nutriment and Rags, having been at least four Times that Value.
>
> I SHALL now therefore humbly propose my own Thoughts; which I hope will not be liable to the least Objection.
>
> I HAVE been assured by a very knowing *American* of my Acquaintance in *London;* that a young healthy Child, well nursed, is, at a Year old, a most delicious, nourishing, and wholesome Food; whether *Stewed, Roasted, Baked,* or *Boiled;* and, I make no doubt, that it will equally serve in a *Fricasie,* or *Ragoust.* . . .
>
> FOR, *First,* as I have already observed, it would greatly lessen the *Number of Papists,* with whom we are yearly overrun; being the principal Breeders of the Nation, as well as our most dangerous Enemies; and who stay at home on Purpose, with a Design to *deliver the Kingdom to the Pretender;* hoping to

Sources: Jonathan Swift, *Gulliver's Travels and Other Writings* (New York: The Modern Library, 1958), pp. 448-90, 492-94, 496; Jonathan Swift, *Gulliver's Travels,* edited by Robert A. Greenberg (New York: W. W. Norton and Company, Inc., 1970), pp. 103-108.

take their Advantage by the Absence *of so many good Protestants,* who have chosen rather to leave their Country, than stay at home, and pay Tithes against their Conscience, to an idolatrous *Episcopal Curate.*

SECONDLY, The poorer Tenants will have something valuable of their own, which, by Law, may be made liable to Distress, and help to pay their Landlord's Rent; their Corn and Cattle being already seized, and *Money a Thing unknown.*

THIRDLY, Whereas the Maintenance of an Hundred Thousand Children, from two Years old, and upwards, cannot be computed at less than ten Shillings a Piece *per Annum,* the Nation's Stock will be thereby encreased Fifty Thousand Pounds *per Annum;* besides the Profit of a new Dish, introduced to the Tables of all *Gentlemen of Fortune* in the Kingdom, who have any Refinement in Taste; and the Money will circulate among ourselves, the Goods being entirely of our own Growth and Manufacture.

FOURTHLY, The constant Breeders, besides the Gain of Eight Shillings *Sterling per Annum,* by the Sale of their Children, will be rid of the Charge of maintaining them after the first Year.

FIFTHLY, This Food would likewise bring great *Custom to Taverns,* where the Vintners will certainly be so prudent, as to procure the best Receipts for dressing it to Perfection; and consequently, have their Houses frequented by all the *fine Gentlemen,* who justly value themselves upon their Knowledge in good Eating; and a skilful Cook, who understands how to oblige his Guests, will contrive to make it as expensive as they please.

SIXTHLY, This would be a great Inducement to Marriage, which all wise Nations have either encouraged by Rewards, or enforced by laws and Penalties. It would encrease the Care and Tenderness of Mothers towards their Children, when they were sure of a Settlement for Life, to the poor Babes, provided in some Sort by the Publick, to their annual Profit instead of Expence. We should soon see an honest Emulation among the married Women, *which of them could bring the fattest Child to the Market.* Men would become as *fond* of their Wives, during the Time of their Pregnancy, as they are now of the *Mares* in Foal, their *Cows* in Calf, or *Sows* when they are ready to farrow; nor offer to beat or kick them, (as it is too *frequent* a Practice) for fear of a Miscarriage.

MANY other Advantages might be enumerated. For instance, the Addition of some Thousand Carcasses in our Exportation of barrelled Beef: The Propagation of *Swines Flesh,* and Improvement in the Art of making good *Bacon;* so much wanted among us by the great Destruction of *Pigs,* too frequent at our Tables, and are no way comparable in Taste, or Magnificence, to a wellgrown fat yearling Child; which, roasted whole, will make a considerable Figure at a *Lord Mayor's Feast,* or any other publick Entertainment. But this, and many others, I omit; being studious of Brevity. . . .

I PROFESS, in the Sincerity of my Heart, that I have not the least personal interest, in endeavouring to promote this necessary Work; having no other Motive than the *publick Good of my Country, by advancing our Trade, providing for Infants, relieving the Poor, and giving some Pleasure to the Rich.* I have no Children, by which I can propose to get a single Penny; the youngest being nine Years old, and my Wife past Child-bearing.

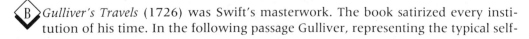

Gulliver's Travels (1726) was Swift's masterwork. The book satirized every institution of his time. In the following passage Gulliver, representing the typical self-satisfied Englishman, has told the King of Brobdingnag about English institutions and customs, and is surprised by the response.

> . . . When I had put an end to these long Discourses, his Majesty in a sixth Audience consulting his Notes, proposed many Doubts, Queries, and Objections, upon every Article. He asked, what Methods were used to cultivate the Minds and Bodies of our young Nobility; and in what kind of Business they commonly spent the first and teachable Part of their Lives. What Course was taken to supply that Assembly, when any noble Family became extinct. What Qualifications were necessary in those who are to be created new Lords: Whether the Humour of the Prince, a Sum of Money to a Court-Lady, or a Prime Minister; or a Design of strengthening a Party opposite to the publick Interest, ever happened to be Motives in those Advancements. What Share of Knowledge these Lords had in the Laws of their Country, and how they came by it, so as to enable them to decide the Properties of their Fellow-Subjects in the last Resort. Whether they were always so free from Avarice, Partialities, or Want, that a Bribe, or some other sinister View, could have no Place among them. Whether those holy Lords I spoke of, were constantly promoted to that Rank upon Account of their Knowledge in religious Matters, and the Sanctity of their Lives; had never been compliers with the Times, while they were common Priests; or slavish prostitute Chaplains to some Nobleman, whose Opinions they continued servilely to follow after they were admitted into that Assembly.
>
> He then desired to know, what Arts were practised in electing those whom I called Commoners. Whether, a Stranger with a strong Purse might not influence the vulgar Voters to chuse him before their own Landlords, or the most considerable Gentleman in the Neighbourhood. How it came to pass, that People were so violently bent upon getting into this Assembly, which I allowed to be a great Trouble and Expence, often to the Ruin of their Families, without any Salary or Pension: Because this appeared such an exalted Strain of Virtue and publick Spirit, that his Majesty seemed to doubt it might possibly not be always sincere: And he desired to know, whether such zealous Gentlemen could have any Views of refunding themselves for the Charges and Trouble they were at, by sacrificing the publick Good to the Designs of a weak and vicious Prince, in Conjunction with a corrupted Ministry. He multiplied his Questions, and sifted me thoroughly upon every Part of this Head; proposing numberless Enquiries and Objections, which I think it not prudent or convenient to repeat.
>
> Upon what I said in relation to our Courts of Justice, his Majesty desired to be satisfied in several Points: And, this I was the better able to do, having been formerly almost ruined by a long Suit in Chancery, which was decreed for me with Costs. He asked, what Time was usually spent in determining between Right and Wrong; and what Degree of Expence. Whether Advocates and Orators had Liberty to plead in Causes manifestly known to be unjust, vexatious, or oppressive. Whether Party in Religion or Politicks were observed to be of any Weight in the Scale of Justice. Whether those pleading Orators were Persons educated in the general Knowledge of Equity; or only in provincial, national, and other local Customs. Whether they or their Judges had any Part in penning those Laws, which they assumed the Liberty of inter-

preting and glossing upon at their Pleasure. Whether they had ever at different Times pleaded for and against the same Cause, and cited Precedents to prove contrary Opinions. Whether they were a rich or a poor Corporation. Whether they received any pecuniary Reward for pleading or delivering their Opinions. And particularly whether they were ever admitted as Members in the lower Senate.

He fell next upon the Management of our Treasury; and said, he thought my Memory had failed me, because I computed our Taxes at about five or six Millions a Year; and when I came to mention the Issues, he found they sometimes amounted to more than double; for, the Notes he had taken were very particular in this Point; because he hoped, as he told me, that the Knowledge of our Conduct might be useful to him; and he could not be deceived in his Calculations. But, if what I told him were true, he was still at a Loss how a Kingdom could run out of its Estate like a private Person. He asked me, who were our Creditors? and, where we found Money to pay them? He wondered to hear me talk of such chargeable and extensive Wars; that, certainly we must be a quarrelsome People, or live among very bad Neighbours; and that our Generals must needs be richer than our Kings. He asked, what Business we had out of our own Islands, unless upon the Score of Trade or Treaty, or to defend the Coasts with our Fleet. Above all, he was amazed to hear me talk of a mercenary standing Army in the Midst of Peace, and among a free People. He said, if we were governed by our own Consent in the Persons of our Representatives, he could not imagine of whom we were afraid, or against whom we were to fight; and would hear my Opinion, whether a private Man's House might not better be defended by himself, his Children, and Family; than by half a Dozen Rascals picked up at a Venture in the Streets, for small Wages, who might get an Hundred Times more by cutting their Throats.

He laughed at my odd Kind of Arithmetick (as he was pleased to call it) in reckoning the Numbers of our People by a Computation drawn from the several Sects among us in Religion and Politicks. He said, he knew no Reason, why those who entertain Opinions prejudicial to the Publick, should be obliged to change, or should not be obliged to conceal them. And, as it was Tyranny in any Government to require the first, so it was Weakness not to enforce the second: For, a Man may be allowed to keep Poisons in his Closet, but not to vend them about as Cordials.

He observed, that among the Diversions of our Nobility and Gentry, I had mentioned Gaming. He desired to know at what Age this Entertainment was usually taken up, and when it was laid down. How much of their Time it employed; whether it ever went so high as to affect their Fortunes. Whether mean vicious People, by their Dexterity in that Art, might not arrive at great Riches, and sometimes keep our very Nobles in Dependance, as well as habituate them to vile Companions; wholly take them from the Improvement of their Minds, and force them by the Losses they received, to learn and practice that infamous Dexterity upon others.

He was perfectly astonished with the historical Account I gave him of our Affairs during the last Century; protesting it was only an Heap of Conspiracies, Rebellions, Murders, Massacres, Revolutions, Banishments; the very worst Effects that Avarice, Faction, Hypocrisy, Perfidiousness, Cruelty, Rage, Madness, Hatred, Envy, Lust, Malice, and Ambition could produce.

His Majesty in another Audience, was at the Pains to recapitulate the Sum of all I had spoken, compared the Questions he made, with the Answers I had given; then taking me into his Hands, and stroaking me gently, delivered himself in these Words, which I shall never forget, nor the Manner he spoke them in. My little Friend *Grildrig;* you have made a most admirable Panegyrick upon your Country. You have clearly proved that Ignorance, Idleness, and Vice are the proper Ingredients for qualifying a Legislator. That Laws are best explained, interpreted, and applied by those whose Interest and Abilities lie in perverting, confounding, and eluding them. I observe among you some Lines of an Institution, which in its Original might have been tolerable; but these half erased, and the rest wholly blurred and blotted by Corruptions. It doth not appear from all you have said, how any one Perfection is required towards the Procurement of any one Station among you; much less that Men are ennobled on Account of their Virtue, that Priests are advanced for their Piety or Learning, Soldiers for their Conduct or Valour, Judges for their Integrity, Senators for the Love of their Country, or Counsellors for their Wisdom. As for yourself (continued the King) who have spent the greatest Part of your Life in travelling; I am well disposed to hope you may hitherto have escaped many Vices of your Country. But, by what I have gathered from your own Relation, and the Answers I have with much Pains wringed and extorted from you; I cannot but conclude the Bulk of your Natives, to be the most pernicious Race of little odious Vermin that Nature ever suffered to crawl upon the Surface of the Earth.

1. Write a précis of Swift's satiric proposal for solving the problem of overpopulation in Ireland. Why and how might the use of satire be an effective weapon against existing views and prejudices?
2. Write a shortened modern version of Gulliver's visit to Brobdingnag based upon a discussion of current political practices.

· · ·

VOLTAIRE

Voltaire (1694-1778), the pen name of François-Marie Arouet, was the most famous *philosophe* of the Enlightenment. His works on social customs, history, philosophy, literature, and politics were well-known, and he challenged the rigid societies in France and on the rest of the European continent in an effort to propigate a doctrine of tolerance and social progress. An admirer of the English, Voltaire associated himself with the science of Bacon and Newton, and with the political philosophy of Locke. Living most of his lifetime outside of France, Voltaire was a critic of arbitrary justice and what he deemed to be unfair and archaic institutions. In his satire *Candide* (1759), Voltaire challenged both authority and blind optimism, as he professed a position of reasonable reform.

A *Candide* opens with an introduction to the young Candide and his teacher Pangloss. The latter was modelled after the philosopher Leibniz. To Voltaire, Pangloss represented the foolishness of a scientist of unbounded optimism whose theory did not permit him to see the world as it is.

In the castle of Baron Thunder-ten-tronckh in Westphalia there lived a youth, endowed by Nature with the most gentle character. His face was the expression of his soul. His judgment was quite honest and he was extremely simple-minded; and this was the reason, I think, that he was named Candide. Old servants in the house suspected that he was the son of the Baron's sister and a decent honest gentleman of the neighborhood, whom this young lady would never marry because he could only prove seventy-one quarterings, and the rest of his genealogical tree was lost, owing to the injuries of time. The Baron was one of the most powerful lords in Westphalia, for his castle possessed a door and windows. His Great Hall was even decorated with a piece of tapestry. The dogs in his stable-yards formed a pack of hounds when necessary; his grooms were his huntsmen; the village curate was his Grand Almoner. They all called him "My Lord," and laughed heartily at his stories. The Baroness weighed about three hundred and fifty pounds, was therefore greatly respected, and did the honors of the house with a dignity which rendered her still more respectable. Her daughter Cunegonde, aged seventeen, was rosy-cheeked, fresh, plump and tempting. The Baron's son appeared in every respect worthy of his father. The tutor Pangloss was the oracle of the house, and little Candide followed his lessons with all the candor of his age and character. Pangloss taught metaphysico-theologo-cosmolonigology. (He proved admirably that there is no effect without a cause and that in this best of all possible worlds.) My Lord the Baron's castle was the best of castles and his wife the best of all possible Baronesses. " 'Tis demonstrated," said he, "that things cannot be otherwise; for, since everything is made for an end, everything is necessarily for the best end. Observe that noses were made to wear spectacles; and so we have spectacles. Legs were visibly instituted to be breeched, and we have breeches. Stones were formed to be quarried and to build castles; and My Lord has a very noble castle; the greatest Baron in the province should have the best house; and as pigs were made to be eaten, we eat pork all the year round; consequently, those who have asserted that all is well talk nonsense; they ought to have said that all is for the best." Candide listened attentively and believed innocently; for he thought Mademoiselle Cunegonde extremely beautiful, although he was never bold enough to tell her so. He decided that after the happiness of being born Baron of Thunder-ten-tronckh, the second degree of happiness was to be Mademoiselle Cunegonde; the third, to see her every day; and the fourth to listen to Doctor Pangloss, the greatest philosopher of the province and therefore of the whole world. One day when Cunegonde was walking near the castle, in a little wood which was called The Park, she observed Doctor Pangloss in the bushes, giving a lesson in experimental physics to her mother's waiting-maid, a very pretty and docile brunette. Mademoiselle Cunegonde had a great inclination for science and

Source: Voltaire, *Candide and Other Writings* (New York: The Modern Library, 1956), pp. 110-12, 186-89.

watched breathlessly the reiterated experiments she witnessed; she observed clearly the Doctor's sufficient reason, the effects and the causes, and returned home very much excited, pensive, filled with the desire of learning, reflecting that she might be the sufficient reason of young Candide and that he might be hers. On her way back to the castle she met Candide and blushed; Candide also blushed. She bade him good-morning in a hesitating voice; Candide replied without knowing what he was saying. Next day, when they left the table after dinner, Cunegonde and Candide found themselves behind a screen; Cunegonde dropped her handkerchief, Candide picked it up; she innocently held his hand; the young man innocently kissed the young lady's hand with remarkable vivacity, tenderness and grace; their lips met, their eyes sparkled, their knees trembled, their hands wandered. Baron Thunder-ten-tronckh passed near the screen, and, observing this cause and effect, expelled Candide from the castle by kicking him in the backside frequently and hard. Cunegonde swooned; when she recovered her senses, the Baroness slapped her in the face; and all was in consternation in the noblest and most agreeable of all possible castles. . . .

B Candide went through many hardships and trials, as Voltaire attacked church, state, and other institutions. At the end of the work the simple hero achieved wisdom and was able to instruct his friends, who include Martin, a pessimist, and the ever-optimistic Pangloss.

. . . Martin . . . concluded that man was born to live in the convulsions of distress or in the lethargy of boredom. Candide did not agree, but he asserted nothing. Pangloss confessed that he had always suffered horribly; but, having once maintained that everything was for the best, he had continued to maintain it without believing it.

One thing confirmed Martin in his detestable principles, made Candide hesitate more than ever, and embarrassed Pangloss. And it was this. One day there came to their farm Paquette and Friar Giroflée, who were in the most extreme misery; they had soon wasted their three thousand piastres, had left each other, made up, quarrelled again, been put in prison, escaped, and finally Friar Giroflée had turned Turk. Paquette continued her occupation everywhere and now earned nothing by it. "I foresaw," said Martin to Candide, "that your gifts would soon be wasted and would only make them the more miserable. You and Cacambo were once bloated with millions of piastres and you are no happier than Friar Giroflée and Paquette." "Ah! Ha!" said Pangloss to Paquette, "so Heaven brings you back to us, my dear child? Do you know that you cost me the end of my nose, an eye and an ear! What a plight you are in! Ah! What a world this is!" This new occurrence caused them to philosophize more than ever.

In the neighborhood there lived a very famous Dervish, who was supposed to be the best philosopher in Turkey; they went to consult him; Pangloss was the spokesman and said; "Master, we have come to beg you to tell us why so strange an animal as man was ever created." "What has it to do with you?" said the Dervish. "Is it your business?" "But, reverend father," said Candide, "there is a horrible amount of evil in the world." "What does it matter," said the Dervish, "whether there is evil or good? When his highness sends a ship to Egypt, does he worry about the comfort or discomfort of the rats in the ship?" "Then what should we do?" said Pangloss. "Hold your tongue," said the Dervish. "I flattered myself," said Pangloss, "that I should discuss with you effects and causes, this best of all possible worlds, the origin of evil, the nature of the soul and pre-established harmony." At these words the Dervish slammed the door in their faces.

During this conversation the news went round that at Constantinople two viziers and the mufti had been strangled and several of their friends impaled. This catastrophe made a prodigious noise everywhere for several hours. As Pangloss, Candide and Martin were returning to their little farm, they came upon an old man who was taking the air under a bower of orange trees at his door. Pangloss, who was as curious as he was argumentative, asked him what was the name of the mufti who had just been strangled. "I do not know," replied the old man. "I have never known the name of any mufti or of any vizier. I am entirely ignorant of the occurrence you mention; I presume that in general those who meddle with public affairs sometimes perish miserably and that they deserve it; but I never inquire what is going on in Constantinople; I content myself with sending there for sale the produce of the garden I cultivate." Having spoken thus, he took the strangers into his house. His two daughters and his two sons presented them with several kinds of sherbet which they made themselves, caymac flavored with candied citron peel, oranges, lemons, limes, pineapples, dates, pistachios and Mocha coffee which had not been mixed with the bad coffee of Batavia and the Isles. After which this good Mussulman's two daughters perfumed the beards of Candide, Pangloss and Martin. "You must have a vast and magnificent estate?" said Candide to the Turk. "I have only twenty acres," replied the Turk. "I cultivate them with my children; and work keeps at bay three great evils: boredom, vice and need."

As Candide returned to his farm he reflected deeply on the Turk's remarks. He said to Pangloss and Martin: "That good old man seems to me to have chosen an existence preferable by far to that of the six kings with whom we had the honor to sup." "Exalted rank," said Pangloss, "is very dangerous, according to the testimony of all philosophers; for Eglon, King of the Moabites, was murdered by Ehud; Absalom was hanged by the hair and pierced by three darts; King Nadab, son of Jeroboam, was killed by Baasha; King Elah by Zimri; Ahaziah by Jehu; Athaliah by Jehoiada; the Kings Jehoiakim, Jeconiah and Zedekiah were made slaves. You know in what manner died Croesus, Astyages, Darius, Denys of Syracuse, Pyrrhus, Perseus, Hannibal, Jugurtha, Ariovistus, Caesar, Pompey, Nero, Otho, Vitellius, Domitian, Richard II of England, Edward II, Henry VI, Richard III, Mary Stuart, Charles I, the three Henrys of France, the Emperor Henry IV. You know . . . " "I also know," said Candide, "that we should cultivate our garden." "You are right," said Pangloss, "for, when man was placed in the Garden of Eden, he was placed there *ut operaretur eum,* to dress it and to keep it; which proves that man was not born for idleness." "Let us work without theorizing," said Martin; " 'tis the only way to make life endurable."

The whole small fraternity entered into this praiseworthy plan, and each started to make use of his talents. The little farm yielded well. Cunegonde was indeed very ugly, but she became an excellent pastry-cook; Paquette embroidered; the old woman took care of the linen. Even Friar Giroflée performed some service; he was a very good carpenter and even became a man of honor; and Pangloss sometimes said to Candide: "All events are linked up in this best of all possible worlds; for, if you had not been expelled from the noble castle, by hard kicks in your backside for love of Mademoiselle Cunegonde, if you had not been clapped into the Inquisition, if you had not wandered about America on foot, if you had not stuck your sword in the Baron, if you had not lost all your sheep from the land of Eldorado, you would not be eating candied citrons and pistachios here." "That's well said," replied Candide, "but we must cultivate our garden."

1. Compare the characters of Pangloss and Candide as they appeared in the beginning of the reading with the way they have changed by the end.
2. A lifetime of wandering finally taught Candide that the world's three great evils were boredom, vice, and need. To counter all three he claimed: "we must cultivate our garden." Explain Candide's point of view and apply it to the conquest of life's "three great evils." How might this be regarded as a critique of his own society by Voltaire?

· · ·

ADAM SMITH

Adam Smith's *An Inquiry into the Nature and Causes of the Wealth of Nations* was the most influential work on economics of the Enlightenment. Still viewed as an apostle of economic liberalism, Smith (1723-90) challenged many of the assumptions of the prevailing mercantilist theories. He recognized that a new economic structure was coming into being in the late eighteenth century, and he believed there was a science of wealth, similar to that of the physical world. The economic sphere, Smith believed, had a natural order, and great progress could be achieved by permitting individuals to pursue their own vision of their economic well-being. He claimed the public good would be enhanced through the workings of individual self-interest.

 Smith placed his emphasis on production and believed that the mercantile system had too many restrictive regulations at the center.

> . . . The general industry of the society never can exceed what the capital of the society can employ. As the number of workmen that can be kept in employment by any particular person must bear a certain proportion to his capital, so the number of those that can be continually employed by all the members of a great society, must bear a certain proportion to the whole capital of that society, and never can exceed that proportion. No regulation of commerce can increase the quantity of industry in any society beyond

Source: Adam Smith, *An Inquiry into the Nature and Causes of the Wealth of Nations* (New York: The Modern Library, 1937), pp. 421, 422-24, 625, 626, 650-51.

what its capital can maintain. It can only divert a part of it into a direction into which it might not otherwise have gone; and it is by no means certain that this artificial direction is likely to be more advantageous to the society than that into which it would have gone of its own accord.

Every individual is continually exerting himself to find out the most advantageous employment for whatever capital he can command. It is his own advantage, indeed, and not that of the society, which he has in view. But the study of his own advantage naturally, or rather necessarily leads him to prefer that employment which is most advantageous to the society.

First, every individual endeavours to employ his capital as near home as he can, and consequently as much as he can in the support of domestic industry; provided always that he can thereby obtain the ordinary, or not a great deal less than the ordinary profits of stock. . . .

Secondly, every individual who employs his capital in the support of domestic industry, necessarily endeavours so to direct that industry, that its produce may be of the greatest possible value.

The produce of industry is what it adds to the subject or materials upon which it is employed. In proportion as the value of this produce is great or small, so will likewise be the profits of the employer. But it is only for the sake of profit that any man employs a capital in the support of industry; and he will always, therefore, endeavour to employ it in the support of that industry of which the produce is likely to be of the greatest value, or to exchange for the greatest quantity either of money or of other goods.

But the annual revenue of every society is always precisely equal to the exchangeable value of the whole annual produce of its industry, or rather is precisely the same thing with that exchangeable value. As every individual, therefore, endeavours as much as he can both to employ his capital in the support of domestic industry, and so to direct that industry that its produce may be of the greatest value; every individual necessarily labours to render the annual revenue of the society as great as he can. He generally, indeed, neither intends to promote the public interest, nor knows how much he is promoting it. By preferring the support of domestic to that of foreign industry, he intends only his own security; and by directing that industry in such a manner as its produce may be of the greatest value, he intends only his own gain, and he is in this, as in many other cases, led by an invisible hand to promote an end which was no part of his intention. Nor is it always the worse for the society that it was no part of it. By pursuing his own interest he frequently promotes that of the society more effectually than when he really intends to promote it. I have never known much good done by those who affected to trade for the public good. It is an affectation, indeed, not very common among merchants, and very few words need be employed in dissuading them from it.

What is the species of domestic industry which his capital can employ, and of which the produce is likely to be of the greatest value, every individual, it is evident, can, in his local situation, judge much better than any statesman or lawgiver can do for him. The statesman, who should attempt to direct private people in what manner they ought to employ their capitals, would not only load himself with a most unnecessary attention, but assume an authority which could safely be trusted, not only to no single person, but to no council or senate whatever, and which would nowhere be so dangerous as in the hands of a man who had folly and presumption enough to fancy himself fit to exercise it.

To give the monopoly of the home-market to the produce of domestic industry, in any particular art or manufacture, is in some measure to direct private people in what manner they ought to employ their capitals, and must, in almost all cases, be either a useless or a hurtful regulation. If the produce of domestic can be brought there as cheap as that of foreign industry, the regulation is evidently useless. If it cannot, it must generally be hurtful. It is the maximum of every prudent master of a family, never to attempt to make at home what it will cost him more to make than to buy. The taylor does not attempt to make his own shoes, but buys them of the shoemaker. The shoemaker does not attempt to make his own clothes, but employs a taylor. The farmer attempts to make neither the one nor the other, but employs those different artificers. All of them find it for their interest to employ their whole industry in a way in which they have some advantage over their neighbours, and to purchase with a part of its produce, or what is the same thing, with the price of a part of it, whatever else they have occasion for.

What is prudence in the conduct of every private family, can scarce be folly in that of a great kingdom. . . .

 B Smith wished to increase the consumption of goods.

. . . Consumption is the sole end and purpose of all production; and the interest of the producer ought to be attended to, only so far as it may be necessary for promoting that of the consumer. The maxim is so perfectly self-evident, that it would be absurd to attempt to prove it. But in the mercantile system, the interest of the consumer is almost constantly sacrificed to that of the producer; and it seems to consider production, and not consumption, as the ultimate end and object of all industry and commerce.

In the restraints upon the importation of all foreign commodities which can come into competition with those of our own growth, or manufacture, the interest of the home-consumer is evidently sacrificed to that of the producer. It is altogether for the benefit of the latter, that the former is obliged to pay that enhancement of price which this monopoly almost always occasions.

It is altogether for the benefit of the producer that bounties are granted upon the exportation of some of his productions. The home-consumer is obliged to pay, first, the tax which is necessary for paying the bounty, and secondly, the still greater tax which necessarily arises from the enhancement of the price of the commodity in the home market. . . .

It cannot be very difficult to determine who have been the contrivers of this whole mercantile system; not the consumers, we may believe, whose interest has been entirely neglected; but the producers, whose interest has been so carefully attended to; and among this latter class our merchants and manufacturers have been by far the principal architects. In the mercantile regulations, which have been taken notice of in this chapter, the interest of our manufacturers has been most peculiarly attended to; and the interest, not so much of the consumers, as that of some other sets of producers, has been sacrificed to it.

A political economist, Smith believed that his new system would increase liberty and freedom.

> . . . It is thus that every system which endeavours, either, by extraordinary encouragements, to draw towards a particular species of industry a greater share of the capital of the society than what would naturally go to it; or, by extraordinary restraints, to force from a particular species of industry some share of the capital which would otherwise be employed in it; is in reality subversive of the great purpose which it means to promote. It retards, instead of accelerating, the progress of the society towards real wealth and greatness; and diminishes, instead of increasing, the real value of the annual produce of its land and labour.
>
> All systems either of preference or of restraint, therefore, being thus completely taken away, the obvious and simple system of natural liberty establishes itself of its own accord. Every man, as long as he does not violate the laws of justice, is left perfectly free to pursue his own interest his own way, and to bring both his industry and capital into competition with those of any other man, or order of men. The sovereign is completely discharged from a duty, in the attempting to perform which he must always be exposed to innumerable delusions, and for the proper performance of which no human wisdom or knowledge could ever be sufficient; the duty of superintending the industry of private people, and of directing it towards the employments most suitable to the interest of the society. According to the system of natural liberty, the sovereign has only three duties to attend to; three duties of great importance, indeed, but plain and intelligible to common understandings: first, the duty of protecting the society from the violence and invasion of other independent societies; secondly, the duty of protecting, as far as possible, every member of the society from the injustice or oppression of every other member of it, or the duty of establishing an exact administration of justice; and, thirdly, the duty of erecting and maintaining certain public works and certain public institutions, which it can never be for the interest of any individual, or small number of individuals, to erect and maintain; because the profit could never repay the expence to any individual or small number of individuals, though it may frequently do much more than repay it to a great society. . . .

1. Outline Smith's ideas on the efficient application of capital by any individual.
2. In what way did Smith believe that the investor is led by an "invisible hand" to work for the benefit of society?
3. Create your own analogy to demonstrate the folly in attempting to regulate investment through tariffs.
4. Why did Smith claim that the mercantile system is mistaken in favouring the producer at the expense of the consumer?
5. Who did he claim is responsible for formulating current mercantile policy?
6. Read Smith's description of the only three duties necessary for the sovereign (government) to perform. How would this view compare with the role of government in the economy today?

■ ■ ■

FREDERICK II

Frederick II of Prussia (reigned 1740-86), known as Frederick the Great, was considered by many of his contemporaries as the model of the enlightened monarch. Concerned with the development of his state, Frederick worked hard at being king and introduced many economic and social reforms to increase the wealth and power of Prussia. An intellectual and a musician, Frederick corresponded with *philosophes* and wrote works for the flute. A military leader and diplomat, he conducted wars, made treaties, and could be ruthless in his attempts to enhance the position of Prussia in Europe and the world. His many essays and memoirs testify to his self-reflection and his attempts, as a practitioner of politics and diplomacy, to build a theory of the modern state.

 In 1781 Frederick reflected on the responsibility and authority of the sovereign.

. . . Princes and monarchs, therefore, are not invested with supreme authority that they may, with impunity, riot in debauchery and voluptuousness. They are not raised by their fellow citizens in order that their pride may pompously display itself, and contemptuously insult simplicity of manners, poverty and wretchedness. Government is not intrusted to them that they may be surrounded by a crowd of useless people, whose idleness engenders every vice.

The ill administration of monarchical government originates in various causes, the source of which is the character of the sovereign. Thus a prince addicted to women suffers himself to be governed by his mistresses, and his favorites, who abuse the ascendancy they have over his mind, commit injustice, protect the most vicious, sell places, and are guilty of other similar acts of infamy. . . .

The sovereign is attached by indissoluble ties to the body of the state; hence it follows that he, by repercussion, is sensible of all the ills which afflict his subjects; and the people, in like manner, suffer from the misfortunes which affect their sovereign. There is but one general good, which is that of the state. If the monarch loses his provinces, he is no longer able as formerly to assist his subjects. If misfortune has obliged him to contract debts, they must be liquidated by the poor citizens; and, in return, if the people are not numerous, and if they are oppressed by poverty, the sovereign is destitute of all resource. These are truths so incontestable that there is no need to insist on them further.

I once more repeat, the sovereign represents the state; he and his people form but one body, which can only be happy as far as united by concord. The prince is to the nation he governs what the head is to the man; it is his duty to see, think, and act for the whole community, that he may procure it every advantage of which it is capable. If it be intended that a monarchical

Source: Louis L. Snyder, editor, *Frederick the Great* (Englewood Cliffs, New Jersey: Prentice-Hall, Inc., 1971), pp. 24-25, 26-28, 43, 44-45, 65-66.

should excel a republican government, sentence is pronounced on the sovereign. He must be active, possess integrity, and collect his whole powers, that he may be able to run the career he has commenced. . . .

There is another interesting object which ought not to be lost sight of, and which, if neglected, would be of irreparable prejudice to good morality; which is that princes are liable too highly to notice persons who are possessed of no other merit than that of great wealth. Honors, so undeservedly bestowed, confirm the people in the vulgar prejudice that wealth only, is necessary to gain respect. Interest and cupidity will then break forth from the curb by which they are restrained. Each will wish to accumulate riches; and, to acquire these, the most iniquitous means will be employed. Corruption increases, takes root, and becomes general. Men of abilities and virtue are despised, and the public honor none but the bastards of Midas, who dazzle by their excessive dissipation and their pomp. To prevent national manners from being perverted to an excess so horrible, the prince ought to be incessantly attentive to distinguish nothing but personal merit, and to show his contempt for that opulence which is destitute of morals and virtue.

As the sovereign is properly the head of a family of citizens, the father of his people, he ought on all occasions to be the last refuge of the unfortunate; to be the parent of the orphan, and the husband of the widow; to have as much pity for the lowest wretch as for the greatest courtiers; and to shed his benefactions over those who, deprived of all other aid, can only find succor in his benevolence. . . .

We ought however to add that the prince who should pursue the laborious route which we have indicated would never attain absolute perfection; because, with all possible good will, he might be deceived in the choice of the persons whom he should employ in administration. Incidents might be depicted under false colors; his orders might not be punctually executed; iniquitous acts might be so concealed as never to arrive at his knowledge; and his ministers, rigorous and consequential, might be too severe, too haughty in their exactions. In fine, it is impossible a monarch should be everywhere, in an extensive kingdom. Such therefore is and must be the destiny of earthly affairs, that the degree of perfection which the happiness of the people requires, as far as it depends on government, never can be attained. Therefore, in this as in everything else, we must of necessity remain satisfied, with that which is the least defective. . . .

B ▷ Frederick had a life-long friendship with Voltaire. In 1736 he wrote his first letter to the *philosophe*.

Sir,
Although I have not the satisfaction of knowing you personally, you are nonetheless known to me by your works. They are treasures of the mind, if the expression may be allowed, and compositions elaborated with so much taste, delicacy, and art, that their beauties appear new each time they are reread. I feel I have discovered in them the character of their ingenious author, who does honor to our age and to the human mind. The great men of modern times will one day be obliged to you, and to you alone, if the dispute con-

cerning the ancients and the moderns should again arise; because you will incline the balance to their side. . . .

Your poems possess qualities which render them respectable and worthy of the admiration and study of good men. They are a course of morality whereby we learn to think and to act. Virtue is painted there in its fairest colors. The idea of true glory is there defined; and you insinuate the taste for knowledge in a manner so fine and so delicate that he who has read your works breathes the ambition of following in your steps. How often have I said to myself: "Wretched man! abandon this burden whose weight exceeds your strength; Voltaire cannot be imitated except by Voltaire himself."

At such moments I have realized that the advantages of birth and that vapor of grandeur with which vanity soothes us is of little service or, to speak truly, of none. These distinctions are foreign to ourselves and but embellish outwardly. How much more preferable are the talents of the mind! How much is due to men whom nature has distinguished by the mere fact that she has created them! She takes pleasure in creating some whom she endows with every capacity needed for the progress of the arts and sciences; 'tis for princes to reward their vigils. Ah! may glory only make use of me to crown your successes! I should fear nothing except that this country is so infertile in laurels that it does not furnish as many as your works deserve.

If I am not so favored by my destiny as to take you into my service, at least I may hope one day to see you, whom I have admired so long and from so far, and to assure you by word of mouth that I am, with all the esteem and consideration due to those who, following the torch of truth, devote their labors to the public, Sir, your affectionate friend,

FRÉDÉRIC P.R. OF PRUSSIA

◇C▷ The friendship between Frederick and Voltaire was a stormy one. However, upon the death of Voltaire in 1778 Frederick delivered a speech in his praise to the Academy of Sciences and Belles Lettres in Berlin.

. . . The cause of Voltaire, supported upon solid foundations, prevailed in all those tribunals where reason was preferred to mystical sophistry. Notwithstanding all the persecutions which he suffered from theological hatred, he always distinguished religion from those who dishonored it; he rendered justice to those ecclesiastics, whose virtues were a real ornament to the Church; and blamed only those scandalous hypocrites, whose morals were a public abomination.

M. de Voltaire, then, passed his life amidst the persecution of those who envied, and the applause of those who admired his greatness. While the invectives of the former were unable to humble his mind, the approbation of the latter did not give him too high an opinion of himself. He was satisfied with enlightening the world, and with inspiring, by his writings, the love of learning and humanity. His morality consisted not merely in delivering good precepts, but in setting a good example. His courage assisted the unhappy family of Calas: he pleaded the cause of Syrvens, and plucked them from the barbarous hands of their judges; he would have raised from the dead the chevalier La Bare, had he possessed the power of working miracles. How delightful is it that a philosopher, from the center of his retreat, should exalt his voice, and become the organ of humanity, in order to compel the judges of men to suspend their unjust decrees? This single stroke in the character of Voltaire, is sufficient to entitle him to a place among the small number of the real benefactors of men. Philosophy and religion unite their strength in recommending the cause of virtue.

Who then acted most like a Christian, the magistrate who cruelly banished a family from their country, or the philosopher who protected and received them; the judge who employed the sword of the law to assassinate an idle and unthinking youth, or the sage who wished to save the life of a young man, and to correct his extravagance: the murderer of Calas, or the protector of a forlorn family?

This, gentlemen, will ever render the memory of Voltaire dear to all who are endowed with a feeling heart, or have been born with bowels of compassion. How precious soever may be the qualities of wit, fancy, genius, and knowledge, those presents of which nature is so rarely lavish; they can never be preferred to acts of beneficence and humanity. We admire the first, but we bless and venerate the second. . . .

1. How did Frederick describe the relationship between the sovereign and the people?
2. What is the prince's duty to the state? to the people?
3. Frederick's letter to Voltaire in 1736 is often described as fan mail. What insights does it give us into the character of the future monarch?
4. What two aspects of Voltaire's character did Frederick praise in his speech on hearing of the philosopher's death? Which of these two did he feel to be more important?

• • •

ENCYCLOPÉDIE

The French *Encyclopédie, ou Dictionnaire raisonne des Sciences, des Arts, and des Métiers* was the compendium of knowledge of the age, edited by Denis Diderot (1713-84) and Jean le Rond d'Alembert (1717-83). The twenty-eight volumes were completed in 1772. In spite of censorship, they reflected the Enlightenment values of liberalism, rationalism, skepticism, and toleration. Many of the articles attacked legal and religious abuses of the day and championed modern science and secularism. Enormously successful, the *Encyclopedia* disseminated Enlightenment ideas far and wide.

 The section on "Intolerance," written by Diderot, was a statement defending Enlightenment values.

. . . Civil intolerance consists in breaking off all dealings with those whose opinions on God and his worship differ from ours, and in persecuting them violently in all sorts of ways.

A few lines taken from the Holy Scriptures, the Church fathers, and the decrees of the councils will suffice to show that whoever is intolerant in this . . . sense is an evil man, a bad Christian, a dangerous subject, a poor statesman, and a bad citizen.

Before we begin to treat this subject, however, we must say to the credit of our Catholic theologians that we have found several who agreed unreservedly with the ideas we shall set forth, ideas in which we follow the most respectable authorities. . . .

Teaching, persuasion, and prayer, these are the only legitimate means of spreading the faith.

Whatever means provoke hate, indignation, and scorn, are blasphemous.

Whatever means awaken the passions and foster self-interest are blasphemous.

Whatever means loosen natural bonds and estrange fathers from children, brothers from brothers, sisters from sisters, are blasphemous.

Whatever means would tend to incite men to rebellion, bring the nations under arms, and drench the earth with blood, are blasphemous.

It is blasphemous to coerce our conscience, the universal arbiter of our actions. Conscience must be enlightened, not constrained.

Men who err in good faith are to be pitied, never punished.

Neither men of good faith nor men of bad faith may be tormented; they must be left to the judgment of God.

If we break off dealings with those we call blasphemous, we will also break off with those we call miserly, indecent, ambitious, irascible, or depraved and will advise others to do the same. It will take only three or four intolerant men to tear apart the entire fabric of society.

If we may tear out one hair of anyone whose opinions differ from ours, we could also claim the whole head, for there is no limit to injustice. Our self-interest, our fanaticism, the occasion or the circumstances will then determine how far we will go in doing harm. . . .

B The article "Philosopher" discussed the Enlightenment ideal.

Nothing is easier to acquire today than the name of philosopher. If a man leads an unobtrusive and withdrawn life, gives the appearance of wisdom, and has read a little, that is enough for him to become known as a philosopher and to gain undeserved distinction.

Others, for whom free thought takes the place of reasoning, look on themselves as the only true philosophers because they have dared to overthrow the sacred bounds set down by religion and have broken the fetters that faith placed on their reason. They are proud of having rid themselves of the prejudices concerning religion which their upbringing instilled in them, and they look with disdain on their fellows as being weak men, slavish spirits and pusillanimous souls who let themselves be frightened by the consequences

Source: Denis Diderot, *et al., Encylopedia,* translated by Nelly S. Hoyt and Thomas Cassirer (Indianapolis: The Bobbs-Merrill Company, Inc., 1965), pp. 147-49, 284-89.

of unbelief, who do not dare for an instant to step outside the circle of established truths or follow new paths, and whose minds are dulled by the yoke of superstition.

But there should be a more accurate conception of a philosopher, and here is how we characterize him.

Other men are impelled to act without either feeling or knowing the causes of their actions; they do not think that there might be such causes. The philosopher, on the contrary, discerns these causes to the best of his ability, often even anticipates them and consciously allows himself to be moved by them: he is a clock which, so to speak, sometimes winds itself. Consequently, he avoids subjects that can produce sentiments in him that are contrary to well-being and a reasonable life, and he seeks those subjects that can arouse feelings suited to the condition in which he finds himself. Reason is to a philosopher what grace is to a Christian. Grace impels the Christian to act, reason impels the philosopher.

Other men are carried away by their passions; their actions are not preceded by reflection: they are men who walk in darkness. A philosopher, on the other hand, even in moments of passion, acts only after reflection; he walks through the night, but he is preceded by a torch.

The philosopher forms his principles from an infinity of individual observations. The common people adopt a principle without thinking of the observations that have produced it; they believe that a maxim exists, so to speak, by itself. The philosopher, however, takes a maxim from its source, he examines its origin, he knows its true worth and uses it only where it is suitable.

For the philosopher truth is not a mistress that corrupts his imagination and therefore appears to him everywhere. He is satisfied if he can bring it to light where he catches a glimpse of it. He does not confuse it with verisimilitude: he accepts as true what is true, as false what is false, as doubtful what is doubtful, and as probable what is merely probable. He goes even further: when he does not have any proper basis, he knows how to suspend judgment, and this is the most perfect trait of the philosopher.

The world is full of very intelligent persons who are always judging. In effect, they are always guessing; for we guess when we judge without knowing whether or not we have sound grounds for judgment. Such people do not know the reach of the human mind and think it can know everything. Thus they think it shameful not to arrive at a decision and imagine that intelligence consists in having opinions. The philosopher believes that it consists in judging well: he is more pleased with himself when he is able to withhold conclusions than he would be if he had made up his mind before perceiving the proper grounds for coming to a decision. Therefore he judges and speaks less, but he judges more accurately and speaks better. He does not avoid the brilliant flashes that naturally come to the mind through a sudden and frequently surprising connection of ideas. This sudden connection is what we commonly call wit. Yet the philosopher in no way actively seeks wit. Instead of such brilliance, he prefers to proceed carefully to perceive his ideas clearly, to know accurately their scope and the connections between them, and thus to avoid taking a wrong turn by carrying too far some particular link between them. It is this ability to distinguish which we call *judgment* and *precise thinking*, and this precision is combined with *flexibility* and *clarity*. The philosopher is not so attached to a system as to be unable to understand the strength of the objections that can be raised against it. The majority of men are so strongly committed to their opinions that they do not even take the trouble to inquire into the opinions of others. The philosopher understands the point of view he rejects, as clearly and to the same extent as his own.

The philosophic spirit is thus characterized by observation and precision and relates everything to its true principles. However, the philosopher cultivates not only the mind; his attention and his preoccupations extend further.

Man is not a monster who should live only in the depths of the sea or the farthest reaches of the forest. The very necessities of life make intercourse with others essential for him. In whatever condition he finds himself, his needs and the desire for well-being oblige him to live in society. Reason demands that he know and study the qualities of sociability and endeavor to acquire them.

Our philosopher does not think that he lives in exile in this world; he does not believe himself to be in enemy territory; he wishes to enjoy as a frugal steward the goods that nature offers him; he wishes to find pleasure in the company of others, and to find pleasure he has to give pleasure, so that he seeks to adapt himself to those with whom he lives by chance or by choice. At the same time he finds what suits him: he is an *honnête homme* who wishes to please others and to render himself useful.

Most nobles, whose dissipations do not leave them enough time for reflection, are without indulgence toward those whom they do not consider their equals. The common run of philosophers who reflect too much, or rather reflect badly, behave in the same manner toward everyone: they flee men, and men avoid them. But our philosopher, who knows how to divide his time between solitude and social intercourse, is full of humanity. He is like the Chremes of Terence who feels that he is human and that humanity itself impels him to take an interest in the good or bad fortune of his neighbor. *Homo sum, humani a me nihil alienum puto.*

There is no need to point out here how scrupulous the philospher is in all matters of honor and probity. One might say that he looks on civil society as a divinity on earth: he offers it incense and honors it with probity, with a painstaking devotion to his duties and a sincere desire not to be a useless or troublesome member of society. Feelings of probity are as much part of the make-up of a philosopher as an enlightened mind. The more reason you find in a man, the more probity you will find in him. In contrast, wherever fanaticism and superstition reign, uncontrolled passions reign too. The temperament of the philosopher is to act out of a feeling for order or according to reason. Because he loves society profoundly, he is concerned, far more than other men, with directing all his efforts toward achieving the ideal of the *honnête homme*. Do not fear that he will engage in acts contrary to probity, when no eyes are watching him. No! Such an action is not in accord with the make-up of the wise man: one might say that he is kneaded with the leaven of rule and order, that he is filled with concern for the good of civil society and that he knows its principles far better than other men. Crime would find too much resistance in him, it would have to destroy too many natural and acquired ideas. His capacity for action resembles, so to speak, the string of a musical instrument that is tuned for a certain tone and could not produce its opposite. He is afraid to fall out of tune with himself, and this reminds me of Velleius' description of Cato of Utica: "He has never done good deeds in order to show that he has done them, but only because it was not in him to do otherwise."

Moreover, in all their actions men seek only their own immediate satisfaction: they are impelled to act by the good, or rather by their present inclination that depends on the elements that constitute their make-up at the moment. Now the philosopher more than anyone else is disposed by his reflections to find a greater attraction and pleasure in living with you, in gaining your trust and esteem, and in fulfilling the duties imposed by friendship and gratitude. These feelings are also nourished in his heart by religion to which he has been brought by the natural light of his reason. To put it another way, wickedness is just as incompatible with the idea of a philosopher as is stupidity, and experience shows us every day that the more rational and enlightened a man is, the more reliable he is and suited to life in society. A fool, said La Rochefoucauld, does not have what it takes to be good. We sin only because the light of our reason is not as strong as our passions, and there is a certain truth in the theological maxim that all sinners are ignorant.

This love of society which is so essential in the philosopher proves the truth of the remark made by the Emperor Antoninus: "How happy the peoples will be when kings will be philosophers, or philosophers kings!"

The philosopher is thus an *honnête homme* who follows reason in all his actions and who combines a reflective and precise mind with the manners and qualities of a sociable man. Graft a prince onto a philosopher of this stamp and you will have a perfect sovereign.

From this it is easy to conclude how far removed the impassive sage of the Stoics is from our philosopher: the philosopher is a man while their sage was only a phantom. They were ashamed of their humanity, he takes pride in his. Their foolish desire was to destroy the passions and raise us above our nature by means of an illusory impassivity; whereas he does not reach out for the illusory honor of destroying the passions, because that is impossible, rather he strives not to be tyrannized by them, to use them to good advantage and reasonably, because that is possible and because reason commands him to do it.

One can see moreover, by all that we have said, how far from being true philosophers are those indolent men who give themselves over to idle meditation and neglect their temporal affairs and everything that we know as *fortune*. The true philosopher is not tormented by ambition; he merely desires the comforts of life. He needs, over and above the bare necessities, the modest superfluity which is a necessity for an *honnête homme* and which alone brings happiness, for it is the foundation of all properties and amenities. Only counterfeit philosophers, with their dazzling maxims, have propagated the false notion that the barest necessities suffice for a philosopher, and they have done so to justify their own indolence.

1. Compare Diderot's lecture on intolerance with the address Frederick the Great gave in honour of Voltaire.
2. Outline, in your own words, the characteristics of the "philosopher" as described in the *Encyclopédie*.

∎ ∎ ∎

CLASSICISM IN ART

The artistic style favoured in the latter part of the Enlightenment was neo-classicism, a belief in looking to the most respected ancients as models for artistic endeavour. Classical themes were pursued as allegories for modern life; the ancient world was seen as a kind of perfect age, which the eighteenth century should strive to reach and, if possible, surpass; style should be taken from works of ancient art, which served as examples. Two of the major art critics of the time were Johann Joachim Winckelmann (1717-68), a German art historian and archaeologist, and Sir Joshua Reynolds (1723-92), an English portrait painter and the first president of the British Royal Academy, which was founded in 1768.

 Winckelmann wrote his *On the Imitation of the Painting and Sculpture of the Greeks* in 1755.

> To the Greek climate we owe the production of taste, and from thence it spread at length over all the politer world. Every invention, communicated for foreigners to that nation, was but the seed of what it became afterwards, changing both its nature and size in a country, chosen, as Plato says, by Minerva, to be inhabited by the Greeks, as productive of every kind of genius.
>
> But this taste was not only original among the Greeks, but seemed also quite peculiar to their country: it seldom went abroad without loss, and was long ere it imparted its kind influences to more distant climes. It was, doubtless, a stranger to the northern zones, when painting and sculpture, those offsprings of Greece, were despised there to such a degree, that the most valuable pieces of Correggio served only for blinds to the windows of the royal stables at Stockholm.
>
> There is but one way for the moderns to become great, and perhaps unequalled; I mean, by imitating the ancients. . . .
>
> It is not only nature which the votaries of the Greeks find in their works, but still more, something superior to nature; ideal beauties, brain-born images, as Proclus says.
>
> The most beautiful body of ours would perhaps be as much inferior to the most beautiful Greek one, . . . The forms of the Greeks, prepared to beauty, by the influence of the mildest and purest sky, became perfectly elegant by their early exercises. . . .
>
> By these exercises the bodies of the Greeks got the great and manly contour observed in their statues, without any bloated corpulency. The young Spartans were bound to appear every tenth day naked before the ephors, who, when they perceived any inclinable to fatness, ordered them a scantier diet; nay,

Sources: David Irwin, editor, *Winckelmann: Writings on Art* (London: Phaidon Press Limited, 1972), pp. 61, 62-64, 65-66, 67-68; Helen Zimmern, editor, *Sir Joshua Reynolds' Discourses* (London: Walter Scott, 1887), pp. 4-5, 10-12, 13-14.

it was one of Pythagoras's precepts, to beware of growing too corpulent; and, perhaps for the same reason, youths aspiring to wrestling-games were, in the remoter ages of Greece, during their trial, confined to a milk diet.

They were particularly cautious in avoiding every deforming custom; and Alcibiades, when a boy, refusing to learn to play on the flute, for fear of its discomposing his features, was followed by all the youths of Athens.

In their dress they were professed followers of nature. No modern stiffening habit, no squeezing stays hindered nature from forming easy beauty; the fair knew no anxiety about their attire. . . .

And must we not then, considering every advantage which nature bestows, or art teaches, for forming, preserving, and improving beauty, enjoyed and applied by the Greeks; must we not then confess, there is the strongest probability that the beauty of their persons excelled all we can have an idea of?

Art claims liberty: in vain would nature produce her noblest offsprings, in a country where rigid laws would choke her progressive growth, as in Egypt, that pretended parent of sciences and arts: but in Greece, where, from their earliest youth, the happy inhabitants were devoted to mirth and pleasure, where narrow-spirited formality never restrained the liberty of manners, the artist enjoyed nature without a veil. . . .

We observe, nevertheless, that the Greek artists in general, submitted to the law prescribed by the Thebans: 'To do, under a penalty, their best in imitating nature.' For, where they could not possibly apply their easy profile, without endangering the resemblance, they followed nature, . . .

But to form a 'just resemblance, and, at the same time, a handsomer one', being always the chief rule they observed, and which Polygnotus constantly went by; they must, of necessity, be supposed to have had in view a more beauteous and more perfect nature. And when we are told, that some artists imitated Praxiteles, who took his concubine Cratina for the model of his Cnidian *Venus;* it is to be understood that they did so, without neglecting these great laws of the art. Sensual beauty furnished the painter with all that nature could give; ideal beauty with the awful and sublime; from that he took the Human, from this the Divine.

Let any one, sagacious enough to pierce into the depths of art, compare the whole system of the Greek figures with that of the moderns, by which, as they say, nature alone is imitated; good heaven! what a number of neglected beauties will he not discover! . . .

Building on this ground, his hand and senses directed by the Greek rule of beauty, the modern artist goes on the surest way to the imitation of nature. The ideas of unity and perfection, which he acquired in meditating on antiquity, will help him to combine, and to ennoble the more scattered and weaker beauties of our nature. Thus he will improve every beauty he discovers in it, and by comparing the beauties of nature with the ideal, form rules for himself.

Then, and not sooner, he, particularly the painter, may be allowed to commit himself to nature, especially in cases where his art is beyond the instruction of the old marbles, to wit, in drapery; then, like Poussin, he may proceed with more liberty. Minds favoured by nature have here a plain way to become originals. . . .

B Reynolds was President of the Royal Academy for many years. He delivered fifteen discourses from 1769 to 1790, which, with one exception, were given on the occasion of the distribution of prizes to students. The lectures constituted the official statement on style and taste of the day. The following selection is taken from the first and second discourses, both delivered in 1769.

. . . One advantage, I will venture to affirm, we shall have in our Academy, which no other nation can boast. We shall have nothing to unlearn. To this praise the present race of Artists have a just claim. As far as they have yet proceeded, they are right. With us the exertions of genius will henceforward be directed to their proper objects. It will not be as it has been in other schools, where he that travelled fastest only wandered farthest from the right way.

Impressed, as I am, therefore, with such a favourable opinion of my associates, in this undertaking, it would ill become me to dictate to any of them. But as these Institutions have so often failed in other nations; and as it is natural to think with regret how much might have been done, I must take leave to offer a few hints, by which those errors may be rectified, and those defects supplied. These the Professors and Visitors may reject or adopt as they shall think proper.

I would chiefly recommend that an implicit obedience to the *Rules of Art*, as established by the practice of the great MASTERS, should be exacted from the *young* Students. That those models, which have passed through the approbation of ages, should be considered by them as perfect and infallible guides; as subjects for their imitation, not their criticism.

I am confident that this is the only efficacious method of making a progress in the Arts; and that he who sets out with doubting, will find life finished before he becomes master of the rudiments. For it may be laid down as a maxim, that he who begins by presuming on his own sense, has ended his studies as soon as he has commenced them. Every opportunity, therefore, should be taken to discountenance that false and vulgar opinion, that rules are the fetters of genius: they are fetters only to men of no genius; as that armour, which upon the strong is an ornament and a defence, upon the weak and misshapen becomes a load, and cripples the body which it was made to protect.

How much liberty may be taken to break through those rules, and, as the poet expresses it,

> "To snatch a grace beyond the reach of art,"

may be a subsequent consideration, when the pupils become masters themselves. It is then, when their genius has received its utmost improvement, that rules may possibly be dispensed with. But let us not destroy the scaffold until we have raised the building. . . .

In speaking to you of the Theory of the Art, I shall only consider it as it has a relation to the *method* of your studies.

Dividing the study of painting into three distinct periods, I shall address you as having passed through the first of them, which is confined to the rudiments; including a facility of drawing any object that presents itself, a tolerable readiness in the management of colours, and an acquaintance with the most simple and obvious rules of composition.

This first degree of proficiency is, in painting, what grammar is in literature, a general preparation for whatever species of the art the student may afterwards choose for his more particular application. The power of drawing, modelling, and using colours is very properly called the Language of the Art; and in this language, the honours you have just received prove you to have made no inconsiderable progress.

When the Artist is once enabled to express himself with some degree of correctness, he must then endeavour to collect subjects for expression; to amass a stock of ideas, to be combined and varied as occasion may require. He is now in the second period of study, in which his business is to learn all that has been known and done before his own time. Having hitherto received instructions from a particular master, he is now to consider the Art itself as his master. He must extend his capacity to more sublime and general instructions. Those perfections which lie scattered among various masters are now united in one general idea, which is henceforth to regulate his taste, and enlarge his imagination. With a variety of models thus before him, he will avoid that narrowness and poverty of conception which attends a bigoted admiration of a single master, and will cease to follow any favourite where he ceases to excel. This period is, however, still a time of subjection and discipline. Though the Student will not resign himself blindly to any single authority, when he may have the advantage of consulting many, he must still be afraid of trusting his own judgment, and of deviating into any track where he cannot find the footsteps of some former master.

The third and last period emancipates the Student from subjection to any authority, but what he shall himself judge to be supported by reason. Confiding now in his own judgment, he will consider and separate those different principles to which different modes of beauty owe their original. In the former period he sought only to know and combine excellence, wherever it was to be found, into one idea of perfection: in this he learns, what requires the most attentive survey, and the most subtle disquisition, to discriminate perfections that are incompatible with each other. . . .

A Student unacquainted with the attempts of former adventurers is always apt to overrate his own abilities; to mistake the most trifling excursions for discoveries of moment, and every coast new to him for a new-found country. If by chance he passes beyond his usual limits, he congratulates his own arrival at those regions which they who have steered a better course have long left behind them.

The productions of such minds are seldom distinguished by an air of originality: they are anticipated in their happiest efforts; and if they are found to differ in any thing from their predecessors, it is only in irregular sallies and trifling conceits. The more extensive, therefore, your acquaintance is with the works of those who have excelled, the more extensive will be your powers of invention; and what may appear still more like a paradox, the more original will be your conceptions. But the difficulty on this occasion is to determine what ought to be proposed as models of excellence, and who ought to be considered as the properest guides.

To a young man just arrived in Italy, many of the present painters of that country are ready enough to obtrude their precepts, and to offer their own performances as examples of that perfection which they affect to recommend.

The modern, however, who recommends himself as a standard, may justly be suspected as ignorant of the true end, and unacquainted with the proper object, of the art which he professes. To follow such a guide will not only retard the Student, but mislead him.

On whom, then, can he rely, or who shall show him the path that leads to excellence? The answer is obvious: those great masters who have travelled the same road with success are the most likely to conduct others. The works of those who have stood the test of ages have a claim to that respect and veneration to which no modern can pretend. The duration and stability of their fame is sufficient to evince that it has not been suspended upon the slender thread of fashion and caprice, but bound to the human heart by every tie of sympathetic approbation.

There is no danger of studying too much the works of those great men. . . .

1. What advantages did Winckelmann feel ancient Greeks brought to their creation of art?
2. What advice does Winckelmann give to "modern" artists?
3. Why, according to Reynolds, must a student adhere to the Rules of Art?
4. Describe the three degrees of proficiency through which any artist must travel in his study.
5. Compare Reynold's concluding thoughts with those of Winckelmann.

2

THE ERA
OF THE FRENCH
REVOLUTION,
1789-1815

T|he last years of the eighteenth century and the first decade and one-half of the nineteenth century witnessed unprecedented social and political transformations, begun by the French Revolution of 1789. It seemed as if the Enlightenment values of equality, rights, and secularism were being tested in all of the West, as class systems were challenged, new constitutions were written, and those who wielded the new political power and authority often abandoned custom for a more creative style of governing. While Europe was at war through most of this period, people in the West began to question their old ties and identities. Many were attracted both to the idea of equal rights and to their nation.

A change in the legitimacy of authority was central to the new social and political movements. All classes in France, in the *cahiers* written just prior to its Revolution, asked about the appropriate relationship between ruler and ruled. Jefferson in America and Sieyès in France stressed the need to abandon the old regime and to establish a new polity. Those who did rebel—in the American colonies and in France—justified their behaviour in documents which dealt with fundamental natural and civil rights. Conservatives, led by Burke, challenged some of the new developments in the name of tradition and inherited wisdom. Liberals, including Paine, argued that rights and democratic institutions were now central to the development of society and the human personality. The figure of Napoleon dominated the early nineteenth century, a new style monarch. For some, he became a political hero; for others, he represented the most dangerous challenge to the traditional culture and organization of the West.

The idea of implementing what was then known as "the rights of man" led Wollstonecraft to write the first major book supporting the rights of women, asking for new attitudes towards females as well as a new type of educational system. The belief in progress was highlighted by Condorcet, whose optimism resulted in a work that predicted a future of indefinite perfection. Using history as his guide, and supporting the universal standard of judgment of the Enlightenment, Condorcet attempted to document and prove a linear historical development.

In art, David was by far the major figure in France. His career and pronouncements raised profound questions about the role of the artist in society and the relationship of the creative artist to the state. Blake, on the other hand, abandoned rationalism for a more mystical and imaginative understanding of human beings and their world, and he challenged what he believed to be the limitations of the neo-classical style and the rules of the artistic establishment.

The ferment of the era of the French Revolution was reflected in strong statements about human nature, values, the relationship of individuals to their community, and the role of the past in shaping the future.

▪ ◈ ▪

RIGHTS AND REVOLUTION

In the late eighteenth century rights and revolution became major concerns as the American and the French revolutions led to a reconsideration of the nature of government, the sources of authority, and the basis of sovereignty. Influenced especially by Locke and Rousseau, revolutionaries in the West sought to justify both their challenge to the old authority and the establishment of a new policy. Major documents included the Declaration of Independence of the American people, the United States Constitution, and the French Declaration of the Rights of Man and of the Citizen.

A) On July 4, 1776, the Second Continental Congress in Philadelphia adopted the Declaration of Independence, justifying the right of revolution in general and giving the reasons why Americans believed they had a right to rebel at that time.

> When, in the course of human events, it becomes necessary for one people to dissolve the political bands which have connected them with another, and to assume, among the powers of the earth, the separate and equal station to which the laws of nature and of nature's God entitle them, a decent respect to the opinions of mankind requires that they should declare the causes which impel them to the separation.
>
> We hold these truths to be self-evident: That all men are created equal; that they are endowed by their Creator with certain unalienable rights; that among these are life, liberty, and the pursuit of happiness; that, to secure these rights, governments are instituted among men, deriving their just powers from the consent of the governed; that whenever any form of government becomes destructive of these ends, it is the right of the people to alter or to abolish it, and to institute new government, laying its foundation on such principles, and organizing its powers in such form, as to them shall seem most likely to effect their safety and happiness. Prudence, indeed, will dictate that governments long established should not be changed for light and transient causes; and accordingly all experience hath shown that mankind are more disposed to suffer, while evils are sufferable, than to right themselves by abolishing the forms to which they are accustomed. But when a long train of abuses and usurpations, pursuing invariably the same object, evinces a design to reduce them under absolute despotism, it is their right, it is their duty, to throw off such government, and to provide new guards for their future security. Such has been the patient sufferance of these colonies; and such is now the necessity which constrains them to alter their former systems of government. The history of the present King of Great Britain is a history of repeated injuries and usurpations, all having in direct object the establishment of an absolute tyranny over these states. To prove this, let facts be submitted to a candid world.

Sources: Bernard Bailyn, *et al.*, *The Great Republic: A History of the American People*, third edition (Lexington, Massachusetts: D. C. Heath and Company, 1985), appendix, pp. v-vi, xvi-xvii; John Hall Stewart, *A Documentary Survey of the French Revolution* (New York: The Macmillan Company, 1951), pp. 113-15.

He has refused his assent to laws, the most wholesome and necessary for the public good.

He has forbidden his governors to pass laws of immediate and pressing importance, unless suspended in their operation till his assent should be obtained; and, when so suspended, he has utterly neglected to attend to them.

He has refused to pass other laws for the accommodation of large districts of people, unless those people would relinquish the right of representation in the legislature, a right inestimable to them, and formidable to tyrants only.

He has called together legislative bodies at places unusual, uncomfortable, and distant from the depository of their public records, for the sole purpose of fatiguing them into compliance with his measures.

He has dissolved representative houses repeatedly, for opposing, with manly firmness, his invasions on the rights of the people.

He has refused for a long time, after such dissolutions, to cause others to be elected; whereby the legislative powers, incapable of annihilation, have returned to the people at large for their exercise; the state remaining, in the mean time, exposed to all the dangers of invasions from without and convulsions within.

He has endeavored to prevent the population of these states; for that purpose obstructing the laws for naturalization of foreigners; refusing to pass others to encourage their migration hither, and raising the conditions of new appropriations of lands.

He has obstructed the administration of justice, by refusing his assent to laws for establishing judiciary powers.

He has made judges dependent on his will alone, for the tenure of their offices, and the amount and payment of their salaries.

He has erected a multitude of new offices, and sent hither swarms of officers to harass our people and eat out their substance.

He has kept among us, in times of peace, standing armies, without the consent of our legislatures.

He has affected to render the military independent of, and superior to, the civil power.

He has combined with others to subject us to a jurisdiction foreign to our constitution, and unacknowledged by our laws, giving his assent to their acts of pretended legislation:

For quartering large bodies of armed troops among us;

For protecting them, by a mock trial, from punishment for any murders which they should commit on the inhabitants of these states;

For cutting off our trade with all parts of the world;

For imposing taxes on us without our consent;

For depriving us, in many cases, of the benefits of trial by jury;

For transporting us beyond seas, to be tried for pretended offenses;

For abolishing the free system of English laws in a neighboring province, establishing therein an arbitrary government, and enlarging its boundaries, so as to render it at once an example and fit instrument for introducing the same absolute rule into these colonies;

For taking away our charters, abolishing our most valuable laws, and altering fundamentally the forms of our governments;

For suspending our own legislatures, and declaring themselves invested with power to legislate for us in all cases whatsoever.

He has abdicated government here, by declaring us out of his protection and waging war against us.

He has plundered our seas, ravaged our coasts, burned our towns, and destroyed the lives of our people.

He is at this time transporting large armies of foreign mercenaries to complete the works of death, desolation, and tyranny already begun with circumstances of cruelty and perfidy scarcely paralleled in the most barbarous ages, and totally unworthy the head of a civilized nation.

He has constrained our fellow-citizens, taken captive on the high seas, to bear arms against their country, to become the executioners of their friends and brethren, or to fall themselves by their hands.

He has excited domestic insurrection among us, and has endeavored to bring on the inhabitants of our frontiers the merciless Indian savages, whose known rule of warfare is an undistinguished destruction of all ages, sexes, and conditions.

In every stage of these oppressions we have petitioned for redress in the most humble terms; our repeated petitions have been answered only by repeated injury. A prince, whose character is thus marked by every act which may define a tyrant, is unfit to be the ruler of a free people.

Nor have we been wanting in our attentions to our British brethren. We have warned them, from time to time, of attempts by their legislature to extend an unwarrantable jurisdiction over us. We have reminded them of the circumstances of our emigration and settlement here. We have appealed to their native justice and magnanimity; and we have conjured them, by the ties of our common kindred, to disavow these usurpations, which would inevitably interrupt our connections and correspondence. They, too, have been deaf to the voice of justice and of consanguinity. We must, therefore, acquiesce in the necessity which denounces our separation, and hold them, as we hold the rest of mankind, enemies in war, in peace friends.

We, therefore, the representatives of the United States of America, in General Congress assembled, appealing to the Supreme Judge of the world for the rectitude of our intentions, do, in the name and by the authority of the good people of these colonies, solemnly publish and declare, that these United Colonies are, and of right ought to be, FREE AND INDEPENDENT STATES; that they are absolved from all allegiance to the British crown, and that all political connection between them and the state of Great Britain is, and ought to be, totally dissolved; and that, as free and independent states, they have full power to levy war, conclude peace, contract alliances, establish commerce, and do all other acts and things which independent states may of right do. And for the support of this declaration, with a firm reliance on the protection of Divine Providence, we mutually pledge to each other our lives, our fortunes, and our sacred honor.

JOHN HANCOCK [*President*]
[*and fifty-five others*]

Successful in war, the Americans adopted a Constitution in 1788. The first ten amendments to the Constitution, known as the Bill of Rights, were discussed by Congress in 1789, and officially adopted in 1791.

ARTICLE I

Congress shall make no law respecting an establishment of religion, or prohibiting the free exercise thereof; or abridging the freedom of speech, or of the press; or of the right of the people peaceably to assemble, and to petition the government for a redress of grievances.

ARTICLE II

A well-regulated militia being necessary to the security of a free State, the right of the people to keep and bear arms shall not be infringed.

ARTICLE III

No soldier shall, in time of peace, be quartered in any house without the consent of the owner, nor in time of war, but in a manner to be prescribed by law.

ARTICLE IV

The right of the people to be secure in their persons, houses, papers, and effects, against unreasonable searches and seizures, shall not be violated, and no warrants shall issue but upon probable cause, supported by oath or affirmation, and particularly describing the place to be searched, and the persons or things to be seized.

ARTICLE V

No person shall be held to answer for a capital, or otherwise infamous crime, unless on a presentment or indictment of a grand jury, except in cases arising in the land or naval forces, or in the militia, when in actual service in time of war or public danger; nor shall any person be subject for the same offense to be twice put in jeopardy of life or limb; nor shall be compelled in any criminal case to be a witness against himself, nor be deprived of life, liberty, or property, without due process of law; nor shall private property be taken for public use without just compensation.

ARTICLE VI

In all criminal prosecutions, the accused shall enjoy the right to a speedy and public trial, by an impartial jury of the State and district wherein the crime shall have been committed, which district shall have been previously ascertained by law, and to be informed of the nature and cause of the accusation; to be confronted with the witnesses against him; to have compulsory process for obtaining witnesses in his favor, and to have the assistance of counsel for his defense.

ARTICLE VII

In suits at common law, where the value in controversy shall exceed twenty dollars, the right of trial by jury shall be preserved, and no fact tried by a jury shall be otherwise reexamined in any court of the United States, than according to the rules of the common law.

ARTICLE VIII

Excessive bail shall not be required, nor excessive fines imposed, nor cruel and unusual punishments inflicted.

ARTICLE IX

The enumeration in the Constitution, of certain rights, shall not be construed to deny or disparage others retained by the people.

ARTICLE X

The powers not delegated to the United States by the Constitution, nor prohibited by it to the States, are reserved to the States respectively, or to the people. . . .

◇C The French National Assembly adopted the Declaration of the Rights of Man and of the Citizen on August 27, 1789. This document, an important and influential statement on rights, was the product of the first constitutional debates in the National Assembly.

The representatives of the French people, organized in National Assembly, considering that ignorance, forgetfulness, or contempt of the rights of man are the sole causes of public misfortunes and of the corruption of governments, have resolved to set forth in a solemn declaration the natural, inalienable, and sacred rights of man, in order that such declaration, continually before all members of the social body, may be a perpetual reminder of their rights and duties; in order that the acts of the legislative power and those of the executive power may constantly be compared with the aim of every political institution and may accordingly be more respected; in order that the demands of the citizens, founded henceforth upon simple and incontestable principles, may always be directed towards the maintenance of the Constitution and the welfare of all.

Accordingly, the National Assembly recognizes and proclaims, in the presence and under the auspices of the Supreme Being, the following rights of man and citizen.

1. Men are born and remain free and equal in rights; social distinctions may be based only upon general usefulness.
2. The aim of every political association is the preservation of the natural and inalienable rights of man; these rights are liberty, property, security, and resistance to oppression.
3. The source of all sovereignty resides essentially in the nation; no group, no individual may exercise authority not emanating expressly therefrom.
4. Liberty consists of the power to do whatever is not injurious to others; thus the enjoyment of the natural rights of every man has for its limits only those that assure other members of society the enjoyment of those same rights; such limits may be determined only by law.
5. The law has the right to forbid only actions which are injurious to society. Whatever is not forbidden by law may not be prevented, and no one may be constrained to do what it does not prescribe.
6. Law is the expression of the general will; all citizens have the right to concur personally, or through their representatives, in its formation; it

must be the same for all, whether it protects or punishes. All citizens, being equal before it, are equally admissible to all public offices, positions, and employments, according to their capacity, and without other distinction than that of virtues and talents.

7. No man may be accused, arrested, or detained except in the cases determined by law, and according to the forms prescribed thereby. Whoever solicit, expedite, or execute arbitrary orders, or have them executed, must be punished; but every citizen summoned or apprehended in pursuance of the law must obey immediately; he renders himself culpable by resistance.

8. The law is to establish only penalties that are absolutely and obviously necessary; and no one may be punished except by virtue of a law established and promulgated prior to the offence and legally applied.

9. Since every man is presumed innocent until declared guilty, if arrest be deemed indispensable, all unnecessary severity for securing the person of the accused must be severely repressed by law.

10. No one is to be disquieted because of his opinions, even religious, provided their manifestation does not disturb the public order established by law.

11. Free communication of ideas and opinions is one of the most precious of the rights of man. Consequently, every citizen may speak, write, and print freely, subject to responsibility for the abuse of such liberty in the cases determined by law.

12. The guarantee of the rights of man and citizen necessitates a public force; such a force, therefore, is instituted for the advantage of all and not for the particular benefit of those to whom it is entrusted.

13. For the maintenance of the public force and for the expenses of administration a common tax is indispensable; it must be assessed equally on all citizens in proportion to their means.

14. Citizens have the right to ascertain, by themselves or through their representatives, the necessity of the public tax, to consent to it freely, to supervise its use, and to determine its quota, assessment, payment, and duration.

15. Society has the right to require of every public agent an accounting of his administration.

16. Every society in which the guarantee of rights is not assured or the separation of powers not determined has no constitution at all.

17. Since property is a sacred and inviolable right, no one may be deprived thereof unless a legally established public necessity obviously requires it, and upon condition of a just and previous indemnity.

1. The Declaration of Independence can be seen as three documents in one. First it is a statement of political philosophy, next a catalogue of grievances, and finally it proclaims the act of independence.
Read carefully through each section of the Declaration and then account for its lasting impact, not only on Americans, but also on other revolutionary groups and activists.

2. The American Revolution has been described as the ''first great victory for the ideas of the Enlightenment.''

Defend this statement with reference to the apparent impact of the ideas of the Enlightenment on the authors of the Declaration of Independence.

3. "Without the Bill of Rights there would be no United States of America." Comment on the view that the Bill of Rights gave the new American Republic its direction and purpose.

4. To what extent is the Declaration of the Rights of Man and of the Citizen a combination of the previous two documents examined in this section?

5. Some critics dismiss the French Declaration for its failure to deal with economic concerns. They call it a document favouring the interests of the bourgeoisie or middle class. What are the implications of this criticism for the future course of the French Revolution?

■ ■ ■

CAHIERS

The *cahiers de doléances*, lists of grievances which preceded the French Revolution of 1789, constitute an important source regarding the ideologies which guided the various groups involved in the revolution. *Cahiers* were drawn up locally and then usually subject to the review of a higher body which chose the representatives to the Estates General. Each estate—the clergy, the nobility, and the third—produced many *cahiers*, which discussed local issues in addition to making general statements on reform, sovereignty, and rights.

The area of Dourdan is in the middle of France. The *cahier* of its clergy was conservative in tone and substance, though it too asked for certain reforms.

> RELIGION
> 1. To preserve in its integrity the precious depository of the Catholic, Apostolic, and Roman religion, the most stable support of the fundamental laws of the State, to effect the enforcement of ordinances concerning the respect which is due churches, sanctification of feast days and Sundays, and, in general, whatever affects public worship. . . .
> 5. Imbued with profound grief at the sight of the appalling deterioration of religion and the depravation of morals in the kingdom, we direct to His Majesty the most ardent and humble representations concerning the disastrous and widely acknowledged cause of this deplorable subversion of all principles. It obviously derives from the disgraceful excess of writings in which the spirit of libertinage, incredulity, and independence prevails, in which faith, modesty, reason, the throne, and the altar are attacked with equal audacity—impious and corrupting books circulated on all sides

Source: John Hall Stewart, *A Documentary Survey of the French Revolution* (New York: The Macmillan Company, 1951), pp. 57, 58, 59, 61-62, 64-67, 69, 70, 73, 75, 76-77, 78, 79-80, 83-84.

with the most revolting profusion and licence, to which the strongest resistance could not be too promptly opposed.

6. Since diversity of religious opinions in the schools for French youth is the greatest danger in the world, His Majesty shall be humbly supplicated also to order all necessary precautions lest there be admitted into any of the universities and academic societies of the kingdom any teacher or member who has not previously given proofs of the greatest ability and of his respectful devotion to the Catholic religion. . . .

CONSTITUTION

1. Since monarchical government is the steadfast constitution of the nation, the most conducive to its internal tranquillity and external security, the most suitable for the extent of its provinces, and the most consistent with the character of its people, who always have distinguished themselves by their love for and devotion to their sovereigns, we will never countenance anything that would tend to alter this form of government. We are inviolably attached to it by the most sacred duties of obedience, by ties of oath and fidelity, by love and respect for our masters, and by the happiness of being subject thereto.

2. We desire that in matters brought under deliberation in the Estates General relative to all orders, voting be by head; but in those concerning more especially one of the three orders, we request that voting be by order. . . .

CIVIL ADMINISTRATION

1. Disposed to second the wishes of the nation, we are inclined zealously to share with all citizens the burden of taxation which we agree to pay as they do, reserving our estates, titles, and honorary rights.

2. The nation shall be supplicated most humbly to assume the present debt of the clergy and, since it was contracted for the service of the State, to consolidate it as a national debt.

3. The King having restored to the nation its former right to vote its own subsidies, a right which the clergy alone had preserved, the general assembly, at its very first meeting, shall decree the continuation of existing taxes until the end of its session, and shall rule definitively on that important matter before its adjournment.

4. His Majesty will be willing to make, in all branches of expenditure, whatever retrenchments his sense of economy and the needs of his people dictate. One part of the taxation should be designated for necessary expenditures, the remainder applied to the payment of interest and liquidation of the national debt.

5. Since every public loan implies a tax, because it must have security, and since the tax must be voted by the nation, every loan would be irregular if not authorized by the national assembly.

6. We request that the provincial assemblies or estates, if they are established, by charged with assessing, equalizing, and collecting the taxes; that such taxes be used, as far as possible, to discharge the obligations of the State in the province where they are collected; that, without distinction, all agents employed in the collection, receipt, custody, and payment thereof be entirely subordinate to the several assemblies. . . .

The nobility of Dourdan requested major changes in its *cahier*.

CONSTITUTION

The citizens comprising the order of the nobility of the *bailliage* of Dourdan consider that, as soon as the Estates General is convened and the assembly constituted, an address should be voted to the King to thank him for the magnanimous act of justice he has just accorded the nation in restoring its rights, and to pledge to him, in the name of all Frenchmen, unlimited gratitude and love, inviolable submission and fidelity to his sacred person, his legitimate authority, and his august royal house. They would doubtless wish to use this liberty first in paying him new homage of their blood and fortune; but they wish more, they wish to contribute with all their power to the personal happiness of His Majesty, as well as to the general welfare of his people, by working in concert with him to bolster the tottering edifice of the French Constitution, by rendering his faithful commons happier through a just distribution of the taxes necessary to the State, by freeing him of the troubles and anxieties which extensive and absolute legislation necessarily entails; finally, by leaving to him only favors to grant and benefits to dispense throughout the free nation that he governs; thus the subjects of all orders, encompassing the Monarch with their liberty, their happiness, and their unlimited devotion, will render him, if possible, still more beloved throughout his realm, and assuredly more respected abroad.

Accordingly, the noble citizens of the *bailliage* of Dourdan request:

That the legislative power reside collectively in the hands of the King and the united nation.

That a formula for the drafting and publication of laws be established, and that it express both the right of the nation and that of the King, in these words, or similar ones: "The free and general Estates of France declare that the general will is _____. Accordingly, the said Estates most respectfully supplicate His Majesty to sanction the said articles by royal approbation _____WE, KING OF FRANCE, upon the request of the Estates General, assembled at _____, have published and do publish _____, have ordered and do order   . Thus we inform all those whom it may concern that they are to take in hand and put into effect all articles above stated, according to their form and tenor; FOR SUCH IS THE OUTCOME OF THE NATIONAL WILL, WHICH HAS RECEIVED THE SEAL OF OUR ROYAL AUTHORITY."

Since the constitutional laws assure each and every one of his liberty, fortune, position, and property, the nobility requests:

That every arbitrary order prejudicial to the liberty of citizens be abolished entirely;

That individual liberty be assured and guaranteed, so that every citizen arrested may be placed in the prisons of the courts which are to take cognizance of his offence within twenty-four hours of the time of his arrest; that, immediately upon his detention, he be permitted to choose a counsel or advocate.

Liberty shall be understood to include the right to come, go, live, and reside wheresoever one pleases, inside or outside the kingdom, without need of permission; referring to the Estates General the determination of cases in which it is necessary to restrict such liberty with regard to leaving the kingdom.

That liberty of the press be granted, upon condition that author and printer are responsible; and the Estates General shall determine the most severe restrictions in order to prevent such liberty from degenerating into licence.

The nobility of the *bailliage* of Dourdan requests, likewise, that, according to the formal wish of His Majesty, no tax be established and no loan be made without the concurrence of the legislative power.

That the administrator of finances be not permitted to make any anticipation or assignment other than on the annual income, under penalty for *lèse-patrie*, the lenders to forfeit all claim.

That any individual convicted of having collected any sum whatsoever in excess of that established by law be declared guilty of embezzlement and sentenced accordingly.

That no citizen be deprived of his rank, employment, or position, except according to a legal judgment.

That all property, whoever be the owner, be inviolable and sacred, property being whatever one owns on public faith and on the affirmation of the law; that no one be deprived thereof except for public interest, and that he then be compensated therefor without delay, and at the highest possible price.

Finally, that ministers henceforth be responsible and accountable to the Estates General.

But if it is magnanimous of the French Monarch to share the legislative power with free subjects, it is at the same time just and necessary that he be invested with all executive power, and that his person be ever sacred.

He must have command of the troops on land and sea, assign military positions, appoint generals and ministers, make peace or war, negotiate treaties of alliance or commerce with foreign powers, convoke, prorogue, and dissolve the Estates General, under the express condition, in case of dissolution, of effecting a new convocation immediately in the form and number approved by the assembled nation.

Finally, the King alone must preserve that right, so kind, so consoling, so worthy of a great monarch, that right to dispense benefits, to encourage virtue by dignities and marks of distinction, and, above all, the right to grant pardon.

The order of nobility desires further that the distinction of three orders in the Estates General be strengthened and regarded as inherent in the Constitution of the French monarchy, and that opinions be given therein only by order.

That in the event, however, that vote by order be absolutely rejected by the Estates General, and the deputy of the *bailliage* of Dourdan see that further resistance to vote by head is useless, he then request that vote by head be taken in the separate chamber of every order and not in the assembly of the three orders united.

That vote by head never take place on matters of particular interest to one of the three orders alone.

That the opposition of one order alone may not delay projects of the other two and result in *veto*, except by at least two-thirds of the votes.

That the Estates General be periodic; that it determine the time of its recurrence and the form of its convocation and composition; that it approve taxation only until its next assembly; and that if it be not convoked by the

King at the established time, all taxes immediately cease to be valid throughout the entire extent of the kingdom.

That the Estates General may not concern itself with any deliberation until, in conjunction with the King, it has passed an act enunciating the Constitution and the rights above mentioned, and constituting, henceforth, the fundamental law of the kingdom. . . .

AGRICULTURE

The nobility of the *bailliage* of Dourdan, firmly convinced of the necessity of protecting agriculture, requests:

That steps be taken to eliminate, as far as possible, the remaining vestiges of the feudal regime, respecting at all times the sacred right of property. . . .

MORALS

That no citizen occupy civil or military positions before the age of twenty, because his life up to that time ought to be devoted to education.

That religion always be the basis of scholastic and moral education. . . .

FINANCES

The nobles regard as decidedly advantageous and even necessary that the first declaration of the Estates General be that, since the nation has the right to consent to taxes, and since all existing taxes are of illegal origin and extension, the Estates General declares them all suppressed by law; that, nevertheless, because of the time required to reorganize this branch of national affairs, and also to avoid possible ill effects on future taxation from an absolute discontinuation of all relations between the taxpayers and the public treasury, the Estates General, desiring that there be no taxes other than those established by the present assembly before its first adjournment, enact provisionally that the present taxes, temporarily authorized, continue to be paid, but only during the present session. . . .

Finally, the nobility declares that, in order to evince its sentiments of esteem, natural equity, and affection for its fellow citizens of the third estate, it wishes to share with them, in proportion to the property and possessions of all orders, whatever imposts and taxes are approved by the nation; claiming to reserve only the sacred rights of property, the prerogatives of rank, honor, and dignity which must appertain to it according to the constitutional principles of the French monarchy.

CLERGY

His Majesty is further supplicated to order that all bishops and beneficiaries reside in their benefices.

That plurality of benefices and charges be proscribed.

That prebends and benefices be set apart for the retirement of *curés* who have performed their ministry worthily for twenty years.

That administration of the sacraments be gratuitious, and that the endowment of *curés*, greater in the cities than in the country districts, be established for these latter at from 1,500 to 1,800 *livres*, and the salary of vicars at from 700 to 1,000 *livres*.

Concerning the question presented by a member of the nobility, and on which he has most zealously insisted, to wit: Whether, assuming that religious matters may be brought to and discussed in the Estates General, it is a court competent to give a decision, and whether the authority of the Estates extends to the spiritual or is confined to the temporal;

The chamber has declared that it believes the Estates General competent concerning discipline but not concerning dogma, and, on the urgent demand of the member of the nobility proposing the question, it has been decreed that it be included in the *cahier*.

NOBILITY

The nobility of the *bailliage* of Dourdan declares that it recognizes only one order of nobility enjoying the same rights.

It requests that nobility no longer be the concomitant of offices which are purely venal and without functions.

That nobility be the reward for distinguished services only.

That neither commerce nor any civil position henceforth be discreditable, provided that such position be not servile.

C ⟩ The *cahier* of the Third Estate discussed fundamental changes required of the old regime.

The order of the third estate of the City, *Bailliage*, and County of Dourdan, imbued with gratitude prompted by the paternal kindness of the King, who deigns to restore its former rights and its former constitution, forgets at this moment its misfortunes and impotence, to harken only to its foremost sentiment and its foremost duty, that of sacrificing everything to the glory of the *Patrie* and the service of His Majesty. It supplicates him to accept the grievances, complaints, and remonstrances which it is permitted to bring to the foot of the throne, and to see therein only the expression of its zeal and the homage of its obedience.

It wishes:

1. That his subjects of the third estate, equal by such status to all other citizens, present themselves before the common father without other distinction which might degrade them.
2. That all the orders, already united by duty and a common desire to contribute equally to the needs of the State, also deliberate in common concerning its needs.
3. That no citizen lose his liberty except according to law; that, consequently, no one be arrested by virtue of special orders, or, if imperative circumstances necessitate such orders, that the prisoner be handed over to the regular courts of justice within forty-eight hours at the latest.
4. That no letters or writings intercepted in the post be the cause of the detention of any citizen, or be produced in court against him, except in case of conspiracy or undertaking against the State.
5. That the property of all citizens be inviolable, and that no one be required to make sacrifice thereof for the public welfare, except upon assurance of indemnification based upon the statement of freely selected appraisers.

6. That, since the maintenance of the commonwealth necessitates an effective revenue, all taxes established since 1614, the year of the last meeting of the Estates General, be confirmed provisionally by His Majesty on the request of the Estates General, and the collection thereof ordered during a limited period of time, not to exceed one year, despite the fact that, owing to lack of consent of the nation, such taxes may be regarded as illegal.

7. That the customary and ordinary charges of the State be regulated; that the expenditure of every department [of the Government], the appointment of all who are employed therein, and the retirement pensions of same be established invariably. . . .

JUSTICE

1. That the administration of justice be reformed, either by restoring strict execution of ordinances, or by reforming the sections thereof that are contrary to the dispatch and welfare of justice.

FINANCES

1. That if the Estates General considers it necessary to preserve the fees of *aides*, such fees be made uniform throughout the entire kingdom and reduced to a single denomination; that, accordingly, all ordinances and declarations in force be evoked . . . ; that the odious tax of *trop-bu* especially, a source of constant annoyance in rural districts, be abolished forever.

2. That the tax of the *gabelle* be eliminated if possible, or that it be regulated among the several provinces of the kingdom . . .

3. That the taxes on hides, which have totally destroyed that branch of commerce and caused it to go abroad, be suppressed forever. . . .

COMMERCE

1. That every regulation which tends to impede the business of citizens be revoked.

MORALS

1. That in the chief towns of every *bailliage* a public school be established, where young citizens may be brought up in the principles of religion and provided with the necessary education by methods authorized by His Majesty on the request of the nation.

2. That in cities and villages schools be established where the poor will be admitted without cost, and instructed in whatever is necessary for them concerning either morals or their individual interests.

3. That livings and benefices for the care of souls henceforth be granted only by competitive examination.

4. That prelates and *curés* be subject to perpetual residence, under penalty of loss of the fruits of their benefices.

5. That, under the same penalty, beneficiaries without a charge be bound to residence during most of the year in the chief town of their benefice, if they have an annual income of 1,000 *livres* or more.

6. That no ecclesiastic hold more than one benefice if such benefice is worth 3,000 *livres* revenue or over; that those in excess of such revenue be declared vacant.

7. That every lottery, the effect of which is to corrupt public morals, every loan involving the element of chance, the effect of which is to encourage speculation and divert funds destined for agriculture and commerce, be proscribed forever.

8. That every community be required to provide for the maintenance of its invalid poor; that, accordingly, all private alms be strictly forbidden; that in every district a charity workshop be established, the funds for which shall be composed of voluntary contributions of individuals and sums which the provincial Estates shall designate therefor, in order to assure constant work for the able-bodied poor.

9. That within the limits of every principal administration a house of correction be established for the confinement of beggars and vagabonds.

10. That all charlatans, and those who have not completed the necessary studies and passed the required examinations, be forbidden to sell drugs or medicines or to practise medicine or surgery, and that the granting of any certificate, permission, or exemption for such purpose be forbidden.

11. That no woman may practise the art of midwifery until she has taken a course in it, has obtained a certificate of competence from a college of surgery, and has been received into the *bailliage*. . . .

13. That the sacraments be administered gratuitously, and contingent fees suppressed.

1. Read each of the submissions from the three Estates. Create a comparative chart of their views dealing with such concerns as: the role of the clergy; attitude towards the king; procedures for voting; taxation; individual rights; education and morals.

2. Based on your findings, comment on the following thesis: "The only thing which the delegates to the Estates General had in common was their opposition to the status quo."

. . .

EMMANUEL JOSEPH SIEYÈS

Emmanuel Joseph Sieyès (1748-1836) was a French clergyman, known as the Abbé Sieyès, prior to the revolution. Sieyès' pamphlet *What is the Third Estate?* appeared in France in January 1789. It was influential in its attack on noble and clerical privileges and in redefining the role of the Third Estate in the nation. Sieyès' concepts of the nation and of sovereignty were instrumental in helping to effect the transition from an Estates-General to a National Assembly in 1789.

Sieyès argued that the Third Estate could consider itself as the nation, in contrast to traditional concepts.

The plan of this book is fairly simple. We must ask ourselves three questions.
1. What is the Third Estate? *Everything*.
2. What has it been until now in the political order? *Nothing*.
3. What does it want to be? *Something*.

We are going to see whether the answers are correct. Meanwhile, it would be improper to say these statements are exaggerated until the supporting evidence has been examined. We shall next examine the measures that have been tried and those that must still be taken for the Third Estate really to become something. Thus, we shall state:
4. What the Ministers have attempted and what even the privileged orders propose to do for it.
5. What ought to have been done.
6. Finally, what remains to be done in order that the Third Estate should take its rightful place.

What does a nation require to survive and prosper? It needs *private* activities and *public* services.

These private activities can all be comprised within four classes of persons:
1. Since land and water provide the basic materials for human needs, the first class, in logical order, includes all the families connected with work on the land.
2. Between the initial sale of goods and the moment when they reach the consumer or user, goods acquire an increased value of a more or less compound nature through the incorporation of varying amounts of labour. In this way human industry manages to improve the gifts of nature and the value of the raw material may be multiplied twice, or ten-fold, or a hundred-fold. Such are the activities of the second class of persons.
3. Between production and consumption, as also between the various stages of production, a variety of intermediary agents intervene, to help producers as well as consumers; these are the dealers and the merchants. Merchants continually compare needs according to place and time and estimate the profits to be obtained from warehousing and transportation; dealers undertake, in the final stage, to deliver the goods on the wholesale and retail markets. Such is the function of the third class of persons.
4. Besides these three classes of useful and industrious citizens who deal with *things* fit to be consumed or used, society also requires a vast number of special activities and of services *directly* useful or pleasant to the *person*. This fourth class embraces all sorts of occupations, from the most distinguished liberal and scientific professions to the lowest of menial tasks.

Such are the activities which support society. But who performs them? The Third Estate.

Source: Emmanuel Joseph Sieyès, *What is the Third Estate?* (London: Pall Mall Press, 1963), pp. 51-57, 62-64, 142-45, 172-73.

Public services can also, at present, be divided into four known categories, the army, the law, the Church and the bureaucracy. It needs no detailed analysis to show that the Third Estate everywhere constitutes nineteen-twentieths of them, except that it is loaded with all the really arduous work, all the tasks which the privileged order refuses to perform. Only the well-paid and honorific posts are filled by members of the privileged order. Are we to give them credit for this? We could do so only if the Third Estate was unable or unwilling to fill these posts. We know the answer. Nevertheless, the privileged have dared to preclude the Third Estate. 'No matter how useful you are', they said, 'no matter how able you are, you can go so far and no further. Honours are not for the like of you.' The rare exceptions, noticeable as they are bound to be, are mere mockery, and the sort of language allowed on such occasions is an additional insult.

When any function is made the prerogative of a separate order among the citizens, has nobody remarked how a salary has to be paid not only to the man who actually does the work, but to all those of the same caste who do not, and also to the entire families of both the workers and the non-workers?

It suffices to have made the point that the so-called usefulness of a privileged order to the public service is a fallacy; that, without help from this order, all the arduous tasks in the service are performed by the Third Estate; that without this order the higher posts could be infinitely better filled; that they ought to be the natural prize and reward of recognised ability and service; and that if the privileged have succeeded in usurping all well-paid and honorific posts, this is both a hateful iniquity towards the generality of citizens and an act of treason to the commonwealth.

Who is bold enough to maintain that the Third Estate does not contain within itself everything needful to constitute a complete nation? It is like a strong and robust man with one arm still in chains. If the privileged order were removed, the nation would not be something less but something more. What then is the Third Estate? All; but an 'all' that is fettered and oppressed. What would it be without the privileged order? It would be all; but free and flourishing. Nothing will go well without the Third Estate; everything would go considerably better without the two others.

It is not enough to have shown that the privileged, far from being useful to the nation, can only weaken and injure it; we must prove further that the nobility is not part of our society at all: it may be a *burden* for the nation, but it cannot be part of it.

The nobility was attacked for being unable to represent the members of the Third Estate.

Let them create as many noblemen as they like; it still remains certain that the moment any citizen is granted privileges against the common laws, he no longer forms part of the common order. His new interest is contrary to the general interest; he becomes incompetent to vote in the name of the People.

According to the same undeniable principle, those who merely hold temporary privileges must also be debarred from representing the Third Estate. Their interest, too, is in greater or lesser part opposed to the common interest;

and although opinion assigns them to the Third Estate and the law does not mention them, the nature of things, stronger than both opinion and the law, sets them irresistibly apart from the common order.

It is objected that to remove from the Third Estate not only those with hereditary privileges, but even those with mere temporary ones, is to try, from sheet wantonness, to weaken that order by depriving it of its more enlightened, courageous and esteemed members.

The last thing I want to do is to diminish the strength or dignity of the Third Estate, since, in my mind, it is completely coincident with my idea of a nation. But can we, whatever our motives, arrange for truth to cease to be truth? If an army has the misfortune to be deserted by its best soldiers, are these the troops it entrusts with the defence of its camp? One cannot say it too often: any privilege runs contrary to common laws; hence, all those who enjoy privileges, without exception, constitute a separate class opposed to the Third Estate. At the same time, I must point out that this should not alarm the friends of the People. On the contrary, it takes us back to the higher national interest by showing the urgent necessity for immediately suppressing all temporary privileges which split the Third Estate and may seem to oblige it to put its destiny in its enemies' hands. . . .

 Sieyès claimed the hope for the future was in the Third Estate.

The Third Estate must now see the direction in which both thought and action are moving, and realise that its sole hope lies in its own intelligence and courage. Reason and justice are on its side; the least it must do is to assure itself of their full support. No, it is too late to work for the conciliation of all parties. What sort of an agreement could one hope for between the energy of the oppressed and the rage of the oppressors? They have dared utter the word *secession*. With it they have threatened both King and People. Heavens! How fortunate it would be for the nation if so desirable a secession could be perpetuated! How easy it would be to do without the privileged! How difficult it will be to induce them to become citizens! . . .

. . . One would have to be blind not to see that our nation has happily seized upon some of these fecund principles that point the way to all that is good, just and useful. It is impossible to ignore them or simply contemplate them in sterile indifference. In these new circumstances, the oppressed classes are naturally the most impressed by the need to put things right; they have acquired most interest in reinstating Justice among men—Justice, that prime virtue, long exiled from this world. It is consequently for the Third Estate to play the leading role in the advance towards national recovery. The Third Estate must, moreover, recognise the danger that unless it improves its status it cannot simply remain as it is. The circumstances do not permit of this faint-hearted calculation. Not to go forwards is to go backwards. . . .

While the aristocrats talk of their honour but pursue their self-interest, the Third Estate, i.e. the nation, will develop its virtue, for if corporate interest is egotism, national interest is virtue. It will suffer the nobles to nourish their expiring vanity on the pleasure of abusing the Third Estate with the most insulting words in the vocabulary of feudalism. The nobles will repeat such words as *commoners*, *peasants* and *villeins*, forgetting that these terms, no matter in what sense one means them, either do not describe the Third Estate as it is to-day or are common to the three orders; forgetting also that, when these words did make sense, ninety-nine per cent of their own number were un-questionably *commoners*, *peasants* and *villeins*, and that the others, necessarily, were brigands. In vain do the privileged classes close their eyes to the revolution which time and events have effected: it is real for all that. There was once a time when the Third Estate was in bondage and the nobility was everything. Now the Third Estate is everything and nobility is only a word. But under cover of this work, however, and based solely on the strength of false opinion, a new and intolerable aristocracy has established itself; and the People has every reason not to want any aristocrats. . . .

Let us now return to our theme.

One final objection is that the privileged, though they may have no right to concern the common will with their privileges, must at least enjoy the political right of representation in their capacity of citizens, like the rest of society does.

However, I have already shown that in becoming privileged they have become the actual enemies of the common interest. Consequently they cannot be charged with providing for it.

To this I would also add that they are at liberty to re-enter the real nation by purging themselves of their unjust privileges, and therefore it is by their own act that they are precluded from exercising political rights. And, finally, their true rights, which are the only ones that can be the concern of the National Assembly, are common both to them *and* the deputies of the assembly. They can therefore reassure themselves with the thought that the deputies cannot harm these interests without injuring themselves.

It is therefore quite certain that only nonprivileged members are competent to be electors to, or deputies in, the National Assembly. The will of the Third Estate will always be good for the generality of citizens; that of the privileged would always be bad for it, unless, neglecting their own interests, they were prepared to vote as simple citizens. But this is the same as voting like the Third Estate itself. Therefore the Third Estate is adequate for everything that can be hoped for from a National Assembly. It follows that the Third Estate, alone, can procure all the promised benefits of the States-General. . . .

1. How effective is Sieyès' opening argument?
2. According to Sieyès, what role did the Third Estate play in the operation of French society?
3. Summarize his argument regarding the relative worth of the Third Estate compared to the other two.
4. How did Sieyès justify his claim that the nobility had no legitimate role in governing the nation?
5. What final message did Sieyès give to the aristocracy?

■ ■ ■

EDMUND BURKE

The most important critic of the French Revolution was Edmund Burke (1729-97). His *Reflections on the Revolution in France* was written in 1790, in reply to those in Britain who supported the activities of the Revolution. Burke had supported the American colonists in their revolution because he believed them to have been agitating for their legitimate rights as British subjects. Now, arguing for the importance of tradition, religion, and established institutions, he claimed that the French had changed so much so fast that chaos and destruction would result. Although he was a strong supporter of government under law and in favour of a monarchy restrained by custom and traditional institutions, Burke became the spokesman for the conservative position in the West.

 Burke understood a constitution to be an inherited system, and believed in the value of using tradition as a guide in social and political affairs.

> . . . You will observe that from Magna Charta to the Declaration of Right it has been the uniform policy of our constitution to claim and assert our liberties as an *entailed inheritance* derived to us from our forefathers, and to be transmitted to our posterity—as an estate specially belonging to the people of this kingdom, without any reference whatever to any other more general or prior right. By this means our constitution preserves a unity in so great a diversity of its parts. We have an inheritable crown, an inheritable peerage, and a House of Commons and a people inheriting privileges, franchises, and liberties from a long line of ancestors.
>
> This policy appears to me to be the result of profound reflection, or rather the happy effect of following nature, which is wisdom without reflection, and above it. A spirit of innovation is generally the result of a selfish temper and confined views. People will not look forward to posterity, who never look backward to their ancestors. Besides, the people of England well know that the idea of inheritance furnishes a sure principle of conservation and a sure principle of transmission, without at all excluding a principle of improvement. It leaves acquisition free, but it secures what it acquires. . . . By a constitutional policy, working after the pattern of nature, we receive, we hold, we transmit our government and our privileges in the same manner in which we enjoy and transmit our property and our lives. The institutions of policy, the goods of fortune, the gifts of providence are handed down to us, and from us, in the same course and order. Our political system is placed in a just correspondence and symmetry with the order of the world and with the mode of existence decreed to a permanent body composed of transitory parts, wherein, by the disposition of a stupendous wisdom, molding together the great mysterious incorporation of the human race, the whole, at one time, is never old or middle-aged or young, but, in a condition of unchangeable constancy, moves on through the varied tenor of perpetual decay, fall, renovation, and

Source: Edmund Burke, *Reflections on the Revolution in France*, edited by Thomas H.D. Mahoney (Indianapolis: The Bobbs-Merrill Company, Inc., 1955), pp. 37-38, 39, 67-70, 97-100, 191-92, 193, 196-97.

progression. Thus, by preserving the method of nature in the conduct of the state, in what we improve we are never wholly new; in what we retain we are never wholly obsolete. . . .

We procure reverence to our civil institutions on the principle upon which nature teaches us to revere individual men: on account of their age and on account of those from whom they are descended. All your sophisters cannot produce anything better adapted to preserve a rational and manly freedom than the course that we have pursued, who have chosen our nature rather than our speculations, our breasts rather than our inventions, for the great conservatories and magazines of our rights and privileges.

 Rights for Burke were inherited, as he attacked the concept of natural rights.

. . . If civil society be made for the advantage of man, all the advantages for which it is made become his right. It is an institution of beneficence; and law itself is only beneficence acting by a rule. Men have a right to live by that rule; they have a right to do justice, as between their fellows, whether their fellows are in public function or in ordinary occupation. They have a right to the fruits of their industry and to the means of making their industry fruitful. They have a right to the acquisitions of their parents, to the nourishment and improvement of their offspring, to instruction in life, and to consolation in death. Whatever each man can separately do, without trespassing upon others, he has a right to do for himself; and he has a right to a fair portion of all which society, with all its combinations of skill and force, can do in his favor. In this partnership all men have equal rights, but not to equal things. He that has but five shillings in the partnership has as good a right to it as he that has five hundred pounds has to his larger proportion. But he has not a right to an equal dividend in the product of the joint stock; and as to the share of power, authority, and direction which each individual ought to have in the management of the state, that I must deny to be amongst the direct original rights of man in civil society, for I have in my contemplation the civil social man, and no other. It is a thing to be settled by convention.

If civil society be the offspring of convention, that convention must be its law. That convention must limit and modify all the descriptions of constitution which are formed under it. Every sort of legislative, judicial, or executory power are its creatures. They can have no being in any other state of things; and how can any man claim under the conventions of civil society rights which do not so much as suppose its existence—rights which are absolutely repugnant to it? One of the first motives to civil society, and which becomes one of its fundamental rules, is *that no man should be judge in his own cause.* By this each person has at once divested himself of the first fundamental right of uncovenanted man, that is, to judge for himself and to assert his own cause. He abdicates all right to be his own governor. He inclusively, in a great measure, abandons the right of self-defense, the first law of nature. Men cannot enjoy the rights of an uncivil and of a civil state together. That he may obtain justice, he gives up his right of determining what it is in points the most essential to him. That he may secure some liberty, he makes a surrender in trust of the whole of it.

Government is not made in virtue of natural rights, which may and do exist in total independence of it, and exist in much greater clearness and in a much greater degree of abstract perfection; but their abstract perfection is their practical defect. By having a right to everything they want everything. Government is a contrivance of human wisdom to provide for human *wants*. Men have a right that these wants should be provided for by this wisdom. Among these wants is to be reckoned the want, out of civil society, of a sufficient restraint upon their passions. Society requires not only that the passions of individuals should be subjected, but that even in the mass and body, as well as in the individuals, the inclinations of men should frequently be thwarted, their will controlled, and their passions brought into subjection. This can only be done *by a power out of themselves*, and not, in the exercise of its function, subject to that will and to those passions which it is its office to bridle and subdue. In this sense the restraints on men, as well as their liberties, are to be reckoned among their rights. But as the liberties and the restrictions vary with times and circumstances and admit to infinite modifications, they cannot be settled upon any abstract rule; and nothing is so foolish as to discuss them upon that principle.

The moment you abate anything from the full rights of men, each to govern himself, and suffer any artificial, positive limitation upon those rights, from that moment the whole organization of government becomes a consideration of convenience. This it is which makes the constitution of a state and the due distribution of its powers a matter of the most delicate and complicated skill. It requires a deep knowledge of human nature and human necessities, and of the things which facilitate or obstruct the various ends which are to be pursued by the mechanism of civil institutions. The state is to have recruits to its strength, and remedies to its distempers. What is the use of discussing a man's abstract right to food or medicine? The question is upon the method of procuring and administering them. In that deliberation I shall always advise to call in the aid of the farmer and the physician rather than the professor of metaphysics.

The science of constructing a commonwealth, or renovating it, or reforming it, is, like every other experimental science, not to be taught a *priori*. . . . The science of government being therefore so practical in itself and intended for such practical purposes—a matter which requires experience, and even more experience than any person can gain in his whole life, however sagacious and observing he may be—it is with infinite caution that any man ought to venture upon pulling down an edifice which has answered in any tolerable degree for ages the common purposes of society, or on building it up again without having models and patterns of approved utility before his eyes. . . .

. . . Thanks to our sullen resistance to innovation, thanks to the cold sluggishness of our national character, we still bear the stamp of our forefathers. We have not (as I conceive) lost the generosity and dignity of thinking of the fourteenth century, nor as yet have we subtilized ourselves into savages. We are not the converts of Rousseau; we are not the disciples of Voltaire; Helvetius has made no progress amongst us. Atheists are not our preachers; madmen are not our lawgivers. We know that *we* have made no discoveries, and we think that no discoveries are to be made, in morality, nor many in the great principles of government, nor in the ideas of liberty, which were understood long before we were born, altogether as well as they will be after the grave has heaped its mold upon our presumption and the silent tomb shall have imposed its law on our pert loquacity. In England we have not yet been completely embowelled of our natural entrails; we still feel within us, and we cherish and cultivate, those inbred sentiments which are the faithful guardians, the active monitors of our duty, the true supporters of all liberal and manly morals. We have not been drawn and trussed, in order that we may be filled, like stuffed birds in a museum, with chaff and rags and paltry blurred shreds of paper about the rights of men. We preserve the whole of our feelings still native and entire, unsophisticated by pedantry and infidelity. We have real hearts of flesh and blood beating in our bosoms. We fear God; we look up with awe to kings, with affection to parliaments, with duty to magistrates, with reverence to priests, and with respect to nobility. Why? Because when such ideas are brought before our minds, it is *natural* to be so affected; because all other feelings are false and spurious and tend to corrupt our minds, to vitiate our primary morals, to render us unfit for rational liberty, and, by teaching us a servile, licentious, and abandoned insolence, to be our low sport for a few holidays, to make us perfectly fit for, and justly deserving of, slavery through the whole course of our lives. . . .

You see, Sir, that in this enlightened age I am bold enough to confess that we are generally men of untaught feelings, that, instead of casting away all our old prejudices, we cherish them to a very considerable degree, and, to take more shame to ourselves, we cherish them because they are prejudices; and the longer they have lasted and the more generally they have prevailed, the more we cherish them. We are afraid to put men to live and trade each on his own private stock of reason, because we suspect that this stock in each man is small, and that the individuals would do better to avail themselves of the general bank and capital of nations and of ages. Many of our men of speculation, instead of exploding general prejudices, employ their sagacity to discover the latent wisdom which prevails in them. If they find what they seek, and they seldom fail, they think it more wise to continue the prejudice, with the reason involved, than to cast away the coat of prejudice and to leave nothing but the naked reason; because prejudice, with its reason, has a motive to give action to that reason, and an affection which will give it permanence. Prejudice is of ready application in the emergency; it previously engages the mind in a steady course of wisdom and virtue and does not leave the man hesitating in the moment of decision skeptical, puzzled, and unresolved. Prejudice renders a man's virtue his habit, and not a series of unconnected acts. Through just prejudice, his duty becomes a part of his nature. . . .

Your literary men and your politicians, and so do the whole clan of the enlightened among us, essentially differ in these points. They have no respect for the wisdom of others, but they pay it off by a very full measure of confidence in their own. With them it is a sufficient motive to destroy an old scheme of things because it is an old one. As to the new, they are in no sort of fear with regard to the duration of a building run up in haste, because duration is no object to those who think little or nothing has been done before their time, and who place all their hopes in discovery. They conceive, very systematically, that all things which give perpetuity are mischievous, and therefore they are at inexpiable war with all establishments. They think that government may vary like modes of dress, and with as little ill effect; that there needs no principle of attachment, except a sense of present convenience, to any constitution of the state. They always speak as if they were of opinion that there is a singular species of compact between them and their magistrates which binds the magistrate, but which has nothing reciprocal in it, but that the majesty of the people has a right to dissolve it without any reason but its will. Their attachment to their country itself is only so far as it agrees with some of their fleeting projects; it begins and ends with that scheme of polity which falls in with their momentary opinion. . . .

The validity of the National Assembly of France was challenged.

> . . . I have taken a view of what has been done by the governing power in France. I have certainly spoken of it with freedom. Those whose principle it is to despise the ancient, permanent sense of mankind and to set up a scheme of society on new principles must naturally expect that such of us who think better of the judgment of the human race than of theirs should consider both them and their devices as men and schemes upon their trial. They must take it for granted that we attend much to their reason, but not at all to their authority. They have not one of the great influencing prejudices of mankind in their favor. They avow their hostility to opinion. Of course, they must expect no support from that influence which, with every other authority, they have deposed from the seat of its jurisdiction.
>
> I can never consider this Assembly as anything else than a voluntary association of men who have availed themselves of circumstances to seize upon the power of the state. They have not the sanction and authority of the character under which they first met. They have assumed another of a very different nature and have completely altered and inverted all the relations in which they originally stood. They do not hold the authority they exercise under any constitutional law of the state. They have departed from the instructions of the people by whom they were sent, which instructions, as the Assembly did not act in virtue of any ancient usage or settled law, were the sole source of their authority. . . .
>
> . . . This Assembly has hardly a year's prescription. We have their own word for it that they have made a revolution. To make a revolution is a measure which, *prima fronte* [on the face of it], requires an apology. To make a revolution is to subvert the ancient state of our country; and no common reasons are called for to justify so violent a proceeding. The sense of mankind authorizes us to examine into the mode of acquiring new power, and to criticize on the use that is made of it, with less awe and reverence than that which is usually conceded to a settled and recognized authority. . . .
>
> At once to preserve and to reform is quite another thing. When the useful parts of an old establishment are kept, and what is superadded is to be fitted to what is retained, a vigorous mind, steady, persevering attention, various powers of comparison and combination, and the resources of an understand-

ing fruitful in expedients are to be exercised; they are to be exercised in a continued conflict with the combined force of opposite vices, with the obstinacy that rejects all improvement and the levity that is fatigued and disgusted with everything of which it is in possession. But you may object—"A process of this kind is slow. It is not fit for an assembly which glories in performing in a few months the work of ages. Such a mode of reforming, possibly, might take up many years." Without question it might; and it ought. It is one of the excellences of a method in which time is amongst the assistants, that its operation is slow and in some cases almost imperceptible. If circumspection and caution are a part of wisdom when we work only upon inanimate matter, surely they become a part of duty, too, when the subject of our demolition and construction is not brick and timber but sentinent beings, by the sudden alteration of whose state, condition, and habits multitudes may be rendered miserable. . . .

1. Contrast Burke's rejection of the "spirit of innovation" with his belief in the free "acquisition" and "conservation" of principles.
2. What advantage did Burke see in the process of handing down institutions and ideas from one generation to the next?
3. Explain Burke's analogy of human beings as "shareholders" in society. How does this compare with the ideas of Rousseau?
4. According to Burke, what is the relationship between the "abstract" concept of natural rights, and the "practical science" of government?
5. Write a précis of Burke's criticisms of the National Assembly in France. Based on your own knowledge of events, comment on his viewpoint.

DEBATE

Take the stance of Burke in opposing the French Revolution. Write a position paper in which you lay out his arguments and refute those of Thomas Paine (cited in the next section of readings). Pair yourself with a student who has completed the same task based on the next set of readings. Stage your own mini-debate on the issue and then, stepping out of role, discuss the strengths and weaknesses of each argument.

▪ ▪ ▪

THOMAS PAINE

The first part of Thomas Paine's *Rights of Man* appeared in early 1791, several months after Edmund Burke's *Reflections* was printed. Thus began the modern argument between radical and conservative, which has continued to the present. Paine (1737-1809) was an Anglo-American whose earlier work *Common Sense* (1776) strongly supported the American rebellion against the British. Now, he wrote to discredit Burke's position on the French Revolution. Paine believed in a political authority that was contractual, as did Burke, but he also supported natural rights and the idea that democratic institutions must be implemented in order to guarantee those rights. The dialogue between Burke and Paine set the tone for the main political debate of the time.

Paine immediately attacked Burke's premises:

. . . There never did, there never will, and there never can exist a parliament, or any description of men, or any generation of men, in any country, possessed of the right or the power of binding and controlling posterity to the *"end of time,"* or of commanding for ever how the world shall be governed, or who shall govern it; and therefore, all such clauses, acts or declarations, by which the makers of them attempt to do what they have neither the right nor the power to do, nor the power to execute, are in themselves null and void.— Every age and generation must be as free to act for itself, *in all cases,* as the ages and generations which preceded it. The vanity and presumption of governing beyond the grave, is the most ridiculous and insolent of all tyrannies. Man has no property in man; neither has any generation a property in the generations which are to follow. The parliament or the people of 1688, or of any other period, has no more right to dispose of the people of the present day, or to bind or to control them *in any shape whatever,* than the parliament or the people of the present day have to dispose of, bind or control those who are to live a hundred or a thousand years hence. Every generation is, and must be, competent to all the purposes which its occasions require. It is the living, and not the dead, that are to be accommodated. When man ceases to be, his power and his wants cease with him; and having no longer any participation in the concerns of this world, he has no longer any authority in directing who shall be its governors, or how its government shall be organized, or how administered.

I am not contending for nor against any form of government, nor for nor against any party here or elsewhere. That which a whole nation chooses to do, it has a right to do. Mr. Burke says, No. Where then *does* the right exist? I am contending for the rights of the *living*, and against their being willed away, and controlled and contracted for, by the manuscript assumed authority of the dead; and Mr. Burke is contending for the authority of the dead over the rights and freedom of the living. There was a time when kings disposed of their crowns by will upon their deathbeds, and consigned the people, like beasts of the field, to whatever successor they appointed. This is now so exploded as scarcely to be remembered, and so monstrous as hardly to be believed: But the parliamentary clauses upon which Mr. Burke builds his political church, are of the same nature. . . .

A greater absurdity cannot present itself to the understanding of man, than what Mr. Burke offers to his readers. He tells them, and he tells the world to come, that a certain body of men, who existed a hundred years ago, made a law; and that there does not now exist in the nation, nor ever will, nor ever can, a power to alter it. Under how many subtleties, or absurdities, has the divine right to govern been imposed on the credulity of mankind! Mr. Burke has discovered a new one, and he has shortened his journey to Rome, by appealing to the power of this infallible parliament of former days; and he produces what it has done, as of divine authority: for that power must certainly be more than human, which no human power to the end of time can alter. . . .

Source: Thomas Paine, *Rights of Man* (Harmondsworth: Penguin Books, 1969), pp. 63-64, 65, 66, 67, 70-71, 72, 73, 90-91, 92-94.

From what, or from whence, does Mr. Burke prove the right of any human power to bind posterity for ever? He has produced his clauses; but he must produce also his proofs, that such a right existed, and show how it existed. If it ever existed, it must now exist; for whatever appertains to the nature of man, cannot be annihilated by man. It is the nature of man to die, and he will continue to die as long as he continues to be born. But Mr. Burke has set up a sort of political Adam, in whom all posterity are bound for ever, he must therefore prove that his Adam possessed such a power, or such a right. . . .

The circumstances of the world are continually changing, and the opinions of men change also; and as government is for the living, and not for the dead, it is the living only that has any right in it. That which may be thought right and found convenient in one age, may be thought wrong and found inconvenient in another. In such cases, Who is to decide, the living, or the dead?

As almost one hundred pages of Mr. Burke's book are employed upon these clauses, it will consequently follow, that if the clauses themselves, so far as they set up an *assumed, usurped* dominion over posterity for ever, are unauthoritative, and in their nature null and void; that all his voluminous inferences and declamation drawn therefrom, or founded thereon, are null and void also: and on this ground I rest the matter. . . .

 Paine claimed that Burke opposed the rights of man and supported privilege and aristocracy.

When a man reflects on the condition which France was in from the nature of her government, he will see other causes for revolt than those which immediately connect themselves with the person or character of Louis XVI. There were, if I may so express it, a thousand despotisms to be reformed in France, which had grown up under the hereditary despotism of the monarchy, and became so rooted as to be in a great measure independent of it. Between the monarchy, the parliament, and the church, there was a *rivalship* of despotism, besides the feudal despotism operating locally, and the ministerial despotism operating everywhere. But Mr. Burke, by considering the King as the only possible object of a revolt, speaks as if France was a village, in which everything that passed must be known to its commanding officer, and no oppression could be acted but what he could immediately control. Mr. Burke might have been in the Bastille his whole life, as well under Louis XVI as Louis XIV and neither the one nor the other have known that such a man as Mr. Burke existed. The despotic principles of the government were the same in both reigns, though the dispositions of the men were as remote as tyranny and benevolence.

What Mr. Burke considers as a reproach to the French Revolution, (that of bringing it forward under a reign more mild than the preceding ones), is one of its highest honours. The revolutions that have taken place in other European countries, have been excited by personal hatred. The rage was against the man, and he became the victim. But, in the same instance of France, we see a revolution generated in the rational contemplation of the rights of man, and distinguishing from the beginning between persons and principles.

But Mr. Burke appears to have no idea of principles, when he is contemplating governments. "Then years ago" (says he) "I could have felicitated France on her having a government, without inquiring what the nature of that government was, or how it was administered." Is this the language of a rational man? Is it the language of a heart feeling as it ought to feel for the rights and happiness of the human race? On this ground, Mr. Burke must compliment all the governments in the world, while the victims who suffer under them, whether sold into slavery, or tortured out of existence, are wholly forgotten. It is power, and not principles, that Mr. Burke venerates; and under this abominable depravity, he is disqualified to judge between them.—Thus much for his opinion as to the occasions of the French Revolution. . . .

Through the whole of Mr. Burke's book I do not observe that the Bastille is mentioned more than once, and that with a kind of implication as if he were sorry it was pulled down, and wished it were built up again. . . .

From his violence and his grief, his silence on some points, and his excess on others, it is difficult not to believe that Mr. Burke is sorry, extremely sorry, that arbitrary power, the power of the Pope, and the Bastille, are pulled down.

Not one glance of compassion, not one commiserating reflection, that I can find throughout this book, has he bestowed on those who lingered out the most wretched of lives, a life without hope, in the most miserable of prisons. It is painful to behold a man employing his talents to corrupt himself. Nature has been kinder to Mr. Burke than he is to her. He is not affected by the reality of distress touching his heart, but by the showy resemblance of it striking his imagination. He pities the plumage but forgets the dying bird. Accustomed to kiss the aristocratical hand that hath purloined him from himself, he degenerates into a composition of art, and the genuine soul of nature forsakes him. His hero or his heroine must be a tragedy-victim expiring in show, and not the real prisoner of misery, sliding into death in the silence of a dungeon.

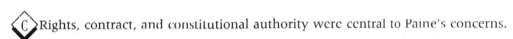 Rights, contract, and constitutional authority were central to Paine's concerns.

. . . Hitherto we have spoken only (and that but in part) of the natural rights of man. We have now to consider the civil rights of man, and to show how the one originates from the other. Man did not enter into society to become *worse* than he was before, nor to have fewer rights than he had before, but to have those rights better secured. His natural rights are the foundation of all his civil rights. But in order to pursue this distinction with more precision, it will be necessary to mark the different qualities of natural and civil rights.

A few words will explain this. Natural rights are those which appertain to man in right of his existence. Of this kind are all the intellectual rights, or rights of the mind, and also all those rights of acting as an individual for his own comfort and happiness, which are not injurious to the natural rights of others.—Civil rights are those which appertain to man in right of his being a member of society. Every civil right has for its foundation, some natural right pre-existing in the individual, but to the enjoyment of which his individual power is not, in all cases, sufficiently competent. Of this kind are all those which relate to security and protection.

From this short review, it will be easy to distinguish between that class of natural rights which man retains after entering into society, and those which he throws into the common stock as a member of society.

The natural rights which he retains, are all those in which the *power* to execute is as perfect in the individual as the right itself. Among this class, as is before mentioned, are all the intellectual rights, or rights of the mind: consequently, religion is one of those rights. The natural rights which are not retained, are all those in which, though the right is perfect in the individual, the power to execute them is defective. They answer not his purpose. A man, by natural right, has a right to judge in his own cause; and so far as the right of mind is concerned, he never surrenders it: But what availeth it him to judge, if he has not power to redress? He therefore deposits this right in the common stock of society, and takes the arm of society, of which he is a part, in preference and in addition to his own. Society *grants* him nothing. Every man is a proprietor in society, and draws on the capital as a matter of right.

From these premises, two or three certain conclusions will follow.

First, That every civil right grows out of a natural right; or, in other words, is a natural right exchanged.

Secondly, That civil power, properly considered as such, is made up of the aggregate of that class of the natural rights of man, which becomes defective in the individual in point of power, and answers not his purpose; but when collected to a focus, becomes competent to the purpose of every one.

Thirdly, That the power produced from the aggregate of natural rights, imperfect in power in the individual, cannot be applied to invade the natural rights which are retained in the individual, and in which the power to execute is as perfect as the right itself.

We have now, in a few words, traced man from a natural individual to a member of society, and shown, or endeavoured to show, the quality of the natural rights retained, and of those which are exchanged for civil rights. Let us now apply these principles to governments.

In casting our eyes over the world, it is extremely easy to distinguish the governments which have arisen out of society, or out of the social compact, from those which have not: but to place this in a clearer light than what a single glance may afford, it will be proper to take a review of the several sources from which governments have arisen, and on which they have been founded.

They may be all comprehended under three heads. First Superstition. Secondly, Power. Thirdly, The common interest of society, and the common rights of man.

The first was a government of priestcraft, the second of conquerors, and the third of reason. . . .

When I contemplate the natural dignity of man; when I feel (for Nature has not been kind enough to me to blunt my feelings) for the honour and happiness of its character, I become irritated at the attempt to govern mankind by force and fraud, as if they were all knaves and fools, and can scarcely avoid disgust at those who are thus imposed upon.

We have now to review the governments which arise out of society, in contradistinction to those which arose out of superstition and conquest.

It has been thought a considerable advance towards establishing the principles of Freedom, to say, that government is a compact between those who govern and those who are governed: but this cannot be true, because it is putting the effect before the cause; for as man must have existed before governments existed, there necessarily was a time when governments did not exist, and consequently there could originally exist no governors to form such a compact with. The fact therefore must be, that the *individuals themselves*, each in his own personal and sovereign right, *entered into a compact with each other* to produce a government: and this is the only mode in which governments have a right to arise, and the only principle on which they have a right to exist.

To possess ourselves of a clear idea of what government is, or ought to be, we must trace it to its origin. In doing this, we shall easily discover that governments must have arisen, either *out* of the people, or *over* the people. Mr. Burke has made no distinction. He investigates nothing to its source, and therefore he confounds everything: but he has signified his intention of undertaking at some future opportunity, a comparison between the constitutions of England and France. As he thus renders it a subject of controversy by throwing the gauntlet, I take him up on his own ground. It is in high challenges that high truths have the right of appearing; and I accept it with the more readiness, because it affords me, at the same time, an opportunity of pursuing the subject with respect to governments arising out of society.

But it will be first necessary to define what is meant by a *constitution*. It is not sufficient that we adopt the word; we must fix also a standard signification to it.

A constitution is not a thing in name only, but in fact. It has not an ideal, but a real existence; and wherever it cannot be produced in a visible form, there is none. A constitution is a thing *antecedent* to a government, and a government is only the creature of a constitution. The constitution of a country is not the act of its government, but of the people constituting a government. It is the body of elements, to which you can refer, and quote article by article; and which contains the principles on which the government shall be established, the manner in which it shall be organized, the powers it shall have, the mode of elections, the duration of parliaments, or by what other name such bodies may be called; the powers which the executive part of the government shall have; and, in fine, everything that relates to the complete organization of a civil government, and the principles on which it shall act, and by which it shall be bound. A constitution, therefore, is to a government, what the laws made afterwards by that government are to a court of judicature. The court of judicature does not make the laws, neither can it alter them; it only acts in conformity to the laws made: and the government is in like manner governed by the constitution.

Can then Mr. Burke produce the English Constitution? If he cannot, we may fairly conclude, that though it has been so much talked about, no such thing as a constitution exists, or ever did exist, and consequently that the people have yet a constitution to form. . . .

The present National Assembly of France is, strictly speaking, the personal social compact.—The members of it are the delegates of the nation in its *original* character; future assemblies will be the delegates of the nation in its *organized* character. The authority of the present Assembly is different to what the authority of future Assemblies will be. The authority of the present one is to form a constitution: the authority of future Assemblies will be to legislate according to the principles and forms prescribed in that constitution; and if experience should hereafter show that alterations, amendments, or additions, are necessary, the constitution will point out the mode by which such things shall be done, and not leave it to the discretionary power of the future government. . . .

1. "The vanity and presumption of governing beyond the grave is the most ridiculous and insolent of all tyrannies." Comment on and evaluate Paine's arguments in support of the "rights of the living" to determine their own form of government.
2. To what extent would you support Paine's opinion of Edmund Burke?
3. Outline Paine's view of the relationship between those natural rights which individuals retain within society and those which are "thrown into the common stock."
4. How did Paine distinguish between a constitution and a government?

DEBATE

Take the stance of Paine and defend the legitimacy of the French Revolution. Write a position paper in which you lay out his arguments and refute those of Edmund Burke. Pair yourself with a student who has completed the same task after the previous set of readings. Stage your own mini-debate on the issue and, then stepping out of role, discuss the strengths and weaknesses of each argument.

• • •

Mary Wollstonecraft

Mary Wollstonecraft (1759-97) wrote the first major feminist work in the modern period, *A Vindication of the Rights of Woman*. Wollstonecraft was a supporter of educational equality and an advocate of women's rights. She lived in Paris during much of the French Revolution and was close to many of its leading figures. A believer in human rights and social progress, Wollstonecraft extended her support of the principles of the Revolution to her own sex, and she argued for a new attitude towards women as part of the belief during the Enlightenment in progress, equality, and reason.

 Wollstonecraft stated that women did not cultivate much of their intellectual potential because of prevailing social attitudes.

> . . . It is vain to expect virtue from women till they are, in some degree, independent of men; nay, it is vain to expect that strength of natural affection,

which would make them good wives and mothers. Whilst they are absolutely dependent on their husbands they will be cunning, mean, and selfish, and the men who can be gratified by the fawning fondness of spaniel-like affection, have not much delicacy, for love is not to be bought, in any sense of the words, its silken wings are instantly shrivelled up when any thing beside a return in kind is sought. Yet whilst wealth encrvates men; and women live, as it were, by their personal charms, how can we expect them to discharge those ennobling duties which equally require exertion and self-denial. . . .

To illustrate my opinion, I need only observe, that when a woman is admired for her beauty, and suffers herself to be so far intoxicated by the admiration she receives, as to neglect to discharge the indispensable duty of a mother, she sins against herself by neglecting to cultivate an affection that would equally tend to make her useful and happy. True happiness, I mean all the contentment, and virtuous satisfaction, that can be snatched in this imperfect state, must arise from well regulated affections; and an affection includes a duty. Men are not aware of the misery they cause, and the vicious weakness they cherish, by only inciting women to render themselves pleasing; they do not consider that they thus make natural and artificial duties clash, by sacrificing the comfort and respectability of a woman's life to voluptuous notions of beauty, when in nature they all harmonize. . . .

It is a melancholy truth; yet such is the blessed effect of civilization! the most respectable women are the most oppressed; and, unless they have understandings far superior to the common run of understandings, taking in both sexes, they must, from being treated like contemptible beings, become contemptible. How many women thus waste life away the prey of discontent, who might have practised as physicians, regulated a farm, managed a shop, and stood erect, supported by their own industry, instead of hanging their heads surcharged with the dew of sensibility, that consumes the beauty to which it at first gave lustre; nay, I doubt whether pity and love are so near akin as poets feign, for I have seldom seen much compassion excited by the helplessness of females, unless they were fair; then, perhaps, pity was the soft handmaid of love, or the harbinger of lust.

How much more respectable is the woman who earns her own bread by fulfilling any duty, than the most accomplished beauty!—beauty did I say?—so sensible am I of the beauty of moral loveliness, or the harmonious propriety that attunes the passions of a well-regulated mind, that I blush at making the comparison; yet I sigh to think how few women aim at attaining this respectability by withdrawing from the giddy whirl of pleasure, or the indolent calm that stupifies the good sort of women it sucks in.

Proud of their weakness, however, they must always be protected, guarded from care, and all the rough toils that dignify the mind.—If this be the fiat of fate, if they will make themselves insignificant and contemptible, sweetly to waste 'life away,' let them not expect to be valued when their beauty fades, for it is the fate of the fairest flowers to be admired and pulled to pieces by the careless hand that plucked them. In how many ways do I wish, from the purest benevolence, to impress this truth on my sex; yet I fear that they

Source: Mary Wollstonecraft, *A Vindication of the Rights of Woman*, edited by Carol H. Poston (New York: W.W. Norton and Company, Inc., 1975), pp. 141, 142, 149, 150, 167, 168-69, 192-94.

will not listen to a truth that dear bought experience has brought home to many an agitated bosom, nor willingly resign the privileges of rank and sex for the privileges of humanity, to which those have no claim who do not discharge its duties. . . .

Would men but generously snap our chains, and be content with rational fellowship instead of slavish obedience, they would find us more observant daughters, more affectionate sisters, more faithful wives, more reasonable mothers—in a word, better citizens. We should then love them with true affection, because we should learn to respect ourselves. . . .

 Equality in education was a major part of Wollstonecraft's reform program.

. . . Let an enlightened nation then try what effect reason would have to bring them back to nature, and their duty; and allowing them to share the advantages of education and government with man, see whether they will become better, as they grow wiser and become free. They cannot be injured by the experiment; for it is not in the power of man to render them more insignificant than they are at present.

To render this practicable, day schools, for particular ages, should be established by government, in which boys and girls might be educated together. . . .

Girls and boys still together? I hear some readers ask: yes. And I should not fear any other consequences than that some early attachment might take place; which, whilst it had the best effect on the moral character of the young people, might not perfectly agree with the views of the parents, for it will be a long time, I fear, before the world will be so far enlightened that parents, only anxious to render their children virtuous, shall allow them to choose companions for life themselves.

Besides, this would be a sure way to promote early marriages, and from early marriages the most salutary physical and moral effects naturally flow. What a different character does a married citizen assume from the selfish coxcomb, who lives, but for himself, and who is often afraid to marry lest he should not be able to live in a certain style. Great emergencies excepted, which would rarely occur in a society of which equality was the basis, a man can only be prepared to discharge the duties of public life, by the habitual practice of those inferiour ones which form the man.

In this plan of education the constitution of boys would not be ruined by the early debaucheries, which now make men so selfish, or girls rendered weak and vain, by indolence, and frivolous pursuits. But, I presuppose, that such a degree of equality should be established between the sexes as would shut out gallantry and coquetry, yet allow friendship and love to temper the heart for the discharge of higher duties.

These would be schools of morality—and the happiness of man, allowed to flow from the pure springs of duty and affection, what advances might not the human mind make? Society can only be happy and free in proportion as it is virtuous; but the present distinctions, established in society, corrode all private, and blast all public virtue. . . .

In her conclusion, Wollstonecraft asked for a "revolution" in the social system and in attitudes towards both sexes.

> . . . That women at present are by ignorance rendered foolish or vicious, is, I think, not to be disputed; and, that the most salutary effects tending to improve mankind might be expected from a REVOLUTION in female manners, appears, at least, with a face of probability, to rise out of the observation. For as marriage has been termed the parent of those endearing charities which draw man from the brutal herd, the corrupting intercourse that wealth, idleness, and folly, produce between the sexes, is more universally injurious to morality than all the other vices of mankind collectively considered. To adulterous lust the most sacred duties are sacrificed, because before marriage, men, by a promiscuous intimacy with women, learned to consider love as a selfish gratification—learned to separate it not only from esteem, but from the affection merely built on habit, which mixes a little humanity with it. Justice and friendship are also set at defiance, and that purity of taste is vitiated which would naturally lead a man to relish an artless display of affection rather than affected airs. But that noble simplicity of affection, which dares to appear unadorned, has few attractions for the libertine, though it be the charm, which by cementing the matrimonial tie, secures to the pledges of a warmer passion the necessary parental attention; for children will never be properly educated till friendship subsists between parents. Virtue flies from a house divided against itself—and a whole legion of devils take up their residence there.
>
> The affection of husbands and wives cannot be pure when they have so few sentiments in common, and when so little confidence is established at home, as must be the case when their pursuits are so different. That intimacy from which tenderness should flow, will not, cannot subsist between the vicious.
>
> Contending, therefore, that the sexual distinction which men have so warmly insisted upon, is arbitrary, I have dwelt on an observation, that several sensible men, with whom I have conversed on the subject, allowed to be well founded; and it is simply this, that the little chastity to be found amongst men, and consequent disregard of modesty, tend to degrade both sexes; and further, that the modesty of women, characterized as such, will often be only the artful veil of wantonness instead of being the natural reflection of purity, till modesty be universally respected.
>
> From the tyranny of man, I firmly believe, the greater number of female follies proceed; and the cunning, which I allow makes at present a part of their character, I likewise have repeatedly endeavoured to prove, is produced by oppression. . . .
>
> Let woman share the rights and she will emulate the virtues of man; for she must grow more perfect when emancipated, or justify the authority that chains such a weak being to her duty. . . .

1. "Would men but generously snap our chains, and be content with rational fellowship instead of slavish obedience, they would find us more observant daughters, more affectionate sisters, more faithful wives, more reasonable

mothers—in a word, better citizens." Reconstruct the arguments used by Wollstonecraft to reach this conclusion.

2. What "revolutionary" changes in education did the author recommend? What social impact did she hope that they would have?

3. Mary Wollstonecraft has often been described as "modern" in her outlook. To what extent have her goals been realized in our own society? To what extent are her arguments still a relevant critique of our society?

■ ■ ■

MARQUIS DE CONDORCET

Antoine-Nicolas de Condorcet (1743-94), a leading mathematician and *philosophe*, wrote, while in hiding from the Reign of Terror of the French Revolution, one of the most influential testaments to optimism, progress, and rationalism to come out of the eighteenth century. His *Sketch for a Historical Picture of the Progress of the Human Mind*, published posthumously in 1795, was an attempt to develop a philosophy of history based on the assumption of human progress. Condorcet believed that humanity was, in his time, at the beginning of its tenth and last stage: this being the establishment of a world where reason and science would be the bases of truth, and where equality, tolerance, and peace would be the foundations of social and political life.

In his introduction Condorcet discussed his belief in using history to understand the nature of human progress and the possibility of "the perfectibility of man."

> Man is born with the ability to receive sensations; to perceive them and to distinguish between the various simple sensations of which they are composed; to remember, recognize and combine them; to compare these combinations; to apprehend what they have in common and the ways in which they differ; to attach signs to them all in order to recognize them more easily and to allow for the ready production of new combinations.
>
> This faculty is developed in him through the action of external objects, that is to say, by the occurrence of certain composite sensations whose constancy or coherence in change are independent of him; through communication with other beings like himself; and finally through various artificial methods which these first developments have led him to invent.
>
> Sensations are attended by pleasure or pain; and man for his part has the capacity to transform such momentary impressions into permanent feelings of an agreeable or disagreeable character, and then to experience these feelings when he either observes or recollects the pleasures and pains of other sentient beings.

Source: Antoine-Nicolas de Condorcet, *Sketch for a Historical Picture of the Progress of the Human Mind*, translated by Jean Barraclough (London: Weidenfeld and Nicolson, 1955), pp. 3-5, 127-28, 136, 163, 179, 184, 193, 194-95, 201-202.

Finally, as a consequence of this capacity and of his ability to form and combine ideas, there arise between him and his fellow-creatures ties of interest and duty, to which nature herself has wished to attach the most precious portion of our happiness and the most painful of our ills.

If one confines oneself to the study and observation of the general facts and laws about the development of these faculties, considering only what is common to all human beings, this science is called metaphysics. But if one studies this development as it manifests itself in the inhabitants of a certain area at a certain period of time and then traces it on from generation to generation, one has the picture of the progress of the human mind. This progress is subject to the same general laws that can be observed in the development of the faculties of the individual, and it is indeed no more than the sum of that development realized in a large number of individuals joined together in a society. What happens at any particular moment is the result of what has happened at all previous moments, and itself has an influence on what will happen in the future.

So such a picture is historical, since it is a record of change and is based on the observation of human societies throughout the different stages of their development. It ought to reveal the order of this change and the influence that each moment exerts upon the subsequent moment, and so ought also to show, in the modifications that the human species has undergone, ceaselessly renewing itself through the immensity of the centuries, the path that it has followed, the steps that it has made towards truth or happiness.

Such observations upon what man has been and what he is today, will instruct us about the means we should employ to make certain and rapid the further progress that his nature allows him still to hope for.

Such is the aim of the work that I have undertaken, and its result will be to show by appeal to reason and fact that nature has set no term to the perfection of human faculties; that the perfectibility of man is truly indefinite; and that the progress of this perfectibility, from now onwards independent of any power that might wish to halt it, has no other limit than the duration of the globe upon which nature has cast us. This progress will doubtless vary in speed, but it will never be reversed as long as the earth occupies its present place in the system of the universe, and as long as the general laws of this system produce neither a general cataclysm nor such changes as will deprive the human race of its present faculties and its present resources. . . .

In his survey of the ninth stage Condorcet elaborated on his belief in reason and science.

. . . This sketch of the progress of philosophy and of the dissemination of enlightenment, whose more general and more evident effects we have already examined, brings us up to the stage when the influence of progress upon public opinion, of public opinion upon nations or their leaders, suddenly ceases to be a slow, imperceptible affair, and produces a revolution in the whole order of several nations, a certain earnest of the revolution that must one day include in its scope the whole of the human race.

After long periods of error, after being led astray by vague or incomplete theories, publicists have at last discovered the true rights of man and how they can all be deduced from the single truth, that *man is a sentient being, capable of reasoning and of acquiring moral ideas.*

They have seen that the maintenance of these rights was the sole object of men's coming together in political societies, and that the social art is the art of guaranteeing the preservation of these rights and their distribution in the most equal fashion over the largest area. It was felt that in every society the means of assuring the rights of the individual should be submitted to certain common rules, but that the authority to choose these means and to determine these rules could belong only to the majority of the members of the society itself; for in making this choice the individual cannot follow his own reason without subjecting others to it, and the will of the majority is the only mark of truth that can be accepted by all without loss of equality.

Each man can in fact genuinely bind himself in advance to the will of the majority which then becomes unanimous; but he can bind only himself; and he cannot engage even himself towards this majority when it fails to respect the rights of the individual, after having once recognized them.

Here we see at once the rights of the majority over society or its members, and the limits of these rights. . . .

At last man could proclaim aloud his right, which for so long had been ignored, to submit all opinions to his own reason and to use in the search for truth the only instrument for its recognition that he has been given. Every man learnt with a sort of pride that nature had not for ever condemned him to base his beliefs on the opinions of others; the superstitions of antiquity and the abasement of reason before the transports of supernatural religion disappeared from society as from philosophy.

Soon there was formed in Europe a class of men who were concerned less with the discovery or development of the truth than with its propagation, men who whilst devoting themselves to the tracking down of prejudices in the hiding places where the priests, the schools, the governments and all long-established institutions had gathered and protected them, made it their life-work to destroy popular errors rather than to drive back the frontiers of human knowledge—an indirect way of aiding its progress which was not less fraught with peril, nor less useful. . . .

All errors in politics and morals are based on philosophical errors and these in turn are connected with scientific errors. There is not a religious system nor a supernatural extravagance that is not founded on ignorance of the laws of nature. The inventors, the defenders of these absurdities could not foresee the successive perfection of the human mind. Convinced that men in their day knew everything that they could ever know and would always believe what they then believed, they confidently supported their idle dreams on the current opinions of their country and their age.

Advances in the physical sciences are all the more fatal to these errors in that they often destroy them without appearing to attack them. . . .

The tenth stage was titled "The Future Progress of the Human Mind."

The time will therefore come when the sun will shine only on free men who know no other master but their reason; when tyrants and slaves, priests and their stupid or hypocritical instruments will exist only in works of history and on the stage; and when we shall think of them only to pity their victims and their dupes; to maintain ourselves in a state of vigilance by thinking on their excesses; and to learn how to recognize and so to destroy, by force of reason, the first seeds of tyranny and superstition, should they ever dare to reappear amongst us.

In looking at the history of societies we shall have had occasion to observe that there is often a great difference between the rights that the law allows its citizens and the rights that they actually enjoy, and, again, between the equality established by political codes and that which in fact exists amongst individuals: and we shall have noticed that these differences were one of the principal causes of the destruction of freedom in the Ancient republics, of the storms that troubled them, and of the weakness that delivered them over to foreign tyrants.

These differences have three main causes: inequality in wealth; inequality in status between the man whose means of subsistence are hereditary and the man whose means are dependent on the length of his life, or, rather, on that part of his life in which he is capable of work; and, finally, inequality in education. . . .

So we might say that a well directed system of education rectifies natural inequality in ability instead of strengthening it, just as good laws remedy natural inequality in the means of subsistence, and just as in societies where laws have brought about this same equality, liberty, though subject to a regular constitution, will be more widespread, more complete than in the total independence of savage life. Then the social art will have fulfilled its aim, that of assuring and extending to all men enjoyment of the common rights to which they are called by nature.

The real advantages that should result from this progress, of which we can entertain a hope that is almost a certainty, can have no other term than that of the absolute perfection of the human race; since, as the various kinds of equality come to work in its favour by producing ampler sources of supply, more extensive education, more complete liberty, so equality will be more real and will embrace everything which is really of importance for the happiness of human beings. . . .

Is there any vicious habit, any practice contrary to good faith, any crime, whose origin and first cause cannot be traced back to the legislation, the institutions, the prejudices of the country wherein this habit, this practice, this crime can be observed? In short will not the general welfare that results from the progress of the useful arts once they are grounded on solid theory, or from the progress of legislation once it is rooted in the truths of political science, incline mankind to humanity, benevolence and justice? In other words, do not all these observations which I propose to develop further in my book, show that the moral goodness of man, the necessary consequence of his constitution, is capable of indefinite perfection like all his other faculties, and that nature has linked together in an unbreakable chain truth, happiness and virtue?

Among the causes of the progress of the human mind that are of the utmost importance to the general happiness, we must number the complete annihilation of the prejudices that have brought about an inequality of rights between the sexes, an inequality fatal even to the party in whose favour it works. It is vain for us to look for a justification of this principle in any differences of physical organization, intellect or moral sensibility between men and women. This inequality has its origin solely in an abuse of strength, and all the later sophistical attempts that have been made to excuse it are vain. . . .

. . . put an end to a principle only too fecund of injustice, cruelty and crime, by removing the dangerous conflict between the strongest and most irrepressible of all natural inclinations and man's duty or the interests of society? Would it not produce what has until now been no more than a dream, national manners of a mildness and purity, formed not by proud asceticism, not by hypocrisy, not by the fear of shame or religious terrors but by freely contracted habits that are inspired by nature and acknowledged by reason?

Once people are enlightened they will know that they have the right to dispose of their own life and wealth as they choose; they will gradually learn to regard war as the most dreadful of scourges, the most terrible of crimes. The first wars to disappear will be those into which usurpers have forced their subjects in defence of their pretended hereditary rights.

Nations will learn that they cannot conquer other nations without losing their own liberty; that permanent confederations are their only means of preserving their independence; and that they should seek not power but security. Gradually mercantile prejudices will fade away: and a false sense of commercial interest will lose the fearful power it once had of drenching the earth in blood and of ruining nations under pretext of enriching them. When at last the nations come to agree on the principles of politics and morality, when in their own better interests they invite foreigners to share equally in all the benefits men enjoy either through the bounty of nature or by their own industry, then all the causes that produce and perpetuate national animosities and poison national relations will disappear one by one; and nothing will remain to encourage or even to arouse the fury of war.

Organizations more intelligently conceived than those projects of eternal peace which have filled the leisure and consoled the hearts of certain philosophers, will hasten the progress of the brotherhood of nations, and wars between countries will rank with assassinations as freakish atrocities, humiliating and vile in the eyes of nature and straining with indelible opprobrium the country or the age whose annals record them. . . .

But are not our physical faculties and the strength, dexterity and acuteness of our senses, to be numbered among the qualities whose perfection in the individual may be transmitted? Observation of the various breeds of domestic animals inclines us to believe that they are, and we can confirm this by direct observation of the human race.

Finally may we not extend such hopes to the intellectual and moral faculties? May not our parents, who transmit to us the benefits or disadvantages of their constitution, and from whom we receive our shape and features, as well as our tendencies to certain physical affections, hand on to us also that part of the physical organization which determines the intellect, the power of the brain, the ardour of the soul or the moral sensibility? Is it not probable that education, in perfecting these qualities, will at the same time influence, modify and perfect the organization itself? Analogy, investigation of the human faculties and the study of certain facts, all seem to give substance to such conjectures which would further push back the boundaries of our hopes.

These are the questions with which we shall conclude this final stage. How consoling for the philosopher who laments the errors, the crimes, the injustices which still pollute the earth and of which he is often the victim is this view of the human race, emancipated from its shackles, released from the empire of fate and from that of the enemies of its progress, advancing with a firm and sure step along the path of truth, virtue and happiness! It is the contemplation of this prospect that rewards him for all his efforts to assist the progress of reason and the defence of liberty. He dares to regard these strivings as part of the eternal chain of human destiny; and in this persuasion he is filled with the true delight of virtue and the pleasure of having done some lasting good which fate can never destroy by a sinister stroke of revenge, by calling back the reign of slavery and prejudice. Such contemplation is for him an asylum, in which the memory of his persecutors cannot pursue him; there he lives in thought with man restored to his natural rights and dignity, forgets man tormented and corrupted by greed, fear or envy; there he lives with his peers in an Elysium created by reason and graced by the purest pleasures known to the love of mankind.

1. What abilities did Condorcet attribute to humanity?
2. How did he argue that the development of these skills is evidence of the "perfectibility" of mankind?
3. What did Condorcet see as the central truth underlying the concept of natural rights? What impact did the discovery of this truth have on society?
4. Outline Condorcet's view of the existence and destruction of "error."
5. How did the author account for the differences between the rights legally granted to citizens and those they actually enjoy?
6. Outline those inequalities and conflicts that Condorcet said would be eliminated when humanity perfects its moral goodness.
7. How did he believe these changes in attitude would affect international relations?
8. Write your own conclusion about Condorcet's arguments with respect to the inevitable progress of the human mind.

• • •

NAPOLEON BONAPARTE

Napoleon Bonaparte (1769-1821), who became Emperor of the French in 1804, claimed to be a "son of the revolution," and set out to conquer Europe and the world. Brilliant and sometimes contradictory, he was viewed during and after his time as a phenomenon who had to be understood as part of the new style of politics introduced by the French Revolution. He was defeated in 1814 and again in 1815 by coalitions of European states. While in exile, Napoleon dictated his memoirs in which he saw himself as a modern hero whose destiny was to bring the benefits of the French Revolution to the world, and who was defeated by reactionaries. His administrative genius and legal reforms had a lasting impact on the development of the modern state, and his new style of rule made him a model for other leaders who followed. His life and his sayings were the subject of much interest and fascination.

 In exile after his defeat, Napoleon dictated and discussed his views on the French Revolution.

> . . . The French Revolution was . . . a general mass movement of the nation against the privileged classes. The French nobility, like that of all Europe, dates from the barbarian invasions which broke up the Roman Empire. In France, the nobles represented the ancient Franks and Burgundians; the rest of the nation, the Gauls. The introduction of the feudal system established the principle that every landed property had a lord. All political rights were exercised by the priests and the nobles. The peasants were enslaved, partly by binding them to the soil.
>
> The progress of civilization and knowledge liberated the people. This new state of affairs caused the prosperity of industry and trade. In the eighteenth century, the larger part of the land, of wealth, and of the fruits of civilization belonged to the people. The nobles, however, still formed a privileged class: they controlled the upper and intermediate courts, they held feudal rights under a great variety of names and forms, they were exempt from contributing to any of the taxes imposed by society, and they had exclusive access to the most honorable employments.
>
> All these abuses stirred the citizens to protest. The chief aim of the Revolution was to destroy all privileges; to abolish manorial courts, justice being an inalienable attribute of the sovereign authority; to suppress all feudal rights as remnants of the people's former slavery; to subject all citizens and all property without distinction to taxation by the State. Finally, the Revolution proclaimed the equality of rights. All citizens could fill all employments, subject only to their talents and the vicissitudes of chance.
>
> The monarchy was made up of provinces annexed to the Crown at various periods. . . . France was not a state but an unamalgamated collection of several states placed side by side. Chance and the events of past centuries had determined the whole. The Revolution, applying its guiding principle of equality to the citizens among themselves as well as to the various territories, destroyed all these petty nations and created a new great nation. There was no more Brittany, no more Normandy, Burgundy, Champagne, Provence, or Lorraine: there was a France. . . .
>
> Whatever had been brought about in the sequence of events since the time of Clovis ceased to exist. These changes were all so favorable to the people that they took hold with the greatest ease: by 1800 there remained not a single memory of the old privileges. . . . In order to trace any existing institution to its origin all that was necessary was to look up the new law that

Source: J. Christopher Herold, ed., *The Mind of Napoleon* (New York: Columbia University Press, 1955), pp. 65-67, 191-93, 272-73.

had established it. Half of the land had changed ownership; the farmers and the bourgeois had become rich. The progress of agriculture, manufactures, and industry passed all our hopes. France offered the spectacle of thirty million inhabitants living within natural limits, forming a single class of citizens governed by a single law, a single organization, a single order. All these changes accorded with the well-being of the nation, with its laws, with justice, and with the spirit of the century.

. . . The counterrevolution [i.e., the reaction that set in after 1815], even if given a free course, must inevitably come to drown in revolution. . . . For henceforth nothing can destroy or efface the grand principles of our Revolution. These great and noble truths must remain forever, so inextricably are they linked to our splendor, our monuments, our prodigious deeds. We have drowned its earlier shame in floods of glory. These truths are henceforth immortal. . . . They live on in England, they illumine America, they are naturalized in France: from this tripod the light will burst upon the world.

These truths will rule the world. They will be the creed, the religion, the morality of all nations. And, no matter what has been said, this memorable era will be linked to my person, because, after all, I have carried its torch and consecrated its principles, and because persecution now has made me its Messiah. . . .

In 1816 Napoleon also discussed his plans for England and his belief in his own destiny.

. . . In my scheme, England was in nature bound to become a mere appendix of France. Nature has made her one of our islands, just like Oléron or Corsica.

. . . I had left open the possibility of a landing [in England]; I had the best army that ever was—the army that was to win at Austerlitz, and with that I have said everything. Four days were enough to reach London. I would not have entered as conqueror but as liberator, a new William of Orange—but more generous and disinterested. The discipline in my army would have been exemplary; it would have behaved in London as if still in Paris. No sacrifices, not even war taxes would have been exacted from the English. We would have appeared to them not as victors but as brothers who had come to restore them to their freedom and their rights. I would have told them to form an assembly and to effect their regeneration by their own efforts; that in political legislation they were our seniors; that we wanted nothing from them except to rejoice in their happiness and prosperity—and I would have been scrupulously faithful to my words. And thus, before a few months had passed, these two nations, these ruthless enemies, would have become united by identical principles, policies, and interests.

From there I would have proceeded to regenerate Europe from the south to the north, under the colors of republicanism—for I was First Consul then—just as I nearly succeeded in doing later, from the north to the south, under monarchic forms. Both these systems could have served equally well, for they tended toward the same end, and both would have been put into operation with firmness, moderation, and good faith. How many known evils, how many evils as yet unknown this poor Europe of ours would have been spared!

There never was a vaster project conceived in the interests of civilization with more generous intent or one that came closer to its realization. And here is the remarkable thing: the obstacles that made me fail did not come from men; they all came from the elements. In the south, the sea has been my undoing; in the north, the burning of Moscow and the cold of winter. Thus water, air, and fire, all of Nature, nothing but Nature—these have been the enemies of a universal regeneration which Nature herself demanded! The problems of Providence are insoluble.

. . . England and France have held the fate of the earth, and especially of European civilization, in their hands. How much evil we have inflicted on each other! How much good we might have done!

Napoleon made heroic claims for himself.

> . . . I have closed the gaping abyss of anarchy, and I have unscrambled chaos. I have cleansed the Revolution, ennobled the common people, and restored the authority of kings. I have stirred all men to competition, I have rewarded merit wherever I found it, I have pushed back the boundaries of greatness. All this, you must admit, is something. Is there any point on which I could be attacked and on which a historian could not take up my defense? My intentions, perhaps? He has evidence enough to clear me. My despotism? He can prove that dictatorship was absolutely necessary. Will it be said that I restricted freedom? He will be able to prove that licence, anarchy, and general disorder were still on our doorstep. Shall I be accused of having loved war too much? He will show that I was always on the defensive. That I wanted to set up a universal monarchy? He will explain that it was merely the fortuitous result of circumstances and that I was led to it step by step by our very enemies. My ambition? Ah, no doubt he will find that I had ambition, a great deal of it—but the grandest and noblest, perhaps, that ever was: the ambition of establishing and consecrating at last the kingdom of reason and the full exercise, the complete enjoyment, of all human capabilities! And in this respect the historian will perhaps find himself forced to regret that such an ambition has not been fulfilled, has not been satisfied. [After a silence the Emperor added:] And yet, my dear Las Cases, these few words hold my whole history.

> . . . Everybody has loved me and hated me; everybody has taken me up, dropped me, and taken me up again. . . . Only this was not all at the same time but at intervals and at various periods. I was like the sun, which crosses the equator as it describes the ecliptic: as soon as I entered each man's clime, I kindled every hope, I was blessed, I was adored; but as soon as I left it, I no longer was understood and contrary sentiments replaced the old ones. . . .

1. Evaluate Napoleon's analysis of both the Revolution and the future of France.
2. "Many historians feel that participants are both the best and worst witnesses of historical events." Account for this statement with reference to the version of history presented by Napoleon.

▪ ▪ ▪

JACQUES-LOUIS DAVID

The art of the period of the French Revolution and Napoleon in France was dominated by the talent and personality of Jacques-Louis David (1748-1825). An excellent painter, David made his reputation in the few years prior to 1789 with works in the neo-classical style, which had strong moral and patriotic themes. During the Revolution he was elected to the Convention. In 1793 he painted portraits commemorating revolutionary martyrs, including one of Marat. After the end of the Reign of Terror, David was imprisoned for a short time, but in the Napoleonic period he became a supporter and painter of the Emperor. His work and life raised important issues about the relationship of the artist to society and the state.

A In August 1793, as a member of the Convention, David supported the closing of the "aristocratic" French Academy of Painting and Sculpture. In November, he proposed to the Convention that a new institution be established.

> In decreeing that those artistic monuments awarded by competition and worthy public recompense shall be judged by a jury named by the people's Representatives, you have paid homage to the unity and indivisibility of the Republic, and you have asked your Committee on Public Education to prepare a list of candidates. Your Committee has, therefore, considered the arts in the light of all those factors by which they should help to spread the progress of the human spirit, and to propagate and transmit to posterity the striking examples of the efforts of a tremendous people who, guided by reason and philosophy, are bringing back to earth the reign of liberty, equality, and law. The arts must therefore contribute forcefully to the education of the public. Too long have tyrants, fearful even of the image of virtue, kept thought itself in chains, encouraged license, and stamped out genius; the arts are the imitation of nature in her most beautiful and perfect form; a feeling natural to man attracts him to the same end . . . Then will those marks of heroism and civic virtue offered the eyes of the people electrify its soul, and plant the seeds of glory and devotion to the fatherland.
>
> Your Committee has decided that, during a period when art, like virtue, must be reborn, to leave the judgment of the productions of genius to artists alone would be to leave them in the rut of habit, in which they crawled before the despotism they flattered. It belongs to those stout souls to whom the study of nature has lent a feeling for truth and grandeur to give a new impulse to the arts and bring them back to the principles of true beauty. Thus he who is gifted with a fine sensibility, though without culture, and the philosopher, the poet, and scholar, each in those different things which make up the art of judging the artist, pupil of nature, are the judges most capable

Sources: Robert Goldwater and Marco Treves, ed., *Artists on Art* (London: John Murray, 1976), pp. 205-206; Lorenz Eitner, *Neoclassicism and Romanticism, 1750-1850* (Englewood Cliffs, New Jersey: Prentice-Hall, Inc., 1970), Volume I, pp. 141-42; Elizabeth Gilmore Holt, ed., *From the Classicists to the Impressionists: Art and Architecture in the Nineteenth Century* (Garden City, New York: Doubleday and Company, Inc., 1966), pp. 5, 6-8.

of representing the tastes and insights of entire people in the task of awarding Republican artists with the palms of glory.

B Also in November 1793, David suggested that a new monument be erected to the French people.

> . . . Unable to usurp God's place in the churches, the kings took possession of their portals. Here they put their effigies, no doubt so that the people's adoration should come to a stop at the entrance of the sanctuary. Accustomed to laying their hands on everything, they had the presumption of competing with God Himself for the incense which men offered Him. You have overthrown these insolent usurpers; laughed to scorn, they now litter the soil which they once stained with their crimes.
>
> Let a monument be raised within the confines of the Commune of Paris, close to the church which the kings once made their Pantheon, to be a reminder to our descendants and the first trophy erected by the Sovereign People in its victory over the tyrants. Let the dismembered fragments of these statues form a lasting monument of the kings' downfall and the people's glory. Let the traveler who passes through this reborn country take back to his homeland the useful lesson: "Once I saw kings in Paris; when I returned, they were no more." (Applause.)
>
> I propose, therefore, that a monument be erected in the square of the Pont Neuf. It is to represent the Giant People, the People of France.
>
> Let this statue, imposing in its strength and simplicity, be inscribed in large letters, on the forehead: *Light*; on the chest: *Nature* and *Truth*; on the arms: *Strength, Courage*. Put in one of its hands the statues of Liberty and Equality embracing one another and ready to traverse the world, in order to show that they are founded on the genius and virtue of the people. And let this statue of the people stand upright and hold in its other hand that terrible club with which the ancients armed their Hercules.
>
> It is up to us to raise such a monument. Other peoples who loved liberty have raised similar ones before us. Not far from our borders lie the bones of the tyrants' slaves who attacked the liberty of the Swiss. Piled into pyramids, they now threaten those impudent kings who would dare to desecrate the land of free men.
>
> Thus we shall pile up in Paris the effigies of the kings and their vile attributes, to serve as the pedestal for the emblem of the French people. . . .

C In 1800 David exhibited his painting *The Battle of Romans and Sabines*, which had been completed in 1799, at a public exhibition, an unusual procedure at that time. The following is part of his justification:

> Antiquity has not ceased to be the great school of modern painters, the source from which they draw the beauties of their art. We seek to imitate the ancient artists, in the genius of their conceptions, the purity of their design, the expressiveness of their features, and the grace of their forms. Could we not take a step further and imitate them also in the customs and institutions established by them to bring their arts to perfection?
>
> For a painter the custom of exhibiting his works before the eyes of his

fellow citizens, in return for which they make individual payment, is not new. . . . the habit of public exhibition of paintings was permitted by the Greeks, and that certainly, when we have to do with the arts, we should not fear to err ourselves if we followed in their footsteps.

In our own time this custom of showing the arts to the public is practised in England and is called *Exhibition*. The pictures of the death of General Wolf and of Lord Chatham, painted by our contemporary, West, and shown by him, won him immense sums. The custom of exhibition existed long before this, and was introduced in the last century by Van Dyck: the public came in crowds to admire his work: he gained by this means a considerable fortune.

Is this not an idea as just as it is wise, which brings to art the means of existing for itself, of supporting itself by its own resources, thus to enjoy the noble independence suited to genius, without which the fire that inspires it is soon extinguished? On the other hand, could there be a more dignified and honourable means of gaining a share of the fruit of his labours than for an artist to submit his works to the judgment of the public and to await the recompense that they will wish to make him. If his work is mediocre, public opinion will soon mete out justice to it. The author, acquiring neither glory nor material reward, would learn by hard experience ways of mending his faults and of capturing the attention of the spectators by more happy conceptions. . . .

. . . If the habit of exhibition could offer to the gifted a means of release from poverty, and if, as a result of this first opportunity, I might help to bring the arts nearer to their true destination which is to serve morality and to elevate the soul, thus extend to the hearts of the spectators those generous sentiments called into being by the productions of the artists! It is a great secret to touch the human heart, and by this means a great impulse might be given to the public energy and to the national character. Who can deny that until now the French people have been strangers to the arts, and that they have lived among them without participating in them? Painting or sculpture offer rare gifts; they become the conquest of a rich man who may have purchased them at a low price. Jealous of his exclusive possession, he admits only a few friends to share a sight forbidden to the rest of society. Now, at least, by favouring the custom of public exhibition, the public, for a modest payment, shares a portion of the riches of genius; they may likewise come to know the arts, to which they are not as indifferent as they affect to believe; their understanding will increase, their taste be formed. Although not experienced enough to pronounce upon the fine points or the difficulties of art, their judgment, constantly inspired by nature and always born of emotion, might often flatter and even enlighten an artist whom they have learned to appreciate.

Moreover, with what regret and grief have men, sincerely devoted to the arts and their country, seen masterpieces of great price pass to foreign nations while their own country, where they were produced, scarcely took notice. Public exhibition would tend to keep such masterpieces in the happy country where they were born; by such means we might hope to see the great days of Greece live again—a land where the artist, satisfied with the sums awarded to him by his fellow citizens, will be happy to make a gift to his countrymen of the masterpieces which they have admired. Having been honoured for his talents, he will end by deserving well of his fellow citizens for his generosity.

I shall doubtless be told that every people has its customs; and that the public exhibition of the arts has never been introduced into France. I answer, in the first place, that I do not undertake to give an explanation of the contradictions of human nature: but I do ask whether it is not true that a dramatic artist gives the greatest possible publicity to his work and receives a portion of the money of the spectators in exchange for the emotions and the varying pleasure he has given them by displaying their passions or their absurdities? I ask if a composer of music, who has given soul and life to a lyric poem, blushes when he shares with the author of the words of the poem, the profits of his creation? Shall what is honourable in one art be humiliating in another? And if the different arts themselves are all members of one family, may not all artists feel themselves as brothers and follow the same laws by which they may arrive at gain and fortune?

I answer again that we must make speed to do what has not yet been done if we wish to do good. What holds us back, then, from introducing into the French Republic a custom which the Greeks and the modern nations have given us? Our old prejudices no longer oppose us in the exercise of public liberty. The nature and the development of our ideas have changed since the Revolution, and we shall not return, I hope, to the false delicacy which had for so long constrained genius. As for myself, I recognize no honour higher than that of having the public as judge. I fear from it neither passion nor partiality: the rewards it bestows are voluntary gifts, witnesses to its taste for the arts: its praise is the free expression of the enjoyment it experiences; such recompense is, without doubt, equal to that of academic times.

The considerations I have proposed as to the custom of public exhibition, of which I shall have been the first to give an example, was especially suggested to me by the wish to obtain for the artists, dedicated to painting, a means by which they might be repaid for the sacrifice of their time and money, and to insure to them a resource against poverty—not seldom their unhappy lot. I have been encouraged and helped in these ideas by the government which, on this occasion, has given me a proof of the remarkable protection it accords to the arts, in furnishing me a place for my exhibition, together with other considerable requirements. I shall have received a most flattering reward if, by the public having come to enjoy my picture, I may have been able to point a useful road to the artist, and, by giving him encouragement, contribute to the advancement of art and to the perfecting of a righteous spirit which we should, without doubt, have for our aim. . . .

1. Although David opposed tyrannical control of the arts, he argued that to "leave the judgment of the productions of genius to artists alone would leave them in a rut." How did David's proposal for artistic approval differ from the traditional method?
2. Evaluate David's justification for the destruction of works of art in the name of the Revolution.
3. Analyse the combination of revolutionary ideals and practical business sense in David's defence of holding a public exhibition.

▪ ▪ ▪

WILLIAM BLAKE

William Blake (1757-1827) was a poet and an artist. He engraved and published nearly all of his major poetry himself, and invented the method of engraving the text and the illustration on the same plate. Opposed to the rationalism and neo-classicism of his time, Blake stressed love and imagination and was interested in the spiritual and the mystical. Though often thought of as an eccentric, he exerted influence on a later generation which became interested in probing a human nature defined by more than reason alone.

Blake owned a copy of Joshua Reynolds' *Discourses*, with whose principles he fundamentally disagreed. The following, written about 1808, is taken from the notes made by Blake in the margins of Reynolds' work.

This Man was Hired to Depress Art.

This is the Opinion of Will Blake: my Proofs of this Opinion are given in the following Notes. . . .

The Arts & Sciences are the Destruction of Tyrannies or Bad Governments. Why should A Good Government endeavour to Depress what is its Chief & only Support?

The Foundation of Empire is Art & Science. Remove them or Degrade them, & the Empire is No More. Empire follows Art & Not Vice Versa as Englishmen suppose. . . .

Reynolds's Opinion was that Genius May be Taught & that all Pretence to Inspiration is a Lie & a Deceit, to say the least of it. For if it is a Deceit, the whole Bible is Madness. This Opinion originates in the Greeks' calling the Muses Daughters of Memory.

The Enquiry in England is not whether a Man has Talents & Genius, But whether he is Passive & Polite & a Virtuous Ass & obedient to Nobelmen's Opinions in Art & Science. If he is, he is a Good Man. If Not, he must be Starved. . . .

It is Evident that Reynolds Wish'd none but Fools to be in the Arts & in order to this, he calls all others Vague Enthusiasts or Madmen.

What has Reasoning to do with the Art of Painting? . . .

Knowledge of Ideal Beauty is Not to be Acquired. It is Born with us. Innate Ideas are in Every Man, Born with him; they are truly Himself. The Man who says that we have No Innate Ideas must be a Fool & Knave, Having No Con-Science or Innate Science. . . .

One Central Form composed of all other Forms being Granted, it does not therefore follow that all other Forms are Deformity.

All Forms are Perfect in the Poet's Mind, but these are not Abstracted nor compounded from Nature, but are from Imagination. . . .

Reynolds Thinks that Man Learns all that he knows. I say on the Contrary that Man Brings All that he has or can have Into the World with him. Man is Born Like a Garden ready Planted & Sown. This World is too poor to produce one Seed.

Source: Geoffrey Keynes, ed., *Poetry and Prose of William Blake* (London: The Nonesuch Library, 1967), pp. 770, 779, 786, 787, 802, 806, 623-24, 626, 633.

The mind is but a barren soil; a soil which is soon exhausted, and will produce no crop, . . .

The mind that could have produced this Sentence must have been a Pitiful, a Pitiable Imbecillity. I always thought that the Human Mind was the most Prolific of All Things & Inexhaustible. I certainly do Thank God that I am not like Reynolds. . . .

It is not in Terms that Reynolds & I disagree. Two Contrary Opinions can never by any Language be made alike. I say, Taste & Genius are Not Teachable or Acquirable, but are born with us. Reynolds says the Contrary. . . .

Demonstration, Similitude & Harmony are Objects of Reasoning. Invention, Identity & Melody are Objects of Intuition. . . .

God forbid that Truth should be Confined to Mathematical Demonstration!

◆B In his *Public Address*, Blake discussed his attitude towards art.

Men think they can Copy Nature as Correctly as I copy Imagination; this they will find Impossible, & all the Copies or Pretended Copiers of Nature, from Rembrandt to Reynolds, believe that Nature becomes to its Victim nothing but Blots & Blurs. Why are Copiers of Nature Incorrect, while Copiers of Imagination are Correct? this is manifest to all. . . .

It is Nonsense for Nobelmen & Gentlemen to offer Premiums for the Encouragement of Art when such Pictures as these can be done without Premiums; let them Encourage what Exists Already, & not endeavour to counteract by tricks; let it no more be said that Empires Encourage Arts, for it is Arts that Encourage Empires. Arts & Artists are Spiritual & laugh at Mortal Contingencies. It is in their Power to hinder Instruction but not to Instruct, just as it is in their Power to Murder a Man but not to make a Man.

Let us teach Buonaparte, & whomsoever else it may concern, That it is not Arts that follow & attend upon Empire, but Empire that attends upon & follows The Arts.

No Man of Sense can think that the Imitation of the Objects of Nature is The Art of Painting, or that such Imitation, which any one may easily perform, is worthy of Notice, much less that such an Art should be the Glory & Pride of a Nation. The Italians laugh at English Connoisseurs, who are most of them such silly Fellows as to believe this. . . .

They say there is no Strait Line in Nature; this Is a Lie, like all that they say. For there is Every Line in Nature. But I will tell them what is Not in Nature. An Even Tint is not in Nature; it produces Heaviness. Nature's Shadows are Ever varying & a Ruled Sky that is quite Even never can Produce a Natural Sky; the same with every Object in a Picture, its Spots are its beauties. Now, Gentlemen Critics, how do you like this? You may rage, but what I say, I will prove by Such Practise & have already done, so that you will rage to your own destruction. . . . A Machine is not a Man nor a Work of Art; it is destructive of Humanity & of Art; the word Machination. . . .

1. Based on the picture presented in this selection of marginal notes, write a brief character sketch of Blake.
2. Compare Blake's views on the nature of art with those of Paine on government.

▪ ◇ ▪

3 ROMANTICISM, NATIONALISM & INDUSTRIALISM, 1815-1848

I n the first half of the nineteenth century a number of new movements appeared in the West, challenging tradition, asserting new values and attitudes towards human nature, and attacking earlier social policy and political ideas.

The period was inaugurated by the new Romanticism, an unco-ordinated movement of literary figures, artists, musicians, and other intellectuals, all of whom felt constrained by traditional values and modes of expression. Romantics valued the individual, a quest for understanding the inner life, reflections on humanity and nature, the spontaneous, the heroic, and the creative life. They looked to exceptional accomplishments and the new, yet also restored the value of myth and religion in the modern world. Abandoning the extreme rationality of the Enlightenment and neo-classicism, they sought to explore all aspects of human nature and human consciousness. Poets such as Wordsworth, Coleridge, and Goethe, artists such as Turner and Delacroix, and critics such as Baudelaire all redefined their fields and brought the new consciousness to public attention.

Nationalism grew to be a major force during the period, as the ideology began to take hold in theory and practice. The nation, an idea revered by those who began the French Revolution, now was viewed as the basis of the state, as culture and political sovereignty began to be equated. In addition, thinkers such as Hegel and Mazzini began to see a people's identity as being fused to their national community. As the state system took on more importance in organizing the West, the doctrine of nationalism became a central ideology.

In politics and philosophy there was some continuity with the liberal Enlightenment tradition. Tocqueville theorized on the nature of egalitarianism and democracy, and Thoreau defended the individual and the right to resist unjust laws in an effort to protect dissent. The philosophy of progress and science, begun during the Enlightenment, was continued by Comte, whose positivist ideas had great influence on methods of social analysis and perceptions of reality.

The first half of the nineteenth century was dominated, above all, by the introduction of the Industrial Revolution, a new way of creating wealth and organizing labour, which began to effect all in the West. The visual symbols became the factory and the railway, and the new political ideology came to be called socialism, which had many varieties. Saint-Simon saw the potential of the Industrial Revolution and asked that it be harnessed and that society be guided by its leaders. Fourier rejected industrial life for a utopian vision of a small community in which life and labour were far more attractive than they were in his own time. Marx and Engels placed the industrial revolution in historical perspective, stressed the importance of economic factors in human society and its organization, saw an inevitable clash of classes, and predicted progress through revolution and the establishment of a new type of society. All socialists rejected the idea that modern life represented the establishment of the value of progress. They all sought a revision of contemporary politics and society. The French novelist Balzac, though not at all sympathetic to liberalism and socialism, wrote a critique of human nature and modern life that paralleled the concerns of many liberal and socialist thinkers.

Most who wrote and thought in this period were impressed with the phenomenon of change. There was a growing understanding that change was the nature of the world, that the comfort of a static, unchanging life would no longer be part of the experience of the West.

WILLIAM WORDSWORTH

William Wordsworth's preface to the second edition (1800) of the *Lyrical Ballads* was the first major critical statement of Romantic poetry and the Romantic movement. The movement challenged the old neo-classical ideal, and it laid a theoretical groundwork for the new literature. In the "Preface," Wordsworth (1770-1850) attacked the beliefs that serious poetry was about the lives of epic heroes, kings and nobles, and that the language of poetry was artificial. On the contrary, Wordsworth asserted that poetry could deal with the feelings of ordinary people, its language could resemble that of everyday life, and the source of literary inspiration was the inner life of the creative poet. The redefinition made by Wordsworth and others, as well as their concern with the relationship between human beings and nature, opened up new literary directions in the early nineteenth century.

In the "Preface," Wordsworth claimed to deal with the lives of common people, as well as with their language.

> . . . The principal object, then, proposed in these poems was to choose incidents and situations from common life, and to relate or describe them, throughout, as far as was possible, in a selection of language really used by men, and, at the same time, to throw over them a certain coloring of imagination, whereby ordinary things should be presented to the mind in an unusual aspect; and further, and above all, to make these incidents and situations interesting by tracing in them, truly though not ostentatiously, the primary laws of our nature: chiefly, as far as regards the manner in which we associate ideas in a state of excitement. Humble and rustic life was generally chosen, because in that condition the essential passions of the heart find a better soil in which they can attain their maturity, are less under restraint, and speak a plainer and more emphatic language; because in that condition of life our elementary feelings co-exist in a state of greater simplicity, and consequently may be more accurately contemplated and more forcibly communicated; because the manners of rural life germinate from those elementary feelings, and, from the necessary character of rural occupations, are more easily comprehended, and are more durable; and, lastly, because in that condition the passions of

Source: M.H. Abrams, *et al., The Norton Anthology of English Literature* (New York: W.W. Norton and Company Inc., 1968), Vol. II, pp. 102-103, 104-105, 107, 110-11.

men are incorporated with the beautiful and permanent forms of nature. The language, too, of these men has been adopted (purified indeed from what appear to be its real defects, from all lasting and rational causes of dislike or disgust) because such men hourly communicate with the best objects from which the best part of language is originally derived; and because, from their rank in society and the sameness and narrow circle of their intercourse, being less under the influence of social vanity, they convey their feelings and notions in simple and unelaborated expressions. Accordingly, such a language, arising out of repeated experience and regular feelings, is a more permanent and a far more philosophical language than that which is frequently substituted for it by poets, who think that they are conferring honor upon themselves and their art, in proportion as they separate themselves from the sympathies of men, and indulge in arbitrary and capricious habits of expression, in order to furnish food for fickle tastes, and fickle appetites, of their own creation. . . .

B Style was opened up to new considerations, as an attempt was made to abandon what was regarded as the rigidity and artificiality of the old ideas.

. . . Having dwelt thus long on the subjects and aim of these poems, I shall request the reader's permission to apprise him of a few circumstances relating to their *style*, in order, among other reasons, that he may not censure me for not having performed what I never attempted. The reader will find the personifications of abstract ideas rarely occur in these volumes, and are utterly rejected, as an ordinary device to elevate the style, and raise it above prose. My purpose was to imitate, and, as far as possible, to adopt the very language of men; and assuredly such personifications do not make any natural or regular part of that language. They are, indeed, a figure of speech occasionally prompted by passion, and I have made use of them as such; but have endeavored utterly to reject them as a mechanical device of style, or as a family language which writers in meter seem to lay claim to by prescription. I have wished to keep the reader in the company of flesh and blood, persuaded that by so doing I shall interest him. Others who pursue a different track will interest him likewise; I do not interfere with their claim, but wish to prefer a claim of my own. There will also be found in these volumes little of what is usually called poetic diction; as much pains has been taken to avoid it as is ordinarily taken to produce it; this has been done for the reason already alleged, to bring my language near to the language of men; and further, because the pleasure which I have proposed to myself to impart is of a kind very different from that which is supposed by many persons to be the proper object of poetry. Without being culpably particular, I do not know how to give my reader a more exact notion of the style in which it was my wish and intention to write than by informing him that I have at all times endeavored to look steadily at my subject; consequently there is, I hope, in these poems little falsehood of description, and my ideas are expressed in language fitted to their respective importance. . . .

Taking up the subject, then, upon general grounds, let me ask what is meant by the word Poet? What is a poet? To whom does he address himself? And what language is to be expected from him?—He is a man speaking to men: a man, it is true, endowed with more lively sensibility, more enthusiasm and tenderness, who has a greater knowledge of human nature, and a more comprehensive soul, than are supposed to be common among mankind; a man pleased with his own passions and volitions, and who rejoices more than other men in the spirit of life that is in him; delighting to contemplate similar volitions and passions as manifested in the goings on of the universe, and habitually impelled to create them where he does not find them. To these qualities he has added a disposition to be affected more than other men by absent things as if they were present; an ability of conjuring up in himself passions which are indeed far from being the same as those produced by real events, yet (especially in those parts of the general sympathy which are pleasing and delightful) do more nearly resemble the passions produced by real events than anything which, from the motions of their own minds merely, other men are accustomed to feel in themselves—whence, and from practice, he has acquired a greater readiness and power in expressing what he thinks and feels, and especially those thoughts and feelings which, by his own choice, or from the structure of his own mind, arise in him without immediate external excitement.

◇C⟩Romantics emphasized spontaneity and the authenticity of the inner life. The first phrase of the following is the most famous of all pronouncements by the Romantics on their poetry.

I have said that poetry is the spontaneous overflow of powerful feelings: it takes its origin from emotion recollected in tranquillity; the emotion is contemplated till, by a species of reaction, the tranquillity gradually disappears, and an emotion, kindred to that which was before the subject of contemplation, is gradually produced, and does itself actually exist in the mind. In this mood successful composition generally begins, and in a mood similar to this it is carried on; but the emotion, of whatever kind, and in whatever degree, from various causes, is qualified by various pleasures, so that in describing any passions whatsoever, which are voluntarily described, the mind will, upon the whole, be in a state of enjoyment. If Nature be thus cautious to preserve in a state of enjoyment a being so employed, the poet ought to profit by the lesson held forth to him, and ought especially to take care that, whatever passions he communicates to his reader, those passions, if his reader's mind be sound and vigorous, should always be accompanied with an over-balance of pleasure. Now the music of harmonious metrical language, the sense of difficulty overcome, and the blind association of pleasure which has been previously received from works of rhyme or meter of the same or similar construction, an indistinct perception perpetually renewed of language closely resembling that of real life, and yet, in the circumstance of meter, differing from it so widely—all these imperceptibly make up a complex feeling of delight, which is of the most important use in tempering the painful feeling always found intermingled with powerful descriptions of the deeper passions. This effect is always produced in pathetic and impassioned poetry; while in lighter compositions the ease and gracefulness with which the poet manages his numbers are themselves confessedly a principal source of the gratification of the reader. All that it is *necessary* to say, however, upon this subject, may be effected by affirming, what few persons will deny, that of two descriptions, either of passions, manners, or characters each of them equally well executed, the one in prose and the other in verse, the verse will be read a hundred times where the prose is read once. . . .

1. Account for Wordsworth's decision to use the lives and language of the common person as a focus for his poetry.
2. Describe Wordsworth's critique of the traditional poetic style and comment on his vision of the ideal poet.
3. Express Wordsworth's definition of poetry in your own words; then comment on his contention that poetry has a longer life than prose.

■ ■ ■

ENGLISH ROMANTIC POETRY

It was in poetry that the Romantic movement found its first expression. The language of poetry is often associated with the Romantic quest for an understanding of the inner life, the attempt to deal with emotion, memory, nature, and the irrational, and the consideration of all aspects of human nature.

A ▷ William Wordsworth's "Tintern Abbey" (the full title is "Lines Composed a Few Miles Above Tintern Abbey on Revisiting the Banks of the Wye During a Tour, July 13, 1798") was the last poem printed in the *Lyrical Ballads* which he and Coleridge published in 1798. Wordsworth (1770-1850) discussed themes related to nature and memory; the relationship between past, present, and future; and human suffering and the human spirit.

Five years have passed; five summers, with the length
Of five long winters! and again I hear
These waters, rolling from their mountain-springs
With a sweet inland murmur.—Once again
Do I behold these steep and lofty cliffs,
Which on a wild secluded scene impress
Thoughts of more deep seclusion; and connect
The landscape with the quiet of the sky.
The day is come when I again repose
Here, under this dark sycamore, and view
These plots of cottage-ground, these orchard-tufts,
Which, at this season, with their unripe fruits,

Among the woods and copses lose themselves,
Nor, with their green and simple hue, disturb
The wild green landscape. Once again I see
These hedge-rows, hardly hedge-rows, little lines
Of sportive wood run wild; these pastoral farms
Green to the very door; and wreathes of smoke
Sent up, in silence, from among the trees,
With some uncertain notice, as might seem,
Of vagrant dwellers in the houseless woods,
Or of some hermit's cave, where by his fire
The hermit sits alone.

Sources: William Wordsworth and Samuel Taylor Coleridge, *Lyrical Ballads, 1798*, edited by W.J.B. Owen (Oxford: Oxford University Press, 1969), pp. 111-17; Samuel Taylor Coleridge, *The Poetical Works of Samuel Taylor Coleridge* (London: Macmillan and Company, Limited, 1914), p. 173; Percy Bysshe Shelley, *Poetical Works* (Oxford: Oxford University Press, 1970), pp. 572-73, 574-75.

Though absent long,
These forms of beauty have not been to me,
As is a landscape to a blind man's eye:
But oft, in lonely rooms, and mid the din
Of towns and cities, I have owed to them,
In hours of weariness, sensations sweet,
Felt in the blood, and felt along the heart,
And passing even into my purer mind
With tranquil restoration:—feelings too
Of unremembered pleasure; such, perhaps,
As may have had no trivial influence
On that best portion of a good man's life;
His little, nameless, unremembered acts
Of kindness and of love. Nor less, I trust,
To them I may have owed another gift,
Of aspect more sublime; that blessed mood,
In which the burthen of the mystery,
In which the heavy and the weary weight
Of all this unintelligible world
Is lighten'd:—that serene and blessed mood,
In which the affections gently lead us on,
Until, the breath of this corporeal frame,
And even the motion of our human blood
Almost suspended, we are laid asleep
In body, and become a living soul:
While with an eye made quiet by the power
Of harmony, and the deep power of joy,
We see into the life of things.

If this
Be but a vain belief, yet, oh! how oft,
In darkness, and amid the many shapes
Of joyless day-light; when the fretful stir
Unprofitable, and the fever of the world,
Have hung upon the beatings of my heart,
How oft, in spirit, have I turned to thee
O sylvan Wye! Thou wanderer through the woods,
How often has my spirit turned to thee!

And now, with gleams of half-extinguish'd thought,
With many recognitions dim and faint,
And somewhat of a sad perplexity,
The picture of the mind revives again:
While here I stand, not only with the sense
Of present pleasure, but with pleasing thoughts
That in this moment there is life and food

For future years. And so I dare to hope
Though changed, no doubt, from what I was, when first
I came among these hills; when like a roe
I bounded o'er the mountains, by the sides
Of the deep rivers, and the lonely streams,
Wherever nature led; more like a man
Flying from something that he dreads, than one
Who sought the thing he loved. For nature then
(The coarser pleasures of my boyish days,
And their glad animal movements all gone by,)
To me was all in all.—I cannot paint
What then I was. The sounding cataract
Haunted me like a passion: the tall rock,
The mountain, and the deep and gloomy wood,
Their colours and their forms, were then to me
An appetite: a feeling and a love,
That had no need of a remoter charm,
By thought supplied, or any interest
Unborrowed from the eye.—That time is past,
And all its aching joys are now no more,
And all its dizzy raptures. Not for this
Faint I, nor mourn nor murmur: other gifts
Have followed, for such loss, I would believe,
Abundant recompence. For I have learned
To look on nature, not as in the hour
Of thoughtless youth, but hearing oftentimes
The still, sad music of humanity,
Not harsh nor grating, though of ample power
To chasten and subdue. And I have felt
A presence that disturbs me with the joy
Of elevated thoughts; a sense sublime
Of something far more deeply interfused,
Whose dwelling is the light of setting suns,
And the round ocean, and the living air,
And the blue sky, and in the mind of man,
A motion and a spirit, that impels
All thinking things, all objects of all thought,
And rolls through all things. Therefore am I still
A lover of the meadows and the woods,
And mountains; and of all that we behold
From this green earth; of all the mighty world
Of eye and ear, both what they half-create,
And what perceive; well pleased to recognize
In nature and the language of the sense,
The anchor of my purest thoughts, the nurse,
The guide, the guardian of my heart, and soul
Of all my moral being. . . .

Samuel Taylor Coleridge (1772-1834) was Wordsworth's close friend and a great poet and literary critic in his own right. His *What is Life?* (1805) dealt with Romantic conceptions of life and death.

RESEMBLES life what once was deem'd of
    light,
Too ample in itself for human sight?
An absolute self—an element un-
    grounded—
All that we see, all colours of all shade

By encroach of darkness made?—
Is very life by consciousness unbounded?
And all the thoughts, pains, joys of
    mortal breath,
A war-embrace of wrestling life and
    death?

 The Romantic movement had a political content and many Romantics supported the ideals of the French Revolution. They also believed in the need for new movements to emancipate the downtrodden and the common person. In 1819, Percy Bysshe Shelley (1792-1822) wrote ''Song to the Men of England'' and ''England in 1819.'' The ''Phantom'' in the latter poem is that of revolution.

SONG TO THE MEN OF ENGLAND

I

MEN of England, wherefore plough
For the lords who lay ye low?
Wherefore weave with toil and care
The rich robes your tyrants wear?

II

Wherefore feed, and clothe, and save,
From the cradle to the grave,
Those ungrateful drones who would
Drain your sweat—nay, drink your
    blood?

III

Wherefore, Bees of England, forge
Many a weapon, chain, and scourge,
That these stingless drones may spoil
The forced produce of your toil?

IV

Have ye leisure, comfort, calm,
Shelter, food, love's gentle balm?
Or what is it ye buy so dear
With your pain and with your fear?

V

The seed ye sow, another reaps;
The wealth ye find, another keeps;
The robes ye weave, another wears;
The arms ye forge, another bears.

VI

Sow seed,—but let no tyrant reap;
Find wealth,—let no impostor heap;
Weave robes,—let not the idle wear;
Forge arms,—in your defence to
    bear.

VII

Shrink to your cellars, holes, and
    cells;
In halls ye deck another dwells.
Why shake the chains ye wrought?
    Ye see
The steel ye tempered glance on ye.

VIII

With plough and spade, and hoe and
    loom,
Trace your grave, and build your
    tomb,
And weave your winding-sheet, till fair
England be your sepulchre.

SONNET: ENGLAND IN 1819

An old, mad, blind, despised, and dying king,—
Princes, the dregs of their dull race, who flow
Through public scorn,—mud from a muddy spring,—
Rulers who neither see, nor feel, nor know,
But leech-like to their fainting country cling,
Till they drop, blind in blood, without a blow,—
A people starved and stabbed in the untilled field,—
An army, which liberticide and prey
Makes as a two-edged sword to all who wield,—
Golden and sanguine laws which tempt and slay;
Religion Christless, Godless—a book sealed;
A Senate,—Time's worst statute unrepealed,—
Are graves, from which a glorious Phantom may
Burst, to illumine our tempestuous day.

1. Write a response to "Tintern Abbey" commenting on the mood and images portrayed. To what extent is the poem characteristic of Wordsworth's view of poetry?
2. Comment on Coleridge's view concerning the relationship between life and death. How is this characteristic of the Romantic view?
3. Compare Shelley's revolutionary poetry with the art of David.
4. What conclusions can you draw from the following statement: "Revolutions are as much the product of the poet's pen and the artist's brush as they are of the gun and paving stone."

▪ ▪ ▪

ROMANTIC ART

Romanticism was an artistic movement as well as a literary one. Artists began to abandon the neo-classicism of David in search of a nature that was authentic, sublime, and full of wonder. Many characteristics of Romanticism were explored by the new generation of artists, which included J.M.W. Turner and John Constable in England, Theodore Géricault, and Eugène Delacroix in France, and Caspar David Friedrich in Germany. They sought to depict a nature that was transcendent and powerful. These artists used poetic symbolism, often were contemporary, rejected urban life, and explored all aspects of human nature.

◇A◇ John Constable (1776-1837) was a great landscape artist and a naturalist. In his paintings he often viewed nature as pastoral and attempted to show it carefully and precisely. His lecture notes and letters have been collected.

Sources: C.R. Leslie, *Memoirs of the Life of John Constable* (London: John Lehmann, 1949), pp. 322, 343, 346-47, 103-104; Eugène Delacroix, *The Journal of Eugène Delacroix*, translated by Walter Pach (New York: Grove Press, Inc., 1961), pp. 68, 173, 334, 336-38; Jonathan Mayne, ed., *Art in Paris, 1845-1862* (London: Phaidon Press Ltd., 1965), pp. 46-47.

. . . I hope to show that ours is a regularly taught profession; that it is *scientific* as well as *poetic*; that imagination alone never did, and never can, produce works that are to stand by a comparison with *realities*; and to show, by tracing the connecting links in the history of landscape painting, that no great painter was ever self taught. . . .

. . . Painting is a science, and should be pursued as an inquiry into the laws of nature. Why, then, may not landscape painting be considered as a branch of natural philosophy, of which pictures are but the experiments?

The young painter, who regardless of present popularity, would leave a name behind him, must become the patient pupil of nature. If we refer to the lives of all who have distinguished themselves in art or science, we shall find they have always been laborious. The landscape painter must walk in the fields with an humble mind. No arrogant man was ever permitted to see nature in all her beauty. If I may be allowed to use a very solemn quotation, I would say most emphatically to the student, 'Remember now thy Creator in the days of thy youth.' The friends of a young artist should not look or hope for precocity. It is often disease only. Quintilian makes use of a beautiful simile in speaking of precocious talent. He compares it to the forward ear of corn that turns yellow and dies before the harvest. Precocity often leads to criticism, sharp, and severe as the feelings are morbid from ill health. Lord Bacon says, 'when a young man becomes a critic, he will find much for his amusement, little for his instruction.' The young artist must receive with deference the advice of his elders, not hastily questioning what he does not yet understand, otherwise his maturity will bear no fruit. The art of seeing nature is a thing almost as much to be acquired as the art of reading the Egyptian hieroglyphics. . . .

. . . That landscape painter who does not make his skies a very material part of his composition, neglects to avail himself of one of his greatest aids. Sir Joshua Reynolds, speaking of the landscapes of Titian, of Salvator, and of Claude, says: 'Even their *skies* seem to sympathize with their subjects.' I have often been advised to consider my sky as *'a white sheet thrown behind the objects.'* Certainly, if the sky is obtrusive, as mine are, it is bad; but if it is evaded, as mine are not, it is worse; it must and always shall with me make an effectual part of the composition. It will be difficult to name a class of landscape in which the sky is not the key note, the standard of scale, and the chief organ of sentiment. You may conceive, then, what a 'white sheet' would do for me, impressed as I am with these notions, and they cannot be erroneous. The sky is the source of light in nature, and governs everything; even our common observations on the weather of every day are altogether suggested by it. The difficulty of skies in painting is very great, both as to composition and execution; because, with all their brilliancy, they ought not to come forward, or, indeed, be hardly thought of any more than extreme distances are; but this does not apply to phenomena or accidental effects of sky, because they always attract particularly. . . .

. . . I should paint my own places best; painting is with me but another word for feeling, . . .

B The major French Romantic artist was Eugène Delacroix (1798-1863). He painted a variety of themes, including literary subjects, the exotic, politics, myth, and nature. Delacroix kept a journal for many of his adult years.

I must eat little and work alone in the evening. I believe that seeing society people, or merely people, from time to time, is not such a danger to work and the progress of the mind as it is claimed to be by many pretended artists; to consort with them is certainly more dangerous. Their whole talk is on a low level; I must return to solitude. . . .

Painting is the trade that takes longest to learn and is the most difficult. It demands erudition like that of the composer, but it also demands execution like that of the violinist. . . .

I see in painters prose writers and poets. Rhyme, measure, the turning of verses which is indispensable and which gives them so much vigor, are analogous to the hidden symmetry, to the equilibrium at once wise and inspired, which governs the meeting or separation of lines and spaces, the echoes of color, etc. This thesis is easy to demonstrate, only one has need of more active organs and a greater sensibility to distinguish error, discord, false relationship among lines and colors, than one needs to perceive that a rhyme is inexact or that a hemistich is clumsily (or badly) hung. But the beauty of verse does not consist of exactitude in obeying rules, when even the most ignorant eyes see at once any lack of attention to them. It resides in a thousand secret harmonies and conventions which make up the power of poetry and which go straight to the imagination; in just the same way the happy choice of forms and the right understanding of their relationship act on the imagination in the art of painting. . . .

What an adoration I have for painting! The mere memory of certain pictures, even when I don't see them, goes through me with a feeling which stirs my whole being like all those rare and interesting memories that one finds at long intervals in one's life, and especially in the very early years of it. . . .

The type of emotion peculiar to painting is, so to speak, *tangible*; poetry and music cannot give it. You enjoy the actual representation of objects as if you really saw them, and at the same time the meaning which the images have for the mind warms you and transports you. These figures, these objects, which seem the thing itself to a certain part of your intelligent being are like a solid bridge on which imagination supports itself to penetrate to the mysterious and profound sensation for which the forms are, so to speak, the hieroglyph, but a hieroglyph far more eloquent than a cold representation, a thing equivalent to no more than a character in the printer's font of type: it is in this sense that the art is sublime, if we compare it to one wherein thought reaches the mind only with the help of letters arranged in an order that has been agreed upon; it is a far more complicated art, if you will (since the font of type is nothing and thought seems to be everything), but a hundred times more expressive if one consider that, independently of the idea, the visible sign, the speaking hieroglyph, a sign without value for the mind in the work of the writer becomes a source of the liveliest enjoyment in the work of the painter. And so, looking upon the spectacle of created things, we have here the satisfaction given by beauty, proportion, contrast, harmony of color, and everything that the eye looks upon with so much pleasure in the outer world—one of the great needs of our nature.

Many people will consider that it is precisely in this simplification of the means of expression that the superiority of literature resides. Such people have never considered with pleasure an arm, a hand, a torso from the antique or from Puget; they care for sculpture even less than painting, and they are strangely deceived if they think that when they have written: *a foot* or *a hand*, they have given to my mind the same emotion as the one I experience when I see a beautiful foot or a beautiful hand. The arts are not algebra, in which the abbreviation of the figures contributes to the success of the problem; success in the arts is by no means a matter of abridging, but of amplifying, if possible, and prolonging the sensation by all possible means. What is the theater? One of the most certain witnesses to man's need for experiencing the largest possible number of emotions at one time. It gathers together all the arts so that each may make us feel their combined effect more strongly; pantomime, costume, and the beauty of the performer double the effect of the word that is spoken or sung. The representation of the place in which the action occurs adds still further to all these types of impression.

It will now be clearer why I have spoken as I have about the *power of painting*. If it possesses but a single moment, it concentrates the *effect* of that moment; the painter is far more the master of that which he wants to express than is the poet or the musician, who is in the hands of interpreters; in a word, if his memory is directed toward fewer aspects of things, he produces an effect which is absolutely one and which can satisfy completely; in addition, the work of the painter is not subject to the same variations, as regards the manner in which it may be understood at different periods. Changing fashion and the prejudices of the moment may cause its value to be looked upon in different ways; but in the end it is always the same, it remains as the artist wanted it to be, whereas the same is not true of things that must pass through the hands of interpreters, as must the works of the theatre. Since the feeling of the artist is no longer there to guide the actors or the singers, the execution can no longer respond to the original intention of the work: the accent disappears, and with it the most delicate part of the impression. Indeed it is a happy author whose work is not mutilated, an affront to which he is exposed even during his lifetime! The mere change of an actor changes the whole physiognomy of a piece.

Charles Baudelaire (1821-67) was a poet who thought deeply about the nature of art and the imagination. For some years he was an art critic as well. In 1846 he wrote on Romanticism.

WHAT IS ROMANTICISM?

Few people today will want to give a real and positive meaning to this word; and yet will they dare assert that a whole generation would agree to join a battle lasting several years for the sake of a flag which was not also a symbol?

If you think back to the disturbances of those recent times, you will see that if but few romantics have survived, it is because few of them discovered romanticism, though all of them sought it sincerely and honestly.

Some applied themselves only to the choice of subjects; but they had not the temperament for their subjects. Others, still believing in a Catholic society, sought to reflect Catholicism in their works. But to call oneself a romantic and to look systematically at the past is to contradict oneself. Some blasphemed the Greeks and the Romans in the name of romanticism: but you can only make Romans and Greeks into romantics if you are one yourself. Many others have been misled by the idea of truth in art, and local colour. Realism had already existed for a long time when that great battle took place, and besides, to compose a tragedy or a picture to the requirements of M. Raoul Rochette is to expose yourself to a flat contradiction from the first comer if he is more learned than M. Raoul Rochette.

Romanticism is precisely situated neither in choice of subjects nor in exact truth, but in a mode of feeling.

They looked for it outside themselves, but it was only to be found within.

For me, Romanticism is the most recent, the latest expression of the beautiful.

There are as many kinds of beauty as there are habitual ways of seeking happiness.

This is clearly explained by the philosophy of progress; thus, as there have been as many ideals as there have been ways in which the peoples of the earth have understood ethics, love, religion, etc., so romanticism will not consist in a perfect execution, but in a conception analogous to the ethical disposition of the age.

It is because some have located it in a perfection of technique that we have had the *rococo* of romanticism, without question the most intolerable of all forms.

Thus it is necessary, first and foremost, to get to know those aspects of nature and those human situations which the artists of the past have disdained or have not known.

To say the word Romanticism is to say modern art—that is, intimacy, spirituality, colour, aspiration towards the infinite, expressed by every means available to the arts.

Thence it follows that there is an obvious contradiction between romanticism and the works of its principal adherents.

Does it surprise you that colour should play such a very important part in modern art? Romanticism is a child of the North, and the North is all for colour; dreams and fairytales are born of the mist. England—that home of fanatical colourists, Flanders and half of France are all plunged in fog; Venice herself lies steeped in her lagoons. As for the painters of Spain, they are painters of contrast rather than colourists.

The South, in return, is all for nature; for there nature is so beautiful and bright that nothing is left for man to desire, and he can find nothing more beautiful to invent than what he sees. There art belongs to the open air: but several hundred leagues to the north you will find the deep dreams of the studio and the gaze of the fancy lost in horizons of grey.

The South is as brutal and positive as a sculptor even in his most delicate compositions; the North, suffering and restless, seeks comfort with the imagination, and if it turns to sculpture, it will more often be picturesque than classical.

1. Contrast Constable's views on artistic expression with those of William Blake.
2. After considering Delacroix's arguments, respond to the following thesis: "Prose, poetry and music have an impact upon humanity, but nothing can match the power of painting."
3. Compare Baudelaire's viewpoint with your understanding of the Romantics you have studied. To what extent would you agree with his analysis?

▪ ▪ ▪

JOHANN WOLFGANG VON GOETHE

Johann Wolfgang von Goethe (1749-1832) was among the great geniuses of the modern period. His literary work is considered the most important in the German language of the last several centuries. He was also a scientist, diplomat, essayist and critic. Goethe's *Faust*, a dramatic tragedy, borrowed its theme from a legend, begun in the sixteenth century, about an exceptional man who strives for universal knowledge and agrees to a pact with the devil in order to obtain it. The themes of the relationship between God, the devil, and human beings, and the role of knowledge and feelings in our lives became important ones in the modern age.

 Near the beginning of the work Mephistopheles, the devil, discusses the hero Faust with the Lord.

> THE LORD. Is there no more that you could add?
> Is finding fault all you can do?
> Is nothing on earth ever right with you?
> MEPHISTOPHELES.
> No, Lord! I find things there, as always, downright bad.
> The human race in all its woes I so deplore
> I hate to plague the poor things any more.
> THE LORD. Do you know Faust?
> MEPHISTOPHELES.   The Doctor?
> THE LORD.   And my servant.
> MEPHISTOPHELES. He serves you in a curious way, I think.
> Not earthly is the poor fool's food and drink.
> An inner ferment drives him far
> And he is half aware that he is mad;
> From heaven he demands the fairest star,

Source: Johann Wolfgang von Goethe, *Faust*, translated by Charles E. Passage (Indianapolis: Bobbs-Merrill Educational Publishing, 1965), pp. 13-15, 19-20, 22-24, 55-56, 59-63.

From earth all peaks of pleasure to be had,
And nothing near and nothing far
Will calm his troubled heart or make it glad.
THE LORD. Though now he serves me but confusedly,
I soon shall guide him on toward what is clear.
The gardener knows, when green comes to the tree,
That flowers and fruit will deck the coming year.
MEPHISTOPHELES. What will you bet you lose him if you give
Me your permission now to steer
Him gently down my path instead?
THE LORD. As long as he on earth may live,
To you such shall not be gainsaid.
Man errs as long as he can strive.
MEPHISTOPHELES. Thank you for that; for with the dead
I never hankered much to be.
It is the plump, fresh cheeks that mean the most to me.
I'm out to corpses calling at my house;
I play the way the cat does with the mouse.
THE LORD. Good, then! The matter is agreed!
Divert this spirit from his primal source,
And if you can ensnare him, lead
Him with you on your downward course;
And stand abashed when you have to confess:
A good man harried in his dark distraction
Can still perceive the ways of righteousness.
MEPHISTOPHELES. All right! It won't be any long transaction.
I have no fears at all for my bet's sake.
And once I've won, let it be understood
You will admit my triumph as you should.
Dust shall he eat, and call it good,
Just like my aunt, the celebrated snake.
THE LORD. There too feel wholly free to try;
Toward your kind I have borne no hate.
Of all the spirits that deny,
The scoffer burdens me with slightest weight.
Man's activeness can all too easily go slack,
He loves to be in ease unqualified;
Hence I set a companion at his side
To goad him like a devil from the back.
But you, true sons of gods, may you
Rejoice in beauty that is full and true!
May that which is evolving and alive
Encompass you in bonds that Love has wrought;
And what exists in wavering semblance, strive
To fix in final permanence of thought.

(*The heavens close, the* ARCHANGELS *disperse.*)

MEPHISTOPHELES. From time to time I like to see the Boss,
　　And with him like to keep things on the level.
　　It's really nice in one of such high class
　　To be so decent with the very Devil.

 Faust is introduced in a section entitled "Night."

FAUST. I've read, alas! through philosophy,
　Medicine and jurisprudence too,
　And, to my grief, theology
　With ardent labor studied through.
　And here I stand with all my lore,
　Poor fool, no wiser than before!
　I'm Master, I'm Doctor, and with my reading
　These ten years now I have been leading
　My scholars on wild-goose hunts, out
　And in, cross-lots, and round about—
　To find that nothing can be known!
　This burns my very marrow and bone.
　I'm shrewder, it's true, than all the tribes
　Of Doctors and Masters and priests and scribes;
　Neither doubts nor scruples now can daunt me,
　Neither hell nor devils now can haunt me—
　But by the same token I lose all delight.
　I don't pretend to know anything aright,
　I don't pretend to have in mind
　Things I could teach to improve mankind.
　Nor have I lands nor treasure hoards,
　Nor honors and splendors the world affords;
　No dog would want to live this way!
　And so I've yielded to magic's sway,
　To see if spirits' force and speech
　Might not bring many a mystery in reach;
　So I no longer need to go
　On saying things that I don't know;
　So I may learn the things that hold
　The world together at its core,
　So I may potencies and seeds behold,
　And trade in empty words no more.

O if, full moon, you did but shine
Your last upon this pain of mine,
Whom I have watched ascending bright
Here at my desk in mid of night;
Then over books and papers here,
Sad friend, you would come into view.
Ah, could I on some mountain height
Rove beneath your mellow light,
Drift on with spirits round mountain caves,
Waft over meadows your dim light laves,
And, clear of learning's fumes, renew
Myself in baths of healing dew!
Am I still in this prison stall?
Accursed, musty hole-in-the-wall,
Where the very light of heaven strains
But dully through the painted panes!
By these enormous book-piles bounded
Which dust bedecks and worms devour,
Which are by sooty charts surrounded
Up to the vaultings where they tower;
With jars shelved round me, and retorts,
With instruments packed in and jammed,
Ancestral junk together crammed—
Such is your world! A world of sorts! . . .
Where can I grasp you, Nature without end?
You breasts, where? Source of all our lives,
On which both heaven and earth depend,
Toward you my withered heart so strives—
You flow, you swell, and must I thirst in vain?

(*Impatiently he turns pages of the book and glimpses the sign of the Earth Spirit.*)

How differently I am affected by this sign!
You, Spirit of the Earth, are nearer me,
I feel more potent energy,
I feel aglow as with new wine.
I feel the strength to brave the world, to go
And shoulder earthly weal and earthly woe,
To wrestle with the tempests there,
In shipwreck's grinding crash not to despair.

Clouds gather over me—
The moon conceals its light—
The lamp has vanished!
Mists rise!—Red lightnings dart and flash
About my head—Down from
The vaulted roof cold horror blows
And seizes me!

Spirit implored, I feel you hovering near. My senses riot in wild commotion!
Reveal yourself! My heart surrenders to you utterly!
Oh how my heart is rent with fear! You must! You must! though it cost life to me!
With new emotion

(He seizes the book and mystically pronounces the sign of the Spirit. A reddish flame flashes. The SPIRIT *appears in the flame.)*

SPIRIT. Who calls me?
FAUST (*cowering*).   Ghastly shape!
SPIRIT.   With might
   You have compelled me to appear,
   You have long sucked about my sphere,
   Now—
FAUST.   No! I cannot bear the sight!
SPIRIT. You begged so breathlessly to bring me near
   To hear my voice and see my face as well;
   I bow before your strong compulsive spell,
   And here I am!—What childish fear
   Besets you, superman! Where is the soul that cried?
   Where is the heart that made and bore a world inside
   Itself and sought amid its gleeful pride
   To be with spirits equal and allied?
   Where are you, Faust, whose voice called out to me,
   Who forced yourself on me so urgently?
   Are you the one who, having felt my breath,
   Now tremble to your being's depth,
   A terrified and cringing worm?
FAUST. Shall I give way before you, thing of flame?
   I am your equal. Faust is my name!
SPIRIT. In tides of life, in action's storm
   I surge as a wave,
   Swaying ceaselessly;
   Birth and the grave,
   An endless sea,
   A changeful flowing,
   A life all glowing:
   I work in the hum of the loom of time
   Weaving the living raiment of godhead sublime.
FAUST. O you who roam the world from end to end,
   Restless Spirit, I feel so close to you! . . .

C The pact between Faust and Mephistopheles is made as Faust wants to learn and experience as much as possible, to strive for knowledge.

FAUST. A knock? Come in! Who now comes bothering me?
MEPHISTOPHELES. It's I.
FAUST.   Come in!
MEPHISTOPHELES.   A third call there must be.
FAUST. Come in, then!

MEPHISTOPHELES.   That's the way I like to hear you.
    We shall, I trust, get on quite well,
    For I have come here to dispel
    Your moods, and as a noble squire be near you,
    Clad all in scarlet and gold braid,
    With my short cape of stiff silk made,
    A rooster feather on my hat,
    A long sharp rapier at my side,
    And I advise you to provide
    Yourself a costume just like that,
    So you, untrammeled and set free,
    Can find out just what life can be.
FAUST. No matter what might be my own attire,
    I would feel life cramped anyway.
    I am too old merely to play,
    Too young to be without desire.
    What can the world give me? Renounce,
    Renounce shalt thou, thou shalt renounce!
    That is the everlasting song
    Dinned in our ears throughout the course
    Of all our lives, which all life long
    Each hour sings until it's hoarse. . . .
MEPHISTOPHELES. You are a man with other men.
    This does not indicate
    That you're to run with the pack;
    I am not one of the great,
    But if you want a track
    Through life together with me,
    I'll adapt myself quite willingly
    To be yours right here and now.
    I am your fellow,
    If it suits you, to the grave,
    I am your servant and your slave.
FAUST. And what am I supposed to do for you?
MEPHISTOPHELES. There's lots of time before that's due.
FAUST. No, no! The Devil is an egoist
    And does not willingly assist
    Another just for God's sake. I insist
    You make all your conditions clear;
    Such a slave is one to fear.
MEPHISTOPHELES. I'll bind myself to be your servant *here*
    And at your beck and call wait tirelessly,
    If when there in the *yonder* we appear
    You will perform the same for me.
FAUST. The yonder is of small concern.
    Once you have smashed this world to pieces,
    The other one may come to be in turn.
    It is out of this earth that my joy springs

And this sun shines upon my sufferings;
Once free of them, this trouble ceases;
Then come what may and as time brings.
About all that I do not wish to hear,
Whether in future there is hate and love
And whether in that yonder sphere
There is a new beneath and new above.

MEPHISTOPHELES. In this mood you dare venture it. Just make
The compact, and I then will undertake
To turn my skills to joy. I'll give you more
Than any man has ever seen before.

FAUST. Poor, sorry Devil, what could you deliver?
Was human mind in lofty aspiration ever
Comprehended by the likes of you?
Do you have food that does not satisfy? Or do
You have red gold that will run through
The hand like quicksilver and away?
A game that none may win who play?
A girl who in my very arms
Will pledge love to my neighbor with her eyes?
Or honor with its godlike charms
Which like a shooting star flashes and dies?
Show me the fruit that rots right on the tree,
And trees that every day leaf out anew!

MEPHISTOPHELES. Such a demand does not daunt me,
Such treasures I can furnish you.
But still the time will come around, good friend,
When we shall want to relish things in peace.

FAUST. If ever I lie down upon a bed of ease,
Then let that be my final end!
If you can cozen me with lies
Into a self-complacency,
Or can beguile with pleasures you devise,
Let that day be the last for me!
This bet I offer!

MEPHISTOPHELES. Done!

FAUST.   And I agree:
If I to any moment say:
Linger on! You are so fair!
Put me in fetters straightaway,
Then I can die for all I care!
Then toll bells for my funeral,
Then of your service you are free,
The clock may stop, the clock hand fall,
And time be past and done for me!

MEPHISTOPHELES. Consider well, we shall remember this.

FAUST. And that would be quite right of you.
I have committed no presumptuousness.

I am a slave no matter what I do,
Yours or another's, we may dismiss.

MEPHISTOPHELES. I will begin right with your doctoral feast
And be your slave this very day.
For life and death's sake, though, just one thing, if I may:
Just write a line or two at least.

FAUST. You ask for written forms, you pedant? Can
You never have known man, or known the word of man?
Is it not enough that by the word I gave
The die of all my days is finally cast?
Does not the world down all its rivers rave,
And should a promise hold me fast?
But this illusion in our hearts is set
And who has ever wanted to uproot it yet?
Happy the man whose heart is true and pure,
No sacrifice he makes will he regret!
A parchment, though, with seal and signature,
That is a ghost at which all people shy.
The word is dead before the ink is dry
And wax and leather hold the mastery.
What, evil spirit, do you want from me?
Bronze, marble, parchment, paper? And then
Am I to write with stylus, chisel, or a pen?
The choice is yours and wholly free.

MEPHISTOPHELES. Why carry on so heatedly
And force your eloquence so high?
Just any little scrap will do;
You sign it with a drop of blood.

FAUST. If that is satisfactory to you,
We'll let it stand at that absurdity.

MEPHISTOPHELES. Blood is a juice of very special kind.

FAUST. I'll honor this pact, you need not be afraid!
The aim of all my strength and mind
Will be to keep this promise I have made.
I puffed myself up far too grand;
In your class I deserve to be.
The mighty Spirit spurned me and
Nature locks herself from me.
The thread of thought is snapped off short,
Knowledge I loathe of every sort.
Let us now sate our ardent passion
In depths of sensuality!
Let miracles of every fashion
Be brought in veils of mystery!
Let us plunge in the flood of time and chance,
Into the tide of circumstance!
Let grief and gratification,
Success and frustration
Spell one another as they can;

> Restless doing is the only way for man.
> MEPHISTOPHELES. There is no goal or limit set.
>   Snatch tidbits as impulse prompts you to,
>   Take on the wing whatever you can get!
>   And may you digest what pleases you.
>   Just help yourself and don't be coy.
> FAUST. But I tell you there is no talk of joy.
>   I vow myself to frenzy, agonies of gratification,
>   Enamored hatred, quickening frustration.
>   Cured of the will to knowledge now, my mind
>   And heart shall be closed to no sorrow any more
>   And all that is the lot of human kind
>   I want to feel down to my senses' core,
>   Grasp with my mind their worst things and their best,
>   Heap all their joys and troubles on my breast,
>   And thus my self to their selves' limits to extend,
>   And like them perish foundering at the end. . . .

1. The original story of Faust depicted a humanist selling his eternal soul in return for worldly knowledge. Goethe has focussed his version of the tale to highlight the inner conflict in all people. Based on the brief excerpt provided, write a modern version of the moral dilemma Faust is confronting.

▪ ▪ ▪

MARY SHELLEY

Mary Shelley's *Frankenstein* (1818) was the creation of a modern myth, having elements of the Faust story, which dealt with the relationship between creator and creation and the idea of the monstrous in all of our lives. Shelley (1797-1851), the daughter of Mary Wollstonecraft, was a young woman when she wrote this gothic tale on a holiday in Italy. Shelley claimed the story grew out of her imagination, in a dream. The tale, subtitled "the modern Prometheus," was about the scientist Dr. Frankenstein, who creates life, and is destroyed by his own work.

◇A◇ In the novel, Frankenstein is the scientist (not the monster, as in most modern film and television versions). In the following passages, he emotionally recounts the horror of his creation of life:

> It was on a dreary night of November, that I beheld the accomplishment of my toils. With an anxiety that almost amounted to agony, I collected the instruments of life around me, that I might infuse a spark of being into the lifeless thing that lay at my feet. It was already one in the morning; the rain pattered dismally against the panes, and my candle was nearly burnt out,

Source: Mary Shelley, *Frankenstein* (Oxford: Oxford University Press, 1969), pp. 57-58, 98-101, 166-67.

when, by the glimmer of the half-extinguished light, I saw the dull yellow eye of the creature open; it breathed hard, and a convulsive motion agitated its limbs.

How can I describe my emotions at this catastrophe, or how delineate the wretch whom with such infinite pains and care I had endeavoured to form? His limbs were in proportion, and I had selected his features as beautiful. Beautiful!—Great God! His yellow skin scarcely covered the work of muscles and arteries beneath; his hair was of a lustrous black, and flowing; his teeth of a pearly whiteness; but these luxuriances only formed a more horrid contrast with his watery eyes, that seemed almost of the same colour as the dun white sockets in which they were set, his shrivelled complexion and straight black lips.

The different accidents of life are not so changeable as the feelings of human nature. I had worked hard for nearly two years, for the sole purpose of infusing life into an inanimate body. For this I had deprived myself of rest and health. I had desired it with an ardour that far exceeded moderation; but now that I had finished, the beauty of the dream vanished, and breathless horror and disgust filled my heart. Unable to endure the aspect of the being I had created, I rushed out of the room, and continued a long time traversing my bed-chamber, unable to compose my mind to sleep. At length lassitude succeeded to the tumult I had before endured; and I threw myself on the bed in my clothes, endeavouring to seek a few moments of forgetfulness. But it was in vain: I slept, indeed, but I was disturbed by the wildest dreams. I thought I saw Elizabeth, in the bloom of health, walking in the streets of Ingolstadt. Delighted and surprised, I embraced her; but as I imprinted the first kiss on her lips, they became livid with the hue of death; her features appeared to change, and I thought that I held the corpse of my dead mother in my arms; a shroud enveloped her form, and I saw the graveworms crawling in the folds of the flannel. I started from my sleep with horror; a cold dew covered my forehead, my teeth chattered, and every limb became convulsed: when, by the dim and yellow light of the moon, as it forced its way through the window shutters, I beheld the wretch—the miserable monster whom I had created. He held up the curtain of the bed; and his eyes, if eyes they may be called, were fixed on me. His jaws opened, and he muttered some inarticulate sounds, while a grin wrinkled his cheeks. He might have spoken, but I did not hear; one hand was stretched out, seemingly to detain me, but I escaped, and rushed down stairs. I took refuge in the courtyard belonging to the house which I inhabited; where I remained during the rest of the night, walking up and down in the greatest agitation, listening attentively, catching and fearing each sound as if it were to announce the approach of the demoniacal corpse to which I had so miserably given life.

Oh! no mortal could support the horror of that countenance. A mummy again endued with animation could not be so hideous as that wretch. . . .

B In the middle of the work, Dr. Frankenstein and the monster meet on Mont Blanc, a favourite place in Romantic literature to depict awe and the sublime. They discuss their relationship, and it is revealed that the monster has deep emotions and feels abandoned by his creator.

. . . I suddenly beheld the figure of a man, at some distance, advancing towards me with superhuman speed. He bounded over the crevices in the ice, among which I had walked with caution; his stature, also, as he approached, seemed to exceed that of man. I was troubled: a mist came over my eyes, and I felt a faintness seize me; but I was quickly restored by the cold gale of the mountains. I perceived, as the shape came nearer (sight tremendous and abhorred?) that it was the wretch whom I had created. I trembled with rage and horror, resolving to wait his approach, and then close with him in mortal combat. He approached; his countenance bespoke bitter anguish, combined with disdain and malignity, while its unearthly ugliness rendered it almost too horrible for human eyes. But I scarcely observed this; rage and hatred had at first deprived me of utterance, and I recovered only to overwhelm him with words expressive of furious detestation and contempt.

'Devil,' I exclaimed, 'do you dare approach me? and do not you fear the fierce vengeance of my arm wreaked on your miserable head? Begone, vile insect! or rather, stay, that I may trample you to dust! and, oh! that I could, with the extinction of your miserable existence, restore those victims whom you have so diabolically murdered!'

'I expected this reception,' said the dæmon. 'All men hate the wretched; how, then, must I be hated, who am miserable beyond all living things! Yet you, my creator, detest and spurn me, thy creature, to whom thou art bound by ties only dissoluble by the annihilation of one of us. You purpose to kill me. How dare you sport thus with life? Do your duty towards me, and I will do mine towards you and the rest of mankind. If you will comply with my conditions, I will leave them and you at peace; but if you refuse, I will glut the maw of death, until it be satiated with the blood of your remaining friends.'

'Abhorred monster! fiend that thou art! the tortures of hell are too mild a vengeance for thy crimes. Wretched devil! you reproach me with your creation; come on, then, that I may extinguish the spark which I so negligently bestowed.'

My rage was without bounds; I sprang on him, impelled by all the feelings which can arm one being against the existence of another.

He easily eluded me, and said—

'Be calm! I entreat you to hear me, before you give vent to your hatred on my devoted head. Have I not suffered enough, that you seek to increase my misery? Life, although it may only be an accumulation of anguish, is dear to me, and I will defend it. Remember, thou hast made me more powerful than thyself; my height is superior to thine; my joints more supple. But I will not be tempted to set myself in opposition to thee. I am thy creature, and I will be even mild and docile to my natural lord and king, if thou wilt also perform thy part, the which thou owest me. Oh, Frankenstein, be not equitable to every other, and trample upon me alone, to whom thy justice, and even thy clemency and affection, is most due. Remember, that I am thy creature;

I ought to be thy Adam; but I am rather the fallen angel, whom thou drivest from joy for no misdeed. Every where I see bliss, from which I alone am irrevocably excluded. I was benevolent and good; misery made me a fiend. Make me happy, and I shall again be virtuous.'

'Begone! I will not hear you. There can be no community between you and me; we are enemies. Begone, or let us try our strength in a fight, in which one must fall.'

'How can I move thee? Will no entreaties cause thee to turn a favourable eye upon thy creature, who implores thy goodness and compassion? Believe me, Frankenstein: I was benevolent; my soul glowed with love and humanity: but am I not alone, miserably alone? You, my creator, abhor me; what hope can I gather from your fellow-creatures, who owe me nothing? they spurn and hate me. The desert mountains and dreary glaciers are my refuge. I have wandered here many days; the caves of ice, which I only do not fear, are a dwelling to me, and the only one which man does not grudge. These bleak skies I hail, for they are kinder to me than your fellow-beings. If the multitude of mankind knew of my existence, they would do as you do, and arm them-selves for my destruction. Shall I not then hate them who abhor me? I will keep no terms with my enemies. I am miserable, and they shall share my wretchedness. Yet it is in your power to recompense me, and deliver them from an evil which it only remains for you to make so great, that not only you and your family, but thousands of others, shall be swallowed up in the whirlwinds of its rage. Let your compassion be moved, and do not disdain me. Listen to my tale: when you have heard that, abandon or commiserate me, as you shall judge that I deserve. But hear me. The guilty are allowed, by human laws, bloody as they are, to speak in their own defence before they are condemned. Listen to me, Frankenstein. You accuse me of murder; and yet you would, with a satisfied conscience, destroy your own creature. Oh, praise the eternal justice of man! Yet I ask you not to spare me: listen to me; and then, if you can, and if you will, destroy the work of your hands.'

'Why do you call to my remembrance,' I rejoined, 'circumstances, of which I shudder to reflect, that I have been the miserable origin and author? Cursed be the day, abhorred devil, in which you first saw light! Cursed (although I curse myself) be the hands that formed you! You have made me wretched beyond expression. You have left me no power to consider whether I am just to you, or not. Begone! relieve me from the sight of your detested form.'

'Thus I relieve thee, my creator,' he said, and placed his hated hands before my eyes, which I flung from me with violence; 'thus I take from thee a sight which you abhor. Still thou canst listen to me, and grant me thy compassion. By the virtues that I once possessed, I demand this from you. Hear my tale; it is long and strange, and the temperature of this place is not fitting to your fine sensations; come to the hut upon the mountain. The sun is yet high in the heavens; before it descends to hide itself behind yon snowy precipices, and illuminate another world, you will have heard my story, and can decide. On you it rests, whether I quit for ever the neighbourhood of man, and lead a harmless life, or become the scourge of your fellow-creatures, and the author of your own speedy ruin.'

Frankenstein agrees to make a mate for the monster, but then has second thoughts. The two remain an inseparable double as a result of this act.

I trembled, and my heart failed within me; when, on looking up, I saw, by the light of the moon, the dæmon at the casement. A ghastly grin wrinkled his lips as he gazed on me, where I sat fulfilling the task which he had allotted to me. Yes, he had followed me in my travels; he had loitered in forests, hid himself in caves, or taken refuge in wide and desert heaths; and he now came to mark my progress, and claim the fulfilment of my promise.

As I looked on him, his countenance expressed the utmost extent of malice and treachery. I thought with a sensation of madness on my promise of creating another like to him, and trembling with passion, tore to pieces the thing on which I was engaged. The wretch saw me destroy the creature on whose future existence he depended for happiness, and, with a howl of devilish despair and revenge, withdrew.

I left the room, and, locking the door, made a solemn vow in my own heart never to resume my labours; and then, with trembling steps, I sought my own apartment. I was alone; none were near me to dissipate the gloom, and relieve me from the sickening oppression of the most terrible reveries.

Several hours passed, and I remained near my window gazing on the sea; it was almost motionless, for the winds were hushed, and all nature reposed under the eye of the quiet moon. A few fishing vessels alone specked the water, and now and then the gentle breeze wafted the sound of voices, as the fishermen called to one another. I felt the silence, although I was hardly conscious of its extreme profundity, until my ear was suddenly arrested by the paddling of oars near the shore, and a person landed close to my house.

In a few minutes after, I hear the creaking of my door, as if some one endeavoured to open it softly. I trembled from head to foot; I felt a presentiment of who it was, and wished to rouse one of the peasants who dwelt in a cottage not far from mine; but I was overcome by the sensation of helplessness, so often felt in frightful dreams, when you in vain endeavour to fly from an impending danger, and was rooted to the spot.

Presently I heard the sound of footsteps along the passage; the door opened, and the wretch whom I dreaded appeared. Shutting the door, he approached me, and said, in a smothered voice—

'You have destroyed the work which you began; what is it that you intend? Do you dare to break your promise? I have endured toil and misery: I left Switzerland with you; I crept along the shores of the Rhine, among its willow islands, and over the summits of its hills. I have dwelt many months in the heaths of England, and among the deserts of Scotland. I have endured incalculable fatigue, and cold, and hunger; do you dare destroy my hopes?'

'Begone! I do break my promise; never will I create another like yourself, equal in deformity and wickedness.'

'Slave, I before reasoned with you, but you have proved yourself unworthy of my condescension. Remember that I have power; you believe yourself miserable, but I can make you so wretched that the light of day will be hateful to you. You are my creator, but I am your master;—obey!' . . .

1. Prepare a position paper for or against the following proposition: "Franken-stein's monster was more human than his creator."
2. Compare Faust and Frankenstein. To what extent did the desire to go beyond human limitations cause the downfall of Dr. Frankenstein?

▪ ▪ ▪

GIUSEPPE MAZZINI

The outstanding figure in the theory and practice of nationalism was Giuseppe Mazzini (1805-72). He believed that nationalism and liberalism could work together for the benefit of all humanity. Mazzini's life was devoted to Italian unity and to the liberation of his fellow Italians from their domination by outsiders. In 1848 and early 1849 he became a leader of the Roman Republic, a revolutionary government which only lasted for a few months. In exile much of his life, Mazzini had great prestige and popularity among European liberals and intellectuals because of his ideals. His beliefs looked to a time when Europeans would live freely, in harmony and peace.

In his *The Duties of Man* (collected essays published in 1860), Mazzini spoke of duties and rights, and of the need to go beyond the idea of individual liberty.

> I want to speak to you of your duties. I want to speak to you, as my heart dictates to me, of the most sacred things which we know—of God, of Humanity, of the Fatherland, of the Family. . . .
>
> Why do I speak to you of your *duties* before speaking to you of your *rights*? Why in a society in which all, voluntarily or involuntarily, oppress you, in which the exercise of all the rights which belong to man is constantly denied you, in which misery is your lot, and what is called happiness is for other classes of men, why do I speak to you of self-sacrifice and not of conquest; of virtue, moral improvement, education, and not of material *well-being*? This is a question which I must answer before going further, because here precisely lies the difference between our school and many others which are being preached to-day in Europe; because, moreover, it is a question which rises readily in the indignant mind of the suffering working-man.
>
> *We are poor, enslaved, unhappy; speak to us of better material conditions, of liberty, of happiness. Tell us if we are doomed to suffer for ever, or if we too may enjoy in our turn. Preach Duty to our masters, to the classes above us which treat us like machines, and monopolise the blessings which belong to all. To us speak of rights; speak of the means of vindicating them; speak of our strength. Wait till we have a recognised existence; then you shall speak to us of duties and of sacrifice.* This is what many of our working-men say, and follow teachers and associations which respond to their desires. They forget one thing only, and that is, that the doctrine which they invoke has been preached for the last fifty years without

Source: Joseph Mazzini, *The Duties of Man and Other Essays* (London: J.M. Dent and Sons, Ltd., 1907), pp. 7-9, 41-42, 49-50, 119, 121-22.

producing the slightest material improvement in the condition of the working-people.

For the last fifty years whatever has been done for the cause of progress and of good against absolute governments and hereditary aristocracies has been done in the name of the Rights of Man; in the name of liberty as the means, and of *well-being* as the object of existence. All the acts of the French Revolution and of the revolutions which followed and imitated it were consequences of a Declaration of the Rights of Man. . . .

. . . Has the condition of the people improved? Have the millions who live by the daily labour of their hands gained the least fraction of the well-being hoped for and promised to them?

No; the condition of the people has not improved; rather it has grown and grows worse in nearly every country, and especially here where I write the price of the necessaries of life has gone on continually rising, the wages of the working-man in many branches of industry falling, and the population multiplying. In nearly every country the lot of workers has become more uncertain, more precarious, and the labour crises which condemn thousands of working-men to idleness for a time have become more frequent. The yearly increase of emigration from one country to another, and from Europe to other parts of the world, and the ever-growing number of beneficent institutions, the increase of poor rates and provisions for the destitute, are enough to prove this. The latter prove also that public attention is waking more and more to the ills of the people; but their inability to lessen those ills to any visible extent points to a no less continual increase of poverty among the classes which they endeavour to help. . . .

 The relationship of human beings to a larger entity, "humanity," was central.

Your first duties, first not in point of time but of importance—because without understanding these you can only imperfectly fulfil the rest—are to Humanity. You have duties as citizens, as sons, as husbands, as fathers—sacred, inviolable duties of which I shall presently speak at length; but what makes these duties sacred and inviolable is the mission, the *duty*, which your nature as *men* imposes on you. You are fathers in order that you may educate *men* to worship and to unfold God's law. You are citizens, you have a country, in order that in a limited sphere, with the concourse of people linked to you already by speech, by tendencies, and by habits, you may labour for the benefit of all *men* whatever they are and may be in the future—a task which each one could ill do by himself, weak and lost amid the immense multitude of his fellow-men. Those who teach morality, limiting its obligations to duties towards family or country, teach you a more or less narrow *egoism* and lead you to what is evil for others and for yourselves. Country and family are like two circles drawn within a greater circle which contains them both; like two steps of a ladder without which you could not climb any higher, but upon which it is forbidden you to stay your feet.

You are *men*; that is, *rational* and *social* creatures *capable, by means of association only, of a progress* to which no one may assign limits; and this is all that we know to-day of the law of life given to Humanity. These characteristics constitute *human nature*, which distinguishes you from the other beings around you and which is entrusted to each of you as a seed to bring to fruit. All your life should tend to the exercise and the regular development of these fundamental faculties of your nature. Whenever you suppress one of these faculties or allow it to be suppressed wholly or in part, you fall from the rank of men to the level of the inferior animals and violate the law of your life, the Law of God. . . .

. . . There is no hope for you except in universal reform and in the brotherhood of all the peoples of Europe, and through Europe of all humanity. I charge you then, O my brothers, by your duty and by your own interest, not to forget that your first duties—duties without fulfilling which you cannot hope to fulfil those owed to family and country—are to Humanity. Let your words and your actions be for all, since God is for all, in His Love and in His Law. In whatever land you may be, wherever a man is fighting for right, for justice, for truth, there is your brother; wherever a man suffers through the oppression of error, of injustice, of tyranny, there is your brother. Free men and slaves, YOU ARE ALL BROTHERS. Origin, law, and goal are one for all of you. Let your creed, your action, the banner beneath which you fight, be likewise one. Do not say, *The language which we speak is different*; tears, actions, martyrdom form a common language for all men, and one which you all understand. Do not say, *Humanity is too vast, and we are too weak.* God does not measure powers, but intentions. Love Humanity. Ask yourselves whenever you do an action in the sphere of your Country, or your family, *If what I am doing were done by all and for all, would it advantage or injure Humanity?* and if your conscience answers, *It would injure Humanity*, desist; desist, even if it seem to you that an immediate advantage for your Country or your family would ensue from your action. Be apostles of this faith, apostles of the brotherhood of nations, and of the unity of the human race—a principle admitted to-day in theory, but denied in practice. Be such apostles wherever and in whatever way you are able. Neither God nor man can demand more of you. But I say to you that by becoming such apostles—even to yourselves only, when you are not able to do more—you will advantage Humanity. God measures the degrees of education which he allows the human race to ascend by the number and the purity of the believers. When you are pure and numerous, God, who numbers you, will open for you the way to action.

 Mazzini stressed the importance of community and association.

To improve yourselves and others—this must be the first aim and the supreme hope of every reform, of every social change. The lot of a *man* is not altered by renovating and embellishing the house in which he lives; where only the body of a slave breathes, and not the soul of a man, all reforms are useless; the neat dwelling, luxuriously furnished, is a whited sepulchre, nothing else. You will never induce the society to which you belong to substitute the system of *association* for that of wages, except by proving that your association will be an instrument of improved production and of collective prosperity. And you can only prove this by showing yourselves capable of founding and maintaining the association by honesty, mutual kindliness, capacity for sacrifice, and love of work. To progress you must show yourselves *capable* of progressing.

Three things are sacred: Tradition, Progress, Association. . . .

I have pointed out to you, to the best of my power, what your Duty is. And the chief and most essential duty of all is to your Country. To secure the freedom and unity of your Country is your duty; and it is also a necessity. The encouragement and the measures of which I have spoken can only be the work of a Free and United Country. The amelioration of your social condition can only result from your participation in the political life of the nation. Without the franchise you will never find true representatives of your aspirations and needs. Without a popular government which, seated in Rome, shall formulate the *Italian Compact*, founded upon the common consent of the nation, and directed to the *progress* of *all* the citizens of the State, there is no hope of better things for you. That day in which, following the example of the French *socialists*, you should separate the *social* from the *political* question and should say: *We can emancipate ourselves whatever may be the form of constitution which rules the Country*, you would yourselves seal the perpetuity of your social servitude.

And I will point out to you, in bidding you farewell, another Duty, not less solemn than that which obliges us to found a Free and United Nation.

Your emancipation can only be founded on the triumph of one principle, the unity of the Human Family. To-day, half of the human family, the half from which we seek inspiration and consolation, the half to which is entrusted the first education of our children, is, by a singular contradiction, declared civilly, politically, and socially unequal, and is excluded from this unity. It is for you who seek your emancipation, in the name of religious truth, to protest in every way and upon every occasion against this negation of unity.

The *emancipation of woman* should be always coupled by you with the *emancipation of the working-man*. It will give your work the consecration of a universal truth.

1. What proof did Mazzini offer to demonstrate that the incessant demand for "rights" has had little success in Europe?
2. Trace the extension of one's duties from family, through nation, to humanity, as seen by Mazzini. Would Michelet agree?
3. Discuss and evaluate Mazzini's concluding argument in which he rejected the pursuit of social gains alone.

■ ■ ■

G.W.F. HEGEL

Georg Wilhelm Friedrich Hegel (1770-1831) was a philosopher of immense influence in many areas, including the theory of knowledge, human nature, and logic. He also had a profound importance in the development of modern ideas on history, nationalism, and social and political change. Hegel's *Lectures on the Philosophy of History* were delivered in the period from 1822 until his death, and were collected by his students and published posthumously. In them, Hegel discussed his concepts of reason, spirit, and freedom, and he developed his idea of dialectical change, which influenced Marx and many other social theorists.

Abstruse and very difficult, Hegel's philosophy of history was predicated on the idea that the past has "reason," its own inherent logic.

> The sole thought which philosophy brings to the treatment of history is the simple concept of *Reason*: that Reason is the law of the world and that, therefore, in world history, things have come about rationally. This conviction and insight is a presupposition of history as such; in philosophy itself it is not presupposed. . . . That this *Idea* or *Reason* is the True, the Eternal, the Absolute Power and that it and nothing but it, its glory and majesty, manifests itself in the world—this, as we said before, has been proved in philosophy and is being presupposed here as proved. . . .
>
> . . . The motion of the solar system proceeds according to immutable laws; these laws are its reason. But neither the sun nor the planets, which according to these laws rotate around it, have any consciousness of it. Thus, the thought that there is Reason in nature, that nature is ruled by universal, unchangeable laws, does not surprise us; we are used to it and make very little of it. . . .
>
> . . . The historical connection of the thought that Reason rules the world with another form of it, well known to us—that of religious truth: that the world is not abandoned to chance and external accident but controlled by *Providence*. I said before that I do not make any demand on your belief in the principle announced; but I think I may appeal to this belief in its religious form, unless the nature of scientific philosophy precludes, as a general rule, the acceptance of any presuppositions; or, seen from another angle, unless the science itself which we want to develop should first give the proof, if not of the truth, at least of the correctness of our principle. The truth that a Providence, that is to say, a divine Providence, presides over the events of the world corresponds to our principle; for divine Providence is wisdom endowed with infinite power which realizes its own aim, that is, the absolute, rational, final purpose of the world. Reason is Thought determining itself in absolute freedom. . . .
>
> . . . To explain history means to reveal the passions of men, their genius, their active powers. This definiteness of Providence is usually called its *plan*. . . .

B Hegel emphasized the importance of the state, as the institution in which the "spirit" actualizes itself.

> . . . Law, morality, the State, and they alone, are the positive reality and satisfaction of freedom. The caprice of the individual is not freedom. It is this caprice which is being limited, the license of particular desires.
>
> The subjective will, passion, is the force which actualizes and realizes. The Idea is the interior; the State is the externally existing, genuinely moral life. It is the union of the universal and essential with the subjective will, and as such it is *Morality*. The individual who lives in this unity has a moral life, a value which consists in this substantiality alone. . . . The laws of ethics are not accidental, but are rationality itself. It is the end of the State to make the

Source: G.W.F. Hegel, *Reason in History*, translated by Robert S. Hartman (Indianapolis: The Bobbs-Merrill Company, Inc., 1953), pp. 11, 13, 14-15, 50, 52-53, 68-71, 94.

substantial prevail and maintain itself in the actual doings of men and in their convictions. It is the absolute interest of Reason that this moral whole exist; and herein lies the justification and merit of heroes who have founded states, no matter how crude. . . .

. . . [The State] is the realization of Freedom, of the absolute, final purpose, and exists for its own sake. All the value man has, all spiritual reality, he has only through the state. For his spiritual reality is the knowing presence to him of his own essence, of rationality, of its objective, immediate actuality present in and for him. Only thus is he truly a consciousness, only thus does he partake in morality, in the legal and moral life of the state. For the True is the unity of the universal and particular will. And the universal in the state is in its laws, its universal and rational provisions. The state is the divine Idea as it exists on earth.

Thus the State is the definite object of world history proper. In it freedom achieves its objectivity and lives in the enjoyment of this objectivity. . . .

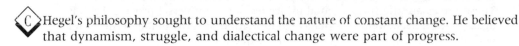

C Hegel's philosophy sought to understand the nature of constant change. He believed that dynamism, struggle, and dialectical change were part of progress.

We have now learned the abstract characteristics of the nature of Spirit, the means which it uses to realize its Idea, and the form which its complete realization assumes in external existence, namely, the State. All that remains for this introduction is to consider the *course of world history*.

Historical change, seen abstractly, has long been understood generally as involving a progress toward the better, the more perfect. Change in nature, no matter how infinitely varied it is, shows only a cycle of constant repetition. In nature nothing new happens under the sun, and in this respect the multiform play of her products leads to boredom. One and the same permanent character continuously reappears, and all change reverts to it. Only the changes in the realm of Spirit create the novel. This characteristic of Spirit suggested to man a feature entirely different from that of nature—the desire toward *perfectibility*. . . .

The principle of *development* implies further that it is based on an inner principle, a presupposed potentiality, which brings itself into existence. This formal determination is essentially the Spirit whose scene, property, and sphere of realization is world history. . . . It proceeds from an inner immutable principle, a simple essence, which first exists as germ. From this simple existence it brings forth out of itself differentiations which connect it with other things. Thus it lives a life of continuous transformation. . . . Thus Spirit is at war with itself. It must overcome itself as its own enemy and formidable obstacle. Development, which in nature is a quiet unfolding, is in Spirit a hard, infinite struggle against itself. What Spirit wants is to attain its own concept. But it hides it from itself and is proud and full of enjoyment in this alienation from itself.

Historical development, therefore, is not the harmless and unopposed simple growth of organic life but hard, unwilling labor against itself. Furthermore, it is not mere formal self-development in general, but the production of an end of determined content. This end we have stated from the beginning: it is Spirit in its essence, the concept of freedom. This is the fundamental object and hence the leading principle of development. Through it the development receives meaning and significance—just as in Roman history Rome is the object and hence the guiding principle of the inquiry into past events. At the same time, however, the events arise out of this object and have meaning and content only with reference to it. . . .

World history, then, represents the phases in the development of the principle whose *content* is the consciousness of freedom. The analysis of its stages in general belongs to Logic. That of its particular, its concrete nature, belongs to the Philosophy of Spirit. Let us only repeat here that the first stage is the immersion of Spirit in natural life, the second its stepping out into the consciousness of its freedom. This first emancipation from nature is incomplete and partial; it issues from immediate naturalness, still refers to it, and hence is still incumbered by it as one of its elements. The third stage is the rising out of this still particular form of freedom into pure universality of freedom, where the spiritual essence attains the consciousness and feeling of itself. These stages are the fundamental principles of the universal process. Each is again, within itself, a process of its own formation. But the detail of this inner dialectic of transition must be left to the sequel.

All we have to indicate here is that Spirit begins with its infinite possibility, but *only* its possibility. As such it contains its absolute content within itself, as its aim and goal, which it attains only as result of its activity. Then and only then has Spirit attained its reality. Thus, in existence, progress appears as an advance from the imperfect to the more perfect. . . .

The result of this process, then, is that the Spirit in objectifying itself and thinking its own being, on the one hand, destroys this (particular) determination of its own being and, on the other hand, grasps its universality. It thus gives a new determination to its principle. The substantial determination of this national spirit is therewith changed; its principle passes into a new and higher one.

It is most important for the full understanding and comprehension of history to grasp and possess the thought of this transition. An individual as unity traverses various stages and remains the same individual. So also a people, up to the stage which is the universal stage of its spirit. In this consists the inner, the conceptual necessity of its change. Here we have the essence, the very soul of the philosophical understanding of history. . . .

1. In your own words, summarize Hegel's belief in the "rational" process of history. How did he relate the "rule of Reason" in human affairs to natural law?
2. Some critics have argued that for Hegel, the individual is subservient to the state. Others claim that the state is simply the product of the collective will which creates an external environment in which the individual may live a rational and moral life. Comment on this debate.
3. In what way did historical change differ from change in nature for Hegel? Is his argument convincing?
4. How did Hegel characterize the struggle towards "perfection"?

5. In the final analysis, what process did Hegel believe moves the Spirit from the realm of possibility to that of attainment?

■ ■ ■

AUGUSTE COMTE

Positivism was a term invented by Auguste Comte (1798-1857) to describe his philosophy. He thought positivism was at the core of the progress of modern times. Positivists believed that the methods of modern science were replacing the old theology and metaphysics. Comte's *Cours de philosophie positive* (1830-42) was an attempt to use the methods of science in all areas of intellectual endeavour and to develop scientific laws for social systems and historical change. Influenced by Montesquieu and Condorcet, Comte's work was an extension of the secularism, progress, and belief in science that characterized the French Enlightenment.

 Comte claimed to have discovered a new "law" of history, which placed positivism on the highest rung of intellectual endeavour.

> In order to explain properly the true nature and peculiar character of the positive philosophy, it is indispensable that we should first take a brief survey of the progressive growth of the human mind viewed as a whole; for no idea can be properly understood apart from its history.
>
> In thus studying the total development of human intelligence in its different spheres of activity, from its first and simplest beginning up to our own time, I believe that I have discovered a great fundamental law, to which the mind is subjected by an invariable necessity. The truth of this law can, I think, be demonstrated both by reasoned proofs furnished by a knowledge of our mental organization, and by historical verification due to an attentive study of the past. This law consists in the fact that each of our principal conceptions, each branch of our knowledge, passes in succession through three different theoretical states: the theological or fictitious state, the metaphysical or abstract state, and the scientific or positive state. In other words, the human mind—by its very nature—makes use successively in each of its researches of three methods of philosophizing, whose characters are essentially different and even radically opposed to each other. We have first the theological method, then the metaphysical method, and finally the positive method. Hence, there are three kinds of philosophy or general systems of conceptions on the aggregate of phenomena which are mutually exclusive of each other. The first is the necessary starting point of human intelligence the third represents its fixed and definitive state; the second is destined to serve only as a transitional method.
>
> In the theological state, the human mind directs its researches mainly toward the inner nature of beings, and toward the first and final causes of all the phenomena that it observes—in a word, toward absolute knowledge. It therefore represents these phenomena as being produced by the direct and con-

Source: Auguste Comte, *Introduction to Positive Philosophy*, edited by Frederick Ferre (Indianapolis: The Bobbs-Merrill Company, Inc., 1970), pp. 1-3, 10, 12-13, 19, 24, 25, 29, 38.

tinuous action of more or less numerous supernatural agents, whose arbitrary intervention explains all the apparent anomalies of the universe.

In the metaphysical state, which is in reality only a simple general modification of the first state, the supernatural agents are replaced by abstract forces, real entities or personified abstractions, inherent in the different beings of the world. These entities are looked upon as capable of giving rise by themselves to all the phenomena observed, each phenomenon being explained by assigning it to its corresponding entity.

Finally, in the positive state, the human mind, recognizing the impossibility of obtaining absolute truth, gives up the search after the origin and hidden causes of the universe and a knowledge of the final causes of phenomena. It endeavours now only to discover, by a well-combined use of reasoning and observation, the actual laws of phenomena—that is to say, their invariable relations of succession and likeness. The explanation of facts, thus reduced to its real terms, consists henceforth only in the connection established between different particular phenomena and some general facts, the number of which the progress of science tends more and more to diminish.

The theological system arrived at its highest form of perfection when it substituted the providential action of a single being for the varied play of the numerous independent gods which had been imagined by the primitive mind. In the same way, the last stage of the metaphysical system consisted in replacing the different special entities by the idea of a single great general entity—nature—looked upon as the sole source of all phenomena. Similarly, the ideal of the positive system, toward which it constantly tends, although in all probability it will never attain such a stage, would be reached if we could look upon all the different phenomena observable as so many particular cases of a single general fact, such as that of gravitation, for example. . . .

B Comte's importance includes being one of the founders of the discipline of sociology, the scientific study of society. He sometimes called it "social physics."

. . . There exists in this respect an invariable and necessary order that our various classes of conceptions have followed, and were bound to follow, in their progressive course; and the exact consideration of this order is the indispensable complement of the fundamental mental law previously enunciated. That order will form the special subject of the next chapter. At present it is sufficient to know that it conforms to the diverse nature of the phenomena, and that it is determined by their degree of generality, of simplicity, and of reciprocal independence—three considerations which, although quite distinct, lead to the same result. Thus, astronomical phenomena, being the most general, the simplest, and the most independent of all others, were the first to be subjected to positive theories; then followed in succession and for the same reasons the phenomena of terrestrial physics, properly so called, those of chemistry, and, finally, those of physiology. . . .

In the four principal categories of natural phenomena enumerated above—astronomical, physical, chemical, and physiological—we notice an important omission relating to social phenomena. Although these are implicitly comprised among physiological phenomena, yet, owing to their importance and the inherent difficulties of their study, they deserve to form a distinct class. This last order of ideas is concerned with the most special, most complicated, and most dependent of all phenomena; it has, therefore, necessarily progressed more slowly than all the preceding orders, even if we do not take into account the more special obstacles to its study which we shall consider later on. However that may be, it is evident that it has not yet been included within the domain of positive philosophy. Theological and metaphysical methods are never used now by anyone in dealing with all the other kinds of phenomena, either as a means of investigation or even as a mode of reasoning. But these discarded methods are, on the contrary, still used exclusively for both purposes in everything that concerns social phenomena, although their insufficiency in this respect has been fully felt already by all good minds, such men being tired of these empty and endless discussions between, e.g., divine right and the sovereignty of the people.

Here, then, is the great, but evidently the only, gap that has to be filled in order to finish the construction of the positive philosophy. Now that the human mind has founded celestial physics, terrestrial physics (mechanical and chemical), and organic physics (vegetable and animal), it only remains to complete the system of observational sciences by the foundation of social physics. . . .

The conceptions which I shall endeavor to present relating to the study of social phenomena, and of which I hope the present chapter has already enabled us to see the germ, cannot be expected to raise social physics at once to the degree of perfection that has been reached by the earlier branches of natural philosophy. Such a hope would be evidently chimerical, seeing that these branches still differ widely from one another in perfectness, as was, indeed, inevitable. But I aim at impressing upon this last branch of our knowledge the same positive character that already marks all the other branches. If this condition is once really fulfilled, the philosophical system of the modern world will be founded at last in its entirety; for there is no observable fact that would not then be included in one or another of the five great categories of astronomical, physical, chemical, physiological, and social phenomena. . . .

 Comte listed several advantages to humanity in pursuing the positive philosophy.

I have now determined, as exactly as possible in a first sketch, the general spirit of a course of positive philosophy. In order to bring out its full character, I must state concisely the principal general advantages that such a work may have—if its essential conditions are fulfilled properly—as regards intellectual progress. I will mention only four. They are fundamental qualities of the positive philosophy.

In the first place, the study of the positive philosophy, by considering the results of the activity of our intellectual faculties, furnishes us with the only really rational means of exhibiting the logical laws of the human mind, which have hitherto been sought by methods so ill calculated to reveal them. . . .

A second consequence, of no less importance and of much more urgent concern, which must immediately result from the establishment of the positive philosophy as defined in this chapter, is the general recasting of our educational system. . . .

The special study of the general traits of the sciences is not only destined to reorganize education, but it will also contribute to the particular progress of the different positive sciences. This constitutes the third fundamental property that I have to point out. . . .

I must draw attention to a fourth and last fundamental property of that which I have called the positive philosophy, and which no doubt deserves our notice more than any other property, for it is today the most important one from a practical point of view. We may look upon the positive philosophy as constituting the only solid basis of the social reorganization that must terminate the crisis in which the most civilized nations have found themselves for so long. . . .

No doubt, when we embrace in our view human labor as a whole, whether theoretical or practical, we must regard our study of nature as intended to furnish us with the true rational basis for acting upon nature. For it is only by knowing the laws of phenomena, and so foreseeing their occurrence, that we are able in active life to make these phenomena modify one another for our advantage. Our direct natural power of acting upon our environment is extremely feeble and wholly disproportioned to our needs. Whenever we succeed in accomplishing anything great, it is due to the fact that our knowledge of natural laws allows us to introduce, among the fixed conditions under whose influence the different phenomena take place, some modifying elements. These, however feeble they may be in themselves, are in certain cases sufficient to turn to our advantage the final results of the sum total of external causes. We may sum up very exactly the general relation of science to art, using these two words in their widest sense, by the following very simple formula: from science comes prevision; from prevision comes action. . . .

1. Outline the three stages through which, according to Comte, the human mind progresses.
2. How did Comte relate the final stages of each mental state?
3. Account for Comte's contention that the means of investigating social phenomena remained at a lower level than that used in scientific investigation.
4. Comment on Comte's analysis of the four properties of positive philosophy. Discuss and evaluate his contention that a scientific approach to social analysis will enable societies to accurately predict future trends and take action to deal with them.

▪ ▪ ▪

HONORÉ DE BALZAC

Honoré de Balzac (1799-1850) called his vast set of novels and stories *The Human Comedy*. It was his intention to use the novel as a means of studying society. His works are both fictional insights in the human condition and a detailed picture of the France of his time. Engels said: "I have learned more from Balzac than from all the works of the historians, economists and professional statisticians of the period taken together." Balzac surveyed the full range of emotion and motivation, and invented a host of characters who represented all social types. Some call him a romantic, others a realist, but there is no question of his influence on all subsequent fiction.

In *Old Goriot* (1834) Balzac opened the novel with a description of the atmosphere and environment of contemporary Paris, as well as some reflections on motivation and chance.

> For the last forty years the elderly Madame Vauquer, *née* de Conflans, has kept a family boarding-house in the Rue Neuve-Sainte-Geneviève between the Latin Quarter and the Faubourg Saint-Marcel. This boarding-house, known as the Maison Vauquer, is open to men and women, young and old, and its respectability has never been questioned by anyone. All the same, no young woman has been seen there for thirty years, and if a young man stays there it is only because his family do not allow him much money. Yet in 1819, the time when this drama begins, an almost penniless girl was living there.
>
> However discredited the word 'drama' may be because of the way it has been overworked and strained and twisted in these days of doleful literature, it must be used here; not that this story is dramatic in the real sense of the word, but perhaps some tears may be shed over it in the reading.
>
> Will it be understood outside Paris? One may doubt it. Only between the heights of Montmartre and Montrouge are there people who can appreciate how exactly, with what close observation, it is drawn from life.
>
> They live in a valley of crumbling stucco and gutters black with mud, a valley full of real suffering and often deceptive joys, and they are so used to sensation that it takes something outrageous to produce a lasting impression. Yet now and then in some overwhelming tragedy evil and good are so strangely mixed that these selfish and self-centred people are forced to pause in their restless pursuit of their own affairs, and their hearts are momentarily touched; but the impression made on them is fleeting, it vanishes as quickly as a delicious fruit melts in the mouth. The chariot of civilization, like the chariot of Juggernaut, is scarcely halted by a heart less easily crushed than the others in its path. It soon breaks this hindrance to its wheel and continues its triumphant course.
>
> And you will show the same insensibility, as you hold this book in your white hand, lying back in a softly cushioned armchair, and saying to yourself, 'Perhaps this one is amusing.' When you have read of the secret sorrows of

Source: Honoré de Balzac, *Old Goriot*, translated by Marion Ayton Crawford (Harmondsworth: Penguin Books, 1951), pp. 27-28, 30, 34, 35, 36, 130-36.

old Goriot you will dine with unimpaired appetite, blaming the author for your callousness, taxing him with exaggeration, accusing him of having given wings to his imagination. But you may be certain that this drama is neither fiction nor romance. *All is true*, so true that everyone can recognize the elements of the tragedy in his own household, in his own heart perhaps.

The lodging-house is Madame Vauquer's own property. It stands at the lower end of the Rue Neuve-Sainte-Geneviève where it slopes so abruptly towards the Rue de l'Arbalète that carriages rarely use it. The absence of wheeled traffic deepens the stillness which prevails in these streets cramped between the domes of the Val-de-Grâce and the Panthéon, two buildings that overshadow them and darken the air with the leaden hue of their dull cupolas. In this district the pavements are dry, the gutters have neither mud nor water, grass grows along the walls. The most carefree passer-by feels depressed where even the sound of wheels is unusual, the houses are gloomy, the walls like a prison. A Parisian straying here would see nothing around him but lodging-houses or institutions, misery or lassitude, the old sinking into the grave or the cheerful young doomed to the treadmill. It is the grimmest quarter of Paris and, it may be said, the least known. . . .

The house itself, three storeys high without counting the attics, is built of hewn stone and washed with that yellow shade which gives a mean look to nearly every house in Paris. The five windows at the front on each floor have small panes, and their blinds are all drawn up to different levels so that the lines are at sixes and sevens. At the side there are two windows, and those on the ground floor are barred with an iron grille. A yard about twenty feet square lies behind the building, inhabited by a happy family of pigs, hens and rabbits, and beyond that there is a shed for fire-wood. The meat-safe is hung up between this shed and the kitchen window, and the greasy water from the sink flows below it. The cook sweeps all the refuse of the house into the Rue Neuve-Sainte-Geneviève through a little door in the yard, and uses floods of water to clean it up for fear of an epidemic.

The ground-floor is well-designed for use as a middle-class boarding-house. The first room is lighted by the two windows facing the street, and may be entered by a French window. A door in this sitting-room leads to a dining-room, which is separated from the kitchen by the well of a staircase, whose wooden steps have coloured waxed tiles set in them.

Nothing could be more depressing than the sight of this sitting-room, with its various chairs upholstered in a haircloth of alternately dull and shiny stripes. In the middle there is a round table with a top of Saint-Anne marble, and on it a white china tea-service with its gilt decoration half worn away, the kind of tea-service that is inevitably found everywhere today. . . .

At the time when this story begins the lodgers numbered seven. . . .

Chance had brought these persons together, but one consideration influenced them all. The two tenants of the second floor paid only seventy-two francs a month. Only in the Faubourg Saint-Marcel, between La Bourbe and La Salpétrière, are such prices to be found, and Madame Couture was the only one in Madame Vauquer's house who did not take advantage of them, which makes it clear that excepting her these boarders must be bearing the weight of a more or less manifest poverty. Moreover the depressing spectacle the interior of the house presented was matched by the clothing of its inmates, who were every bit as dilapidated. The men wore coats whose original colour was unimaginable, shoes like those left abandoned in the gutters in smart districts, frayed linen, clothes which were only the shadow of their former selves. The women had old-fashioned dresses, dyed and faded and redyed again, darned old lace, gloves shiny with long use, collars which were always discoloured and frills frayed at the edges. But although their clothes were of such a kind, they nearly all possessed solidly built bodies, constitutions which had withstood the storms of life. Although their cold, hard faces were worn, like those on coins withdrawn from circulation, their withered mouths were armed with avid teeth. These lodgers made one feel the aura shed by dramas, dramas over and done with or still being acted; not the kind of drama played behind the footlights in front of painted canvas, but living dramas acted in silence, icy dramas which seared the heart, on which no curtain is rung down. . . .

B One of Balzac's most powerful characters was Vautrin, a thief in hiding known as Cheat-Death. He befriends a young law student, Eugène Rastignac, in the boarding house and, in a Faustian scene, Vautrin offers Eugène advice about the world and a pact.

'If I talk to you like this about the world it's because it has given me reason to do so, I know it well. Do you think I blame it? Not at all. It has always been like this. Moralists will never change it. Man is no angel. He is sometimes more of a hypocrite and sometimes less, and then fools say that he has or has not principles. I don't think the rich are any worse than the masses: men are much the same at the top, the bottom, and in the middle of the social scale. In a million of this herd of human cattle there are ten sharp fellows to be found who climb above everything, even above laws; I am one of them. You, if you're above the common herd, go straight forward with your head high. But you will have to fight against envy, slander, mediocrity, against the whole world. Napoleon came up against a Minister of War called Aubry who just failed to send him to the Colonies. Sound yourself! See if you will be able to get up every morning with a will more determined than it was the night before. In that case I am going to make you an offer that nobody would refuse. Mind what I say.

'You see I have a fancy. My notion is to go and live the patriarchal life on a great estate, say a hundred thousand acres, in the United States of America, in the deep South. I intend to be a planter, to have slaves, earn a few nice little millions selling my cattle, my tobacco, my timber, living like a monarch, doing as I like, leading a life unimaginable by people here where we live crouched in a burrow made of stone and plaster. I am a great poet. My poems are not written: they are expressed in action and in feeling, I possess at this moment fifty thousand francs, which would give me scarcely forty niggers. I need two hundred thousand francs, for I want two hundred niggers to carry out my idea of the patriarchal life properly. Negroes, you see, are children ready-made that you can do what you like with, without a nosy Public Prosecutor coming to ask you questions about them. With this black capital, in ten years I shall have three or four millions. If I succeed no one will say to me, ''Who are you?'' I shall be Mr. Four-Millions, American citizen. I shall be fifty years of age, not yet rotten; I shall enjoy myself in my own fashion.

'In one word, if I find you an heiress worth a million will you give me two hundred thousand francs? Twenty per cent commission; well, is that too much? You will make your little wife love you. Once married you will make a show of uneasiness and remorse, you will go about with a long face for a couple of weeks. Then one night after some tomfoolery you will confess to your wife between two kisses that you have debts amounting to two hundred thousand francs, and call her ''Darling!'' This farce is played every day by young fellows of the highest rank. A young woman does not refuse her purse to the man who captures her heart. Do you think that you will be a loser by it? Not you. You will find a way to make up your two hundred thousand francs again by a stroke of business. With your capital and your sharp wits you will pile up a fortune as large as your heart could wish. *Ergo* in six months you will have made us all happy, yourself, a sweet wife, and your old Papa Vautrin, not to speak of your family, blowing on their fingers in the winter-time for want of fire-wood. Don't let my offer, or what I ask for either, startle you. Out of sixty fashionable marriages taking place in Paris forty-seven are made on similar terms. The Chamber of Notaries forced Monsieur—'

'What must I do?' said Rastignac, eagerly interrupting him.

'Practically nothing,' Vautrin replied, with an involuntary movement of delight like the suppressed exclamation of an angler feeling a bite at the end of his line. 'Mark this well. The heart of a poor unfortunate and unhappy girl is the thirstiest of sponges to soak up love, a parched sponge which expands as soon as a drop of tenderness falls on it. To court a young woman you meet in circumstances of loneliness, despair and poverty, when she has no suspicion of the wealth in store for her; by Heaven! it's like having a sequence of five and a quatorze at piquet, it's knowing the numbers in the lottery beforehand, it's playing the stock market with secret information. On a solid foundation you are building an indestructible marriage. When the girl comes into millions she will throw them at your feet like pebbles. ''Take them, my dearest Adolphe!'' she will say, or ''Take them, my dearest Alfred!'' or ''Eugène,'' or anyone who has had the wit to sacrifice himself for her. By ''sacrifice'' I mean selling your old coat in order to eat mushrooms on toast with her at the Cadran-Bleu and go on afterwards to the Ambigu-Comique in the evening, or pawning your watch to give her a shawl. I needn't say anything to you about scribbling love-letters to her, or the sentimental monkey-tricks that go down so well with women, such as sprinkling drops of water on your writing-paper like tears when you are separated from her: you seem to me to be perfectly well acquainted with the lingo of the heart.

'Paris, you see, is like a forest in the New World where a score of savage tribes, the Illinois, the Hurons, struggle for existence: each group lives on what it can get by hunting throughout society. You are a hunter of millions; to capture them you employ snares, limed twigs, decoys. There are many ways of hunting. Some hunt heiresses, others catch their prey by shady financial transactions; some fish for souls, others sell their clients bound hand and foot. The man who comes back with his gamebag well lined is welcomed, fêted, received into good society. Let us be just to this hospitable place, here you have to do with the most accommodating city in the world. If the proud aristocracies of all the capitals of Europe refuse to give a blackguard millionaire admittance to their ranks, Paris holds out her arms to him, runs to his parties, eats his dinners and clinks glasses with his infamy.'

'But where should I find such a girl?' said Eugène.

'She is there, before your eyes, and yours already!'

'Mademoiselle Victorine?'

'Precisely.'

'Say that again!'

'She loves you already, your little Baroness de Rastignac!'

'She hasn't got a sou,' said Eugène in astonishment.

'Ah! now we're coming to it. Another word or two and everything will be clear. Father Taillefer is an old scoundrel who is credited with having murdered one of his friends during the Revolution; he is one of my brave boys who are independent in their views. He is a banker, senior partner in the firm of Frédéric Taillefer and Company. He has only one son and means to leave all he possesses to him, to the prejudice of Victorine. Such injustices don't please me. I'm like Don Quixote, I like to defend the weak against the strong. If it were the will of Heaven to take his son from him Taillefer would acknowledge his daughter. He would want to have someone or other to leave his money to, it's a weakness of human nature, and he's not likely to have any more children, I know. Victorine is gentle and sweet, she will soon twist her father round her little finger, and make him spin like a humming-top with the whip of sentiment! She will appreciate your devotion too much to forget you and you will marry her. For my part I will take the rôle of Providence upon myself: I'll persuade the will of Heaven to act in the right way. I have a friend I've done some very good turns to, a colonel in the Army of the Loire who has just been transferred into the Garde Royale. He's a man who listens to my advice, and he turned ultra-royalist: he isn't one of those idiots who stick to their opinions. If I have one more piece of advice to give you, my sweet lad, it is this—don't stick any more firmly to your opinions than to your work. When you are asked for them, sell them. A man who boasts of never changing his opinions is a man who forces himself to move always in a straight line, a simpleton who believes he is infallible. There are no such things as principles, there are only events; there are no laws, there are only circumstances: the man who is wiser than his fellows accepts events and circumstances in order to turn them to his own ends. If there were fixed principles and laws nations would not change them as easily as we change our shirts. The individual is not expected to be more scrupulous than the nation. The man who has rendered least service to France is the uncompromising La Fayette, yet he is a fetish, venerated because he has always seen everything in blacks and whites; at best he's good enough to be put in the Conservatoire among the machines, labelled like the rest of the exhibits: while Talleyrand, the tortuous Talleyrand, the prince at whom everyone has a stone to fling, who has sufficient contempt for humanity to spit as many vows as it asks for in its face, was the man who saved France from being torn to pieces at the Congress of Vienna—they fling mud at him and they owe him laurel wreaths. Oh! I know what's going on in the world. I hold the key to many men's secrets. That's enough, I shall hold an unalterable opinion when I find three minds agreed on the application of a principle, and I shall wait a long time! There are not three judges in the law-courts with the same opinion about a point of law.

'Well, to return to my man,—he would put Christ back on the cross if I told him to. At a single word from his Papa Vautrin he will pick a quarrel with that scamp who doesn't send so much as a five-franc piece to his sister, and'—Vautrin rose to his feet, took up a defensive posture like a fencing-master, and then lunged. '—and underground!' he added.

'Oh, horrible!' said Eugène. 'You're joking, Monsieur Vautrin, aren't you? You must be!'

'Now, now, keep cool!' said the man. 'Don't behave like a child. Still, if it amuses you, you can stamp your foot and fly into a rage. You can call me a scoundrel, a scalawag, a rapscallion, a ruffian, only don't call me a blackleg or a spy. Go ahead, fire your broadside. I forgive you, it's so natural at your age. I was like that myself once. Only, consider: you will do worse some day. You will go and flirt with some pretty woman, and you will take her money. The thought has entered your mind, of course,' said Vautrin, 'for how are you to get on if your love-making doesn't bring you money? Virtue, my dear student, is indivisible: it either is, or it is not. They tell us to do penance for our sins: that's a fine system which rids you of a crime by an act of contrition! You seduce a woman in order to set your foot on some rung of the social ladder, you stir up dissension among the children of a family, you stoop to all the shameful practices that are employed, under the rose or openly, for the sake of pleasure or personal advantage: do you believe those are works of faith, hope and charity? Why should the toff who robs a boy of half his fortune in a night get off with two months in prison, while the poor devil who steals a hundred-franc note with aggravating circumstances is sent to penal servitude? Those are your laws. There isn't a clause in them which doesn't touch absurdity. The honey-tongued man in yellow gloves has committed many a murder, he sheds no blood, but his victim sweats blood for him all the same; the other rascal opened a door with a jemmy: dark deeds both of them! Between what I propose and what you will one day do there's no difference, bar the bloodshed. And you believe in absolute standards in that world! Despise men then, and look for the holes you can slip through in the Law's net. The secret of great fortunes with no apparent source is a forgotten crime, forgotten because it was properly carried out.'

'Oh, don't say any more! I don't want to listen to you, you make me doubt myself. At this moment I only know what I feel.'

'As you please, my fine fellow. I thought you were tougher,' said Vautrin. 'I won't say any more. Just one thing though.' He stared hard at the student. 'You know my secret,' he said.

'A young man who refuses you will know he must forget it.'

'That's well said. I'm pleased with you. Anyone else, you know, will be less scrupulous. Bear in mind what I want to do for you. I'll give you a fortnight to decide about my offer. You can take it or leave it.' . . .

1. "I have learned more from Balzac than from all the works of the historians, economists and professional statisticians of the period taken together."

Account for this statement with reference to the insights presented by Balzac in this brief excerpt.

2. Compare the discussion held between Vautrin and Eugène with that of Mephistopheles and Faust.

3. Comment on the following statement by Vautrin: "There are no such things as principles, there are only events; there are no laws, there are only circumstances; the man who is wiser than his fellows accepts events and circumstances in order to turn them to his own ends."

・ ・ ・

JEREMY BENTHAM

Jeremy Bentham (1748-1832) was the philosopher most closely associated with utilitarianism, the social and political philosophy that was based on providing for "the greatest happiness of the greatest number." Bentham was a reformer, and he hoped to use the law to broaden public participation in government and to develop legislation which would provide for an amelioration of social conditions. The utilitarian movement had great influence on the political development of Great Britain in the early nineteenth century.

Bentham wrote his *Constitutional Code* between 1820 and 1832. In the introduction he discussed the "greatest happiness" principle.

> . . . When I say the greatest happiness of the whole community, ought to be the end or object of pursuit, in every branch of the law—of the political rule of action, and of the constitutional branch in particular, what is it that I express?—this and no more, namely that it is my wish, my desire, to see it taken for such, by those who, in the community in question, are actually in possession of the powers of government; taken for such, on the occasion of every arrangement made by them in the exercise of such their powers, so that their endeavours shall be, to render such their cause of action contributory to the obtainment of that same end. . . .
>
> In saying, as above, the proper end of government is the greatest happiness of all, or in case of competition, the greatest happiness of the greatest number, it seems to me that I have made a declaration of peace and goodwill to all men.
>
> On the other hand, were I to say, the proper end of government is the greatest happiness of some one, naming him, or of some few, naming them, it seems to me that I should be making a declaration of war against all men, with the exception of that one, or of those few. . . .
>
> This being the basis on which all legislation and all morality rests, these few words written in hopes of clearing away all obscurity and ambiguity, all

Source: *The Works of Jeremy Bentham*, edited by John Bowring (New York: Russell and Russell, 1962), Volume IX, pp. 4, 5-6, 7, 9, 10.

doubts and difficulties, will not, I hope, be regarded as misapplied, or applied in waste.

The right and proper end of government in every political community, is the greatest happiness of all the individuals of which it is composed, say, in other words, the greatest happiness of the greatest number. . . .

The *actual* end of government is, in every political community, the greatest happiness of those, whether one or many, by whom the powers of government are exercised.

In general terms, the proof of this position may be referred to particular experience, as brought to view by the history of all nations.

This experience may be termed *particular*, inasmuch as the particular class of rulers is the only class concerned in it, to which it bears reference. This may be called the experimental or practical proof.

For further proof, reference may be made to the general, indeed the all-comprehensive, principle of human nature. The position which takes this fact for its subject, may be termed an axiom, and may be expressed in the words following.

In the general tenor of life, in every human breast, self-regarding interest is predominant over all other interests put together. More shortly thus,— Self-regard is predominant,—or thus,—Self-preference has place everywhere.

This position may, to some eyes, present itself in the character of an axiom: as such self-evident, and not standing in need of proof. To others, as a position or proposition which, how clearly soever true, still stands in need of proof.

To deliver a position in the character of an axiom, is to deliver it under the expectation that, either it will not be controverted at all, or that he by whom it is controverted, will not, in justification of the denial given by him to it, be able to advance anything by which the unreasonableness of his opinion or pretended opinion, will not be exposed. Of this stamp are the axioms laid down by Euclid. In the axioms so laid down by him, nothing of dogmatism will, it is believed, be found.

By the principle of self-preference, understand that propensity in human nature, by which, on the occasion of every act he exercises, every human being is led to pursue that line of conduct which, according to his view of the case, taken by him at the moment, will be in the highest degree contributory to his own greatest happiness, whatsoever be the effect of it, in relation to the happiness of other similar beings, any or all of them taken together. For the satisfaction of those who may doubt, reference may be made to the *existence* of the species as being of itself a proof, and *that* a conclusive one. For after exception made of the case of children not arrived at the age of which they are capable of going alone, or adults reduced by infirmity to a helpless state; take any two individuals, A and B, and suppose the whole care of the happiness of A confined to the breast of B, A himself not having any part in it; and the whole care of the happiness of B confined to the breast of A, B himself not having any part in it, and this to be the case throughout, it will soon appear that, in this state of things, the species could not continue in existence, and that a few months, not to say weeks or days, would suffice for the annihilation of it. . . .

Note that, if in the situation of ruler, the truth of this position, held good in no more than a bare majority, of the whole number of instances, it would suffice for every practical purpose, in the character of a ground for all political arrangements; in the character of a consideration, by which the location of the several portions of the aggregate mass of political power should be determined; for, in the way of induction, it is only by the greater, and not the lesser number of instances, that the general conclusion can reasonably be determined; in a word, mathematically speaking, the probability of a future contingent event, is in the direct ratio of the number of instances in which an event of the same sort has happened, to the number of those in which it has not happened; it is in this direct ratio, and not in the inverse.

If such were the condition of human beings, that the happiness of no one being came in competition with that of any other,—that is to say, if the happiness of each, or of any one, could receive increase to an unlimited amount, without having the effect of producing decrease in the happiness of any other, then the above expression might serve without limitation or explanation. But on every occasion, the happiness of every individual is liable to come into competition with the happiness of every other. If, for example, in a house containing two individuals, for the space of a month, there be a supply of food barely sufficient to continue for that time; not merely the happiness of each, but the existence of each, stands in competition with, and is incompatible with the existence of the other.

Hence it is, that to serve for all occasions, instead of saying the greatest happiness of all, it becomes necessary to use the expression, the greatest happiness of the greatest number.

If, however, instead of the word *happiness*, the word *interest* is employed, the phrase *universal interest* may be employed as corresponding indifferently to the interest of the greatest number, or to the interest of all. . . .

 Bentham asked about the best form of government.

What, then, is the best *form* of government? This question may itself be clothed in an indefinite number of forms. What is the most eligible? what is the most desirable? what is the most expedient? what is the most right and proper? and so on. . . .

In every community in which a constitutional code, generally acknowledged to be in force, is in existence, a really existing constitutional branch of law, and with it, as the offspring of it, a constitution, is so far in existence.

In no community in which no constitutional code thus generally acknowledged to be in force, is in existence, is any such branch of law as a constitutional branch, or any such thing as a constitution, really in existence.

In a community in which, as above, no such thing as a constitution is really to be found, things to each of which the name of a constitution is given, are to be found in endless multitudes. On each occasion, the thing designated by the phrase "the constitution," is a substitute for a constitution—a substitute framed by the imagination of the person by whom this phrase is uttered, framed by him, and, of course, adapted to that which, in his mind, is the purpose of the moment, whatsoever that purpose be; in so far as that purpose is the promoting the creation or preservation of an absolutely monarchical form of government, the constitution thus imagined and invented by him is of the absolutely monarchical cast; in so far as that purpose is the promoting the creation or preservation of a limitedly monarchical form of government, it is of the limitedly monarchical cast; in so far as the purpose is the creation of preservation of a democratical form of government, it is of the democratic cast.

The Anglo-American United States have a constitution. They have a constitutional code; the constitution is the system of arrangements delineated in that code.

It has for its object the greatest happiness of the greatest number, and in pursuit of that object, the powers of government are allotted by it to the greatest number.

The French and Spanish nations have constitutions. The English monarchy has no constitution, for it has no all-comprehensive constitutional code, nor in short, any constitutional code whatsoever generally acknowledged as such; nor by any one individual of the whole community acknowledged as such. Hence, so it is, that of the assertion contained in the phrases, "excellent constitution,"—"matchless constitution," an assertion by which every endeavour to produce the effect of the worst constitution possible is so naturally accompanied, no disproof can be opposed otherwise than by the assertion of a plain and universally notorious matter of fact, viz.—that the English people have no constitution at all belonging to them. England, not having any constitution at all, has no excellent, no matchless constitution; for nothing has no properties. If ever it has a constitution, that constitution will most probably be a democratical one; for nothing less than an insurrection on the part of the greatest number, will suffice to surmount and subdue so vast a power as that which is composed of the conjunct action of force, intimidation, corruption, and delusion. . . .

Under an absolute monarchy, the constitutional branch of the law has, for its sole actual end, the greatest happiness of the one individual, in whose hands without division, the whole of the supreme operative power is lodged.

For decency's sake, the end thus actually and exclusively pursued, is not the end professed and declared to be pursued. For the designation of the end actually pursued, regard for decency and conciseness, substitutes, on each occasion, one or another of a small assortment of phrases: preservation of order, preservation of legitimacy, for example.

Under a limited monarchy, the constitutional branch of law has, for its actual object, a more complex object; viz. the greatest happiness of the monarch, coupled with, and limited by, the greatest happiness of the conjunctly or subordinately ruling few, by whose respective powers the limitations that are applied to the power of the monarch, are applied.

Under a representative democracy, the constitutional branch of law has, for its actual end, the greatest happiness of the greatest number. . . .

1. What did Bentham identify as the "proper end of government"?
2. How did he say this compares with the actual end of government?
3. Outline the limitations that Bentham contended changed the concept of universal happiness to one of universal interest.
4. Comment on the criteria which Bentham presented for judging governments.
5. What role did a constitution play in the formation of government?

6. Using the principles of universal happiness, how did Bentham rate the principal types of government existing in his day?

• • •

ALEXIS DE TOCQUEVILLE

Alexis de Tocqueville (1805-59) was the most astute commentator of his time on liberalism, equality, and democracy. In 1831 he visited the United States on a commission from the French government to study the penal system. The result was not only that report, but two volumes on social equality and political democracy in the United States entitled *Democracy in America* (1835, 1840). Tocqueville valued individual freedom and believed the trend to democracy, the rule of the majority, was inevitable in the modern world. But he was also concerned with preventing "democratic despotism" and the "tyranny of the majority."

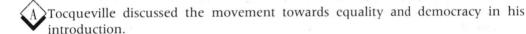 Tocqueville discussed the movement towards equality and democracy in his introduction.

> Among the novel objects that attracted my attention during my stay in the United States, nothing struck me more forcibly than the general equality of condition among the people. I readily discovered the prodigious influence that this primary fact exercises on the whole course of society; it gives a peculiar direction to public opinion and a peculiar tenor to the laws; it imparts new maxims to the governing authorities and peculiar habits to the governed.
>
> I soon perceived that the influence of this fact extends far beyond the political character and the laws of the country, and that it has no less effect on civil society than on the government; it creates opinions, gives birth to new sentiments, founds novel customs, and modifies whatever it does not produce. The more I advanced in the study of American society, the more I perceived that this equality of condition is the fundamental fact from which all others seem to be derived and the central point at which all my observations constantly terminated. . . .
>
> . . . The scene is now changed. Gradually the distinctions of rank are done away with; the barriers that once severed mankind are falling; property is divided, power is shared by many, the light of intelligence spreads, and the capacities of all classes tend towards equality. Society becomes democratic, and the empire of democracy is slowly and peaceably introduced into institutions and customs. . . .
>
> There is one country in the world where the great social revolution that I am speaking of seems to have nearly reached its natural limits. It has been effected with ease and simplicity; say rather that this country is reaping the fruits of the democratic revolution which we are undergoing, without having had the revolution itself.

Source: Alexis de Tocqueville, *Democracy in America* (New York: Vintage Books, 1945), Volume I, pp. 3, 9, 14-15, 269-72, Volume II, pp. 99-100, 102-103.

The emigrants who colonized the shores of America in the beginning of the seventeenth century somehow separated the democratic principle from all the principles that it had to contend with in the old communities of Europe, and transplanted it alone to the New World. It has there been able to spread in perfect freedom and peaceably to determine character of the laws by influencing the manners of the country.

It appears to me beyond a doubt that, sooner or later, we shall arrive, like the Americans, at an almost complete equality of condition. But I do not conclude from this that we shall ever be necessarily led to draw the same political consequences which the Americans have derived from a similar social organization I am far from supposing that they have chosen the only form of government which a democracy may adopt; but as the generating cause of laws and manners in the two countries is the same, it is of immense interest for us to know what it has produced in each of them.

It is not, then, merely to satisfy a curiosity, however legitimate, that I have examined America; my wish has been to find there instruction by which we may ourselves profit. Whoever should imagine that I have intended to write a panegyric would be strangely mistaken, and on reading this book he will perceive that such was not my design; nor has it been my object to advocate any form of government in particular, for I am of the opinion that absolute perfection is rarely to be found in any system of laws. I have not even pretended to judge whether the social revolution, which I believe to be irresistible, is advantageous or prejudicial to mankind. I have acknowledged this revolution as a fact already accomplished, or on the eve of its accomplishment; and I have selected the nation, from among those which have undergone it, in which its development has been the most peaceful and the most complete, in order to discern its natural consequences and to find out, if possible, the means of rendering it profitable to mankind. I confess that in America I saw more than America; I sought there the image of democracy itself, with its inclinations, its character, its prejudices, and its passions, in order to learn what we have to fear or to hope from its progress. . . .

B Justice, right, the will of the majority—all were important. Yet, Tocqueville found some dangers in majority rule and he believed that power must submit to institutional restraints.

I hold it to be an impious and detestable maxim that, politically speaking, the people have a right to do anything; and yet I have asserted that all authority originates in the will of the majority. Am I, then, in contradiction with myself?

A general law, which bears the name of justice, has been made and sanctioned, not only by a majority of this or that people, but by a majority of mankind. The rights of every people are therefore confined within the limits of what is just. A nation may be considered as a jury which is empowered to represent society at large and to apply justice, which is its law. Ought such a jury, which represents society, to have more power than the society itself whose laws it executes?

When I refuse to obey an unjust law, I do not contest the right of the majority to command, but I simply appeal from the sovereignty of the people to the sovereignty of mankind. Some have not feared to assert that a people can never outstep the boundaries of justice and reason in those affairs which are peculiarly its own; and that consequently full power may be given to the majority by which it is represented. But this is the language of a slave.

A majority taken collectively is only an individual, whose opinions, and frequently whose interests, are opposed to those of another individual, who is styled a minority. If it be admitted that a man possessing absolute power may misuse that power by wronging his adversaries, why should not a majority be liable to the same reproach? Men do not change their characters by uniting with one another; nor does their patience in the presence of obstacles increase with their strength. For my own part, I cannot believe it; the power to do everything, which I should refuse to one of my equals, I will never grant to any number of them.

I do not think that, for the sake of preserving liberty, it is possible to combine several principles in the same government so as really to oppose them to one another. The form of government that is usually termed *mixed* has always appeared to me a mere chimera. Accurately speaking, there is no such thing as a *mixed government*, in the sense usually given to that word, because in all communities some one principle of action may be discovered which preponderates over the others. England in the last century, which has been especially cited as an example of this sort of government, was essentially an aristocratic state, although it comprised some great elements of democracy; for the laws and customs of the country were such that the aristocracy could not but preponderate in the long run and direct public affairs according to its own will. The error arose from seeing the interests of the nobles perpetually contending with those of the people, without considering the issue of the contest, which was really the important point. When a community actually has a mixed government—that is to say, when it is equally divided between adverse principles—it must either experience a revolution or fall into anarchy.

I am therefore of the opinion that social power superior to all others must always be placed somewhere; but I think that liberty is endangered when this power finds no obstacle which can retard its course and give it time to moderate its own vehemence.

Unlimited power is in itself a bad and dangerous thing. Human beings are not competent to exercise it with discretion. God alone can be omnipotent, because his wisdom and his justice are always equal to his power. There is no power on earth so worthy of honor in itself or clothed with rights so sacred that I would admit its uncontrolled and all-predominant authority. When I see that the right and the means of absolute command are conferred on any power whatever, be it called a people or a king, an aristocracy or a democracy, a monarchy or a republic, I say there is the germ of tyranny, and I seek to live elsewhere, under other laws.

In my opinion, the main evil of the present democratic institutions of the United States does not arise, as is often asserted in Europe, from their weakness, but from their irresistible strength. I am not so much alarmed at the excessive liberty which reigns in that country as at the inadequate securities which one finds there against tyranny.

When an individual or a party is wronged in the United States, to whom can he apply for redress? If to public opinion, public opinion constitutes the majority; if to the legislature, it represents the majority and implicitly obeys it; if to the executive power, it is appointed by the majority and serves as a passive tool in its hands. The public force consists of the majority under arms; the jury is the majority invested with the right of hearing judicial cases; and in certain states even the judges are elected by the majority. However iniquitous or absurd the measure of which you complain, you must submit to it as well as you can.

If, on the other hand, a legislative power could be so constituted as to represent the majority without necessarily being the slave of its passions, an executive so as to retain a proper share of authority, and a judiciary so as to remain independent of the other two powers, a government would be formed which would still be democratic while incurring scarcely any risk of tyranny.

I do not say that there is a frequent use of tyranny in America at the present day; but I maintain that there is no sure barrier against it, and that the causes which mitigate the government there are to be found in the circumstances and the manners of the country more than in its laws. . . .

A distinction must be drawn between tyranny and arbitrary power. Tyranny may be exercised by means of the law itself, and in that case it is not arbitrary; arbitrary power may be exercised for the public good, in which case it is not tyrannical. Tyranny usually employs arbitrary means, but if necessary it can do without them.

In the United States the omnipotence of the majority, which is favorable to the legal despotism of the legislature, likewise favors the arbitrary authority of the magistrate. The majority has absolute power both to make the laws and to watch over their execution; and as it has equal authority over those who are in power and the community at large, it considers public officers as its passive agents and readily confides to them the task of carrying out its designs. . . .

C ▷ Tocqueville believed "democratic nations show a more ardent and enduring love of equality than of liberty."

. . . It is possible to imagine an extreme point at which freedom and equality would meet and blend. Let us suppose that all the people take a part in the government, and that each one of them has an equal right to take part in it. As no one is different from his fellows, none can exercise a tyrannical power; men will be perfectly free because they are all entirely equal; and they will all be perfectly equal because they are entirely free. To this ideal state democratic nations tend. This is the only complete form that equality can assume upon earth; but there are a thousand others which, without being equally perfect, are not less cherished by those nations.

The principle of equality may be established in civil society without prevailing in the political world. There may be equal rights of indulging in the same pleasures, of entering the same professions, of frequenting the same places; in a word, of living in the same manner and seeking wealth by the same means, although all men do not take an equal share in the government.

A kind of equality may even be established in the political world though there should be no political freedom there. A man may be the equal of all his countrymen save one, who is the master of all without distinction and who selects equally from among them all the agents of his power. Several other combinations might be easily imagined by which very great equality would be united to institutions more or less free or even to institutions wholly without freedom.

Although men cannot become absolutely equal unless they are entirely free, and consequently equality, pushed to its furthest extent, may be confounded with freedom, yet there is good reason for distinguishing the one from the other. The taste which men have for liberty and that which they feel for equality are, in fact, two different things; and I am not afraid to add that among democratic nations they are two unequal things. . . .

Democratic nations are at all times fond of equality, but there are certain epochs at which the passion they entertain for it swells to the height of fury. This occurs at the moment when the old social system, long menaced, is overthrown after a severe internal struggle, and the barriers of rank are at length thrown down. At such times men pounce upon equality as their booty, and they cling to it as to some precious treasure which they fear to lose. The passion for equality penetrates on every side into men's hearts, expands there, and fills them entirely. Tell them not that by this blind surrender of themselves to an exclusive passion they risk their dearest interests; they are deaf. Show them not freedom escaping from their grasp while they are looking another way; they are blind, or rather they can discern but one object to be desired in the universe. . . .

I think that democratic communities have a natural taste for freedom; left to themselves, they will seek it, cherish it, and view any privation of it with regret. But for equality their passion is ardent, insatiable, incessant, invincible; they call for equality in freedom and if they cannot obtain that, they still call for equality in slavery. They will endure poverty, servitude, barbarism, but they will not endure aristocracy.

This is true at all times, and especially in our own day. All men and all powers seeking to cope with this irresistible passion will be overthrown and destroyed by it. In our age freedom cannot be established without it, and despotism itself cannot reign without its support.

1. Summarize Tocqueville's argument that America (the United States) simply illustrated the general trend toward social equality already present in Europe.
2. Account for Tocqueville's distinction between democracy and majority rule, and outline his concern with regard to the dangers inherent in the latter.
3. Tocqueville commented that citizens in a democratic state may be consumed by such a passion for equality, that they may sacrifice their freedom in the process. Explain the reasoning behind this seemingly contradictory point of view. Do you agree?

■ ■ ■

HENRY DAVID THOREAU

Henry David Thoreau (1817-62) was an American author and naturalist who championed individualism. He lived a life that challenged materialism and tried to get at what was basic to the human spirit. Thoreau wrote eloquently about life on the rivers and in the woods, as he regularly took himself away from civilization to a style of living based upon essentials. His political essay "Civil Disobedience" (1849) was the result of his staying in prison overnight for refusing to pay a tax supporting the Mexican War. Thoreau's emphasis on what was basic and his defense of his principles had great influence on later movements in favour of political freedom, including those led by Gandhi and Martin Luther King.

 In *Walden* (1854) Thoreau described his life by the pond from 1845 to 1847.

> I went to the woods because I wished to live deliberately, to front only the essential facts of life, and see if I could not learn what it had to teach and not, when I came to die, discover that I had not lived. I did not wish to live what was not life, living is so dear, nor did I wish to practise resignation, unless it was quite necessary. I wanted to live deep and suck out all the marrow of life, to live so sturdily and Spartan-like as to put to rout all that was not life, to cut a broad swath and shave close, to drive life into a corner, and reduce it to its lowest terms, and, if it proved to be mean, why then to get the whole and genuine meanness of it, and publish its meanness to the world; or if it were sublime, to know it by experience, and be able to give a true account of it in my next excursion. For most men, it appears to me, are in a strange uncertainty about it, whether it is of the devil or of God, and have *somewhat hastily* concluded that it is the chief end of man here to "glorify God and enjoy him forever."
>
> Still we live meanly, like ants; though the fable tells us that we were long ago changed into men; like pygmies we fight with cranes; it is error upon error, and clout upon clout, and our best virtue has for its occasion a superfluous and evitable wretchedness. Our life is frittered away by detail. An honest man has hardly need to count more than his ten fingers, or in extreme cases he may add his ten toes, and lump the rest. Simplicity, simplicity, simplicity! I say, let your affairs be as two or three, and not a hundred or a thousand; instead of a million count half a dozen, and keep your accounts on your thumb nail. In the midst of this chopping sea of civilized life, such are the clouds and storms and quicksands and thousand-and-one items to be allowed for, that a man has to live, if he would not founder and go to the bottom and not make his port at all, by dead reckoning and he must be a great calculator indeed who succeeds. Simplify, simplify. Instead of three meals a day, if it be necessary eat but one; instead of a hundred dishes, five; and reduce other things in proportion. . . .

Source: Henry David Thoreau, *Walden and Other Writings*, edited by Joseph Wood Krutch (New York: Bantam Books, 1962), pp. 172-73, 174, 177-78, 85-86, 88, 92, 94, 96-97.

Why should we live with such hurry and waste of life? We are determined to be starved before we are hungry. Men say that a stitch in time saves nine, and so they take a thousand stitches to-day to save nine to-morrow. As for *work*, we haven't any of any consequence. We have the Saint Vitus' dance, and cannot possibly keep our heads still. . . .

Let us spend one day as deliberately as Nature, and not be thrown off the track by every nutshell and mosquito's wing that falls on the rails. Let us rise early and fast, or break fast, gently and without perturbation; let company come and let company go, let the bells ring and the children cry,—determined to make a day of it. Why should we knock under and go with the stream? Let us not be upset and overwhelmed in that terrible rapid and whirlpool called a dinner, situated in the meridian shallows. Weather this danger and you are safe, for the rest of the way is down hill. With unrelaxed nerves, with morning vigor, sail by it, looking another way, tied to the mast like Ulysses. If the engine whistles, let it whistle till it is hoarse for its pains. If the bell rings, why should we run? We will consider what kind of music they are like. Let us settle ourselves and work and wedge our feet downward through the mud and slush of opinion, and prejudice, and tradition, and delusion, and appearance, that alluvion which covers the globe, through Paris and London, through New York and Boston and Concord, through church and state, through poetry and philosophy and religion, till we come to a hard bottom and rocks in place, which we can call *reality*, and say, This is, and no mistake; and then begin, having a *point d'appui*, below freshet and frost and fire, a place where you might found a wall or a state, or set a lamp-post safely, or perhaps a gauge, not a Nilometer, but a Realometer, that future ages might know how deep a freshet of shams and appearances had gathered from time to time. If you stand right fronting and face to face to a fact, you will see the sun glimmer on both its surfaces, as if it were a cimeter, and feel its sweet edge dividing you through the heart and marrow, and so you will happily conclude your mortal career. Be it life or death, we crave only reality. If we are really dying, let us hear the rattle in our throats and feel cold in the extremities; if we are alive, let us go about our business.

Time is but the stream I go a-fishing in. I drink at it; but while I drink I see the sandy bottom and detect how shallow it is. Its thin current slides away, but eternity remains. I would drink deeper; fish in the sky, whose bottom is pebbly with stars. . . .

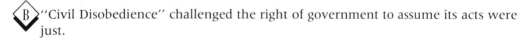 "Civil Disobedience" challenged the right of government to assume its acts were just.

I heartily accept the motto,—"That government is best which governs least;" and I should like to see it acted up to more rapidly and systematically. Carried out, it finally amounts to this, which also I believe,—"That government is best which governs not at all;" and when men are prepared for it, that will be the kind of government which they will have. Government is at best but an expedient; but most governments are usually, and all governments are sometimes, inexpedient. The objections which have been brought against a standing army, and they are many and weighty, and deserve to prevail, may also at last be brought against a standing government. The standing army is only an arm of the standing government. The government itself, which is only the mode which the people have chosen to execute their will, is equally liable to be abused and perverted before the people can act through it. Witness the present Mexican war, the work of comparatively a few individuals using the standing government as their tool; for, in the outset, the people would not have consented to this measure.

. . . Governments show thus how successfully men can be imposed on, even impose on themselves, for their own advantage. It is excellent, we must all allow. Yet this government never of itself furthered any enterprise, but by the alacrity with which it got out of its way. *It* does not keep the country free. *It* does not settle the West. *It* does not educate. The character inherent in the American people has done all that has been accomplished; and it would have done somewhat more, if the government had not sometimes got in its way. For government is an expedient by which men would fain succeed in letting one another alone; and, as has been said, when it is most expedient, the governed are most let alone by it. Trade and commerce, if they were not made of India-rubber, would never manage to bounce over the obstacles which legislators are continually putting in their way; and, if one were to judge these men wholly by the effects of their actions and not partly by their intentions, they would deserve to be classed and punished with those mischievous persons who put obstructions on the railroads.

But, to speak practically and as a citizen, unlike those who call themselves no-government men, I ask for, not at once no government, but *at once* a better government. Let every man make known what kind of government would command his respect, and that will be one step toward obtaining it.

After all, the practical reason why, when the power is once in the hands of the people, a majority are permitted, and for a long period continue, to rule is not because they are most likely to be in the right, nor because this seems fairest to the minority, but because they are physically the strongest. But a government in which the majority rule in all cases cannot be based on justice, even as far as men understand it. Can there not be a government in which majorities do not virtually decide right and wrong, but conscience?— in which majorities decide only those questions to which the rule of expediency is applicable? Must the citizen ever for a moment, or in the least degree, resign his conscience to the legislator? Why has every man a conscience, then? I think that we should be men first, and subjects afterward. It is not desirable to cultivate a respect for the law, so much as for the right. The only obligation which I have a right to assume is to do at any time what I think right. . . .

All men recognize the right of revolution; that is, the right to refuse allegiance to, and to resist, the government, when its tyranny or its inefficiency are great and unendurable. But almost all say that such is not the case now. But such was the case, they think, in the Revolution of '75. If one were to tell me that this was a bad government because it taxed certain foreign commodities brought to its ports, it is most probable that I should not make an ado about it, for I can do without them. All machines have their friction; and possibly this does enough good to counterbalance the evil. At any rate, it is a great evil to make a stir about it. But when the friction comes to have its machine, and oppression and robbery are organized, I say, let us not have such a machine any longer. In other words, when a sixth of the population of a nation which has undertaken to be the refuge of liberty are slaves, and a whole country is unjustly overrun and conquered by a foreign army, and subjected to military law, I think that it is not too soon for honest men to rebel and revolutionize. What makes this duty the more urgent is the fact the country so overrun is not our own, but ours is the invading army. . . .

 Injustice, thought Thoreau, must be met by an unwillingness to acquiesce.

. . . Unjust laws exist: shall we be content to obey them, or shall we endeavor to amend them, and obey them until we have succeeded, or shall we transgress them at once? Men generally, under such a government as this, think that they ought to wait until they have persuaded the majority to alter them. They think that, if they should resist, the remedy would be worse than the evil. But it is the fault of the government itself that the remedy *is* worse than the evil. *It* makes it worse. Why is it not more apt to anticipate and provide for reform? Why does it not cherish its wise minority? Why does it cry and resist before it is hurt? Why does it not encourage its citizens to be on the alert to point out its faults, and *do* better than it would have them? Why does it always crucify Christ, and excommunicate Copernicus and Luther, and pronounce Washington and Franklin rebels?

One would think, that a deliberate and practical denial of its authority was the only offense never contemplated by government; else, why has it not assigned its definite, its suitable and proportionate penalty? If a man who has no property refuses but once to earn nine shillings for the state, he is put in prison for a period unlimited by any law that I know, and determined only by the discretion of those who placed him there; but if he should steal ninety times nine shillings from the state, he is soon permitted to go at large again. . . .

Under a government which imprisons any unjustly, the true place for a just man is also a prison. The proper place to-day, the only place which Massachusetts has provided for her freer and less desponding spirits, is in her prisons, to be put out and locked out of the State by her own act, as they have already put themselves out by their principles. It is there that the fugitive slave, and the Mexican prisoner on parole, and the Indian come to plead the wrongs of his race should find them; on that separate, but more free and honorable ground, where the State places those who are not *with* her, but *against* her,—the only house in a slave State in which a free man can abide with honor. If any think that their influence would be lost there, and their voices no longer afflict the ear of the State, that they would not be as an enemy within its walls, they do not know by how much truth is stronger than error, nor how much more eloquently and effectively he can combat injustice who has experienced a little in his own person. Cast your whole vote, not a strip of paper merely, but your whole influence. A minority is powerless while it conforms to the majority; it is not even a minority then; but it is irresistible when it clogs by its whole weight. If the alternative is to keep all just men in prison, or give up war and slavery, the State will not hesitate which to choose. If a thousand men were not to pay their tax-bills this year, that would not be a violent and bloody measure, as it would be to pay them, and enable the State to commit violence and shed innocent blood. This is, in fact, the definition of a peaceable revolution, if any such is possible. If the tax-gatherer, or any other public officer, asks me, as one has done, "But what shall I do?" my answer is, "If you really wish to do anything, resign your office." When the subject has refused allegiance, and the officer has resigned his office, then the revolution is accomplished. But even suppose blood should flow. Is there not a sort of blood shed when the conscience is wounded? Through this wound a man's real manhood and immortality flow out, and he bleeds to an everlasting death. I see this blood flowing now. . . .

Some years ago, the State met me in behalf of the Church, and commanded me to pay a certain sum toward the support of a clergyman whose preaching my father attended, but never I myself. "Pay," it said, "or be locked up in the jail." I declined to pay. But, unfortunately, another man saw fit to pay it. I did not see why the schoolmaster should be taxed to support the priest, and not the priest the schoolmaster; for I was not the State's schoolmaster, but I supported myself by voluntary subscription. I did not see why the lyceum should not present its tax-bill, and have the State to back its demand, as well as the Church. However, at the request of the selectmen, I condescended to make some such statement as this in writing:—"Know all men by these presents, that I, Henry Thoreau, do not wish to be regarded as a member of any incorporated society which I have not joined." This I gave to the town clerk; and he has it. The State, having thus learned that I did not wish to be regarded as a member of that church, has never made a like demand on me since; though it said that it must adhere to its original presumption that time. If I had known how to name them, I should then have signed off in detail from all the societies which I never signed on to; but I did not know where to find a complete list.

I have paid no poll-tax for six years. I was put into a jail once on this account, for one night; and, as I stood considering the walls of solid stone, two or three feet thick, the door of wood and iron, a foot thick, and the iron grating which strained the light, I could not help being struck with the foolishness of that institution which treated me as if I were mere flesh and blood and bones, to be locked up. I wondered that it should have concluded at length that this was the best use it could put me to, and had never thought to avail itself of my services in some way. I saw that, if there was a wall of stone between me and my townsmen, there was a still more difficult one to climb or break through before they could get to be as free as I was. I did not for a moment feel confined, and the walls seemed a great waste of stone and mortar. I felt as if I alone of all my townsmen had paid my tax. They plainly did not know how to treat me, but behaved like persons who are underbred. In every threat and in every compliment there was a blunder; for they thought that my chief desire was to stand the other side of that stone wall. I could not but smile to see how industriously they locked the door on my meditations, which followed them out again without let or hindrance, and *they* were really all that was dangerous. As they could not reach me, they had resolved to punish my body; just as boys, if they cannot come at some person against whom they have a spite, will abuse his dog. I saw that the State was half-witted, that it was timid as a lone woman with her silver spoons, and that it did not know its friends from its foes, and I lost all my remaining respect for it, and pitied it.

Thus the State never intentionally confronts a man's sense, intellectual or moral, but only his body, his senses. It is not armed with superior wit or honesty, but with superior physical strength. I was not born to be forced. I will breathe after my own fashion. Let us see who is the strongest. What force has a multitude? They only can force me who obey a higher law than I. They force me to become like themselves. I do not hear of *men* being *forced* to live this way or that by masses of men. What sort of life were that to live? When I meet a government which says to me, "Your money or your life," why should I be in haste to give it my money? It may be in a great strait, and not know what to do: I cannot help that. It must help itself; do as I do. It is not worth the while to snivel about it. I am not responsible for the successful working of the machinery of society. I am not the son of the engineer. I perceive that, when an acorn and a chestnut fall side by side, the one does not remain inert to make way for the other, but both obey their own laws, and spring and grow and flourish as best they can, till one, perchance, overshadows and destroys the other. If a plant cannot live according to its nature, it dies; and so a man. . . .

1. In *Walden*, Thoreau strikes a responsive chord to those in modern society who would step back from the hectic pace of life. How relevant and viable are Thoreau's views in the post-industrial age?
2. Compare Thoreau's view of majority rule with the view of Tocqueville on the same subject. What parallels do you find between the two writers?
3. Protesters in the 1960s found much support in Thoreau's ideas. Apply the principles and concerns laid out in this reading to the issues of the 1960s.
4. "Unjust laws exist: shall we be content to obey them, or shall we endeavor to amend them, and obey them until we have succeeded, or shall we transgress them at once?" Using modern examples, answer Thoreau's question. Be certain in your response to either directly refute or support the point of view put forward in this excerpt.

■ ■ ■

HENRI DE SAINT-SIMON

The early nineteenth century saw the development of socialism as a political and social philosophy. Among the first major thinkers associated with the new idea was Claude Henri, Comte de Saint-Simon (1760-1825). Known now as a utopian socialist, he believed the French Revolution had helped to destroy an outmoded social and political order. He felt that the new system ought to reflect advances in commerce and industry. The new leaders should be the scientists and industrialists, replacing theologians, kings, and aristocrats. Saint-Simon envisioned an organic society, in which all groups would benefit from the establishment of an economic and social system in accord with advances in knowledge and industry.

In 1814 Saint-Simon and his pupil Augustin Thierry presented a plan for *The Reorganization of the European Community*. Here they discussed their ideas on society and social change and their belief in progress.

What will be the character of our own century? Till now, it has none. Will it simply continue on the lines laid down by the preceding century? Will our writers be nothing but echoes of the last of these philosophers? I do not think so. The progress of the human spirit, the need for universal institutions which the upheavals of Europe make so desperately urgent—all this tells me that the examination of the great political questions will be the aim of the intellectual enquiries of our times.

The philosophy of the last century was revolutionary; that of the nineteenth century must be constructive. Lack of institutions leads to the destruction of all society; outworn institutions prolong the ignorance and the prejudices of the times which produced them. Shall we be forced to choose between barbarism and stupidity? Writers of the nineteenth century, you alone can avert this frightful dilemma!

The social order has been overturned because it no longer corresponded with the level of enlightenment; it is for you to create a better order. The body politic has been dissolved; it is for you to reconstitute it. Such a task is difficult, no doubt, but it is not beyond your powers; you govern opinion, and opinion governs the world. Sustained by the hope of performing a useful service, I dare to attempt the task of a pioneer; and in this first essay I shall try to review the conditions of Europe and the means of reorganizing it. A ruler who claims to be great must foster the arts and sciences. This axiom, repeated so many times, expresses vaguely a truth which has not yet been fully grasped. The only kings who have exercised a powerful influence on the world have been those who, yielding to the movement of their age, have followed the lines marked out for them by the writings of their contemporaries. . . .

Just as revolutions in States, when they come about through the progress of enlightenment, bring a better order, so the political crisis which has dissolved the European body politic was, at the same time, paving the way for a better organization. This reorganization cannot be achieved suddenly, at one stroke; for outworn institutions only gradually collapse, and better ones are only gradually built; they rise and fall slowly and insensibly. . . .

It is essential to admit to the House of Commons of the European Parliament, i.e. one of the two active powers of the European constitution, only such men as by their wide contacts, emancipation from purely local customs, their occupations which are cosmopolitan in aim rather than national, are better able to arrive quickly at this wider point of view which makes the corporate will, and at the common interest which should be also the corporate interest of the European parliament.

Men of business, scientists, magistrates, and administrators are the only classes who should be summoned to form the House of Commons of the great parliament. It is a fact that whatever common interests exist in the

Source: Henri de Saint-Simon, *Social Organization, the Science of Man, and Other Writings,* edited by Felix Markham (New York: Harper and Row, 1952), pp. 29, 32, 47, 68, 72-75, 76-79.

European community can be traced to the sciences, arts, law, commerce, administration, and industry.

For every million persons in Europe who know how to read and write there should sit as their representatives in the House of Commons of the great parliament, a man of business, a scientist, an administrator and a lawyer. . . .

. . . There will come a time, without doubt, when all the peoples of Europe will feel that questions of common interest must be dealt with before coming down to national interests; then evils will begin to lessen, troubles abate, wars die out. That is the ultimate direction in which we are steadily progressing; it is there that the progress of the human mind will carry us. But which is more worthy of man's prudence—to hasten towards it, or to let ourselves be dragged there?

Poetic imagination has put the Golden Age in the cradle of the human race, amid the ignorance and brutishness of primitive times; it is rather the Iron Age which should be put there. The Golden Age of the human race is not behind us but before us; it lies in the perfection of the social order. Our ancestors never saw it; our children will one day arrive there; it is for us to clear the way.

In 1819 Saint-Simon speculated on the differences between the old order and the new.

Suppose that France suddenly lost fifty of her best physicists, chemists, physiologists, mathematicians, poets, painters, sculptors, musicians, writers; fifty of her best mechanical engineers, civil and military engineers, artillery experts, architects, doctors, surgeons, apothecaries, seamen, clockmakers; fifty of her best bankers, two hundred of her best business men, two hundred of her best farmers, fifty of her best ironmasters, arms manufacturers, tanners, dyers, miners, clothmakers, cotton manufacturers, silk-makers, linen-makers, manufacturers of hardware, of pottery and china, of crystal and glass, ship chandlers, carriers, printers, engravers, goldsmiths, and other metal-workers; her fifty best masons, carpenters, joiners, farriers, locksmiths, cutlers, smelters, and a hundred other persons of various unspecified occupations, eminent in the sciences, fine arts, and professions; making in all the three thousand leading scientists, artists, and artisans of France.

These men are the Frenchmen who are the most essential producers, those who make the most important products, those who direct the enterprises most useful to the nation, those who contribute to its achievements in the sciences, fine arts and professions. They are in the most real sense the flower of French society; they are, above all Frenchmen, the most useful to their country, contribute most to its glory, increasing its civilization and prosperity. The nation would become a lifeless corpse as soon as it lost them. It would immediately fall into a position of inferiority compared with the nations which it now rivals, and would continue to be inferior until this loss had been replaced, until it had grown another head. It would require at least a generation for France to repair this misfortune; for men who are distinguished in work of positive ability are exceptions, and nature is not prodigal of exceptions, particularly in this species.

Let us pass on to another assumption. Suppose that France preserves all the men of genius that she possesses in the sciences, fine arts and professions, but has the misfortune to lose in the same day Monsieur the King's brother, Monseigneur le duc d'Angoulême, Monseigneur le duc de Berry, Monseigneur le duc d'Orléans, Monseigneur le duc de Bourbon, Madame la duchesse d'Angoulême, Madame la duchesse de Berry, Madame la duchesse d'Orléans, Madame la duchesse de Bourbon, and Mademoiselle de Condé. Suppose that France loses at the same time all the great officers of the royal household, all the ministers (with or without portfolio), all the councillors of state, all the chief magistrates, marshals, cardinals, archbishops, bishops, vicars-general, and canons, all the prefects and sub-prefects, all the civil servants, and judges, and, in addition, ten thousand of the richest proprietors who live in the style of nobles.

This mischance would certainly distress the French, because they are kind-hearted, and could not see with indifference the sudden disappearance of such a large number of their compatriots. But this loss of thirty-thousand individuals, considered to be the most important in the State, would only grieve them for purely sentimental reasons and would result in no political evil for the State.

In the first place, it would be very easy to fill the vacancies which would be made available. There are plenty of Frenchmen who could fill the function of the King's brother as well as can Monsieur; plenty who could take the place of a Prince. . . . There are plenty of Frenchwomen who would be as good princesses as Madame la duchesse d'Angoulême, . . .

The ante-chambers of the palace are full of courtiers ready to take the place of the great household officials. The army has plenty of soldiers who would be as good leaders as our present Marshals. How many clerks there are who are as good as our ministers? How many administrators who are capable of managing the affairs of the departments better than the existing prefects and sub-prefects? How many barristers who are as good lawyers as our judges? How many vicars as expert as our cardinals, archbishops, bishops, vicars-general, and canons? As for the ten thousand aristocratic landowners, their heirs could need no apprenticeship to do the honours of their drawing-rooms as well as they.

The prosperity of France can only exist through the effects of the progress of the sciences, fine arts and professions. The Princes, the great household officials, the Bishops, Marshals of France, prefects and idle landowners contribute nothing directly to the progress of the sciences, fine arts and professions. Far from contributing they only hinder, since they strive to prolong the supremacy existing to this day of conjectural ideas over positive science. They inevitably harm the prosperity of the nation by depriving, as they do, the scientists, artists and artisans of the high esteem to which they are properly entitled. They are harmful because they expend their wealth in a way which is of no direct use to the sciences, fine arts, and professions: they are harmful because they are a charge on the national taxation, to the amount of three or four hundred millions under the heading of appointments, pensions, gifts, compensations, for the upkeep of their activities which are useless to the nation.

These suppositions underline the most important fact of present politics: they provide a point of view from which we can see this fact in a flash in all its extent; they show clearly, though indirectly, that our social organization is seriously defective: that men still allow themselves to be governed by violence and ruse, and that the human race (politically speaking) is still sunk in immorality.

The scientists, artists, and artisans, the only men whose work is of positive utility to society, and cost it practically nothing, are kept down by the princes and other rulers who are simply more or less incapable bureaucrats. Those who control honours and other national awards owe, in general, the supremacy they enjoy, to the accident of birth, to flattery, intrigue and other dubious methods.

Those who control public affairs share between them every year one half of the taxes, and they do not even use a third of what they do not pocket personally in a way which benefits the citizen.

These suppositions show that society is a world which is upside down.

The nation holds as a fundamental principle that the poor should be generous to the rich, and that therefore the poorer classes should daily deprive themselves of necessities in order to increase the superfluous luxury of the rich.

The most guilty men, the robbers on a grand scale, who oppress the mass of the citizens, and extract from them three or four hundred millions a year, are given the responsibility of punishing minor offences against society.

Ignorance, superstition, idleness and costly dissipation are the privilege of the leaders of society, and men of ability, hard-working and thrifty, are employed only as inferiors and instruments.

To sum up, in every sphere men of greater ability are subject to the control of men who are incapable. From the point of view of morality, the most immoral men have the responsibility of leading the citizens towards virtue; from the point of view of distributive justice, the most guilty men are appointed to punish minor delinquents.

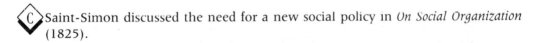

C Saint-Simon discussed the need for a new social policy in *On Social Organization* (1825).

The mechanism of social organization was inevitably very complicated so long as the majority of individuals remained in a state of ignorance and improvidence which rendered them incapable of administering their own affairs. In this state of incomplete intellectual development they were swayed by brutal passions which urged them to revolt and every kind of anarchy.

In such a situation, which was the necessary prelude to a better social order, it was necessary for the minority to be organized on military lines, to obtain a monopoly of legislation, and so to keep all power to itself, in order to hold the majority in tutelage and subject the nation to strong discipline. Thus the main energies of the community have till now been directed to maintaining itself as a community, and any efforts directed to improving the moral and physical welfare of the nation have necessarily been regarded as secondary.

To-day this state of affairs can and should be completely altered. The main effort should be directed to the improvement of our moral and physical welfare; only a small amount of force is now required to maintain public order, since the majority have become used to work (which eliminates disorder) and now consists of men who have recently proved that they are capable of administering property, whether in land or money.

As the minority no longer has need of force to keep the proletarian class in subordination, the course which it should adopt is as follows:

1. A policy by which the proletariat will have the strongest interest in maintaining public order.
2. A policy which aims at making the inheritance of landed property as easy as possible.
3. A policy which aims at giving the highest political importance to the workers.

Such a policy is quite simple and obvious, if one takes the trouble to judge the situation by one's own intelligence, and to shake off the yoke enforced on our minds by the political principles of our ancestors—principles which were sound and useful in their own day, but are no longer applicable to present circumstances. The mass of the population is now composed of men (apart from exceptions which occur more or less equally in every class) who are capable of administering property whether in land or in money, and therefore we can and must work directly for the improvement of the moral and physical welfare of the community.

The most direct method of improving the moral and physical welfare of the majority of the population is to give priority in State expenditure to ensuring work for all fit men, to secure their physical existence; spreading throughout the proletarian class a knowledge of positive science; ensuring for this class forms of recreation and interests which will develop their intelligence.

We must add to this the measures necessary to ensure that the national wealth is administered by men most fitted for it, and most concerned in its administration, that is to say the most important industrialists.

Thus the community, by means of these fundamental arrangements, will be organized in a way which will completely satisfy reasonable men of every class.

There will no longer be a fear of insurrection, and consequently no longer a need to maintain large standing armies to suppress it; no longer a need to spend enormous sums on a police force; no longer a fear of foreign danger, for a body of thirty millions of men who are a contented community would easily repel attack, even if the whole human race combined against them.

We might add that neither princes nor peoples would be so mad as to attack a nation of thirty millions who displayed no aggressive intentions against their neighbours, and were united internally by mutual interests.

Furthermore, there would no longer be a need for a system of police-spying in a community in which the vast majority had an interest in maintaining the established order.

The men who brought about the Revolution, the men who directed it, and the men who, since 1789 and up to the present day, have guided the nation, have committed a great political mistake. They have all sought to improve the governmental machine, whereas they should have subordinated it and put administration in the first place.

They should have begun by asking a question the solution of which is simple and obvious. They should have asked who, in the present state of morals and enlightenment, are the men most fitted to manage the affairs of the nation. They would have been forced to recognize the fact that the scientists, artists and industrialists, and the heads of industrial concerns are the men who possess the most eminent, varied, and most positively useful ability, for the guidance of men's minds at the present time. They would have recognized the fact that the work of the scientists, artists, and industrialists is that which, in discovery and application, contributes most to national prosperity.

They would have reached the conclusion that the scientists, artists and leaders of industrial enterprises are the men who should be entrusted with administrative power, that is to say, with the responsibility for managing the national interests; and that the functions of government should be limited to maintaining public order. . . .

1. Outline Saint-Simon's view of the challenge facing Europeans at the beginning of the nineteenth century.
2. Comment on Saint-Simon's scathing attack on French society. Summarize the author's basic thesis in a single sentence.
3. Thoreau wrote the following in "Civil Disobedience": "That government is best which governs least." How would Saint-Simon respond to this proposition?

• • •

CHARLES FOURIER

Charles Fourier (1772-1837) was one of the most eccentric and interesting utopian thinkers of modern times. A socialist and egalitarian, Fourier took delight in inventing a language to describe his ideas. He was a visionary who hoped for a time of great accomplishment and happiness for all human beings. Fourier was hostile to contemporary society, and he rejected the modern industrial world as unattractive and cruel to human nature. He intended to liberate all the "passions" in a communal life where people enjoyed their labour in a spirit of friendship and craftmanship. A number of communities were founded on his principles by individuals interested in experimenting with a new ideal. Fourier also deeply influenced later thinkers through his insightful critique of the problems of contemporary civilization.

 Fourier was angry at some of the excesses of industrial society.

Authors of the uncertain sciences, who pretend to labour for the good of the human race, do you believe that six hundred million barbarians and savages form no part of the human race? Yet they suffer; well, what have you done for them? Nothing. Your systems are only applicable to civilisation.

Far from succeeding in civilising and uniting the human race, your theories gain only the profound contempt of the barbarians, and your customs excite only the irony of the savage; his strongest imprecation against an enemy is to wish him our fate, and to say to him: "May you be reduced to working a field!" Words which may be regarded as a malediction uttered by Nature itself. Yes, civilised industry is reproved by Nature, since it is abhorred by free peoples who would embrace it at once if it accorded with the passions of man. . . .

It is, above all, in industrial policy that our century displays its pride; proud of some material strides, it does not perceive that it is retrograding politically, and that its rapid advance is that of the crab, which moves, but moves backward.

Industrialism is the latest of our scientific chimeras; it is the mania of producing in confusion, without any system of proportional compensation, without any guarantee to the producer or wage-earner that he will participate in the increase of wealth; accordingly, we find the industrial regions sprinkled with beggars to as great, or, perhaps, a greater extent than those countries which are indifferent to this sort of progress. . . .

Industry offers a subversion far more striking; this is the *opposition of the two kinds of interest, collective and individual.* Every person engaged in an industry is at war with the mass, and malevolent toward it from personal interest. A physician wishes his fellow-citizens good, genuine cases of fevers, and an attorney good lawsuits in every family. An architect has need of a good conflagration which should reduce a quarter of the city to ashes, and a glazier desires a good hail-storm which should break all the panes of glass. A tailor, a shoemaker, wishes the public to use only poorly-dyed stuffs and shoes made of bad leather, so that a triple amount may be consumed,—for the benefit of trade; that is their refrain. A court of justice regards it opportune that France continues to commit a hundred and twenty thousand crimes and actionable offences, that number being necessary to maintain the criminal courts. It is thus that in civilised industry every individual is in intentional war against the mass; necessary result of anti-associative industry or an inverted world. We shall see this absurdity disappear in the associative *régime*, where each individual will find his advantage only in that of the mass. . . .

 Labour was important, for that is how we spend much of our time and obtain some of our identity. Fourier asked for a new set of conditions.

In the civilised mechanism we find everywhere composite unhappiness instead of composite charm. Let us judge of it by the case of labour. It is, says the Scripture very justly, a punishment of man: Adam and his issue are condemned to earn their bread by the sweat of their brow. That, already, is an affliction; but this labour, this ungrateful labour upon which depends the earning of our miserable bread, we cannot even get it! a labourer lacks the

Source: Charles Fourier, *Design for Utopia: Selected Writings of Charles Fourier,* translated by Julia Franklin (New York: Schocken Books, 1971), pp. 82, 83, 86-87, 163-65, 188-89, 193, 200.

labour upon which his maintenance depends,—he asks in vain for a tribulation! He suffers a second, that of obtaining work at times whose fruit is his master's and not his, or of being employed in duties to which he is entirely unaccustomed. . . . The civilised labourer suffers a third affliction through the maladies with which he is generally stricken by the excess of labour demanded by his master. . . . He suffers a fifth affliction, that of being despised and treated as a beggar because he lacks those necessaries which he consents to purchase by the anguish of repugnant labour. He suffers, finally, a sixth affliction, in that he will obtain neither advancement nor sufficient wages, and that to the vexation of present suffering is added the perspective of future suffering and of being sent to the gallows should he demand that labour which he may lack to-morrow.

Labour, nevertheless, forms the delight of various creatures, such as beavers, bees, wasps, ants, which are entirely at liberty to prefer inertia: but God has provided them with a social mechanism which attracts to industry, and causes happiness to be found in industry. Why should he not have accorded us the same favour as these animals? What a difference between their industrial condition and ours! A Russian, an Algerian, work from fear of the lash or the bastinado; an Englishman, a Frenchman, from fear of the famine which stalks close to his poor household; the Greeks and the Romans, whose freedom has been vaunted to us, worked as slaves, and from fear of punishment, like the negroes in the colonies to-day.

Associative labour, in order to exert a strong attraction upon people, will have to differ in every particular from the repulsive conditions which render it so odious in the existing state of things. It is necessary, in order that it become attractive, that associative labour fulfil the following seven conditions:

1. That every labourer be a partner, remunerated by dividends and not by wages.
2. That every one, man, woman, or child, be remunerated in proportion to the three faculties, *capital, labour*, and *talent*.
3. That the industrial sessions be varied about eight times a day, it being impossible to sustain enthusiasm longer than an hour and a half or two hours in the exercise of agricultural or manufacturing labour.
4. That they be carried on by bands of friends, united spontaneously, interested and stimulated by very active rivalries.
5. That the workshops and husbandry offer the labourer the allurements of elegance and cleanliness.
6. That the division of labour be carried to the last degree, so that each sex and age may devote itself to duties that are suited to it.
7. That in this distribution, each one, man, woman, or child, be in full enjoyment of the right to labour or the right to engage in such branch of labour as they may please to select, provided they give proof of integrity and ability.

Finally, that, in this new order, people possess a guarantee of well-being, of a minimum sufficient for the present and the future, and that this guarantee free them from all uneasiness concerning themselves and their families.

We find all these properties combined in the associative mechanism, whose discovery I make public. . . .

Association and co-operation were the keys to the good life under "Harmonism," the society which would supplant the ills of "Civilization."

The sense of ownership is the most powerful lever known, to electrify the civilised; one may, without exaggeration, estimate the product of labour of an owner as double when compared with servile or wage labour. We see facts in proof of this every day; workmen, shockingly slow and awkward when working for wages, become phenomena of diligence as soon as they labour on their own account.

The first problem, therefore, which ought to be studied in political economy is how to transform all wage-earners into co-interested or associated proprietors.

A poor man, in Harmony, if he own but part of a share, but one-twentieth, is proprietor of the entire district, *in participation*: he can say, "our lands, our palace, our mansions, our forests, our works, our factories." All is his property; he is interested in the whole of the personal and landed possessions.

If, under existing conditions, a forest is deteriorated, a hundred peasants will look upon it with indifference. The forest is simple property; it belongs exclusively to the lord; they rejoice at what may be prejudicial to him, and will secretly exert themselves to increase the damage. If a torrent sweeps the land away, three-fourths of the inhabitants own none along the banks, and laugh at the havoc. Frequently, they rejoice to see the water ravage the patrimony of a rich neighbour, whose property is simple, devoid of bonds of union with the body of the inhabitants, and inspiring them with no interest whatever.

In Harmony, where the interests are combined, and where each one is a partner, even if only to the extent of getting a share of the proceeds allotted to labour, each one always desires the prosperity of the whole district; each one suffers from the harm which befals even the smallest portion of it. Thus, already through personal interest, good-will is general among the members, and this results solely from their not being wage-workers but co-interested; . . .

The luxury of Harmony, or the eighth period, is corporative; each one is anxious to give brilliance to the groups and Series which he favours. . . .

If corporate bodies, even in civilisation, are averse to the appearance of poverty, it may readily be conceived that in Harmony they are averse even to the appearance of mediocrity. . . .

The secret of the *unity of interest*, therefore, lies in Association. The three classes, being associated and united in interest, would forget their hatred; and that the more readily because the opportunities for attractive labour would put an end to the drudgery of the people and the disdain of the rich for inferiors, whose labours, now become enticing, they would share. There would be an end to the envy with which the poor regard the idle, who reap without having sown: there would no longer be any idlers, or poor, and social anti-pathies would disappear with the causes which produced them. . . .

1. What evidence did Fourier give to justify his claim that "every person engaged in industry is at war with the mass"?
2. Summarize the characteristics of the "associative mechanism" which Fourier saw as taking the place of the exploitation of labour in his day.

3. Outline the benefits which Fourier envisioned in the creation of a "unity of interest." In what ways was Fourier a thinker who supported the idea of progress?

• • •

Karl Marx ◆ Friedrich Engels

Karl Marx (1818-83) and Friedrich Engels (1820-95) were friends and collaborators who were appalled at the price paid by many human beings to make industrial society work. In the 1840s they began their analysis of capitalism, the middle-class, and contemporary society with a critique of the conditions of working life. This analysis was to have a profound influence on future social thought. In the *Manifesto of the Communist Party* of February 1848, the most influential work in the history of socialism, the two men summarized their position on the idea of historical development, the importance of the economic mode of production, the role of class struggle, and the nature of social and political change.

A. Engels' father was a wealthy German manufacturer, and the son went to Manchester, England in 1842 to work in one of the branches of his father's business. He stayed until 1844 and in that year wrote *The Condition of the Working Class in England*. In the book he catalogued the horrible conditions of labour during the industrial revolution and placed the blame on the system and on the bourgeoisie.

> No one can be complacent about a situation which injures and cripples so many workers for the benefit of a single class. It is tragic that so many industrious workers are injured in the factories and are condemned to a lifetime of poverty and hunger. Their middle-class employers must bear the sole responsibility for this disgraceful state of affairs.
>
> A fine list of diseases and injuries due solely to the revolting greed of the middle classes! Simply in order to fill the pockets of the bourgeoisie, women are rendered unfit to bear children, children are crippled, while grown men are stunted and maimed. The health of whole generations of workers is undermined, and they are racked with diseases and infirmities. Let us recall a few of the more barbarous cases [brought to light by the Factories Enquiry Commission's Reports.] Stuart reports that children were dragged naked out of bed by overseers and driven with blows and kicks to the factories, their clothes over their arms. Blows had at first aroused them from their slumbers, but before long they were asleep again over their work. A case is reported of a wretched child being roused by a shout from the foreman, when the machinery had stopped working. Still half asleep, the child, with eyes still closed, automatically went through the motions of working the silent machine. We read of children who were too tired [when the day's work was over] to go

Sources: Friedrich Engels, *The Condition of the Working Class in England* (Oxford: Basil Blackwell, 1971), pp. 188, 189, 311-12, 312-13; Robert Tucker, ed., *The Marx-Engels Reader*, second edition (New York: W.W. Norton and Company, Inc., 1978), pp. 74, 473-74, 475, 476, 477, 478, 479, 480-82, 483, 484, 486, 488, 490-91, 500.

home, but hid themselves under the wool in the drying room, only to be driven from the factory by blows from a strap. We read of hundreds of children who come home from the factory every evening so tired that they cannot eat their supper from lack of sleep and lack of appetite. Their parents found them on their knees at their bedside, where they had fallen asleep while saying their prayers. . . . Should one not detest the middle classes, who so hypocritically boast of their humanity and sacrifice, while really they are concerned solely with filling their pockets? . . .

. . . When I speak of the 'bourgeoisie' in this chapter I am referring not only to the middle class proper but also to the so-called aristocracy. This is because the privileges enjoyed by the aristocracy affect their relations with the middle classes rather than with the workers. Since all other privileges sink into insignificance when coupled with the privilege of property, the workers regard both bourgeoisie and aristocracy together as a single property-owning class. The only difference between the middle classes (in the narrower sense) and the aristocracy is this: the former come into direct contact with the factory workers, some of the miners and (if they are farmers) with the agricultural labourers. But the latter have relations only with certain miners and with the farm workers [but not with the factory operatives].

I have never seen so demoralized a social class as the English middle classes. They are so degraded by selfishness and moral depravity as to be quite incapable of salvation. And here I refer to the bourgeoisie proper . . . The middle classes have a truly extraordinary conception of society. They really believe that all human beings (themselves excluded) and indeed all living things and inanimate objects have a real existence only if they make money or help to make it. Their sole happiness is derived from gaining a quick profit. They feel pain only if they suffer a financial loss. Every single human quality with which they are endowed is grossly debased by selfish greed and love of gain. Admittedly the English middle classes make good husbands and family men. They have also all sorts of so-called 'private virtues'. In the ordinary daily affairs of life they seem to be as respectable and as decent as the members of any other middle class. One finds them better than Germans to deal with in business. The English do not condescend to that petty haggling which characterises the German trader with his pathetically limited horizon. But what is the use of all that? When all comes to all what really matters to the Englishman is his own interest and above all his desire to make money.

One day I walked with one of these middle-class gentlemen into Manchester. I spoke to him about the disgraceful unhealthy slums and drew his attention to the disgusting condition of that part of the town in which the factory workers lived. I declared that I had never seen so badly built a town in my life. He listened patiently and at the corner of the street at which we parted company he remarked: 'And yet there is a great deal of money made here. Good morning, Sir'. . . .

The middle classes in England have become the slaves of the money they worship. Even the English language is permeated by the one idea that dominates the waking hours of the bourgeoisie. People see 'valued' in terms of hard cash. They say of a man: 'He is worth £10,000', and by that they mean that he possesses that sum. Anyone who has money is 'respectable'. He belongs to 'the better sort of people'. He is said to be 'influential', which means that what he says carried weight in the circles in which he moves. The spirit of petty bargaining permeates the whole language. Everything is expressed in commercial terms or in the categories of the science of economics. The English judge every aspect of life in terms of 'supply and demand'. The English middle classes believe in absolutely unbridled freedom of competition, consequently the principle of 'laissez faire' is allowed to dominate government and administration, medicine, education and even religion—for the authority of the Established Church is rapidly declining. The bourgeoisie believe that free competition should be absolutely unchecked. The State should have no power whatsoever to interfere with this holy principle. The bourgeois ideal is a society in which there is no 'State' at all to exercise any authority—a state of anarchy comparable with that in friend Stirner's 'society', where everybody can exploit everybody else to their heart's content. But the English middle classes cannot do without the State just as they cannot do without the workers. They need the State to keep the workers in order. Nevertheless the bourgeoisie do everything to prevent the State from interfering in any way with their own affairs. . . .

B Marx, in 1844, discussed the concept of the alienation of labour.

What, then, constitutes the alienation of labour?

First, the fact that labour is *external* to the worker, i.e., it does not belong to his essential being; that in his work, therefore, he does not affirm himself but denies himself, does not feel content but unhappy, does not develop freely his physical and mental energy but mortifies his body and ruins his mind. The worker therefore only feels himself outside his work, and in his work feels outside himself. He is at home when he is not working, and when he is working he is not at home. His labour is therefore not voluntary, but coerced; it is *forced labour*. It is therefore not the satisfaction of a need; it is merely a *means* to satisfy needs external to it. Its alien character emerges clearly in the fact that as soon as no physical or other compulsion exists, labour is shunned like the plague. External labour, labour in which man alienates himself, is a labour of self-sacrifice, of mortification. Lastly, the external character of labour for the worker appears in the fact that it is not his own, but someone else's, that it does not belong to him, that in it he belongs, not to himself, but to another. Just as in religion the spontaneous activity of the human imagination, of the human brain and the human heart, operates independently of the individual—that is, operates on him as an alien, divine or diabolical activity—in the same way the worker's activity is not his spontaneous activity. It belongs to another, it is the loss of his self. . . .

C *The Manifesto of the Communist Party* was a powerful polemic based upon an analysis of historical change.

A spectre is haunting Europe—the spectre of Communism. All the Powers of old Europe have entered into a holy alliance to exorcise this spectre: Pope and Czar, Metternich and Guizot, French Radicals and German police-spies.

Where is the party in opposition that has not been decried as Communistic by its opponents in power? Where the Opposition that has not hurled back the branding reproach of Communism, against the more advanced opposition parties, as well as against its reactionary adversaries?

Two things result from this fact.

I. Communism is already acknowledged by all European Powers to be itself a Power.

II. It is high time that Communists should openly, in the face of the whole world, publish their views, their aims, their tendencies, and meet this nursery tale of the Spectre of Communism with a Manifesto of the party itself.

To this end, Communists of various nationalities have assembled in London, and sketched the following Manifesto, to be published in the English, French, German, Italian, Flemish and Danish languages.

The history of all hitherto existing society is the history of class struggles.

Freeman and slave, patrician and plebeian, lord and serf, guild-master and journeyman, in a word, oppressor and oppressed, stood in constant opposition to one another, carried on an uninterrupted, now hidden, now open fight, a fight that each time ended, either in a revolutionary re-constitution of society at large, or in the common ruin of the contending classes.

In the earlier epochs of history, we find almost everywhere a complicated arrangement of society into various orders, a manifold gradation of social rank. In ancient Rome we have patricians, knights, plebeians, slaves; in the Middle Ages, feudal lords, vassals, guild-masters, journeymen, apprentices, serfs; in almost all of these classes, again, subordinate gradations.

The modern bourgeois society that has sprouted from the ruins of feudal society has not done away with clash antagonisms. It has but established new classes, new conditions of oppression, new forms of struggle in place of the old ones.

Our epoch, the epoch of the bourgeoisie, possesses, however, this distinctive feature: it has simplified the class antagonisms: Society as a whole is more and more splitting up into two great hostile camps, into two great classes directly facing each other: Bourgeoisie and Proletariat. . . .

◆ The bourgeoisie was the controlling class in industrial society, and Marx and Engels praised it in the *Manifesto* as a historical advance.

We see, therefore, how the modern bourgeoisie is itself the product of a long course of development, of a series of revolutions in the modes of production and of exchange.

Each step in the development of the bourgeoisie was accompanied by a corresponding political advance of that class. An oppressed class under the sway of the feudal nobility, an armed and self-governing association in the mediaeval commune; here independent urban republic (as in Italy and Germany), there taxable "third estate" of the monarchy (as in France), afterwards, in the period of manufacture proper, serving either the semi-feudal or the absolute monarchy as a counterpoise against the nobility, and, in fact, corner-stone of the great monarchies in general, the bourgeoisie has at last, since the establishment of Modern Industry and of the world-market, conquered for itself, in the modern representative State, exclusive political sway. The executive of the modern State is but a committee for managing the common affairs of the whole bourgeoisie.

The bourgeoisie, historically, has played a most revolutionary part.

The bourgeoisie, wherever it has got the upper hand, has put an end to all feudal, patriarchal, idyllic relations. . . .

The bourgeoisie has stripped of its halo every occupation hitherto honoured and looked up to with reverent awe. It has converted the physician, the lawyer, the priest, the poet, the man of science, into its paid wage-labourers.

The bourgeoisie has torn away from the family its sentimental veil, and has reduced the family relation to a mere money relation.

The bourgeoisie has disclosed how it came to pass that the brutal display of vigour in the Middle Ages, which Reactionists so much admire, found its fitting complement in the most slothful indolence. It has been the first to show what man's activity can bring about. It has accomplished wonders far surpassing Egyptian pyramids, Roman aqueducts, and Gothic cathedrals; it has conducted expeditions that put in the shade all former Exoduses of nations and crusades.

The bourgeoisie cannot exist without constantly revolutionising the instruments of production, and thereby the relations of production, and with them the whole relations of society. . . .

The bourgeoisie has through its exploitation of the world-market given a cosmopolitan character to production and consumption in every country. . . .

The bourgeoisie, by the rapid improvement of all instruments of production, by the immensely facilitated means of communication, draws all, even the most barbarian, nations into civilisation. . . .

The bourgeoisie has subjected the country to the rule of the towns. It has created enormous cities, has greatly increased the urban population as compared with the rural, and has thus rescued a considerable part of the population from the idiocy of rural life. . . .

The bourgeoisie, during its rule of scarce one hundred years, has created more massive and more colossal productive forces than have all preceding generations together. Subjection of Nature's forces to man, machinery, application of chemistry to industry and agriculture, steam-navigation, railways, electric telegraphs, clearing of whole continents for cultivation, canalisation of rivers, whole populations conjured out of the ground—what earlier century had even a presentiment that such productive forces slumbered in the lap of social labour?

We see then: the means of production and of exchange, on whose foundation the bourgeoisie built itself up, were generated in feudal society. At a certain stage in the development of these means of production and of exchange, the conditions under which feudal society produced and exchanged, the feudal organisation of agriculture and manufacturing industry, in one word, the feudal relations of property became no longer compatible with the already developed productive forces; they became so many fetters. They had to be burst asunder; they were burst asunder.

Into their place stepped free competition, accompanied by a social and political constitution adapted to it, and by the economical and political sway of the bourgeois class. . . .

 The two men theorized that the proletariat will develop consciousness, overthrow the bourgeoisie, and establish a new society.

But not only has the bourgeoisie forged the weapons that bring death to itself; it has also called into existence the men who are to wield those weapons— the modern working class—the proletarians.

In proportion as the bourgeoisie, *i.e.,* capital, is developed, in the same proportion is the proletariat, the modern working class, developed—a class of labourers, who live only so long as they find work, and who find work only so long as their labour increases capital. These labourers, who must sell themselves piece-meal, are a commodity, like very other article of commerce, and are consequently exposed to all the vicissitudes of competition, to all the fluctuations of the market.

Owing to the extensive use of machinery and to division of labour, the work of the proletarians has lost all individual character, and consequently, all charm for the workman. He becomes an appendage of the machine, and it is only the most simple, most monotonous, and most easily acquired knack, that is required of him. . . .

Modern industry has converted the little workshop of the patriarchal master into the great factory of the industrial capitalist. Masses of labourers, crowded into the factory, are organised like soldiers. As privates of the industrial army they are placed under the command of a perfect hierarchy of officers and sergeants. Not only are they slaves of the bourgeois class, and of the bourgeois State; they are daily and hourly enslaved by the machine, by the over-looker, and, above all, by the individual bourgeois manufacturer himself. The more openly this despotism proclaims gain to be its end and aim, the more petty, the more hateful and the more embittering it is. . . .

The proletariat goes through various stages of development. With its birth begins its struggle with the bourgeoisie. At first the contest is carried on by individual labourers, then by the workpeople of a factory, then by the operatives of one trade, in one locality, against the individual bourgeois who directly exploits them. They direct their attacks not against the bourgeois conditions of production, but against the instruments of production themselves; they destroy imported wares that compete with their labour, they smash to pieces machinery, they set factories ablaze, they seek to restore by force the vanished status of the workman of the Middle Ages.

At this stage the labourers still form an incoherent mass scattered over the whole country, and broken up by their mutual competition. If anywhere they unite to form more compact bodies, this is not yet the consequence of their own active union, but of the union of the bourgeoisie, which class, in order to attain its own political ends, is compelled to set the whole proletariat in motion, and is moreover yet, for a time, able to do so. At this stage, therefore, the proletarians do not fight their enemies, but the enemies of their enemies, the remnants of absolute monarchy, the landowners, the non-industrial bourgeois, the petty bourgeoisie. Thus the whole historical movement is concentrated in the hands of the bourgeoisie; every victory so obtained is a victory for the bourgeoisie.

But with the development of industry the proletariat not only increases in number; it becomes concentrated in greater masses, its strength grows, and it feels that strength more. The various interests and conditions of life within the ranks of the proletariat are more and more equalised, in proportion as machinery obliterates all distinctions of labour, and nearly everywhere reduces wages to the same low level. The growing competition among the bourgeois, and the resulting commercial crises, make the wages of the workers ever more fluctuating. The unceasing improvement of machinery, ever more rapidly developing, makes their livelihood more and more precarious; the collisions between individual workmen and individual bourgeois take more and more the character of collisions between two classes. Thereupon the workers begin to form combinations (Trade Unions) against the bourgeois; they club together in order to keep up the rate of wages; they found permanent associations in order to make provision beforehand for these occasional revolts. Here and there the contest breaks out into riots.

Now and then the workers are victorious, but only for a time. The real fruit of their battles lies, not in the immediate result, but in the ever-expanding union of the workers. This union is helped on by the improved means of communication that are created by modern industry and that place the workers of different localities in contact with one another. It was just this contact that was needed to centralise the numerous local struggles, all of the same character, into one national struggle between classes. But every class struggle is a political struggle. And that union, to attain which the burghers of the Middle Ages, with their miserable highways, required centuries, the modern proletarians, thanks to railways, achieve in a few years.

This organisation of the proletarians into a class, and consequently into a political party, is continually being upset again by the competition between the workers themselves. But it ever rises up again, stronger, firmer, mightier. It compels legislative recognition of particular interests of the workers, by taking advantage of the divisions among the bourgeoisie itself. Thus the ten-hours' bill in England was carried.

Altogether collisions between the classes of the old society further, in many ways, the course of development of the proletariat. The bourgeoisie finds itself involved in a constant battle. At first with the aristocracy; later on, with those portions of the bourgeoisie itself, whose interests have become antagonistic to the progress of industry; at all times, with the bourgeoisie of foreign countries. In all these battles it sees itself compelled to appeal to the proletariat, to ask for its help, and thus, to drag it into the political arena. The bourgeoisie itself, therefore, supplies the proletariat with its own elements of political and general education, in other words, it furnishes the proletariat with weapons for fighting the bourgeoisie.

Further, as we have already seen, entire sections of the ruling classes are, by the advance of industry, precipitated into the proletariat, or are at least threatened in their conditions of existence. These also supply the proletariat with fresh elements of enlightenment and progress.

Finally, in times when the class struggle nears the decisive hour, the process of dissolution going on within the ruling class, in fact within the whole range of society, assumes such a violent, glaring character, that a small section of the ruling class cuts itself adrift, and joins the revolutionary class, the class that holds the future in its hands. Just as, therefore, at an earlier period, a section of the nobility went over to the bourgeoisie, so now a portion of the bourgeoisie goes over to the proletariat, and in particular, a portion of the bourgeois ideologists, who have raised themselves to the level of comprehending theoretically the historical movement as a whole.

Of all the classes that stand face to face with the bourgeoisie today, the proletariat alone is a really revolutionary class. The other classes decay and finally disappear in the face of Modern Industry; the proletariat is its special and essential product. . . .

The aims of the communists, then one of the many branches of socialism, were made clear:

In what relation do the Communists stand to the proletarians as a whole?

The Communists do not form a separate party opposed to other working-class parties.

They have no interests separate and apart from those of the proletariat as a whole.

They do not set up any sectarian principles of their own, by which to shape and mould the proletarian movement. . . .

The immediate aim of the Communists is the same as that of all the other proletarian parties: formation of the proletariat into a class, overthrow of the bourgeois supremacy, conquest of political power by the proletariat. . . .

The distinguishing feature of Communism is not the abolition of property generally, but the abolition of bourgeois property. But modern bourgeois private property is the final and most complete expression of the system of producing and appropriating products, that is based on class antagonisms, on the exploitation of the many by the few.

In this sense, the theory of the Communists may be summed up in the single sentence: Abolition of private property. . . .

You are horrified at our intending to do away with private property. But in your existing society, private property is already done away with for nine-tenths of the population; its existence for the few is solely due to its non-existence in the hands of those nine-tenths. You reproach us, therefore, with intending to do away with a form of property, the necessary condition for whose existence is the non-existence of any property for the immense majority of society. . . .

The Communists are further reproached with desiring to abolish countries and nationality.

The working men have no country. We cannot take from them what they have not got. Since the proletariat must first of all acquire political supremacy, must rise to be the leading class of the nation, must constitute itself *the* nation, it is, so far, itself national, though not in the bourgeois sense of the word.

National differences and antagonisms between peoples are daily more and more vanishing, owing to the development of the bourgeoisie, to freedom of commerce, to the world-market, to uniformity in the mode of production and in the conditions of life corresponding thereto.

The supremacy of the proletariat will cause them to vanish still faster. United action, of the leading civilised countries at least, is one of the first conditions for the emancipation of the proletariat. . . .

We have seen above, that the first step in the revolution by the working class, is to raise the proletariat to the position of ruling class, to win the battle of democracy.

The proletariat will use its political supremacy to wrest, by degrees, all capital from the bourgeoisie, to centralise all instruments of production in the hands of the State, *i.e.*, of the proletariat organised as the ruling class; and to increase the total of productive forces as rapidly as possible.

Of course, in the beginning, this cannot be effected except by means of despotic inroads on the rights of property, and on the conditions of bourgeois production; by means of measures, therefore, which appear economically insufficient and untenable, but which, in the course of the movement, out-strip themselves, necessitate further inroads upon the old social order, and are unavoidable as a means of entirely revolutionising the mode of production.

These measures will of course be different in different countries.

Nevertheless in the most advanced countries, the following will be pretty generally applicable.

1. Abolition of property in land and application of all rents of land to public purposes.
2. A heavy progressive or graduated income tax.
3. Abolition of all right of inheritance.
4. Confiscation of the property of all emigrants and rebels.
5. Centralisation of credit in the hands of the State, by means of a national bank with State capital and an exclusive monopoly.
6. Centralisation of the means of communication and transport in the hands of the State.
7. Extension of factories and instruments of production owned by the State; the bringing into cultivation of waste-lands, and the improvement of the soil generally in accordance with a common plan.
8. Equal liability of all to labour. Establishment of industrial armies, especially for agriculture.
9. Combination of agriculture with manufacturing industries; gradual abolition of the distinction between town and country, by a more equable distribution of the population over the country.
10. Free education for all children in public schools. Abolition of children's factory labour in its present form. Combination of education with industrial production, &c., &c.

When, in the course of development, class distinctions have disappeared, and all production has been concentrated in the hands of a vast association of the whole nation, the public power will lose its political character. Political power, properly so called, is merely the organised power of one class for oppressing another. If the proletariat during its contest with the bourgeoisie is compelled, by the force of circumstances, to organise itself as a class, if, by means of a revolution, it makes itself the ruling class, and, as such, sweeps away by force the old conditions of production, then it will, along with these conditions, have swept away the conditions for the existence of class antagonisms and of classes generally, and will thereby have abolished its own supremacy as a class.

In place of the old bourgeois society, with its classes and class antagonisms, we shall have an association, in which the free development of each is the condition for the free development of all. . . .

In short, the Communists everywhere support every revolutionary movement against the existing social and political order of things.

In all these movements they bring to the front, as the leading question in each, the property question, no matter what its degree of development at the time.

Finally, they labour everywhere for the union and agreement of the democratic parties of all countries.

The Communists disdain to conceal their views and aims. They openly declare that their ends can be attained only by the forcible overthrow of all existing social conditions. Let the ruling classes tremble at a Communistic revolution. The proletarians have nothing to lose but their chains. They have a world to win.

WORKING MEN OF ALL COUNTRIES, UNITE!

1. Contrast the lives of the members of the proletariat with those of the middle class as described by Engels.
2. How did Marx describe the alienation of a labourer from his work?
3. Comment on the vision of history as one of perpetual class struggle, as put forward in the opening of the *Manifesto*.
4. ''The bourgeoisie during its rule of scarce one hundred years, has created more massive and more colossal productive forces than have all preceeding generations together.'' Account for this statement with specific reference to the accomplishments of the bourgeoisie as laid out in the *Manifesto*. Why did Marx and Engels see the development of the bourgeoisie as progressive?
5. Trace the development of the proletariat from a disorganized group of industrial workers, to a unified class in opposition to the bourgeoisie.
6. Carefully précis the views and recommendations of the Communists of 1848. To what extent would their policies seem radical today? Comment on the impact of the ideas contained in the *Manifesto* on the working class as described by Engels in Reading (a).

4

IDEOLOGY, CULTURE & SOCIETY IN THE WEST, 1848-1880

I n the middle of the nineteenth century the West experienced major political revolutions and ideas about the nation-state were created and refined. The year 1848 was the most revolutionary in modern Western history and in the period from 1848 to 1880 modern Italy and Germany were created, the United States underwent a crisis of national identity, and other states, France and Russia among them, underwent internal changes of major dimensions. These developments were reflected in thought: in the important considerations of Marx and Engels on the nature of history and society; in the attempts by Lincoln and Bismarck to define the role of the nation-state; in the varied ideologies of liberalism, anarchism, socialism, and nationalism.

Evolution was a major new synthesis, and it changed thinking about human nature, values, and humanity's relationship to nature. Preceded by the theories of Malthus and Spencer, Darwin's work of 1859 was the most significant event in biological thinking of the last two centuries. Some used Darwin's theories as a basis for discussions about the relationship between the individual and the community. All thought was affected by the considerations on science and Catholicism retrenched and officially challenged the new trends.

In the arts, a key concept was that of realism, exemplified by Flaubert in the novel and Courbet in the visual arts. Writers such as Dickens and Turgenev also came to play a part in social criticism, challenging prevailing conditions and attitudes. In some cases, writers challenged the very assumptions guiding the century: Dostoyevsky asked about the role of mysticism, suffering and inner emotion in our lives; Sand attacked the relationships between the classes and the sexes; and Baudelaire developed a new poetic language of symbolism which stimulated the imagination.

The mid-nineteenth century was a rich and varied period of cultural activity in the West—vibrant, creative, secure and self-reflective.

KARL MARX

Karl Marx (1818-83) elaborated and further developed his thought on the relationships between history, economics, social structure, politics, and the human personality in his works after 1848. He was also deeply concerned with contemporary events and tried to understand them in the context of his new synthesis. In all of Marx's works there was an interweaving of the practical and the theoretical which was one of the basic assumptions of his thought.

Source: Robert C. Tucker, ed., *The Marx-Engels Reader*, second edition (New York: W.W. Norton and Company, 1978), pp. 595, 596, 597-98, 616, 512, 516, 517-19, 543-44.

⟨A⟩In late 1851 and early 1852 Marx wrote *The Eighteenth Brumaire of Louis Bonaparte*. This was an attempt to explain how the grandeur of the possibility of the French Revolution of 1848 could result in the rule and authority of what he termed a "grotesque mediocrity." Like all of Marx's major works, *The Eighteenth Brumaire* is also important for its speculations on the nature of history.

Hegel remarks somewhere that all great, world-historical facts and personages occur, as it were, twice. He has forgotten to add: the first time as tragedy, the second as farce. . . .

Men make their own history, but they do not make it just as they please; they do not make it under circumstances chosen by themselves, but under circumstances directly found, given and transmitted from the past. The tradition of all the dead generations weighs like a nightmare on the brain of the living. And just when they seem engaged in revolutionising themselves and things, in creating something entirely new, precisely in such epochs of revolutionary crisis they anxiously conjure up the spirits of the past to their service and borrow from them names, battle slogans and costumes in order to present the new scene of world history in this time-honoured disguise and this borrowed language. Thus Luther donned the mask of the Apostle Paul, the Revolution of 1789 to 1814 draped itself alternately as the Roman Republic and the Roman Empire, and the Revolution of 1848 knew nothing better to do than to parody, in turn, 1789 and the revolutionary tradition of 1793 to 1795. In like manner the beginner who has learnt a new language always translates it back into his mother tongue, but he has assimilated the spirit of the new language and can produce freely in it only when he moves in it without remembering the old and forgets in it his ancestral tongue. . . .

From 1848 to 1851 only the ghost of the old revolution walked. . . . An entire people, which had imagined that by a revolution it had increased its power of action, suddenly finds itself set back into a dead epoch and, in order that no doubt as to the relapse may be possible, the old data again arise, the old chronology, the old names, the old edicts, which have long become a subject of antiquarian erudition, and the old henchmen, who had long seemed dead and decayed. . . .

The social revolution of the nineteenth century cannot draw its poetry from the past, but only from the future. It cannot begin with itself, before it has stripped of all superstition in regard to the past. Earlier revolutions required world-historical recollections in order to drug themselves concerning their own content. In order to arrive at its content, the revolution of the nineteenth century must let the dead bury their dead. There the phrase went beyond the content; here the content goes beyond the phrase. . . .

Bourgeois revolutions, like those of the eighteenth century, storm more swiftly from success to success; their dramatic effects outdo each other; men and things seem set in sparkling brilliants; ecstasy is the everyday spirit: but they are short lived; soon they have attained their zenith, and a long depression lays hold of society before it learns soberly to assimilate the results of its storm and stress period. Proletarian revolutions, on the other hand, like those of the nineteenth century, criticise themselves constantly, interrupt themselves continually in their own course, come back to the apparently accomplished in order to begin it afresh, deride with unmerciful thoroughness the inadequacies, weaknesses and paltrinesses of their first attempts, seem to throw down their adversary only in order that he may draw new strength from the earth and rise again more gigantic before them, recoil ever and anon from the indefinite prodigiousness of their own aims, until the situation has been created which makes all turning back impossible, . . .

Bonaparte would like to appear as the patriarchal benefactor of all classes. But he cannot give to one class without taking from another. . . .

B The First International (actually called The Working Men's International Association) was founded in 1864, as a society to include all workers in a single movement. Marx delivered the Inaugural Address.

WORKING MEN,

It is a great fact that the misery of the working masses has not diminished from 1848 to 1864, and yet this period is unrivalled for the development of its industry and the growth of its commerce. . . .

After the failure of the Revolutions of 1848, all party organisations and party journals of the working classes were, on the Continent, crushed by the iron hand of force, the most advanced sons of labour fled in despair to the Transatlantic Republic, and the short-lived dreams of emancipation vanished before an epoch of industrial fever, moral marasme, and political reaction. The defeat of the Continental working classes, partly owed to the diplomacy of the English Government, acting then as now in fraternal solidarity with the Cabinet of St. Petersburg, soon spread its contagious effects to this side of the Channel. . . .

And yet the period passed since the Revolutions of 1848 has not been without its compensating features. We shall here only point to two great facts.

After a thirty years' struggle, fought with most admirable perseverance, the English working classes, improving a momentaneous split between the land-lords and money-lords, succeeded in carrying the Ten Hours' Bill. The immense physical, moral and intellectual benefits hence accruing to the factory operatives, half-yearly chronicled in the reports of the inspectors of factories, are now acknowledged on all sides. Most of the Continental governments had to accept the English Factory Act in more or less modified forms, and the English Parliament itself is every year compelled to enlarge its sphere of action. . . .

But there was in store a still greater victory of the political economy of labour over the political economy of property. We speak of the co-operative movement, especially the co-operative factories raised by the unassisted efforts of a few bold "hands." The value of these great social experiments cannot be over-rated. By deed, instead of by argument, they have shown that production on a large scale, and in accord with the behests of modern science, may be carried on without the existence of a class of masters employing a class of hands; that to bear fruit, the means of labour need not be monopolised as a means of dominion over, and of extortion against, the labouring man himself; and that, like slave labour, like serf labour, hired labour is but a transitory and inferior form, destined to disappear before associated labour plying its toil with a willing hand, a ready mind, and a joyous heart. In

England, the seeds of the co-operative system were sown by Robert Owen; the working men's experiments, tried on the Continent, were, in fact, the practical upshot of the theories, not invented, but loudly proclaimed, in 1848. . . .

One element of success they possess—numbers; but numbers weigh only in the balance, if united by combination and led by knowledge. Past experience has shown how disregard of that bond of brotherhood which ought to exist between the workmen of different countries, and incite them to stand firmly by each other in all their struggles for emancipation, will be chastised by the common discomfiture of their incoherent efforts. This thought prompted the working men of different countries assembled on September 28, 1864, in public meeting at St. Martin's Hall, to found the International Association. . . .

Proletarians of all countries, Unite!

C Marx could be as angry at his critics on the left as he was at his enemies on the right. One of the most influential revolutionaries of the nineteenth century was the Russian Mikhail Bakunin. In 1874-75, Marx discussed Bakunin's work *Statehood and Anarchy*. As he sometimes did, Marx would quote from his critic and then make his own comments.

> "Or, if one looks at this question from a national point of view, we may suppose that for the Germans, the Slavs for the same reason will enter into the same slavish subordination to the victorious German proletariat as the latter will now enjoy with respect to its own bourgeoisie." [Bakunin]

> Schoolboy drivel! A radical social revolution is connected with certain historical conditions of economic development; the latter are its presupposition. Therefore it is possible only where the industrial proletariat, together with capitalist production, occupies at least a substantial place in the mass of the people. And in order for it to have any chance at all of being victorious, it must be capable, *mutatis mutandis*, of doing at least as much directly for the peasant as the French bourgeoisie did during its revolution for the French peasant of that time. A fine idea, that the rule of the workers includes the enslavement of agricultural labor! But here appears the innermost thought of Herr Bakunin. He understands absolutely nothing about social revolution; all he knows are its political phrases. For him its economic requisites do not exist. Since all hitherto existing economic formations, developed or undeveloped, have included the enslavement of the working person (whether in the form of the wage worker, the peasant, etc.), he thinks that a *radical revolution* is possible under all these formations. Not only that! He wants a European social revolution, resting on the economic foundation of capitalist production, to take place on the level of the Russian or Slavic agricultural and pastoral peoples and not to overstep that level; although he does see that *navigation* creates a difference between the brothers, but only *navigation*, for that is a difference all politicians know about! *Will power* and not economic conditions is the basis of his social revolution. . . .

1. "The tradition of all the dead generations weighs like a nightmare on the brain of the living." Account for Marx's view that human progress had often been trapped by the patterns of the past.

2. Contrast in Marxist terms the difference between bourgeois and proletarian revolutions.

3. Outline the gains which, according to Marx, the proletariat had made in the fifteen years after the 1848 revolutions.

4. Marx criticized Bakunin for understanding "absolutely nothing about social revolution." Based on your understanding of events in the twentieth century, how accurate was Marx's assessment?

■ ■ ■

FRIEDRICH ENGELS

Friedrich Engels (1820-95) gave Marx both intellectual and emotional support. He was Marx's only collaborator.

A At the funeral of his friend in 1883, Engels delivered an address at the graveside, summing up what he believed to have been Marx's accomplishments.

> On the 14th of March, at a quarter to three in the afternoon, the greatest living thinker ceased to think. He had been left alone for scarcely two minutes, and when we came back we found him in his armchair, peacefully gone to sleep—but for ever.
>
> An immeasurable loss has been sustained both by the militant proletariat of Europe and America, and by historical science, in the death of this man. The gap that has been left by the departure of this mighty spirit will soon enough make itself felt.
>
> Just as Darwin discovered the law of development of organic nature, so Marx discovered the law of development of human history: the simple fact, hitherto concealed by an overgrowth of ideology, that mankind must first of all eat, drink, have shelter and clothing, before it can pursue politics, science, art, religion, etc.; that therefore the production of the immediate material means of subsistence and consequently the degree of economic development attained by a given people or during a given epoch form the foundation upon which the state institutions, the legal conceptions, art, and even the ideas on religion, of the people concerned have been evolved, and in the light of which they must, therefore, be explained, instead of *vice versa*, as had hitherto been the case.
>
> But that is not all. Marx also discovered the special law of motion governing the present-day capitalist mode of production and the bourgeois society that this mode of production has created. The discovery of surplus value suddenly threw light on the problem, in trying to solve which all previous investigations, of both bourgeois economists and socialist critics, had been groping in the dark.

Source: Robert C. Tucker, ed., *The Marx-Engels Reader,* second edition (New York: W.W. Norton and Company, 1978), pp. 681-82, 699, 700, 701-702, 713, 715-16.

Two such discoveries would be enough for one lifetime. Happy the man to whom it is granted to make even one such discovery. But in every single field which Marx investigated—and he investigated very many fields, none of them superficially—in every field, even in that of mathematics, he made independent discoveries.

Such was the man of science. But this was not even half the man. Science was for Marx a historically dynamic, revolutionary force. However great the joy with which he welcomed a new discovery in some theoretical science whose practical application perhaps it was as yet quite impossible to envisage, he experienced quite another kind of joy when the discovery involved immediate revolutionary changes in industry, and in historical development in general. . . .

For Marx was before all else a revolutionist. His real mission in life was to contribute, in one way or another, to the overthrow of capitalist society and of the state institutions which it had brought into being, to contribute to the liberation of the modern proletariat, which *he* was the first to make conscious of its own position and its needs, conscious of the conditions of its emancipation. . . .

. . . Marx was the best hated and most calumniated man of his time. Governments, both absolutist and republican, deported him from their territories. Bourgeois, whether conservative or ultra-democratic, vied with one another in heaping slanders upon him. All this he brushed aside as though it were cobweb, ignoring it, answering only when extreme necessity compelled him. And he died beloved, revered and mourned by millions of revolutionary fellow workers—from the mines of Siberia to California, in all parts of Europe and America—and I make bold to say that though he may have had many opponents he had hardly one personal enemy.

His name will endure through the ages, and so also will his work!

◆B Engels published his own summary of Marxian thought, *Socialism: Utopian and Scientific* in 1880. The work became the most important popular statement of Marx's ideas and vision.

The new facts [of the nineteenth century] made imperative a new examination of all past history. Then it was seen that *all* past history, with the exception of its primitive stages, was the history of class struggles; that these warring classes of society are always the products of the modes of production and of exchange—in a word, of the *economic* conditions of their time; that the economic structure of society always furnishes the real basis, starting from which we can alone work out the ultimate explanation of the whole superstructure of juridical and political institutions as well as of the religious, philosophical, and other ideas of a given historical period. . . .

From that time forward socialism was no longer an accidental discovery of this or that ingenious brain, but the necessary outcome of the struggle between two historically developed classes—the proletariat and the bourgeoisie. Its task was no longer to manufacture a system of society as perfect as possible, but to examine the historico-economic succession of events from which these classes, and their antagonism had of necessity sprung, and to discover in the economic conditions thus created the means of ending the conflict. But the socialism of earlier days was as incompatible with this materialistic conception as the conception of Nature of the French materialists was with dialectics and modern natural science. The socialism of earlier days certainly criticised the existing capitalistic mode of production and its consequences. But it could not explain them, and, therefore, could not get the mastery of them. It could only simply reject them as bad. The more strongly this earlier socialism denounced the exploitation of the working class, inevitable under capitalism, the less able was it clearly to show in what this exploitation consisted and how it arose. But for this it was necessary—(1) to present the capitalistic method of production in its historical connection and its inevitableness during a particular historical period, and therefore, also, to present its inevitable downfall; and (2) to lay bare its essential character, which was still a secret. This was done by the discovery of *surplus value*. It was shown that the appropriation of unpaid labour is the basis of the capitalist mode of production and of the exploitation of the worker that occurs under it; that even if the capitalist buys the labour power of his labourer at its full value as a commodity on the market, he yet extracts more value from it than he paid for; and that in the ultimate analysis this surplus value forms those sums of value from which are heaped up the constantly increasing masses of capital in the hands of the possessing classes. The genesis of capitalist production and the production of capital were both explained.

These two great discoveries, the materialistic conception of history and the revelation of the secret of capitalistic production through surplus value, we owe to Marx. With these discoveries socialism became a science. . . .

The present structure of society—this is now pretty generally conceded—is the creation of the ruling class of today, of the bourgeoisie. The mode of production peculiar to the bourgeoisie, known, since Marx, as the capitalist mode of production, was incompatible with the feudal system, with the privileges it conferred upon individuals, entire social ranks and local corporations, as well as with the hereditary ties of subordination which constituted the framework of its social organisation. The bourgeoisie broke up the feudal system and built upon its ruins the capitalist order of society, the kingdom of free competition, of personal liberty, of the equality, before the law, of all commodity owners, of all the rest of the capitalist blessings. Thenceforward the capitalist mode of production could develop in freedom. Since steam, machinery, and the making of machines by machinery transformed the older manufacture into modern industry, the productive forces evolved under the guidance of the bourgeoisie developed with a rapidity and in a degree unheard of before. But just as the older manufacture, in its time, and handicraft, becoming more developed under its influence, had come into collision with the feudal trammels of the guilds, so now modern industry, in its more complete development, comes into collision with the bounds within which the capitalistic mode of production holds it confined. The new productive forces have already outgrown the capitalistic mode of using them. And this conflict between productive forces and modes of production is not a conflict engendered in the mind of man, like that between original sin and divine justice. It exists, in fact, objectively, outside us, independently of the will and actions even of the men that have brought it on. Modern socialism is nothing but the reflex, in thought, of this conflict in fact; its ideal reflection in the minds, first, of the class directly suffering under it, the working class. . . .

At the end of the work, Engels discussed the future and its meaning.

Whilst the capitalist mode of production more and more completely trans forms the great majority of the population into proletarians, it creates the power which, under penalty of its own destruction, is forced to accomplish this revolution. Whilst it forces on more and more the transformation of the vast means of production, already socialised, into state property, it shows itself the way to accomplishing this revolution. *The proletariat seizes political power and turns the means of production into state property.*

But, in doing this, it abolishes itself as proletariat, abolishes all class dis tinctions and class antagonisms, abolishes also the state as state. Society thus far, based upon class antagonisms, had need of the state. That is, of an organisation of the particular class which was *pro tempore* the exploiting class, an organisation for the purpose of preventing any interference from without with the existing conditions of production, and, therefore, especially, for the purpose of forcibly keeping the exploited classes in the condition of oppression corresponding with the given mode of production (slavery, serfdom, wage-labour). The state was the official representative of society as a whole; the gathering of it together into a visible embodiment. But it was this only in so far as it was the state of that class which itself represented, for the time being, society as a whole: in ancient times, the state of slaveowning citizens; in the Middle Ages, the feudal lords; in our own time, the bourgeoisie. When at last it becomes the real representative of the whole of society, it renders itself unnecessary. As soon as there is no longer any social class to be held in subjection; as soon as class rule, and the individual struggle for existence based upon our present anarchy in production, with the collisions and excesses arising from these, are removed, nothing more remains to be repressed, and a special repressive force, a state, is no longer necessary. The first act by virtue of which the state really constitutes itself the representative of the whole of society—this is, at the same time, its last independent act as a state. State interference in social relations becomes, in one domain after another, superfluous, and then dies out of itself; the government of persons is replaced by the administration of things, and by the conduct of processes of production. The state is not "abolished." *It dies out.* This gives the measure of the value of the phrase *"a free state,"* but as to its justifiable use at times by agitators, and as to its ultimate scientific insufficiency; and also of the demands of the so-called anarchists for the abolition of the state out of hand. . . .

The socialised appropriation of the means of production does away, not only with the present artificial restrictions upon production, but also with the positive waste and devastation of productive forces and products that are at the present time the inevitable concomitants of production, and that reach their height in the crises. Further, it sets free for the community at large a mass of means of production and of products, by doing away with the senseless extravagance of the ruling classes of today and their political representatives. The possibility of securing for every member of society, by means of socialised production, an existence not only fully sufficient materially, and becoming day by day more full, but an existence guaranteeing to all the free development and exercise of their physical and mental faculties—this possibility is now for the first time here, but *it is here.*

With the seizing of the means of production by society, production of commodities is done away with, and, simultaneously, the mastery of the product over the producer. Anarchy in social production is replaced by systematic, definite organisation. The struggle for individual existence disappears. Then for the first time man, in a certain sense, is finally marked off from the rest of the animal kingdom, and emerges from mere animal conditions of existence into really human ones. The whole sphere of the conditions of life which environ man, and which have hitherto ruled man, now comes under the dominion and control of man, who for the first time becomes the real, conscious lord of Nature, because he has now become master of his own social organisation. The laws of his own social action, hitherto standing face to face with man as laws of Nature foreign to, and dominating him, will then be used with full understanding, and so mastered by him. Man's own social organisation, hitherto confronting him as a necessity imposed by Nature and history, now becomes the result of his own free action. The extraneous objective forces that have hitherto governed history pass under the control of man himself. Only from that time will man himself, more and more consciously, make his own history—only from that time will the social causes set in movement by him have, in the main and in a constantly growing measure, the results intended by him. It is the ascent of man from the kingdom of necessity to the kingdom of freedom. . . .

1. Imagine that you are a newspaper reporter at Marx's graveside. Comment on the image of Marx as depicted by Engels.
2. Write your own obituary of Marx, making it about the same length as Engel's speech.
3. Explain Marx's "two great discoveries" and account for their impact on socialist thought.
4. What eventual changes in the human condition did Engels forsee resulting from the destruction of capitalism?
5. Why did Engels believe that human beings, in his time, finally had the possibility of creating their own history?

▪ ▪ ▪

JOHN STUART MILL

John Stuart Mill (1806-73) was among the greatest liberals of the period, as well as being a logician and political economist. Much of his life was spent trying to define and confirm the rights of the individual, without losing sight that we all live in a community and have social responsibilities.

Mill discussed the issue of personal freedom and social obligations in *On Liberty* (1859).

The object of this Essay is to assert one very simple principle, as entitled to govern absolutely the dealings of society with the individual in the way of compulsion and control, whether the means used be physical force in the form of legal penalties, or the moral coercion of public opinion. That principle is, that the sole end for which mankind are warranted, individually or collectively, in interfering with the liberty of action of any of their number, is self-protection. That the only purpose for which power can be rightfully exercised over any member of a civilised community, against his will, is to prevent harm to others. His own good, either physical or moral, is not a sufficient warrant. He cannot rightfully be compelled to do or forbear because it will be better for him to do so, because it will make him happier, because, in the opinions of others, to do so would be wise, or even right. These are good reasons for remonstrating with him, or reasoning with him, or persuading him, or entreating him, but not for compelling him, or visiting him with any evil in case he do otherwise. To justify that, the conduct from which it is desired to deter him must be calculated to produce evil to some one else. The only part of the conduct of any one, for which he is amenable to society, is that which concerns others. In the part which merely concerns himself, his independence is, of right, absolute. Over himself, over his own body and mind, the individual is sovereign. . . .

. . . there is a sphere of action in which society, as distinguished from the individual, has, if any, only an indirect interest; comprehending all that portion of a person's life and conduct which affects only himself, or if it also affects others, only with their free, voluntary, and undeceived consent and participation. When I say only himself, I mean directly, and in the first instance; for whatever affects himself, may affect others *through* himself; and the objection which may be grounded on this contingency, will receive consideration in the sequel. This, then, is the appropriate region of human liberty. It comprises, first, the inward domain of consciousness; demanding liberty of conscience in the most comprehensive sense; liberty of thought and feeling; absolute freedom of opinion and sentiment on all subjects, practical or speculative, scientific, moral, or theological. The liberty of expressing and publishing opinions may seem to fall under a different principle, since it belongs to that part of the conduct of an individual which concerns other people; but, being almost of as much importance as the liberty of thought itself, and resting in great part on the same reasons, is practically inseparable from it. Secondly, the principle requires liberty of tastes and pursuits; of framing the plan of our life to suit our own character; of doing as we like, subject to such consequences as may follow: without impediment from our fellow-creatures, so long as what we do does not harm them, even though they should think our conduct foolish, perverse, or wrong. Thirdly, from this liberty of each individual, follows the liberty, within the same limits, of combination among individuals; freedom to unite, for any purpose not involving harm to others:

Sources: John Stuart Mill, *On Liberty*, edited by David Spitz (New York: W.W. Norton and Company, 1975), pp. 10-11, 13-14, 105, 106; John Stuart Mill, *Considerations on Representative Government*, edited by Currin V. Shields (New York: The Liberal Arts Press, 1958), pp. 103-104, 127-28; John Stuart Mill, *The Subjection of Women* (Cambridge, Massachusetts: The M.I.T. Press, 1970), pp. 21, 22, 79-81, 82.

the persons combining being supposed to be of full age, and not forced or deceived.

No society in which these liberties are not, on the whole, respected, is free, whatever may be its form of government; and none is completely free in which they do not exist absolute and unqualified. The only freedom which deserves the name, is that of pursuing our own good in our own way, so long as we do not attempt to deprive others of theirs, or impede their efforts to obtain it. Each is the proper guardian of his own health, whether bodily, or mental and spiritual. Mankind are greater gainers by suffering each other to live as seems good to themselves, than by compelling each to live as seems good to the rest. . . .

 Mill was influenced by and indebted to Alexis de Tocqueville for some of his conclusions on the nature of freedom, community and democracy.

To determine the point at which evils, so formidable to human freedom and advancement, begin, or rather at which they begin to predominate over the benefits attending the collective application of the force of society, under its recognised chiefs, for the removal of the obstacles which stand in the way of its well-being; to secure as much of the advantages of centralised power and intelligence as can be had without turning into governmental channels too great a proportion of the general activity—is one of the most difficult and complicated questions in the art of government. It is, in a great measure, a question of detail, in which many and various considerations must be kept in view, and no absolute rule can be laid down. But I believe that the practical principle in which safety resides, the ideal to be kept in view, the standard by which to test all arrangements intended for overcoming the difficulty, may be conveyed in these words: the greatest dissemination of power consistent with efficiency; but the greatest possible centralisation of information, and diffusion of it from the centre. Thus, in municipal administration, there would be, as in the New England States, a very minute division among separate officers, chosen by the localities, of all business which is not better left to the persons directly interested; but besides this, there would be, in each department of local affairs, a central superintendence, forming a branch of the general government. . . .

. . . A government cannot have too much of the kind of activity which does not impede, but aids and stimulates, individual exertion and development. The mischief begins when, instead of calling forth the activity and powers of individuals and bodies, it substitutes its own activity for theirs; when, instead of informing, advising, and, upon occasion, denouncing, it makes them work in fetters, or bids them stand aside and does their work instead of them. The worth of a State, in the long run, is the worth of the individuals composing it; and a State which postpones the interests of *their* mental expansion and elevation, to a little more of administrative skill, or of that semblance of it which practice gives, in the details of business; a State which dwarfs its men, in order that they may be more docile instruments in its hands even for beneficial purposes—will find that with small men no great thing can really be accomplished; and that the perfection of machinery to which it has sacrificed everything, will in the end avail it nothing, for want of the vital power which, in order that the machine might work more smoothly, it has preferred to banish.

 In *Considerations on Representative Government* Mill discussed democracy in the context of the times.

. . . In a really equal democracy every or any section would be represented, not disproportionately, but proportionately. A majority of the electors would always have a majority of the representatives, but a minority of the electors would always have a minority of the representatives. Man for man they would be as fully represented as the majority. Unless they are, there is not equal government, but a government of inequality and privilege: one part of the people rule over the rest; there is a part whose fair and equal share of influence in the representation is withheld from them, contrary to all just government, but, above all, contrary to the principle of democracy, which professes equality as its very root and foundation. . . .

Such a representative democracy as has now been sketched, representative of all, and not solely of the majority—in which the interests, the opinions, the grades of intellect which are outnumbered would nevertheless be heard, and would have a chance of obtaining by weight of character and strength of argument an influence which would not belong to their numerical force— this democracy, which is alone equal, alone impartial, alone the government of all by all, the only true type of democracy, would be free from the greatest evils of the falsely-called democracies which now prevail, and from which the current idea of democracy is exclusively derived. But even in this democracy, absolute power, if they chose to exercise it, would rest with the numerical majority; and these would be composed exclusively of a single class, alike in biases, prepossessions, and general modes of thinking, and a class, to say no more, not the most highly cultivated. The constitution would, therefore, still be liable to the characteristic evils of class government: in a far less degree, assuredly, than that exclusive government by a class which now usurps the name of democracy, but still under no effective restraint except what might be found in the good sense, moderation, and forbearance of the class itself. If checks of this description are sufficient, the philosophy of constitutional government is but solemn trifling. All trust in constitutions is grounded on the assurance they may afford, not that the depositaries of power will not, but that they cannot, misemploy it. Democracy is not the ideally best form of government unless this weak side of it can be strengthened, unless it can be so organized that no class, not even the most numerous, shall be able to reduce all but itself to political insignificance and direct the course of legislation and administration by its exclusive class interest. The problem is to find the means of preventing this abuse, without sacrificing the characteristic advantages of popular government.

Mill always claimed he was indebted to his wife, Harriet Taylor, for many of his ideas, and there is much critical speculation on how deeply Mrs. Mill, who died in 1858, collaborated with her husband on some of his works, including the essay which became *On Liberty*. Mill's work *The Subjection of Women* (1871) is concerned with the emancipation of women, and is a tribute to Harriet Taylor's influence and to Mill's willingness to break from earlier social stereotypes.

> The social subordination of women thus stands out an isolated fact in modern social institutions; a solitary breach of what has become their fundamental law; a single relic of an old world of thought and practice exploded in everything else, but retained in the one thing of most universal interest; . . .
>
> The least that can be demanded is, that the question should not be considered as prejudged by existing fact and existing opinion, but open to discussion on its merits, as a question of justice and expediency: the decision on this, as on any of the other social arrangements of mankind, depending on what an enlightened estimate of tendencies and consequences may show to be most advantageous to humanity in general, without distinction of sex. . . .
>
> What is now called the nature of women is an eminently artificial thing—the result of forced repression in some directions, unnatural stimulation in others. It may be asserted without scruple, that no other class of dependents have had their character so entirely distorted from its natural proportions by their relation with their masters; for, if conquered and slave races have been, in some respects, more forcibly repressed, whatever in them has not been crushed down by an iron heel has generally been let alone, and if left with any liberty of development, it has developed itself according to its own laws; but in the case of women, a hot-house and stove cultivation has always been carried on of some of the capabilities of their nature, for the benefit and pleasure of their masters. . . .
>
> . . . The law of servitude in marriage is a monstrous contradiction to all the principles of the modern world, and to all the experience through which those principles have been slowly and painfully worked out. It is the sole case, now that negro slavery has been abolished, in which a human being in the plentitude of every faculty is delivered up to the tender mercies of another human being, in the hope forsooth that this other will use the power solely for the good of the person subjected to it. Marriage is the only actual bondage known to our law. There remain no legal slaves, except the mistress of every house.
>
> It is not, therefore, on this part of the subject, that the question is likely to be asked, *Cui bono?* We may be told that the evil would outweigh the good, but the reality of the good admits of no dispute. In regard, however, to the larger question, the removal of women's disabilities—their recognition as the equals of men in all that belongs to citizenship—the opening to them of all honourable employments, and of the training and education which qualifies for those employments—there are many persons for whom it is not enough that the inequality has no just or legitimate defence; they require to be told what express advantage would be obtained by abolishing it.
>
> To which let me first answer, the advantage of having the most universal and pervading of all human relations regulated by justice instead of injustice.

The vast amount of this gain to human nature, it is hardly possible, by any explanation or illustration, to place in a stronger light than it is placed by the bare statement, to anyone who attaches a moral meaning to words. All the selfish propensities, the self-worship, the unjust self-preference, which exist among mankind, have their source and root in, and derive their principal nourishment from, the present constitution of the relation between men and women. Think what it is to a boy, to grow up to manhood in the belief that without any merit or any exertion of his own, though he may be the most frivolous and empty or the most ignorant and stolid of mankind, by the mere fact of being born a male he is by right the superior of all and every one of an entire half of the human race: including probably some whose real superiority to himself he has daily or hourly occasion to feel; but even if in his whole conduct he habitually follows a woman's guidance, still, if he is a fool, she thinks that of course she is not, and cannot be, equal in ability and judgment to himself; and if he is not a fool, he does worse—he sees that she is superior to him, and believes that, notwithstanding her superiority, he is entitled to command and she is bound to obey. What must be the effect on his character, of this lesson? And men of the cultivated classes are often not aware how deeply it sinks into the immense majority of male minds. For, among right-feeling and well-bred people, the inequality is kept as much as possible out of sight; above all, out of sight of the children. As much obedience is required from boys to their mother as to their father: they are not permitted to domineer over their sisters, nor are they accustomed to see these postponed to them, but the contrary; the compensations of the chivalrous feeling being made prominent, while the servitude which requires them is kept in the background. Well brought-up youths in the higher classes thus often escape the bad influences of the situation in their early years, and only experience them when, arrived at manhood, they fall under the dominion of facts as they really exist. Such people are little aware, when a boy is differently brought up, how early the notion of his inherent superiority to a girl arises in his mind; how it grows with his growth and strengthens with his strength; how it is inoculated by one schoolboy upon another; how early the youth thinks himself superior to his mother, owing her perhaps forbearance, but no real respect; and how sublime and sultan-like a sense of superiority he feels above all, over the woman whom he honours by admitting her to a partnership of his life. Is it imagined that all this does not pervert the whole manner of existence of the man, both as an individual and as a social being? It is an exact parallel to the feeling of a hereditary king that he is excellent above others by being born a king, or a noble by being born a noble. The relation between husband and wife is very like that between lord and vassal, except that the wife is held to more unlimited obedience than the vassal was. . . .

. . . The principle of the modern movement in morals and politics, is that conduct, and conduct alone, entitles to respect: that not what men are, but what they do, constitutes their claim to deference; that, above all, merit, and not birth, is the only rightful claim to power and authority. If no authority, not in its nature temporary, were allowed to one human being over another, society would not be employed in building up propensities with one hand which it has to curb with the other. The child would really, for the first time in man's existence on earth, be trained in the way he should go, and when he was old there would be a chance that he would not depart from it. But so long as the right of the strong to power over the weak rules in the very heart of society, the attempt to make the equal right of the weak the principle of its outward actions will always be an uphill struggle; for the law of justice, which is also that of Christianity, will never get possession of men's inmost sentiments; they will be working against it, even when bending to it.

The second benefit to be expected from giving to women the free use of their faculties, by leaving them the free choice of their employments, and opening to them the same field of occupation and the same prizes and encouragements as to other human beings, would be that of doubling the mass of mental faculties available for the higher service of humanity. . . .

1. What did Mill identify as the only justification for society interfering with the life of an individual? Do you agree?
2. Explain the three basic liberties that Mill believes arise from his basic principle.
3. Comment on Mill's basic definition of freedom. What criticisms might he direct at modern democratic societies?
4. Compare Mill's view of the role of government in society with that of Marx and Engels.
5. "Democracy is not the ideally best form of government . . . unless it can be so organized that no class, not even the most numerous, shall be able to reduce all but itself to political insignificance." Account for this statement with reference to Mill's observations regarding the dangers of the tyranny of the majority.
6. Outline the argument in which Mill equated the treatment of women with legalized slavery.
7. Comment on Mill's description of the socialization process, which implants the concept of sexual inequality in people's minds.
8. To what extent do you feel that Mill's charges against his society are still valid today?

▪ ▪ ▪

ABRAHAM LINCOLN

Abraham Lincoln (1809-65), president of the United States during its Civil War, was a nationalist who believed in a strong central government and a libertarian who espoused and defended a doctrine of freedom. A politician who always worked within the realm of the possible, Lincoln was also self-reflective and eloquent in his public statements about slavery, the relationship of government to the governed, and the nature of the nation and the state. Assassinated in 1865, Lincoln's ideals and concepts influenced all of the West.

A Lincoln headed the Republican Party, which opposed the extension of slavery in the United States. His reflections on the issue before his presidency represent a groping with many major questions about human beings and their relationship to society and political authority. In an address in 1860 in New York, Lincoln questioned the attitudes of those who supported the cause of the South and slavery.

Your purpose, then, plainly stated, is, that you will destroy the government, unless you be allowed to construe and enforce the Constitution as you please, on all points in dispute between you and us. You will rule or ruin in all events. . . .

. . . But you will not abide the election of a Republican president! In that supposed event, you say, you will destroy the Union; and then, you say, the great crime of having destroyed it will be upon us! That is cool. A highwayman holds a pistol to my ear, and mutters through his teeth, "Stand and deliver, or I shall kill you, and then you will be a murderer!"

To be sure, what the robber demanded of me—my money—was my own; and I had a clear right to keep it; but it was no more my own than my vote is my own; and the threat of death to me, to extort my money, and the threat of destruction to the Union, to extort my vote, can scarcely be distinguished in principle.

A few words now to Republicans. *It is exceedingly desirable that all parts of this great confederacy shall be at peace, and in harmony, one with another. Let us Republicans do our part to have it so. Even though much provoked, let us do nothing through passion and ill temper. Even though the Southern people will not so much as listen to us, let us calmly consider their demands, and yield to them if, in our deliberate view of our duty, we possibly can.* Judging by all they say and do, and by the subject and nature of their controversy with us, let us determine, if we can, what will satisfy them. . . .

These natural, and apparently adequate means all failing, what will convince them? This, and this only: cease to call slavery *wrong*, and join them in calling it *right*. And this must be done thoroughly—done in *acts* as well as in *words*. Silence will not be tolerated—we must place ourselves avowedly with them. Senator Douglas' new sedition law must be enacted and enforced, suppressing all declarations that slavery is wrong, whether made in politics, in presses, in pulpits, or in private. We must arrest and return their fugitive slaves with greedy pleasure. We must pull down our free state constitutions. The whole atmosphere must be disinfected from all taint of opposition to slavery, before they will cease to believe that all their troubles proceed from us.

I am quite aware they do not state their case precisely in this way. Most of them would probably say to us, "Let us alone, *do* nothing to us, and *say* what you please about slavery." But we do let them alone—have never disturbed them—so that, after all, it is what we say, which dissatisfies them. They will continue to accuse us of doing, until we cease saying.

I am also aware they have not, as yet, in terms, demanded the overthrow of our free-state constitutions. Yet those constitutions declare the wrong of

Source: *Abraham Lincoln, Selected Speeches, Messages, and Letters,* edited by T. Harry Williams (New York: Rinehart and Company, Inc., 1957), pp. 126, 128, 129-30, 143-44, 146-48.

slavery, with more solemn emphasis, than do all other sayings against it; and when all these other sayings shall have been silenced, the overthrow of these constitutions will be demanded, and nothing be left to resist the demand. It is nothing to the contrary, that they do not demand the whole of this just now. Demanding what they do, and for the reason they do, they can voluntarily stop nowhere short of this consummation. Holding, as they do, that slavery is morally right, and socially elevating, they cannot cease to demand a full national recognition of it, as a legal right, and a social blessing.

Nor can we justifiably withhold this, on any ground save our conviction that slavery is wrong. If slavery is right, all words, acts, laws, and constitutions against it, are themselves wrong, and should be silenced, and swept away. If it is right, we cannot justly object to its nationality—its universality; if it is wrong, they cannot justly insist upon its extension—its enlargement. All they ask, we could readily grant, if we thought slavery right; all we ask, they could as readily grant, if they thought it wrong. Their thinking it right, and our thinking it wrong, is the precise fact upon which depends the whole controversy. Thinking it right, as they do, they are not to blame for desiring its full recognition, as being right; but, thinking it wrong, as we do, can we yield to them? Can we cast our votes with their view, and against our own? In view of our moral, social, and political responsibilities, can we do this?

Wrong as we think slavery is, we can yet afford to let it alone where it is, because that much is due to the necessity arising from its actual presence in the nation; but can we, while our votes will prevent it, allow it to spread into the national territories, and to overrun us here in these free states? If our sense of duty forbids this, then let us stand by our duty, fearlessly and effectively. Let us be diverted by none of those sophistical contrivances wherewith we are so industriously plied and belabored—contrivances such as groping for some middle ground between the right and the wrong, vain as the search for a man who should be neither a living man nor a dead man—such as a policy of "don't care" on a question about which all true men do care—such as Union appeals beseeching true Union men to yield to Disunionists, reversing the divine rule, and calling, not the sinners, but the righteous to repentance—such as invocations to Washington, imploring men to unsay what Washington said, and undo what Washington did.

Neither let us be slandered from our duty by false accusations against us, nor frightened from it by menaces of destruction to the government nor of dungeons to ourselves. LET US HAVE FAITH THAT RIGHT MAKES MIGHT, AND IN THAT FAITH, LET US, TO THE END, DARE TO DO OUR DUTY AS WE UNDERSTAND IT.

 Lincoln's First Inaugural Address in March 1861 was a defence of the idea of union.

All profess to be content in the Union, if all constitutional rights can be maintained. Is it true, then, that any right, plainly written in the Constitution, has been denied? I think not. Happily the human mind is so constituted, that no party can reach to the audacity of doing this. Think, if you can, of a single instance in which a plainly written provision of the Constitution has ever been denied. If, by the mere force of numbers, a majority should deprive a minority of any clearly written constitutional right, it might, in a moral point of view, justify revolution—certainly would, if such right were a vital one. But such is not our case. All the vital rights of minorities, and of individuals, are so plainly assured to them, by affirmations and negations, guaranties and prohibitions, in the Constitution, that controversies never arise concerning them. But no organic law can ever be framed with a provision specifically applicable to every question which may occur in practical administration. No foresight can anticipate, nor any document of reasonable length contain express provisions for all possible questions. Shall fugitives from labor be surrendered by national or by state authority? The Constitution does not expressly say. *May* Congress prohibit slavery in the territories? The Constitution does not expressly say. *Must* Congress protect slavery in the territories? The Constitution does not expressly say.

From questions of this class spring all our constitutional controversies, and we divide upon them into majorities and minorities. If the minority will not acquiesce, the majority must, or the government must cease. There is no other alternative; for continuing the government, is acquiescence on one side or the other. If a minority, in such case, will secede rather than acquiesce, they make a precedent which in turn, will divide and ruin them; for a minority of their own will secede from them, whenever a majority refuses to be controlled by such minority. For instance, why may not any portion of a new confederacy, a year or two hence, arbitrarily secede again, precisely as portions of the present Union now claim to secede from it. All who cherish disunion sentiments, are now being educated to the exact temper of doing this. Is there such perfect identity of interests among the states to compose a new Union, as to produce harmony only, and prevent renewed secession?

Plainly, the central idea of secession, is the essence of anarchy. A majority, held in restraint by constitutional checks, and limitations, and always changing easily, with deliberate changes of popular opinions and sentiments, is the only true sovereign of a free people. Whoever rejects it, does, of necessity, fly to anarchy or to despotism. Unanimity is impossible; the rule of a minority, as a permanent arrangement, is wholly inadmissible; so that, rejecting the majority principle, anarchy, or despotism in some form, is all that is left. . . .

This country, with its institutions, belongs to the people who inhabit it. Whenever they shall grow weary of the existing government, they can exercise their *constitutional* right of amending it, or their *revolutionary* right to dismember, or overthrow it. I cannot be ignorant of the fact that many worthy, and patriotic citizens are desirous of having the national Constitution amended. While I make no recommendation of amendments. I fully recognize the rightful authority of the people over the whole subject, to be exercised in either of the modes prescribed in the instrument itself; and I should, under existing circumstances, favor, rather than oppose, a fair opportunity being afforded the people to act upon it.

I will venture to add that, to me, the convention mode seems preferable, in that it allows amendments to originate with the people themselves, instead of only permitting them to take, or reject, propositions, originated by others, not especially chosen for the purpose, and which might not be precisely such, as they would wish to either accept or refuse. I understand a proposed amendment to the Constitution—which amendment, however, I have not seen, has passed Congress, to the effect that the federal government, shall never interfere with the domestic institutions of the states, including that of persons held to service. To avoid misconstruction of what I have said, I depart from my purpose not to speak of particular amendments, so far as to say that, holding such a provision to now be implied constitutional law, I have no objection to its being made express, and irrevocable.

The chief magistrate derives all his authority from the people, and they have conferred none upon him to fix terms for the separation of the states. The people themselves can do this also if they choose; but the executive, as such, has nothing to do with it. His duty is to administer the present government, as it came to his hands, and to transmit it, unimpaired by him, to his successor.

Why should there not be a patient confidence in the ultimate justice of the people? Is there any better, or equal hope, in the world? In our present differences, is either party without faith of being in the right? If the Almighty Ruler of nations, with his eternal truth and justice, be on your side of the North, or on yours of the South, that truth, and that justice, will surely prevail, by the judgment of this great tribunal, the American people.

By the frame of the government under which we live, this same people have wisely given their public servants but little power for mischief; and have, with equal wisdom, provided for the return of that little to their own hands at very short intervals.

While the people retain their virtue, and vigilance, no administration, by any extreme of wickedness or folly, can very seriously injure the government, in the short space of four years.

My countrymen, one and all, think calmly and well, upon this whole subject. Nothing valuable can be lost by taking time. If there be an object to *hurry* any of you, in hot haste, to a step which you would never take deliberately, that object will be frustrated by taking time; but no good object can be frustrated by it. Such of you as are now dissatisfied, still have the old Constitution unimpaired, and, on the sensitive point, the laws of your own framing under it; while the new administration will have no immediate power, if it would, to change either. If it were admitted that you who are dissatisfied, hold the right side in the dispute, there still is no single good reason for precipitate action. Intelligence, patriotism, Christianity, and a firm reliance on Him, who has never yet forsaken this favored land, are still competent to adjust, in the best way, all our present difficulty.

In *your* hands, my dissatisfied fellow-countrymen, and not in *mine*, is the momentous issue of civil war. The government will not assail *you*. You can have no conflict, without being yourselves the aggressors. *You* have no oath registered in Heaven to destroy the government, while *I* shall have the most solemn one to "preserve, protect and defend" it.

I am loath to close. We are not enemies, but friends. We must not be enemies. Though passion may have strained, it must not break our bonds of affection. The mystic chords of memory, stretching from every battlefield, and patriot grave, to every living heart and hearthstone, all over this broad land, will yet swell the chorus of the Union, when again touched, as surely they will be, by the better angels of our nature.

In 1863 Lincoln delivered his Gettysburg Address, a short speech summing up his position on the United States in the midst of the Civil War.

> Four score and seven years ago our fathers brought forth on this continent, a new nation, conceived in liberty, and dedicated to the proposition that all men are created equal.
>
> Now we are engaged in a great civil war, testing whether that nation, or any nation so conceived and so dedicated, can long endure. We are met on a great battlefield of that war. We have come to dedicate a portion of that field, as a final resting place for those who here gave their lives that that nation might live. It is altogether fitting and proper that we should do this.
>
> But, in a larger sense, we cannot dedicate—we cannot consecrate—we cannot hallow—this ground. The brave men, living and dead, who struggled here, have consecrated it, far above our poor power to add or detract. The world will little note, nor long remember what we say here, but it can never forget what they did here. It is for us the living, rather, to be dedicated here to the unfinished work which they who fought here have thus far so nobly advanced. It is rather for us to be here dedicated to the great task remaining before us—that from these honored dead we take increased devotion—that we here highly resolve that these dead shall not have died in vain—that this nation, under God, shall have a new birth of freedom—and that government of the people, by the people, for the people, shall not perish from the earth.

1. Assess Lincoln's 1860 address as a political speech. To what extent does he overstate the position of his opponents in order to characterize his own position as one of rational compromise?
2. Comment on Lincoln's use of the American Constitution as a means of controlling political passions.
3. Contrast the political position of the campaigning politician in excerpt (a) with that of the elected president in excerpt (b).
4. According to Lincoln, the Civil War was primarily a conflict in defence of the principles of liberalism. Respond to this statement, in your own words.

• • •

OTTO VON BISMARCK

Otto von Bismarck (1815-98) was one of the creators of the modern state as the leading figure in German unification and in the establishment and maintenance of the state system after 1871. Bismarck, a Prussian, was a believer in the importance of the state, and he did everything possible to centralize authority. Yet he was also a man of restraint, whose doctrine would not permit him to seek a univeral empire or to go beyond nationalist ends. As a practicioner of *Realpolitik*, and in his speeches and reflections, Bismarck articulated many of the concepts which have played a major role in guiding states in the modern world.

During his early years as the political leader of Prussia, Bismarck insisted that force and power must be understood and used. The following is from a speech of 1862:

> Our blood is too hot; we prefer to wear armor which is too heavy for our slender body; but we should use it nonetheless. The eyes of Germany are fixed not upon Prussia's liberalism, but upon her armed might. Bavaria, Würtemberg, and Baden may indulge in liberal experiments; therefore, no one will assign to them Prussia's role. Prussia must harbor and maintain her strength for the favorable moment—a moment which has already, on one occasion, slipped by; Prussia's boundaries, as drawn by the Vienna treaties, are not suitable for a healthy state life. The great questions of the day will not be decided by speeches or by majority decisions—that was the mistake of 1848 and 1849—but by blood and iron!

Bismarck's alliance "system" was his most famous accomplishment. In his memoirs he discussed some of the considerations that guided his policy.

> The triple alliance which I originally sought to conclude after the peace of Frankfort, and about which I had already sounded Vienna and St. Petersburg, from Meaux, in September 1870, was an alliance of the three Emperors with the further idea of bringing into it monarchical Italy. It was designed for the struggle which, as I feared, was before us; between the two European tendencies which Napoleon called Republican and Cossack, and which I, according to our present ideas, should designate on the one side as the system of order on a monarchical basis, and on the other as the social republic to the level of which the anti-monarchical development is wont to sink, either slowly or by leaps and bounds, until the conditions thus created become intolerable, and the disappointed populace are ready for a violent return to monarchical institutions in a Caesarean form. I consider that the task of escaping from this *circulus vitiosus*, or, if possible, of sparing the present generation and their children an entrance into it, ought to be more closely incumbent on the strong existing monarchies, those monarchies which still have a vigorous life, than any rivalry over the fragments of nations which people the Balkan peninsula. If the monarchical governments have no understanding of the necessity for holding together in the interests of political and social order, but make themselves subservient to the chauvinistic impulses of their subjects, I fear that the international revolutionary and social struggles which will have to be fought out will be all the more dangerous, and take such a form that the victory on the part of monarchical order will be more difficult. . . .
>
> . . . The idea of coalitions gave me nightmares. We had waged victorious wars against two of the European Great Powers; everything depended on inducing at least one of the two mighty foes whom we had beaten in the field to renounce the anticipated design of uniting with the other in a war of revenge. To all who knew history and the character of the Gallic race, it

Sources: Thomas C. Mendenhall, *et al.*, *The Quest for a Principle of Authority in Europe, 1715-Present: Select Problems in Historical Interpretation* (New York: Holt, Rinehart and Winston, 1948), p. 220; Otto von Bismarck, *Bismarck: The Man and the Statesman* (being the reflections and reminiscences of Otto von Bismarck) (London: Smith, Elder, and Co., 1898), Volume II, pp. 248-49, 252, 253, 267, 270-71, 278-79, 280-81.

was obvious that that Power could not be France, and if a secret treaty of Reichstadt was possible without our consent, without our knowledge, so also was a renewal of the old coalition . . . of France, Austria, and Russia, whenever the elements which it represented, and which beneath the surface were still present in Austria, should gain the ascendency there. . . .

This situation demanded an effort to limit the range of the possible anti-German coalition by means of treaty arrangements placing our relations with at least one of the Great Powers upon a firm footing. The choice could only lie between Austria and Russia, for the English constitution does not admit of alliances of assured permanence, and a union with Italy alone did not promise an adequate counterpoise to a coalition of the other three Great Powers, even supposing her future attitude and formation to be considered independently not only of French but also of Austrian influence. The area available for the formation of the coalition would therefore be narrowed till only the alternative remained which I have indicated. . . .

Even in the last century it was perilous to reckon on the constraining force of the text of a treaty of alliance when the conditions under which it had been written were changed; to-day it is hardly possible for the government of a great Power to place its resources unreservedly at the disposal of a friendly state when the sentiment of the people disapproves it. No longer, therefore, does the text of a treaty afford the same securities as in the days of the 'cabinet wars,' which were waged with armies of from 30,000 to 60,000 men; a family war, such as Frederick William II waged on behalf of his brother-in-law in Holland, could hardly to-day be put upon the European stage, nor could the conditions preliminary to such a war as Nicholas waged on Hungary be readily again found. Nevertheless the plain and searching words of a treaty are not without influence on diplomacy when it is concerned with precipitating or averting a war; nor are even treacherous and violent governments usually inclined to an open breach of faith, so long as the *force majeure* of imperative interests does not intervene. . . .

. . . All contracts between great states cease to be unconditionally binding as soon as they are tested by 'the struggle for existence.' No great nation will ever be induced to sacrifice its existence on the altar of fidelity to contract when it is compelled to choose between the two. The maxim 'ultra posse nemo obligatur' holds good in spite of all treaty formulas whatsoever, nor can any treaty guarantee the degree of zeal and the amount of force that will be devoted to the discharge of obligations when the private interest of those who lie under them no longer reinforces the text and its earliest interpretation. If, then, changes were to occur in the political situation of Europe of such a kind as to make an anti-German policy appear *salus publica* for Austria-Hungary, public faith could no more be expected to induce her to make an act of self-sacrifice than we saw gratitude do during the Crimean war, though the obligation was perhaps stronger than any can be established by the wax and parchment of a treaty.

An alliance under legislative sanction would have realised the constitutional project which hovered before the minds of the most moderate members of the assembly of the Paulskirche, both those who stood for the narrower Imperial-German and those who represented the wider Austro-German confederation; but the very reduction of such a scheme to contractual form would militate against the durability of its mutual obligations. The example of Austria between 1850 and 1866 was a warning to me that the political changes which such arrangements essay to control outrun the credits which independent states can assure to one another in the course of their political transactions. I think, therefore, that to ensure the durability of a written treaty it is indispensable that the variable element of political interest, and the perils involved therein, should not be left out of account. The German alliance is the best calculated to secure for Austria a peaceful and conservative policy. . . .

We must and can honourably maintain the alliance with the Austro-Hungarian monarchy; it corresponds to our interests, to the historical traditions of Germany, to the public opinion of our people. The influences and forces under and amid which the future policy of Vienna must be shaped are, however, more complex than with us, by reason of the manifold diversity of the nationalities the divergence of their aspirations and activities, the influence of the clergy, and the temptations to which the Danubian countries are exposed in the Balkan and Black Sea latitudes.

We cannot abandon Austria, but neither can we lose sight of the possibility that the policy of Vienna may willy-nilly abandon us. The possibilities which in such a case remain open to us must be clearly realised and steadily borne in mind by German statesmen before the critical moment arrives, nor must their action be determined by prejudice or misunderstanding, but by an entirely dispassionate weighing of the national interests. . . .

International policy is a fluid element which under certain conditions will solidify, but on a change of atmosphere reverts to its original diffuse condition. The clause *rebus sic stantibus* is tacitly understood in all treaties that involve performance. The Triple Alliance is a strategic position, which in the face of the perils that were imminent at the time when it was concluded was politic, and, under the prevailing conditions, feasible. It has been from time to time prolonged, and may be yet further prolonged, but eternal duration is assured to no treaty between Great Powers; and it would be unwise to regard it as affording a permanently stable guarantee against all the possible contingencies which in the future may modify the political, material, and moral conditions under which it was brought into being. It has the significance of a strategic position adopted after strict scrutiny of the political situation of Europe at the time when it was concluded, but it no more constitutes a foundation capable of offering perennial resistance to time and change than did many another alliance (triple or quadruple) of recent centuries, and in particular the Holy Alliance and the German Confederation. It does not dispense us from the attitude of *toujours en vedette*.

1. How would Bismarck's view of nation-building compare with that of Mazzini?
2. "For Bismarck, alliances were a product of the time and circumstance under which they were concluded. No nation should ever remain committed to an alliance against its own national interests." React to this statement with reference to the impact of the commitments of the Triple Alliance on German foreign policy in 1914.

▪ ▪ ▪

PIUS IX

The term of office of Pope Pius IX (reigned 1846-78) was among the most important for the Roman Catholic Church in modern times. In an era of nationalism and secularism, Pius IX came to see himself as a defender of tradition and orthodoxy. Though he began as a moderate liberal, the events of the revolutions of 1848 turned him into a dogmatist and an ultramontane, one who believed in a church which was centralized under the authority of the institution of the Papacy. Pius IX believed that the Catholic Church was endangered by modern trends, and he rejected them all in a position of non-compromise. Pope during the Italian *Risorgimento*, Pius witnessed the decline of his secular authority while he tried to buttress the spiritual authority of the Papacy.

 In 1864 Pius IX issued *The Syllabus of Errors*, a document which challenged virtually the whole intellectual and political development of the West since the end of the middle ages.

> [It is an error] that there exists no Divine Power, Supreme Being, Wisdom and Providence, distinct from the Universe. . . . That the prophecies and miracles narrated in Holy Scripture are the fictions of poets. . . .

> . . . [It is an error] that the Church ought to tolerate the errors of philosophy; leaving to philosophy the care of their correction. That the decrees of the Apostolic See and of the Roman Congregations fetter the free progress of science. That the method and principles, by which the old scholastic Doctors cultivated Theology, are no longer suitable to the demands of the age. . . .

> [It is an error] that every man is free to embrace and profess the religion he shall believe true, guided by the light of reason. . . . That the eternal salvation may (at least) be hoped for, of all those who are not at all in the true Church of Christ. That Protestantism is nothing more than another form of the same true Christian religion; in which it is possible to please God equally as in the Catholic Church. . . .

> [It is an error] that the Roman Pontiffs and Oecumenical Councils have exceeded the limits of their power, have usurped the rights of princes, and have even committed errors in defining matters of faith and morals. That the Church has not the power of availing herself of force, or of any direct or indirect temporal power. . . . That ecclesiastical jurisdiction for the temporal causes—whether civil or criminal—of the clergy, ought by all means to be abolished. . . . That National Churches can be established, after being withdrawn and separated from the authority of the holy Pontiff. That many Pontiffs have, by their arbitrary conduct, contributed to the division of the Church into Eastern and Western.

> . . . [It is an error] that the civil government—even when exercised by an infidel sovereign—possesses an indirect and negative power over religious

Source: Henry Bettenson, editor, *Documents of the Christian Church* (Oxford: Oxford University Press, 1963), pp. 382-84, 384-85.

affairs; and possesses, not only the right called that of *exequatur*, but also that of the (so-called) *appellatio ab abusu*. . . . That the best theory of civil society requires that popular schools, open to the children of all classes, should be freed from all ecclesiastical authority. . . . That the Church ought to be separated from the State, and the State from the Church.

. . . [It is an error] that knowledge of philosophical matters, and of morals, and civil laws, may be and should be independent of Divine and ecclesiastical authority. . . . That it is allowable to refuse obedience to legitimate princes; nay more, to rise in insurrection against them. . . .

. . . [It is an error] that the abrogation of the temporal power of which the Apostolic See is possessed, would be the greatest contribution to the liberty and prosperity of the Church. . . .

[It is an error] that in the present day, it is no longer necessary that the Catholic religion be held as the only religion of the State, to the exclusion of all other modes of worship: whence it has been wisely provided by the law, in some countries nominally Catholic, that persons coming to reside therein shall enjoy the free exercise of their own worship. . . . That the Roman Pontiff can, and ought to, reconcile himself to, and agree with, progress, liberalism, and modern civilization.

B Pius IX called the First Vatican Council in 1869. It was the first Council of the Roman Catholic Church to meet since the Council of Trent was called in 1545 to respond to the challenge of the Reformation. In 1870, the Council proclaimed the new dogma of papal infallibility.

. . . We [i.e. Pope Pius IX], adhering faithfully to the tradition received from the beginning of the Christian faith—with a view to the glory of our Divine Saviour, the exaltation of the Catholic religion, and the safety of Christian peoples (the sacred Council approving), teach and define as a dogma divinely revealed: That the Roman Pontiff, when he speaks *ex cathedra* (that is, when—fulfilling the office of Pastor and Teacher of all Christians—on his supreme Apostolical authority, he defines a doctrine concerning faith or morals to be held by the Universal Church), through the divine assistance promised him in blessed Peter, is endowed with that infallibility, with which the Divine Redeemer has willed that His Church—in defining doctrine concerning faith or morals—should be equipped: And therefore, that such definitions of the Roman Pontiff of themselves—and not by virtue of the consent of the Church—are irreformable. If any one shall presume (which God forbid!) to contradict this our definition; let him be anathema.

1. Pius IX states that it is an error to think "that the Roman Pontiff can, and ought to, reconcile himself to, and agree with, progress, liberalism, and modern civilization." Analyse the reasons behind the Roman Catholic Church issuing such a statement in the late nineteenth century.
2. In what way was the dogma of papal infallibility the final defence to the challenge first raised by Galileo?

• • •

THOMAS MALTHUS

While Thomas Malthus (1766-1834) wrote his most influential work *An Essay on the Principle of Population* in 1798, its influence was felt most in the middle of the nineteenth century. Charles Darwin wrote in his *Autobiography* that upon reading "Malthus on *Population* [in 1838] . . . , it at once struck me that under [certain] circumstances favourable variations would tend to be preserved, and unfavourable ones to be destroyed. The result of this would be the formation of new species. Here, then, I had at last got a theory by which to work . . . "

A Malthus' theory was a formula that was important in considering social progress as well as evolution.

. . . I think I may fairly make two postulata.

First, That food is necessary to the existence of man.

Secondly, That the passion between the sexes is necessary and will remain nearly in its present state.

These two laws, ever since we have had any knowledge of mankind, appear to have been fixed laws of our nature, and, as we have not hitherto seen any alteration in them, we have no right to conclude that they will ever cease to be what they now are, without an immediate act of power in that Being who first arranged the system of the universe, and for the advantage of his creatures, still executes, according to fixed laws, all its various operations.

I do not know that any writer has supposed that on this earth man will ultimately be able to live without food. But Mr. Godwin has conjectured that the passion between the sexes may in time be extinguished. As, however, he calls this part of his work a deviation into the land of conjecture, I will not dwell longer upon it at present than to say that the best arguments for the perfectibility of man are drawn from a contemplation of the great progress that he has already made from the savage state and the difficulty of saying where he is to stop. But towards the extinction of the passion between the sexes, no progress whatever has hitherto been made. It appears to exist in as much force at present as it did two thousand or four thousand years ago. There are individual exceptions now as there always have been. But, as these exceptions do not appear to increase in number, it would surely be a very unphilosophical mode of arguing, to infer merely from the existence of an exception, that the exception would, in time, become the rule, and the rule the exception.

Assuming then, my postulata as granted, I say that the power of population is indefinitely greater than the power in the earth to produce subsistence for man.

Population, when unchecked, increases in a geometrical ratio. Subsistence increases only in an arithmetical ratio. A slight acquaintance with numbers will shew the immensity of the first power in comparison of the second.

Source: Thomas Robert Malthus, *An Essay on the Principle of Population*, edited by Philip Appleman (New York: W.W. Norton and Company, 1976), pp. 19-21, 60-61.

By that law of our nature which makes food necessary to the life of man, the effects of these two unequal powers must be kept equal.

This implies a strong and constantly operating check on population from the difficulty of subsistence. This difficulty must fall some where and must necessarily be severely felt by a large portion of mankind.

Through the animal and vegetable kingdoms, nature has scattered the seeds of life abroad with the most profuse and liberal hand. She has been comparatively sparing in the room and the nourishment necessary to rear them. The germs of existence contained in this spot of earth, with ample food and ample room to expand in, would fill millions of worlds in the course of a few thousand years. Necessity, that imperious all pervading law of nature, restrains them within the prescribed bounds. The race of plants and the race of animals shrink under this great restrictive law. And the race of man cannot, by any efforts of reason, escape from it. Among plants and animals its effects are waste of seed, sickness, and premature death. Among mankind, misery and vice. The former, misery, is an absolutely necessary consequence of it. Vice is a highly probable consequence, and we therefore see it abundantly prevail, but it ought not, perhaps, to be called an absolutely necessary consequence. The ordeal of virtue is to resist all temptation to evil.

This natural inequality of the two powers of population and of production in the earth and that great law of our nature which must constantly keep their effects equal form the great difficulty that to me appears insurmountable in the way to the perfectibility of society. All other arguments are of slight and subordinate consideration in comparison of this. I see no way by which man can escape from the weight of this law which pervades all animated nature. No fancied equality, no agrarian regulations in their utmost extent, could remove the pressure of it even for a single century. And it appears, therefore, to be decisive against the possible existence of a society, all the members of which should live in ease, happiness, and comparative leisure, and feel no anxiety about providing the means of subsistence for themselves and families.

Consequently, if the premises are just, the argument is conclusive against the perfectibility of the mass of mankind. . . .

B Malthus was himself influenced by Condorcet's *Sketch for a Historical Picture of the Progress of the Human Mind.*

The last question which Mr. Condorcet proposes for examination is the organic perfectibility of man. He observes that if the proofs which have been already given and which, in their development, will receive greater force in the work itself, are sufficient to establish the indefinite perfectibility of man upon the supposition of the same natural faculties and the same organization which he has at present, what will be the certainty, what the extent of our hope, if this organization, these natural faculties themselves, are susceptible of amelioration?

From the improvement of medicine, from the use of more wholesome food and habitations, from a manner of living which will improve the strength of the body by exercise without impairing it by excess, from the destruction of the two great causes of the degradation of man, misery and too great riches, from the gradual removal of transmissible and contagious disorders by the improvement of physical knowledge, rendered more efficacious by the progress of reason and of social order, he infers that though man will not absolutely become immortal, yet that the duration between his birth and natural death will increase without ceasing, will have no assignable term, and may properly be expressed by the word indefinite. He then defines this word to mean either a constant approach to an unlimited extent, without ever reaching it, or an increase in the immensity of ages to an extent greater than any assignable quantity.

But surely the application of this term in either of these senses to the duration of human life is in the highest degree unphilosophical and totally unwarranted by any appearances in the laws of nature. Variations from different causes are essentially distinct from a regular and unretrograde increase. The average duration of human life will to a certain degree vary from healthy or unhealthy climates, from wholesome or unwholesome food, from virtuous or vicious manners, and other causes, but it may be fairly doubted whether there is really the smallest perceptible advance in the natural duration of human life since first we have had any authentic history of man. The prejudices of all ages have indeed been directly contrary to this supposition, and though I would not lay much stress upon these prejudices, they will in some measure tend to prove that there has been no marked advance in an opposite direction. . . .

1. Outline Malthus' basic contention with regard to the relationship between the growth of population and food production. Comment on his conclusions concerning the impact of this relationship on the "perfectibility of the mass of mankind."
2. Contrast the apparent optimism of Condorcet with the views expressed by Malthus.

■ ■ ■

Charles Darwin

Charles Darwin (1809-82) was the giant of the natural sciences of the nineteenth century. His work *The Origin of Species by Means of Natural Selection or the Preservation of Favoured Races in the Struggle for Life*, published in 1859, caused an immediate sensation and changed the dialogue about how we think about human nature, nature itself, and biological relations. His concept of evolution and the supporting material he presented to substantiate it have shaped research in the biological sciences for over a century.

 In the first edition of *The Origin of Species* Darwin discussed what he intended to do.

When on board H.M.S. *Beagle*, as naturalist, I was much struck with certain facts in the distribution of the inhabitants of South America, and in the geological relations of the present to the past inhabitants of that continent. These facts seemed to me to throw some light on the origin of species—that mystery of mysteries, as it has been called by one of our greatest philosophers. . . .

In considering the Origin of Species, it is quite conceivable that a naturalist, reflecting on the mutual affinities of organic beings, on their embryological relations, their geographical distribution, geological succession, and other such facts, might come to the conclusion that each species had not been independently created, but had descended, like varieties, from other species. Nevertheless, such a conclusion, even if well founded, would be unsatisfactory, until it could be shown how the innumerable species inhabiting this world have been modified, so as to acquire that perfection of structure and coadaptation which most justly excites our admiration. Naturalists continually refer to external conditions, such as climate, food &c., as the only possible cause of variation. In one very limited sense, as we shall hereafter see, this may be true; but it is preposterous to attribute to mere external conditions, the structure, for instance, of the woodpecker, with its feet, tail, beak, and tongue, so admirably adapted to catch insects under the bark of trees. In the case of the misseltoe, which draws its nourishment from certain trees, which has seeds that must be transported by certain birds, and which has flowers with separate sexes absolutely requiring the agency of certain insects to bring pollen from one flower to the other, it is equally preposterous to account for the structure of this parasite, with its relations to several distinct organic beings, by the effects of external conditions, or of habit, or of the volition of the plant itself. . . .

It is, therefore, of the highest importance to gain a clear insight into the means of modification and coadaptation. At the commencement of my observations it seemed to me probable that a careful study of domesticated animals and of cultivated plants would offer the best chance of making out this obscure problem. Nor have I been disappointed; in this and in all other perplexing cases I have invariably found that our knowledge, imperfect though it be, of variation under domestication, afforded the best and safest clue. I may venture to express my conviction of the high value of such studies, although they have been very commonly neglected by naturalists.

From these considerations, I shall devote the first chapter of this Abstract to Variation under Domestication. We shall thus see that a large amount of hereditary modification is at least possible; and, what is equally or more important, we shall see how great is the power of man in accumulating by his Selection successive slight variations. I will then pass on to the variability of species in a state of nature; but I shall, unfortunately, be compelled to treat this subject far too briefly, as it can be treated properly only by giving long catalogues of facts. We shall, however, be enabled to discuss what circumstances are most favourable to variation. In the next chapter the Struggle for

Source: Charles Darwin, *The Origin of Species*, edited by J.W. Burrow (Harmondsworth: Penguin Books, 1968), pp. 65, 66-69, 116-17, 119, 169-70, 455, 456, 458-60; *Darwin*, edited by Philip Appleman (New York: W.W. Norton and Company, 1970), pp. 264-65, 275-76.

Existence amongst all organic beings throughout the world, which inevitably follows from their high geometrical powers of increase, will be treated of. This is the doctrine of Malthus, applied to the whole animal and vegetable kingdoms. As many more individuals of each species are born than can possibly survive; and as, consequently, there is a frequently recurring struggle for existence, it follows that any being, if it vary however slightly in any manner profitable to itself, under the complex and sometimes varying conditions of life, will have a better chance of surviving, and thus be *naturally selected*. From the strong principle of inheritance, any selected variety will tend to propagate its new and modified form.

This fundamental subject of Natural Selection will be treated at some length in the fourth chapter; and we shall then see how Natural Selection almost inevitably causes much Extinction of the less improved forms of life, and induces what I have called Divergence of Character. In the next chapter I shall discuss the complex and little known laws of variation and of correlation of growth. . . .

No one ought to feel surprise at much remaining as yet unexplained in regard to the origin of species and varieties, if he makes due allowance for our profound ignorance in regard to the mutual relations of all the beings which live around us. Who can explain why one species ranges widely and is very numerous, and why another allied species has a narrow range and is rare? Yet these relations are of the highest importance, for they determine the present welfare, and, as I believe, the future success and modification of every inhabitant of this world. Still less do we know of the mutual relations of the innumerable inhabitants of the world during the many past geological epochs in its history. Although much remains obscure, and will long remain obscure, I can entertain no doubt, after the most deliberate study and dispassionate judgement of which I am capable, that the view which most naturalists entertain, and which I formerly entertained—namely, that each species has been independently created—is erroneous. I am fully convinced that species are not immutable; but that those belonging to what are called the same genera are lineal descendants of some other and generally extinct species, in the same manner as the acknowledged varieties of any one species are the descendants of that species. Furthermore, I am convinced that Natural Selection has been the main but not exclusive means of modification.

B Darwin's discussion on the struggle for existence was among his most controversial sections.

A struggle for existence inevitably follows from the high rate at which all organic beings tend to increase. Every being, which during its natural lifetime produces several eggs or seeds, must suffer destruction during some period of its life, and during some season or occasional year, otherwise, on the principle of geometrical increase, its numbers would quickly become so inordinately great that no country could support the product. Hence, as more individuals are produced than can possibly survive, there must in every case be a struggle for existence, either one individual with another of the same species, or with the individuals of distinct species, or with the physical conditions of life. It is the doctrine of Malthus applied with manifold force to the whole animal and vegetable kingdoms; for in this case there can be no artificial increase of food, and no prudential restraint from marriage. Although some species may be now increasing, more or less rapidly, in numbers, all cannot do so, for the world would not hold them.

There is no exception to the rule that every organic being naturally increases at so high a rate, that if not destroyed, the earth would soon be covered by the progeny of a single pair. Even slow-breeding man has doubled in twenty-five years, and at this rate, in a few thousand years, there would literally not be standing room for his progeny. . . .

In looking at Nature, it is most necessary to keep the foregoing considerations always in mind—never to forget that every single organic being around us may be said to be striving to the utmost to increase in numbers; that each lives by a struggle at some period of its life; that heavy destruction inevitably falls either on the young or old, during each generation or at recurrent intervals. Lighten any check, mitigate the destruction ever so little, and the number of the species will almost instantaneously increase to any amount. The face of Nature may be compared to a yielding surface, with ten thousand sharp wedges packed close together and driven inwards by incessant blows, sometimes one wedge being struck, and then another with greater force. . . .

 Natural selection came to be a term used in many areas, and unsettled many in its assumption that nature is not always benign.

If during the long course of ages and under varying conditions of life, organic beings vary at all in the several parts of their organisation, and I think this cannot be disputed; if there be, owing to the high geometrical powers of increase of each species, at some age, season, or year, a severe struggle for life, and this certainly cannot be disputed; then, considering the infinite complexity of the relations of all organic beings to each other and to their conditions of existence, causing an infinite diversity in structure, constitution, and habits, to be advantageous to them, I think it would be a most extraordinary fact if no variation ever had occurred useful to each being's own welfare, in the same way as so many variations have occurred useful to man. But if variations useful to any organic being do occur, assuredly individuals thus characterised will have the best chance of being preserved in the struggle for life; and from the strong principle of inheritance they will tend to produce offspring similarly characterised. This principle of preservation, I have called, for the sake of brevity, Natural Selection. Natural selection, on the principle of qualities being inherited at corresponding ages, can modify the egg, seed, or young, as easily as the adult. Amongst many animals, sexual selection will give its aid to ordinary selection, by assuring to the most vigorous and best adapted males the greatest number of offspring. Sexual selection will also give characters useful to the males alone, in their struggles with other males.

Whether natural selection has really thus acted in nature, in modifying and adapting the various forms of life to their several conditions and stations, must be judged of by the general tenour and balance of evidence given in the following chapters. But we already see how it entails extinction; and how largely extinction has acted in the world's history, geology plainly declares. Natural selection, also, leads to divergence of character; for more living beings can be supported on the same area the more they diverge in structure, habits, and constitution, of which we see proof by looking at the inhabitants of any small spot or at naturalised productions. Therefore during the modification of the descendants of any one species, and during the incessant struggle of all species to increase in numbers, the more diversified these descendants become, the better will be their chance of succeeding in the battle of life. Thus the small differences distinguishing varieties of the same species, will steadily tend to increase till they come to equal the greater differences between species of the same genus, or even of distinct genera. . . .

 Darwin knew that he was changing things, that he was making a "revolution."

When the views entertained in this volume on the origin of species, or when analogous views are generally admitted, we can dimly foresee that there will be a considerable revolution in natural history. . . .

A grand and almost untrodden field of inquiry will be opened, on the causes and laws of variation, on correlation of growth, on the effects of use and disuse, on the direct action of external conditions, and so forth. . . .

In the distant future I see open fields for far more important researches. Psychology will be based on a new foundation, that of the necessary acquirement of each mental power and capacity by gradation. Light will be thrown on the origin of man and his history.

Authors of the highest eminence seem to be fully satisfied with the view that each species has been independently created. To my mind it accords better with what we know of the laws impressed on matter by the Creator, that the production and extinction of the past and present inhabitants of the world should have been due to secondary causes, like those determining the birth and death of the individual. When I view all beings not as special creations, but as the lineal descendants of some few beings which lived long before the first bed of the Silurian system was deposited, they seem to me to become ennobled. Judging from the past, we may safely infer that not one living species will transmit its unaltered likeness to a distant futurity. And of the species now living very few will transmit progeny of any kind to a far distant futurity; for the manner in which all organic beings are grouped, shows that the greater number of species of each genus, and all the species of many genera, have left no descendants, but have become utterly extinct. We can so far take a prophetic glance into futurity as to fortell that it will be the common and widely-spread species, belonging to the larger and dominant groups, which will ultimately prevail and procreate new and dominant species. As all the living forms of life are the lineal descendants of those which lived long before the Silurian epoch, we may feel certain that the ordinary succession by generation has never once been broken, and that no cataclysm has desolated the whole world. Hence we may look with some confidence to a secure future of equally inappreciable length. And as natural selection works solely by and for the good of each being, all corporeal and mental endowments will tend to progress towards perfection.

It is interesting to contemplate an entangled bank, clothed with many plants of many kinds, with birds singing on the bushes, with various insects flitting about, and with worms crawling through the damp earth, and to reflect that these elaborately constructed forms, so different from each other, and dependent on each other in so complex a manner, have all been produced by laws acting around us. These laws, taken in the largest sense, being Growth with Reproduction; Inheritance which is almost implied by reproduction; Variability from the indirect and direct action of the external conditions of life, and from use and disuse; a Ratio of Increase so high as to lead to a Struggle for Life, and as a consequence to Natural Selection, entailing Divergence of Character and the Extinction of less-improved forms. Thus, from the war of nature, from famine and death, the most exalted object which we are capable of conceiving, namely, the production of the higher animals, directly follows. There is grandeur in this view of life, with its several powers, having been originally breathed into a few forms or into one; and that, whilst this planet has gone cycling on according to the fixed law of gravity, from so simple a beginning endless forms most beautiful and most wonderful have been, and are being, evolved.

⬦E⬦ While Darwin tried to steer clear of controversy surrounding theology and social systems, he followed *The Origin of Species* with another massive and important work in 1871, *The Descent of Man*. Here he speculated on human nature.

. . . The main conclusion here arrived at, and now held by many naturalists who are well competent to form a sound judgment, is that man is descended from some less highly organised form. The grounds upon which this conclusion rests will never be shaken, for the close similarity between man and the lower animals in embryonic development, as well as in innumerable points of structure and constitution, both of high and of the most trifling importance,—the rudiments which he retains, and the abnormal reversions to which he is occasionally liable,—are facts which cannot be disputed. They have long been known, but until recently they told us nothing with respect to the origin of man. Now when viewed by the light of our knowledge of the whole organic world, their meaning is unmistakable. The great principle of evolution stands up clear and firm, when these groups or facts are considered in connection with others, such as the mutual affinities of the members of the same group, their geographical distribution in past and present times, and their geological succession. It is incredible that all these facts should speak falsely. He who is not content to look, like a savage, at the phenomena of nature as disconnected, cannot any longer believe that man is the work of a separate act of creation. He will be forced to admit that the close resemblance of the embryo of man to that, for instance of a dog—the construction of his skull, limbs and whole frame on the same plan with that of other mammals, independently of the uses to which the parts may be put—the occasional re-appearance of various structures, for instance of several muscles, which man does not normally possess, but which are common to the Quadrumana—and a crowd of analogous facts—all point in the plainest manner to the conclusion that man is the co-descendant with other mammals of a common progenitor. . . .

The belief in God has often been advanced as not only the greatest, but the most complete of all the distinctions between man and the lower animals. It is however impossible, as we have seen, to maintain that this belief is innate or instinctive in man. On the other hand a belief in all-pervading spiritual agencies seems to be universal; and apparently follows from a considerable advance in man's reason, and from a still greater advance in his faculties of imagination, curiosity and wonder. I am aware that the assumed instinctive belief in God has been used by many persons as an argument for His existence. But this is a rash argument, as we should thus be compelled to believe in the existence of many cruel and malignant spirits, only a little more powerful than man; for the belief in them is far more general than in a beneficent Deity. The idea of a universal and beneficent Creator does not seem to arise in the mind of man, until he has been elevated by long-continued culture. . . .

I am aware that the conclusions arrived at in this work will be denounced by some as highly irreligious; but he who denounces them is bound to shew why it is more irreligious to explain the origin of man as a distinct species by descent from some lower form, through the laws of variation and natural selection, than to explain the birth of the individual through the laws of ordinary reproduction. The birth both of the species and of the individual are equally parts of that grand sequence of events, which our minds refuse to accept as the result of blind chance. The understanding revolts at such a conclusion, whether or not we are able to believe that every slight variation of structure,—the union of each pair in marriage,—the dissemination of each seed,—and other such events, have all been ordained for some special purpose. . . .

The advancement of the welfare of mankind is a most intricate problem: all ought to refrain from marriage who cannot avoid abject poverty for their children; for poverty is not only a great evil, but tends to its own increase by leading to recklessness in marriage. On the other hand, as Mr. Galton has remarked, if the prudent avoid marriage, whilst the reckless marry, the inferior members tend to supplant the better members of society. Man, like every other animal, has no doubt advanced to his present high condition through a struggle for existence consequent on his rapid multiplication; and if he is to advance still higher, it is to be feared that he must remain subject to a severe struggle. Otherwise he would sink into indolence, and the more gifted men would not be more successful in the battle of life than the less gifted. Hence our natural rate of increase, though leading to many and obvious evils, must not be greatly diminished by any means. There should be open competition for all men; and the most able should not be prevented by laws or customs from succeeding best and rearing the largest number of offspring. Important as the struggle for existence has been and even still is, yet as far as the highest part of man's nature is concerned there are other agencies more important. For the moral qualities are advanced, either directly or indirectly, much more through the effects of habit, the reasoning powers, instruction, religion, &c., than through natural selection; though to this latter agency may be safely attributed the social instincts, which afforded the basis for the development of moral sense.

The main conclusion arrived at in this work, namely, that man is descended from some lowly organised form, will, I regret to think, be highly distasteful to many. But there can hardly be a doubt that we are descended from barbarians. The astonishment which I felt on first seeing a party of Fuegians on a wild and broken shore will never be forgotten by me, for the reflection at once rushed into my mind—such were our ancestors. These men were absolutely naked and bedaubed with paint, their long hair was tangled, their mouths, frothed with excitement, and their expression was wild, startled, and distrustful. They possessed hardly any arts, and like wild animals lived on what they could catch; they had no government, and were merciless to every one not of their own small tribe. He who has seen a savage in his native land will not feel much shame, if forced to acknowledge that the blood of some more humble creature flows in his veins. For my own part I would as soon be descended from that heroic little monkey, who braved his dreaded enemy in order to save the life of his keeper, or from that old baboon, who descending from the mountains, carried away in triumph his young comrade from a crowd of astonished dogs—as from a savage who delights to torture his enemies, offers up bloody sacrifices, practises infanticide without remorse, treats his wives like slaves, knows no decency, and is haunted by the grossest superstitions.

Man may be excused for feeling some pride at having risen, though not through his own exertions, to the very summit of the organic scale; and the fact of his having thus risen, instead of having been aboriginally placed there, may give him hope for a still higher destiny in the distant future. But we are not here concerned with hopes or fears, only with the truth as far as our reason permits us to discover it; and I have given the evidence to the best of my ability. We must, however, acknowledge, as it seems to me, that man with all his noble qualities, with sympathy which feels for the most debased, with benevolence which extends not only to other men but to the humblest living creature, with his god-like intellect which has penetrated into the movements and constitution of the solar system—with all these exalted powers—Man still bears in his bodily frame the indelible stamp of his lowly origin.

1. Based on his summary in reading (a), comment on the process by which Darwin reached his conclusions.
2. Explain Darwin's "struggle for existence" in terms of Malthus' theories of population growth.
3. "In the final analysis survival in the process of natural selection depends more on cooperation than on competition." Discuss this statement with regard to Darwin's view of the impact of natural selection on the development of species.
4. In spite of Darwin's assertion that "not one living species will transmit its unaltered likeness to a distant futurity," many people in the nineteenth century used his theories as a basis for racism. Using the arguments put forward by Darwin, refute this use of his ideas to support racial superiority.
5. Account for Darwin's contention that it is no more irreligious to believe in natural selection than it is to believe in human reproduction.

▪ ▪ ▪

HERBERT SPENCER

Herbert Spencer (1820-1903) did much to popularize the concept of evolution and Darwinian ideas. Yet, he is important in his own right as one of the great synthesizers of the nineteenth century. He believed in science, evolution, and progress; and he made contributions to fields as diverse as history, biology, sociology, and anthropology. Influenced by Comte as well as Darwin, Spencer became an important figure in Europe in the decades of the 1860s and 1870s and, even when his reputation waned there, he was influential in the United States through the rest of the century.

 Spencer developed his concept of evolution in society prior to Darwin's publication of *The Origin of Species* in 1859. He has some claim to originality. In 1857 Spencer wrote about progress.

> Now, we propose in the first place to show, that this law of organic progress is the law of all progress. Whether it be in the development of the Earth, in the development of Life upon its surface, in the development of Society, of Government, of Manufactures, of Commerce, of Language, Literature, Science, Art, this same evolution of the simple into the complex, through successive differentiations, holds throughout. From the earliest traceable cosmical changes down to the latest results of civilization, we shall find that the transformation of the homogeneous into the heterogeneous, is that in which Progress essentially consists. . . .
>
> Whether an advance from the homogeneous to the heterogeneous is or is not displayed in the biological history of the globe, it is clearly enough displayed in the progress of the latest and most heterogeneous creature—Man. It is alike true that, during the period in which the Earth has been peopled, the human organism has grown more heterogeneous among the civilized divisions of the species; and that the species, as a whole, has been growing more heterogeneous in virtue of the multiplication of races and the differentiation of these races from each other. . . .
>
> Observe, now, however, a further consequence. There must arise not simply a tendency towards the differentiation of each race of organisms into several races; but also a tendency to the occasional production of a somewhat higher organism. Taken in the mass these divergent varieties which have been caused by fresh physical conditions and habits of life, will exhibit changes quite indefinite in kind and degree; and changes that do not necessarily constitute an advance. Probably in most cases the modified type will be neither more nor less heterogeneous than the original one. In some cases the habits of life adopted being simpler than before, a less heterogeneous structure will result: there will be a retrogradation. But it *must* now and then occur, that some division of a species, falling into circumstances which give it rather more

Sources: Herbert Spencer, *On Social Evolution: Selected Writings*, edited by J.D.Y. Peel (Chicago: University of Chicago Press, 1972), pp. 40, 48-49, 52; Herbert Spencer, *Essays on Education* (London: J.M. Dent and Sons, 1911), pp. 42-44.

complex experiences, and demand actions somewhat more involved, will have certain of its organs further differentiated in proportionately small degrees,—will become slightly more heterogeneous.

Thus, in the natural course of things, there will from time to time arise an increased heterogeneity both of the Earth's flora and fauna, and of individual races included in them. Omitting detailed explanations, and allowing for the qualifications which cannot here be specified, we think it is clear that geological mutations have all along tended to complicate the forms of life, whether regarded separately or collectively. The same causes which have led to the evolution of the Earth's crust from the simple into the complex, have simultaneously led to a parallel evolution of the Life upon its surface. In this case, as in previous ones, we see that the transformation of the homogeneous into the heterogeneous is consequent upon the universal principle, that every active force produces more than one change. . . .

If the advance of Man towards greater heterogeneity is traceable to the production of many effects by one cause, still more clearly may the advance of Society towards greater heterogeneity be so explained. Consider the growth of an industrial organization. When, as must occasionally happen, some individual of a tribe displays unusual aptitude for making an article of general use—a weapon, for instance—which was before made by each man for himself, there arises a tendency towards the differentiation of that individual into a maker of such weapons. His companions—warriors and hunters all of them,— severally feel the importance of having the best weapons that can be made; and are therefore certain to offer strong inducements to this skilled individual to make weapons for them. He, on the other hand, having not only an unusual faculty, but an unusual liking, for making such weapons (the talent and the desire for any occupation being commonly associated), is predisposed to fulfil these commissions on the offer of an adequate reward: especially as his love of distinction is also gratified. This first specialization of function, once commenced, tends ever to become more decided. . . .

. . . It will be seen that as in each event of to-day, so from the beginning, the decomposition of every expended force into several forces has been perpetually producing a higher complication; that the increase of heterogeneity so brought about is still going on, and must continue to go on; and that thus Progress is not an accident, not a thing within human control, but a beneficent necessity.

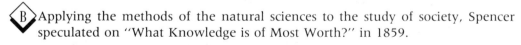

B Applying the methods of the natural sciences to the study of society, Spencer speculated on "What Knowledge is of Most Worth?" in 1859.

We conclude, then, that for discipline, as well as for guidance, science is of chiefest value. In all its effects, learning the meanings of things, is better than learning the meanings of words. Whether for intellectual, moral, or religious training, the study of surrounding phenomena is immensely superior to the study of grammars and lexicons.

Thus to the question we set out with—What knowledge is of most worth?— the uniform reply is—Science. This is the verdict on all the counts. For direct self-preservation, or the maintenance of life and health, the all-important knowledge is—Science. For that indirect self-preservation which we call gaining a livelihood, the knowledge of greatest value is—Science. For the due discharge of parental functions, the proper guidance is to be found only in—Science. For that interpretation of national life, past and present, without which the citizen cannot rightly regulate his conduct, the indispensable key is—Science. Alike for the most perfect production and highest enjoyment of art in all its forms, the needful preparation is still—Science. And for purposes of discipline—intellectual, moral, religious—the most efficient study is, once more—Science. The question which at first seemed so perplexed, has become, in the course of our inquiry, comparatively simple. We have not to estimate the degrees of importance of different orders of human activity, and different studies as severally fitting us for them; since we find that the study of Science, in its most comprehensive meaning, is the best preparation for all these orders of activity. We have not to decide between the claims of knowledge of great though conventional value, and knowledge of less though intrinsic value; seeing that the knowledge which proves to be of most value in all other respects, is intrinsically most valuable: its worth is not dependent upon opinion, but is as fixed as is the relation of man to the surrounding world. Necessary and eternal as are its truths, all Science concerns all mankind for all time. Equally at present and in the remotest future, must it be of incalculable importance for the regulation of their conduct, that men should understand the science of life, physical, mental, and social; and that they should understand all other science as a key to the science of life.

And yet this study, immensely transcending all other in importance, is that which, in an age of boasted education, receives the least attention. While what we call civilisation could never have arisen had it not been for science, science forms scarcely an appreciable element in our so-called civilised training. Though to the progress of science we owe it, that millions find support where once there was food only for thousands; yet of these millions but a few thousands pay any respect to that which has made their existence possible. Though increasing knowledge of the properties and relations of things has not only enabled wandering tribes to grow into populous nations, but has given to the countless members of these populous nations, comforts and pleasures which their few naked ancestors never even conceived, or could have believed, yet is this kind of knowledge only now receiving a grudging recognition in our highest educational institutions. To the slowly growing acquaintance with the uniform co-existences and sequences of phenomena—to the establishment of invariable laws, we owe our emancipation from the grossest superstitions. But for science we should be still worshipping fetishes; or, with hecatombs of victims, propitiating diabolical deities. And yet this science, which, in place of the most degrading conceptions of things, has given us some insight into the grandeurs of creation, is written against in our theologies and frowned upon from our pulpits.

Paraphrasing an Eastern fable, we may say that in the family of knowledges, Science is the household drudge, who, in obscurity, hides unrecognised perfections. To her has been committed all the works; by her skill, intelligence, and devotion, have all conveniences and gratifications been obtained; and while ceaselessly ministering to the rest, she has been kept in the background, that her haughty sisters might flaunt their fripperies in the eyes of the world. The parallel holds yet further. For we are fast coming to the *dénouement*, when the positions will be changed; and while these haughty sisters sink into merited neglect, Science, proclaimed as highest alike in worth and beauty, will reign supreme.

1. "For Spencer the differentiation and specialization of Darwin's theories of natural adaptation, were nowhere more evident than in the progress of humanity." Account for this statement in terms of Spencer's explanation of the heterogeneous development of human society.
2. Summarize Spencer's arguments in support of his thesis that the study of science should be the prime focus of education. Do you agree?

▪ ▪ ▪

GUSTAVE FLAUBERT

Many critics believe the "modern" novel was created by the Frenchman Gustave Flaubert (1821-80), and that the most influential work of fiction of the nineteenth century is Flaubert's *Madame Bovary*. In his style Flaubert often was a "realist," one who tries to describe things with great accuracy; yet he used metaphor and allusion, and his writing incorporates the voice of the narrator. Flaubert's novel created a scandal when it was published in 1857, partly because of its frank statements about human emotion and sensuality, and in part because it challenged many of the public beliefs of middle-class society.

Flaubert's main character was Emma Bovary, a country girl who married a doctor as a way of realizing her dreams about love and romance. Flaubert described the young Emma and the contrast between her ideals and the life she led.

> . . . At the convent there was an old spinster who came for a week every month to look after the linen. As a member of an ancient noble family ruined by the Revolution she was a protégée of the archdiocese; and she ate at the nuns' table in the refectory and always stayed for a chat with them before returning upstairs to her work. The girls often slipped out of study-hall to pay her a visit. She had a repertoire of eighteenth-century love songs, and sang them in a low voice as she sewed. She told stories, kept the girls abreast of the news, did errands for them in the city, and to the older ones would surreptitiously lend one of the novels she always carried in her apron pocket— novels of which the good spinster herself was accustomed to devour long

Source: Gustave Flaubert, *Madame Bovary*, trans. Francis Steegmuller (New York: The Modern Library, 1957), pp. 41-45, 88-89, 368-70.

chapters in the intervals of her task. They were invariably about love affairs, lovers, mistresses, harassed ladies swooning in remote pavilions. Couriers were killed at every relay, horses ridden to death on every page; there were gloomy forests, broken hearts, vows, sobs, tears and kisses, skiffs in the moonlight, nightingales in thickets; the noblemen were all brave as lions, gentle as lambs, incredibly virtuous, always beautifully dressed, and wept copiously on every occasion. For six months, when she was fifteen, Emma begrimed her hands with this dust from old lending libraries. Later, reading Walter Scott, she became infatuated with everything historical and dreamed about oaken chests and guardrooms and troubadours. She would have liked to live in some old manor, like those long-waisted chatelaines who spent their days leaning out of fretted Gothic casements, elbow on parapet and chin in hand, watching a white-plumed knight come galloping out of the distance on a black horse. At that time she worshipped Mary Queen of Scots, and venerated women illustrious or ill-starred. In her mind Joan of Arc, Héloïse, Agnès Sorel, La Belle Ferronière and Clémence Isaure stood out like comets on the shadowy immensity of history; and here and there (though less clearly outlined than the others against the dim background, and quite unrelated among themselves) were visible also St. Louis and his oak, the dying Bayard, certain atrocities of Louis XI, bits of the Massacre of St. Bartholomew, the plumed crest of Henri IV, and, always, the memory of the hotel plates glorifying Louis XIV.

The sentimental songs she sang in music class were all about little angels with golden wings, madonnas, lagoons, gondoliers—mawkish compositions that allowed her to glimpse, through the silliness of the words and the indiscretions of the music, the alluring, phantasmagoric realm of genuine feeling. Some of her schoolmates brought to the convent the keepsake albums they had received as New Year's gifts. They had to hide them—it was very exciting; they could be read only at night, in the dormitory. Careful not to harm the lovely satin bindings, Emma stared bedazzled at the names of the unknown authors—counts or viscounts, most of them—who had written their signatures under their contributions.

She quivered as she blew back the tissue paper from each engraving: it would curl up into the air, then sink gently down against the page. Behind a balcony railing a young man in a short cloak clasped in his arms a girl in a white dress, a chatelaine bag fastened to her belt; or there were portraits of unidentified aristocratic English beauties with blond curls, staring out at you with their wide light-colored eyes from under great straw hats. Some were shown lolling in carriages, gliding through parks; their greyhound ran ahead, and two little grooms in white knee breeches drove the trotting horses. Others, dreaming on sofas, an opened letter lying beside them, gazed at the moon through a window that was half open, half draped with a black curtain. Coy maidens with tears on their cheeks kissed turtledoves through the bars of Gothic bird cages; or, smiling, their cheeks practically touching their own shoulders, they pulled the petals from daisies with pointed fingers that curved up at the ends like Eastern slippers. Then there were sultans with long pipes swooning under arbors in the arms of dancing girls; there were Giaours, Turkish sabres, fezzes. And invariably there were blotchy, pale landscapes of fantastic countries: pines and palms growing together, tigers on the right, a lion on the left, Tartar minarets on the horizon, Roman ruins in the foreground, a few kneeling camels—all of it set in a very neat and orderly virgin forest, with a great perpendicular sunbeam quivering in the water; and standing out on the water's surface—scratched in white on the steel-gray background—a few widely spaced floating swans.

The bracket lamp above Emma's head shone down on those pictures of every corner of the world as she turned them over one by one in the silence of the dormitory, the only sound, coming from the distance, that of some belated cab on the boulevards.

When her mother died, she wept profusely for several days. She had a memorial picture made for herself from the dead woman's hair; and in a letter filled with sorrowful reflections on life that she sent to Les Bertaux, she begged to be buried, when her time came, in the same grave. Her father thought she must be ill, and went to see her. Emma was privately pleased to feel that she had so very quickly attained this ideal of ethereal languor, inaccessible to mediocre spirits. So she let herself meander along Lamartinian paths, listening to the throbbing of harps on lakes, to all the songs of dying swans, to the falling of every leaf, to the flight of pure virgins ascending to heaven, and to the voice of the Eternal speaking in the valleys. Gradually these things began to bore her, but she refused to admit it and continued as before, first out of habit, then out of vanity; until one day she discovered with surprise that the whole mood had evaporated, leaving her heart as free of melancholy as her brow was free of wrinkles.

The good nuns, who had been taking her vocation quite for granted, were greatly surprised to find that Mademoiselle Rouault was apparently slipping out of their control. And indeed they had so deluged her with prayers, retreats, novenas and sermons, preached so constantly the respect due the saints and the martyrs, and given her so much good advice about modest behavior and the saving of her soul, that she reacted like a horse too tightly reined: she balked, and the bit fell from her teeth. In her enthusiasms she had always looked for something tangible: she had loved the church for its flowers, music for its romantic words, literature for its power to stir the passions; and she rebelled before the mysteries of faith just as she grew ever more restive under discipline, which was antipathetic to her nature. When her father took her out of school no one was sorry to see her go. The Mother Superior, indeed, remarked that she had lately been displaying a certain lack of reverence toward the community.

Back at home, Emma at first enjoyed giving orders to the servants, then grew sick of country life and longed to be back in the convent. By the time Charles first appeared at Les Bertaux she thought that she was cured of illusions—that she had nothing more to learn, and no great emotions to look forward to.

But in her eagerness for a change, or perhaps overstimulated by this man's presence, she easily persuaded herself that love, that marvelous thing which had hitherto been like a great rosy-plumaged bird soaring in the splendors of poetic skies, was at last within her grasp. And now she could not bring herself to believe that the uneventful life she was leading was the happiness of which she had dreamed.

Another main character in the novel is Monsieur Homais, a pharmacist who is a hypocrite and who represents the new culture of "science" and rationalism coming out of the Enlightenment.

> "Bravo!" cried the pharmacist. "Go ahead! Keep sending your daughters to confession to strapping fellows like that! But if I were the government I'd have every priest bled once a month. Yes, a fine generous phlebotomy every month, Madame, in the interests of morals and decency."
>
> "That's enough, Monsieur Homais! You've no respect for religion!"
>
> "On the contrary. I'm a very religious man, in my own way, far more so than all these people with their mummeries and their tricks. I worship God, I assure you! I believe in a Supreme Being, a Creator. Whoever he is—and what difference does it make?—he put us here on earth to fulfill our duties as citizens and parents. But I don't have to go into church and kiss silver platters and hand over my money to fatten up a lot of rascals that eat better than you and I! To him, one can do full honor in a forest, a field—or merely by gazing up at the ethereal vault, like the ancients. My God is the God of Socrates, of Franklin, of Voltaire, of Béranger! My credo is the credo of Rousseau! I adhere to the immortal principles of '89! I have no use for the kind of God who goes walking in his garden with a stick, sends his friends to live in the bellies of whales, gives up the ghost with a groan and then comes back to life three days later! Those things aren't only absurd in themselves, Madame—they're completely opposed to all physical laws. It goes to prove, by the way, that priests have always wallowed in squalid ignorance and have wanted nothing better than to drag the entire world down to their own level."
>
> As he ended, he glanced about in search of an audience: for a moment, during his outburst, he had had the illusion that he was addressing the village council. But the mistress of the inn was no longer listening to him: . . .

Emma's quest is doomed to failure, because of her own inadequacies as well as the social limitations of her time. Caught in a world of middle-class banality, she does not have the inner resources to transcend it. She takes her own life.

> She slowly turned her face, and seemed overjoyed at suddenly seeing the purple stole—doubtless recognizing, in this interval of extraordinary peace, the lost ecstasy of her first mystical flights and the first visions of eternal bliss.
>
> The priest stood up and took the crucifix; she stretched out her head like someone thirsting; and pressing her lips to the body of the God-Man, she imprinted on it, with every ounce of her failing strength, the most passionate love-kiss she had ever given. Then he recited the *Misereatur* and the *Indulgentiam*, dipped his right thumb in the oil, and began the unctions. First he anointed her eyes, once so covetous of all earthly luxuries; then her nostrils, so gluttonous of caressing breezes and amorous scents; then her mouth, so prompt to lie, so defiant in pride, so loud in lust; then her hands, that had thrilled to voluptuous contacts; and finally the soles of her feet, once so swift when she had hastened to slake her desires, and now never to walk again.
>
> The curé wiped his fingers, threw the oil-soaked bits of cotton into the fire, and returned to the dying woman, sitting beside her and telling her that now

she must unite her sufferings with Christ's and throw herself on the divine mercy.

As he ended his exhortations he tried to have her grasp a blessed candle, symbol of the celestial glories soon to surround her. Emma was too weak, and couldn't close her fingers: but for Monsieur Bournisien the candle would have fallen to the floor.

Yet she was no longer so pale, and her face was serene, as though the sacrament had cured her.

The priest didn't fail to point this out: he even explained to Bovary that the Lord sometimes prolonged people's lives when He judged it expedient for their salvation; and Charles remembered another day, when, similarly close to death, she had received communion.

"Perhaps there's hope after all," he thought.

And indeed, she looked all about her, slowly, like someone waking from a dream; then, in a distinct voice, she asked for her mirror, and she remained bowed over it for some time, until great tears flowed from her eyes. Then she threw back her head with a sigh, and sank onto the pillow.

At once her breast began to heave rapidly. Her tongue hung at full length from her mouth; her rolling eyes grew dim like the globes of two lamps about to go out; and one might have thought her dead already but for the terrifying, ever-faster movement of her ribs, which were shaken by furious gasps, as though her soul were straining violently to break its fetters. Félicité knelt before the crucifix, and even the pharmacist flexed his knees a little. Monsieur Canivet stared vaguely out into the square. Bournisien had resumed his praying, his face bowed over the edge of the bed and his long black cassock trailing out behind him into the room. Charles was on the other side, on his knees, his arms stretched out toward Emma. He had taken her hands, and was pressing them, shuddering at every beat of her heart, as at the tremors of a falling ruin. As the death-rattle grew louder, the priest speeded his prayers: they mingled with Bovary's stifled sobs, and at moments everything seemed drowned by the monotonous flow of Latin syllables that sounded like the tolling of a bell.

Suddenly from out on the sidewalk came a noise of heavy wooden shoes and the scraping of a stick, and a voice rose up, a raucous voice singing:

> *A clear day's warmth will often move*
> *A lass to stray in dreams of love.*

Emma sat up like a galvanized corpse, her hair streaming, her eyes fixed and gaping.

> *To gather up the stalks of wheat*
> *The swinging scythe keeps laying by,*
> *Nanette goes stooping in the heat*
> *Along the furrow where they lie.*

"The blind man!" she cried.

Emma began to laugh—a horrible, frantic, desperate laugh—fancying that she saw the beggar's hideous face, a figure of terror looming up in the darkness of eternity.

*The wind blew very hard that day
And snatched her petticoat away!*

A spasm flung her down on the mattress. Everyone drew close. She had ceased to exist.

1. Discuss the character of Emma Bovary. How did her dreams turn into a nightmare? Some critics see Emma as a victim of her society. Do you agree?
2. Is Monsieur Homais characteristic of the middle class of the nineteenth century? Would Balzac or Marx agree with this view?
3. Flaubert used the character of the blind man as the person who reveals the truth. Comment on the attitude of the other characters in the passage.

▪ ▪ ▪

GUSTAVE COURBET

Gustave Courbet (1819-77) was the most important realist painter of his time, as he broke with traditions insisting that paintings be either historical or romantic. Courbet painted ordinary people, though he did so in a style that often borrowed from epic themes. In 1851 he showed his *Stonebreakers* and *Funeral at Ornans* at the Salon and angered many critics. Both paintings dealt with everyday life, the former treating two peasants and their work as fully integrated, the latter depicting a funeral as a village event. The poor were given prominence and Courbet attempted to accurately depict village life. In 1855 Courbet's *Studio of the Painter* was rejected for a show held at the Exposition Universelle in Paris. The artist then set about holding his own exhibition. Courbet's work opened the world of art to new themes, and he was influential in getting critics and other artists to question their assumptions about the purpose and meaning of art.

In 1855, at his private exhibition, Courbet discussed his work and the idea of realism.

The title of Realist was thrust upon me just as the title of Romantic was imposed upon the men of 1830. Titles have never given a true idea of things: if it were otherwise, the works would be unnecessary.

Without expanding on the greater or lesser accuracy of a name which nobody, I should hope, can really be expected to understand, I will limit myself to a few words of elucidation in order to cut short the misunderstandings.

I have studied, outside of any system and without prejudice, the art of the ancients and the art of the moderns. I no more wanted to imitate the one than to copy the other; nor, furthermore, was it my intention to attain the trivial goal of *art for art's sake*. No! I simply wanted to draw forth from a complete acquaintance with tradition the reasoned and independent consciousness of my own individuality.

Source: Linda Nochlin, ed., *Realism and Tradition in Art: 1848–1900* (Englewood Cliffs, New Jersey: Prentice-Hall, Inc., 1966), pp. 33-34, 34-36.

To know in order to be able to create, that was my idea. To be in a position to translate the customs, the ideas, the appearance of my epoch, according to my own estimation; to be not only a painter, but a man as well; in short, to create living art—this is my goal.

B ▷ Courbet wrote a letter to his students in 1861, discussing his positions on the relationships between the teacher and the pupil, and between the artist and his times.

GENTLEMEN AND COLLEAGUES:

You were anxious to open a studio of painting where you would be able to continue your education as artists without restraint, and you were eager to suggest that it be placed under my direction.

Before making any reply, I have to get things straight with you about that word *direction*. I can't lay myself open to making it a question of teacher and students between us.

I must explain to you what I recently had the occasion to tell the congress at Antwerp: I do not have, I cannot have, pupils.

I, who believe that every artist should be his own teacher, cannot dream of setting myself up as a professor.

I cannot teach my art, nor the art of any school whatever, since I deny that art can be taught, or, in other words, I maintain that art is completely individual, and is, for each artist, nothing but the talent issuing from his own inspiration and his own studies of tradition.

I say in addition that, in my opinion, for an artist art or talent can only be a way of applying his own personal abilities to the ideas and objects of the time in which he lives.

Above all, the art of painting can only consist of the representation of objects which are visible and tangible for the artist.

An epoch can only be reproduced by its own artists, I mean by the artists who lived in it. I hold the artists of one century basically incapable of reproducing the aspect of a past or future century—in other words, of painting the past or the future.

It is in this sense that I deny the possibility of historical art applied to the past. Historical art is by nature contemporary. Each epoch must have its artists who express it and reproduce it for the future. An age which has not been capable of expressing itself through its own artists has no right to be represented by subsequent artists. This would be a falsification of history.

The history of an era is finished with that era itself and with those of its representatives who have expressed it. It is not the task of modern times to add anything to the expression of former times, to ennoble or embellish the past. What has been, has been. The human spirit must always begin work afresh in the present, starting off from acquired results. One must never start out from foregone conclusions, proceeding from synthesis to synthesis, from conclusion to conclusion.

The real artists are those who pick up their age exactly at the point to which it has been carried by preceding times. To go backward is to do nothing;

it is pure loss; it means that one has neither understood nor profited by the lessons of the past. This explains why the archaic schools of all kinds are brought down to the most barren compilations.

I maintain, in addition, that painting is an essentially *concrete* art and can only consist of the representation of *real and existing* things. It is a completely physical language, the words of which consist of all visible objects; an object which is *abstract*, not visible, non-existent, is not within the realm of painting.

Imagination in art consists in knowing how to find the most complete expression of an existing thing, but never in inventing or creating that thing itself.

The beautiful exists in nature and may be encountered in the midst of reality under the most diverse aspects. As soon as it is found there, it belongs to art, or rather, to the artist who knows how to see it there. As soon as beauty is real and visible, it has its artistic expression from these very qualities. Artifice has no right to amplify this expression; by meddling with it, one only runs the risk of perverting and, consequently, of weakening it. The beauty provided by nature is superior to all the conventions of the artist.

Beauty, like truth, is a thing which is relative to the time in which one lives and to the individual capable of understanding it. The expression of the beautiful bears a precise relation to the power of perception acquired by the artist.

Here are my basic ideas about art. With such ideas, to think of the possibility of opening a school for the teaching of conventional principles would be going back to the incomplete, received notions which have everywhere directed modern art up to this point. . . .

It is not possible to have schools for painting; there are only painters. Schools have no use except for discerning the analytic procedures of art. No school is capable of pressing on to a synthesis in isolation. Painting *cannot*, without falling into abstraction, let a partial aspect of art dominate, whether it be drawing, color, composition, or any other one of the extraordinary multiplicity of means the totality of which alone constitutes this art.

I am, therefore, unable to open a school, to form pupils, to teach this or that partial tradition of art.

I can only explain to some artists, who would be my collaborators and not my pupils, the method by which, in my opinion, one becomes a painter, by which I myself have tried to become one since my earliest days, leaving to each person the complete control of his individuality, the full liberty of his own expression in the application of this method. To achieve this aim, the organization of a communal studio, recalling those extremely fruitful collaborations of the studios of the Renaissance, could certainly be useful and contribute to the opening of the era of modern painting, and I would eagerly give myself to everything you want of me in order to attain this goal.

With deepest sincerity,

GUSTAVE COURBET

1. Courbet wanted "to create living art." Contrast his artistic goal with that of the Romantic painters.
2. Account for Courbet's advocacy of a communal approach to art education rather than that of the traditional teacher and student relationship.

▪ ▪ ▪

IVAN TURGENEV

Ivan Turgenev (1818-83) was the most popular and well-known Russian writer in the West in the mid-nineteenth century. Turgenev, like many Russian intellectuals, believed that his country was in need of major reforms, especially with regard to serfdom and the class system. While he wrote lyrical novels in the style of realism, Turgenev also used his writing to challenge the *status quo* in Russia, criticizing traditional institutions and the social structure, and advocating change along the lines of the major Western states. His novel *Fathers and Sons* (1862), published just after the legal emancipation of the serfs, caused a critical storm as Turgenev, introducing the idea of nihilism, wrote of the break between the generations and of the difficulty of making meaningful changes in Russian society. His anti-hero, Bazarov, became a controversial figure in the many discussions about where Russia ought to head.

In the novel Bazarov is contrasted with Pavel Petrovich Kirsanov, a representative of the "old" Russia.

> Arkady went up to his uncle and again felt the perfumed moustaches brush his cheeks. Pavel Petrovich sat down at the table. He was wearing an elegant suit cut in the English fashion, and a gay little fez graced his head. The fez and the carelessly knotted cravat carried a suggestion of the more free life in the country but the stiff collar of his shirt—not white, it is true, but striped as is correct for morning wear—stood up as inexorably as ever against his well-shaved chin.
>
> 'But where is your new friend?' he asked Arkady.
>
> 'Not in the house; he usually gets up early and goes off somewhere. The great thing is not to pay any attention to him: he can't stand ceremony.'
>
> 'Yes, that is obvious.' Taking his time, Pavel Petrovich began buttering his bread. 'Is he staying with us for long?'
>
> 'That depends. He's stopping here on his way to his father's.'
>
> 'And where does his father live?'
>
> 'In the same province as ourselves, about sixty miles from here. He owns a smallish estate. He used to be an army doctor.'
>
> 'Tut, tut, tut! Of course. I kept wondering where I had heard that name before: Bazarov? Nikolai, don't you remember, there was a surgeon called Bazarov in our father's division?'
>
> 'I believe there was.'

Source: Ivan Turgenev, *Fathers and Sons* (Harmondsworth: Penguin Books, 1965), pp. 93-99, 121-29.

'Yes, yes, to be sure. So that surgeon will be this fellow's father. H'm!' Pavel Petrovich pulled his moustaches. 'Well, and this Monsieur Bazarov, what is he exactly?' he inquired with deliberation.

'What is Bazarov?' Arkady smiled. 'Would you like me to tell you, uncle, what he is exactly?'

'Please do, nephew.'

'He is a nihilist!'

'A what?' asked Nikolai Petrovich, while his brother lifted his knife in the air with a small piece of butter on the tip and remained motionless.

'He is a nihilist,' repeated Arkady.

'A nihilist,' said Nikolai Petrovich. 'That comes from the Latin *nihil—nothing*, I imagine; the term must signify a man who . . . who recognizes nothing?'

'Say—who respects nothing,' put in Pavel Petrovich, and set to work with the butter again.

'Who looks at everything critically,' observed Arkady.

'Isn't that exactly the same thing?' asked Pavel Petrovich.

'No, it's not the same thing. A nihilist is a person who does not take any principle for granted, however much that principle may be revered.'

'Well, and is that a good thing?' interrupted Pavel Petrovich.

'It depends on the individual, my dear uncle. It's good in some cases and very bad in others.'

'Indeed. Well, I can see this is not our cup of tea. We of the older generation think that without principles' (Pavel Petrovich pronounced the word as if it were French, whereas Arkady put the stress on the first syllable)—'without principles taken as you say on trust one cannot move an inch or draw a single breath. *Vous avez changé tout cela*, may God grant you health and a general's rank, but we shall be content to look on and admire *Messieurs les* . . . what was it?' . . .

 Finally, the two men clash directly:

The skirmish took place that very day, at tea time. Pavel Petrovich came down to the sitting-room, irritable and determined, prepared to do battle. He was only waiting for a pretext to rush upon the enemy but the pretext was a long time presenting itself. Bazarov never said much in the presence of the 'old Kirsanovs' (that was how he spoke of the brothers), and that evening he felt out of sorts as he sipped one cup of tea after another in silence. Pavel Petrovich was consumed with impatience; at last his wish was granted.

The conversation turned to one of the neighbouring landowners. 'A complete rotter, a third-rate aristocrat,' Bazarov, who had met him in Petersburg, remarked dispassionately.

'Permit me to inquire,' began Pavel Petrovich, his lips trembling, 'in your opinion are the words "rotter" and "aristocrat" synonymous?'

'I said "third-rate aristocrat",' replied Bazarov, lazily taking a sip of tea.

'Precisely; but I imagine you hold the same opinion of true aristocrats as you do of third-rate ones. I think it my duty to tell you that I do not share that opinion. I venture to assert that everyone knows I am a man of liberal views and devoted to progress; but for that very reason I respect aristocrats—

genuine ones. Kindly remember, sir' (at these words Bazarov raised his eyes to Pavel Petrovich)—'kindly remember, sir,' he repeated with acrimony, 'the English aristocracy. They never yield one iota of their rights, and for that reason they respect the rights of others; they demand the fulfilment of obligations due to them, and therefore they fulfil their own obligations to others. The aristocracy has given England her freedom and maintains it for her.'

'You're harping on an old tune,' Bazarov retorted, 'but what are you trying to prove by it?'

'*Phthis*, my dear sir.' (When Pavel Petrovich was angry he would deliberately say 'phthis' and 'phthat', though he knew perfectly well that the dictionary allowed of no such words. This odd habit was a legacy from the period of Alexander I. The exquisites of those days, on the rare occasions when they spoke their own language, said 'phthis' and 'phthat', as much as to say, 'We, of course, are Russian born, at the same time we are important personages who can dispense with grammatical rules.') 'I am seeking to prove *phthis*— without a sense of proper pride, without a sense of self-respect—and these feelings are highly developed in the aristocrat—there can be no firm foundation for the social . . . *bien public* . . . the social fabric. It is personal character that matters, my dear sir: a man's personal character must be as strong as a rock, since everything else is built up on it. I am very well aware, for instance, that you are pleased to ridicule my habits, my way of dressing, my punctiliousness, in fact. But those very things proceed from a sense of self-respect, from a sense of duty—yes, sir, of duty. I may live in the country, in the wilds of the country, but I do not let myself go, I respect myself as a human being.'

'Allow me, Pavel Petrovich,' Bazarov put in, 'you say you respect yourself and you sit with your arms folded: what sort of benefit does that do the *bien public*? If you didn't respect yourself, you'd do just the same.'

Pavel Petrovich turned pale.

'That is quite another matter. I am not under the slightest obligation to explain to you why I sit with folded arms, as you are pleased to put it. I merely wish to say that aristocratism is a principle, and only immoral or silly people can live in our age without principles. I said as much to Arkady the day after he came home, and I repeat it to you now. Isn't that so, Nikolai?'

Nikolai Petrovich nodded assent, while Bazarov exclaimed:

'Aristocratism, liberalism, progress, principles—think of it, what a lot of foreign . . . and useless words! To a Russian they're not worth a straw.'

'What, in your opinion, does he need? To hear you talk we might all be living outside human society, beyond its laws. Doesn't the logic of history demand. . . .'

'What has that logic to do with us? We can get on without that too.'

'What do you mean?'

'Just that. You don't need logic, I suppose, to put a piece of bread in your mouth when you're hungry? We've no time for such abstractions!'

Pavel Petrovich threw up his hands.

'After that I fail to understand you. You insult the Russian people. How you can decline to recognize principles and precepts passes my comprehension. What other basis for conduct in life have we got?'

'I've told you already, uncle, that we don't recognize any authorities,' Arkady interposed.

'We base our conduct on what we recognize as useful,' Bazarov went on. 'In these days the most useful thing we can do is to repudiate—and so we repudiate.'

'Everything?'

'Everything.'

'What? Not only art, poetry . . . but also . . . I am afraid to say it . . .'

'Everything,' Bazarov repeated with indescribable composure.

Pavel Petrovich stared at him. He had not expected this; while Arkady positively glowed with satisfaction.

'However, if I may say so,' began Nikolai Petrovich, 'you repudiate everything, or, to put it more precisely, you are destroying everything. . . . But one must construct too, you know.'

'That is not our affair. . . . The ground must be cleared first.'

'The present condition of the people requires it,' added Arkady pompously. 'We are bound to carry out these requirements, we have no right to indulge in the gratification of our personal egoism.'

This last sentence obviously did not please Bazarov: it smacked of philosophy, that is, of romanticism, for Bazarov considered philosophy synonymous with romanticism; but he did not judge it necessary to contradict his young disciple.

'No, no!' Pavel Petrovich cried with sudden vehemence. 'I cannot believe that you two really know the Russian people, that you represent their needs and aspirations! No, the Russians are not what you imagine them to be. They hold tradition sacred, they are a patriarchal people—they cannot live without faith . . .'

'I am not going to dispute that,' Bazarov interrupted. 'I'm even ready to agree that there you are right.'

'But if I am right . . .'

'It still proves nothing.'

'Exactly, it proves nothing,' echoed Arkady with the assurance of a practised chess-player who has anticipated an apparently dangerous move on the part of his opponent, and so is not in the least disconcerted.

'What do you mean—it proves nothing?' muttered Pavel Petrovich, dumbfounded. 'You must be going against your own people then?'

'And what if we are?' shouted Bazarov. 'The people believe that when it thunders the prophet Elijah is riding across the sky in his chariot. Well? Am I to agree with them? Besides, if they are Russian, so am I.'

'No, you are no Russian after what you have just said! I must decline to recognize you as a Russian.'

'My grandfather tilled the soil,' answered Bazarov with supercilious pride. 'Ask any of your peasants which of us—you or me—he would more readily acknowledge as a fellow-countryman. You don't even know how to talk to them.'

'While you talk to them and despise them at the same time.'

'Why not, if they deserve to be despised. You find fault with my attitude, but who told you I stumbled on it by chance—that it was not the product of that very national spirit which you are so anxious to defend?'

'What an ideal! A fat lot of use nihilists are!'

'Of use or not, it's not for us to decide. After all, you consider yourself of some use in the world.'

'Gentlemen, gentlemen, no personalities, please!' cried Nikolai Petrovich, getting up.

Pavel Petrovich smiled, and laying his hand on his brother's shoulder made him sit down again.

'Do not worry,' he said. 'I shall not forget myself, thanks to that very sense of dignity which is so savagely assailed by Mr—by Dr Bazarov. If you will allow me,' he continued, turning to Bazarov again, 'perhaps you think your doctrine is a novelty? That is quite a mistake. The materialism you preach has gained currency more than once and has always proved bankrupt . . .'

'Another foreign term!' Bazarov interrupted him. He was beginning to lose his temper, and his face had gone a coarse coppery colour. 'In the first place, we preach nothing: that's not our way . . .'

'What do you do, then?'

'This is what we do. Not so very long ago we were saying that our officials took bribes, that we had no roads, no trade, no impartial courts of justice . . .'

'Oh, I see, you are accusers—that, I think, is the right name. Well, I too should agree with many of your criticisms, but . . .'

'Then we realized that just to keep on and on talking about our social diseases was a waste of time, and merely led to a trivial doctrinaire attitude. We saw that our clever men, our so-called progressives and reformers never accomplished anything, that we were concerning ourselves with a lot of nonsense, discussing art, unconscious creative work, parliamentarianism, the bar, and the devil knows what, while all the time the real question was getting daily bread to eat, when the most vulgar superstitions are stifling us, when our industrial enterprises come to grief solely for want of honest men at the top, when even the emancipation of the serfs—the emancipation the government is making such a fuss about—is not likely to be to our advantage, since those peasants of ours are only too glad to rob even themselves to drink themselves silly at the gin-shop.'

'So,' Pavel Petrovich interrupted him—'so you were convinced of all this and decided not to do anything serious yourselves.'

'And decided not to do anything serious,' Bazarov repeated grimly. He suddenly felt vexed with himself for having spoken so freely in front of this member of the upper class.

'But to confine yourselves to abuse?'

'To confine ourselves to abuse.'

'And that is called nihilism?'

'And that is called nihilism,' Bazarov repeated again, this time with marked insolence.

Pavel Petrovich screwed up his eyes slightly.

'So that's it,' he muttered in a voice that was curiously calm. 'Nihilism's a panacea for every ill, and you—you are our saviours and heroes. Very well. But why do you abuse other people, even other accusers like yourselves? Aren't you just talking like all the rest?'

'We may have our faults but we are not guilty of that one,' muttered Bazarov through his teeth.

'What then? Are you doing anything? Are you preparing for action?'

Bazarov did not answer. Pavel Petrovich quivered but at once regained control of himself.

'H'm! . . . Action, destruction . . .' he went on. 'But how can you destroy without even knowing why?'

'We destroy because we are a force,' remarked Arkady.

Pavel Petrovich looked at his nephew and laughed.

'Yes, a force, and therefore not accountable to anyone,' said Arkady, drawing himself up.

'Wretched boy!' groaned Pavel Petrovich, now no longer in a state to restrain himself. 'Can't you realize the kind of thing you are encouraging in Russia with your miserable creed? No, it's enough to try the patience of an angel! A force! You might as well say that the wild Kalmuck and the Mongolian represent a force—but what is that to us? Civilization is what we value, yes, yes, my good sir: its fruits are precious to us. And don't tell me those fruits are of no importance: the meanest penny-a-liner—*un barbouilleur*, a piano-player who makes five farthings an evening—even they are of more use than you, because they stand for civilization and not crude Mongolian force! You fancy yourselves advanced, but your proper home is a Kalmuck tent! A force! And finally, my forceful gentlemen, remember this: there are only four men and a half of you, whereas the others number millions who won't let you trample their most sacred beliefs underfoot—it is they who will crush you!'

'If they do crush us, it will serve us right,' observed Bazarov. 'But we shall see what we shall see. We're not so few as you suppose.'

'What? Do you seriously think you can take on the whole nation?'

'A penny candle, you know, set Moscow on fire,' Bazarov responded.

'I see. First an almost Satanic pride, then gibes—so that is what attracts the young, that is what wins the inexperienced hearts of boys! Look, there is one sitting beside you, ready to worship the ground beneath your feet. Look at him.' (Arkady turned away and scowled.) 'And this plague has already spread far and wide. I am told that in Rome our artists never set foot in the Vatican. Raphael they practically regard as a fool because, if you please, he is an authority. Yet they themselves are so impotent and sterile that their imagination cannot rise above *Girl at the Fountain*, try as they may. And the girl is abominably drawn. They are fine fellows to your mind, are they not?'

'To my mind,' retorted Bazarov, 'Raphael's not worth a brass farthing; and they are no better.'

'Bravo! Bravo! Do you hear, Arkady . . . that is how young men of today should express themselves! And if you come to think of it, how could they fail to follow you! In the old days young people had to study. If they did not want to be thought ignorant they had to work hard whether they liked it or not. But now they need only say, "Everything in the world is rubbish!"—and the trick's done. The young men are simply delighted. Whereas they were only sheep's heads before, now they have suddenly blossomed out as nihilists!'

'Your vaunted sense of your own dignity has let you down,' Bazarov remarked phlegmatically, while Arkady went hot all over and his eyes flashed. 'Our argument has gone too far . . . we'd better stop. I shall be prepared to agree with you,' he added, getting up, 'when you can show me a single institution of contemporary life, private or public, which does not call for absolute and ruthless repudiation.'

'I can confront you with a million such,' cried Pavel Petrovich. 'A million! Now take the Peasant Commune, for example.'

A cold sneer twisted Bazarov's face.

'Well, so far as the commune is concerned,' he said, 'you had better discuss that with your brother. I should think he has seen by now what the commune is like in reality—its mutual responsibility, sobriety and the like.'

'Take the family, then—the family as it exists among our peasants!' shouted Pavel Petrovich.

'I suggest you had better not investigate that too closely either. You have, I suppose, heard of the way the head of the family can select his daughters-in-law? Listen to me, Pavel Petrovich, give yourself a couple of days to think it over—you're not likely to come on anything straight away. Go through the various classes of society and scrutinize them carefully, and in the mean-time Arkady and I will—'

'Jeer at everything,' broke in Pavel Petrovich.

'No, go and dissect frogs. Come along, Arkady. Good-bye for the present, gentlemen!'

The two friends went out, leaving the brothers alone, speechless and just looking at each other. . . .

1. Read the debate between the aristocrat Pavel Petrovich and the nihilist Bazarov. Assume for a moment that Bazarov and Arkady had not gone off at that moment to dissect frogs. Extend the debate for another page, creating arguments that might have been used by each side.

▪ ▪ ▪

CHARLES DICKENS

Charles Dickens (1812-70) was a prolific novelist who wrote works of great popularity which, with humour and pathos, vividly depicted life in Victorian society. In *Hard Times* (1854) Dickens dealt with many contemporary issues, including education, class, the role of women and, above all, the horrors, both personal and environmental, of the new industrial Britain.

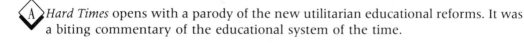 *Hard Times* opens with a parody of the new utilitarian educational reforms. It was a biting commentary of the educational system of the time.

'Now, what I want is, Facts. Teach these boys and girls nothing but Facts. Facts alone are wanted in life. Plant nothing else, and root out everything else. You can only form the minds of reasoning animals upon Facts: nothing else will ever be of any service to them. This is the principle on which I bring

Source: Charles Dickens, *Hard Times,* (Harmondsworth: Penguin Books, 1969), pp. 47-50, 64, 108-13.

◀Diego Velázquez (1599-1660), *Las Meninas* (The Maids of Honour), 1656 ▪ *Velázquez' painting is one of the masterpieces of the baroque period. The painter is in the work, on the left, and the king and queen are reflected in the mirror. While seeming to be a painting of an ordinary moment in the life of the Spanish court, the work explores the nature of reality, our ability to depict the visual world, the use of the mirror as a symbol and a metaphor, and the use of light and space. Paintings were no longer fixed and static, but reflected a reality constantly in transformation.*

▪ ◇ ▪

▼Antoine Watteau (1684-1721), *A Pilgrimage to Cythera*, 1717 ▪ *Watteau's work signalled a shift from the baroque to the rococo, a more playful, delicate and fragile style, which also stressed movement and change. His paintings were called fêtes galantes, elegant entertainments, in recognition of their lighter moods and subjects. Here, pilgrims come to the island of love, where Venus, shown as a statue on the right, is said to have risen from the sea.*

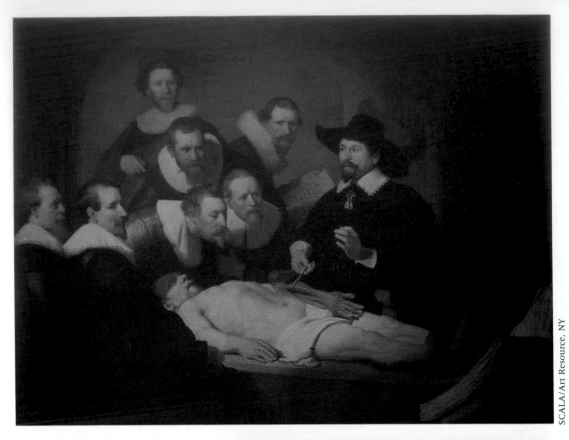

▲Rembrandt van Rijn (1606-69), *The Anatomy Lesson of Dr. Tulp*, 1632 • *Rembrandt was the master of chiaroscuro, the use of light and shade to depict human emotion and drama. In* The Anatomy Lesson *he showed a teacher and his students engaged in learning about the human body – a moment of profound importance. Rembrandt gave each of his subjects a personality; here the corpse is invested with dignity. A group portrait, it also deals with the connection between life and death.*

▶Jan Vermeer (1632-75), *The Love Letter*, 1666 • *Vermeer brought the viewer into the interior world of domestic life and emotion. Here a woman receives a letter and is about to open it. The drama is framed through the doorway, and light radiates from the interior. On the wall behind are paintings within the painting, as Vermeer brings us further into the inner meaning of the moment.*

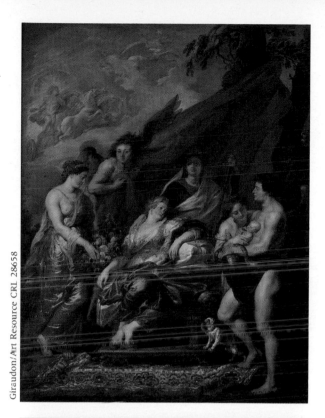

◀Peter Paul Rubens (1577-1640), *The Birth of Louis XIII*, c. 1621-24 • *Rubens was commissioned by the Queen of France, Marie de' Medici, to complete a series of paintings for a grand residence she was having built in Paris. This work was the eighth of twenty-one paintings about Marie's life. It used classical themes and a baroque style to show the Queen at the center being given her son, the future Louis XIII, by the allegorical figure of Health.*

◀Hyacinthe Rigaud (1659-1743), *Portrait of Louis XIV*, 1701 • *Rigaud painted the Sun King, Louis XIV, at the height of his power. Louis, a person of prestige and grandeur, is surrounded by symbols of his authority.*

►Nicolas Poussin (1594-1665), *The Rape of the Sabine Women,* c. 1635 ▪ *Poussin was the major painter in the classical style in the seventeenth century. He used themes taken from ancient and biblical history and mythology, and valued the principles of reason, order, and symmetry. His paintings often had a close relationship to literature, depicting human history and emotion, and presenting lessons about human nature and behaviour.*

►Jacques-Louis David (1748-1825), *The Oath of the Horatii,* 1784 ▪ *Led by David, neo-classicism came to be the accepted style of painting in the last half of the eighteenth century. In this work, David depicted a moment of civic dedication and sacrifice that was both heroic and tragic. Three young men pledge their lives to defend their city, while the intricate family relationships among the two warring cities foreshadows tragedy, whatever the outcome. David's work was seen as a protest against political and social circumstances in the France of* the ancien régime.

◀Francisco Goya (1746-1828), *The Third of May, 1808,* 1814 • *Goya commemorated an uprising in Spain in opposition to the occupation of the country by France during the Napoleonic period. Those being shot by the anonymous soldiers of the firing squad were viewed as martyrs to national liberation and political liberty, as the light shines on the lower-class victims of oppression.*

◀Eugène Delacroix (1798-1863), *Liberty Leading the People,* 1830 • *Delacroix celebrated the French Revolution of 1830 against the authoritarian rule of the Bourbon Charles X. Liberty is shown as an allegorical figure, leading various social types to revolt in defence of their rights. Delacroix linked political revolution with Romanticism in a painting, which greatly influenced the imagery and symbolism of later generations.*

▲John Constable (1776-1837), *The Hay Wain*, 1821 • *Constable wished to base his landscapes on the precise observation and rendering of nature. A Romantic, he painted many scenes of pastoral countrysides in which human beings integrated into the natural environment.*

▲Joseph Mallord William Turner (1775-1851), *Rain, Steam, and Speed: The Great Western Railway*, 1844 ▪ *Turner was interested in colour and atmosphere, and his paintings captured a nature in which change was the rule. In this work he united the early industrial revolution with a rendering of nature. The perspective of the painting was also unusual, as the railway seems to be moving off the painting.*

▼Claude Monet (1840-1926), *La Gâre Saint-Lazare*, 1877 ▪ *Monet, an impressionist, painted the Saint-Lazare railway station several times, in order to deal with a world of light and colour which constantly created a new visual reality. For Monet, and many others in the nineteenth century, the railway was the symbol of modernity and part of the recording of contemporary life.*

▲Theodore Gericault (1791-1824), *Raft of the Medusa*, 1818-19 • *Gericault based this painting upon a real event, the shipwreck of the ship* Medusa *in 1816. He attempted to depict human suffering and horror in revealing a humanity bound together, caught in a moment between despair and hope. This work, shown in the Salon of 1819, publicized many of the new Romantic ideas about the form and subject of painting.*

▼Gustave Courbet (1819-77), *The Burial at Ornans*, 1849 • *Courbet helped to define realism in paintings which dealt with ordinary people and their lives. Here, a village funeral is shown to be a social event as well as a sacred one. When challenged about the content of his paintings, Courbet replied: ''Show me an angel and I'll paint one. . . .''*

▲Claude Monet, *Impression, Sunrise*, 1872 ▪ *In 1874 a group of painters, including Cézanne, Degas, Monet, Morisot, and Pissarro, put on their own exhibition, after having been rejected by the official Salon. One of Monet's contributions was this controversial painting, attacked by the critics, the title of which gave the impressionist movement its name. In all of his paintings, Monet tried to capture a moment in light and form.*

◀Edgar Degas (1834-1917), *The Star or The Dancer on the Stage*, 1878 ▪ *Degas' paintings of ballerinas captured the grace and movement of the dance. Here, he gave the viewer the perspective from a box above the stage, and the star ballerina is seen in a moment of motion.*

▲Edouard Manet (1832-83), *Claude Monet Painting on His Boat*, 1874 ▪ *Manet's work helped to bring painting outdoors, in an attempt to capture light and colour as they actually appeared to the observer. Like all the impressionists, Manet helped to lighten the canvas and painted his own world, rather than historical or classical themes.*

▶Edouard Manet, *Portrait of Émile Zola*, 1868 ▪ *The author Zola, a defender of the new radical art of the nineteenth century, was painted by Manet, at his desk. Over the desk are three images: a Japanese print, which indicates the profound influence of Japanese art forms on the impressionists; an etching of a painting by Velázquez; and a copy of Manet's own* Olympia *of 1863, whose frank sensuality scandalized the public.*

IA ORANA MARIA

▲Georges Seurat (1859-91), *Sunday Afternoon on the Island of La Grande Jatte, 1884-86* • *Seurat's paintings emanate out of the impressionist movement but have come to be called neo-impressionist in acknowledgment of his attempt to carefully and scientifically analyse colour and light. His method was calculated to produce a formula for the relationships between colours and to virtually eliminate the observer. He said: ''[Others] see poetry in what I have done. No, I apply my method, and that is all there is to it.''*

◀Paul Gauguin (1848-1903), *Ia Orana Maria, 1891* • *Gauguin abandoned his family and, eventually, Europe, in an effort to introduce new values into painting. He derived these values from a primitive world that he believed was more in touch with the essentials of human nature than was middle-class Western society. Ia Orana Maria was painted in Tahiti; its title means the same as Ave Maria. The native woman and her son are likened to the Virgin and Child in a canvas of brilliant colour, which reinterpreted Western artistic values.*

255

▲Vincent van Gogh (1853-90), *The Potato Eaters*, 1885 ▪ *Van Gogh broke new ground in painting, as he used the experiences of his inner and outer lives as the subjects of his work.* The Potato Eaters *reflected his deep feeling for the poor, and he ennobled these tillers of the soil. Van Gogh here depicts the poor at a meal, which has the quality of a sacred ritual.*

▼Vincent van Gogh, *Starry Night*, 1889 ▪ *Oil on canvas, 29 x 36¹/₄'' (73.7 x 92.1 cm) Van Gogh used his painting to express his emotions, a profound inner world in which he, as an individual, confronted himself in relation to the universe. His work became more and more expressive, as he boldly used colour and vivid brushstrokes. In* Starry Night *the universe is seen as a galaxy of whirl and light. A mysterious cypress tree grows beyond the finite village.*

▲ Paul Ceźanne (1839-1906), *Jas de Bouffan*, 1885-87 ▪ *Cézanne's post-impressionist paintings came to be experiments in form and colour, as he investigated the external world in a new way. He sought the permanent order in nature, and tried to capture its timelessness. In a letter he wrote: ". . . treat nature by the cylinder, the sphere, the cone, everything in proper perspective so that each side of an object or a plane is directed toward a central point."*

◀ Pablo Picasso (1881-1973), *Les Desmoiselles d'Avignon*, 1907 ▪ *Oil on canvas, 8' x 7'8'' (243.9 x 233.7 cm) A landmark in the history of art, this painting introduced many of the ideas incorporated into the movement called cubism: objects, people, and space were seen as geometrical forms and were depicted in symbolic modes; primitive sculpture was used as a model, as a powerful means of getting at essentials, ending the reliance on refined European ideas of painting; traditional perspective was abandoned.*

► Marcel Duchamp (1887-1968), *Nude Descending a Staircase, No. 2,* 1912 ▪ *Attacked by critics and the public, Duchamp's painting created a scandal when it was shown in North America in 1913. The title, seemingly traditional, is in contrast with the dynamic, almost mechanical, depiction of movement, done by using a number of interlaced images, as if in a motion picture. Duchamp soon became a leader of the Dada movement, which began in 1916, and which challenged all of the conventional beliefs of Western civilization.*

► Umberto Boccioni (1882-1916), *Dynamism of a Human Body,* 1913 ▪ *Growing out of literature, futurism was a movement that attacked all tradition and glorified speed and power. In art, futurists took some of the ideas of cubism and sought to create paintings and sculptures that captured the dynamism of the modern. They wished to put the spectator inside the painting, and stressed simultaneity. "A galloping horse," said Boccioni, "has not four legs; it has twenty."*

Hermitage Muse um, Leningrad

▲Henri Matisse (1869-1954), *Dance,
1909* ▪ *Matisse, in the early twentieth century,
became interested in new possibilities of using colour as a means of organizing a painting, as well
as making a symbolic statement. In* Dance *he
painted the pure joy of the activity by using only
a few colours on what is obviously a flat surface,
developing the rhythm of movement. Reducing the
activity to essentials gave the painting a power
beyond that of traditional representational art.*

▼Salvador Dali (1904-   ), *The Persistence of
Memory, 1931* ▪ *Oil on canvas, 9¹/₂ x 13'' (24.1
x 33 cm)* ▪ *The surrealist movement extended the
findings and methods of psychoanalysis into art.
Surrealists investigated the world of dreams and
the unconscious as a means of revealing the inner
life of human beings. Dali's paintings, careful in
their precise rendering of strange landscapes, were
meant to disturb and arouse viewers. The symbolism of time and its distortions is here used to
depict the relationship between time, memory,
our own lives, and eternity.*

Collection, The Museum of Modern Art, New York. Given anonymously.

▲Pablo Picasso, *Guernica*, 1937 ▪ *One of the most moving and profound anti-war paintings ever created, Picasso's* Guernica *used modern techniques to depict the horror, suffering, and tragedy of modern warfare. It was painted after the Spanish city of Guernica was bombed by German aircraft supporting the fascist Spanish forces during the Spanish Civil War. The terror-bombing, the first time saturation bombing was used on a civilian population, was successful, as the city was destroyed and many of its citizens were killed. Outraged and angered, Picasso used the event to paint this mural, a universal statement against war.*

▼Jackson Pollock (1912-56), *Number 6*, 1949 ▪ *Pollock's paintings, part of the movement called abstract expressionism, marked the final break with traditional perspective in the twentieth century, begun earlier by Picasso, Duchamp, and Boccioni. Pollock used paint as the medium itself, and the canvas which resulted was a statement about how the painter used the paint to create an object. Full of the personal power of its creator, Pollock's paintings opened new possibilities and demanded new critical criteria about the nature and meaning of art.*

The Museum of Fine Arts, Houston. Gift of D. and J. de Menil.

260

up my own children, and this is the principle on which I bring up these children. Stick to Facts, sir!'

The scene was a plain, bare, monotonous vault of a schoolroom, and the speaker's square forefinger emphasized his observations by underscoring every sentence with a line on the schoolmaster's sleeve. The emphasis was helped by the speaker's square wall of a forehead, which had his eyebrows for its base, while his eyes found commodious cellarage in two dark caves, overshadowed by the wall. The emphasis was helped by the speaker's mouth, which was wide, thin, and hard set. The emphasis was helped by the speaker's voice, which was inflexible, dry, and dictatorial. The emphasis was helped by the speaker's hair, which bristled on the skirts of his bald head, a plantation of firs to keep the wind from its shining surface, all covered with knobs, like the crust of a plum pie, as if the head had scarcely warehouse-room for the hard facts stored inside. The speaker's obstinate carriage, square coat, square legs, square shoulders—nay, his very neckcloth, trained to take him by the throat with an unaccommodating grasp, like a stubborn fact, as it was—all helped the emphasis.

'In this life, we want nothing but Facts, sir; nothing but Facts!'

The speaker, and the schoolmaster, and the third grown person present, all backed a little, and swept with their eyes the inclined plane of little vessels then and there arranged in order, ready to have imperial gallons of facts poured into them until they were full to the brim.

Thomas Gradgrind, sir. A man of realities. A man of fact and calculations. A man who proceeds upon the principle that two and two are four, and nothing over, and who is not to be talked into allowing for anything over. Thomas Gradgrind, sir—peremptorily Thomas—Thomas Gradgrind. With a rule and a pair of scales, and the multiplication table always in his pocket, sir, ready to weigh and measure any parcel of human nature, and tell you exactly what it comes to. It is a mere question of figures, a case of simple arithmetic. You might hope to get some other nonsensical belief into the head of George Gradgrind, or Augustus Gradgrind, or John Gradgrind, or Joseph Gradgrind (all supposititious, non-existent persons), but into the head of Thomas Gradgrind—no, sir!

In such terms Mr Gradgrind always mentally introduced himself, whether to his private circle of acquaintance, or to the public in general. In such terms, no doubt, substituting the words 'boys and girls', for 'sir', Thomas Gradgrind now presented Thomas Gradgrind to the little pitchers before him, who were to be filled so full of facts.

Indeed, as he eagerly sparkled at them from the cellarage before mentioned, he seemed a kind of cannon loaded to the muzzle with facts, and prepared to blow them clean out of the regions of childhood at one discharge. He seemed a galvanizing apparatus, too, charged with a grim mechanical substitute for the tender young imaginations that were to be stormed away.

'Girl number twenty,' said Mr Gradgrind, squarely pointing with his square forefinger, 'I don't know that girl. Who is that girl?'

'Sissy Jupe, sir,' explained number twenty, blushing, standing up, and curtseying.

'Sissy is not a name,' said Mr Gradgrind. 'Don't call yourself Sissy. Call yourself Cecilia.'

'It's father as calls me Sissy, sir,' returned the young girl in a trembling voice, and with another curtsey.

'Then he has no business to do it,' said Mr Gradgrind. 'Tell him he mustn't. Cecilia Jupe. Let me see. What is your father?'

'He belongs to the horse-riding, if you please, sir.'

Mr Gradgrind frowned, and waved off the objectionable calling with his hand.

'We don't want to know anything about that, here. You mustn't tell us about that, here. Your father breaks horses, don't he?'

'If you please, sir, when they can get any to break, they do break horses in the ring, sir.'

'You mustn't tell us about the ring, here. Very well, then. Describe your father as a horsebreaker. He doctors sick horses, I dare say?'

'Oh yes, sir.'

'Very well, then. He is a veterinary surgeon, a farrier and horsebreaker. Give me your definition of a horse.'

(Sissy Jupe thrown into the greatest alarm by this demand.)

'Girl number twenty unable to define a horse!' said Mr Gradgrind, for the general behoof of all the little pitchers. 'Girl number twenty possessed of no facts, in reference to one of the commonest of animals! Some boy's definition of a horse. Bitzer, yours.'

The square finger, moving here and there, lighted suddenly on Bitzer, perhaps because he chanced to sit in the same ray of sunlight which, darting in at one of the bare windows of the intensely whitewashed room, irradiated Sissy. For, the boys and girls sat on the face of the inclined plane in two compact bodies, divided up the centre by a narrow interval; and Sissy, being at the corner of a row on the sunny side, came in for the beginning of a sunbeam, of which Bitzer, being at the corner of a row on the other side, a few rows in advance, caught the end. But, whereas the girl was so dark-eyed and dark-haired, that she seemed to receive a deeper and more lustrous colour from the sun when it shone upon her, the boy was so light-eyed and light-haired that the self-same rays appeared to draw out of him what little colour he ever possessed. His cold eyes would hardly have been eyes, but for the short ends of lashes which, by bringing them into immediate contrast with something paler than themselves, expressed their form. His short-cropped hair might have been a mere continuation of the sandy freckles on his forehead and face. His skin was so unwholesomely deficient in the natural tinge, that he looked as though, if he were cut, he would bleed white.

'Bitzer,' said Thomas Gradgrind. 'Your definition of a horse.'

'Quadruped. Graminivorous. Forty teeth, namely twenty-four grinders, four eye-teeth, and twelve incisive. Sheds coat in the spring; in marshy countries, sheds hoofs, too. Hoofs hard, but requiring to be shod with iron. Age known by marks in mouth.' Thus (and much more) Bitzer.

'Now girl number twenty,' said Mr Gradgrind. 'You know what a horse is.' . . .

B The concern with "fact" took control of the landscape of industrial society, believed Dickens. His description of Coketown, his imaginary industrial town, was a condemnation of the human dimension of the necessities of factory life.

> Coketown, to which Messrs Bounderby and Gradgrind now walked, was a triumph of fact; it had no greater taint of fancy in it than Mrs Gradgrind herself. Let us strike the key-note, Coketown, before pursuing our tune.
>
> It was a town of red brick, or of brick that would have been red if the smoke and ashes had allowed it; but, as matters stood it was a town of unnatural red and black like the painted face of a savage. It was a town of machinery and tall chimneys, out of which interminable serpents of smoke trailed themselves for ever and ever, and never got uncoiled. It had a black canal in it, and a river that ran purple with ill-smelling dye, and vast piles of building full of windows where there was a rattling and a trembling all day long, and where the piston of the steam-engine worked monotonously up and down, like the head of an elephant in a state of melancholy madness. It contained several large streets all very like one another, and many small streets still more like one another, inhabited by people equally like one another, who all went in and out at the same hours, with the same sound upon the same pavements, to do the same work, and to whom every day was the same as yesterday and tomorrow, and every year the counterpart of the last and the next. . . .

C The cruelty of life in industrial society is illustrated by the contrast between Josiah Bounderby, the owner of the factory, and Stephen Blackpool, one of the workers. Blackpool, tied down in a loveless marriage to an alcoholic, consults with Bounderby about the possibility of a divorce. (It should be noted that the divorce laws in England in 1854, on grounds other than adultery, were a complicated and expensive process, as described by Bounderby. Dickens' work was one of the many pleas for reform, which came in acts passed in 1857 and 1878.)

> Stephen came out of the hot mill into the damp wind and cold wet streets, haggard and worn. He turned from his own class and his own quarter, taking nothing but a little bread as he walked along, towards the hill on which his principal employer lived, in a red house with black outside shutters, green inside blinds, a black street door, up two white steps, BOUNDERBY (in letters very like himself) upon a brazen plate, and a round brazen door-handle underneath it like a brazen full-stop.
>
> Mr Bounderby was at his lunch. So Stephen had expected. Would his servant say that one of the Hands begged leave to speak to him? Message in return, requiring name of such Hand. Stephen Blackpool. There was nothing troublesome against Stephen Blackpool; yes, he might come in.
>
> Stephen Blackpool in the parlour. Mr Bounderby (whom he just knew by sight), at lunch on chop and sherry. Mrs Sparsit netting at the fire-side, in a side-saddle attitude, with one foot in a cotton stirrup. It was a part, at once of Mrs Sparsit's dignity and service, not to lunch. She supervised the meal

officially, but implied that in her own stately person she considered lunch a weakness.

'Now, Stephen,' said Mr Bounderby, 'what's the matter with *you*?'

Stephen made a bow. Not a servile one—these Hands will never do that! Lord bless you, sir, you'll never catch them at that, if they have been with you twenty years!—and, as a complimentary toilet for Mrs Sparsit, tucked his neckerchief ends into his waistcoat.

'Now, you know,' said Mr Bounderby, taking some sherry, 'we have never had any difficulty with you, and you have never been one of the unreasonable ones. You don't expect to be set up in a coach and six, and to be fed on turtle soup and venison, with a gold spoon, as a good many of 'em do!' Mr Bounderby always represented this to be the sole, immediate, and direct object of any Hand who was not entirely satisifed; 'and therefore I know already that you have not come here to make a complaint. Now, you know, I am certain of that, beforehand.'

'No, sir, sure I ha' not coom for nowt o' th' kind.'

Mr Bounderby seemed agreeably surprised, notwithstanding his previous strong conviction. 'Very well,' he returned. 'You're a steady Hand, and I was not mistaken. Now, let me hear what it's all about. As it's not that, let me hear what it is. What have you got to say? Out with it, lad!'

Stephen happened to glance towards Mrs Sparsit. 'I can go, Mr Bounderby, if you wish it,' said that self-sacrificing lady, making a feint of taking her foot out of the stirrup.

Mr Bounderby stayed her, by holding a mouthful of chop in suspension before swallowing it, and putting out his left hand. Then, withdrawing his hand and swallowing his mouthful of chop, he said to Stephen:

'Now, you know, this good lady is a born lady, a high lady. You are not to suppose because she keeps my house for me, that she hasn't been very high up the tree—ah, up at the top of the tree! Now, if you have got anything to say that can't be said before a born lady, this lady will leave the room. If what you have got to say *can* be said before a born lady, this lady will stay where she is.'

'Sir, I hope I never had nowt to say, not fitten for a born lady to year, sin' I were born mysen,' was the reply, accompanied with a slight flush.

'Very well,' said Mr Bounderby, pushing away his plate, and leaning back. 'Fire away!'

'I ha' coom,' Stephen began, raising his eyes from the floor, after a moment's consideration, 'to ask yo yor advice. I need't overmuch. I were married on Eas'r Monday nineteen year sin, long and dree. She were a young lass— pretty enow—wi' good accounts of herseln. Well! She went bad—soon. Not along of me. Gonnows I were not a unkind husband to her.'

'I have heard all this before,' said Mr Bounderby. 'She took to drinking, left off working, sold the furniture, pawned the clothes, and played old Gooseberry.'

'I were patient wi' her.'

('The more fool you, I think,' said Mr Bounderby, in confidence to his wine-glass.)

'I were very patient wi' her. I tried to wean her fra't, ower and ower agen. I tried this, I tried that, I tried t'other. I ha' gone home, many's the time, and found all vanished as I had in the world, and her without a sense left to bless herseln lying on bare ground. I ha' dun't not once, not twice—twenty time!'

Every line in his face deepened as he said it, and put in its affecting evidence of the suffering he had undergone.

'From bad to worse, from worse to worsen. She left me. She disgraced herseln everyways, bitter and bad. She coom back, she coom back, she coom back. What could I do t' hinder her? I ha' walked the streets nights long, ere ever I'd go home. I ha' gone t' th' brigg, minded to fling myseln ower, and ha' no more on't. I ha' bore that much, that I were owd when I were young.'

Mrs Sparsit, easily ambling along with her netting-needles, raised the Coriolanian eyebrows and shook her head, as much as to say, 'The great know trouble as well as the small. Please to turn your humble eye in My direction.'

'I ha' paid her to keep awa' fra' me. These five year I ha' paid her. I ha' gotten decent fewtrils about me agen. I ha' lived hard and sad, but not ashamed and fearfo' a' the minnits o' my life. Last night, I went home. There she lay upon my har-stone! There she is!'

In the strength of his misfortune, and the energy of his distress, he fired for the moment like a proud man. In another moment, he stood as he had stood all the time— his usual stoop upon him; his pondering face addressed to Mr Bounderby, with a curious expression on it, half shrewd, half perplexed, as if his mind were set upon unravelling something very difficult; his hat held tight in his left hand, which rested on his hip; his right arm, with a rugged propriety and force of action, very earnestly emphasizing what he said: not least so when it always paused, a little bent, but not withdrawn, as he paused.

'I was acquainted with all this, you know,' said Mr Bounderby, 'except the last clause, long ago. It's a bad job, that's what it is. You had better had been satisfied as you were, and not have got married. However, it's too late to say that.'

'Was it an unequal marriage, sir, in point of years?' asked Mrs Sparsit.

'You hear what this lady asks. Was it an unequal marriage in point of years, this unlucky job of yours?' said Mr Bounderby.

'Not e'en so. I were one-and-twenty myseln; she were twenty nighbut.'

'Indeed, sir?' said Mrs Sparsit to her Chief, with great placidity. 'I inferred, from its being so miserable a marriage, that it was probably an unequal one in point of years.'

Mr Bounderby looked very hard at the good lady in a sidelong way that had an odd sheepishness about it. He fortified himself with a little more sherry.

'Well? Why don't you go on?' he then asked, turning rather irritably on Stephen Blackpool.

'I ha' coom to ask yo, sir, how I am to be ridded o' this woman.' Stephen infused a yet deeper gravity into the mixed expression of his attentive face. Mrs Sparsit uttered a gentle ejaculation, as having received a moral shock.

'What do you mean?' said Bounderby, getting up to lean his back against the chimney-piece. 'What are you talking about? You took her for better for worse.'

'I mun' be ridden o' her. I cannot bear't nommore. I ha' lived under't so long, for that I ha' had'n the pity and comforting words o' th' best lass living or dead. Haply, but for her, I should ha' gone hottering mad.'

'He wishes to be free, to marry the female of whom he speaks, I fear, sir,' observed Mrs Sparsit in an undertone, and much dejected by the immorality of the people.

'I do. The lady says what's right. I do. I were a coming to't. I ha' read i' th' papers that great fok (fair faw 'em a'! I wishes 'em no hurt!) are not bonded together for better for worse so fast, but that they can be set free fro' *their* misfortnet marriages, an marry ower agen. When they dunnot agree, for that their tempers is ill-sorted, they had rooms o' one kind an another in their houses, above a bit, and they can live asunders. We fok ha' only one room, an we can't. When that won't do, they ha' gowd an other cash, an they can say "This for yo, an that for me," an they can go their separate ways. We can't. Spite o' all that, they can be set free for smaller wrongs than mine. So, I mun be ridden o' this woman, an I want t'know how?'

'No how,' returned Mr Bounderby.

'If I do her any hurt, sir, there's a law to punish me?'

'Of course there is.'

'If I flee from her, there's a law to punish me?'

'Of course there is.'

'If I marry t'oother dear lass, there's a law to punish me?'

'Of course there is.'

'If I was to live wi' her an not marry her—saying such a thing could be, which it never could or would, an her so good—there's a law to punish me, in every innocent child belonging to me?'

'Of course there is.'

'Now, a' God's name,' said Stephen Blackpool, 'show me the law to help me!'

'Hem! There's a sanctity in this relation of life,' said Mr Bounderby, 'and— and—it must be kept up.'

'No no, dunnot say that, sir. 'Tan't kep' up that way. Not that way. 'Tis kep' down that way. I'm a weaver, I were in a fact'ry when a chilt, but I ha' gotten een to see wi' and eern to year wi'. I read in th' papers every 'Sizes, every Sessions—and you read too—I know it!—with dismay—how th' sup- posed unpossibility o' ever getting unchained from one another, at any price, on any terms, brings blood upon this land, and brings many common married fok to battle, murder, and sudden death. Let us ha' this, right understood. Mine's a grievous case, an I want—if yo will be so good—t'know the law that helps me.'

'Now, I tell you what!' said Mr Bounderby, putting his hands in his pockets. 'There *is* such a law.'

Stephen, subsiding into his quiet manner, and never wandering in his attention, gave a nod.

'But it's not for you at all. It costs money. It costs a mint of money.'

How much might that be? Stephen calmly asked.

'Why, you'd have to go to Doctors' Commons with a suit, and you'd have to go to a court of Common Law with a suit, and you'd have to go to the House of Lords with a suit, and you'd have to get an Act of Parliament to enable you to marry again, and it would cost you (if it was a case of very plain-sailing), I suppose from a thousand to fifteen hundred pound,' said Mr Bounderby. 'Perhaps twice the money.'

'There's no other law?'

'Certainly not.'

'Why then, sir,' said Stephen, turning white, and motioning with that right hand of his, as if he gave everything to the four winds, ''*tis* a muddle. 'Tis just a muddle a'toogether, an the sooner I am dead, the better.' . . .

1. What, according to Dickens, are the problems of the educational system in England during his time?
2. Based on the picture painted by Dickens in *Hard Times*, write a description of life for the working-class in industrial England.

▪ ▪ ▪

FYODOR DOSTOYEVSKY

The novels of Fyodor Dostoyevsky (1821-81) are among the most profound investigations of our inner life. A Russian, Dostoyevsky challenged much of the materialism and belief in progress in the West in the nineteenth century. With a view of human nature that was willful, mystical, and centered on suffering as one of the fundamentals of human experience, Dostoyevsky explored religious belief and the power of love. In his search for meaning and motivation, he rejected the image of human beings as rational creatures.

Dostoyevsky's *Notes from Underground* (1864) is a work in which his nameless anti-hero lashes out against the ideals of his time.

> Gentlemen, of course I'm joking, and I know I am not doing it very successfully, but you know you mustn't take everything I say for a joke. I may be joking with clenched teeth. Gentlemen, there are some questions that torment me; answer them for me. For example, here you are wanting to wean man from his old habits and correct his will to make it conform to the demands of science and common sense. But how do you know that you not only can, but ought to remake man like that? What makes you conclude that it is absolutely *necessary* to correct man's volition in that way? In short, how do you know that such a correction will be good for man? And, to sum the whole thing up, why are you so *certain* that not flying in the face of his real, normal interests, certified by the deductions of reason and arithmetic, is really always for his good and must be a law for all mankind? After all, for the time being it is only your supposition. Even if we assume it as a rule of logic, it may not be a law for all mankind at all. Perhaps you think I'm mad, gentlemen? Let me make a reservation. I agree that man is an animal predominantly constructive, foredoomed to conscious striving towards a goal, and applying himself to the art of engineering, that is to the everlasting and unceasing

Sources: Fyodor Dostoyevsky, *Notes from Underground and The Double* (Harmondsworth: Penguin Books, 1972), pp. 39-41; Fyodor Dostoyevsky, *The Brothers Karamazov* (New York: Signet, 1957), pp. 240-43.

construction of a road—*no matter where it leads*, and that the main point is not *where* it goes, but that it should go somewhere, and that a well-conducted child, even if he despises the engineering profession, should not surrender to that disastrous sloth which, as is well known, is the mother of all vices. Man loves construction and the laying out of roads, that is indisputable. But how is it that he is so passionately disposed to destruction and chaos? Tell me that! But on this subject I should like to put in two words of my own. Doesn't his passionate love for destruction and chaos (and nobody can deny that he is sometimes devoted to them; that is a fact), arise from his instinctive fear of attaining his goal and completing the building he is erecting? For all you know, perhaps it is only from a distance that he likes the building, and from close to he doesn't like it at all; perhaps, he only likes building it, not living in it, and leave it afterwards *aux animaux domestiques*, such as ants, sheep, etc. Ants' likes and dislikes are quite different. They have remarkable buildings of the same sort, that remain eternally undestroyed—ant-hills.

All respectable ants begin with the ant-hill, and they will probably end with it too, which does great credit to their constancy and their positive character. But man is a fickle and disreputable creature and perhaps, like a chess-player, is interested in the process of attaining his goal rather than the goal itself. And who knows, (nobody can say with certainty), perhaps man's sole purpose in this world consists in this uninterrupted process of attainment, or in other words in living, and not specifically in the goal, which of course must be something like twice two is four, that is, a formula; but after all, twice two is four is not life, gentlemen, but the beginning of death. At least, man has always feared this $2 \times 2 = 4$ formula, and I still fear it. We may suppose a man may do nothing but search for such equations, crossing the oceans and dedicating his life to the quest; but succeeding, really finding them—I swear he will be afraid of that. Really, he will feel that if he finds them, he will have nothing left to search for. When workmen have finished work, they at least receive their money, they go and spend it in the pub, they get hauled off to the police-station—that's enough to occupy them for a week. But where can mankind go? To say the least, something uncomfortable is to be noticed in man on the achievement of similar goals. He likes progress towards the goal, but he does not altogether care for the achievement of it, and that, of course, is ridiculous. In short, mankind is comically constructed; all this plainly amounts to a joke. But $2 \times 2 = 4$ is nevertheless an intolerable thing. Twice two is four is, in my opinion, nothing but impudence. 'Two and two make four' is like a cocky young devil standing across your path with arms akimbo and a defiant air. I agree that two and two make four is an excellent thing; but to give everything its due, two and two make five is also a very fine thing.

And why are you so firmly and triumphantly certain that only what is normal and positive—in short, only well-being—is good for man? Is reason mistaken about what is good? After all, perhaps prosperity isn't the only thing that pleases mankind, perhaps he is just as attracted to suffering. Perhaps suffering is just as good for him as prosperity. Sometimes a man is intensely, even passionately, attached to suffering—that is a fact. About this there is no need to consult universal history: ask yourself, if you are a man and have ever lived even in some degree. As for my own personal opinion, I find it somehow unseemly to love only well-being. Whether it's a good thing or a bad thing, smashing things is also sometimes very pleasant. I am not here standing up for suffering, or for well-being either. I am standing out for my own caprices and for having them guaranteed when necessary. There is no place for suffering in farces, for example, I know that. It is quite inconceivable in a millennium: suffering is doubt, negation, and what sort of millennium would it be of which one could have any doubts? All the same, I am certain that man will never deny himself destruction and chaos. Suffering—after all, that is the sole cause of consciousness. Although I declared to begin with that in my opinion consciousness is man's supreme misfortune, I know that man loves it and would not change it for any gratification. Consciousness is infinitely greater than, for example, two and two make four. After twice two is achieved there will of course be nothing left to do, much less to learn. All that will then be possible will be to shut off one's five senses and immerse oneself in meditation. But with consciousness, even if it has the same result, I mean that there will be nothing to do, at least one could sometimes resort to self-flagellation, and that stimulates, at any rate. It may be retrograde, but all the same it's better than nothing. . .

◆B◆ In his last novel, *The Brothers Karamazov* (1880), Dostoyevsky dealt with the issues of injustice, evil, struggle, and faith. One section, called "The Grand Inquisitor," is an allegory about human life, in which people are seen as striving for freedom but needing authority. The tale is told by Ivan, a rationalist, to his brother, Alyosha, a monk. It is an exploration of the paradoxes inherent in the dichotomies of freedom and authority, and reason and faith.

Alyosha had listened in silence. Toward the end he was greatly moved and seemed several times on the point of interrupting, but he restrained himself. Now his words came with a rush.

"But . . . that's absurd!" he cried. "Your poem is in praise of Jesus, not in blame of Him—as you meant it to be. And who will believe you about freedom? Is that the way to understand it? That's not the idea of it in the Orthodox Church . . . That's Rome, and not even the whole of Rome, it's false—those are the worst Catholics, the Inquisitors, the Jesuits! . . . And there could not be such a fantastic creature as your Inquisitor. What are these sins of mankind they take on themselves? Who are these keepers of the mystery who have taken some curse upon themselves for the happiness of mankind? When have they been seen? We know the Jesuits. They are spoken ill of, but surely they are not what you describe? They are not that at all, not at all. . . . They are simply the Romish army for the earthly sovereignty of the world in the future, with the Pontiff of Rome for Emperor . . . That's their ideal, but there's no sort of mystery about it. . . . It's simple lust for power, for filthy earthly gain, for domination—something like a universal serfdom with them as masters— that's all they stand for. They don't even believe in God perhaps. Your suffering Grand Inquisitor is a mere fantasy."

"Wait, wait," laughed Ivan. "How upset you are! A fantasy you say, let it be so! Of course it's a fantasy. But let me say: do you really think that the Roman Catholic movement of the last centuries is actually nothing but the lust for power, for filthy earthly gain? Is that Father Paissy's teaching?''

"No, no, on the contrary, Father Paissy did once say something rather the same as you . . . But of course it's not the same, not at all the same." Alyosha quickly corrected himself.

"A precious admission, in spite of your 'not at all the same.' I ask you why your Jesuits and Inquisitors have united simply for vile material gain? Why can there not be among them one martyr oppressed by great sorrow and loving humanity? You see, only suppose that there was one such man among all those who desire nothing but filthy material gain—if there's only one like my old Inquisitor, who had himself eaten roots in the desert and made frenzied efforts to subdue his flesh to make himself free and perfect. But yet all his life he loved humanity, and suddenly his eyes were opened, and he saw that it is no great moral blessedness to attain perfection and freedom, if at the same time one gains the conviction that millions of God's creatures have been created as a mockery, that they will never be capable of using their freedom, that these poor rebels can never turn into giants to complete the tower, that it was not for such geese that the great idealist dreamt his dream of harmony. Seeing all that he turned back and joined—the clever people. Surely that could have happened?"

"Joined whom, what clever people?" cried Alyosha, completely carried away. "They have no such great cleverness and no mysteries and secrets. . . . Perhaps nothing but atheism, that's all their secret. Your Inquisitor does not believe in God, that's his secret!"

"What if he doesn't believe in God! At last you have guessed it. It's perfectly true that that's the whole secret. But isn't that suffering, at least for a man like that, who has wasted his whole life in the desert and yet could not shake off his incurable love of humanity? In his old age he reached the clear conviction that nothing but the advice of the great dread spirit could build up any tolerable sort of life for the feeble, unruly 'incomplete, empirical creatures created in jest.' And so, convinced of this, he sees that he must follow the council of the wise spirit, the dread spirit of death and destruction, and accept lying and deception, and lead men consciously to death and destruction. He sees that he must deceive them all the way so that they may not notice where they are being led, that the poor blind creatures may at least on the way think themselves happy. And note, the deception is in the name of Him in whose ideal the old man had so fervently believed all his life. Is not that tragic? And if only one such stood at the head of the whole army 'filled with the lust for power only for the sake of filthy gain'—would not one such be enough to make a tragedy? More than that, one such standing at the head is enough to create the actual leading idea of the Roman Church with all its armies and Jesuits, its highest idea. I tell you frankly that I firmly believe that there has always been such a man among those who stood at the head of the movement. Who knows, there may have been some such even among the Roman Popes. Who knows, perhaps the spirit of that accursed old man who loves mankind so obstinately in his own way, is to be found even now in a whole multitude of such old men, existing not by chance but by agreement. Perhaps these old men formed a secret league long ago for the guarding of the mystery, to guard it from the weak and the unhappy, so as to make them happy. No doubt it is so and so it must be indeed. I believe that even among the Masons there's something of the same mystery and that that's why the Catholics detest the Masons. They feel that the Masons are breaking up the unity of the idea, while it is so essential that there should be one flock and one shepherd. . . . But from the way I defend my idea you might think that I am angry at your criticism. Enough of it."

"Maybe you are a Mason yourself!" said Alyosha suddenly. "You don't believe in God," he added, speaking this time very sorrowfully. He felt that his brother was looking at him ironically. "How does your poem end?" he asked, suddenly looking down. "Or was that the end?"

"I meant to end it like this. When the Inquisitor stopped speaking he waited some time for his Prisoner to answer him. His silence weighed down upon him. He saw that the Prisoner had listened carefully all the time, looking gently in his face. But evidently he did not want to reply. The old man longed for Him to say something, however bitter and terrible. But He suddenly approached the old man in silence and softly kissed him on the forehead. That was his answer. The old man shuddered. His lips moved. He went to the door, opened it and said to Him: 'Go, and come no more. . . . Come not at all, never, never!' And he let Him out into the dark alleys of the town. The Prisoner went away."

"And the old man?"

"The kiss glows in his heart, but the old man holds to his idea."

"And you with him, you too?" cried Alyosha sadly.

Ivan laughed.

"Why, it's all nonsense. Alyosha. It's only a senseless poem of a senseless student, who could never write two lines of verse. Why do you take it so seriously? Surely you don't think I am going straight off to the Jesuits, to join the men who are correcting His work? Good Lord, it's no business of mine. I told you, all I want is to live on to thirty, and then . . . dash the cup to the ground!"

"But the little sticky leaves, and the precious tombs, and the blue sky, and the woman you love! How will you live, how will you love them?" Alyosha asked sorrowfully. "With such a hell in your heart and your head, how can you? No, that's just what you are going away for, to join them . . . if not, you will kill yourself, you can't endure it!"

"There is a strength to endure everything," Ivan said with a cold smile.

"What strength?"

"The strength of the Karamazovs—the strength of the Karamazov baseness."

"To sink into debauchery? To stifle your soul with corruption?"

"Possibly even that . . . only perhaps till I am thirty I will escape it, and then."

"How will you escape it? By what will you escape it? That's impossible with your ideas."

"In the Karamazov way."

" 'Everything is lawful,' you mean? Everything is lawful, is that it?"

Ivan scowled, and all at once turned strangely pale. "Ah, you're repeating yesterday's phrase, which so offended Miusov—and which Dmitri pounced upon so naively and paraphrased!" He smiled queerly. "Yes, if you like, 'everything is lawful' since the word has been said. I won't deny it. And Dmitri's version isn't bad."

Alyosha looked at him in silence.

"I thought that in going away from here I would at least have you," Ivan said suddenly with unexpected feeling. "But now I see that there is no place for me even in your heart, my dear hermit. The formula, 'all is lawful,' I won't renounce. Will you renounce me for that?"

Alyosha got up, went to him and softly kissed him on the forehead.

"That's plagiarism," cried Ivan, highly delighted. "You stole that from my poem. But thank you. Come, Alyosha, it's time we were going, both of us." . . .

1. "Humanity's struggle is its goal. As a result, man fears ever reaching perfection, for without that struggle, life would cease to have meaning." Comment on this attitude as reflected by Dostoyevsky and contrast its thesis with the ideas of Condorcet.

▪ ▪ ▪

GEORGE SAND

George Sand (1804-76), born Amantine Lucile Aurore Dupin, was regarded by many European intellectuals as the most remarkable woman of her age. By the time she was thirty she had written a major novel, which argued against traditional marriage and in favour of the emancipation of women, and had begun a life in which she supported herself by her writing. Sand had a succession of lovers, including, for nine years, the great composer Frédéric Chopin. Starting as a romantic novelist, Sand became a socialist and a democrat. In 1848 she became involved in the provisional government in France as the editor of its major bulletin. Sand published an immense amount, and also carried on a voluminous correspondence with her friends, many of whom were the major thinkers of the day. Her own life and work became a touchstone for a new view of the role of women in society.

A In March 1848, Sand discussed the divisions in France during the revolution of 1848, and outlined her beliefs in the "Letter to the Rich."

> The great fear—or pretext—of the aristocracy at this hour is communism. If it were possible to laugh at such a serious moment, we would find this fear really amusing. By the word "communism," they really mean the people, their needs, their hopes. Let us not be confused: the people are the people, communism is the calumniated, misunderstood future of the people.
>
> The ruse is useless: it is the people who upset and worry you, the Republic whose development you fear, and the idea of rights for all that you cannot bear without discomfort or resentment. . . .

Source: Joseph Barry, translator and editor, *George Sand: In her own words* (Garden City, New York: Anchor Books, 1979), pp. 373-75, 354-55, 405, 410-13.

This phantom which you dare not even face you have chosen to all "communism." You are terrified by an idea because there are groups who believe in this idea, because this belief will one day spread and, little by little, change the whole social structure. Supposing its triumph to be near, do you not realize that, whether you reveal your fear and aversion, whether you cover your eyes with your hands so as not to see it, or whether, summoning your courage, you succeed in provoking blind hatred against it, you are only going to give this idea an importance, a cohesion, and a luster it does not yet pretend to have? You are still yesterday's men, you still believe that you can defend your viewpoint by bitter, hostile struggle. You are making an unthinkable error. Can you not understand that the equality to which you, as well as the people, are entitled can only be achieved through liberty? I should also invoke fraternity, if I could believe that there was among you a heart so hard as not to understand that this word carries within itself its own definition—health of the soul. . . .

Alas, no! The people are not communist. And yet France is destined to become communist within a century. Among the people communism has reached an infinitely small minority. Now, you know that if majorities represent the truths of the present, then minorities represent those of the future. Therefore we should show regard and respect for minorities and give them freedom. Refused these things, they become hostile; they may even become dangerous; we are reduced to controlling them by force; and they either suffer martyrdom or seek revenge.

Martyrdom morally kills those who inflict it, just as revenge physically kills those who suffer it. So allow communism to live in peace, for it will develop more rapidly in war, and you can only inspire its followers with wisdom, restraint, and patience by allowing them freedom to present their theories. If these are crazy and unjust, do not worry; the people will discard them with cheerful common sense, just as the monarchy was discarded. If they are worthy and can be gradually applied, you yourself will be obliged to recognize them, since, instead of threatening existing property rights, they insure their continuation for as long as is necessary. . . .

 Sand wrote to a friend on August 1, 1848 about the failure of the French Revolution of 1848.

There are two kinds of property, just as there are two kinds of lives. There is private property, as there is private and individual life. And there is common, public property, as there is a common, public life—that is to say, social life, the life of human relations. All societies have always recognized common, public property and sanctified it in their laws. No society is possible without such property.

It has been characteristic of private property, of its abuse and exaggeration, to give rise to extreme inequalities of condition. However good and legitimate it may be in itself, it has to find its remedy in the wide and wise enlargement of common property. Common property, of course, includes highways, railroads, canals, mines, revenues—everything that cannot be monopolized by private individuals without an unwarranted encroachment upon the wealth of all. Such encroachment nevertheless took place during the reign of speculation and unrestrained individualism. The riches of all became the object of speculation of the privileged class and today this class claims more loudly than ever to be proprietor of the property of the state. . . .

Thus, there must be two kinds of communism. I have drawn your attention to the errors and excesses of one, which I have never had nor could I ever have any part in defending. And there is social communism, which only demands fundamental common rights and the progressive extension, suitably adapted to circumstances, of these rights. No reasonable creature can reject *this* communism, although the word, perverted by blindly progressive sects and by blind enemies of progress, has become a badge one can wear when one wishes to be attacked by the unintelligent, the profligate, the swindlers and fools of all kinds.

Because of their instinctive understanding of this communism but because they promoted it piecemeal, without clarity or commitment, the government of the period from February to May [1848] failed. By rejecting it with bias, prejudice, and self-interest, the majority of the Assembly brought on the June disasters. The June insurrectionists probably did not know what they were fighting for. The force of circumstance, physical and spiritual unrest, led them inevitably to be roused by leaders with no social ideas, as far as I know, and who are even suspected of having been the agents of foreign powers, of royal pretenders, and of extreme bourgeois reactionaries.

C Sand had much to say about the place of women in nineteenth century society. In 1837, she wrote the following:

Women are given a deplorable education. This is men's greatest crime against them. Men have introduced abuses everywhere, monopolizing the advantages of the most consecrated institutions. They have played upon even the most innocent and legitimate feelings. They have succeeded in bringing about the enslavement and degradation of women, a condition which today they claim was instituted by God and is part of unchanging law.

D In 1848 Sand discussed the dilemmas surrounding the legal relations between men and women at that time.

Should women participate one day in political life? Yes, one day. Here I agree with you. But is that day near? No, I do not think so. For the condition of women to be changed, society must first be changed radically.

Perhaps we already agree on these two questions. But this raises a third question. Some women ask, If society is to be changed, must not women intervene politically in public affairs from this very moment? I make so bold as to reply that they must not, because social conditions are such that women could not honorably and honestly exercise a political mandate.

As women are under the tutelage and domination of men through marriage, they cannot possibly give guarantees of political independence unless they individually, and in defiance of laws and customs, break this tutelage hallowed by custom and law.

Thus it seems senseless to me, and I ask forgiveness of those of my sex who have thought necessary to follow this line, to begin where one should end and end where one should begin. . . .

To leave no ambiguity about these considerations I am bringing forward, I shall express my whole thought concerning this famous emancipation of women, so much discussed of late.

I believe it to be easily and immediately realizable, in so far as the present state of our customs allows. It consists simply in giving back to women the civil rights which marriage alone deprives them of, which remaining single alone maintains for them. This detestable error of our legislation places woman under the covetous domination of man and transforms a married woman into an eternal minor; it might induce most young women never to marry, if they had the slightest idea about civil legislation at the time they give up their rights. It is strange that the guardians of the old order ostentatiously attach to their lying slogan the words of "family" and "property," since the marriage pact, as admired and proclaimed by them, totally destroys the property rights of one whole sex. Either property or marriage is not as holy as they declare, for two equally holy things cannot logically cancel out each other. . . .

Until civil equality is enshrined in the law there will certainly be exceptional and intolerable abuses of marital authority. The housewife and mother, still a minor at the age of eighty, is certainly in a ridiculous and humiliating situation. It is certain that the despotic powers attributed to the husband give him the right to refuse to provide for the material welfare of his wife and children; the right to commit adultery outside the home; the right to control alone, without his wife, the education of their children; a right to corrupt the latter through bad example or principles—for instance, by giving them his mistresses as governesses as has been known in illustrious families; the right to command the household and give orders to servants and maids; especially the right to insult his wife; the right to turn out the wife's parents while imposing on her his own; the right to reduce her to the hardships of poverty while squandering away her rightful income or capital on prostitutes; the right to beat her and have her complaints rejected by a court of law, if she fails to produce witnesses or recoils in the face of scandal; finally, the right to dishonor her by unjust suspicions as well as to have her punished for misbehavior. All these rights are barbarous, abominable, and inhumane, and I would go so far as to say that they are the sole cause of the infidelities, quarrels, scandals, and crimes which so often defile the sanctuary of the family, and they will continue to defile it, O poor human beings, until you do away with the scaffold and prison chains for criminals, with insults and domestic slavery, with prison and public shame for unfaithful wives. Until that day, women will always have the vices of the oppressed, that is to say, the cunning ruses of slaves; and those among you who are not in a position to be tyrants will be what so many are today: the ridiculous slaves of these tyrants' vengeful slaves. . . .

Yes, civil equality, equality in marriage, equality in the family—that is what you should ask for, indeed demand. . . . No man should obey a woman—that would be monstrous; no man should give orders to a woman—that is despicable.

1. Outline Sand's rationale for not interfering with communism, in her "Letter to the Rich" of France.

2. Explain Sand's definition of social communism.
3. Compare Sand's opinion on the treatment of women in society with that of Mill's. In the face of such arguments, account for the continued suppression of women's rights in the nineteenth century.

• • •

CHARLES BAUDELAIRE

Some of the most important poetry of the nineteenth century was written by Charles Baudelaire (1821-67). Interested in the exotic and the imagination, Baudelaire published *Les fleurs du mal* in 1857 to a cry of scandal and obscenity from a public that found it difficult to understand his intentions. Baudelaire wished poetry to be totally different from prose, to be a language of connotation and a vehicle of personal creativity. His concern with evil and the unusual set him apart from many of his contemporaries, and his use of symbolic language required a new critical sensibility. However, his influence was enormous, and many later poets have acknowledged their debt to Baudelaire as a pioneer in the possibilities of language and in the freeing of poetry from traditional constraints.

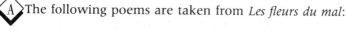 The following poems are taken from *Les fleurs du mal*:

PREFACE

Folly and error, sin and avarice
Work on our bodies, occupy our thoughts,
And we ourselves sustain our sweet regrets
As mendicants nourish their worms and lice.

Our wrongs are stubborn, our repentance base;
We lavishly pay for confessions,
And to the muddy path gaily return,
Thinking that vile tears will our sins erase.

Our evil's pillow Satan Trismegist
Our ravished senses at his leisure lulls,
And all the precious metal of our wills
Is vaporized by this arch-scientist.

The Devil holds our strings in puppetry!
In objects vile we find attraction;
Each day we sink nearer perdition,
Unhorrified, through rank obscurity.

Source: Charles Baudelaire, *Selected Poems*, translated and introduced by Joanna Richardson (Harmondsworth: Penguin Books, 1975), pp. 27-28, 47, 111-12.

As some poor libertine will bite and kiss
The bruised breast of an ancient courtesan,
We catch a passing pleasure clandestine,
Like an old orange squeeze out all its juice.

And, like a million helminths swarming, dense,
A world of Demons tipple in our brains,
And, when we breathe, Death in our lungs remains,
River invisible, with dull complaints.

If rape and dagger, fire and hellebore
Have not yet prinked out with designs ornate
The common canvas of our wretched fate,
It is, alas, that our faint soul demurs.

And yet among the jackals, panthers, hounds,
The monkeys, serpents, vultures, scorpions,
The beasts which howl and growl and crawl and scream
And in our heinous zoo of sins abound,

There's one more hideous, evil, obscene!
Though it makes no great gesture, no great cry,
It would lay waste the earth quite willingly,
And in a yawn engulf creation.

Boredom! Its eyes with tears unwilling shine,
It dreams of scaffolds, smoking its cheroot.
Reader, you know this monster delicate,
—Double-faced reader,—kinsman,—brother mine!

The Enemy

My youth was nothing but a sombre storm,
Shot through from time to time by brilliant sun;
Thunder and rain such havoc did perform
That there remain few fruits vermilion.

Now I have reached the autumn of my mind,
I must with spade and rake turn gardener,
Restore again the inundated ground,
Where water hollows holes like sepulchres.

And who knows if my reverie's new flowers
Will in this soil washed like a sandy shore
Find mystic aliment to make them bloom?

—O sorrow, sorrow! Time eats life away,
The Foe obscure which does our hearts consume
Grows stronger from our blood and our decay!

AUTUMN SONG

i

Soon we shall plunge into the shadows cold;
Farewell, the brilliance of brief summers gone!
Already I can hear the sad trees felled,
The wood resounding on the courtyard stone.

All winter will return into my soul:
Hate, anger, horror, toil, and sudden chill,
And, like the sun in its antarctic hell,
My heart, a red and frozen block, is still.

I listen, trembling, to each log that falls;
The scaffold being built echoes less dull.
My spirit broken like a citadel
By heavy battering-rams infallible.

I feel, lulled by these blows monotonous,
As if, quickly, a coffin were nailed down.
For whom?—Summer is dead; here autumn is!
This strange sound echoes as for someone gone.

ii

I love the greenish light of your long eyes,
Sweet beauty, but today all saddens me,
No love or hearth or boudoir satisfies
My soul like radiant sunshine on the sea.

Yet love me, tender heart! A mother be,
Though for a sinner, for a thankless man;
Be mistress, sister, sweetness transitory
Of splendid autumn or of setting sun.

Brief task! The grave awaits me, avidly!
O let me on your lap my head incline,
Lament the incandescent summer day,
Savour the golden sweetness of decline.

1. Identify several images and themes in Baudelaire's poems, and compare
   them with those used by contemporary poets and songwriters.

▪ ◇ ▪

At the end of the nineteenth and the beginning of the twentieth century, Western tradition was challenged as it had not been since the Renaissance. Not content with revising and developing earlier ideas, writers and artists in all areas often rejected many of the assumptions that had guided the West, including the rationality of human nature, the objectivity of science, and the ability of human beings to make choices from sets of alternatives based upon reason. Fresh concepts were opened up and new emphasis was placed on the role of myth and in exploring the depths of our inner life. A drastic revision about the nature of humanity and our understanding of and relationship to the world occured at that time.

The irrational and the importance of our inner life was explored anew. Nietzsche demanded a new philosophy, one based on will rather than reason. He influenced many thinkers who called for a new, more creative understanding of evolution and human development, as well as Sorel, who emphasized the role of violence and myth in our social and political lives. At the same time, Van Gogh, in his artistic endeavour, explored his own inner life as a means of understanding all of humanity.

The period was a liberal and constitutional era in the politics of the West, as the franchise was broadened and the middle-class gained more economic, political, and social power. Chekhov recorded the eventual demise of the old aristocracy, while Ibsen challenged bourgeois values and institutions as being artificial and restrictive. The novelist Zola investigated the life of the great under-class, those who did manual work to keep society going, and he had compassion for the poor and the people who did not benefit during a time in which more wealth existed than ever before. In social and political philosophy, Bernstein, in western Europe, revised Marxist ideas to put them into conformity with his value of a developing social democracy; Lenin, in eastern Europe, insisted that the Marxist tradition not abandon its revolutionary tactics and its ultimate goals.

In this period the major work of two of the most seminal and influential figures in modern history was begun. Einstein put forth his idea of relativity and changed the way we think about the physical world and our relationship to it. Freud developed psychoanalysis and his theories about the human personality which restructured the dialogue about human nature. Both men not only challenged the tradition they inherited; they transformed it forever and in their broad areas set the tone for the next century of development.

The First World War seemed to ratify the work of the radical intellectuals who had revised, and sometimes abandoned, much of their cultural heritage. This war was a great tragedy for the whole of civilization, four years of death and destruction without precedent in human history. Writers and artists of the war responded with sensitive and personal works, sometimes with the view that in the midst of such enormous horror it might be necessary to start again. The creativity of many of those who worked in this period, Nietzsche, Einstein and Freud among them, came to form the basis of twentieth century thought.

▪ ◈ ▪

FRIEDRICH NIETZSCHE

Rejecting both traditional religion and modern science as the bases of truth and meaning, Friedrich Nietzsche (1844-1900) demanded that philosophy in the West open itself to different ideas. He emphasized myth, art, and individual will, as he abandoned much of the inherited philosophical tradition from the ancient world and the Judeo-Christian tradition. Nietzsche found contemporary morality to be limiting to human potential. He praised the superior individual, disliked democracy and nationalism, and challenged the validity of the Christian conception of the deity. His work, a sometimes startling probe into all that was human, introduced much that became characteristic of the twentieth century.

In *Beyond Good and Evil* (1885), Nietzsche turned around the usual conceptions of truth and falsehood, philosophy and dogma.

> The falseness of a given judgment does not constitute an objection against it, so far as we are concerned. It is perhaps in this respect that our new language sounds strangest. The real question is how far a judgment furthers and maintains life, preserves a given type, possibly cultivates and trains a given type. We are, in fact, fundamentally inclined to maintain that the falsest judgments are the most indispensable to us, that man cannot live without accepting the logical fictions as valid, without measuring reality against the purely invented world of the absolute, the immutable, without constantly falsifying the world by means of numeration. That getting along without false judgments would amount to getting along without life, negating life. To admit untruth as a necessary condition of life: this implies, to be sure, a perilous resistance against customary value-feelings. A philosophy that risks it nonetheless, if it did nothing else, would by this alone have taken its stand beyond good and evil.
>
> What tempts us to look at all philosophers half suspiciously and half mockingly is not so much that we recognize again and again how innocent they are, how often and how easily they make mistakes and lose their way, in short their childishness and childlike-ness—but rather that they are not sufficiently candid, though they make a great virtuous noisy to-do as soon as the problem of truthfulness is even remotely touched upon. Every one of them pretends that he has discovered and reached his opinions through the self-development of cold, pure, divinely untroubled dialectic (in distinction to the mystics of every rank who, more honest and fatuous, talk about "inspiration"), whereas, at bottom, a pre-conceived dogma, a notion, an "institution," or mostly a heart's desire, made abstract and refined, is defended by them with arguments sought after the fact. They are all of them lawyers (though wanting to be called anything but that), and for the most part quite sly defenders of their prejudices which they christen "truths"—*very* far removed they are from the courageous conscience which admits precisely this; . . .

Sources: Friedrich Nietzsche, *Beyond Good and Evil* (Chicago: Henry Regnery Company, 1955), pp. 4-5, 47-49, 174-75; Friedrich Nietzsche, *The Birth of Tragedy* [and] *The Genealogy of Morals* (Garden City, New York: Doubleday and Company, Inc., 1956), pp. 11, 298-99.

One must test oneself to see if one is meant for independence and for command. And one must do it at the right time. Never avoid your tests, though they may be the most dangerous game you can play, and in the end are merely tests at which you are the only witness and the sole judge. Never remain tied up with a person—not even the most beloved. Every person is a prison and a tight corner. Never remain tied up with a fatherland—not even when it most suffers and needs help (it is somewhat less difficult to untie one's heart for a victorious fatherland). Never remain tied up with compassion—not even compassion for a superior human being into whose rare torture and helplessness chance has given us an insight. Nor with a science, not even if it lures us with the most precious findings that seem to have been stored up for us alone. Never remain tied up with our own emancipation, that delicious bird-like distance and strangeness which soars ever higher and sees more and more spread out below; the danger of things that fly. Nor with our own virtues which would sacrifice the whole of us to some one thing, to our hospitality, for example. This is the danger of dangers to superior and lavish souls who spend themselves extravagantly and almost indifferently, turning the virtue of liberality into a vice. One must know how to *conserve* oneself. That is the most rigorous test of independence.

A new species of philosopher is coming up over the horizon. I risk baptizing them with a name that is not devoid of peril. As I read them (as they allow themselves to be read—for it is characteristic of their type that they wish to remain riddles in some sense), these philosophers of the future have a right (perhaps also a wrong!) to be called: *Experimenters*. This name itself is only an experiment, and, if you will, a temptation.

Will they be new friends of "truth," these coming philosophers? Most probably, for all philosophers thus far have loved their truths. But surely they will not be dogmatists. It must run counter to their pride and their taste that their truth should be a truth for everyman, this having been the secret wish and ultimate motive of all dogmatic striving. "My judgment is *my* judgment, to which hardly anyone else has a right," is what the philosopher of the future will say. One must get rid of the bad taste of wishing to agree with many others. "Good" is no longer good in the mouth of my neighbor. And how could there be a "common good"! The expression contradicts itself: what can be common cannot have much value. In the end it must be as it always was: great things remain for the great; abysses for the deep; delicacies and tremors for the subtle; and, all in all, all things rare for the rare!— . . .

 Nietzsche attacked democracy and nationalism.

Call it "civilization" or "humanization" or "progress"—this present-day distinction which is being sought for Europeans; or call it simply, without praise or blame, by its political formula: the democratic movement in Europe. Behind all the moral and political foregrounds which such formulas designate, there is going on an immense *physiological* process whose current is running strong. The process of the mutual assimilation of Europeans, their growing separation from the conditions which give rise to climatically determined and caste-bound races, their increasing independence of any *definite* milieu that would seek to inscribe itself on their bodies and souls with centuries of unvarying demands. In other words, the gradual appearance of an essentially supra-national and nomadic type of human being who, physiologically speaking, has a maximum of adaptability as his typical excellence. This process of the "European in progress" might be slowed up by some great relapses, but it would more than gain in vehemence and depth what it might lose in time. The still raging storm and stress of "national feelings" is one of these forces, likewise the presently emerging anarchism. The whole process will probably end with results least expected by its naive furtherers and admirers, the apostles of "modern ideas." The same new conditions which will, on the average, bring about an equalization and mediocritization of man, a useful, hardworking, adaptable herd-animal of many uses, are also disposed in the highest degree to the creation of exceptional men of most dangerous and fascinating quality. For while the adaptability which is constantly tested in changing conditions and which begins its work anew with each generation, almost with each decade, offers no possibility for a *powerful type*; while the total impression that these future Europeans will make will probably be one of manifold, gossipy, willpower-poor and extremely employable workers who *need* a boss, a master who gives them commands, as they need their daily bread; while in other words, the democratization of Europe will amount to the creation of a type prepared in the subtlest sense for *slavery*—the individual, meanwhile, the exceptional case, the *strong* man, will turn out to be stronger and richer than he has probably ever been, thanks to the lack of prejudice in his schooling, thanks to the enormous varied practice he can get in skills and disguises. I meant to say that the democratization of Europe is at the same time an involuntary arrangement for the training of tyrants—taking the word in every sense, including its most intellectual. . . .

C Conventional morality and religion were challenged through the image of Dionysos, a Greek god of fertility and wine, who was associated with dancing, ecstasy, and the abandonment of rational limits.

As for morality, on the other hand, could it be anything but a will to deny life, a secret instinct of destruction, a principle of calumny, a reductive agent— the beginning of the end?—and, for that very reason, the Supreme Danger? Thus it happened that in those days, with this problem book, my vital instincts turned against ethics and founded a radical counterdoctrine, slanted esthetically, to oppose the Christian libel on life. But it still wanted a name. Being a philologist, that is to say a man of *words*, I christened it rather arbitrarily— for who can tell the real name of the Antichrist?—with the name of a Greek god, Dionysos. . . .

D The "ascetic" ideal, one of self-sacrifice and giving up one's own will, was challenged by Nietzsche in one of his last major works, *The Genealogy of Morals* (1887).

Until the advent of the ascetic ideal, man, the animal *man*, had no meaning at all on this earth. His existence was aimless; the question, "Why is there such a thing as man?" could not have been answered; man willed neither himself nor the world. Behind every great human destiny there rang, like a refrain, an even greater "In vain!" Man knew that something was lacking; a great vacuum surrounded him. He did not know how to justify, to explain, to affirm himself. His own meaning was an unsolved problem and made him suffer. He also suffered in other respects, being altogether an ailing animal, yet what bothered him was not his suffering but his inability to answer the question "What is the meaning of my trouble?" Man, the most courageous animal, and the most inured to trouble, does not deny suffering *per se*: he wants it, he seeks it out, provided that it can be given a meaning. Finally the ascetic ideal arose to give it meaning—its only meaning, so far. But any meaning is better than none and, in fact, the ascetic ideal has been the best stopgap that ever existed. Suffering had been interpreted, the door to all suicidal nihilism slammed shut. No doubt that interpretation brought new suffering in its wake, deeper, more inward, more poisonous suffering: it placed all suffering under the perspective of *guilt*. . . . All the same, man had saved himself, he had achieved a meaning, he was no longer a leaf in the wind, a plaything of circumstances, of "crass casualty": he was now able to will something—no matter the object or the instrument of his willing; the will itself had been saved. We can no longer conceal from ourselves what exactly it is that this whole process of willing, inspired by the ascetic ideal, signifies— this hatred of humanity, of animality, of inert matter; this loathing of the senses, of reason even; this fear of beauty and happiness; this longing to escape from illusion, change, becoming, death, and from longing itself. It signifies, let us have the courage to face it, a will to nothingness, a revulsion from life, a rebellion against the principal conditions of living. And yet, despite everything, it is and remains a *will*. Let me repeat, now that I have reached the end, what I said at the beginning: man would sooner have the void for his purpose than be void of purpose. . . .

1. Account for Nietzsche's attitude with respect to the acceptance of the existence of "untruth."
2. In *Beyond Good and Evil* what criticisms are laid against the traditional approach to philosophy?
3. Comment on Nietzsche's argument that individuals must know how to "conserve" themselves.
4. Respond to Nietzsche's contention that the furtherance of democratic institutions would result in both the "mediocritization of man" and the emergence of a new class of tyrants.
5. Using the arguments put forward by Nietzsche, defend the following: "Man would sooner have the void for his purpose than be void of purpose."

▪ ▪ ▪

VINCENT VAN GOGH

The life of Vincent van Gogh (1853-90) was described by Pablo Picasso as "one which is the archetype of our times: . . . an essentially solitary and tragic adventure." Now recognized as one of the most profound and talented artists in the history of the West, Van Gogh was ignored in his own lifetime by the general public. He knew many languages and was very intelligent, but he was subject to extremes of excitement and sadness, which made it difficult for him to maintain continuing social relationships. He had great compassion for his fellow human beings and started as a lay preacher, but found it difficult to sustain that work. His thread to normal life was his brother Theo, who gave him emotional and financial support. Vincent wrote hundreds of letters to Theo recording his quest for an art which many believe reflected the innermost feelings of humanity and which became a testament to human creativity.

 Van Gogh, in 1882, wrote to his brother, giving some thoughts on art and life.

I approve of principles and think them worth while only when they develop into actions, and I think it well to reflect and to try to be conscientious, because this strengthens a man's energy and unites his different activities into a whole. Those people whom you describe would, I think, be more stable if they thought more about what they were going to do, but for the rest I greatly prefer them to those people who air their principles without taking the slightest trouble or even thinking of putting them into practice. For the latter have no use for their most beautiful principles, and the former are just the people who, if they begin to live with energy and reflection, might achieve something great. For great things are not done just by impulse, but are a series of small things put together.

What is drawing? How does one learn it? It is working through an invisible iron wall that seems to stand between what one *feels* and what one *can do*. How is one to get through that wall—since pounding against it is of no use? One must undermine the wall and drill through it slowly and patiently, in my opinion. And, look here, how can one continue such a work assiduously without being disturbed or distracted from it—unless one reflects and regulates one's life according to principles? And it is the same with other things as it is with art. Great things are not accidental, but they certainly must be *willed*. Whether a man's principles originate in actions or the actions in principles is something which seems to me insoluble, and as little worth decision as the question of which came first, the chicken or the egg. But I consider it of very positive and great value that one must try to develop one's power of reflection and will.

I am very curious to know whether you will find something in the figures I am making now when you eventually see them. That is also a question like the one about the chicken and the egg—must one make figures after a composition is found, or must one combine the separate figures into a composition which follows from them? I think that the result would be pretty much the same provided one *works*.

I conclude the same way you ended your letter: that we have in common a liking for looking behind the scenes in a theater; or, in other words, we both are inclined to analyze things. It is, I believe, exactly the quality one needs for painting—in painting or drawing one must exert that power. It may be that to some extent nature has endowed us with a gift (but you certainly

Source: *The Complete Letters of Vincent van Gogh* (Greenwich, Connecticut, New York Graphic Society, 1959), Volume I, pp. 469-70, Volume II, pp. 367-68, 369-72, Volume III, pp. 54-55, 58.

have it, and so do I—for that perhaps we are indebted to our childhood in Brabant and to surroundings which contributed more than is usually the case to our learning to think) but it is especially later on that the artistic feeling develops and ripens through work. I do not know *how* you might become a very good painter, but I certainly believe that it is in you and might be developed. . . .

I think you will see what I mean in the picture of the potato eaters, . . . It is very dark, however, and in the white, for instance, hardly any white has been used, but simply the neutral color, which is made by mixing red, blue, yellow, for instance vermilion, Paris blue and Naples yellow.

Therefore that color is in itself a pretty dark gray, but in the picture it looks white.

I'll tell you why I do it that way. Here the subject is a gray interior, lit by a little lamp.

The dirty linen tablecloth, the smoky wall, the dirty caps in which the women have worked in the field—*when seen through the eyelashes* in the light of the lamp, all this proves to be *very dark* gray; and the lamp, though a yellow-reddish glow, is even lighter—even a great deal—than the white in question.

As to the flesh colors—I know quite well that considered superficially, that is without thinking about it, they seem *what is called* flesh color.

But when starting the picture, I tried to paint them that way, with yellow ocher, red ocher and white, for instance.

But that was much, much *too light* and was decidedly wrong.

What was to be done? All the heads were finished, and even finished with great care, but I immediately repainted them, inexorably, and the color they are painted in now is like *the color of a very dusty potato, unpeeled of course.* . . .

 In 1885, Van Gogh discussed his painting, *The Potato Eaters.*

I want to tell you that I am working on the potato eaters, and I have painted new studies of the heads; the hands especially are greatly changed.

What I am trying to do most is to bring *life* into it. . . .

I will not send the potato eaters unless *I know for sure* there is *something* in it.

But I am getting on with it, and I think there are completely different things in it than you can ever have seen in my work. At least, so distinctly.

I mean the life especially. I paint this *from memory on the picture itself.* But you know yourself how many times I have painted these heads!

And then I drop in every night to correct some details on the spot.

But in the picture I give free scope to my own head in the sense of *thought* or imagination, which is not so much the case in *studies*, where no creative process is allowed, but where one finds food for one's imagination in reality, in order to make it exact. . . .

But the most difficult things—the heads, the hands, and the ensemble— are finished. Perhaps you will now find in it what you wrote some time ago, that though it is personal, yet it will remind you of other painters—with a certain family resemblance. Which you did not find in my studies then, but I think if you compare my studies with other studies, there would also be a resemblance. . . .

As to the potato eaters, it is a picture that will show well in gold, I am sure of that, but it would show as well on a wall, papered in the deep color of ripe corn.

It simply cannot be seen without such a setting.

It does not show up well against a dark background, and not at all against a dull background. That's because it gives a glimpse of a very gray interior. In reality too it stands in a gold frame, as it were, because the hearth and the glow of the fire on the white wall would be nearer to the spectator, now they are outside the picture, but in reality they throw the whole thing into perspective.

I repeat, it must be shut off by framing it in something of a deep gold or brass color.

If you yourself want to see it as it must be seen, don't forget this, please. This putting it next to a gold tone gives, at the same time, a brightness *to spots where you would not expect it*, and takes away the marbled aspect it gets when unfortunately placed against a dull or black background. The shadows are painted in blue, and a gold color puts life into this. . . .

I have tried to emphasize that those people, eating their potatoes in the lamplight, have dug the earth with those very hands they put in the dish, and so it speaks of *manual labor*, and how they have honestly earned their food.

I have wanted to give the impression of a way of life quite different from that of us civilized people. Therefore I am not at all anxious for everyone to like it or to admire it at once.

All winter long I have had the threads of this tissue in my hands, and have searched for the ultimate pattern; and though it has become a tissue of rough, coarse aspect, nevertheless the threads have been chosen carefully and according to certain rules. And it might prove to be a real *peasant picture. I know it is*. But he who prefers to see the peasants in their Sunday-best may do as he likes. I personally am convinced I get better results by painting them in their roughness than by giving them a conventional charm.

I think a peasant girl is more beautiful than a lady, in her dusty, patched blue skirt and bodice, which get the most delicate hues from weather, wind and sun. But if she puts on a lady's dress, she loses her peculiar charm. A peasant is more real in his fustian clothes in the fields than when he goes to church on Sunday in a kind of dress coat.

In the same way it would be wrong, I think, to give a peasant picture a certain conventional smoothness. If a peasant picture smells of bacon, smoke, potato steam—all right, that's not unhealthy; if a stable smells of dung—all right, that belongs to a stable; if the field has an odor of ripe corn or potatoes or of guano or manure—that's healthy, especially for city people.

Such pictures may *teach* them something. But to be perfumed is not what a peasant picture needs. . . .

Painting peasant life is a serious thing, and I should reproach myself if I did not try to make pictures which will rouse serious thoughts in those who think seriously about art and about life. . . .

. . . one must paint the peasants as being one of them, as feeling, thinking as they do.

Because one cannot help being the way one is. . . .

Van Gogh wrote the following in 1888:

It seems that in the book *My Religion*, Tolstoi implies that whatever happens in the way of violent revolution, there will also be a private and secret revolution in men, from which a new religion will be born, or rather something altogether new, which will have no name, but which will have the same effect of comforting, of making life possible, which the Christian religion used to have. It seems to me that the book ought to be very interesting.

In the end we shall have had enough of cynicism and skepticism and humbug, and we shall want to live more musically. How will that come about, and what will we really find? It would be interesting to be able to prophesy, but it is even better to be able to feel that kind of foreshadowing, instead of seeing absolutely nothing in the future beyond the disasters that are all the same bound to strike the modern world and civilization like terrible lightning, through a revolution or a war, or the bankruptcy of worm-eaten states. If we study Japanese art, we see a man who is undoubtedly wise, philosophic and intelligent, who spends his time doing what? In studying the distance between the earth and the moon? No. In studying Bismarck's policy? No. He studies a single blade of grass.

But this blade of grass leads him to draw every plant and then the seasons, the wide aspects of the countryside, then animals, then the human figure. So he passes his life, and life is too short to do the whole.

Come now, isn't it almost a true religion which these simple Japanese teach us, who live in nature as though they themselves were flowers?

And you cannot study Japanese art, it seems to me, without becoming much gayer and happier, and we must return to nature in spite of our education and our work in a world of convention. . . .

I envy the Japanese the extreme clearness which everything has in their work. It is never tedious, and never seems to be done too hurriedly. Their work is as simple as breathing, and they do a figure in a few sure strokes with the same ease as if it were as simple as buttoning your coat.

Oh! someday I must manage to do a figure in a few strokes. That will keep me busy all winter. Once I can do that, I shall be able to do people strolling on the boulevards, in the street, and heaps of new subjects. While I have been writing this letter I have drawn about a dozen. I am on the track of it, but it is very complicated because what I am after is that in a few strokes the figure of a man, a woman, a child, a horse, a dog, shall have a head, a body, legs, all in the right proportion. . . .

. . . More and more I come to think that the true and right way in the picture trade is to follow one's taste, what one has learned from the masters, in short, one's faith. *It is no easier*, I am convinced, to make a good picture than it is to find a diamond or a pearl: it means taking trouble, and you risk your life for it as a dealer or as an artist. Then once you have some good stones, you must never doubt yourself again, but boldly fix your price and stick to it. Meanwhile, however . . . but still this thought encourages me to work, even while I naturally still suffer at having to spend money. But this idea of the pearl came to me in the midst of my suffering, and I should not be surprised if it did you good, too, during periods of discouragement. There are as few good pictures as good diamonds. . . .

1. Select two or three of Van Gogh's paintings, including *The Potato Eaters*. Using his own words, create an accompanying commentary that could be used to stimulate discussion of his work.
2. From his letters, discuss how Van Gogh viewed his art as a means of investigating and illuminating human nature.

. . .

LEO TOLSTOY

Lev (Leo) Nikolaevich Tolstoy (1828-1910) was a great writer of fiction who came to believe in a moral regeneration through a mystical form of Christianity. Tolstoy had sympathy with the Russian peasant and hoped for a society in which basic peasant virtues would be understood by the aristocracy, and the division between the rich and poor, spiritual as well as material, would be ended. At times he supported non-violent resistance to authority, and the ideal of a utopian religious community. With his powerful intellectual gifts, he wrote important and influential works of fiction, including the vast work centered on Napoleon's invasion of Russia, *War and Peace* (1869).

In the First Epilogue to *War and Peace* Tolstoy reflected on the nature of history.

Seven years had passed. The storm-tossed sea of European history had subsided within its shores and seemed to have become calm. But the mysterious forces that move humanity (mysterious because the laws of their motion are unknown to us) continued to operate.

Though the surface of the sea of history seemed motionless, the movement of humanity went on as unceasingly as the flow of time. Various groups of people formed and dissolved, the coming formation and dissolution of kingdoms and displacement of peoples was in course of preparation.

The sea of history was not driven spasmodically from shore to shore as previously. It was seething in its depths. Historic figures were not borne by the waves from one shore to another as before. They now seemed to rotate on one spot. The historical figures at the head of armies, who formerly reflected the movement of the masses by ordering wars, campaigns, and battles, now reflected the restless movement by political and diplomatic combinations, laws, and treaties. . . .

The activity of Alexander or of Napoleon cannot be called useful or harmful, for it is impossible to say for what it was useful or harmful. If that activity

Sources: Leo Tolstoy, *War and Peace*, translated by Louise and Aylmer Maude (New York: Oxford University Press, 1933), pp. 1253, 1256-58, 1260, 1264; Hans Kohn, ed. *The Modern World: 1848 to the Present* (New York: The Macmillan Company, 1963), pp. 145-46, 147, 149-51.

displeases somebody, this is only because it does not agree with his limited understanding of what is good. Whether the preservation of my father's house in Moscow, or the glory of the Russian arms, or the prosperity of the Petersburg and other universities, or the freedom of Poland or the greatness of Russia, or the balance of power in Europe, or a certain kind of European culture called "progress" appear to me to be good or bad, I must admit that besides these things the action of every historic character has other more general purposes inaccessible to me.

But let us assume that what is called science can harmonize all contradictions and possesses an unchanging standard of good and bad by which to try historic characters and events; let us say that Alexander could have done everything differently; let us say that with guidance from those who blame him and who profess to know the ultimate aim of the movement of humanity, he might have arranged matters according to the program his present accusers would have given him—of nationality, freedom, equality, and progress (these, I think, cover the ground). Let us assume that this program was possible and had then been formulated, and that Alexander had acted on it. What would then have become of the activity of all those who opposed the tendency that then prevailed in the government—an activity that in the opinion of the historians was good and beneficent? Their activity would not have existed: there would have been no life, there would have been nothing.

If we admit that human life can be ruled by reason, the possibility of life is destroyed.

If we assume as the historians do that great men lead humanity to the attainment of certain ends—the greatness of Russia or of France, the balance of power in Europe, the diffusion of the ideas of the Revolution, general progress, or anything else—then it is impossible to explain the facts of history without introducing the conceptions of *chance* and *genius*.

If the aim of the European wars at the beginning of the nineteenth century had been the aggrandizement of Russia, that aim might have been accomplished without all the preceding wars and without the invasion. If the aim was the aggrandizement of France, that might have been attained without the Revolution and without the Empire. If the aim was the dissemination of ideas, the printing press could have accomplished that much better than warfare. If the aim was the progress of civilization, it is easy to see that there are other ways of diffusing civilization more expedient than by the destruction of wealth and of human lives.

B Tolstoy introduced the concept of chance into human development.

Why did it happen in this and not in some other way?

Because it happened so! "*Chance* created the situation; *genius* utilized it," says history.

But what is *chance*? What is *genius*?

The words *chance* and *genius* do not denote any really existing thing and therefore cannot be defined. Those words only denote a certain stage of understanding of phenomena. I do not know why a certain event occurs; I think that I cannot know it; so I do not try to know it and I talk about *chance*. I see a force producing effects beyond the scope of ordinary human agencies; I do not understand why this occurs and I talk of *genius*.

To a herd of rams, the ram the herdsman drives each evening into a special enclosure to feed and that becomes twice as fat as the others must seem to be a genius. And it must appear an astonishing conjunction of genius with a whole series of extraordinary chances that this ram, who instead of getting into the general fold every evening goes into a special enclosure where there are oats—that this very ram, swelling with fat, is killed for meat.

But the rams need only cease to suppose that all that happens to them happens solely for the attainment of their sheepish aims; they need only admit that what happens to them may also have purposes beyond their ken, and they will at once perceive a unity and coherence in what happened to the ram that was fattened. Even if they do not know for what purpose they are fattened, they will at least know that all that happened to the ram did not happen accidentally, and will no longer need the conceptions of *chance* or *genius*.

Only by renouncing our claim to discern a purpose immediately intelligible to us, and admitting the ultimate purpose to be beyond our ken, may we discern the sequence of experiences in the lives of historic characters and perceive the cause of the effect they produce (incommensurable with ordinary human capabilities), and then the words *chance* and *genius* become superfluous.

We need only confess that we do not know the purpose of the European convulsions and that we know only the facts—that is, the murders, first in France, then in Italy, in Africa, in Prussia, in Austria, in Spain, and in Russia— and that the movements from the west to the east and from the east to the west form the essence and purpose of these events, and not only shall we have no need to see exceptional ability and genius in Napoleon and Alexander, but we shall be unable to consider them to be anything but like other men, and we shall not be obliged to have recourse to *chance* for an explanation of those small events which made these people what they were, but it will be clear that all those small events were inevitable.

By discarding a claim to knowledge of the ultimate purpose, we shall clearly perceive that just as one cannot imagine a blossom or seed for any single plant better suited to it than those it produces, so it is impossible to imagine any two people more completely adapted down to the smallest detail for the purpose they had to fulfill, than Napoleon and Alexander with all their antecedents. . . .

As the sun and each atom of ether is a sphere complete in itself, and yet at the same time only a part of a whole too immense for man to comprehend, so each individual has within himself his own aims and yet has them to serve a general purpose incomprehensible to man.

A bee settling on a flower has stung a child. And the child is afraid of bees and declares that bees exist to sting people. A poet admires the bee sucking from the chalice of a flower and says it exists to suck the fragrance of flowers. A beekeeper, seeing the bee collect pollen from flowers and carry it to the hive, says that it exists to gather honey. Another beekeeper who has studied the life of the hive more closely says that the bee gathers pollen dust to feed the young bees and rear a queen, and that it exists to perpetuate its race. A botanist notices that the bee flying with the pollen of a male flower to a pistil fertilizes the latter, and sees in this the purpose of the bee's existence. Another, observing the migration of plants, notices that the bee helps in this work, and may say that in this lies the purpose of the bee. But the ultimate purpose of the bee is not exhausted by the first, the second, or any of the processes the human mind can discern. The higher the human intellect rises in the discovery of these purposes, the more obvious it becomes that the ultimate purpose is beyond our comprehension.

All that is accessible to man is the relation of the life of the bee to other manifestations of life. And so it is with the purpose of historic characters and nations.

1. Account for Tolstoy's contention that reliance on the concepts of "chance" and "genius" are merely humanity's inability to accept a higher purpose in the progress of historical events.
2. How would Comte or Condorcet respond to Tolstoy's view of historical change?

. . .

HENRIK IBSEN

The dramas of the Norwegian playwright Henrik Ibsen (1828-1906) shocked and disturbed theatregoers at the end of the nineteenth century, as he sharply criticized contemporary bourgeois life and institutions. Searching for a means of dramatizing modern life, Ibsen developed a naturalistic style, in which the play unfolded in a manner resembling life itself. In challenging his time, Ibsen was especially critical of modern marriage and was sympathetic to the plight of women who were restricted from developing their intelligence and realizing their potential. He insisted that drama must deal with the major social issues of the day.

In Ibsen's *A Doll House* (1879), the main character, Nora, is trapped in a marriage in which she is an object and treated as a child by her husband, Helmer. She rebels, and insists on having her own life. The sound of the door slamming shut at the end of the play was for many critics the beginning of modern drama.

HELMER. You loved me the way a wife ought to love her husband. It's simply the means that you couldn't judge. But you think I love you any the less for not knowing how to handle your affairs? No, no—just lean on me; I'll guide you and teach you. I wouldn't be a man if this feminine helplessness didn't make you twice as attractive to me. You musn't mind those sharp words I said—that was all in the first confusion of thinking my world had collapsed. I've forgiven you, Nora; I swear I've forgiven you.

NORA. My thanks for your forgiveness. (*She goes out through the door, right.*)

HELMER. No, wait—(*Peers in.*) What are you doing in there?

NORA (*inside*). Getting out of my costume.

HELMER (*by the open door*). Yes, do that. Try to calm yourself and collect your thoughts again, my frightened little songbird. You can rest easy now; I've got wide wings to shelter you with. (*Walking about close by the door.*) How snug and nice our home is, Nora. You're safe here; I'll keep you like a hunted dove I've rescued out of a hawk's claws. I'll bring peace to your poor, shuddering heart. Gradually it'll happen, Nora; you'll see. Tomorrow all this will look different to you; then everything will be as it was. I won't have to go on repeating I forgive you; you'll feel it for yourself. How can you imagine I'd ever conceivably want to disown you—or even blame you in any way? Ah, you don't know a man's heart, Nora. For a man there's something indescribably sweet and satisfying in knowing he's forgiven his wife—and forgiven her out of a full and open heart. It's as if she belongs to him in two ways now: in a sense he's given her fresh into the world again, and she's become his wife and his child as well. From now on that's what you'll be to me—you little, bewildered, helpless thing. Don't be afraid of anything, Nora; just open your heart to me, and I'll be conscience and will to you both— (NORA *enters in her regular clothes.*) What's this? Not in bed? You've changed your dress?

NORA. Yes, Torvald. I've changed my dress.

HELMER. But why now, so late?

NORA. Tonight I'm not sleeping.

HELMER. But Nora dear—

NORA (*looking at her watch*). It's still not so very late. Sit down, Torvald; we have a lot to talk over. (*She sits at one side of the table.*)

HELMER. Nora—what is this? That hard expression—

NORA. Sit down. This'll take some time. I have a lot to say.

HELMER (*sitting at the table directly opposite her*). You worry me, Nora. I don't understand you.

NORA. No, that's exactly it. You don't understand me. And I've never understood you either—until tonight. No, don't interrupt. You can just listen to what I say. We're closing out accounts, Torvald.

HELMER. How do you mean that?

Source: Henrik Ibsen, *Four Major Plays* (New York: New American Library, 1965), pp. 107-14.

NORA (*after a short pause*). Doesn't anything strike you about our sitting here like this?

HELMER. What's that?

NORA. We've been married now eight years. Doesn't it occur to you that this is the first time we two, you and I, man and wife, have ever talked seriously together?

HELMER. What do you mean—seriously?

NORA. In eight whole years—longer even—right from our first acquaintance, we've never exchanged a serious word on any serious thing.

HELMER. You mean I should constantly go and involve you in problems you couldn't possibly help me with?

NORA. I'm not talking of problems. I'm saying that we've never sat down seriously together and tried to get to the bottom of anything.

HELMER. But dearest, what good would that ever do you?

NORA. That's the point right there: you've never understood me. I've been wronged greatly, Torvald—first by Papa, and then by you.

HELMER. What! By us—the two people who've loved you more than anyone else?

NORA (*shaking her head*). You never loved me. You've thought it fun to be in love with me, that's all.

HELMER. Nora, what a thing to say!

NORA. Yes, it's true now, Torvald. When I lived at home with Papa, he told me all his opinions, so I had the same ones too; or if they were different I hid them, since he wouldn't have cared for that. He used to call me his doll-child, and he played with me the way I played with my dolls. Then I came into your house—

HELMER. How can you speak of our marriage like that?

NORA (*unperturbed*). I mean, then I went from Papa's hands into yours. You arranged everything to your own taste, and so I got the same taste as you—or I pretended to; I can't remember. I guess a little of both, first one, then the other. Now when I look back, it seems as if I'd lived here like a beggar—just from hand to mouth. I've lived by doing tricks for you, Torvald. But that's the way you wanted it. It's a great sin what you and Papa did to me. You're to blame that nothing's become of me.

HELMER. Nora, how unfair and ungrateful you are! Haven't you been happy here?

NORA. No, never, I thought so—but I never have.

HELMER. Not—not happy!

NORA. No, only lighthearted. And you've always been so kind to me. But our home's been nothing but a playpen. I've been your doll-wife here, just as at home I was Papa's doll-child. And in turn the children have been my dolls. I thought it was fun when you played with me, just as they thought it fun when I played with them. That's been our marriage, Torvald.

HELMER. There's some truth in what you're saying—under all the raving exaggeration. But it'll all be different after this. Playtime's over; now for the schooling.

NORA. Whose schooling—mine or the children's?

HELMER. Both yours and the children's, dearest.

NORA. Oh, Torvald, you're not the man to teach me to be a good wife to you.

HELMER. And you can say that?

NORA. And I—how am I equipped to bring up children?

HELMER. Nora!

NORA. Didn't you say a moment ago that that was no job to trust me with?

HELMER. In a flare of temper! Why fasten on that?

NORA. Yes, but you were so very right. I'm not up to the job. There's another job I have to do first. I have to try to educate myself. You can't help me with that. I've got to do it alone. And that's why I'm leaving you now.

HELMER (jumping up). What's that?

NORA. I have to stand completely alone, if I'm ever going to discover myself and the world out there. So I can't go on living with you.

HELMER. Nora, Nora!

NORA. I want to leave right away. Kristine should put me up for the night—

HELMER. You're insane! You've no right! I forbid you!

NORA. From here on, there's no use forbidding me anything. I'll take with me whatever is mine. I don't want a thing from you, either now or later.

HELMER. What kind of madness is this!

NORA. Tomorrow I'm going home—I mean, home where I came from. It'll be easier up there to find something to do.

HELMER. Oh, you blind, incompetent child!

NORA. I must learn to be competent, Torvald.

HELMER. Abandon your home, your husband, your children! And you're not even thinking what people will say.

NORA. I can't be concerned about that. I only know how essential this is.

HELMER. Oh, it's outrageous. So you'll run out like this on your most sacred vows.

NORA. What do you think are my most sacred vows?

HELMER. And I have to tell you that! Aren't they your duties to your husband and children?

NORA. I have other duties equally sacred.

HELMER. That isn't true. What duties are they?

NORA. Duties to myself.

HELMER. Before all else, you're a wife and a mother.

NORA. I don't believe in that anymore. I believe that, before all else, I'm a human being, no less than you—or anyway, I ought to try to become one. I know the majority thinks you're right, Torvald, and plenty of books agree with you, too. But I can't go on believing what the majority says, or what's written in books. I have to think over these things myself and try to understand them.

HELMER. Why can't you understand your place in your own home? On a point like that, isn't there one everlasting guide you can turn to? Where's your religion?

NORA. Oh, Torvald, I'm really not sure what religion is.

HELMER. What—?

NORA. I only know what the minister said when I was confirmed. He told me religion was this thing and that. When I get clear and away by myself,

I'll go into that problem too. I'll see if what the minister said was right, or, in any case, if it's right for me.

HELMER. A young woman your age shouldn't talk like that. If religion can't move you, I can try to rouse your conscience. You do have some moral feeling? Or, tell me—has that gone too?

NORA. It's not easy to answer that, Torvald. I simply don't know. I'm all confused about these things. I just know I see them so differently from you. I find out, for one thing, that the law's not at all what I'd thought—but I can't get it through my head that the law is fair. A woman hasn't a right to protect her dying father or save her husband's life! I can't believe that.

HELMER. You talk like a child. You don't know anything of the world you live in.

NORA. No, I don't. But now I'll begin to learn for myself. I'll try to discover who's right, the world or I.

HELMER. Nora, you're sick; you've got a fever. I almost think you're out of your head.

NORA. I've never felt more clearheaded and sure in my life.

HELMER. And—clearheaded and sure—you're leaving your husband and children?

NORA. Yes.

HELMER. Then there's only one possible reason.

NORA. What?

HELMER. You no longer love me.

NORA. No. That's exactly it.

HELMER. Nora! You can't be serious!

NORA. Oh, this is so hard, Torvald—you've been so kind to me always. But I can't help it. I don't love you anymore.

HELMER (*struggling for composure*). Are you also clearheaded and sure about that?

NORA. Yes, completely. That's why I can't go on staying here.

HELMER. Can you tell me what I did to lose your love?

NORA. Yes, I can tell you. It was this evening when the miraculous thing didn't come—then I knew you weren't the man I'd imagined.

HELMER. Be more explicit; I don't follow you.

NORA. I've waited now so patiently eight long years—for my Lord, I know miracles don't come every day. Then this crisis broke over me, and such a certainty filled me: now the miraculous event would occur. While Krogstad's letter was lying out there, I never for an instant dreamed that you could give in to his terms. I was so utterly sure you'd say to him: go on, tell your tale to the whole wide world. And when he'd done that—

HELMER. Yes, what then? When I'd delivered my own wife into shame and disgrace—!

NORA. When he'd done that, I was so utterly sure that you'd step forward, take the blame on yourself and say I am the guilty one.

HELMER. Nora—!

NORA. You're thinking I'd never accept such a sacrifice from you? No, of course not. But what good would my protests be against you? That was the miracle I was waiting for, in terror and hope. And to stave that off, I would have taken my life.

HELMER. I'd gladly work for you day and night, Nora—and take on pain and deprivation. But there's no one who gives up honor for love.

NORA. Millions of women have done just that.

HELMER. Oh, you think and talk like a silly child.

NORA. Perhaps. But you neither think nor talk like the man I could join myself to. When your big fright was over—and it wasn't from any threat against me, only for what might damage you—when all the danger was past, for you it was just as if nothing had happened. I was exactly the same, your little lark, your doll, that you'd have to handle with double care now that i'd turned out so brittle and frail. (*Gets up.*) Torvald—in that instant it dawned on me that for eight years I've been living here with a stranger, and that I'd even conceived three children—oh, I can't stand the thought of it! I could tear myself to bits.

HELMER (*heavily*). I see. There's a gulf that's opened between us—that's clear. Oh, but Nora, can't we bridge it somehow?

NORA. The way I am now, I'm no wife for you.

HELMER. I have the strength to make myself over.

NORA. Maybe—if your doll gets taken away.

HELMER. But to part! To part from you! No, Nora, no—I can't imagine it.

NORA (*going out, right*). All the more reason why it has to be. (*She reenters with her coat and a small overnight bag, which she puts on a chair by the table.*)

HELMER. Nora, Nora, not now! Wait till tomorrow.

NORA. I can't spend the night in a strange man's room.

HELMER. But couldn't we live here like brother and sister—

NORA. You know very well how long that would last. (*Throws her shawl about her.*) Good-bye, Torvald. I won't look in on the children. I know they're in better hands than mine. The way I am now, I'm no use to them.

HELMER. But someday, Nora—someday—?

NORA. How can I tell? I haven't the least idea what'll become of me.

HELMER. But you're my wife, now and wherever you go.

NORA. Listen, Torvald—I've heard that when a wife deserts her husband's house just as I'm doing, then the law frees him from all responsibility. In any case, I'm freeing you from being responsible. Don't feel yourself bound, any more than I will. There has to be absolute freedom for us both. Here, take your ring back. Give me mine.

HELMER. That too?

NORA. That too.

HELMER. There it is.

NORA. Good. Well, now it's all over. I'm putting the keys here. The maids know all about keeping up the house—better than I do. Tomorrow, after I've left town, Kristine will stop by to pack up everything that's mine from home. I'd like those things shipped up to me.

HELMER. Over! All over! Nora, won't you ever think about me?

NORA. I'm sure I'll think of you often, and about the children and the house here.

HELMER. May I write you?

NORA. No—never. You're not to do that.

HELMER. Oh, but let me send you—

NORA. Nothing. Nothing.

HELMER. Or help you if you need it.

NORA. No. I accept nothing from strangers.

HELMER. Nora—can I never be more than a stranger to you?

NORA (*picking up the overnight bag*). Ah, Torvald—it would take the greatest miracle of all—

HELMER. Tell me the greatest miracle!

NORA. You and I both would have to transform ourselves to the point that— Oh, Torvald, I've stopped believing in miracles.

HELMER. But I'll believe. Tell me! Transform ourselves to the point that—?

NORA. That our living together could be a true marriage. (*She goes out down the hall.*)

HELMER (*sinks down on a chair by the door, face buried in his hands*). Nora! Nora! (*Looking about and rising.*) Empty. She's gone. (*A sudden hope leaps in him.*) The greatest miracle—?

(*From below, the sound of a door slamming shut.*)

1. Although *A Doll House* was written in 1879, the sentiments expressed by Nora would be more typically heard a century or more later. Contrast Helmer and Nora to show how they represent differing nineteenth century views on the role of women in society.

• • •

ANTON CHEKHOV

Anton Chekhov (1860-1904) was a dramatist and writer of short stories whose works, while detailing everyday life and the nuances of human relationships, also recorded the passing of an age in Russia and in Europe. Chekhov's plays depicted the lives of the privileged aristocracy and landowning class in Czarist Russia. He suggested that the days of the old regime must inevitably end as the new social era transformed institutions. In Chekhov's plays the ruling class is morally empty, clinging to the old forms while realizing their world is passing away. Chekhov, like the nineteenth century Russian novelist Turgenev, had the wonderful capacity of combining an exploration into human relationships while writing about social transformation.

Chekhov called his last play, *The Cherry Orchard* (1904), a "comedy," but the director realized it was also a "serious drama of Russian life." Set on an estate in provincial Russia, it contrasted Lopakhin, a merchant, with the landholding class.

> LYUBOV ANDREYEVNA: Is this really me sitting here? [*Laughs.*] I feel like jumping about and waving my arms. [*Buries her face in her hands.*] What if it's only a dream! God knows I love my country, love it dearly. I couldn't look out the train window, I was crying so! [*Through tears*] But I must drink

Source: Anton Chekhov, *Chekhov: The Major Plays* (New York: New American Library, 1964), pp. 324-27, 357, 364-67, 380.

my coffee. Thank you, Firs, thank you, my dear old friend. I'm so glad you're still alive.

FIRS: The day before yesterday.

GAYEV: He's hard of hearing.

LOPAKHIN: I must go now, I'm leaving for Kharkov about five o'clock. It's so annoying! I wanted to have a good look at you, and have a talk. You're as splendid as ever.

PISHCHIK [*breathing heavily*]: Even more beautiful. . . . Dressed like a Parisienne. . . . There goes my wagon, all four wheels!

LOPAKHIN: Your brother here, Leonid Andreich, says I'm a boor, a money-grubber, but I don't mind. Let him talk. All I want is that you should trust me as you used to, and that your wonderful, touching eyes should look at me as they did then. Merciful God! My father was one of your father's serfs, and your grandfather's, but you yourself did so much for me once, that I've forgotten all that and love you as if you were my own kin—more than my kin.

LYUBOV ANDREYEVNA: I can't sit still, I simply cannot. [*Jumps up and walks about the room in great excitement.*] I cannot bear this joy. . . . Laugh at me, I'm silly. . . . My dear little bookcase . . . [*Kisses bookcase.*] my little table . . .

GAYEV: Nurse died while you were away.

LYUBOV ANDREYEVNA [*sits down and drinks coffee*]: Yes, God rest her soul. They wrote me.

GAYEV: And Anastasy is dead. Petrushka Kosoi left me and is now with the police inspector in town. [*Takes a box of hard candies from his pocket and begins to suck one.*]

PISHCHIK: My daughter, Dashenka . . . sends her regards . . .

LOPAKHIN: I wish I could tell you something very pleasant and cheering. [*Glances at his watch.*] I must go directly, there's no time to talk, but . . . well, I'll say it in a couple of words. As you know, the cherry orchard is to be sold to pay your debts. The auction is set for August twenty-second, but you need not worry, my dear, you can sleep in peace, there is a way out. This is my plan. Now, please listen! Your estate is only twenty versts from town, the railway runs close by, and if the cherry orchard and the land along the river were cut up into lots and leased for summer cottages, you'd have, at the very least, an income of twenty-five thousand a year.

GAYEV: Excuse me, what nonsense!

LYUBOV ANDREYEVNA: I don't quite understand you, Yermolai Alekseich.

LOPAKHIN: You will get, at the very least, twenty-five rubles a year for a two-and-a-half-acre lot, and if you advertise now, I guarantee you won't have a single plot of ground left by autumn, everything will be snapped up. In short, I congratulate you, you are saved. The site is splendid, the river is deep. Only, of course, the ground must be cleared . . . you must tear down all the old outbuildings, for instance, and this house, which is worthless, cut down the old cherry orchard—

LYUBOV ANDREYEVNA: Cut it down? Forgive me, my dear, but you don't know what you are talking about. If there is one thing in the whole province that is interesting, not to say remarkable, it's our cherry orchard.

LOPAKHIN: The only remarkable thing about this orchard is that it is very big. There's a crop of cherries every other year, and then you can't get rid of them, nobody buys them.

GAYEV: This orchard is even mentioned in the *Encyclopedia*.

LOPAKHIN [*glancing at his watch*]: If we don't think of something and come to a decision, on the twenty-second of August the cherry orchard, and the entire estate, will be sold at auction. Make up your minds! There is no other way out, I swear to you. None whatsoever.

FIRS: In the old days, forty or fifty years ago, the cherries were dried, soaked, marinated, and made into jam, and they used to—

GAYEV: Be quiet, Firs.

FIRS: And they used to send cartloads of dried cherries to Moscow and Kharkov. And that brought in money! The dried cherries were soft and juicy in those days, sweet, fragrant. . . . They had a method then . . .

LYUBOV ANDREYEVNA: And what has become of that method now?

FIRS: Forgotten. Nobody remembers. . . .

PISHCHIK: How was it in Paris? What's it like there? Did you eat frogs?

LYUBOV ANDREYEVNA: I ate crocodiles.

PISHCHIK: Think of that now!

LOPAKHIN: There used to be only the gentry and the peasants living in the country, but now these summer people have appeared. All the towns, even the smallest ones, are surrounded by summer cottages. And it is safe to say that in another twenty years these people will multiply enormously. Now the summer resident only drinks tea on his porch, but it may well be that he'll take to cultivating his acre, and then your cherry orchard will be a happy, rich, luxuriant—

GAYEV [*indignantly*]: What nonsense! . . .

B The old landowner, Lyubov Andreyevna, understands the symbolism of the cherry orchard in her life.

LYUBOV ANDREYEVNA [*In great agitation*]: Why isn't Leonid here? If only I knew whether the estate had been sold or not! The disaster seems to me so incredible that I don't even know what to think, I'm lost. . . . I could scream this very instant . . . I could do something foolish. Save me, Petya. Talk to me, say something. . . .

TROFIMOV: Whether or not the estate is sold today—does it really matter? That's all done with long ago; there's no turning back, the path is overgrown. Be calm, my dear. One must not deceive oneself; at least once in one's life one ought to look the truth straight in the eye.

LYUBOV ANDREYEVNA: What truth? You can see where there is truth and where there isn't, but I seem to have lost my sight, I see nothing. You boldly settle all the important problems, but tell me, my dear boy, isn't it because you are young and have not yet had to suffer for a single one of your problems? You boldly look ahead, but isn't it because you neither see nor expect anything dreadful, since life is still hidden from your young eyes? You're bolder, more honest, deeper than we are, but think about it, be just a little bit magnanimous, and spare me. You see, I was born here, my mother and father lived here, and my grandfather. I love this house, without the cherry orchard my life has no meaning for me, and if it must be sold, then sell me with the orchard. . . . [*Embraces* TROFIMOV *and kisses him on the forehead.*] And my son was drowned here. . . . [*Weeps.*] Have pity on me, you good, kind man. . . .

C ▷It is Lopakhin who is the winner, though Chekhov was ambiguous about the results.

[*Voices in the ballroom: "Lopakhin has come! Yermolai Alekseich!"* PISHCHIK *enters.*]

PISHCHIK: As I live and breathe! [*Kisses* LOPAKHIN.] There is a whiff of cognac about you, dear soul. And we've been making merry here, too.

[*Enter* LYUBOV ANDREYEVNA.]

LYUBOV ANDREYEVNA: Is that you, Yermolai Alekseich? What kept you so long? Where's Leonid?

LOPAKHIN: Leonid Andreich arrived with me, he's coming . . .

LYUBOV ANDREYEVNA [*agitated*]: Well, what happened? Did the sale take place? Tell me!

LOPAKHIN [*embarrassed, fearing to reveal his joy*]: The auction was over by four o'clock. . . . We missed the train, had to wait till half past nine. [*Sighing heavily*] Ugh! My head is swimming. . . .

[*Enter* GAYEV; *he carries his purchases in one hand and wipes away his tears with the other.*]

LYUBOV ANDREYEVNA: Lyonya, what happened? Well, Lyonya? [*Impatiently, through tears.*] Be quick, for God's sake!

GAYEV [*not answering her, simply waves his hand. To* FIRS, *weeping*]: Here, take these. . . . There's anchovies, Kerch herrings. . . . I haven't eaten anything all day. . . . What I have been through! [*The click of billiard balls is heard through the open door to the billiard room, and* YASHA's *voice: "Seven and eighteen!"* GAYEV's *expression changes, he is no longer weeping.*] I'm terribly tired. Firs, help me change. [*Goes through the ballroom to his own room, followed by* FIRS.]

PISHCHIK: What happened at the auction? Come on, tell us!

LYUBOV ANDREYEVNA: Is the cherry orchard sold?

LOPAKHIN: It's sold.

LYUBOV ANDREYEVNA: Who bought it?

LOPAKHIN: I bought it. [*Pause*]

[LYUBOV ANDREYEVNA *is overcome; she would fall to the floor if it were not for the chair and table near which she stands.* VARYA *takes the keys from her belt and throws them on the floor in the middle of the drawing room and goes out.*]

LOPAKHIN: I bought it! Kindly wait a moment, ladies and gentlemen, my head is swimming, I can't talk. . . . [*Laughs.*] We arrived at the auction, Deriganov was already there. Leonid Andreich had only fifteen thousand, and straight off Deriganov bid thirty thousand over and above the mortgage. I saw how the land lay, so I got into the fight and bid forty. He bid forty-five. I bid fifty-five. In other words, he kept raising it by five thousand, and I by ten. Well, it finally came to an end. I bid ninety thousand above the mortgage, and it was knocked down to me. The cherry orchard is now mine! Mine! [*Laughs uproariously.*] Lord! God in heaven! The cherry orchard is mine!

Tell me I'm drunk, out of my mind, that I imagine it. . . . [*Stamps his feet.*] Don't laugh at me! If my father and my grandfather could only rise from their graves and see all that has happened, how their Yermolai, their beaten, half-literate Yermolai, who used to run about barefoot in winter, how that same Yermolai has bought an estate, the most beautiful estate in the whole world! I bought the estate where my father and grandfather were slaves, where they weren't even allowed in the kitchen. I'm asleep, this is just some dream of mine, it only seems to be. . . . It's the fruit of your imagination, hidden in the darkness of uncertainty. . . . [*Picks up the keys, smiling tenderly.*] She threw down the keys, wants to show that she's not mistress here any more. . . . [*Jingles the keys.*] Well, no matter. [*The orchestra is heard tuning up.*] Hey, musicians, play, I want to hear you! Come on, everybody, and see how Yermolai Lopakhin will lay the ax to the cherry orchard, how the trees will fall to the ground! We're going to build summer cottages, and our grandsons and great-grandsons will see a new life here. . . . Music! Strike up!

[*The orchestra plays.* LYUBOV ANDREYEVNA *sinks into a chair and weeps bitterly.*]

LOPAKHIN [*reproachfully*]: Why didn't you listen to me, why? My poor friend, there's no turning back now. [*With tears*] Oh, if only all this could be over quickly, if somehow our discordant, unhappy life could be changed!

PISHCHIK [*takes him by the arm; speaks in an undertone*]: She's crying. Let's go into the ballroom, let her be alone. . . . Come on. . . . [*Leads him into the ballroom.*]

LOPAKHIN: What's happened? Musicians, play so I can hear you! Let everything be as I want it! [*Ironically*] Here comes the new master, owner of the cherry orchard! [*Accidentally bumps into a little table, almost upsetting the candelabrum.*] I can pay for everything! [*Goes out with* PISHCHIK.]

[*There is no one left in either the drawing room or the ballroom except* LYUBOV ANDREYEVNA, *who sits huddled up and weeping bitterly. The music plays softly.* ANYA *and* TROFIMOV *enter hurriedly.* ANYA *goes to her mother and kneels before her.* TROFIMOV *remains in the doorway of the ballroom.*]

ANYA: Mama! . . . Mama, you're crying! Dear, kind, good Mama, my beautiful one, I love you . . . I bless you. The cherry orchard is sold, it's gone, that's true, true, but don't cry, Mama, life is still before you, you still have your good, pure soul. . . . Come with me, come, darling, we'll go away from here! . . . We'll plant a new orchard, more luxuriant than this one. You will see it and understand; and joy, quiet, deep joy, will sink into your soul, like the evening sun, and you will smile, Mama! Come, darling, let us go. . . .

D The old servant is the only one who remains at the end of the play.

[*The stage is empty. There is the sound of doors being locked, then of the carriages driving away. It grows quiet. In the stillness there is the dull thud of an ax on a tree, a forlorn, melancholy sound. Footsteps are heard. From the door on the right* FIRS *appears. He is dressed as always in a jacket and white waistcoat, and wears slippers. He is ill.*]

FIRS [*goes to the door and tries the handle*]: Locked. They have gone. . . . [*Sits down on the sofa.*] They've forgotten me. . . . Never mind . . . I'll sit here awhile. . . . I expect Leonid Andreich hasn't put on his fur coat and has gone off in his overcoat. [*Sighs anxiously.*] And I didn't see to it. . . . When they're young, they're green! [*Mumbles something which cannot be understood.*] I'll lie down awhile. . . . There's no strength left in you, nothing's left, nothing. . . . Ach, you . . . addlepate! [*Lies motionless.*]

[*A distant sound is heard that seems to come from the sky, the sound of a snapped string mournfully dying away. A stillness falls, and nothing is heard but the thud of the ax on a tree far away in the orchard.*]

1. "In *The Cherry Orchard*, Chekhov has created a microcosm of the social upheavals of the period." Comment on this statement with reference to the changes reflected in the reading, especially with reference to class and social relations.

• • •

ÉMILE ZOLA

Émile Zola (1840-1902), a novelist, was deeply concerned with social issues, especially the plight of the poor in the modern industrial world. He wrote many novels, including a series of twenty about the history of a family, *Les Rougon-Macquart*, subtitled "the natural and social history of a family under the [French] Second Empire." Zola claimed that the novelist was a scientist who records the life of his day, but in his works there is much ideology, subtle characterization, and often a lyricism not at all associated with an objective approach. Zola was also active in the politics of his day, including his defence of civil rights in his pamphlet *J'Accuse* (1898) during the episode of the Dreyfus Affair.

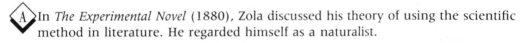

In *The Experimental Novel* (1880), Zola discussed his theory of using the scientific method in literature. He regarded himself as a naturalist.

Returning to the novel, we see here equally that the writer is part observer and part experimenter. In him the observer provides the facts as he has seen them, decides the point of departure, establishes the firm ground on which the characters will move and phenomena develop. Then the experimenter appears and sets up the experiment, I mean to say causes the characters to move and act in a particular story, in order to show that the succession of facts will be such as the determination of the phenomena that are being studied demands. At this point, it is nearly always what Claude Bernard calls an experiment "to see what happens." . . . The problem is to know what a certain passion acting in certain surroundings will produce from the point of view of the individual, and from that of society; and an experimental novel, . . . is simply the official report of the experiment that the writer now repeats before the eyes of the public. The whole operation consists of taking facts

Sources: Eugen Weber, ed., *Paths to the Present* (New York: Dodd, Mead and Company, Inc., 1966), pp. 167-69, 171-72; Émile Zola, *Germinal* (Harmondsworth: Penguin Books, 1954), pp. 271-77, 278-82, 495-499.

from life, then of studying their structure by acting upon them through alterations of circumstances and surroundings, without ever deviating from the laws of nature. At the end, there is knowledge of man, scientific knowledge, in its individual and social operation.

No doubt we are far from the certainties of chemistry, and even of physiology. We do not yet know the reagent that will discompose passions and allow them to be analyzed. Often, in this study, I shall have occasion to recall that the experimental novel is younger than experimental medicine, itself hardly born. But I am not concerned to note established results, I only want to expound a method clearly. If the experimental novelist still fumbles through the most obscure and complex of sciences, this does not prevent the existence of science. It cannot be denied that the naturalist novel, as we conceive it at the moment, is a true experiment that the writer carries out on man, helping himself by observation. . . .

But we see how things begin to clear when one takes this point of view of the experimental method applied in the novel, and applied with all the scientific precision that the subject can stand today. One foolish objection brought up against us naturalist writers is that we want to be solely photographers. We can protest as much as we like that we accept character, temperament, self-expression, we are still answered by inane arguments about the impossibility of being strictly true to life, about the need to arrange facts in order to create a work of art. Well! with the application of the experimental method to the novel, there is no more cause for dispute. The idea of experiment carries with it the idea of modification. We do start with true facts, which provide our firm base; but to show the structure of facts we have to produce and direct the phenomena; that is our share of imagination and talent in the work. Thus, without having to fall back on questions of form, of style, that I shall examine later, I note right away that, when we use experimental methods in our novels, we must modify nature without departing from it. If we remember the definition: "Observation shows, experiment teaches," we can begin by claiming for our books this lofty lesson of experiment.

The writer, far from being diminished, grows here in singular fashion. An experiment, even the simplest, is always based on an idea, itself born of an observation. . . . Thus, instead of binding the writer within narrow limits, the experimental method leaves him free to use all his intelligence as a thinker and all his talent as a creator. He will have to see, to understand, to invent. An observed fact must generate the idea of the experiment to follow, of the novel to be written, in order to get at the complete knowledge of a truth. Then, having discussed and decided the plan of the experiment, he will always judge its results with the freedom of a man who accepts only facts consistent with the determinism of phenomena. He has started from doubt to arrive at absolute knowledge; and he only stops doubt when the structure of passion, which he has taken to pieces and put together again, functions according to the laws that nature established. There is no vaster, freer task for the human mind. We shall see below the wretchedness of the scholastics, of the systematizers, of the theoreticians of idealism, when compared to the experimenters' triumph.

I sum up this first part by repeating that naturalist writers observe and experiment, and that all their labors arise from the position of doubt they take up before little-known truths, unexplained phenomena, until suddenly, one day, an experimental idea awakes their talent and incites them to set up an experiment in order to analyze the facts and master them. . . .

. . . Man is not alone, he lives in society, in a social environment and, hence, for us writers, this social environment endlessly modifies the phenomena. Our real task, our essential study, is right there, in the reciprocal effects of society on the individual and the individual on society. For the physiologist, the external and the internal environment are purely chemical and physical, and this allows him to find their laws quite easily. We have not yet reached the point of proving that the social environment is also only chemical and physical. Yet it certainly is, or, rather, it is the variable product of a group of living beings who are absolutely subject to the chemical and physical laws that rule both matter and living bodies. Hence, we shall see that one may affect the social environment by affecting the phenomena that have been mastered in man. And this is what constitutes the experimental novel: to grasp the mechanism of phenomena in man, to show the structure of intellectual and sensual events such as physiology makes known to us, under the influence of heredity and environmental circumstances, then to show the living man in the social surroundings which he has himself created, which he modifies every day, and in the midst of which he undergoes in his turn a continuous transformation. Thus, we find support in physiology, we take isolated man from the hands of the physiologist, in order to carry forward the solution of the problem and to resolve scientifically the question of knowing how men behave in society.

These general ideas are sufficient to guide us for the moment. Later, when science has advanced further, when the experimental novel has furnished decisive results, some critic will say more precisely what I only sketched out today.

[At this point] the experimental novel is a consequence of the scientific evolution of our time; it continues and completes physiology which is itself based on chemistry and physics; it substitutes for the study of abstract, metaphysical man the study of natural man, subject to physico-chemical laws and determined by the influence of his environment; it is, in a word, the literature of our scientific age, just as classic and romantic literature corresponded to an age of scholasticism and theology. . . .

B Zola's novels were very popular in his day. His *Germinal* (1885) was about the struggle of the poor in mining regions of France. In it the workers decide their only hope is to strike.

The Plan-des-Dames was a great clearing recently opened up by tree-felling. It was on a gentle slope, girt by lofty trees, magnificent beeches whose straight, regular trunks surrounded it with a white colonnade flecked with green lichens. Some of the fallen giants still lay on the grass, while to the left a pile of sawn logs stood in a geometrical cube. With the coming of evening the cold had sharpened, and the frozen mosses crackled under foot. At ground level it was quite dark already, but the higher branches showed up against the pale sky, in which the rising full moon would soon dim the stars.

Nearly three thousand mining folk had come to the meeting-place, a milling crowd of men, women, and children gradually pouring into the clearing and overflowing into the undergrowth. Latecomers were still arriving, and the sea of faces wrapped in shadow stretched as far as the nearby beeches. A hum of conversation rose from it like a stormy wind in the still, frozen forest.

Étienne stood at the top, looking down the slope, with Rasseneur and Maheu. A dispute had broken out and their voices could be heard in sudden bursts. . . .

The dispute had arisen because Rasseneur wanted to proceed constitutionally by electing officers. He was still smarting from his defeat at the Bon Joyeux, and he had sworn to have his revenge, counting on regaining his former prestige with the rank and file of the miners and not merely with the delegates. Étienne thought that a committee was outrageous and ridiculous here in the forest. Since they were hunted down like wolves they must act like revolutionaries and savages.

Seeing that the argument might go on for ever, he took control of the crowd at once by standing on a felled trunk and shouting:

'Comrades! comrades!'

The confused murmur died down like a long-drawn-out sigh. While Maheu silenced Rasseneur's protests, Étienne went on in stentorian tones:

'Comrades, since we are forbidden to speak, since they put the police on to us as though we were thieves, we have come here to thrash the matter out! We are free here, we are at home, and nobody will come and shut us up, any more than you can the birds and animals!'

He was answered by a thunder of cries and exclamations.

'Yes, yes the forest is ours, we've a right to talk here. . . . Go on!'

Étienne stood still for a moment on his log. The moon was still too low on the horizon, and only lit the topmost branches, so that the crowd, which had gradually calmed down into complete silence, was still lost in shadow. He too looked black, and stood out above the crowd at the top of the slope like a dark pillar.

Slowly he raised one arm and began; but his voice no longer thundered, for he had adopted the frigid tones of a simple representative of the people making his report. Now at last he was able to work in the speech which the police had cut short at the Bon Joyeux. He began with a rapid history of the strike, making a point of expressing it with scientific eloquence—facts, nothing but facts. He spoke first of his dislike of strikes; the miners had not wanted this one, the directors had provoked them with their new scale of payment for timbering. Then he reminded them of the first approach made by their delegates to the manager, and of the bad faith of the Administration; and then, later, at the time of their second deputation, the tardy concession, the two centimes given back after they had tried to steal them. So now here they were: he quoted figures to show that the provident fund was exhausted, gave details of the allocation of the help that had been sent, devoted a few sentences to excusing the International, Pluchart, and the others for not having done more for them in the middle of all their preoccupations in the struggle for world conquest. So the situation was daily going from bad to worse, the Company had given them back their cards and was threatening to take on workers from Belgium, moreover they had intimidated the weaker brethren and had persuaded a number of miners to go back to work. He still spoke in a monotonous tone, as though to drive home the seriousness of his news; he told of the victory of famine and the death of hope, the struggle that had reached the culminating frenzy of courage. Then suddenly, without raising his voice, he concluded:

'It is in these circumstances, mates, that you must come to a decision tonight. Do you want the strike to go on? And if so, what do you propose to do to beat the Company?'

A great silence fell from the starry sky. In the darkness the unseen crowd held its peace at these heartbreaking words, and a sigh of despair was the only sound that could be heard through the trees.

But already Étienne was speaking again, in a different voice. He was no longer the secretary of an Association, but a leader, an apostle bringing the gospel of truth. Were there any cowards among them who would break their word? Why, they would have suffered for a whole month in vain and go back to the pits hanging their heads, back once again to face the never-ending agony! Wouldn't it be better to die at once in an attempt to destroy the tyranny of capital starving the workers? Wasn't it a stupid game that they had had quite enough of, this business of always submitting under the lash of hunger until it came to the point when once again hunger drove even the meekest of them to revolt? He showed how the miners were exploited and were the only ones to suffer from these disastrous crises, reduced to starvation whenever the exigencies of competition brought down prices. No! the timbering scale was unacceptable, it was only a disguised economy, they meant to rob each man of one hour of his working day. This time it had gone too far, and the time was coming for the downtrodden worms to turn and see justice done.

He paused, with arms outstretched. The word justice shook the crowd, and a burst of applause passed over it like the rustle of dry leaves. Voices shouted:

'Justice! it's high time. . . . Justice!'

Gradually Étienne was warming up. He lacked Rasseneur's facile stream of words. Often he was at a loss, and had to use tortuous sentences from which he emerged with an effort emphasized by a forward lunge of his shoulders. But when he was pulled up in this way he found simple, energetic images which struck home to his audience, whilst his movements, those of a workman on the job, elbows now well back and now thrust forward to strike out with his fists, his jaw suddenly jutting out as though to bite, had an extraordinary effect upon his mates. As they all said, he was not very big but he made you listen.

'The wage system is a new form of slavery,' he went on in a still more ringing voice. 'The mine should belong to the miner, like the sea to the fisherman and the earth to the peasant. . . . Do you understand? The mine is yours—yours, for you have all paid for it with a hundred years of blood and misery!'

He faced up squarely to the thorny legal question, and lost his way in the maze of special regulations on mines. The sub-soil belonged to the nation just as much as the soil. It was only a hateful privilege that handed over the monopoly to the Companies, and this was all the more shameful in the case of Montsou, where the so-called legality of the concessions was complicated by agreements made ages ago with owners of ancient fiefs according to the old custom of Hainault. The mining folk had only to reconquer their own possessions, he said, as with a wave of the hand he took in the whole country, beyond the forest. Just then the moon rose clear of the topmost branches and lit him up. When the crowd, still in darkness, saw his figure standing out white, distributing fortunes with open hands, they burst out again into prolonged applause.

'Yes, yes, quite right! . . . Bravo!'

Then Étienne trotted out his favourite subject, the collectivization of the means of production, as he said more than once in a phrase the pedantic jargon of which pleased him mightily. His own evolution was now complete. He had started from the sentimental fraternity of the novice, the need to reform the wage system, and now he had reached the political theory of abolishing wages altogether. Since the Bon Joyeux meeting his collectivisim, from being vague and humanitarian, had hardened into a complicated programme each point of which he could argue scientifically. As a first point he affirmed that liberty could only be gained by the destruction of the State. Then, when the people had the government in their own hands, reforms could begin: return to the primitive community, substitution of a free and equal family for the morally oppressive one, absolute civil, political, and economic equality individual independence guaranteed thanks to the possession of the tools for work and of the whole output, and finally free technical education paid for out of collective funds. That involved a total recasting of the old corrupt society: he attacked marriage and the right to bequeath property, limited everybody's personal fortune and overthrew the iniquitous monument of dead centuries with the same repeated sweeping gesture of the harvester striking down the ripe corn with his scythe; then with the other hand he built humanity of tomorrow, an edifice of truth and justice rising in the dawn of the twentieth century. Reason tottered before this mental effort and left only the obsession of the fanatic. Gone were the scruples of his human feeling and common sense, and nothing seemed simpler than the realization of this brave new world: he had foreseen everything and he referred to it as though it were a machine he could fix up in a couple of hours, and neither fire nor blood counted.

'It is our turn now,' he yelled in a final crescendo. 'It is our turn to have power and wealth!'

Acclamations roared towards him from the depths of the forest. By now the moon lit up the whole clearing and picked out the isolated points in the sea of heads, far off into the dim recesses of the glades between the tall grey trunks. Here, in the icy winter night, was a whole people in a white heat of passion, with shining eyes and parted lips, famished men, women, and children let loose to pillage the wealth of ages, the wealth of which they had been dispossessed. They no longer felt the cold, for these burning words had warmed them to the vitals. They were uplifted in a religious ecstasy, like the feverish hope of the early Christians expecting the coming reign of justice.

Many obscure phrases had baffled them, they were far from understanding these technical and abstract arguments, but their very obscurity and abstract nature broadened still further the field of promises and carried them away into hallucinations. What a wonderful dream! To be the masters and suffer no more! To enjoy life at last!

'That's right, by God! Our turn now! Death to the exploiters!'

The women were hysterical. Maheude forgot her usual calm and yielded to the intoxication of hunger, la Levaque was yelling, Ma Brûlé, beside herself, was waving her witch's arms, Philomène was shaking herself to pieces in a fit of coughing, and Mouquette was so worked up that she was shouting endearments at the speaker. Amongst the men, Maheu was quite won over and had exclaimed with impatience at Pierron trembling on one side of him and Levaque talking too much on the other, whilst the scoffers, Zacharie and Mouquet, feeling ill at ease, tried to raise a giggle by saying how amazed they were that the comrade could say so much without having a drink. But the biggest noise of all came from the wood-pile, on which Jeanlin was shouting and egging on Bébert and Lydie by brandishing the basket containing Poland.

The clamour rose again. Étienne was tasting the heady wine of popularity. This was power that he was holding in his hands, materialized in the three thousand breasts whose hearts were beating at his bidding. . . .

. . . to everybody's amazement old Bonnemort could be seen standing on a log and holding forth in the midst of the uproar. Until then Mouque and he had stood there absorbed, appearing, as they always did, to be musing on far-off things. Probably he was overcome by one of those garrulous fits which suddenly came and stirred up the past so violently that his memories welled up and poured out of his mouth for hours. A deep silence had fallen, and they listened to this old man, this ghostly spectre in the moonlight and as he was telling things with no obvious bearing on the discussion, long stories that nobody could understand, the amazement grew. He was talking about his own young days, the death of his two uncles who were crushed in a fall at Le Voreux, then he went on to the pneumonia that had carried off his wife. But through it all he clung to his point: things had never gone well in the past and they never would in the future. For example, they had had a meeting in the forest, five hundred of them, because the king would not reduce working hours; but then he stopped short and began the story of another strike—he'd seen so many of them, he had! And they all finished up under these here trees in the Plan-des-Dames, or else at the Charbonnerie, or further off still, over Saut-du-Loup way. Sometimes it was freezing, sometimes it was blazing. One night it had rained so hard that they had gone home without saying anything. And the king's soldiers arrived and it ended up with shooting.

'We put our hands up like this, and swore never to go back. Oh, I've sworn, I have. . . . oh, yes, I've sworn!'

The crowd was gaping in uncomfortable amazement when Étienne, who had been watching the scene, leaped on to the fallen tree and stood beside the old man. He had recognized Chaval among his friends in the front row, and the thought that Catherine must be there too had put new fire into him, and a desire to be applauded in front of her.

'Comrades, you have just heard, here is one of our old friends and that's what he has suffered, and what our children will suffer it we don't have it out once and for all with these thieves and murderers.'

His rage was terrifying. Never had he spoken so vehemently. With one arm he supported old Bonnemort, displaying him like a flag of misery and grief, crying for vengeance. In rapid phrases he went back to the first of the Maheus, and told of the whole of this family done to death in the pit, victimized by the Company, hungrier than ever after a hundred years of toil; and then by contrast he pictured the bellies of the directors sweating money, the great crowd of shareholders kept like whores for a century, doing nothing, just enjoying their bodies. Wasn't it terrible to think of? A whole race of people dying down in the pits, sons after their fathers, so that bribes could be given to Ministers and generations of noble lords and bourgeois could give grand parties or sit and grow fat by their own firesides! He had studied miners' occupational diseases and now brought them all out with horrible details: anaemia, scrofula, black bronchitis, choking asthma, paralysing rheumatism. They, poor devils, were just machine-fodder, they were penned like cattle in housing estates, the big Companies were gradually dominating their whole lives, regulating slavery, threatening to enlist all the nation's workers, millions of hands to increase the wealth of a thousand idlers. But the ignorant miner, the mere brute buried in the bowels of the earth, was a thing of the past. In the depths of the mine an army was springing up, a harvest of citizens germinating like seeds that would break through the earth one sunny day. And then they would know whether, after forty years' service, they could dare to offer a hundred and fifty francs as a pension to an old man of sixty, spitting coal and with legs swollen with the water of the coal-face. Yes, labour would call capital to account, capital, that impersonal god, unknown to the worker, crouching somewhere in his mysterious tabernacle whence he sucked the blood of the poor starving devils he lived on! They would go and hunt him out, and make him show his face in the glare of fires, they would drown him in blood, this disgusting hog, this monstrous idol gorged with human flesh!

He stopped, but his arms remained stretched out into space, pointing at the enemy over there, somewhere, wherever he might be in the world. This time the clamour raised by the crowd was so loud that the bourgeois of Montsou heard it and looked anxiously towards Vandame, thinking it was some terrible landslide. Night birds flew up out of the woods and soared into the moonlit sky.

He wanted an immediate decision.

'Comrades, what have you decided? Do you vote for going on with the strike?'

'Yes, yes,' roared the voices.

'Then what steps are you going to take? If any blacklegs go down the pit tomorrow we are bound to be beaten.'

The voices rose again like a hurricane:

'Death to all blacklegs!'

'Very well, then, you have decided to hold them to their duty and sworn word. This is what we could do: go to the pits, our presence will stop the blacklegs, and we could show the Company that we are all in agreement and will die rather than surrender.'

'Right-oh! to the pits, to the pits!'

All the time he had been speaking Étienne had been looking for Catherine among the pale, roaring faces down there. No, she could not be there. But Chaval he could still see, making a point of sneering and shrugging his shoulders, consumed with jealousy and ready to sell himself for a little of Étienne's popularity.

'And if there are any informers amongst our numbers, mates,' Étienne went on, 'let them look out, for we know who they are. Yes, I can see some Vandame men who haven't left their pit.'

'Is that for my benefit?' asked Chaval with a fine show of bravado.

'Yours or anybody else's. But, as it's you who have spoken, you might as well understand that those who have got something to eat are quite a different thing from those who go hungry. You are working at Jean-Bart. . . . '

A mocking voice broke in:

'Oh, he works, does he? No, he's got a woman who works for him.'

Chaval went scarlet and swore.

'Christ! aren't we allowed to work, then?'

'No!' shouted Étienne, 'not when your mates are going through hell for the good of all. We are not going to let people crawl over to the bosses' side just to do themselves a good turn. If the strike had been general we should have been the masters long before this. Ought a single Vandame man to have gone down when Montsou was out? The trump card would be if the whole area stopped work—at Monsieur Deneulin's same as here. Do you see? they're all blacklegs on the coal-faces at Jean-Bart. You are all traitors!'

The crowd round Chaval was getting dangerous; fists were being brandished and cries of death were heard. He had turned pale. But in his furious determination to get the better of Étienne, he suddenly had an idea.

'Just you listen to me now! You come to Jean-Bart tomorrow and see for yourselves whether I am working! We are all on your side, and that's what I was sent here to say. The furnaces have got to be put out, and the enginemen must come out too. And if the pumps give out, all the better! The water will burst up the pits and the whole bloody lot.'

He was wildly applauded in his turn, and from then on even Étienne was edged into the background, as speaker after speaker mounted the fallen trunk, waved his arms about in the din and threw out the wildest proposals. It was now a paroxysm of blind faith, the impatience of a religious sect, weary of waiting for a miracle and determined to provoke one itself. These people, light-headed with hunger, saw red, had visions of fire and blood in a glorious apotheosis out of which universal happiness was rising before their eyes. The peaceful moonlight bathed this surging swell, and the clamour for blood was hemmed in on all sides by the deep silence of the forest. The frozen moss crackled under foot, whilst the beeches, standing tall and strong, spreading the delicate tracery of their branches black against the sky, were blind and deaf to the poor wretches moving at their feet.

There was some pushing in the crowd, and Maheude found herself next to her husband, and both of them, crazed by the long-drawn-out exasperation of the past months, were backing up Levaque who was going one better than everybody else and demanding the heads of the engineers. Pierron had vanished. Bonnemort and Mouque, both talking at once, were saying vague and terrible things that nobody could hear. Zacharie, just for fun, was agitating for the demolition of the churches, whilst Mouquet was banging the ground with his *crosse*, just to add to the row. The women were quite off their heads: la Levaque, hands on hips, was going for Philomène, whom she accused of laughing; Mouquette talked of putting the police out of action by kicking them up the so-and-so; Ma Brûlé, who had been cuffing Lydie for being without her basket or any salad either, was aiming punches into the air, for all the bosses she would have liked to get hold of. For a moment Jeanlin had been overcome with panic, Bébert having heard from a fellow that Madame Rasseneur had seen them take Poland; but he soon decided to go back and let the rabbit loose at the door of the Avantage, and set about yelling louder than ever, opening and brandishing his new knife and proudly making the blade gleam.

'Comrades! comrades!' Étienne was repeating, at the end of his tether, hoarse with trying get a moment's silence in order to come to some definite decision.

At last he got their attention.

'Comrades! tomorrow morning at Jean-Bart; is that settled?'

'Yes, yes, to Jean-Bart! Death to the traitors!'

The three thousand voices rose to heaven in a tempest, and died away in the pure light of the moon.

The end of *Germinal* considers the future and our ability to shape events.

Back in the open air, Étienne walked along the road absorbed in a welter of confused thoughts. But he also took deep breaths of the pure air and rejoiced in the space and sky. The sun was mounting triumphant over the horizon and the whole countryside was awakening to a new and happy day. From east to west across the measureless plain everything was bathed in a golden haze, and on all sides life was springing up warm and vigorous. Its youthful ectasy was made up of the rustling sounds of earth, the song of birds and the murmur of streams and woods. It was good to be alive; the old world meant to live through another spring.

Full of this hope, he slackened his pace and let his eyes wander from right to left, taking in the gaiety of the new season. He thought about himself, and knew that he was now strong, matured by his hard experience down in the pit. His apprenticeship was over, and he was going forth fully armed as a fighting missionary of the revolution, having declared war on society, for he had seen it and condemned it . . . . Was Darwin right, then, was this world nothing but a struggle in which the strong devoured the weak so that the species might advance in strength and beauty? The question disturbed him although as a self-styled scientist he could only settle it one way. But his misgivings were dispelled by one idea, a most attractive ambition: to go on with his old cherished examination of basic theory on the first occasion when he spoke in public. For if one class had to be devoured, surely the people, vigorous and young, must devour the effete and luxury-loving bourgeoisie? A new society needed new blood. In this expectation of a new invasion of barbarians regenerating the decayed nations of the old world, he rediscovered his absolute faith in a coming revolution, and this time it would be the real one, whose fires would cast their red glare over the end of this epoch even as the rising sun was now drenching the sky in blood . . . .

Deep down underfoot the picks were still obstinately hammering away. All his comrades were there, he could hear them following his every step. Beneath this field of beet was it not Maheude, bent double at her task, whose hoarse gasps for breath were coming up to him, mingled with the whirring of the ventilator? To left and to right far away into the distance he thought he could recognize other friends under the corn, the hedges and young trees. The April sun was now well up in the sky, shedding its glorious warming rays on the teeming earth. Life was springing from her fertile womb, buds were bursting into leaf and the fields were quickening with fresh green grass. Everywhere seeds were swelling and lengthening, cracking open the plain in their upward thrust for warmth and light. The sap was rising in abundance with whispering voices, the germs of life were opening with a kiss. On and on, ever more insistently, his comrades were tapping, tapping, as though they too were rising through the ground. On this youthful morning, in the fiery rays of the sun, the whole country was alive with this sound. Men were springing up, a black avenging host was slowly germinating in the furrows, thrusting upwards for the harvests of future ages. And very soon their germination would crack the earth asunder.

1. Evaluate Zola's concept of the experimental novel in terms of the application of the scientific method to writing.
2. Apply Zola's definition of the experimental novel to the first selection from *Germinal*. How far did the novel follow his theory?
3. Using both excerpts from *Germinal*, defend the following assertion by Zola: "Instead of binding the writer within narrow limits, the experimental method leaves him free to use all his intelligence as a thinker and all his talent as a creator."

▪ ▪ ▪

EDUARD BERNSTEIN

Eduard Bernstein (1850-1932) was the major "revisionist" of orthodox Marxism. He was an important figure in the theory and development of social democracy. Bernstein was in exile from Germany from 1878 until 1901, leaving after Germany passed anti-socialist laws. In Switzerland and then in England he wrote about his new ideas, which are contained in his major work, *Evolutionary Socialism* (1899). Bernstein believed Marx and Engels were wrong in predicting the collapse of capitalism, and he wished to reform the existing political and social system by legal means. He worked to unite democracy and socialism into a single idea, and his was a philosophy that appealed to many in western Europe.

 Bernstein summed up his ideas in the preface to the 1909 English edition of *Evolutionary Socialism*.

The present book has not only had its history, it has also in some way made a little history. Called forth by the circumstances described in the preface to the German edition, it created at its appearance a fair stir inside and outside German social democracy. . . .

. . . the views put forward in the book have received the bye-name of REVISIONISM, and although some of those who are called REVISIONISTS in German social democracy hold on several points of views different from mine, the book can, all in all, be regarded as an exposition of the theoretical and political tendencies of the German social democratic revisionists. . . .

. . . Unable to believe in finalities at all, I cannot believe in a final aim of socialism. But I strongly believe in the socialist movement, in the march forward of the working classes, who step by step must work out their emancipation by changing society from the domain of a commercial landholding oligarchy to a real democracy which in all its departments is guided by the interests of those who work and create.

 Capitalism will not necessarily fall, claimed Bernstein in the book.

. . . If the universal crisis is the inherent law of capitalistic production, it must prove its reality now or in the near future. Otherwise the proof of its inevitableness hovers in the air of abstract speculation. . . .

. . . Unless unforeseen external events bring about a general crisis—and as we have said that can happen any day—there is no urgent reason for concluding that such a crisis will come to pass for purely economic reasons. Local and partial depressions are unavoidable; general stagnation is not unavoidable with the present organisation and extension of the world market, and particularly with the great extension of the production of articles of food. The latter phenomenon is of peculiar importance for our problem. Perhaps nothing has contributed so much to the mitigation of commercial crises or to the stopping of their increase as the fall of rent and of the price of food.

 Democratic socialism and liberalism had a relationship for Bernstein. He believed that socialists had to abandon their revolutionary posture and move to an evolutionary point of view.

. . . nearly all who use the word democracy to-day understand by it more than a mere form of government. We shall come much nearer to the definition if we express ourselves negatively, and define democracy as an absence of class government, as the indication of a social condition where a political privilege belongs to no one class as opposed to the whole community. By that the explanation is already given as to why a monopolist corporation is in principle anti-democratic. This negative definition has, besides, the advantage that it gives less room than the phrase "government by the people" to the idea of the oppression of the individual by the majority which is absolutely repugnant to the modern mind. To-day we find the oppression of the minority by the majority "undemocratic," although it was originally held to be quite

Source: Eduard Bernstein, *Evolutionary Socialism* (New York: Schocken Books, 1961), pp. xxi-xxii, 87, 93-94, 142-43, 153-54, 166, 202, 203-204.

consistent with government by the people. The idea of democracy includes, in the conception of the present day, a notion of justice—an equality of rights for all members of the community, and in that principle the rule of the majority, to which in every concrete case the rule of the people extends, finds its limits. The more it is adopted and governs the general consciousness, the more will democracy be equal in meaning to the highest possible degree of freedom for all. . . .

Liberalism had historically the task of breaking the chains which the fettered economy and the corresponding organisations of law of the middle ages had imposed on the further development of society. That it at first strictly maintained the form of bourgeois liberalism did not stop it from actually expressing a very much wider-reaching general principle of society whose completion will be socialism.

Socialism will create no new bondage of any kind whatever. The individual is to be free, not in the metaphysical sense, as the anarchists dreamed —i.e., free from all duties towards the community— but free from every economic compulsion in his action and choice of a calling. Such freedom is only possible for all by means of organisation. In this sense one might call socialism "organising liberalism," for when one examines more closely the organisations that socialism wants and how it wants them, he will find that what distinguishes them above all from the feudalistic organisations, outwardly like them, is just their liberalism, their democratic constitution, their accessibility. Therefore the trade union, striving after an arrangement similar to a guild, is, in the eyes of the socialist, the product of self-defence against the tendency of capitalism to overstock the labour market; but, at the same time, just on account of its tendency towards a guild, and to the degree in which that obtains, is it an unsocialistic corporate body. . . .

. . . Even where socialist parties have originally taken the same hypotheses for the starting point of their work, they have found themselves obliged in the course of time to adapt their activity to the special conditions of their country. At a given moment, therefore, one can probably set up general political principles of social democracy with a claim that they apply to all countries, but no programme of action applicable for all countries is possible.

As shown above, democracy is a condition of socialism to a much greater degree than is usually assumed, i.e., it is not only the means but also the substance. Without a certain amount of democratic institutions or traditions, the socialist doctrine of the present time would not indeed be possible. There would, indeed, be a workers' movement, but no social democracy. The modern socialist movement—and also its theoretic explanation—is actually the product of the influence of the great French Revolution and of the conceptions of right which through it gained general acceptance in the wages and labour movement. . . .

My proposition, "To me that which is generally called the ultimate aim of socialism is nothing, but the movement is everything," has often been conceived as a denial of every definite aim of the socialist movement, . . . I expressed the conviction that with the continuance of free development, the English working classes would certainly increase their demands, but would desire nothing that could not be shown each time to be necessary and attainable beyond all doubt. That is at the bottom nothing else than what I say to-day. And if anyone wishes to bring up against me the advances in social democracy made since then in England, I answer that with this extension a development of the English social democracy has gone hand in hand from the Utopian, revolutionary sect, as Engels repeatedly represented it to be, to the party of political reform which we now know. No socialist capable of thinking, dreams to-day in England of an imminent victory for socialism by means of a violent revolution—none dreams of a quick conquest of Parliament by a revolutionary proletariat. But they rely more and more on work in the municipalities and other self-governing bodies. The early contempt for the trade union movement has been given up; a closer sympathy has been won for it and, here and there also, for the co-operative movement.

And the ultimate aim? Well, that just remains an ultimate aim. ''The working classes have no fixed and perfect Utopias to introduce by means of a vote of the nation. They know that in order to work out their own emancipation— and with it that higher form of life which the present form of society irresistibly makes for by its own economic development—they, the working classes, have to pass through long struggles, a whole series of historical processes, by means of which men and circumstances will be completely transformed. They have no ideals to realise, they have only to set at liberty the elements of the new society which have already been developed in the womb of the collapsing bourgeois society.'' So writes Marx in *Civil War in France*. I was thinking of this utterance, not in every point, but in its fundamental thought in writing down the sentence about the ultimate aim. For after all what does it say but that the movement, the series of processes, is everything, whilst every aim fixed beforehand in its details is immaterial to it. . . .

1. Create a hypothetical conversation between Bernstein and Karl Marx in which the two men debate their contrasting views of socialism.

▪ ▪ ▪

GEORGES SOREL

Georges Sorel (1847-1922) challenged the idea that politics was an activity pursued by rational individuals who sought happiness. He believed, like Nietszche, that human beings were guided by a kind of will, through which they defined themselves and which demanded great energy. Sorel also introduced myth as part of the substance of modern politics, as he claimed that people were often motivated by the irrational, which took the form of a social and political myth. Attacking democracy and parliaments, Sorel praised action and violence as means of social change and political metamorphoses. While his position was rejected by those who supported social democracy and various forms of liberalism, Sorel's ideas, called syndicalism, appealed to anarchists and, later, to fascists.

In his *Reflections on Violence* (1908), Sorel discussed the aims of syndicalism.

. . . Syndicalists do not propose to reform the State, as the men of the eighteenth century did; they want to destroy it, because they wish to realise this idea of Marx's that the Socialist revolution ought not to culminate in the replacement of one governing authority by another minority. The Syndicalists outline their doctrine still more clearly when they give it a more ideological aspect, and declare themselves antipatriotic—following the example of the *Communist Manifesto*.

It is impossible that there should be the slightest understanding between Syndicalists and official Socialists on this question; the latter, of course, speak of breaking up everything, but they attack men in power rather than power itself; they hope to possess the State forces, and they are aware that on the day when they control the Government they will have need of an army; they will carry on foreign politics, and consequently they in their turn will have to praise the feeling of devotion to the fatherland. . . .

Thus it cannot any longer be contested that there is an absolute opposition between revolutionary Syndicalism and the State; this opposition takes in France the particularly harsh form of antipatriotism, because the politicians have devoted all their knowledge and ability to the task of spreading confusion in people's minds about the essence of Socialism. On the plane of patriotism there can be no compromises and halfway positions; it is therefore on this plane that the Syndicalists have been forced to take their stand when middle-class people of every description employed all their powers of seduction to corrupt Socialism and to alienate the workers from the revolutionary idea. They have been led to deny the idea of patriotism by one of those necessities which are met with at all times in the course of history, and which philosophers have sometimes great difficulty in explaining—because the choice is imposed by external conditions, and not freely made for reasons drawn from the nature of things. This character of historical necessity gives to the existing antipatriotic movement a strength which it would be useless to attempt to dissimulate by means of sophistries.

We have the right to conclude from the preceding analysis that Syndicalist violence, perpetrated in the course of strikes by proletarians who desire the overthrow of the State, must not be confused with those acts of savagery . . . of the State . . . We have the right to hope that a Socialist revolution carried out by pure Syndicalists would not be defiled by the abominations which sullied the middle-class revolutions.

 Sorel did not believe in reform, but in violent confrontation and in the importance of myth—in this case the "myth of the general strike."

It is here that the rôle of violence in history appears to us as singularly great, for it can, in an indirect manner, so operate on the middle class as to awaken them to a sense of their own class sentiment. Attention has often been drawn to the danger of certain acts of violence which comprised *admirable social*

Source: Georges Sorel, *Reflections on Violence*, translated by T.E. Hulme (New York: Collier Books, 1961), pp. 116-18, 90-92, 122-25, 126.

works, disgusted employers who were disposed to arrange the happiness of their workmen, and developed egoism where the most noble sentiments formerly reigned.

To repay with *black ingratitude* the *benevolence* of those who would protect the workers, to meet with insults the homilies of the defenders of human fraternity, and to reply by blows to the advances of the propagators of social peace—all that is assuredly not in conformity with the rules of the fashionable Socialism . . . but it is a very practical way of indicating to the middle class that they must mind their own business and only that.

I believe also that it may be useful to thrash the orators of democracy and the representatives of the Government, for in this way you insure that none shall retain any illusions about the character of acts of violence. But these acts can have historical value only if they are the *clear and brutal expression of the class war*: the middle classes must not be allowed to imagine that, aided by cleverness, social science, or high-flown sentiments, they might find a better welcome at the hands of the proletariat.

The day on which employers perceive that they have nothing to gain by works which promote social peace, or by democracy, they will understand that they have been ill-advised by the people who persuaded them to abandon their trade of creators of productive forces for the noble profession of educators of the proletariat. Then there is some chance that they may get back a part of their energy, and that moderate or conservative economics may appear as absurd to them as they appeared to Marx. In any case, the separation of classes being more clearly accentuated, the proletarian movement will have some chance of developing with greater regularity than to-day.

The two antagonistic classes therefore influence each other in a partly indirect but decisive manner. Capitalism drives the proletariat into revolt, because in daily life the employers use their force in a direction opposed to the desire of their workers; but the future of the proletariat is not entirely dependent on this revolt; the working classes are organised under the influence of other causes, and Socialism, inculcating in them the revolutionary idea, prepares them to suppress the hostile class. Capitalist force is at the base of all this process, and its action is automatic and inevitable. Marx supposed that the middle class had no need to be incited to employ force, but we are to-day faced with a new and very unforeseen fact—a middle class which seeks to weaken its own strength. Must we believe that the Marxian conception is dead? By no means, for proletarian violence comes upon the scene just at the moment when the conception of social peace is being held up as a means of moderating disputes; proletarian violence confines employers to their rôle of producers, and tends to restore the separation of the classes, just when they seemed on the point of intermingling in the democratic marsh.

Proletarian violence not only makes the future revolution certain, but it seems also to be the only means by which the European nations—at present stupefied by humanitarianism—can recover their former energy. This kind of violence compels capitalism to restrict its attentions solely to its material rôle and tends to restore to it the warlike qualities which it formerly possessed. A growing and solidly organised working class can compel the capitalist class to remain firm in the industrial war; if a united and revolutionary proletariat confronts a rich middle class, eager for conquest, capitalist society will have reached its historical perfection. . . .

. . . Syndicalism endeavours to employ methods of expression which throw a full light on things, which put them exactly in the place assigned to them by their nature, and which bring out the whole value of the forces in play. . . . in short, the movements of the revolted masses must be represented in such a way that the soul of the revolutionaries may receive a deep and lasting impression.

These results could not be produced in any very certain manner by the use of ordinary language; use must be made of a body of images which, *by intuition alone*, and before any considered analyses are made, is capable of evoking as an undivided whole the mass of sentiments which corresponds to the different manifestations of the war undertaken by Socialism against modern society. The Syndicalists solve this problem perfectly, by concentrating the whole of Socialism in the drama of the general strike; there is thus no longer any place for the reconciliation of contraries in the equivocations of the professors; everything is clearly mapped out, so that only one interpretation of Socialism is possible. . . .

Neither do I attach any importance to the objections made to the general strike based on considerations of a practical order. The attempt to construct hypotheses about the nature of the struggles of the future and the means of suppressing capitalism, on the model furnished by history, is a return to the old methods of the Utopists. There is no process by which the future can be predicted scientifically, nor even one which enables us to discuss whether one hypothesis about it is better than another; it has been proved by too many memorable examples that the greatest men have committed prodigious errors in thus desiring to make predictions about even the least distant future.

And yet without leaving the present, without reasoning about this future, which seems for ever condemned to escape our reason, we should be unable to act at all. Experience shows that the *framing of a future, in some indeterminate time*, may, when it is done in a certain way, be very effective, and have very few inconveniences; this happens when the anticipations of the future take the form of those myths, which enclose with them, all the strongest inclinations of a people, of a party or of a class, inclinations which recur to the mind with the insistence of instincts in all the circumstances of life; and which give an aspect of complete reality to the hopes of immediate action by which, more easily than by any other method, men can reform their desires, passions, and mental activity. We know, moreover, that these social myths in no way prevent a man profiting by the observations which he makes in the course of his life, and form no obstacle to the pursuit of his normal occupations. . . .

A knowledge of what the myths contain in the way of details which will actually form part of the history of the future is then of small importance; they are not astrological almanacs; it is even possible that nothing which they contain will ever come to pass,—as was the case with the catastrophe expected by the first Christians. In our own daily life, are we not familiar with the fact that what actually happens is very different from our preconceived notion of it? And that does not prevent us from continuing to make resolutions. Psychologists say that there is heterogeneity between the ends in view and the ends actually realised: the slightest experience of life reveals this law to us, which Spencer transferred into nature, to extract therefrom his theory of the multiplication of effects.

The myth must be judged as a means of acting on the present; any attempt to discuss how far it can be taken literally as future history is devoid of sense. *It is the myth in its entirety which is alone important*: its parts are only of interest in so far as they bring out the main idea. . . .

1. In what way did Sorel distinguish the aims and tactics of syndicalism from those of socialism?
2. Sorel believed that violence is essential to restore productive energy to society. Do you agree?
3. Account for Sorel's view that it is the essence of myth that is important rather than its accuracy as a blueprint for the future.

▪ ▪ ▪

VLADIMIR LENIN

Vladimir Ilyich Ulyanov Lenin (1870-1924) became the most important political theorist and practioner of Marxism in the twentieth century. Lenin was a revolutionary in a Russia that he believed to be so backward and reactionary that no reform would be meaningful. In exile from the Czarist authorities, Lenin led the Bolshevik faction which took control of Russia during the uprisings in 1917. He then set out to transform Russia into a communist state. Deeply concerned with the plight of the Russian lower classes, Lenin and his followers believed that the country needed radical change along the lines laid down by Marx.

In *What Is to Be Done?* (1902), Lenin discussed his aims. He was the inventor of the new style political party, a group of dedicated professional revolutionaries who would work to end the existing authority by any means.

> The question arises, what should political education consist in? Can it be confined to the propaganda of working-class hostility to the autocracy? Of course not. It is not enough to *explain* to the workers that they are politically oppressed (any more than it is to *explain* to them that their interests are antagonistic to the interests of the employers). Agitation must be conducted with regard to every concrete example of this oppression (as we have begun to carry on agitation round concrete examples of economic oppression). Inasmuch as *this* oppression affects the most diverse classes of society, inasmuch as it manifests itself in the most varied spheres of life and activity—vocational, civic, personal, family, religious, scientific, etc., etc.—is it not evident that *we*

Source: Robert C. Tucker, editor, *The Lenin Anthology* (New York: W.W. Norton and Company, Inc., 1975), pp. 36, 38, 56-57, 58, 140-41, 243-46, 267.

shall not be fulfilling our task of developing the political consciousness of the workers if we do not *undertake* the organisation of the *political exposure* of the autocracy *in all its aspects?* In order to carry on agitation round concrete instances of oppression, these instances must be exposed (as it is necessary to expose factory abuses in order to carry on economic agitation). . . .

Revolutionary Social-Democracy has always included the struggle for reforms as part of its activities. But it utilises "economic" agitation for the purpose of presenting to the government, not only demands for all sorts of measures, but also (and primarily) the demand that it cease to be an autocratic government. Moreover, it considers it its duty to present this demand to the government on the basis, not of the economic struggle *alone*, but of all manifestations in general of public and political life. In a word, it subordinates the struggle for reforms, as the part to the whole, to the revolutionary struggle for freedom and for socialism. . . .

In our time only a party that will *organise* really *nation-wide* exposures can become the vanguard of the revolutionary forces. The word "nation-wide" has a very profound meaning. The overwhelming majority of the non-working-class exposers (be it remembered that in order to become the vanguard, we must attract other classes) are sober politicians and level-headed men of affairs. They know perfectly well how dangerous it is to "complain" even against a minor official, let alone against the "omnipotent" Russian government. And they will come *to us* with their complaints only when they see that these complaints can really have effect, and that we represent *a political force*. In order to become such a force in the eyes of outsiders, much persistent and stubborn work is required to *raise* our own consciousness, initiative, and energy. To accomplish this it is not enough to attach a "vanguard" label to rearguard theory and practice.

But if we have to undertake the organisation of a really nation-wide exposure of the government, in what way will then the class character of our movement be expressed?—the overzealous advocate of "close organic contact with the proletarian struggle" will ask us, as indeed he does. The reply is manifold: we Social-Democrats will organise these nation-wide exposures; all questions raised by the agitation will be explained in a consistently Social-Democratic spirit, without any concessions to deliberate or undeliberate distortions of Marxism; the all-round political agitation will be conducted by a party which unites into one inseparable whole the assault on the government in the name of the entire people, the revolutionary training of the proletariat, and the safeguarding of its political independence, the guidance of the economic struggle of the working class, and the utilisation of all its spontaneous conflicts with its exploiters which rouse and bring into our camp increasing numbers of the proletariat. . . .

B In *Two Tactics of Social-Democracy in the Democratic Revolution*, written during the 1905 revolution in Russia, Lenin discussed his goal of moving beyond a liberal revolution to a proletarian one.

The democratic revolution is bourgeois in nature. The slogan of a general redistribution, or "land and freedom"—that most widespread slogan of the peasant masses, downtrodden and ignorant, yet passionately yearning for light and happiness—is a bourgeois slogan. But we Marxists should know that there is not, nor can there be, any other path to real freedom for the proletariat and the peasantry, than the path of bourgeois freedom and bourgeois progress. We must not forget that there is not, nor can there be at the present time, any other means of bringing socialism nearer, than complete political liberty, than a democratic republic, than the revolutionary-democratic dictatorship of the proletariat and the peasantry. As representatives of the advanced and only revolutionary class, revolutionary without any reservations, doubts, or looking back, we must confront the whole of the people with the tasks of the democratic revolution as extensively and boldly as possible and with the utmost initiative. To disparage these tasks means making a travesty of theoretical Marxism, distorting it in philistine fashion, while in practical politics it means placing the cause of the revolution into the hands of the bourgeoisie, which will inevitably recoil from the task of consistently effecting the revolution. The difficulties that lie on the road to complete victory of the revolution are very great. No one will be able to blame the proletariat's representatives if, when they have done everything in their power, their efforts are defeated by the resistance of reaction, the treachery of the bourgeoisie, and the ignorance of the masses. But everybody, and, above all, the class-conscious proletariat, will condemn Social-Democracy if it curtails the revolutionary energy of the democratic revolution and dampens revolutionary ardour because it is afraid to win, because it is actuated by the consideration: lest the bourgeoisie recoil.

Revolutions are the locomotives of history, said Marx. Revolutions are festivals of the oppressed and the exploited. At no other time are the mass of the people in a position to come forward so actively as creators of a new social order, as at a time of revolution. At such times the people are capable of performing miracles, if judged by the limited, philistine yardstick of gradualist progress. But it is essential that leaders of the revolutionary parties, too, should advance their aims more comprehensively and boldly at such a time, so that their slogans shall always be in advance of the revolutionary initiative of the masses, serve as a beacon, reveal to them our democratic and socialist ideal in all its magnitude and splendour, and show them the shortest and most direct route to complete, absolute, and decisive victory. Let us leave to the opportunists of the . . . bourgeoisie the task of inventing roundabout, circuitous paths of compromise, out of fear of the revolution and of the direct path. If we are forcibly compelled to drag ourselves along such paths we shall be able to fulfill our duty in petty, everyday work also. But first let the choice of path be decided in ruthless struggle. We shall be traitors, betrayers of the revolution, if we do not use this festive energy of the masses and their revolutionary ardour to wage a ruthless and self-sacrificing struggle for the direct and decisive path. Let the bourgeois opportunists contemplate the future reaction with craven fear. The workers will not be intimidated either by the thought that reaction intends to be terrible, or that the bourgeoisie proposes to recoil. The workers do not expect to make deals; they are not asking for petty concessions. What they are striving towards is ruthlessly to crush the reactionary forces, i.e., to set up a *revolutionary-democratic dictatorship of the proletariat and the peasantry.*

Of course, in stormy times greater dangers threaten the ship of our Party than in periods of the smooth "sailing" of liberal progress, which means the painfully steady sucking of the working class's life-blood by its exploiters. Of course, the tasks of the revolutionary-democratic dictatorship are infinitely more difficult and more complex than the tasks of an "extreme opposition," or of an exclusively parliamentary struggle. But whoever is consciously capable of preferring smooth sailing and the course of safe "opposition" in the present revolutionary situation had better abandon Social-Democratic work for a while, had better wait until the revolution is over, until the festive days have passed, when humdrum, everyday life starts again, and his narrow routine standards no longer strike such an abominably discordant note, or constitute such an ugly distortion of the tasks of the advanced class.

At the head of the whole people, and particularly of the peasantry—for complete freedom, for a consistent democratic revolution, for a republic! At the head of all the toilers and the exploited—for socialism! Such in practice must be the policy of the revolutionary proletariat, such is the class slogan which must permeate and determine the solution of every tactical problem, every practical step of the workers' party during the revolution.

C Lenin was opposed to Russia's participation in the First World War. In his influential *Imperialism, the Highest Stage of Capitalism* (1916), he put forth the thesis that the war was the result of capitalist expansion.

We must now try to sum up, to draw together the threads of what has been said above on the subject of imperialism. Imperialism emerged as the development and direct continuation of the fundamental characteristics of capitalism in general. But capitalism only became capitalist imperialism at a definite and very high stage of its development, when certain of its fundamental characteristics began to change into their opposites, when the features of the epoch of transition from capitalism to a higher social and economic system had taken shape and revealed themselves in all spheres. Economically, the main thing in this process is the displacement of capitalist free competition by capitalist monopoly. Free competition is the basic feature of capitalism, and of commodity production generally; monopoly is the exact opposite of free competition, but we have seen the latter being transformed into monopoly before our eyes, creating large-scale industry and forcing out small industry, replacing large-scale by still larger-scale industry, and carrying concentration of production and capital to the point where out of it has grown and is growing monopoly: cartels, syndicates and trusts, and merging with them, the capital of a dozen or so banks, which manipulate thousands of millions. At the same time the monopolies, which have grown out of free competition, do not eliminate the latter, but exist above it and alongside it, and thereby give rise to a number of very acute, intense antagonisms, frictions, and conflicts. Monopoly is the transition from capitalism to a higher system.

If it were necessary to give the briefest possible definition of imperialism we should have to say that imperialism is the monopoly stage of capitalism. Such a definition would include what is most important, for, on the one hand, finance capital is the bank capital of a few very big monopolist banks, merged with the capital of the monopolist associations of industrialists; and, on the other hand, the division of the world is the transition from a colonial policy which has extended without hindrance to territories unseized by any capitalist power, to a colonial policy of monopolist possession of the territory of the world, which has been completely divided up.

But very brief definitions, although convenient, for they sum up the main points, are nevertheless inadequate, since we have to deduce from them some especially important features of the phenomenon that has to be defined. And so, without forgetting the conditional and relative value of all definitions in general, which can never embrace all the concatenations of a phenomenon in its full development, we must give a definition of imperialism that will include the following five of its basic features:

(1) the concentration of production and capital has developed to such a high stage that it has created monopolies which play a decisive role in economic life; (2) the merging of bank capital with industrial capital, and the creation, on the basis of this "finance capital," of a financial oligarchy; (3) the export of capital as distinguished from the export of commodities acquires exceptional importance; (4) the formation of international monopolist capitalist associations which share the world among themselves, and (5) the territorial division of the whole world among the biggest capitalist powers is completed. Imperialism is capitalism at that stage of development at which the dominance of monopolies and finance capital is established; in which the export of capital has acquired pronounced importance; in which the division of the world among the international trusts has begun, in which the division of all territories of the globe among the biggest capitalist powers has been completed. . . .

. . . The characteristic feature of imperialism is *not* industrial *but* finance capital. It is not an accident that in France it was precisely the extraordinarily rapid development of finance capital, and the weakening of industrial capital, that from the eighties onwards gave rise to the extreme intensification of annexationist (colonial) policy. The characteristic feature of imperialism is precisely that it strives to annex *not only* agrarian territories, but even most highly industrialized regions (German appetite for Belgium; French appetite for Lorraine), because (1) the fact that the world is already partitioned obliges those contemplating a *redivision* to reach out for *every kind* of territory, and (2) an essential feature of imperialism is the rivalry between several great powers in the striving for hegemony, i.e., for the conquest of territory, not so much directly for themselves as to weaken the adversary and undermine *his* hegemony. (Belgium is particularly important for Germany as a base for operations against Britain; Britain needs Baghdad as a base for operations against Germany, etc.) . . .

. . . the only conceivable basis under capitalism for the division of spheres of influence, interests, colonies, etc., is a calculation of the *strength* of those participating, their general economic, financial, military strength, etc. And the strength of these participants in the division does not change to an equal degree, for the *even* development of different undertakings, trusts, branches of industry, or countries is impossible under capitalism. Half a century ago Germany was a miserable, insignificant country, if her capitalist strength is compared with that of the Britain of that time; Japan compared with Russia in the same way. Is it "conceivable" that in ten or twenty years' time the relative strength of the imperialist powers will have remained *un*changed? It is out of the question.

Therefore, in the realities of the capitalist system, . . . alliances, no matter what form they may assume, whether of one imperialist coalition against another, or of a general alliance embracing *all* the imperialist powers, are *inevitably* nothing more than a "truce" in periods between wars. Peaceful alliances prepare the ground for wars, and in their turn grow out of wars; the one conditions the other, producing alternating forms of peaceful and non-peaceful struggle on *one and the same* basis of imperialist connections and relations within world economics and world politics. . . .

1. Outline the proposals identified by Lenin as being necessary for the organization of a nation-wide revolutionary movement. Have other movements in the twentieth century adopted Lenin's tactics?
2. Outline Lenin's views of the differences between bourgeois and proletariat revolutions.
3. Comment on Lenin's belief that imperialism was supported by finance capitalism and was based less on the desire to acquire territory than it was on the wish to keep an enemy from doing so. In your view, how much was the diplomacy before the First World War related to economic considerations?

■ ■ ■

ALBERT EINSTEIN

Albert Einstein (1879-1955) is widely regarded to be the most important scientific thinker since Newton. His concepts and ideas have transformed the way we all see the world. Einstein made many contributions to thermodynamics, mechanics, and to quantum theory, but he is best known for the introduction of the theory of relativity in 1905. In using the idea of relativity as a means of dealing with all physical phenomena, he changed the fundamental principles by which we understand the physical universe. Instead of space and time, the speed of light became the new "absolute." Einstein was always aware that his work had enormous implications in the field of epistemology, the theory of knowledge. He recognized that he and his scientific colleagues were changing our perception of how we understand and relate to the world.

In his "Autobiographical Notes" (1949), Einstein discussed how we think and the nature of concepts and propositions.

What, precisely, is "thinking"? When, at the reception of sense-impressions, memory-pictures emerge, this is not yet "thinking." And when such pictures form series, each member of which calls forth another, this too is not yet

Source: Paul Arthur Schilpp, ed., *Albert Einstein: Philosopher-Scientist* (New York: Tudor Publishing Company, 1951), pp. 7, 9, 11, 13, 19, 21, 25, 31, 33, 81, 83.

"thinking." When, however, a certain picture turns up in many such series, then—precisely through such return—it becomes an ordering element for such series, in that it connects series which in themselves are unconnected. Such an element becomes an instrument, a concept. I think that the transition from free association or "dreaming" to thinking is characterized by the more or less dominating rôle which the "concept" plays in it. It is by no means necessary that a concept must be connected with a sensorily cognizable and reproducible sign (word); but when this is the case thinking becomes by means of that fact communicable.

With what right—the reader will ask—does this man operate so carelessly and primitively with ideas in such a problematic realm without making even the least effort to prove anything? My defense: all our thinking is of this nature of a free play with concepts; the justification for this play lies in the measure of survey over the experience of the senses which we are able to achieve with its aid. The concept of "truth" can not yet be applied to such a structure; to my thinking this concept can come in question only when a far-reaching agreement (convention) concerning the elements and rules of the game is already at hand.

For me it is not dubious that our thinking goes on for the most part without use of signs (words) and beyond that to a considerable degree unconsciously. For how, otherwise, should it happen that sometimes we "wonder" quite spontaneously about some experience? This "wondering" seems to occur when an experience comes into conflict with a world of concepts which is already sufficiently fixed in us. Whenever such a conflict is experienced hard and intensively it reacts back upon our thought world in a decisive way. The development of this thought world is in a certain sense a continuous flight from "wonder."

A wonder of such nature I experienced as a child of 4 or 5 years, when my father showed me a compass. That this needle behaved in such a determined way did not at all fit into the nature of events, which could find a place in the unconscious world of concepts (effect connected with direct "touch"). I can still remember—or at least believe I can remember—that this experience made a deep and lasting impression upon me. Something deeply hidden had to be behind things. What man sees before him from infancy causes no reaction of this kind; he is not surprised over the falling of bodies, concerning wind and rain, nor concerning the moon or about the fact that the moon does not fall down, nor concerning the differences between living and non-living matter.

At the age of 12 I experienced a second wonder of a totally different nature: in a little book dealing with Euclidian plane geometry, which came into my hands at the beginning of a schoolyear. Here were assertions, as for example the intersection of the three altitudes of a triangle in one point, which—though by no means evident—could nevertheless be proved with such certainty that any doubt appeared to be out of the question. This lucidity and certainty made an indescribable impression upon me. That the axiom had to be accepted unproved did not disturb me. In any case it was quite sufficient for me if I could peg proofs upon propositions the validity of which did not seem to me to be dubious. For example I remember that an uncle told me the Pythagorean theorem before the holy geometry booklet had come into my hands. After much effort I succeeded in "proving" this theorem on the basis of the similarity of triangles; in doing so it seemed to me "evident" that the relations of the sides of the right-angled triangles would have to be completely determined by one of the acute angles. Only something which did not in similar fashion seem to be "evident" appeared to me to be in need of any proof at all. Also, the objects with which geometry deals seemed to be of no different type than the objects of sensory perception, "which can be seen and touched." This primitive idea . . . rests obviously upon the fact that the relation of geometrical concepts to objects of direct experience (rigid rod, finite interval, etc.) was unconsciously present.

If thus it appeared that it was possible to get certain knowledge of the objects of experience by means of pure thinking, this "wonder" rested upon an error. Nevertheless, for anyone who experiences it for the first time, it is marvellous enough that man is capable at all to reach such a degree of certainty and purity in pure thinking as the Greeks showed us for the first time to be possible in geometry.

Now that I have allowed myself to be carried away sufficiently to interrupt my scantily begun obituary, I shall not hesitate to state here in a few sentences my epistemological credo, although in what precedes something has already incidentally been said about this. This credo actually evolved only much later and very slowly and does not correspond with the point of view I held in younger years.

I see on the one side the totality of sense-experiences, and, on the other, the totality of the concepts and propositions which are laid down in books. The relations between the concepts and propositions among themselves and each other are of a logical nature, and the business of logical thinking is strictly limited to the achievement of the connection between concepts and propositions among each other according to firmly laid down rules, which are the concern of logic. The concepts and propositions get "meaning," viz., "content," only through their connection with sense-experiences. The connection of the latter with the former is purely intuitive, not itself of a logical nature. The degree of certainty with which this connection, viz., intuitive combination, can be undertaken, and nothing else, differentiates empty phantasy from scientific "truth." The system of concepts is a creation of man together with the rules of syntax, which constitute the structure of the conceptual systems. . . .

A proposition is correct if, within a logical system, it is deduced according to the accepted logical rules. A system has truth-content according to the certainty and completeness of its co-ordination-possibility to the totality of experience. A correct proposition borrows its "truth" from the truth-content of the system to which it belongs. . . .

⬦**B** Einstein believed that Newton's laws were not sufficient. They were not the final foundation of physics.

Now to the field of physics as it presented itself at that time. In spite of all the fruitfulness in particulars, dogmatic rigidity prevailed in matters of principles: In the beginning (if there was such a thing) God created Newton's laws of motion together with the necessary masses and forces. This is all;

everything beyond this follows from the development of appropriate mathematical methods by means of deduction.

We must not be surprised, therefore, that, so to speak, all physicists of the last century saw in classical mechanics a firm and final foundation for all physics, yes, indeed, for all natural science, . . .

Before I enter upon a critique of mechanics as the foundation of physics, something of a broadly general nature will first have to be said concerning the points of view according to which it is possible to criticize physical theories at all. The first point of view is obvious: the theory must not contradict empirical facts. . . .

The factor which finally succeeded, after long hesitation, to bring the physicists slowly around to give up the faith in the possibility that all of physics could be founded upon Newton's mechanics, was the electrodynamics of Faraday and Maxwell. . . .

. . . Newton, forgive me; you found the only way which, in your age, was just about possible for a man of highest thought- and creative power. The concepts, which you created, are even today still guiding our thinking in physics, although we now know that they will have to be replaced by others farther removed from the sphere of immediate experience, if we aim at a profounder understanding of relationships. . . .

C Physics was thought of as a conceptual study.

Physics is an attempt conceptually to grasp reality as it is thought independently of its being observed. In this sense one speaks of "physical reality." In pre-quantum physics there was no doubt as to how this was to be understood. In Newton's theory reality was determined by a material point in space and time; in Maxwell's theory, by the field in space and time. In quantum mechanics it is not so easily seen. . . .

1. What is the relationship between concepts and sense experiences as outlined by Einstein?
2. Respond to Einstein's comments on the limitations of Newtonian physics and its difference from relativity and quantum physics.

. . .

POETRY OF THE FIRST WORLD WAR

The poetry and prose written during and about the First World War (1914-18) is among the most pessimistic and horrific writing in the history of the West. The war, which saw millions killed and wounded, put an end for many to the notions of optimism and progress which the West had supported since the Enlightenment. Starting out as a patriotic enterprise, the war period became a nightmare for a civilization previously secure in its belief that it was advanced. It was in the many trenches of the First World War that the values of the Western tradition were challenged by a widening voice.

Anna Akhmatova (1889-1966) wrote her poem "July 1914" just prior to the outbreak of war, during a month when all Europe was wondering about the outcome of the newest and most dangerous diplomatic "crisis."

July 1914

I

All month a smell of burning, of dry peat
smouldering in the bogs.
Even the birds have stopped singing,
the aspen does not tremble.

The god of wrath glares in the sky,
the fields have been parched since Easter.
A one-legged pilgrim stood in the yard
with his mouth full of prophecies:

'Beware of terrible times . . . the earth
opening for a crowd of corpses.
Expect famine, earthquakes, plagues,
and heavens darkened by eclipses.

'But our land will not be divided
by the enemy at his pleasure:
the Mother-of-God will spread
a white shroud over these great sorrows.'

II

From the burning woods drifts
the sweet smell of juniper.
Widows grieve over their brood,
the village rings with their lamentation.

If the land thirsted, it was not in vain,
nor were the prayers wasted;
for a warm red rain soaks
the trampled fields.

Low, low hangs the empty sky,
tender is the voice of the supplicant:
'They wound Thy most holy body,
They are casting lots for Thy garments.'

Isaac Rosenberg's "August 1914" dealt with the life that will be missed and the new experience of youth. Rosenberg (1890-1918) was killed in the war.

August 1914

What in our lives is burnt
In the fire of this?
The heart's dear granary?
The much we shall miss?

Three lives hath one life—
Iron, honey, gold.
The gold, the honey gone—
Left is the hard and cold.

Iron are our lives
Molten right through our youth.
A burnt space through ripe fields
A fair mouth's broken tooth.

Source: Jon Silkin, ed., *The Penguin Book of First World War Poetry,* second edition (Harmondsworth: Penguin Books, 1981), pp. 260-61, 207-208, 182-83.

C Wilfred Owen's "Dulce Et Decorum Est" reflected the war experience and the anger of its participants. Owen (1893-1918) died one week before the armistice ending the war. The Latin phrase at the end of the poem, which includes its ironic title, translates: "It is sweet and proper to die for one's country."

Dulce Et Decorum Est

Bent double, like old beggars under sacks,
Knock-kneed, coughing like hags, we cursed through sludge,
Till on the haunting flares we turned our backs
And towards our distant rest began to trudge.
Men marched asleep. Many had lost their boots
But limped on, blood-shod. All went lame; all blind;
Drunk with fatigue; deaf even to the hoots
Of gas shells dropping softly behind.

Gas! GAS! Quick, boys!—An ecstasy of fumbling,
Fitting the clumsy helmets just in time;
But someone still was yelling out and stumbling,
And flound'ring like a man in fire or lime . . .
Dim, through the misty panes and thick green light,
As under a green sea, I saw him drowning.

In all my dreams, before my helpless sight,
He plunges at me, guttering, choking, drowning.

If in some smothering dreams you too could pace
Behind the wagon that we flung him in,
And watch the white eyes writhing in his face,
His hanging face, like a devil's sick of sin;
If you could hear, at every jolt, the blood
Come gargling from the froth-corrupted lungs,
Obscene as cancer, bitter as the cud
Of vile, incurable sores on innocent tongues,—
My friend, you would not tell with such high zest
To children ardent for some desperate glory,
The old Lie: Dulce et decorum est
Pro patria mori.

1. Compare these poems, in style and content, with those of the Romantics one century earlier.
2. Why does Owen use the Latin phrase in his poem and in its title?

• • •

ART AND THE ARTISTIC TRADITION

A number of art movements grew in the late nineteenth and early twentieth century, all devoted to a new exploration of how the artist could depict and understand human nature. Some groups celebrated the irrational and instinctual, and rejected much of the artistic tradition of the West. Two such movements were Futurism, which tried to revolutionize the arts in the decade before the First World War, and Dadaism, which, during and after the war, pointed out the nonsense and absurdity in much of modern life.

 Futurism was full of destruction and violence, rejecting the past and living in and for the present. Powerful as it was, Futurism became associated with the activism and political elitism of Fascism. Filippo Tommaso Marinetti (1876-1944) wrote "The Foundation of Futurism" in 1909.

FUTURISTIC MANIFESTO
1. We want to sing the love of danger, the habit of danger and of temerity.
2. The essential elements of our poetry will be courage, daring, and revolt.
3. Literature having up to now magnified thoughtful immobility, ecstasy, and sleep, we want to exalt the aggressive gesture, the feverish insomnia, the athletic step, the perilous leap, the box on the ear, and the fisticuff.
4. We declare that the world's wonder has been enriched by a fresh beauty: the beauty of speed. A racing car with its trunk adorned by great exhaust pipes like snakes with an explosive breath . . . a roaring car that seems to be driving under shrapnel, is more beautiful than the *Victory of Samothrace*.
5. We want to sing the man who holds the steering wheel, whose ideal stem pierces the Earth, itself launched on the circuit of its orbit.
6. The poet must expend himself with warmth, refulgence, and prodigality, to increase the enthusiastic fervor of the primordial elements.
7. There is no more beauty except in struggle. No masterpiece without an aggressive character. Poetry must be a violent attack against the unknown forces, summoning them to lie down before man.
8. We stand on the far promontory of centuries! . . . What is the use of looking behind us, since our task is to smash the mysterious portals of the impossible? Time and Space died yesterday. We live already in the absolute, since we have already created the eternal omnipresent speed.
9. We want to glorify war—the only hygiene of the world—militarism, patriotism, the anarchist's destructive gesture, the fine Ideas that kill, and the scorn of woman.
10. We want to demolish museums, libraries, fight against moralism, feminism, and all opportunistic and utilitarian cowardices.
11. We shall sing the great crowds tossed about by work, by pleasure, or revolt; the many-colored and polyphonic surf of revolutions in modern

Source: Eugen Weber, *Paths to the Present* (New York: Dodd, Mead and Company, Inc., 1966), pp. 244-46, 248-51, 253.

capitals; the nocturnal vibration of the arsenals and the yards under their violent electrical moons; the gluttonous railway stations swallowing smoky serpents; the factories hung from the clouds by the ribbons of their smoke; the bridges leaping like athletes hurled over the diabolical cutlery of sunny rivers; the adventurous steamers that sniff the horizon; the broad-chested locomotives, prancing on the rails like great steel horses curbed by long pipes, and the gliding flight of airplanes whose propellers snap like a flag in the wind, like the applause of an enthusiastic crowd.

It is in Italy that we launch this manifesto of tumbling and incendiary violence, this manifesto through which today we set up *Futurism*, because we want to deliver Italy from its gangrene of professors, of archaeologists, of guides, and of antiquarians.

Italy has been too long a great secondhand brokers' market. We want to rid it of the innumerable museums that cover it with innumerable cemeteries.

Museums, cemeteries! . . . Truly identical in the sinister jostling of bodies that do not know each other. Great public dormitories where one sleeps forever side by side with beings hated or unknown. Reciprocal ferocity of painters and of sculptors killing each other with line and color in the same gallery.

They can be visited once a year as the dead are visited once a year. . . . We can accept that much! We can even conceive that flowers may once a year be left for *la Gioconda!* . . . But we cannot admit that our sorrows, our fragile courage, our anxiety may be taken through there every day! . . . Do you want to be poisoned? Do you want to rot?

What can one find in an old painting beside the embarrassing contortions of the artist trying to break the barriers that are impassable to his desire to wholly express his dream?

To admire an old painting is to pour our sensitiveness into a funeral urn, instead of throwing it forward by violent casts of creation and action. Do you mean thus to waste the best of you in a useless admiration of the past that must necessarily leave you exhausted, lessened, trampled?

As a matter of fact the daily frequentation of museums, of libraries and of academies (those cemeteries of wasted efforts, those calvaries of crucified dreams, those catalogues of broken impulses! . . .) is for the artist what the prolonged tutelage of parents is for intelligent young men, drunk with their talent and their ambitious will.

For the dying, the invalid, the prisoner, it will do. Since the future is forbidden them, there may be a salve for their wounds in the wonderful past. . . . But we want nothing of it—we the young, the strong, the living *Futurists!*

Let the good incendiaries come with their carbonized fingers! . . . Here they are! Here they are! . . . Set the library stacks on fire! Turn the canals in their course to flood the museum vaults! . . . There go the glorious canvases, floating adrift! Take up the picks and the hammers! Undermine the foundations of the venerable cities!

The oldest among us are not yet thirty; this means that we have at least ten years to carry out our task. When we are forty, let those younger and more valiant than us kindly throw us into the waste basket like useless manuscripts! . . . They will come after us from afar, from everywhere, prancing on the light rhythm of their first poems, clawing the air with their crooked fingers, sniffing at academy gates the good scent of our rotting intellects already intended for the catacombs of libraries.

But we shall not be there. They will find us at last, on some winter night, out in the country, under a sad hangar on which the monotonous rain strums, crouching by our trembling planes, warming our hands over the miserable fire of our books of today gaily blazing under the scintillating flight of their images.

They will gather in a mob around us, panting with anguish and spite, and all exasperated by our untiring courage will bound forward to kill us with the more hatred for the love and admiration in their hearts. And Injustice, strong and wholesome, will glitter radiantly in their eyes. For art can be nothing but violence, cruelty and injustice.

The oldest among us are not yet thirty and yet we have already squandered great treasures, treasures of energy, of love, of courage and eager will, hastily, deliriously, countlessly, breathlessly, with both hands.

Look at us! We are not out of breath. . . . Our heart is not in the least tired! For it feeds on fire, on hatred, on speed! . . . You find it surprising? That is because you do not even remember having lived!—Up on the crest of the world, once more we hurl our challenge to the stars!

Your objections? Enough! Enough! I know them! Fair enough! We know well enough what our fine, false intelligence asserts.—We are only, it says, the summary and the extension of our forebears.—Perhaps! Let it be so! . . . What does it matter? . . . But we don't want to listen! Beware of repeating these infamous words! Rather, look up!

Up on the crest of the world, once more we hurl our challenge to the stars!

B⟩ The Dada movement was founded in 1916 by Tristan Tzara (1896-1945) and others. It was an outgrowth of anarchism and surrealism. Dadaism began as a reaction to the destruction and horrors associated with the First World War, and it was a critique of a civilization that seemed to be bent on destruction. In 1918 Tzara wrote in a *Dada Manifesto*:

DADA SIGNIFIES NOTHING
If one thinks it futile, if one wastes one's time for a word that signifies nothing . . .

Thus was DADA born of a need for independence, of suspicion for the community. Those who belong to us keep their freedom. We recognize no theory. We have enough of the cubist and futuristic academies: laboratories of formalistic ideas. Does one engage in art to earn money and stroke the pretty bourgeois? The rhymes ring with the assonance of coin, the modulation glides along the curve of a stomach seen in profile. All the groups of artists, riding on different comets, have come to this bank in the end. The door opens on the possibilities of wallowing in cushions and in food.
Here we anchor in fat ground. Here we have the right to proclaim for we have known the thrills and the awakening. Returning drunk with energy we

drive the trident into the indifferent flesh. We are streams of maledictions in tropical abundance of vertiginous vegetations, resin and rain is our sweat, we bleed and burn the thirst, our blood is strength.

Cubism was born of a simple way of seeing things: Cézanne painted a cup twenty inches below his eyes, the cubists look at it from above, others complicate the appearance by taking a perpendicular section and placing it soberly beside. (I do not forget the creators, nor the great issues of the subject which they finally settled.) The futurist sees the same cup in successive movement of objects one beside the other and maliciously adds a few force-lines. That does not prevent the canvas being a good or bad painting destined for the investment of intellectual capital.

The new painter creates a world, whose elements are also its means, a sober and definite work without a theme. The new artist protests: he no longer paints (symbolic and illusionistic reproduction) but creates directly in stone, wood, iron, tin, it being possible to turn the rocks of locomotive organisms in every direction by the limpid wind of monetary sensation. All pictural or plastic work is useless; let it be a monster that scares the servile spirits, not sweetly-sick to decorate the refectories of animals in human garb, illustrations of this dismal fable of humanity.

A painting is the art of causing two geometrical lines established as being parallel to meet on a canvas, before our eyes, in a reality which transposes into a world of other conditions and possibilities. This work is neither specified nor defined in the work, it belongs in its innumerable variations to the beholder. For its creator it is without cause and without theory. *Order = disorder; self = non-self; affirmative = negation*: supreme illuminations of an absolute art. Absolute in purity of cosmic and orderly chaos, eternal in the globule second without duration without respiration without light without verification. I like an ancient work for its novelty. There is only the contrast that binds us to the past. The writers that teach morality and discuss or improve the psychological fundamental principle have, apart from a hidden desire for gain, a ridiculous understanding of life, which they have classified, divided, canalized; they insist on seeing the categories dance to their tune. Their readers sneer and go on: what's the use? . . .

The philosophy is the question: where to begin to look at life, god, ideas, or other phantoms. All one looks at is false. I do not consider the relative result more important than the choice between cake and cherries after dinner. The way of taking a quick look at the other side of a question in order to indirectly impose one's opinion is called dialectics, that is to haggle the spirit of french fried potatoes while dancing the method around.

If I cry:

Ideal, ideal, ideal,

Knowledge, Knowledge, Knowledge,

Bangbang, bangbang, bangbang,

I have given a fair account of progress, law, morality, and all the other fine qualities that different very intelligent people have discussed in so many books, in order to conclude in the end that, all the same, everyone has danced after his own personal bangbang, and that he is right because of his bangbang, satisfaction of sickly curiosity; . . . The philosophers like to add to this element:

The power to observe. But, as a matter of fact, this magnificent quality of the mind is the proof of its impotence. We observe, we look from one or more points of view, we choose them from among the millions that exist. Experience is also a result of chance and individual faculties. Science disgusts me as soon as it becomes speculation-cum-system, loses its useful character—which is so useless—but at least individual. I loathe fat objectivity and harmony, this science that finds everything in its place. Carry on kids, humanity . . . Science says that we are the servants of nature: everything is fine, make love and break your necks. Carry on kids, humanity, pretty bourgeois and virginal journalists. . . . I am against systems, the most acceptable of systems is that of having none on principle. . . .

. . . But if life is a bad joke, without aim or initial delivery, and because we think we have to extricate ourselves properly from it, like washed chrysanthemums, we have proclaimed a single ground for understanding: art. It does not matter that we, knights of the spirit, have been singing to it for centuries. Art afflicts no one and those who know how to go about it will receive caresses and a splendid opportunity to fill the country with their conversation. Art is a private thing, the artist makes it for himself; a comprehensible work is a journalist's product, . . .

I proclaim the opposition of all the cosmic faculties to this gonorrhea of a putrid sun produced by the factories of philosophical thought, the fierce, implacable struggle, with all the means of

DADAIST DISGUST
Every product of disgust apt to become a negation of the family, is *dada*; protest with the fists of all one's being in destructive action: DADA; knowledge of all the means up to now rejected by the sex chaste with facile compromise and manners: *DADA*; abolition of logic, dance of the impotents of creation: DADA; of all hierarchy and social equation set up for the values by our valets: *DADA*; every object, all the objects, the sentiments and the obscurities, the phantoms and the precise clash of parallel lines, are means in our struggle: DADA; abolition of memory: DADA; abolition of archaeology: DADA; abolition of prophets: DADA; abolition of the future: DADA; absolute undisputable belief in every god that is the immediate product of spontaneity: *DADA*; elegant and unprejudiced leap from one harmony to the other sphere; trajectory of a word cast like an emphatic record cry; respect of all individualities in their monetary folly: serious, timorous, timid, ardent, forceful, decisive, enthusiastic; stripping one's church of all heavy and useless accessories; spitting out like a luminous cascade the unkindly or loving thought, or pampering it—with the lively satisfaction of knowing that it doesn't matter either way—with the same intensity in the thicket, unblemished by insects for the wellborn blood, and gilded by bodies of archangels, of one's soul. Liberty: DADA DADA DADA, shriek of the shriveled colors, blending of the contraries and of all the contradictions, the grotesqueries, the inconsistencies: LIFE.

1. "At first glance the rejection of the past, the incitement to violence, and the excitement of expression all seem to point to a similarity between Futurism

and Dadaism. Upon careful re-examination, however, their differences become clearly apparent." Comment on this statement with reference to both the manifestos of the two movements and examples of the artistic products of each.

. . .

SIGMUND FREUD

Sigmund Freud (1856-1939) is the individual who has most changed our understanding of the human personality in the twentieth century. Freud, a medical doctor, decided that the cause of some of the physical illnesses of his patients was grounded in their mental life. He became a controversial figure at the end of the nineteenth century, as he began an exploration of the inner life of human beings, which opened up questions of neuroses, psychoses, and sexuality. He introduced such terms as ego, id, super-ego, repression, and sublimation into the clinical and common languages. Freud argued that each human being had a deep inner life, which needed to be understood if we were ever to comprehend the nature of humanity. He explored areas which have been thought unimportant or had been ignored, and he coined a new terminology about the human personality, which changed the way we talk and think about ourselves. No serious thinker since Freud's time could ignore the issues raised by his fertile and original mind.

 In 1900 Freud published his *The Interpretation of Dreams*. In it, he discussed his belief that dreams have meaning in the lives of both children and adults.

> We find ourselves in the full daylight of a sudden discovery. Dreams are not to be likened to the unregulated sounds that rise from a musical instrument struck by the blow of some external force instead of by a player's hand; they are not meaningless, they are not absurd; they do not imply that one portion of our store of ideas is asleep while another portion is beginning to wake. On the contrary, they are psychical phenomena of complete validity—fulfilments of wishes; they can be inserted into the chain of intelligible waking mental acts; they are constructed by a highly complicated activity of the mind . . . .
>
> It is easy to prove that dreams often reveal themselves without any disguise as fulfilments of wishes; so that it may seem surprising that the language of dreams was not understood long ago. For instance, there is a dream that I can produce in myself as often as I like—experimentally, as it were. If I eat anchovies or olives or any other highly salted food in the evening, I develop thirst during the night which wakes me up. But my waking is preceded by a dream; and this always has the same content, namely, that I am drinking.

Sources: Sigmund Freud, *The Interpretation of Dreams*, translated by James Strachey (New York: Avon Books, 1965), pp. 155, 156-57, 159-60, 165-66, 647; Sigmund Freud, *The Origin and Development of Psychoanalysis* (Chicago: Henry Regnery Company, 1965), pp. 20-28, 42-46.

I dream I am swallowing down water in great gulps, and it has the delicious taste that nothing can equal but a cool drink when one is parched with thirst. Then I wake up and have to have a real drink. This simple dream is occasioned by the thirst which I become aware of when I wake. The thirst gives rise to a wish to drink, and the dream shows me that wish fulfilled. In doing so it is performing a function—which it was easy to divine. I am a good sleeper and not accustomed to be woken by any physical need. If I can succeed in appeasing my thirst by *dreaming* that I am drinking, then I need not wake up in order to quench it. This, then, is a dream of convenience. Dreaming has taken the place of action, as it often does elsewhere in life. Unluckily my need for water to quench my thirst cannot be satisfied by a dream in the same way as my thirst for revenge against my friend Otto and Dr. M.; but the good intention is there in both cases. Not long ago this same dream of mine showed some modification. I had felt thirsty even before I fell asleep, and I had emptied a glass of water that stood on the table beside my bed. A few hours later during the night I had a fresh attack of thirst, and this had inconvenient results. In order to provide myself with some water I should have had to get up and fetch the glass standing on the table by my wife's bed. I therefore had an appropriate dream that my wife was giving me a drink out of a vase; this vase was an Etruscan cinerary urn which I had brought back from a journey to Italy and had since given away. But the water in it tasted so salty (evidently because of the ashes in the urn) that I woke up. It will be noticed how conveniently everything was arranged in this dream. Since its only purpose was to fulfil a wish; it could be completely egoistical. A love of comfort and convenience is not really compatible with consideration for other people. The introduction of the cinerary urn was probably yet another wish-fulfilment. I was sorry that the vase was no longer in my possession—just as the glass of water on my wife's table was out of my reach. The urn with its ashes fitted in, too, with the salty taste in my mouth which had now grown stronger and which I knew was bound to wake me. . . .

The wish-fulfilment can be detected equally easily in some other dreams which I have collected from normal people. A friend of mine, who knows my theory of dreams and has told his wife of it, said to me one day: 'My wife has asked me to tell you that she had a dream yesterday that she was having her period. You can guess what that means.' I could indeed guess it. The fact that this young married woman dreamt that she was having her period meant that she had missed her period. I could well believe that she would have been glad to go on enjoying her freedom a little longer before shouldering the burden of motherhood. It was a neat way of announcing her first pregnancy. Another friend of mine wrote and told me that, not long before, his wife had dreamt that she had noticed some milk stains on the front of her vest. This too was an announcement of pregnancy, but not of a first one. The young mother was wishing that she might have more nourishment to give her second child than she had had for her first.

A young woman had been cut off from society for weeks on end while she nursed her child through an infectious illness. After the child's recovery, she had a dream of being at a party at which, among others, she met Alphonse Daudet, Paul Bourget, and Marcel Prévost; they were all most affable to her and highly amusing. All of the authors resembled their portraits, except Marcel

Prévost, of whom she had never seen a picture; and he looked like . . . the disinfection officer who had fumigated the sick-room the day before and who had been her first visitor for so long. Thus it seems possible to give a complete translation of the dream: 'It's about time for something more amusing than this perpetual sick-nursing.'

These examples will perhaps be enough to show that dreams which can only be understood as fulfilments of wishes and which bear their meaning upon their faces without disguise are to be found under the most frequent and various conditions. They are mostly short and simple dreams, which afford a pleasant contrast to the confused and exuberant compositions that have in the main attracted the attention of the authorities. Nevertheless, it will repay us to pause for a moment over these simple dreams. We may expect to find the very simplest forms of dreams in *children*, since there can be no doubt that their psychical productions are less complicated than those of adults. Child psychology, in my opinion, is destined to perform the same useful services for adult psychology that the investigation of the structure or development of the lower animals has performed for research into the structure of the higher classes of animals. Few deliberate efforts have hitherto been made to make use of child psychology for this purpose. . . .

I do not myself know what animals dream of. But a proverb, to which my attention was drawn by one of my students, does claim to know. 'What,' asks the proverb, 'do geese dream of?' And it replies: 'Of maize.' The whole theory that dreams are wish-fulfilments is contained in these two phrases.

It will be seen that we might have arrived at our theory of the hidden meaning of dreams most rapidly merely by following linguistic usage. It is true that common language sometimes speaks of dreams with contempt. (The phrase *'Träume sind Schäume* [Dreams are froth]' seems intended to support the scientific estimate of dreams.) But, on the whole, ordinary usage treats dreams above all as the blessed fulfillers of wishes. If ever we find our expectation surpassed by the event, we exclaim in our delight: 'I should never have imagined such a thing even in my wildest dreams.'

. . . If we restrict ourselves to the minimum of new knowledge which has been established with certainty, we can still say this of dreams: they have proved that *what is suppressed continues to exist in normal people as well as abnormal, and remains capable of psychical functioning*. Dreams themselves are among the manifestations of this suppressed material; this is so theoretically in every case, and it can be observed empirically in a great number of cases at least, and precisely in cases which exhibit most clearly the striking peculiarities of dream-life. In waking life the suppressed material in the mind is prevented from finding expression and is cut off from internal perception owing to the fact that the contradictions present in it are eliminated—one side being disposed of in favour of the other; but during the night, under the sway of an impetus towards the construction of compromises, this suppressed material finds methods and means of forcing its way into consciousness. . . .

The interpretation of dreams is the royal road to a knowledge of the unconscious activities of the mind.

By analysing dreams we can take a step forward in our understanding of the composition of that most marvellous and most mysterious of all instruments. Only a small step, no doubt; but a beginning. . . .

◆B▷ Freud gave several lectures at Clark University in the United States in 1910, explaining his new ideas. These lectures have been collected as *The Origin and Development of Psychoanalysis*. In them, Freud described the beginnings of the technique of psychoanalysis.

Since I could not alter the psychic state of most of my patients at my wish, I directed my efforts to working with them in their normal state. This seems at first sight to be a particularly senseless and aimless undertaking. The problem was this: to find out something from the patient that the doctor did not know and the patient himself did not know. How could one hope to make such a method succeed? The memory of a very noteworthy and instructive proceeding came to my aid, which I had seen in Bernheim's clinic at Nancy. Bernheim showed us that persons put in a condition of hypnotic somnambulism, and subjected to all sorts of experiences, had only apparently lost the memory of those somnambulic experiences, and that their memory of them could be awakened even in the normal state. If he asked them about their experiences during somnambulism, they said at first that they did not remember, but if he persisted, urged, assured them that they did know, then every time the forgotten memory came back.

Accordingly I did this with my patients. When I had reached in my procedure with them a point at which they declared that they knew nothing more, I would assure them that they did know, that they must just tell it out, and I would venture the assertion that the memory which would emerge at the moment that I laid my hand on the patient's forehead would be the right one. In this way I succeeded, without hypnosis, in learning from the patient all that was necessary for a construction of the connection between the forgotten pathogenic scenes and the symptoms which they had left behind. This was a troublesome and in its length an exhausting proceeding, and did not lend itself to a finished technique. But I did not give it up without drawing definite conclusions from the data which I had gained. I had substantiated the fact that the forgotten memories were not lost. They were in the possession of the patient, ready to emerge and form associations with his other mental content, but hindered from becoming conscious, and forced to remain in the unconscious by some sort of a force. The existence of this force could be assumed with certainty, for in attempting to drag up the unconscious memories into the consciousness of the patient, in opposition to this force, one got the sensation of his own personal effort striving to overcome it. One could get an idea of this force, which maintained the pathological situation, from the resistance of the patient.

It is on this idea of *resistance* that I based my theory of the psychic processes of hystericals. It had been found that in order to cure the patient it was necessary that this force should be overcome. Now with the mechanism of the cure as a starting point, quite a definite theory could be constructed. These same forces, which in the present situation as resistances opposed the emergence of the forgotten ideas into consciousness, must themselves have caused the forgetting, and repressed from consciousness the pathogenic experiences. I called this hypothetical process "repression" (*Verdrangung*), and considered that it was proved by the undeniable existence of resistance.

But now the question arose: what were those forces, and what were the conditions of this repression, in which we were now able to recognize the pathogenic mechanism of hysteria? . . . In all those experiences, it had happened that a wish had been aroused, which was in sharp opposition to the other desires of the individual, and was not capable of being reconciled with the ethical, æsthetic and personal pretensions of the patient's personality. There had been a short conflict, and the end of this inner struggle was the repression of the idea which presented itself to consciousness as the bearer of this irreconcilable wish. This was, then, repressed from consciousness and forgotten. The incompatibility of the idea in question with the "ego" of the patient was the motive of the repression, the ethical and other pretensions of the individual were the repressing forces. The presence of the incompatible wish, or the duration of the conflict, had given rise to a high degree of mental pain; this pain was avoided by the repression. This latter process is evidently in such a case a device for the protection of the personality.

I will not multiply examples, but will give you the history of a single one of my cases, in which the conditions and the utility of the repression process stand out clearly enough. Of course for my purpose I must abridge the history of the case and omit many valuable theoretical considerations. It is that of a young girl, who was deeply attached to her father, who had died a short time before, and in whose care she had shared . . . When her older sister married, the girl grew to feel a peculiar sympathy for her new brother-in-law, which easily passed with her for family tenderness. This sister soon fell ill and died, while the patient and her mother were away. The absent ones were hastily recalled, without being told fully of the painful situation. As the girl stood by the bedside of her dead sister, for one short moment there surged up in her mind an idea, which might be framed in these words: "Now he is free and can marry me." We may be sure that this idea, which betrayed to her consciousness her intense love for her brother-in-law, of which she had not been conscious, was the next moment consigned to repression by her revolted feelings. The girl fell ill with severe hysterical symptoms, and, when I came to treat the case, it appeared that she had entirely forgotten that scene at her sister's bedside and the unnatural, egoistic desire which had arisen in her. She remembered it during the treatment, reproduced the pathogenic moment with every sign of intense emotional excitement, and was cured by this treatment.

Perhaps I can make the process of repression and its necessary relation to the resistance of the patient, more concrete by a rough illustration, which I will derive from our present situation.

Suppose that here in this hall and in this audience, whose exemplary stillness and attention I cannot sufficiently commend, there is an individual who is creating a disturbance, and, by his ill-bred laughing, talking, by scraping his feet, distracts my attention from my task. I explain that I cannot go on with my lecture under these conditions, and thereupon several strong men among you get up, and, after a short struggle, eject the disturber of the peace from the hall. He is now "repressed," and I can continue my lecture. But in order that the disturbance may not be repeated, in case the man who has just been thrown out attempts to force his way back into the room, the gentlemen who have executed my suggestion take their chairs to the door and establish themselves there as a "resistance," to keep up the repression. Now, if you transfer both locations to the psyche, calling this "consciousness," and the outside the "unconscious," you have a tolerably good illustration of the process of repression. . . .

New questions at once arise in great number from our theory. The situation of psychic conflict is a very frequent one; an attempt of the ego to defend itself from painful memories can be observed everywhere, and yet the result is not a mental fission. We cannot avoid the assumption that still other conditions are necessary, if the conflict is to result in dissociation. I willingly concede that with the assumption of "repression" we stand, not at the end, but at the very beginning of a psychological theory. But we can advance only one step at a time, and the completion of our knowledge must await further and more thorough work . ,

Remember that with the ejection of the rowdy and the establishment of the watchers before the door, the affair is not necessarily ended. It may very well happen that the ejected man, now embittered and quite careless of consequences, gives us more to do. He is no longer among us, we are free from his presence, his scornful laugh, his half-audible remarks, but in a certain sense the repression has miscarried, for he makes a terrible uproar outside, and by his outcries and by hammering on the door with his fists interferes with my lecture more than before. Under these circumstances it would be hailed with delight if possibly our honored president, Dr. Stanley Hall, should take upon himself the rôle of peacemaker and mediator. He would speak with the rowdy on the outside, and then turn to us with recommendation that we let him in again, provided he would guarantee to behave himself better. On Dr. Hall's authority we decide to stop the repression, and now quiet and peace reign again. This is in fact a fairly good presentation of the task devolving upon the physician in the psychoanalytic therapy of neuroses. To say the same thing more directly: we come to the conclusion, from working with hysterical patients and other neurotics, that they have not fully succeeded in repressing the idea to which the incompatible wish is attached. They have, indeed, driven it out of consciousness and out of memory, and apparently saved themselves a great amount of psychic pain, *but in the unconscious the suppressed wish still exists*, only waiting for its chance to become active, and finally succeeds in sending into consciousness, instead of the repressed idea, a disguised and unrecognizable surrogate-creation (*Ersatzbildung*), to which the same painful sensations associate themselves that the patient thought he was rid of through his repression. This surrogate of the suppressed idea—the symptom—is secure against further attacks from the defenses of the ego, and instead of a short conflict there originates now a permanent suffering. We can observe in the symptom, besides the tokens of its disguise, a remnant of traceable similarity with the originally repressed idea; the way in which the surrogate is built up can be discovered during the psychoanalytic treatment of the patient, and for his cure the symptom must be traced back over the same route to the repressed idea. If this repressed material is once more made part of the conscious mental functions—a process which supposes the overcoming of considerable resistance—the psychic conflict which then arises, the same which the patient wished to avoid, is made capable of a happier termination, under the guidance of the physician, than is offered by repression. There are several possible suitable decisions which can bring conflict and neurosis to a happy end; in particular cases the attempt may be made to combine several of these. Either the personality of the patient may be convinced that he has been wrong in rejecting the pathogenic wish, and he may be made to accept it either wholly or in part; or this wish may itself be directed to a higher goal which is free from objection, by what is called sublimation (*Sublimierung*); or the rejection may be recognized as rightly motivated, and the automatic and therefore insufficent mechanism of repression be reinforced by the higher, more characteristically human mental faculties: one succeeds in mastering his wishes by conscious thought.

Forgive me if I have not been able to present more clearly these main points of the treatment which is today known as "psychoanalysis." The difficulties do not lie merely in the newness of the subject. . . .

. . . I may now pass to that group of everyday mental phenomena whose study has become a technical help for psychoanalysis.

These are the bungling of acts (*Fehlhandlungen*) among normal men as well as among neurotics, to which no significance is ordinarily attached; the forgetting of things which one is supposed to know and at other times really does know (for example the temporary forgetting of proper names); mistakes in speaking (*Versprechen*), which occur so frequently; analogous mistakes in writing (*Verschreiben*) and in reading (*Verlesen*), the automatic execution of purposive acts in wrong situations (*Vergreifen*) and the loss or breaking of objects, etc. These are trifles, for which no one has ever sought a psychological determination, which have passed unchallenged as chance experiences, as consequences of absent-mindedness, inattention and similar conditions. Here, too, are included the acts and gestures executed without being noticed by the subject, to say nothing of the fact that he attaches no psychic importance to them; as playing and trifling with objects, humming melodies, handling one's person and clothing and the like.

These little things, the bungling of acts, like the symptomatic and chance acts (*Symptom- und Zufallshandlungen*) are not so entirely without meaning as is generally supposed by a sort of tacit agreement. They have a meaning, generally easy and sure to interpret from the situation in which they occur, and it can be demonstrated that they either express impulses and purposes which are repressed, hidden if possible from the consciousness of the individual, or that they spring from exactly the same sort of repressed wishes and complexes which we have learned to know already as the creators of symptoms and dreams.

It follows that they deserve the rank of symptoms, and their observation, like that of dreams, can lead to the discovery of the hidden complexes of the psychic life. With their help one will usually betray the most intimate of his secrets. If these occur so easily and commonly among people in health, with whom repression has on the whole succeeded fairly well, this is due to their insignificance and their inconspicuous nature. But they can lay claim to high theoretic value, for they prove the existence of repression and surrogate creations even under the conditions of health. You have already noticed that the psychoanalyst is distinguished by an especially strong belief in the determination of the psychic life. For him there is in the expressions of the psyche nothing trifling, nothing arbitrary and lawless, he expects everywhere a widespread motivation, where customarily such claims are not made; more than that, he is even prepared to find a manifold motivation of these psychic expressions, while our supposedly inborn causal need is satisfied with a single psychic cause.

Now keeping in mind the means which we possess for the discovery of the hidden, forgotten, repressed things in the soul life: the study of the irruptive ideas called up by free association, the patient's dreams, and his bungled and symptomatic acts; and adding to these the evaluation of other phenomena which emerge during the psychoanalytic treatment, on which I shall later make a few remarks under the heading of "transfer" (*Uebertragung*, you will come with me to the conclusion that our technique is already sufficiently efficacious for the solution of the problem of how to introduce the pathogenic psychic material into consciousness, and so to do away with the suffering brought on by the creation of surrogate symptoms.

The fact that by such therapeutic endeavors our knowledge of the mental life of the normal and the abnormal is widened and deepened, can of course only be regarded as an especial attraction and superiority of this method.

I do not know whether you have gained the impression that the technique through whose arsenal I have led you is a peculiarly difficult one. I consider that on the contrary for one who has mastered it, it is quite adapted for use. But so much is sure, that it is not obvious, that it must be learned no less than the histological or the surgical technique.

You may be surprised to learn that in Europe we have heard very frequently judgments passed on psychoanalysis by persons who knew nothing of its technique and had never practised it, but who demanded scornfully that we show the correctness of our results. There are among these people some who are not in other things unacquainted with scientific methods of thought, who for example would not reject the result of a microscopical research because it cannot be confirmed with the naked eye in anatomical preparations, and who would not pass judgment until they had used the microscope. But in matters of psychoanalysis circumstances are really more unfavorable for gaining recognition. Psychoanalysis will bring the repressed in mental life to conscious acknowledgement, and everyone who judges it is himself a man who has such repressions, perhaps maintained only with difficulty. It will consequently call forth the same resistances from him as from the patient, and this resistance can easily succeed in disguising itself as intellectual rejection, and bring forward arguments similar to those from which we protect our patients by the basic principles of psychoanalysis. It is not difficult to substantiate in our opponents the same impairment of intelligence produced by emotivity which we may observe every day with our patients. The arrogance of consciousness which for example rejects dreams so lightly, belongs—quite generally—to the strongest protective apparatus which guards us against the breaking through of the unconscious complexes, and as a result it is hard to convince people of the reality of the unconscious, and to teach them anew what their conscious knowledge contradicts.

1. Comment on Freud's argument categorizing dreaming as a form of wish fulfilment.
2. Using Freud's example as a model, create your own analogy of the process of repression.
3. Account for Freud's opinion of those who could not accept the findings of psychoanalysis.

6

THE WEST IN TRIAL & CRISIS, 1918–1945

F rom world war to world war, with a massive depression in between, the period from 1918 to 1945 was time when the West questioned its own viability as a society and a culture, while at the same time seeking new norms. After the First World War there was a widespread belief that the West was in crisis. Major poets during the era underscored the sense of futility and impending violence, as Eliot and Yeats wrote about the banality of our lives and the harshness of the new collective experience. Ortega y Gasset challenged the values of mass society and saw them as ushering in a new era of barbarism.

Both communism and fascism became alternatives to the old liberalism and democracy. Lenin's Bolsheviks were now in power in the Soviet Union, developing a new collective society; in Italy, Germany, and elsewhere, fascists grabbed public authority and institutionalized totalitarian, sometimes racist, states. Some intellectuals were attracted by the new communism of the Soviet Union, though the realities of the 1930s disillusioned and ultimately alienated many from its doctrines. The violence, irrationality, and excesses of fascists disturbed many people and brought to the fore new, much darker, considerations about human empathy and human nature. A literature of dissent grew. Writers such as Orwell sought to develop a viable and humane social democracy as the only reasonable political alternative to the seemingly overpowering authoritarianism.

The literature of the period was full of attempts to explore the new sense of a more complex and irrational human nature. Zamyatin stressed the difficulties and importance of developing personal relationships and avoiding cultural ossification. Mann and Brecht wrote about human beings in crisis, caught sometimes in an irrationalism that seemed overwhelming, or facing authority with little or no support.

It was an era in which the ambiguities and complexities of human relationships were explored. Freud continued his quest for an understanding of the human psyche and the conflict between personal desire and social constraint. His work implied that however limited we were, we could, with great difficulty and even some personal pain, take control of our own lives. Others saw some hope in conscious human action. In economics, Keynes claimed that we need not be at the mercy of impersonal forces beyond our control. The new theological formulations of Buber stressed the importance of personal relationships in participating in the religious experience. And the diary of the young Anne Frank, written during the Holocaust, insisted on a hopeful view of the future and on responsibility for one's own self.

What emerged from the three decades from the First World War to the close of the Second was a view of human nature that was far more complex than ever before. This included a sense that individuals must assert their own values, a fear that technology will overwhelm us, and a new belief that Europe and the West, so long secure and at the center of world affairs, needed to re-examine itself fully, critically, and without illusions.

• ◇ •

POETRY OF THE INTER-WAR PERIOD

In the period after the First World War, poets, like visual artists, experimented with new forms and attempted to deal with the alienation and anger of a civilization that saw itself as being in crisis and spiritually empty. Often, the poets used new and different language as a means of signalling their dislocation from tradition and to try to get at the core of the feeling of their time.

A T.S. Eliot (1888-1965) wrote "The Love Song of J. Alfred Prufrock" (1917) as a dramatic monologue, and the poem contrasts the banality of Prufrock's life with the ideals he abandoned.

THE LOVE SONG OF J. ALFRED PRUFROCK

s'io credesse che mia risposta fosse
A persona che mai tornasse al mondo,
Questa fiamma staria senza piu scosse.
Ma perciocche giammai di questo fondo
Non torno vivo alcun, s'i'odo il vero,
Senza tema d'infamia ti rispondo. [1]

Let us go then, you and I,
When the evening is spread out against the sky
Like a patient etherized upon a table;
Let us go, through certain half-deserted streets,
The muttering retreats
Of restless nights in one-night cheap hotels
And sawdust restaurants with oyster shells:
Streets that follow like a tedious argument
Of insidious intent
To lead you to an overwhelming question . . .
Oh, do not ask, "What is it?"
Let us go and make our visit.

In the room the women come and go
Talking of Michelangelo.

The yellow fog that rubs its back upon the windowpanes,
The yellow smoke that rubs its muzzle on the windowpanes
Licked its tongue into the corners of the evening,
Lingered upon the pools that stand in drains,
Let fall upon its back the soot that falls from chimneys,
Slipped by the terrace, made a sudden leap,
And seeing that it was a soft October night,
Curled once about the house, and fell asleep.

And indeed there will be time
For the yellow smoke that slides along the street,
Rubbing its back upon the windowpanes;
There will be time, there will be time
To prepare a face to meet the faces that you meet;

Sources: M.H. Abrams, *et al.*, *The Norton Anthology of English Literature*, revised (New York: W.W. Norton and Company Inc., 1968), Volume II, pp. 1773-76, 1582-83, 1894-96; Anna Akhmatova, *Poems*, translated by Lyn Coffin (New York: W.W. Norton and Company, 1983), pp. 58-59.

There will be time to murder and create,
And time for all the works and days of hands
That lift and drop a question on your plate;
Time for you and time for me,
And time yet for a hundred indecisions,
And for a hundred visions and revisions,
Before the taking of a toast and tea.

In the room the women come and go
Talking of Michelangelo.

And indeed there will be time
To wonder, "Do I dare?" and, "Do I dare?"
Time to turn back and descend the stair,
With a bald spot in the middle of my hair—
(They will say: "How his hair is growing thin!")
My morning coat, my collar mounting firmly to the chin,
My necktie rich and modest, but asserted by a simple pin—
(They will say: "But how his arms and legs are thin!")
Do I dare
Disturb the universe?
In a minute there is time
For decisions and revisions which a minute will reverse.

For I have known them all already, known them all—
Have known the evenings, mornings, afternoons,
I have measured out my life with coffee spoons;
I know the voices dying with a dying fall
Beneath the music from a farther room.
      So how should I presume?

And I have known the eyes already, known them all—
The eyes that fix you in a formulated phrase,
And when I am formulated, sprawling on a pin,
When I am pinned and wriggling on the wall,
Then how should I begin
To spit out all the butt-ends of my days and ways?
      And how should I presume?

And I have known the arms already, known them all—
Arms that are braceleted and white and bare
(But in the lamplight, downed with light brown hair!)
Is it perfume from a dress
That makes me so digress?
Arms that lie along a table, or wrap about a shawl.
      And should I then presume?
      And how should I begin?

                    . . . . .

Shall I say, I have gone at dusk through narrow streets
And watched the smoke that rises from the pipes
Of lonely men in shirt-sleeves, leaning out of windows? . . .

I should have been a pair of ragged claws
Scuttling across the floors of silent seas.

                    . . . . .

And the afternoon, the evening, sleeps so peacefully!
Smoothed by long fingers,
Asleep . . . tired . . . or it malingers,
Stretched on the floor, here beside you and me.
Should I, after tea and cakes and ices,
Have the strength to force the moment to its crisis?
But though I have wept and fasted, wept and prayed,

Though I have seen my head (grown slightly bald) brought in upon
      a platter,
I am no prophet—and here's no great matter;
I have seen the moment of my greatness flicker,
And I have seen the eternal Footman hold my coat, and snicker,
And in short, I was afraid.

And would it have been worth it, after all,
After the cups, the marmalade, the tea,
Among the porcelain, among some talk of you and me,
Would it have been worth while,
To have bitten off the matter with a smile,
To have squeezed the universe into a ball
To roll it toward some overwhelming question,
To say: "I am Lazarus, come from the dead,
Come back to tell you all, I shall tell you all"—
If one, settling a pillow by her head,
     Should say: "That is not what I meant at all.
     That is not it, at all."

And would it have been worth it, after all,
Would it have been worth while,
After the sunsets and the dooryards and the sprinkled streets,
After the novels, after the teacups, after the skirts that trail along
     the floor—
And this, and so much more?—
It is impossible to say just what I mean!
But as if a magic lantern threw the nerves in patterns on a
     screen:
Would it have been worth while
If one, settling a pillow or throwing off a shawl,
And turning toward the window, should say:
     "That is not it at all,
     That is not what I meant, at all."

       . . . . .

No! I am not Prince Hamlet, nor was meant to be;
Am an attendant lord, one that will do
To swell a progress, start a scene or two,
Advise the prince; no doubt, an easy tool,
Deferential, glad to be of use,
Politic, cautious, and meticulous;
Full of high sentence, but a bit obtuse;
At times, indeed, almost ridiculous—
Almost, at times, the Fool.

I grow old . . . I grow old . . .
I shall wear the bottoms of my trousers rolled.

Shall I part my hair behind? Do I dare to eat a peach?
I shall wear white flannel trousers, and walk upon the beach.
I have heard the mermaids singing, each to each.

I do not think that they will sing to me.

I have seen them riding seaward on the waves
Combing the white hair of the waves blown back
When the wind blows the water white and black.

We have lingered in the chambers of the sea
By sea-girls wreathed with seaweed red and brown
Till human voices wake us, and we drown.

Footnote: [1] "If I thought that my reply would be to one who would never return to the world, this flame would stay without further movement; but since none has ever returned alive from this depth, if what I hear is true, I answer you without fear of infamy." Dante, *Inferno* xxvii, 61-66.

B In "The Second Coming" (1921), William Butler Yeats expressed what many believed after the First World War: a harsh, dark, iron age had arrived, the beginnings of a new, less hopeful time.

THE SECOND COMING

Turning and turning in the widening gyre
The falcon cannot hear the falconer;
Things fall apart; the center cannot hold;
Mere anarchy is loosed upon the world,
The blood-dimmed tide is loosed, and everywhere
The ceremony of innocence is drowned;
The best lack all conviction, while the worst
Are full of passionate intensity.

Surely some revelation is at hand;
Surely the Second Coming is at hand.
The Second Coming! Hardly are those words out

When a vast image out of *Spiritus Mundi*
Troubles my sight: somewhere in sands of the desert
A shape with lion body and the head of a man,
A gaze blank and pitiless as the sun,
Is moving its slow thighs, while all about it
Reel shadows of the indignant desert birds.
The darkness drops again; but now I know
That twenty centuries of stony sleep
Were vexed to nightmare by a rocking cradle,
And what rough beast, its hour come round at last,
Slouches towards Bethlehem to be born?

C W.H. Auden (1907-73), in "Spain 1937," wrote about the experience of the Spanish Civil War. That conflict was viewed by many in Europe and the West as a testing time for democracy against the rising tide of fascism.

SPAIN 1937

Yesterday all the past. The language of size
Spreading to China along the trade routes; the diffusion
        Of the counting-frame and the cromlech;
Yesterday the shadow-reckoning in the sunny climates.

Yesterday the assessment of insurance by cards,
The divination of water; yesterday the invention
        Of cart wheels and clocks, the taming of
Horses; yesterday the bustling world of the navigators.

Yesterday the abolition of fairies and giants;
The fortress like a motionless eagle eyeing the valley,
        The chapel built in the forest;
Yesterday the carving of angels and of frightening gargoyles.

The trial of heretics among the columns of stone;
Yesterday the theological feuds in the taverns
        And the miraculous cure at the fountain;
Yesterday the Sabbath of Witches. But today the struggle.

Yesterday the installation of dynamos and turbines;
The construction of railways in the colonial desert;
        Yesterday the classic lecture
On the origin of Mankind. But today the struggle.

Yesterday the belief in the absolute value of Greek;
The fall of the curtain upon the death of a hero;
        Yesterday the prayer to the sunset,
And the adoration of madmen. But today the struggle.

As the poet whispers, startled among the pines
Or, where the loose waterfall sings, compact, or upright
        On the crag by the leaning tower:
"O my vision. O send me the luck of the sailor."

And the investigator peers through his instruments
At the inhuman provinces, the virile bacillus
        Or enormous Jupiter finished:
"But the lives of my friends. I inquire, I inquire."

And the poor in their fireless lodgings dropping the sheets
Of the evening paper: "Our day is our loss. O show us
        History the operator, the
Organizer, Time the refreshing river."

And the nations combine each cry, invoking the life
That shapes the individual belly and orders
        The private nocturnal terror:
"Did you not found once the city-state of the sponge,

"Raise the vast military empires of the shark
And the tiger, establish the robin's plucky canton?
        Intervene. O descend as a dove or
A furious papa or a mild engineer: but descend."

And the life, if it answers at all, replies from the heart
And the eyes and the lungs, from the shops and squares of the city:
        "O no, I am not the Mover,
Not today, not to you. To you I'm the
"Yes-man, that bar-companion, the easily-duped:
I am whatever you do; I am your vow to be
        Good, your humorous story;
I am your business voice; I am your marriage.

"What's your proposal? To build the Just City? I will.
I agree. Or is it the suicide pact, the romantic
        Death? Very well, I accept, for
I am your choice, your decision: yes, I am Spain."

Many have heard it on remote peninsulas,
On sleepy plains, in the aberrant fishermen's islands,
        In the corrupt heart of the city;
Have heard and migrated like gulls or the seeds of a flower.

They clung like burrs to the long expresses that lurch
Through the unjust lands, through the night, through the alpine tunnel;

They floated over the oceans;
They walked the passes: they came to present their lives.

On that arid square, that fragment nipped off from hot
Africa, soldered so crudely to inventive Europe,
      On that tableland scored by rivers,
Our fever's menacing shapes are precise and alive.

Tomorrow, perhaps, the future: the research on fatigue
And the movements of packers; the gradual exploring of all the
      Octaves of radiation;
Tomorrow the enlarging of consciousness by diet and breathing.

Tomorrow the rediscovery of romantic love;
The photographing of ravens; all the fun under
      Liberty's masterful shadow;
Tomorrow the hour of the pageant-master and the musician.

Tomorrow, for the young, the poets exploding like bombs,
The walks by the lake, the winter of perfect communion;
      Tomorrow the bicycle races
Through the suburbs on summer evenings: but today the struggle.

Today the inevitable increase in the chances of death;
The conscious acceptance of guilt in the fact of murder;
      Today the expending of powers
On the flat ephemeral pamphlet and the boring meeting.

Today the makeshift consolations; the shared cigarette;
The cards in the candle-lit barn and the scraping concert,
      The masculine jokes; today the
Fumbled and unsatisfactory embrace before hurting.

The stars are dead; the animals will not look:
We are left alone with our day, and the time is short and
      History to the defeated
May say Alas but cannot help or pardon.

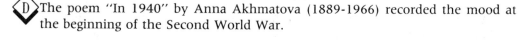 The poem "In 1940" by Anna Akhmatova (1889-1966) recorded the mood at the beginning of the Second World War.

In 1940

1.

When they bury an epoch,
No psalms are read while the coffin settles,
The grave will be adorned with a rock,
With bristly thistles and nettles.
Only the gravediggers dig and fill,
Working with zest. Business to do!
And it's so still, my God, so still,
You can hear time passing by you.

And later, like a corpse, it will rise
Ride the river in spring like a leaf,—
But the son doesn't recognize
His mother, the grandson turns away in grief,
Bowed heads do not embarrass,
Like a pendulum goes the moon.

Well, this is the sort of silent tune
That plays in fallen Paris.

2. To Londoners

The twenty-fourth drama by William Shakespeare
Time is writing with a careless hand.
Since we partake of the feast of fear,
We'd rather read Hamlet, Caesar, Lear,
By the river of lead where today we stand,
Or carry Juliet, sweet as a kiss,
To her grave, with songs and torches to lead,
Or tremble in darkness as in an abyss
With a hired killer Macbeth will need,—
Only . . . not this, not this, not this,
This we don't have the strength to read!

5.

I warn you, that's the way things are:
This is my final lifetime.
Not as a swallow, reed, or star,
Not as a bell to ring or chime,
Not as the water in a spring,
Not as a maple, branch or beam—
I won't alarm those who are living,
I won't appear in anyone's dream,
Unappeased and unforgiving.

1. Select two of the poetry selections. Using the images presented in the pieces, put your choices into their historical context and perspective.

■ ■ ■

SURREALISM

Surrealism was a literary and artistic movement that evolved out of a number of avant-garde ideas, including those of Dadaism. It was a rebellion against the *status quo* and attacked many established beliefs and institutions. Linking artistic creativity to the unconscious, surrealists attempted, through symbolism, to arrive at an understanding of human nature in its many forms. The movement made its greatest contributions in the visual arts, in the works of such artists as de Chirico, Dali, and Magritte.

In 1924 André Breton (1896-1966) wrote a *Manifesto of Surrealism*, which described the nature and goals of the movement and attacked a view of the world governed only by reason and logic.

> We are still living under the reign of logic: this, of course, is what I have been driving at. But in this day and age logical methods are applicable only to

Source: André Breton, *Manifestos of Surrealism* (Ann Arbor: The University of Michigan Press, 1972), pp. 9-10, 14, 26.

solving problems of secondary interest. The absolute rationalism that is still in vogue allows us to consider only facts relating directly to our experience. Logical ends, on the contrary, escape us. It is pointless to add that experience itself has found itself increasingly circumscribed. It paces back and forth in a cage from which it is more and more difficult to make it emerge. It too leans for support on what is most immediately expedient, and it is protected by the sentinels of common sense. Under the pretense of civilization and progress, we have managed to banish from the mind everything that may rightly or wrongly be termed superstition, or fancy; forbidden is any kind of search for truth which is not in conformance with accepted practices. It was, apparently, by pure chance that a part of our mental world which we pretended not to be concerned with any longer—and, in my opinion by far the most important part—has been brought back to light. For this we must give thanks to the discoveries of Sigmund Freud. On the basis of these discoveries a current of opinion is finally forming by means of which the human explorer will be able to carry his investigations much further, authorized as he will henceforth be not to confine himself solely to the most summary realities. The imagination is perhaps on the point of reasserting itself, of reclaiming its rights. If the depths of our mind contain within it strange forces capable of augmenting those on the surface, or of waging a victorious battle against them, there is every reason to seize them—first to seize them, then, if need be, to submit them to the control of our reason. The analysts themselves have everything to gain by it. But it is worth noting that no means has been designated a priori for carrying out this undertaking, that until further notice it can be construed to be the province of poets as well as scholars, and that its success is not dependent upon the more or less capricious paths that will be followed. . . .

. . . I believe in the future resolution of these two states, dream and reality, which are seemingly so contradictory, into a kind of absolute reality, a *surreality*, if one may so speak. It is in quest of this surreality that I am going, certain not to find it but too unmindful of my death not to calculate to some slight degree the joys of its possession.

A story is told according to which Saint-Pol-Roux, in times gone by, used to have a notice posted on the door of his manor house in Camaret, every evening before he went to sleep, which read: THE POET IS WORKING.

A great deal more could be said, but in passing I merely wanted to touch upon a subject which in itself would require a very long and much more detailed discussion; I shall come back to it. At this juncture, my intention was merely to mark a point by noting the *hate of the marvelous* which rages in certain men, this absurdity beneath which they try to bury it. Let us not mince words: the marvelous is always beautiful, anything marvelous is beautiful, in fact only the marvelous is beautiful. . . .

Breton attempted to define surrealism:

. . . I am defining it once and for all:

SURREALISM, *n*. Psychic automatism in its pure state, by which one proposes to express—verbally, by means of the written word, or in any other manner—the actual functioning of thought. Dictated by thought, in the absence of any control exercised by reason, exempt from any aesthetic or moral concern.

ENCYCLOPEDIA. *Philosophy.* Surrealism is based on the belief in the superior reality of certain forms of previously neglected associations, in the omnipotence of dream, in the disinterested play of thought. It tends to ruin once and for all all other psychic mechanisms and to substitute itself for them in solving all the principal problems of life. . . .

1. Respond to Breton's attack on the cold rule of logic. Did his thought have any precedents?
2. Using artistic examples to support your view, write your own definition of surrealism.

• • •

VLADIMIR LENIN

Vladimir Lenin (1870-1924) arrived in Russia in April 1917, several weeks after the revolution which overthrew the Czar and installed a provisional government. Leader of the Bolsheviks, Lenin was in opposition to the new government. In November 1917 he led a *coup d'état*, which placed him and his followers in power. Lenin's political leadership was determined and daring, and he managed to guide the new Soviet state through a civil war and economic hardship. He died in January 1924, not having fully settled many of the theoretical issues and practical problems about the new communist state.

In 1917 Lenin wrote *State and Revolution*, in which he discussed the road to be taken from democracy to communism.

Previously the question was put as follows: to achieve its emancipation, the proletariat must overthrow the bourgeoisie, win political power and establish its revolutionary dictatorship.

Now the question is put somewhat differently: the transition from capitalist society—which is developing towards communism—to communist society is impossible without a "political transition period," and the state in this period can only be the revolutionary dictatorship of the proletariat.

What, then, is the relation of this dictatorship to democracy?

We have seen that the *Communist Manifesto* simply places side by side the two concepts: "to raise the proletariat to the position of the ruling class" and "to win the battle of democracy." On the basis of all that has been said above, it is possible to determine more precisely how democracy changes in the transition from capitalism to communism.

In capitalist society, providing it develops under the most favourable conditions, we have a more or less complete democracy in the democratic republic. But this democracy is always hemmed in by the narrow limits set by capitalist exploitation, and consequently always remains, in effect, a democracy for the minority, only for the propertied classes, only for the rich. Freedom in capitalist society always remains about the same as it was in the

Source: *The Lenin Anthology*, edited by Robert C. Tucker (New York: W.W. Norton and Company, Inc., 1975), pp. 372-75, 735-36, 738-39.

ancient Greek republics: freedom for the slave-owners. Owing to the conditions of capitalist exploitation, the modern wage slaves are so crushed by want and poverty that "they cannot be bothered with democracy," "cannot be bothered with politics"; in the ordinary, peaceful course of events, the majority of the population is debarred from participation in public and political life . . . .

Democracy for an insignificant minority, democracy for the rich—that is the democracy of capitalist society. If we look more closely into the machinery of capitalist democracy, we see everywhere, in the "petty"—supposedly petty—details of the suffrage (residential qualification, exclusion of women, etc.), in the technique of the representative institutions, in the actual obstacles to the right of assembly (public buildings are not for "paupers"!), in the purely capitalist organisation of the daily press, etc., etc.—we see restriction after restriction upon democracy. These restrictions, exceptions, exclusions, obstacles for the poor seem slight, especially in the eyes of one who has never known want himself and has never been in close contact with the oppressed classes in their mass life (and nine out of ten, if not ninety-nine out of a hundred, bourgeois publicists and politicians come under this category); but in their sum total these restrictions exclude and squeeze out the poor from politics, from active participation in democracy. . . .

And the dictatorship of the proletariat, i.e., the organisation of the vanguard of the oppressed as the ruling class for the purpose of suppressing the oppressors, cannot result merely in an expansion of democracy. *Simultaneously* with an immense expansion of democracy, which *for the first time* becomes democracy for the poor, democracy for the people, and not democracy for the money-bags, the dictatorship of the proletariat imposes a series of restrictions on the freedom of the oppressors, the exploiters, the capitalists. We must suppress them in order to free humanity from wage slavery, their resistance must be crushed by force; it is clear that there is no freedom and no democracy where there is suppression and where there is violence.

Engels expressed this splendidly in his letter to Bebel when he said . . . that "the proletariat needs the state, not in the interests of freedom but in order to hold down its adversaries, and as soon as it becomes possible to speak of freedom the state as such ceases to exist."

Democracy for the vast majority of the people, and suppression by force, i.e., exclusion from democracy, of the exploiters and oppressors of the people—this is the change democracy undergoes during the *transition* from capitalism to communism.

Only in communist society, when the resistance of the capitalists has been completely crushed, when the capitalists have disappeared, when there are no classes (i.e., when there is no distinction between the members of society as regards their relation to the social means of production), *only* then "the state . . . ceases to exist," and "*it becomes possible to speak of freedom.*" Only then will a truly complete democracy become possible and be realised, a democracy without any exceptions whatever. And only then will democracy begin to *wither away*, owing to the simple fact that, freed from capitalist slavery, from the untold horrors, savagery, absurdities and infamies of capitalist exploitation, people will gradually *become accustomed* to observing the elementary rules of social intercourse that have been known for centuries and repeated for thousands of years in all copy-book maxims. They will become accustomed to observing them without force, without coercion, without subordination, *without the special apparatus* for coercion called the state.

The expression "the state *withers away*" is very well chosen, for it indicates both the gradual and the spontaneous nature of the process . . . .

And so in capitalist society we have a democracy that is curtailed, wretched, false, a democracy only for the rich, for the minority. The dictatorship of the proletariat, the period of transition to communism, will for the first time create democracy for the people, for the majority, along with the necessary suppression of the exploiters, of the minority. Communism alone is capable of providing really complete democracy, and the more complete it is, the sooner it will become unnecessary and wither away of its own accord.

In other words, under capitalism we have the state in the proper sense of the word, that is, a special machine for the suppression of one class by another, and, what is more, of the majority by the minority. Naturally, to be successful, such an undertaking as the systematic suppression of the exploited majority by the exploiting minority calls for the utmost ferocity and savagery in the matter of suppressing, it calls for seas of blood, through which mankind is actually wading its way in slavery, serfdom and wage labour.

Furthermore, during the *transition* from capitalism to communism suppression is *still* necessary, but it is now the suppression of the exploiting minority by the exploited majority. A special apparatus, a special machine for suppression, the "state," is *still* necessary, but this is now a transitional state. It is no longer a state in the proper sense of the word; for the suppression of the minority of exploiters by the majority of the wage slaves of *yesterday* is comparatively so easy, simple and natural a task that it will entail far less bloodshed than the suppression of the risings of slaves, serfs or wage-labourers, and it will cost mankind far less. And it is compatible with the extension of democracy to such an overwhelming majority of the population that the need for a *special machine* of suppression will begin to disappear. Naturally, the exploiters are unable to suppress the people without a highly complex machine for performing this task, but *the people* can suppress the exploiters even with a very simple "machine," almost without a "machine," without a special apparatus, by the simple *organisation of the armed people* (such as the Soviets of Workers' and Soldiers' Deputies, we would remark, running ahead).

Lastly, only communism makes the state absolutely unnecessary, for there is *nobody* to be suppressed—"nobody" in the sense of a *class*, of a systematic struggle against a definite section of the population. We are not utopians, and do not in the least deny the possibility and inevitability of excesses on the part of *individual persons*, or the need to stop *such* excesses. In the first place, however, no special machine, no special apparatus of suppression, is needed for this; this will be done by the armed people themselves, as simply and as readily as any crowd of civilised people, even in modern society, interferes to put a stop to a scuffle or to prevent a woman from being assaulted. And, secondly, we know that the fundamental social cause of excesses, which consist in the violation of the rules of social intercourse, is the exploitation of the people, their want and their poverty. With the removal of this chief cause, excesses will inevitably begin to "*wither away.*" We do not know how quickly and in what succession, but we do know they will wither away. With their withering away the state will also *wither away*.

Without building utopias, Marx defined more fully what can be defined *now* regarding this future, namely, the difference between the lower and higher places (levels, stages) of communist society.

 Lenin was concerned with political leadership and the transition to a new, different state. In 1923 he wrote about the need to overcome bureaucratic thinking.

. . . in the matter of our state apparatus we should now draw the conclusion from our past experience that it would be better to proceed more slowly.

Our state apparatus is so deplorable, not to say wretched, that we must first think very carefully how to combat its defects, bearing in mind that these defects are rooted in the past, which, although it has been overthrown, has not yet been overcome, has not yet reached the stage of a culture that has receded into the distant past. I say culture deliberately, because in these matters we can only regard as achieved what has become part and parcel of our culture, of our social life, our habits. We might say that the good in our social system has not been properly studied, understood, and taken to heart; it has been hastily grasped at; it has not been verified or tested, corroborated by experience, and not made durable, etc. Of course, it could not be otherwise in a revolutionary epoch, when development proceeded at such breakneck speed that in a matter of five years we passed from tsarism to the Soviet system.

It is time we did something about it. We must show sound scepticism for too rapid progress, for boastfulness, etc. We must give thought to testing the steps forward we proclaim every hour, take every minute and then prove every second that they are flimsy, superficial and misunderstood. The most harmful thing here would be haste. The most harmful thing would be to rely on the assumption that we know at least something, or that we have any considerable number of elements necessary for the building of a really new state apparatus, one really worthy to be called socialist, Soviet, etc.

No, we are ridiculously deficient of such an apparatus, and even of the elements of it, and we must remember that we should not stint time on building it, and that it will take many, many years.

What elements have we for building this apparatus? Only two. First, the workers who are absorbed in the struggle for socialism. These elements are not sufficiently educated. They would like to build a better apparatus for us, but they do not know how. They cannot build one. They have not yet developed the culture required for this; and it is culture that is required. Nothing will be achieved in this by doing things in a rush, by assault, by vim or vigour, or in general, by any of the best human qualities. Secondly, we have elements of knowledge, education and training, but they are ridiculously inadequate compared with all other countries.

Here we must not forget that we are too prone to compensate (or imagine that we can compensate) our lack of knowledge by zeal, haste, etc.

In order to renovate our state apparatus we must at all costs set out, first, to learn, secondly, to learn, and thirdly, to learn, and then see to it that learning shall not remain a dead letter, or a fashionable catch-phrase (and we should admit in all frankness that this happens very often with us), that learning shall really become part of our very being, that it shall actually and fully become a constituent element of our social life. In short, we must not make the demands that are made by bourgeois Western Europe, but demands that are fit and proper for a country which has set out to develop into a socialist country . . . .

We have been bustling for five years trying to improve our state apparatus, but it has been mere bustle, which has proved useless in these five years, or even futile, or even harmful. This bustle created the impression that we were doing something, but in effect it was only clogging up our institutions and our brains.

It is high time things were changed.

We must follow the rule: Better fewer, but better. We must follow the rule: Better get good human material in two or even three years than work in haste without hope of getting any at all . . . .

In substance, the matter is as follows:

Either we prove now that we have really learned something about state organisation (we ought to have learned something in five years), or we prove that we are not sufficiently mature for it. If the latter is the case, we had better not tackle the task . . . .

1. "Lenin took the rhetoric of the Communist Manifesto, and made it into a concrete reality." Account for this statement with reference to the relationship between the writings of Marx and Lenin.
2. Compare Lenin's vision of the state with the reality that eventually emerged under Stalin.

■ ■ ■

YEVGENY ZAMYATIN

Yevgeny Zamyatin (1884-1937), a Russian novelist and essayist, was deeply concerned with the nature of social and political power and the problem of totalitarianism. He was trained as a naval engineer and was involved in the unsuccessful Russian revolution of 1905. Zamyatin became a writer while pursuing his work in shipbuilding and was in England at the time of the March 1917 revolution. Returning to Russia, he questioned the Soviet state and the direction of the new authorities after the Bolsheviks took power. Zamyatin insisted that the writer had an obligation to act as a social critic and conscience. His novel *We* (1920), and other writings, got him into difficulties with Soviet authorities who demanded artistic conformity. Zamyatin was given permission to leave Russia in 1931. He died six years later in exile in Paris.

Zamyatin's *We* is a futuristic novel denouncing totalitarianism. He believed that a state based on technological models stifled human nature and human creativity.

The novel, which was written in the form of personal journal entries by a scientist, D-503, has never been published in the Soviet Union.

I have just looked over what I had written yesterday, and I see that I did not express myself clearly enough. Of course, it is all entirely clear to any of us. But perhaps you, the unknown readers to whom the *Integral* will bring my notes, have reached only that page in the great book of civilization that our ancestors read some nine hundred years ago. Perhaps you do not know even about such elementary things as the Table of Hours, the Personal Hour, the Maternity Norm, the Green Wall, and the Benefactor. It seems to me ridiculous yet very difficult to speak about all this. It is as if a writer of, say, the twentieth century had to explain in his novel the meaning of "coat," or "apartment," or "wife." Yet, if his novel were to be translated for savages, how could he avoid explaining what a "coat" meant?

I am certain that a savage would look at the "coat" and wonder, "What is it for? It's only a hindrance." It seems to me that your response may be exactly the same when I tell you that none of us has been beyond the Green Wall since the Two Hundred Years' War.

But, my dear readers, a man must think, at least a little. It helps. After all, it is clear that the entire history of mankind, insofar as we know it, is the history of transition from nomadic to increasingly settled forms of existence. And does it not follow that the most settled form (ours) is at the same time the most perfect (ours)? People rushed about from one end of the earth to the other only in prehistoric times, when there were nations, wars, commerce, discoveries of all sorts of Americas. But who needs that now? What for?

I admit, the habit of such settled existence was not achieved easily, or all at once. During the Two Hundred Years' War, when all the roads fell into ruin and were overgrown with grass, it must at first have seemed extremely inconvenient to live in cities cut off from one another by green jungles. But what of it? After man's tail dropped off, it must have been quite difficult for him at first to learn to drive off flies without its aid. In the beginning he undoubtedly missed his tail. But now—can you imagine yourself with a tail? Or can you imagine yourself in the street naked, without a coat? (For you may still be trotting about in "coats.") And so it is with me: I cannot imagine a city that is not clad in a Green Wall; I cannot imagine a life that is not regulated by the figures of our Table.

The Table . . . At this very moment, from the wall in my room, its purple figures on a field of gold stare tenderly and sternly into my eyes. Involuntarily, my mind turns to what the ancients called an "icon," and I belong to compose poems or prayers (which are the same thing). Oh, why am I not a poet, to render fitting praise to the Table, the heart and pulse of the One State!

As schoolchildren we all read (perhaps you have, too) that greatest literary monument to have come down to us from ancient days—"The Railway Guide." But set it side by side with our Table, and it will be as graphite next to a diamond: both consist of the same element—carbon—yet how eternal, how

Sources: Yevgeny Zamyatin, *We*, translated by Mirra Ginsburg (New York: Bantam Books, 1972), pp. 10-14, 39-40, 88-90; Yevgeny Zamyatin, *A Soviet Heretic*, edited and translated by Mirra Ginsburg (Chicago: The University of Chicago Press, 1970), pp. 108-109, 112.

transparent is the diamond, how it gleams! Whose breath will fail to quicken as he rushes clattering along the pages of "The Railway Guide"? But our Table of Hours! Why, it transforms each one of us into a figure of steel, six-wheeled hero of a mighty epic poem. Every morning, with six-wheeled precision, at the same hour and the same moment, we—millions of us—get up as one. At the same hour, in million-headed unison, we start work; and in million-headed unison we end it. And, fused into a single million-handed body, at the same second, designated by the Table, we lift our spoons to our mouths. At the same second, we come out for our walk, go to the auditorium, go to the hall for Taylor exercises, fall asleep. . . .

I shall be entirely frank: even we have not yet found an absolute, precise solution to the problem of happiness. Twice a day, from sixteen to seventeen, and from twenty-one to twenty-two, the single mighty organism breaks up into separate cells; these are the Personal Hours designated by the Table. In these hours you will see modestly lowered shades in the rooms of some; others will walk with measured tread along the avenue, as though climbing the brass stairs of the March; still others, like myself now, are at their desks. But I am confident—and you may call me an idealist and dreamer—I am confident that sooner or later we shall fit these Personal Hours as well into the general formula. Some day these 86,400 seconds will also be entered in the Table of Hours.

I have read and heard many incredible things about those times when people still lived in a free, i.e., unorganized, savage condition. But most incredible of all, it seems to me, is that the state authority of that time—no matter how rudimentary—could allow men to live without anything like our Table, without obligatory walks, without exact regulation of mealtimes, getting up and going to bed whenever they felt like it. Some historians even say that in those times the street lights burned all night, and people walked and drove round in the streets at all hours of the night.

Try as I may, I cannot understand it. After all, no matter how limited their intelligence, they should have understood that such a way of life was truly mass murder—even if slow murder. The state (humaneness) forbade the killing of a single individual, but not the partial killing of millions day by day. To kill one individual, that is, to diminish the total sum of human lives by fifty years, was criminal. But to diminish the sum of human lives by fifty million years was not considered criminal. Isn't that absurd? Today, any ten-year-old will solve this mathematical-moral problem in half a minute. They, with all their Kants taken together, could not solve it (because it never occurred to any of the Kants to build a system of scientific ethics, i.e., ethics based on subtraction, addition, division, and multiplication).

And wasn't it absurd that the state (it dared to call itself a state!) could leave sexual life without any semblance of control? As often and as much as anyone might wish. . . . Totally unscientific, like animals. And blindly, like animals, they bore their young. Isn't it ridiculous: to know agriculture, poultry-breeding, fish-breeding (we have exact information that they knew all this), yet fail to go on to the ultimate step of this logical ladder—child-breeding; fail to establish such a thing as our Maternal and Paternal Norms.

It is so absurd, so unbelievable, that I am afraid, as I write this, that you, my unknown readers, will think me a malicious joker. I am afraid you may decide that I am merely trying to mock you, telling you utter nonsense with a straight face.

But, to begin with, I am incapable of jokes, for every joke contains a lie as an implicit function. Secondly, our One State Science asserts that this was how the ancients lived, and our State Science never errs. Besides, where would state logic have come from at a time when men were living in the condition of freedom—the condition of animals, apes, the herd? What could be expected of them, when even in our time the wild, apelike echo still occasionally rises from somewhere below, from some shaggy depth?

Fortunately, only on rare occasions. Fortunately, there are only small accidents of detail, which can easily be repaired without halting the eternal, grandiose movement of the entire Machine. And to expel the warped bolt, we have the skilled, heavy hand of the Benefactor and the experienced eyes of the Guardians. . . .

The bell for bedtime: it is past twenty-two. Until tomorrow.

B But D-503 discovers that personal happiness may be as important as absorption into the whole. The idea of the irrational conquering the rational is represented by the concept of the square root of minus one. D-503 is told that he has a "soul."

How long ago it was—during my school years—when I first encountered $\sqrt{-1}$. A vivid memory, as though cut out of time: the brightly lit spherical hall, hundreds of round boys' heads, and Plapa, our mathematics teacher. We nicknamed him Plapa. He was badly worn out, coming apart, and when the monitor plugged him in, the loudspeakers would always start with "Pla-pla-pla-tsh-sh-sh," and only then go on to the day's lesson. One day Plapa told us about irrational numbers, and, I remember, I cried, banged my fists on the table, and screamed, "I don't want $\sqrt{-1}$! Take $\sqrt{-1}$. out of me!" This irrational number had grown into me like something foreign, alien, terrifying. It devoured me—it was impossible to conceive, to render harmless, because it was outside *ratio*.

And now again $\sqrt{-1}$. I've just glanced through my notes, and it is clear to me: I have been dodging lying to myself—merely to avoid seeing the $\sqrt{-1}$. It's nonsense that I was sick, and all the rest of it. I could have gone there. A week ago, I am sure, I would have gone without a moment's hesitation. But now? Why?

Today, too. Exactly at sixteen-ten I stood before the sparkling glass wall. Above me, the golden, sunny, pure gleam of the letters on the sign over the Office. Inside, through the glass, I saw the long line of bluish unifs. Faces glowing like icon lamps in an ancient church: they had come to perform a great deed, to surrender upon the altar of the One State their loved ones, their friends, themselves. And I—I longed to join them, to be with them. And could not: my feet were welded deep into the glass slabs of the pavement, and I stood staring dully, incapable of moving from the spot. . . .

I followed obediently, swinging my unnecessary, alien arms. It was impossible to raise my eyes; I walked all the way through a crazy, upside-down world: some strange machines, their bases up; people glued antipodally to the ceiling; and, lower still, beneath it all, the sky locked into the thick glass of the pavement. I remember: what I resented most of all was that, for this last time in my life, I was seeing everything in this absurdly upside-down unreal state. But it was impossible to raise my eyes.

We stopped. A staircase rose before me. Another step, and I would see the figures in white medical smocks, the huge, mute Bell. . . .

With an enormous effort, I finally tore my eyes away from the glass under-foot, and suddenly the golden letters of MEDICAL OFFICE burst into my face. At that moment it had not even occurred to me to wonder why he had spared me, why he had brought me here instead of to the Operational Section. At a single bound I swung across the steps, slammed the door firmly behind me, and took a deep breath. I felt: I had not breathed since morning, my heart had not been beating—and it was only now that I had taken my first breath, only now that the sluices in my breast had opened. . . .

There were two of them: one short, with tubby legs, weighing the patients with his eyes as though lifting them on horns; the other paper-thin, with gleaming scissor-lips, his nose a finest blade. . . . The same one.

I rushed to him as to someone near and dear, mumbling about insomnia, dreams, shadows, a yellow world. The scissor-lips gleamed, smiled.

"You're in a bad way! Apparently, you have developed a soul."

A soul? That strange, ancient, long-forgotten word. We sometimes use the words "soul-stirring," "soulless," but "soul" . . . ?

"Is it . . . very dangerous?" I muttered.

"Incurable," the scissors snapped.

"But . . . what, essentially, does it mean. I somehow don't . . . don't understand it."

"Well, you see . . . How can I explain it to you? . . . You are a mathematician, aren't you?"

"Yes."

"Well, then—take a plane, a surface—this mirror, say. And on this surface are you and I, you see? We squint against the sun. And here, the blue electric spark inside that tube, and there—the passing shadow of an acro. All of it only on the surface, only momentary. But imagine this impermeable sub-stance softened by some fire; and nothing slides across it any more, everything enters into it, into this mirror world that we examined with such curiosity when we were children. Children are not so foolish, I assure you. The plane has acquired volume, it has become a body, a world, and everything is now inside the mirror—inside you: the sun, the blast of the whirling propeller, your trembling lips, and someone else's. Do you understand? The cold mirror reflects, throws back, but this one absorbs, and everything leaves its trace—forever. A moment, a faint line on someone's face—and it remains in you forever. Once you heard a drop fall in the silence, and you hear it now. . . ."

"Yes, yes, exactly. . . . " I seized his hand. I heard it now—drops falling slowly from the washstand faucet. And I knew: this was forever. "But why, why suddenly a soul? I've never had one, and suddenly . . . Why . . . No one else has it, and I . . . ?"

I clung even more violently to the thin hand; I was terrified of losing the lifeline.

"Why? Why don't you have feathers, or wings—only shoulder blades, the base for wings? Because wings are no longer necessary, we have the aero, wings would only interfere. Wings are for flying, and we have nowhere else to fly: we have arrived, we have found what we had been searching for. Isn't that so?"

I nodded in confusion. He looked at me with a scalpel-sharp laugh. The other heard it, pattered in from his office on his tubby feet, lifted my paper-thin doctor, lifted me on his horn-eyes.

"What's the trouble? A soul? A soul, you say? What the devil! We'll soon return to cholera if you go on that way. I told you" (raising the paper-thin one on his horns) "—I told you, we must cut out imagination. In everyone. . . . Extirpate imagination. Nothing but surgery, nothing but surgery will do. . . . " . . .

◈ C ◈ In 1923 Zamyatin wrote an essay, "On Literature, Revolution, Entropy, and Other Matters." Here he contrasted revolution and stagnation, and demanded that literature take a critical stance on the side of change.

The law of revolution is red, fiery, deadly; but this death means the birth of new life, a new star. And the law of entropy is cold, ice blue, like the icy interplanetary infinities. The flame turns from red to an even, warm pink, no longer deadly, but comfortable. The sun ages into a planet, convenient for highways, stores, beds, prostitutes, prisons: this is the law. And if the planet is to be kindled into youth again, it must be set on fire, it must be thrown off the smooth highway of evolution: this is the law.

The flame will cool tomorrow, or the day after tomorrow (in the Book of Genesis days are equal to years, ages). But someone must see this already today, and speak heretically today about tomorrow. Heretics are the only (bitter) remedy against the entropy of human thought.

When the flaming, seething sphere (in science, religion, social life, art) cools, the fiery magma becomes coated with dogma—a rigid, ossified, motionless crust. Dogmatization in science, religion, social life, or art is the entropy of thought. What has become dogma no longer burns; it only gives off warmth—it is tepid, it is cool. Instead of the Sermon on the Mount, under the scorching sun, to up-raised arms and sobbing people, there is drowsy prayer in a magnificent abbey. Instead of Galileo's "But still, it turns!" there are dispassionate computations in a well-heated room in an observatory. On the Galileos, the epigones build their own structures, slowly, bit by bit, like corals. This is the path of evolution—until a new heresy explodes the crush of dogma and all the edifices of the most enduring stone which have been raised upon it.

Explosions are not very comfortable. And therefore the exploders, the heretics, are justly exterminated by fire, by axes, by words. To every today, to every evolution, to the laborious, slow, useful, most useful, creative, coral-building work, heretics are a threat. Stupidly, recklessly, they burst into today from tomorrow; they are romantics. . . . It is just to chop off the head of a heretical literature which challenges dogma; this literature is harmful.

But harmful literature is more useful than useful literature, for it is anti-entropic, it is a means of combating calcification, sclerosis, crust, moss, quiescence. It is utopian, absurd.

. . . Heretics are necessary to health; if there are no heretics, they should be invented. . . .

A new form is not intelligible to everyone; many find it difficult. Perhaps. The ordinary, the banal is, of course, simpler, more pleasant, more comfortable. Euclid's world is very simple, and Einstein's world is very difficult—but it is no longer possible to return to Euclid. No revolution, no heresy is comfortable or easy. For it is a leap, it is a break in the smooth evolutionary curve, and a break is a wound, a pain. But the wound is necessary: most of mankind suffers from hereditary sleeping sickness, and victims of this sickness (entropy) must not be allowed to sleep, or it will be their final sleep, death.

The same disease often afflicts artists and writers: they sink into satiated slumber in forms once invented and twice perfected. And they lack the strength to wound themselves, to cease loving what they once loved, to leave their old, familiar apartments filled with the scent of laurel leaves and walk away into the open field, to start anew.

Of course, to wound oneself is difficult, even dangerous. But for those who are alive, living today as yesterday and yesterday as today is still more difficult.

1. Respond to the view of life in a totalitarian state as depicted by Zamyatin. Summarize his portrait and comment on his use of the novel to criticize the social system.
2. What argument did Zamyatin make for revolutionary change? How might his views have been affected by World War I and the Russian Revolution?

• • •

The West and Communism

As an ideology, communism was attractive to many Western intellectuals in the 1920s and 1930s who believed that liberal democracy was failing and who were deeply troubled by the rise of fascism. Many were attracted by the ideals and the rhetoric of communism, and many believed the Russian Revolution was an event heralding a new, more just future. Disillusionment set in during the Stalinist period, as evidence of purges, killings, torture, deception, and hypocrisy piled up. The Communist Party, a new-style political organization demanding loyalty and obedience, had won many in the 1920s; by the end of the 1930s a large number left the Party, their faith shaken by events. Still, the attraction of communism testified to a hope for a new idealism during a harsh and difficult period.

Arthur Koestler (1904-83) was a novelist and essayist born in Hungary who lived in many areas of Europe before settling in England. He joined the Communist Party in 1931 and left it in 1938. He described the experience of being "converted" to communism.

I was ripe to be converted as a result of my personal case-history; thousands of other members of the intelligentsia and the middle classes of my generation were ripe for it by virtue of other personal case-histories; but however much these differed from case to case, they had a common denominator: the rapid disintegration of moral values, of the pre-1914 pattern of life in post-war Europe, and the simultaneous lure of the new revelation which had come from the East.

I joined the Party (which to this day has remained 'the' Party for all of us who once belonged to it) in 1931, at the beginning of that short-lived period of optimism, of that abortive spiritual renaissance, later known as the Pink Decade. The stars of that treacherous dawn were Barbusse, Romain Rolland, Gide and Malraux in France: Piscator, Becher, Renn, Brecht, Eisler, Saeghers in Germany; Auden, Isherwood, Spender in England; Dos Passos, Upton Sinclair, Steinbeck, in the United States. The cultural atmosphere was saturated with Progressive Writers' congresses, experimental theatres, committees for Peace and against Fascism, societies for cultural relations with the U.S.S.R., Russian films and *avant-garde* magazines. It looked indeed as if the Western world, convulsed by the aftermath of war, scourged by inflation, depression, unemployment and the absence of a faith to live for, was at last going to 'clear from the head the masses of impressive rubbish;—Rally the lost and trembling forces of the will—Gather them up and let them loose upon the earth—Till they construct at last a human justice. (Auden.) The new star of Bethlehem had risen in the East; and for a modest sum, Intourist was prepared to allow you a short and well-focused glimpse of the Promised Land. . . .

Gradually I learnt to distrust my mechanistic preoccupation with facts and to regard the world around me in the light of dialectic interpretation. It was a satisfactory and indeed blissful state; once you had assimilated the technique you were no longer disturbed by facts; they automatically took on the proper colour and fell into their proper place. Both morally and logically, the Party was infallible: morally, because its aims were right, that is, in accord with the Dialectic of History, and these aims justified all means; logically, because the Party was the vanguard of the proletariat, and the proletariat the embodiment of the active principle in History.

Opponents of the Party, from straight reactionaries to Social-Fascists, were products of their environment; their ideas reflected the distortions of bourgeois society. Renegades from the Party were lost souls, fallen out of grace; to argue with them, even to listen to them, meant trafficking with the powers of Evil. . . .

Not only our thinking, but also our vocabulary was reconditioned. Certain words were taboo—for instance, 'lesser evil' or 'spontaneous'; the latter, because 'spontaneous manifestations of the revolutionary class-consciousness' were part of Trotsky's theory of the Permanent Revolution. Other words and turns of phrase became favourite stocks-in-trade. I mean not only the obvious words of Communist jargon like 'the toiling masses,' but words like

Source: Arthur Koestler, *et al.*, *The God That Failed* (London: The Right Book Club, n.d.), pp. 30, 43, 53-55, 104-105, 116-19, 193-98.

'concrete' or 'sectarian' ('you must put your question into a more concrete form, comrade'; 'you are adopting a left-sectarian attitude, comrade'); and even such abstruse words as 'herostratic.' In one of his works Lenin had mentioned Herostratus, the Greek who burnt down a temple because he could think of no other way of achieving fame. Accordingly, one often heard and read phrases like 'the criminally herostratic madness of the counter-revolutionary wreckers of the heroic efforts of the toiling masses in the Fatherland of the Proletariat to achieve the second Five Year Plan in four years.'

According to their vocabulary and favourite clichés, you could smell out at once people with Trotskyite, Reformist, Brandlerite, Blanquist and other deviations. And vice versa, Communists betrayed themselves by their vocabulary to the police, and later to the Gestapo. I know of one girl whom the Gestapo had picked up almost at random, without any evidence against her, and who was caught out on the word 'concrete.' The Gestapo Commissar had listened to her with boredom, half-convinced that his underlings had blundered in arresting her—until she used the fatal word for the second time. The Commissar pricked his ears. 'Where did you pick up that expression?' he asked. The girl, until that moment quite self-possessed, became rattled, and, once rattled, she was lost.

Our literary, artistic and musical tastes were similarly reconditioned. Lenin had said somewhere that he had learnt more about France from Balzac's novels than from all history books put together. Accordingly, Balzac was the greatest writer of all times, whereas other novelists of the past merely reflected 'the distorted values of the decaying society which had produced them.' On the Art Front the guiding principle of the period was Revolutionary Dynamism. A picture without a smoking factory chimney or a tractor in it was escapist; on the other hand, the slogan 'dynamism' left sufficient scope for cubist, expressionist, and other experimental styles. This changed a few years later when Revolutionary Dynamism was superseded by Socialist Realism; henceforth everything modern and experimental became branded as 'bourgeois formalism' expressing 'the putrid corruption of capitalist decay.' In both music and drama, the chorus was regarded at that time as the highest form of expression, because it reflected a collective, as opposed to a bourgeois-individualistic, approach. As individual *personæ* could not be altogether abolished on the stage, they had to be stylized, typified, depersonalized. . . . Psychology became greatly simplified: there were two recognized emotive impulses: class solidarity and the sexual urge. The rest was 'bourgeois metaphysics'; or, like ambition and the lust for power, 'products of competitive capitalist economy.' . . .

 The Italian novelist Ignazio Silone (1900-78) helped found the Italian Communist Party in 1921. He left in 1930.

For me to join the party of proletarian revolution was not just a simple matter of signing up with a political organization; it meant a conversion, a complete dedication. Those were still the days when to declare oneself a Socialist or a Communist was equivalent to throwing oneself to the winds, and meant breaking with one's parents and not finding a job. If the material consequences were harsh and hard, the difficulties of spiritual adaptation were no less painful. My own internal world, the 'Middle Ages' which I had inherited and which were rooted in my soul, and from which, in the last analysis, I had derived my initial aspiration to revolt, were shaken to their foundations, as though by an earthquake. Everything was thrown into the melting-pot, everything became a problem. Life, death, love, good, evil, truth, all changed their meaning or lost it altogether. It is easy enough to court danger when one is no longer alone; but who can describe the dismay of once and for all renouncing one's faith in the individual immortality of the soul? It was too serious for me to be able to discuss it with anyone; my Party comrades would have found it a subject for mockery, and I no longer had any other friends. So, unknown to anyone, the whole world took on a different aspect. How men are to be pitied.

The conditions of life imposed on the Communists by the Fascist conquest of the State were very hard. But they also served to confirm some of the Communists' political theses and provided an opportunity to create a type of organization which was in no way incompatible with the Communist mentality. So I too had to adapt myself, for a number of years, to living like a foreigner in my own country. One had to change one's name, abandon every former link with family and friends, and live a false life to remove any suspicion of conspiratorial activity. The Party became family, school, church, barracks; the world that lay beyond it was to be destroyed and built anew. The psychological mechanism whereby each single militant becomes progressively identified with the collective organization is the same as that used in certain religious orders and military colleges, with almost identical results. Every sacrifice was welcomed as a personal contribution to the 'price of collective redemption'; and it should be emphasized that the links which bound us to the Party grew steadily firmer, not in spite of the dangers and sacrifices involved, but because of them. This explains the attraction exercised by Communism on certain categories of young men and of women, on intellectuals, and on the highly sensitive and generous people who suffer most from the wastefulness of bourgeois society. Anyone who thinks he can wean the best and most serious-minded young people away from Communism by enticing them into well-warmed halls to play billiards, starts from an extremely limited and unintelligent conception of mankind. . . .

Before I left Moscow an Italian working man came to see me. He had been a refugee in Russia for some years to avoid the long term of imprisonment to which a Fascist tribunal had sentenced him. (He is still, I believe, a Communist to-day). He came to complain of the humiliating conditions of the workers in the Moscow factory to which he was attached. He was ready to put up with the material shortages of every kind since to remedy them was clearly beyond the power of individuals, but he could not understand why the workmen were entirely at the mercy of the factory directorate and had no effective organization to protect their interests; why, in this respect also, they should be much worse off than in capitalist countries. Most of the much-vaunted rights of the working class were purely theoretical.

In Berlin, on my way back, I read in the paper that the Executive of the Communist International had severely rebuked Trotsky for a document he had prepared about recent events in China. I went to the offices of the German Communist Party and asked Thälmann for an explanation. 'This is untrue,' I said to him sharply.

But he explained that the statutes of the International authorized the Presidium, in case of urgency, to adopt any resolution in the name of the Executive . . . .

Realization came, however, slowly and with difficulty, during the course of the succeeding years. And to this day I go on thinking it over, trying to understand better. If I have written books, it has been to try and understand and to make others understand. I am not at all certain that I have reached the end of my efforts. The truth is this: the day I left the Communist Party was a very sad one for me, it was like a day of deep mourning, the mourning for my lost youth. And I come from a district where mourning is worn longer than elsewhere. It is not easy to free oneself from an experience as intense as that of the underground organization of the Communist Party. Something of it remains and leaves a mark on the character which lasts all one's life. One can, in fact, notice how recognizable the ex-Communists are. They constitute a category apart, like ex-priests and ex-regular officers. The number of ex-Communists is legion to-day. 'The final struggle,' I said jokingly to Togliatti recently, 'will be between the Communists and the ex-Communists.'

However, I carefully avoided, after I had left the Communist Party, ending up in one of the many groups and splinter-groups of ex-Communists; and I have never regretted this in any way, as I know well the kind of fate which rules over these groups and splinter-groups, and makes little sects of them which have all the defects of official Communism, the fanaticism, the centralization, the abstraction, without the qualities and advantages which the latter derives from its vast working-class following. The logic of opposition at all costs has carried many ex-Communists far from their starting-points, in some cases as far as Fascism.

Consideration of the experience I have been through has led me to a deepening of the motives for my separation which go very much further than the circumstantial ones by which it was produced. But my faith in Socialism, to which I think I can say my entire life bears testimony, has remained more alive than ever in me. In its essence it has gone back to what it was when I first revolted against the old social order; a refusal to admit the existence of destiny, an extension of the ethical impulse from the restricted individual and family sphere to the whole domain of human activity, a need for effective brotherhood, an affirmation of the superiority of the human person over all the economic and social mechanisms which oppress him. As the years have gone by there has been added to this an intuition of man's dignity and a feeling of reverence for that which in man is always trying to outdistance itself, and lies at the root of his eternal disquiet. But I do not think that this kind of Socialism is in any way peculiar to me. The 'mad truths' recorded above are older than Marxism; towards the second half of the last century they took refuge in the workers' movement born of industrial capitalism, and continue to remain one of its most tenacious founts of inspiration. I have repeatedly expressed my opinion on the relations between the Socialist Movement and the theories of Socialism: these relations are by no means rigid or immutable. With the development of new studies the theories may go out of fashion or be discarded, but the movement goes on. It would be inaccurate, however, with regard to the old quarrel between the doctrinaires and the empiricists of the workers' movement, to include me among the latter. I do not conceive Socialist policy as tied to any particular theory, but to a faith. The more Socialist theories claim to be 'scientific,' the more transitory they are: but Socialist values are permanent. The distinction between theories and values is not sufficiently recognized, but it is fundamental. On a group of theories one can found a school; but on a group of values one can found a culture, a civilization, a new way of living together among men.

 André Gide (1869-1951), a French novelist, went to Russia in 1936 full of hope and came back disillusioned.

Amongst all workers and artisans in the Soviet Union it is the writer who is most favoured and indulged. The immense privileges that I was offered amazed and terrified me and I was afraid of being seduced and corrupted. I did not go to the Soviet Union for the sake of benefits and those that I saw were glaring. But that did not prevent my criticism since the most-favoured position enjoyed by writers in Russia—better than in any other country in the world— was granted only to the right-thinking. That was a danger signal to me and I was immediately on my guard. The price exacted is the total surrender of all opposition, and opposition in the Soviet Union is merely the exercise of free criticism. I discovered that a certain distinguished member of the Academy of Sciences had just been released from prison, whose sole crime had been independence of judgment, and when foreign scientists tried to get in touch with him, they were always told that he was indisposed. Another was dismissed from his professorship and denied laboratory facilities for having expressed scientific opinions which did not tally with current Soviet doctrine, and he was obliged to write a public letter of recantation to avoid deportation. It is a characteristic trait of despotism to be unable to suffer independence and to tolerate only servility. However just his brief, woe betide the Soviet lawyer who rises to defend an accused whom the authorities wish to see convicted. Stalin allows only praise and approbation and soon he will be surrounded only by those who cannot put him in the wrong since they have no opinions whatsoever. His portrait is seen everywhere, his name is on everyone's lips and praise of him occurs in every public speech. Is all this the result of worship, love or fear? Who can say? I remember, on the way to Tiflis, as we went through Gori—the little village where he was born—I thought it would be a kind and courteous attention to send him a personal message as an expression of gratitude for the warm welcome we had received in the Soviet Union where we had been treated everywhere with lavish hospitality. I thought that no better opportunity would occur again, so I had the car stopped at the post office and I handed in a telegram which began: 'Passing through Gori on our wonderful trip I feel the impulse to send you'— but here the translator paused and said that he could not transmit such a message, that 'you,' when addressed to Stalin, was not sufficient. It was not decent, he declared, and something must be added. He suggested 'You leader of the workers' or else 'You Lord of the people.' It seemed to me absurd and

I said that Stalin must surely be above such flattery, but all in vain. Nothing would budge him and he would not transmit the telegram unless I agreed to the emendation. I reflected sadly that such formalities contribute to erect an insuperable barrier between Stalin and his subjects. I was also frequently obliged to make additions or alterations in the speeches I delivered in the course of my visit. They explained to me that a word like 'destiny' must always be preceded by the epithet 'glorious' when it referred to the destiny of the Soviet Union; on the other hand they requested me to delete the adjective 'great' when it qualified a king, since a monarch can never be 'great'! At Leningrad I was invited to address a society of students and writers and I submitted my script beforehand to the committee; but I was informed that what I had intended to say would be considered unseemly since it was not in the Party line. The ensuing difficulties were so many and so tortuous that I eventually abandoned the project of the address, which ran as follows: 'I have often been invited to give my views on contemporary Soviet Literature and I would like to explain why I have hitherto refused to express an opinion. This will permit me to clarify and amplify certain statements which I made in the Red Square in Moscow on the occasion of Gorky's funeral. I spoke then of the new problems which the very success of the Revolution had provoked and I said it would be to the eternal credit of the Soviet Union to have resuscitated them for our consideration. As the future of civilization is closely linked with whatever solution is found for them in Russia, it seems to me profitable to raise them again here. The majority, even when it comprises the best elements, never appreciates what is new or difficult in a work of art, but only what can readily be recognized—that is to say what is most commonplace. It must be remembered that there are revolutionary as well as bourgeois commonplaces and clichés. It is also essential to realize that what gives quality to a work of art and brings it immortality is never what comes from the revolution nor what reflects its doctrine, however noble it may be. A work of art will survive only by what is truly original in it, by the new questions it asks or anticipates, and by the answers that it gives to questions which have not yet been formulated. I greatly fear that many of the works of art impregnated with the purest Marxist doctrine—to which indeed they owe their contemporary success—will, for posterity, smack only of the laboratory. The only works of art which will survive oblivion are those which have risen superior to contemporary pre-occupations. Now that the Revolution is triumphant, art runs a grave risk—as grave as any under the most calamitous oppressions—the danger of becoming an orthodoxy. What triumphant revolution needs to grant, above all else, to the artist is freedom. Without complete freedom art loses all its significance and worth. . . . I personally believe that it is precisely the works which flatter and approve which are of poor educational worth and that a culture, if it is to progress, must ignore them. As for the literature which confines itself to reflecting society, I have already said what I think of it. To remain in constant self-contemplation and self-admiration may be one stage in the development of a young society, but it would indeed be regrettable and tragic if this first stage were to remain the final and only one.' . . .

Deplorable and unsatisfactory as the state of affairs in the Soviet Union is, I would have remained silent if I could have been assured of any faint progress towards something better. It is because I have reached the firm conviction that the Soviet Union is sliding down the slope that I had hoped to see it ascend, and because it has abandoned, one after another—and always for the most specious reasons—the liberties gained by the great Revolution after so much hardship and bloodshed. It is because I see it dragging in its wake to irreparable chaos the Communist Parties of other countries that I consider it my duty to speak openly.

No question of party loyalty can restrain me from speaking frankly, for I place truth above the Party. I know well that in Marxist doctrine there is no such thing as truth—at least not in any absolute sense—there is only relative truth. I believe, however, that in so serious a matter it is criminal to lead others astray, and urgent to see matters as they are, not as we would wish them to be—or had hoped that they might be. The Soviet Union has deceived our fondest hopes and shown us tragically in what treacherous quicksand an honest revolution can founder. The same old capitalist society has been re-established, a new and terrible despotism crushing and exploiting man, with all the abject and servile mentality of serfdom. Russia, like Demophoon, has failed to become a God and she will never now arise from the fires of the Soviet ordeal.

1. Comment on Koestler's depiction of the attitudes of initiates to communism and the process of their indoctrination. Describe his bias as illustrated in these observations.
2. Outline, according to Silone, the conflict between socialist values and socialist theories.
3. Describe the role of the arts in the Soviet Union as depicted by Gide. Give reasons for the decision of the state to take such a restrictive view on free expression.

• • •

Fascism

Fascism, which grew during the inter-war period, was related to the difficult social and economic circumstances existing at that time. There were many fascist movements, though no single coherent ideology. All were anti-democratic and anti-communist, and regarded liberalism as a philosophy unsuited to the new era. Fascists adopted nationalism to their purposes and became the defenders of an authoritarian, dictatorial nation-state. The leader of the movement was glorified as the embodiment of all that was best in the people. Violent, irrational, and totalitarian, fascism attracted many who believed traditional democracy could no longer address their problems and who feared the growth and spread of communism.

 Benito Mussolini (1883-1945) was the "Duce," the leader of fascist Italy, from 1922 to 1945. He was the author of an article on the nature of fascism.

Fascism is now clearly defined not only as a régime but as a doctrine. This means that Fascism, exercising its critical faculties on itself and on others, has studied from its own special standpoint and judged by its own standards all the problems affecting the material and intellectual interests now causing such grave anxiety to the nations of the world, and is ready to deal with them by its own policies.

First of all, as regards the future development of mankind,—and quite apart from all present political considerations—Fascism does not, generally speaking, believe in the possibility or utility of perpetual peace. It therefore discards pacifism as a cloak for cowardly supine renunciation in contra-distinction to self-sacrifice. War alone keys up all human energies to their maximum tension and sets the seal of nobility on those peoples who have the courage to face it. All other tests are substitutes which never place a man face to face with himself before the alternative of life or death. Therefore all doctrines which postulate peace at all costs are incompatible with Fascism. Equally foreign to the spirit of Facism, even if accepted as useful in meeting special political situations—are all internationalistic or League superstructures which, as history shows, crumble to the ground whenever the heart of nations is deeply stirred by sentimental, idealistic or practical considerations. Fascism carries this anti-pacifistic attitude into the life of the individual. "I don't care a damn" (*me ne frego*)—the proud motto of the fighting squads scrawled by a wounded man on his bandages, is not only an act of philosophic stoicism, it sums up a doctrine which is not merely political: it is evidence of a fighting spirit which accepts all risks. It signifies a new style of Italian life. The Fascist accepts and loves life; he rejects and despises suicide as cowardly. Life as he understands it means duty, elevation, conquest; life must be lofty and full, it must be lived for oneself but above all for others, both near bye and far off, present and future. . . .

That the vicissitudes of economic life—discoveries of raw materials, new technical processes, scientific inventions—have their importance, no one denies; but that they suffice to explain human history to the exclusion of other factors is absurd. Fascism believes now and always in sanctity and heroism, that is to say in acts in which no economic motive—remote or immediate— is at work. Having denied historic materialism, which sees in men mere puppets on the surface of history, appearing and disappearing on the crest of the waves while in the depths the real directing forces move and work, Fascism also denies the immutable and irreparable character of the class struggle which is the natural outcome of this economic conception of history; above all it denies that the class struggle is the preponderating agent in social transformations. . . .

After socialism, Fascism trains its guns on the whole block of democratic ideologies, and rejects both their premises and their practical applications and implements. Fascism denies that numbers, as such, can be the determining factor in human society; it denies the right of numbers to govern by means of periodical consultations; it asserts the irremediable and fertile and benef-

Sources: Benito Mussolini, *Fascism: Doctrine and Institutions* (New York: Howard Fertig, 1968), pp. 18-19, 20, 21, 23, 25-26, 27-28, 29-31; Adolph Hitler, *Mein Kampf*, translated by Ralph Manheim (London: Hutchinson, and Co. Ltd., 1969), pp. 258-59, 260-61, 262-63, 272-73, 402, 403, 405-406, 408, 410.

icent inequality of men who cannot be levelled by any such mechanical and extrinsic device as universal suffrage. Democratic régimes may be described as those under which the people are, from time to time, deluded into the belief that they exercise sovereignty, while all the time real sovereignty resides in and is exercised by other and sometimes irresponsible and secret forces. Democracy is a kingless régime infested by many kings who are sometimes more exclusive, tyrannical, and destructive than one, even if he be a tyrant. . . .

. . . In rejecting democracy Fascism rejects the absurd conventional lie of political equalitarianism, the habit of collective irresponsibility, the myth of felicity and indefinite progress. But if democracy be understood as meaning a régime in which the masses are not driven back to the margin of the State, then the writer of these pages has already defined Fascism as an organised, centralised, authoritarian democracy.

Fascism is definitely and absolutely opposed to the doctrines of liberalism, both in the political and the economic sphere. . . .

The Fascist negation of socialism, democracy, liberalism, should not, however, be interpreted as implying a desire to drive the world backwards to positions occupied prior to 1789, a year commonly referred to as that which opened the demo-liberal century. History does not travel backwards. . . .

A party governing a nation "totalitarianly" is a new departure in history. There are no points of reference nor of comparison. From beneath the ruins of liberal, socialist, and democratic doctrines, Fascism extracts those elements which are still vital. It preserves what may be described as "the acquired facts" of history; it rejects all else. That is to say, it rejects the idea of a doctrine suited to all times and to all people. Granted that the XIXth century was the century of socialism, liberalism, democracy, this does not mean that the XXth century must also be the century of socialism, liberalism, democracy. Political doctrines pass; nations remain. We are free to believe that this is the century of authority, a century tending to the "right", a Fascist century. If the XIXth century was the century of the individual (liberalism implies individualism) we are free to believe that this is the "collective" century, and therefore the century of the State. . . .

The key-stone of the Fascist doctrine is its conception of the State, of its essence, its functions, and its aims. For Fascism the State is absolute, individuals and groups relative. Individuals and groups are admissable in so far as they come within the State. Instead of directing the game and guiding the material and moral progress of the community, the liberal State restricts its activities to recording results. The Fascist State is wide awake and has a will of its own . . . .

If liberalism spells individualism, Fascism spells government. The Fascist State is, however, a unique and original creation. It is not reactionary but revolutionary, for it anticipates the solution of certain universal problems which have been raised elsewhere, in the political field by the splitting-up of parties, the usurpation of power by parliaments, the irresponsibility of assemblies; in the economic field by the increasingly numerous and important functions discharged by trade-unions and trade associations with their disputes and ententes, affecting both capital and labor; in the ethical field by the need felt for order, discipline, obedience to the moral dictates of patriotism.

Fascism desires the State to be strong and organic, based on broad foundations of popular support. The Fascist State lays claim to rule in the economic field no less than in others; it makes its action felt throughout the length and breadth of the country by means of its corporative, social, and educational institutions, and all the political, economic, and spiritual forces of the nation, organised in their respective associations, circulate within the State.

A State based on millions of individuals who recognise its authority, feel its action, and are ready to serve its ends is not the tyrannical state of a mediaeval lordling. It has nothing in common with the despotic States existing prior to or subsequent to 1789. Far from crushing the individual, the Fascist State multiplies his energies, just as in a regiment a soldier is not diminished but multiplied by the number of his fellow soldiers . . . .

The Fascist State expresses the will to exercise power and to command . . . . Fascism sees in the imperialistic spirit—i.e. in the tendency of nations to expand—a manifestation of their vitality. In the opposite tendency, which would limit their interests to the home country, it sees a symptom of decadence. Peoples who rise or rearise are imperialistic; renunciation is characteristic of dying peoples. The Fascist doctrine is that best suited to the tendencies and feelings of a people which, like the Italian, after lying fallow during centuries of foreign servitude, is now reasserting itself in the world.

But imperialism implies discipline, the coordination of efforts, a deep sense of duty and a spirit of self-sacrifice . . . .

Never before have the peoples thirsted for authority, direction, order, as they do now. If each age has its doctrine, then innumerable symptoms indicate that the doctrine of our age is the Fascist. That it is vital is shown by the fact that it has aroused a faith; that this faith has conquered souls is shown by the fact that Fascism can point to its fallen heroes and its martyrs.

Fascism has now acquired throughout the world that universality which belongs to all doctines which by achieving self-expression represent a moment in the history of human thought.

B Adolph Hitler (1889-1945) was the leader of the racist National Socialist (Nazi) state in Germany from 1933 to 1945. His racism, anti-Semitism, and his totalitarian beliefs were made plain in his work *Mein Kampf* (My Struggle), a large work full of anger, bigotry, hatred, and elitism, which was published in two parts in 1925 and 1926.

Any crossing of two beings not at exactly the same level produces a medium between the level of the two parents. This means: the offspring will probably stand higher than the racially lower parent, but not as high as the higher one. Consequently, it will later succumb in the struggle against the higher level. Such mating is contrary to the will of Nature for a higher breeding of all life. The precondition for this does not lie in associating superior and inferior, but in the total victory of the former. The stronger must dominate and not blend with the weaker, thus sacrificing his own greatness. Only the born weakling can view this as cruel, but he after all is only a weak and limited man; for if this law did not prevail, any conceivable higher development of organic living beings would be unthinkable. . . .

The result of all racial crossing is therefore in brief always the following:

(a) Lowering of the level of the higher race;

(b) Physical and intellectual regression and hence the beginning of a slowly but surely progressing sickness.

To bring about such a development is, then, nothing else but to sin against the will of the eternal creator.

And as a sin this act is rewarded.

When man attempts to rebel against the iron logic of Nature, he comes into struggle with the principles to which he himself owes his existence as a man. And this attack must lead to his own doom.

Here, of course, we encounter the objection of the modern pacifist, as truly Jewish in its effrontery as it is stupid! 'Man's role is to overcome Nature!'

Millions thoughtlessly parrot this Jewish nonsense and end up by really imagining that they themselves represent a kind of conqueror of Nature; though in this they dispose of no other weapon than an idea, and at that such a miserable one, that if it were true no world at all would be conceivable. . . .

All great cultures of the past perished only because the originally creative race died out from blood poisoning.

The ultimate cause of such a decline was their forgetting that all culture depends on men and not conversely; hence that to preserve a certain culture the man who creates it must be preserved. This preservation is bound up with the rigid law of necessity and the right to victory of the best and stronger in this world.

Those who want to live, let them fight, and those who do not want to fight in this world of eternal struggle do not deserve to live.

Even if this were hard—that is how it is! Assuredly, however, by far the harder fate is that which strikes the man who thinks he can overcome Nature, but in the last analysis only mocks her. Distress, misfortune, and diseases are her answer.

The man who misjudges and disregards the racial laws actually forfeits the happiness that seems destined to be his. He thwarts the triumphal march of the best race and hence also the precondition for all human progress, and remains, in consequence, burdened with all the sensibility of man, in the animal realm of helpless misery. . . .

The mightiest counterpart to the Aryan is represented by the Jew. In hardly any people in the world is the instinct of self-preservation developed more strongly than in the so-called 'chosen'. Of this, the mere fact of the survival of this race may be considered the best proof. Where is the people which in the last two thousand years has been exposed to so slight changes of inner disposition, character, etc., as the Jewish people? What people, finally, has gone through greater upheavals than this one—and nevertheless issued from the mightiest catastrophes of mankind unchanged? What an infinitely tough will to live and preserve the species speaks from these facts!

The mental qualities of the Jew have been schooled in the course of many centuries. Today he passes as 'smart', and this in a certain sense he has been at all times. But his intelligence is not the result of his own development, but of visual instruction through foreigners. For the human mind cannot climb to the top without steps; for every step upward he needs the foundation of the past, and this in the comprehensive sense in which it can be revealed only in general culture. . . .

Since the Jew—for reasons which will at once become apparent—was never in possession of a culture of his own, the foundations of his intellectual work were always provided by others. His intellect at all times developed through the cultural world surrounding him.

The reverse process never took place. . . .

Adolph Hitler <u>*Mein Kampf*</u>

⟨C⟩ Rejecting majority rule and parliamentary democracy, Hitler believed in a "folkish" state and in the importance of leadership.

The folkish National Socialist state sees its chief task in *educating and preserving the bearer of the state*. It is not sufficient to encourage the racial elements as such, to educate them and finally instruct them in the needs of practical life; the state must also adjust its own organisation to this task. . . .

A philosophy of life which endeavours to reject the democratic mass idea and give this earth to the best people—that is, the highest humanity—must logically obey the same aristocratic principle within this people and make sure that the leadership and the highest influence in this people fall to the best minds. Thus, it builds, not upon the idea of the majority, but upon the idea of personality.

Anyone who believes today that a folkish National Socialist state must distinguish itself from other states only in a purely mechanical sense, by a superior construction of its economic life—that is, by a better balance between rich and poor, or giving broad sections of the population more right to influence the economic process, or by fairer wages by elimination of excessive wage differentials—has not gone beyond the most superficial aspect of the matter and has not the faintest idea of what we call a philosophy. . . .

A human community appears well organised only if it facilitates the labours of these creative forces in the most helpful way and applies them in a manner beneficial to all. The most valuable thing about the invention itself, whether it lie in the material field or in the world of ideas, is primarily the inventor as a personality. Therefore, to employ him in a way benefiting the totality is the first and highest task in the organisation of a national community. Indeed, the organisation itself must be a realisation of this principle. Thus, also, it is redeemed from the curse of mechanism and becomes a living thing. *It must itself be an embodiment of the endeavour to place thinking individuals above the masses, thus subordinating the latter to the former.*

Consequently, the organisation must not only not prevent the emergence of thinking individuals from the mass; on the contrary, it must in the highest degree make this possible and easy by the nature of its own being. In this it must proceed from the principle that the salvation of mankind has never lain in the masses, but in its creative minds, which must therefore really be regarded as benefactors of the human race. To assure them of the most decisive influence and facilitate their work is in the interest of the totality. Assuredly this interest is not satisfied, and is not served by the domination of the unintelligent or incompetent, in any case uninspired masses, but solely by the leadership of those to whom Nature has given special gifts for this purpose.

The selection of these minds, as said before, is primarily accomplished by the hard struggle for existence. Many break and perish, thus showing that they are not destined for the ultimate, and in the end only a few appear to be chosen. In the fields of thought, artistic creation, even, in fact, of economic life, this selective process is still going on today, though, especially in the latter field, it faces a grave obstacle. The administration of the state and likewise the power embodied in the organised military might of the nation are also dominated by these ideas. Here, too, the idea of personality is everywhere dominant—its authority downward and its responsibility towards the higher personality above. Only political life has today completely turned away from this most natural principle. While all human culture is solely the result of the individual's creative activity, everywhere, and particularly in the highest *leadership* of the national community, the *principle of the value of the majority* appears decisive, and from that high place begins to gradually poison all life; that is, in reality to dissolve it. The destructive effect of the Jew's activity in other national bodies is basically attributable only to his eternal efforts to undermine the position of the personality in the host-peoples and to replace it by the mass. Thus, the organising principle of Aryan humanity is replaced by the destructive principle of the Jew. He becomes 'a ferment of decomposition' among peoples and races, and in the broader sense a dissolver of human culture. . . .

The folkish philosophy is basically distinguished from the Marxist philosophy by the fact that it not only recognises the value of race, but with it the importance of the personality, which it therefore makes one of the pillars of its entire edifice. . . .

. . . The folkish state must free all leadership and especially the highest— that is, the political leadership—entirely from the parliamentary principle of majority rule—in other words, mass rule—and instead absolutely guarantee the right of the personality.

From this the following realisation results:

The best state constitution and state form is that which, with the most unquestioned certainty, raises the best minds in the national community to leading position and leading influence. . . .

This principle—absolute responsibility unconditionally combined with absolute authority—will gradually breed an élite of leaders such as today, in this era of irresponsible parliamentarianism, is utterly inconceivable.

Thus, the political form of the nation will be brought into agreement with that law to which it owes its greatness in the cultural and economic field.

1. Précis, in your own words, Mussolini's definition of fascism.
2. Using the arguments put forward in the excerpt, comment on Mussolini's assertion that "the XIXth century was the century of the individual . . . [this is] the century of the State."
3. What evidence appears in Hitler's comments in *Mein Kampf* that foreshadows the racist policies of the future Third Reich?
4. Comment on Hitler's argument that the state must be organized so the political leadership is free from majority interference.

▪ ▪ ▪

THOMAS MANN

Thomas Mann (1875-1955) was a novelist, short-story writer and essayist whose work helped shape the culture of the twentieth century. His stories and novels dealt with all of the themes of the century, including the complex issue of the role of the irrational in our lives, human motivation, and myth. In the novels *The Magic Mountain* (1922) and *Doctor Faustus* (1947), Mann explored the dichotomies of imagination and reason, and myth and history. Leaving Germany in 1933 because of the politics of the Nazi era, Mann was a major figure in asserting the importance and lasting value of the humanistic tradition in the West.

⬧A⬧ Mann wrote the story "Mario and the Magician" in 1929, as an exploration of the new facism and irrationality of the time. He used a magician, a charismatic figure named Cipolla, to demonstrate the role of the irrational in people's lives, and to capture the social and political atmosphere. In the story a German family visits an Italian resort and has an unpleasant experience. They decide to go to the magic show for amusement.

> It had got to a quarter past nine, it got to almost half past. It was natural that we should be nervous. When would the children get to bed? It had been a mistake to bring them, for now it would be very hard to suggest breaking off their enjoyment before it had got well under way. The stalls had filled in time; all Torre, apparently, was there: the guests of the Grand Hotel, the guests of Villa Eleonora, familiar faces from the beach. We heard English and German and the sort of French that Rumanians speak with Italians. Madame Angiolieri herself sat two rows behind us, with her quiet, bald-headed spouse, who kept stroking his moustache with the two middle fingers of his right hand. Everybody had come late, but nobody too late. Cipolla made us wait for him.
>
> He made us wait. That is probably the way to put it. He heightened the suspense by his delay in appearing. And we could see the point of this, too—only not when it was carried to extremes. Towards half past nine the audience began to clap—an amiable way of expressing justifiable impatience, evincing as it does an eagerness to applaud. For the little ones, this was a joy in itself—all children love to clap. From the popular sphere came loud cries of *"Pronti!"* *"Cominciamo!"* And lo, it seemed now as easy to begin as before it had been hard. A gong sounded, greeted by the standing rows with a many-voiced "Ah-h!" and the curtains parted. They revealed a platform furnished more like a schoolroom than like the theatre of a conjuring performance—largely because of the blackboard in the left foreground. There was a common yellow hat-stand, a few ordinary straw-bottomed chairs, and further back a little round table holding a water carafe and glass, also a tray with a liqueur glass and a flask of pale yellow liquid. We had still a few seconds of time to let

Source: Thomas Mann, *Death in Venice and Seven Other Stories*, translated by H.T. Lowe-Porter (New York: Vintage Books, 1930), pp. 148-53, 163-67, 175-81.

these things sink in. Then, with no darkening of the house, Cavaliere Cipolla made his entry.

He came forward with a rapid step that expressed his eagerness to appear before his public and gave rise to the illusion that he had already come a long way to put himself at their service—whereas, of course, he had only been standing in the wings. His costume supported the fiction. A man of an age hard to determine, but by no means young; with a sharp, ravaged face, piercing eyes, compressed lips, small black waxed moustache, and a so-called imperial in the curve between mouth and chin. He was dressed for the street with a sort of complicated evening elegance, in a wide black pelerine with velvet collar and satin lining; which, in the hampered state of his arms, he held together in front with his white-gloved hands. He had a white scarf round his neck; a top hat with a curving brim sat far back on his head. Perhaps more than anywhere else the eighteenth century is still alive in Italy, and with it the charlatan and mountebank type so characteristic of the period. Only there, at any rate, does one still encounter really well-preserved specimens. Cipolla had in his whole appearance much of the historic type; his very clothes helped to conjure up the traditional figure with its blatantly, fantastically foppish air. His pretentious costume sat upon him, or rather hung upon him, most curiously, being in one place drawn too tight, in another a mass of awkward folds. There was something not quite in order about his figure, both front and back—that was plain later on. But I must emphasize the fact that there was not a trace of personal jocularity or clownishness in his pose, manner, or behaviour. On the contrary, there was complete seriousness, an absence of any humorous appeal; occasionally even a cross-grained pride, along with that curious, self-satisfied air so characteristic of the deformed. None of all this, however, prevented his appearance from being greeted with laughter from more than one quarter of the hall.

All the eagerness had left his manner. The swift entry had been merely an expression of energy, not of zeal. Standing at the footlights he negligently drew off his gloves, to display long yellow hands, one of them adorned with a seal ring with a lapis-lazuli in a high setting. As he stood there, his small hard eyes, with flabby pouches beneath them, roved appraisingly about the hall, not quickly, rather in a considered examination, pausing here and there upon a face with his lips clipped together, not speaking a word. Then with a display of skill as surprising as it was casual, he rolled his gloves into a ball and tossed them across a considerable distance into the glass on the table. Next from an inner pocket he drew forth a packet of cigarettes; you could see by the wrapper that they were the cheapest sort the government sells. With his fingertips he pulled out a cigarette and lighted it, without looking, from a quick-firing benzine lighter. He drew the smoke deep into his lungs and let it out again, tapping his foot, with both lips drawn in an arrogant grimace and the grey smoke streaming out between broken and saw-edged teeth.

With a keenness equal to his own his audience eyed him. The youths at the rear scowled as they peered at this cocksure creature to search out his secret weaknesses. He betrayed none. In fetching out and putting back the cigarettes his clothes got in his way. He had to turn back his pelerine, and in so doing revealed a riding-whip with a silver claw-handle that hung by a leather thong from his left forearm and looked decidedly out of place. You could see that he had on not evening clothes but a frock-coat, and under this, as he lifted it to get at his pocket, could be seen a striped sash worn about the body. Somebody behind me whispered that this sash went with his title of Cavaliere. I give the information for what it may be worth—personally, I never heard that the title carried such insignia with it. Perhaps the sash was sheer pose, like the way he stood there, without a word, casually and arrogantly puffing smoke into his audience's face.

People laughed, as I said. The merriment had become almost general when somebody in the "standing seats," in a loud, dry voice, remarked: "*Buona sera.*"

Cipolla cocked his head. "Who was that?" asked he, as though he had been dared. "Who was that just spoke? Well? First so bold and now so modest? *Paura*, eh?" He spoke with a rather high, asthmatic voice, which yet had a metallic quality. He waited.

"That was me," a youth at the rear broke into the stillness, seeing himself thus challenged. He was not far from us, a handsome fellow in a woollen shirt, with his coat hanging over one shoulder. He wore his surly, wiry hair in a high, dishevelled mop, the style affected by the youth of the awakened Fatherland; it gave him an African appearance that rather spoiled his looks. "*Bè*! That was me. It was your business to say it first, but I was trying to be friendly."

More laughter. The chap had a tongue in his head. "*Ha sciolto la scilin-guágnolo*," I heard near me. After all, the retort was deserved.

"Ah, bravo!" answered Cipolla. "I like you, *giovanotto*. Trust me, I've had my eye on you for some time. People like you are just in my line. I can use them. And you are the pick of the lot, that's plain to see. You do what you like. Or is it possible you have ever not done what you liked—or even, maybe, what you didn't like? What somebody else liked, in short? Hark ye, my friend, that might be a pleasant change for you, to divide up the willing and the doing and stop tackling both jobs at once. Division of labour, *sistema americano, sa!* For instance, suppose you were to show your tongue to this select and honourable audience here—your whole tongue, right down to the roots?"

"No, I won't," said the youth, hostilely. "Sticking out your tongue shows a bad bringing-up."

"Nothing of the sort," retorted Cipolla. "You would only be *doing* it. With all due respect to your bringing-up, I suggest that before I count ten, you will perform a right turn and stick out your tongue at the company here further than you knew yourself that you could stick it out."

He gazed at the youth, and his piercing eyes seemed to sink deeper into their sockets. "*Uno!*" said he. He had let his riding-whip slide down his arm and made it whistle once through the air. The boy faced about and put out his tongue, so long, so extendedly, that you could see it was the very uttermost in tongue which he had to offer. Then turned back, stony-faced, to his former position.

"That was me," mocked Cipolla, with a jerk of his head towards the youth. "*Bè*! That was me." Leaving the audience to enjoy its sensations, he turned towards the little round table, lifted the bottle, poured out a small glass of what was obviously cognac, and tipped it up with a practised hand.

The children laughed with all their hearts. They had understood practically nothing of what had been said, but it pleased them hugely that something so funny should happen, straightaway, between that queer man up there and somebody out of the audience. They had no preconception of what an "evening" would be like and were quite ready to find this a priceless beginning. As for us, we exchanged a glance and I remember that involuntarily I made with my lips the sound that Cipolla's whip had made when it cut the air. For the rest, it was plain that people did not know what to make of a preposterous beginning like this to a sleight-of-hand performance. They could not see why the *giovanotto*, who after all in a way had been their spokesman, should suddenly have turned on them to vent his incivility. They felt that he had behaved like a silly ass and withdrew their countenances from him in favour of the artist, who now came back from his refreshment table and addressed them as follows:

"Ladies and gentlemen," said he, in his wheezing, metallic voice, "you saw just now that I was rather sensitive on the score of the rebuke this hopeful young linguist saw fit to give me"—"*questo linguista di belle speranze*" was what he said, and we all laughed at the pun. "I am a man who sets some store by himself, you may take it from me. And I see no point in being wished a good-evening unless it is done courteously and in all seriousness. For anything else there is no occasion. When a man wishes me a good-evening he wishes himself one, for the audience will have one only if I do. So this lady-killer of Torre di Venere" (another thrust) "did well to testify that I have one tonight and that I can dispense with any wishes of his in the matter. I can boast of having good evenings almost without exception. One not so good does come my way now and again, but very seldom. My calling is hard and my health not of the best. I have a little physical defect which prevented me from doing my bit in the war for the greater glory of the Fatherland. It is perforce with my mental and spiritual parts that I conquer life—which after all only means conquering oneself. . . ."

◆ B ▷ Mario, a young waiter whom the family knows, is called to the stage by the magician.

Mario obeyed. I can see him now going up the stairs to Cipolla, who continued to beckon him, in that droll, picture-book sort of way. He hesitated for a moment at first; that, too, I recall quite clearly. During the whole evening he had lounged against a wooden pillar at the side entrance, with his arms folded, or else with his hands thrust into his jacket pockets. He was on our left, near the youth with the militant hair, and had followed the performance attentively, so far as we had seen, if with no particular animation and God knows how much comprehension. He could not much relish being summoned thus, at the end of the evening. But it was only too easy to see why he obeyed. After all, obedience was his calling in life; and then, how should a simple lad like him find it within his human capacity to refuse compliance to a man so throned and crowned as Cipolla at that hour? Willy-nilly he left his column and with a word of thanks to those making way for him he mounted the steps with a doubtful smile on his full lips.

Picture a thickest youth of twenty years, with clipt hair, a low forehead, and heavy-lidded eyes of an indefinite grey, shot with green and yellow. These things I knew from having spoken with him, as we often had. There was a saddle of freckles on the flat nose, the whole upper half of the face retreated behind the lower, and that again was dominated by thick lips that parted to show the salivated teeth. These thick lips and the veiled look of the eyes lent the whole face a primitive melancholy—it was that which had drawn us to him from the first. In it was not the faintest trace of brutality—indeed, his hands would have given the lie to such an idea, being unusually slender and delicate even for a southerner. They were hands by which one liked being served.

We knew him humanly without knowing him personally, if I may make that distinction. We saw him nearly every day, and felt a certain kindness for his dreamy ways, which might at times be actual inattentiveness, suddenly transformed into a redeeming zeal to serve. His mien was serious, only the children could bring a smile to his face. It was not sulky, but uningratiating, without intentional effort to please—or, rather, it seemed to give up being pleasant in the conviction that it could not succeed. We should have remembered Mario in any case, as one of those homely recollections of travel which often stick in the mind better than more important ones. But of his circumstances we knew no more than that his father was a petty clerk in the Municipio and his mother took in washing.

His white waiter's-coat became him better than the faded striped suit he wore, with a gay coloured scarf instead of a collar, the ends tucked into his jacket. He neared Cipolla, who however did not leave off that motion of his finger before his nose, so that Mario had to come still closer, right up to the chair-seat and the master's legs. Whereupon the latter spread out his elbows and seized the lad, turning him so that we had a view of his face. Then gazed him briskly up and down, with a careless, commanding eye.

"Well, *ragazzo mio*, how comes it we make acquaintance so late in the day? But believe me, I made yours long ago. Yes, yes, I've had you in my eye this long while and known what good stuff you were made of. How could I go and forget you again? Well, I've had a good deal to think about. . . . Now tell me, what is your name? The first name, that's all I want."

"My name is Mario," the young man answered, in a low voice.

"Ah, Mario. Very good. Yes, yes, there is such a name, quite a common name, a classic name too, one of those which preserve the heroic traditions of the Fatherland. *Bravo! Salve!*" And he flung up his arm slantingly above his crooked shoulder, palm outward, in the Roman salute. He might have been slightly tipsy by now, and no wonder; but he spoke as before, clearly, fluently, and with emphasis. Though about this time there had crept into his voice a gross, autocratic note, and a kind of arrogance was in his sprawl.

"Well, now, Mario *mio*," he went on, "it's a good thing you came this evening, and that's a pretty scarf you've got on; it is becoming to your style of beauty. It must stand you in good stead with the girls, the pretty pretty girls of Torre—"

From the row of youths, close by the place where Mario had been standing, sounded a laugh. It came from the youth with the militant hair. He stood there, his jacket over his shoulder, and laughed outright, rudely and scornfully.

Mario gave a start. I think it was a shrug, but he may have started and then hastened to cover the movement by shrugging his shoulders, as much as to say that the neckerchief and the fair sex were matters of equal indifference to him.

The Cavaliere gave a downward glance.

"We needn't trouble about him," he said. "He is jealous, because your scarf is so popular with the girls, maybe partly because you and I are so friendly up here. Perhaps he'd like me to put him in mind of his colic—I could do it free of charge. Tell me, Mario. You've come here this evening for a bit of fun—and in the daytime you work in an ironmonger's shop?"

"In a café," corrected the youth.

"Oh, in a café. That's where Cipolla nearly came a cropper! What you are is a cup-bearer, a Ganymede—I like that, it is another classical allusion—*Salvietta*!" Again the Cavaliere saluted, to the huge gratification of his audience.

Mario smiled too. "But before that," he interpolated, in the interest of accuracy. "I worked for a while in a shop in Portoclemente." He seemed visited by a natural desire to assist the prophecy by dredging out its essential features.

"There, didn't I say so? In an ironmonger's shop?"

"They kept combs and brushes," Mario got round it.

"Didn't I say that you were not always a Ganymede? Not always at the sign of the serviette? Even when Cipolla makes a mistake, it is a kind that makes you believe in him. Now tell me: Do you believe in me?"

An indefinite gesture.

"A half-way answer," commented the Cavaliere. "Probably it is not easy to win your confidence. Even for me, I can see, it is not so easy. I see in your features a reserve, a sadness, *un tratto di malinconia* . . . tell me" (he seized Mario's hand persuasively) "have you troubles?"

"*Nossignore*," answered Mario, promptly and decidedly.

"You *have* troubles," insisted the Cavaliere, bearing down the denial by the weight of his authority. "Can't I see? Trying to pull the wool over Cipolla's eyes, are you? Of course, about the girls—it is a girl, isn't it? You have love troubles?"

Mario gave a vigorous head-shake. And again the *giovanotto's* brutal laugh rang out. The Cavaliere gave heed. His eyes were roving about somewhere in the air: but he cocked an ear to the sound, then swung his whip backwards, as he had once or twice before in his conversation with Mario, that none of his puppets might flag in their zeal. The gesture had nearly cost him his new prey: Mario gave a sudden start in the direction of the steps. But Cipolla had him in his clutch.

"Not so fast," said he. "That would be fine, wouldn't it? So you want to skip, do you, Ganymede, right in the middle of the fun, or, rather, when it is just beginning? Stay with me, I'll show you something nice. I'll convince you. You have no reason to worry, I promise you. This girl—you know her and others know her too—what's her name? Wait! I read the name in your eyes, it is on the tip of my tongue and yours too—"

"Silvestra!" shouted the *giovanotto* from below.

The Cavaliere's face did not change.

"Aren't there the forward people?" he asked, not looking down, more as in undisturbed converse with Mario. "Aren't there the young fighting-cocks that crow in season and out? Takes the word out of your mouth, the conceited fool, and seems to think he has some special right to it. Let him be. But Silvestra, your Silvestra—ah, what a girl that is! What a prize! Brings your heart into your mouth to see her walk or laugh or breathe, she is so lovely. And her round arms when she washes, and tosses her head back to get the hair out of her eyes! An angel from paradise!"

Mario started at him, his head thrust forward. He seemed to have forgotten the audience, forgotten where he was. The red rings round his eyes had got larger, they looked as though they were painted on. His thick lips parted.

"And she makes you suffer, this angel," went on Cipolla, "or, rather, you make yourself suffer for her—there is a difference, my lad, a most important difference, let me tell you. There are misunderstandings in love, maybe nowhere else in the world are there so many. I know what you are thinking: what does this Cipolla, with his little physical defect, know about love? Wrong, all wrong, he knows a lot. He has a wide and powerful understanding of its workings, and it pays to listen to his advice. But let's leave Cipolla out, cut him out altogether and think only of Silvestra, your peerless Silvestra! What! Is she to give any young gamecock the preference, so that he can laugh while you cry? To prefer him to a chap like you, so full of feeling and so sympathetic? Not very likely, is it? It is impossible—we know better, Cipolla and she. If I were to put myself in her place and choose between the two of you, a tarry lout like that—a codfish, a sea-urchin—and a Mario, a knight of the serviette, who moves among gentlefolk and hands round refreshments with an air— my word, but my heart would speak in no uncertain tones—it knows to whom I gave it long ago. It is time that he should see and understand, my chosen one! It is time that you see me and recognize me, Mario, my beloved! Tell me, who am I?"

It was grisly, the way the betrayer made himself irresistible, wreathed and coquetted with his crooked shoulder, languished with the puffy eyes, and showed his splintered teeth in a sickly smile. And alas, at his beguiling words, what was come of our Mario? It is hard for me to tell, hard as it was for me to see; for here was nothing less than an utter abandonment of the inmost soul, a public exposure of timid and deluded passion and rapture. He put his hands across his mouth, his shoulders rose and fell with his pantings. He could not, it was plain, trust his eyes and ears for joy, and the one thing he forgot was precisely that he could not trust them. "Silvestra!" he breathed, from the very depths of his vanquished heart.

"Kiss me!" said the hunchback. "Trust me, I love thee. Kiss me here." And with the tip of his index finger, hand, arm, and little finger outspread, he pointed to his cheek, near the mouth. And Mario bent and kissed him.

It had grown very still in the room. That was a monstrous moment, grotesque and thrilling, the moment of Mario's bliss. In that evil span of time, crowded with a sense of the illusiveness of all joy, one sound became audible, and that not quite at once, but on the instant of the melancholy and ribald meeting between Mario's lips and the repulsive flesh which thrust itself forward for his caress. It was the sound of a laugh, from the *giovanotto* on our left. It broke into the dramatic suspense of the moment, coarse, mocking, and yet—or I must have been grossly mistaken—with an undertone of compassion for the poor bewildered, victimized creature. It had a faint ring of that *"Poveretto"* which Cipolla had declared was wasted on the wrong person, when he claimed the pity for his own.

The laugh still rang in the air when the recipient of the caress gave his whip a little swish, low down, close to his chair-leg, and Mario started up and flung himself back. He stood in that posture staring, his hands one over the other on those desecrated lips. Then he beat his temples with his clenched fists, over and over; turned and staggered down the steps, while the audience applauded, and Cipolla sat there with his hands in his lap, his shoulders shaking. Once below, and even while in full retreat, Mario hurled himself round with legs flung wide apart; one arm flew up, and two flat shattering detonations crashed through applause and laughter.

There was instant silence. Even the dancers came to a full stop and stared about, struck dumb. Cipolla bounded from his seat. He stood with his arms spread out, slanting as though to ward everybody off, as though next moment he would cry out: "Stop! Keep back! Silence! What was that?" Then, in that instant, he sank back in his seat, his head rolling on his chest; in the next he had fallen sideways to the floor, where he lay motionless, a huddled heap of clothing, with limbs awry.

The commotion was indescribable. Ladies hid their faces, shuddering, on the breasts of their escorts. There were shouts for a doctor, for the police. People flung themselves on Mario in a mob, to disarm him, to take away the weapon that hung from his fingers—that small, dull-metal, scarcely pistol-shaped tool with hardly any barrel—in how strange and unexpected a direction had fate levelled it!

And now—now finally, at last—we took the children and led them towards the exit, past the pair of *carabinieri* just entering. Was that the end, they wanted to know, that they might go in peace? Yes, we assured them, that was the end. An end of horror, a fatal end. And yet a liberation—for I could not, and I cannot, but find it so!

1. How does Mann depict power in his story?
2. Account for Mann's assertion that the killing of Cipolla was an act of liberation for Mario and the rest of the audience.

▪ ▪ ▪

JOSÉ ORTEGA Y GASSET

The Spanish philosopher José Ortega y Gasset (1883-1955) was deeply concerned with the problems of liberalism and democracy in the twentieth century. Ortega believed that mass society was opposed to traditional culture and civilization, and that fascism and communism were reflections of the rise of the masses to power. To some his concerns were too traditional and elitist a response to the problems of the inter-war period. Yet in his writings, Ortega defended the humanist tradition of the West, while pointing out some of its paradoxes and contradictions. His essay "The Revolt of the Masses" (1930) was one of the first important probes into the dilemmas of mass society and culture.

 Ortega claimed that a major new feature of the twentieth century was the rise of the masses to power.

There is one fact which, whether for good or ill, is of utmost importance in the public life of Europe at the present moment. This fact is the accession of the masses to complete social power. As the masses, by definition, neither should nor can direct their own personal existence, and still less rule society in general, this fact means that actually Europe is suffering from the greatest crisis that can afflict peoples, nations, and civilisation. Such a crisis has occurred more than once in history. Its characteristics and its consequences are well known. So also is its name. It is called the rebellion of the masses. In order to understand this formidable fact, it is important from the start to avoid giving to the words "rebellion," "masses," and "social power" a meaning exclusively or primarily political. Public life is not solely political, but equally, and even primarily, intellectual, moral, economic, religious, it comprises all our collective habits, including our fashions both of dress and of amusement. . . .

Strictly speaking, the mass, as a psychological fact, can be defined without waiting for individuals to appear in mass formation. In the presence of one individual we can decide whether he is "mass" or not. The mass is all that which sets no value on itself—good or ill—based on specific grounds, but which feels itself "just like everybody," and nevertheless is not concerned about it; is, in fact, quite happy to feel itself as one with everybody else. Imagine a humble-minded man who, having tried to estimate his own worth on specific grounds—asking himself if he has any talent for this or that, if he excels in any direction—realises that he possesses no quality of excellence. Such a man will feel that he is mediocre and commonplace, ill-gifted, but will not feel himself "mass."

When one speaks of "select minorities" it is usual for the evil-minded to twist the sense of this expression, pretending to be unaware that the select man is not the petulant person who thinks himself superior to the rest, but the man who demands more of himself than the rest, even though he may not fulfil in his person those higher exigencies. For there is no doubt that the most radical division that it is possible to make of humanity is that which splits it into two classes of creatures: those who make great demands on themselves, piling up difficulties and duties; and those who demand nothing special of themselves, but for whom to live is to be every moment what they already are, without imposing on themselves any effort towards perfection; mere buoys that float on the waves. This reminds me that orthodox Buddhism is composed of two distinct religions: one, more rigorous and difficult, the other easier and more trivial: the Mahayana—"great vehicle" or "great path"— and the Hinayana—"lesser vehicle" or "lesser path." The decisive matter is

Source: José Ortega y Gasset, *The Revolt of the Masses* (New York: W.W. Norton and Company, 1957), pp. 11, 14-17, 18, 49-51, 91-92, 94.

whether we attach our life to one or the other vehicle, to a maximum or a minimum of demands upon ourselves.

The division of society into masses and select minorities is, then, not a division into social classes, but into classes of men, and cannot coincide with the hierarchic separation of "upper" and "lower" classes. It is, of course, plain that in these "upper" classes, when and as long as they really are so, there is much more likelihood of finding men who adopt the "great vehicle," whereas the "lower" classes normally comprise individuals of minus quality. But, strictly speaking, within both these social classes, there are to be found mass and genuine minority. As we shall see, a characteristic of our times is the predominance, even in groups traditionally selective, of the mass and the vulgar. Thus, in the intellectual life, which of its essence requires and pre-supposes qualification, one can note the progressive triumph of the pseudo-intellectual, unqualified, unqualifiable, and, by their very mental texture, disqualified. Similarly, in the surviving groups of the "nobility," male and female. On the other hand, it is not rare to find to-day amongst working men, who before might be taken as the best example of what we are calling "mass," nobly disciplined minds.

There exist, then, in society, operations, activities, and functions of the most diverse order, which are of their very nature special, and which consequently cannot be properly carried out without special gifts. For example: certain pleasures of an artistic and refined character, or again the functions of government and of political judgment in public affairs. Previously these special activities were exercised by qualified minorities, or at least by those who claimed such qualification. The mass asserted no right to intervene in them; they realised that if they wished to intervene they would necessarily have to acquire those special qualities and cease being mere mass. They recognised their place in a healthy dynamic social system.

If we now revert to the facts indicated at the start, they will appear clearly as the heralds of a changed attitude in the mass. They all indicate that the mass has decided to advance to the foreground of social life, to occupy the places, to use the instruments and to enjoy the pleasures hitherto reserved to the few. It is evident, for example, that the places were never intended for the multitude, for their dimensions are too limited, and the crowd is continuously overflowing; thus manifesting to our eyes and in the clearest manner the new phenomenon: the mass, without ceasing to be mass, is supplanting the minorities. . . .

. . . *The characteristic of the hour is that the commonplace mind, knowing itself to be commonplace, has the assurance to proclaim the rights of the commonplace and to impose them wherever it will.* As they say in the United States: "to be different is to be indecent." The mass crushes beneath it everything that is different, everything that is excellent, individual, qualified and select. Anybody who is not like everybody, who does not think like everybody, runs the risk of being eliminated. And it is clear, of course, that this "everybody" is not "everybody." "Everybody" was normally the complex unity of the mass and the divergent, specialised minorities. Nowadays, "everybody" is the mass alone. Here we have the formidable fact of our times, described without any concealment of the brutality of its features.

For Ortega, the new population growth had important consequences.

The key to this analysis is found when, returning to the starting-point of this essay, we ask ourselves: "Whence have come all these multitudes which nowadays fill to overflowing the stage of history?" . . .

The fact is this: from the time European history begins in the VIth Century up to the year 1800—that is, through the course of twelve centuries—Europe does not succeed in reaching a total population greater than 180 million inhabitants. Now, from 1800 to 1914—little more than a century—the population of Europe mounts from 180 to 460 millions! I take it that the contrast between these figures leaves no doubt as to the prolific qualities of the last century. In three generations it produces a gigantic mass of humanity which, launched like a torrent over the historic area, has inundated it. This fact, I repeat, should suffice to make us realise the triumph of the masses and all that is implied and announced by it. Furthermore, it should be added as the most concrete item to that rising of the level of existence which I have already indicated.

But at the same time this fact proves to us how unfounded is our admiration when we lay stress on the increase of new countries like the United States of America. We are astonished at this increase, which has reached to 100 millions in a century, when the really astonishing fact is the teeming fertility of Europe. Here we have another reason for correcting the deceptive notion of the Americanisation of Europe. Not even that characteristic which might seem specifically American—the rapidity of increase in population—is peculiarly such. Europe has increased in the last century much more than America. America has been formed from the overflow of Europe.

But although this fact . . . is not as well known as it should be, the confused idea of a considerable population increase in Europe was widespread enough to render unnecessary insistence on it. In the figures cited, then, it is not the increase of population which interests me, but the fact that by the contrast with the previous figures the dizzy rapidity of the increase is brought into relief. This is the point of importance for us at the moment. For that rapidity means that heap after heap of human beings have been dumped on to the historic scene at such an accelerated rate, that it has been difficult to saturate them with traditional culture. And in fact, the average type of European at present possesses a soul, healthier and stronger it is true than those of the last century, but much more simple. Hence, at times he leaves the impression of a primitive man suddenly risen in the midst of a very old civilisation. In the schools, which were such a source of pride to the last century, it has been impossible to do more than instruct the masses in the technique of modern life; it has been found impossible to educate them. They have been given tools for an intenser form of existence, but no feeling for their great historic duties; they have been hurriedly inoculated with the pride and power of modern instruments, but not with their spirit. Hence they will have nothing to do with their spirit, and the new generations are getting ready to take over command of the world as if the world were a paradise without trace of former footsteps, without traditional and highly complex problems. . . .

Ortega feared the growth of a new kind of primitivism in the modern era.

Advanced civilisation is one and the same thing as arduous problems. Hence, the greater the progress, the greater danger it is in. Life gets gradually better, but evidently also gradually more complicated. Of course, as problems become more complex, the means of solving them also become more perfect. But each new generation must master these perfected means. Amongst them—to come to the concrete—there is one most plainly attached to the advance of a civilisation, namely, that it have a great deal of the past at its back, a great deal of experience; in a word: history. Historical knowledge is a technique of the first order to preserve and continue a civilisation already advanced. Not that it affords positive solutions to the new aspect of vital conditions—life is always different from what it was—but that it prevents us committing the ingenuous mistakes of other times. But if, in addition to being old and, therefore, beginning to find life difficult, you have lost the memory of the past, and do not profit by experience, then everything turns to disadvantage. Well, it is my belief that this is the situation of Europe. The most "cultured" people to-day are suffering from incredible ignorance of history. I maintain that at the present day, European leaders know much less history than their fellows of the XVIIIth, even of the XVIIth Century. That historical knowledge of the governing minorities—governing *sensu lato*—made possible the prodigious advance of the XIXth Century. Their policy was thought out—by the XVIIIth Century—precisely in order to avoid the errors of previous politics, thought out in view of those errors and embraced in its substance the whole extent of experience. But the XIXth Century already began to lose "historic culture," although during the century the specialists gave it notable advance as a science. To this neglect is due in great part its peculiar errors, which to-day press upon us. In the last third of the century there began—though hidden from sight—that involution, that retrogression towards barbarism, that is, towards the ingenuousness and primitivism of the man who has no past, or who has forgotten it.

Hence, Bolshevism and Fascism, the two "new" attempts in politics that are being made in Europe and on its borders, are two clear examples of essential retrogression. Not so much by the positive content of their doctrine, which, taken in isolation, naturally has its partial truth—what is there in the universe which has not some particle of truth?—as on account of the *anti*-historic, anachronistic way in which they handle the rational elements which the doctrine contains. Typical movements of mass-men, directed, as all such are, by men who are mediocrities, improvised, devoid of a long memory and a "historic conscience," they behave from the start as if they already belonged to the past, as if, though occurring at the present hour, they were really fauna of a past age. . . .

Both Bolshevism and Fascism are two false dawns; they do not bring the morning of a new day, but of some archaic day, spent over and over again: they are mere primitivism. And such will all movements be which fall into the stupidity of starting a boxing-match with some portion or other of the past, instead of proceeding to digest it. No doubt an advance must be made on the liberalism of the XIXth Century. But this is precisely what cannot be done by any movement such as Fascism, which declares itself anti-liberal.

Because it was that fact—the being anti-liberal or non-liberal—which constituted man previous to liberalism. And as the latter triumphed over its opposite, it will either repeat its victory time and again, or else everything—liberalism and anti-liberalism—will be annihilated in the destruction of Europe. There is an inexorable chronology of life. In it liberalism is posterior to anti-liberalism, or what comes to the same, is more vital than it, just as the gun is more of a weapon than the lance. . . .

1. In what way did Ortega distinguish between "social classes" and "classes of men"?
2. What danger did the author see in the growing predominance of the "mass" in European society?
3. Account for Ortega's statement that the average European "leaves the impression of a primitive man suddenly risen in the midst of a very old civilisation."
4. Comment on Ortega's assertion that Fascism and Bolshevism were both primitive and anti-historic movements.

. . .

GEORGE ORWELL

George Orwell (1903-50) has come to be best known for his novels *Animal Farm* (1945) and *1984* (1949). During the period between the First and Second World Wars, Orwell worked in the British Imperial Civil Service and then wrote much fiction, literary criticism, and social commentary. Orwell became a democratic socialist and began his penetrating and relentless criticism of all systems, including fascism and bolshevism, which limited freedom and supported tyranny. He worried about the ability of liberal democracy to respond to contemporary problems, given the realities of the Depression. Orwell had great compassion for the poor, was opposed to the class system of his native Britain, and worked to expose and correct social problems.

Orwell wrote *The Road to Wigan Pier* in 1937, during the Great Depression, after having lived for some time among the poor mining class in England. He showed his compassion and honesty in detailing their lives, and insisted that the labour of the miners must be understood and counted in society.

> Watching coal-miners at work, you realize momentarily what different universes different people inhabit. Down there where coal is dug it is a sort of world apart which one can quite easily go through life without ever hearing about. Probably a majority of people would even prefer not to hear about it. Yet it is the absolutely necessary counterpart of our world above. Practically everything we do, from eating an ice to crossing the Atlantic, and from baking a loaf to writing a novel, involves the use of coal, directly or indirectly. For

Source: George Orwell, *The Road to Wigan Pier* (Harmondsworth: Penguin Books, 1962), pp. 29-31, 45-47, 64-65, 188-90, 202-204.

all the arts of peace coal is needed; if war breaks out it is needed all the more. In time of revolution the miner must go on working or the revolution must stop, for revolution as much as reaction needs coal. Whatever may be happening on the surface, the hacking and shovelling have got to continue without a pause, or at any rate without pausing for more than a few weeks at the most. In order that Hitler may march the goosestep, that the Pope may denounce Bolshevism, that the cricket crowds may assemble at Lord's, that the Nancy poets may scratch one another's backs, coal has got to be forthcoming. But on the whole we are not aware of it; we all know that we 'must have coal', but we seldom or never remember what coal getting involves. Here am I, sitting writing in front of my comfortable coal fire. It is April but I still need a fire. Once a fortnight the coal cart drives up to the door and men in leather jerkins carry the coal indoors in stout sacks smelling of tar and shoot it clanking into the coal-hole under the stairs. It is only very rarely, when I make a definite mental effort, that I connect this coal with that far-off labour in the mines. It is just 'coal'—something that I have got to have; black stuff that arrives mysteriously from nowhere in particular, like manna except that you have to pay for it. You could quite easily drive a car right across the north of England and never once remember that hundreds of feet below the road you are on the miners are hacking at the coal. Yet in a sense it is the miners who are driving your car forward. Their lamp-lit world down there is as necessary to the daylight world above as the root is to the flower.

It is not long since conditions in the mines were worse than they are now. There are still living a few very old women who in their youth have worked underground, with a harness round their waists and a chain that passed between their legs, crawling on all fours and dragging tubs of coal. They used to go on doing this even when they were pregnant. And even now, if coal could not be produced without pregnant women dragging it to and fro, I fancy we should let them do it rather than deprive ourselves of coal. But most of the time, of course, we should prefer to forget that they were doing it. It is so with all types of manual work; it keeps us alive, and we are oblivious of its existence. More than anyone else, perhaps, the miner can stand as the type of the manual worker, not only because his work is so exaggeratedly awful, but also because it is vitally necessary and yet so remote from our experience, so invisible, as it were, that we are capable of forgetting it as we forget the blood in our veins. In a way it is even humiliating to watch coal-miners working. It raises in you a momentary doubt about your own status as an 'intellectual' and a superior person generally. For it is brought home to you, at least while you are watching, that it is only because miners sweat their guts out that superior persons can remain superior. You and I and the editor of the *Times Lit. Supp.*, and the Nancy poets and the Archbishop of Canterbury and Comrade X, author of *Marxism for Infants*—all of us *really* owe the comparative decency of our lives to poor drudges underground, blackened to the eyes, with their throats full of coal dust, driving their shovels forward with arms and belly muscles of steel.

 Orwell's description of industrial towns recalled that of Dickens a century earlier.

As you walk through the industrial towns you lose yourself in labyrinths of little brick houses blackened by smoke, festering in planless chaos round miry alleys and little cindered yards where there are stinking dust-bins and lines of grimy washing and half-ruinous w.c.s. The interiors of these houses are always very much the same, though the number of rooms varies between two or five. All have an almost exactly similar living-room, ten or fifteen feet square, with an open kitchen range; in the larger ones there is a scullery as well, in the smaller ones the sink and copper are in the living-room. At the back there is the yard, or part of a yard shared by a number of houses, just big enough for the dustbin and the w.c. Not a single one has hot water laid on. You might walk, I suppose, through literally hundreds of miles of streets inhabited by miners, every one of whom, when he is in work, getting black from head to foot every day, without ever passing a house in which one could have a bath. It would have been very simple to install a hot-water system working from the kitchen range, but the builder saved perhaps ten pounds on each house by not doing so, and at the time when these houses were built no one imagined that miners wanted baths.

For it is to be noted that the majority of these houses are old, fifty or sixty years old at least, and great numbers of them are by any ordinary standard not fit for human habitation. They go on being tenanted simply because there are no others to be had. And that is the central fact about housing in the industrial areas: not that the houses are poky and ugly, and insanitary and comfortless, or that they are distributed in incredibly filthy slums round belching foundries and stinking canals and slag-heaps that deluge them with sulphurous smoke—though all this is perfectly true—but simply that there are not enough houses to go round. . . .

. . . But in the industrial areas the mere difficulty of getting hold of a house is one of the worst aggravations of poverty. It means that people will put up with anything—any hole and corner slum, any misery of bugs and rotting floors and cracking walls, any extortion of skinflint landlords and blackmailing agents—simply to get a roof over their heads. I have been into appalling houses, houses in which I would not live a week if you paid me, and found that the tenants had been there twenty and thirty years and only hoped they might have the luck to die there. In general these conditions are taken as a matter of course, though not always. Some people hardly seem to realize that such things as decent houses exist and look on bugs and leaking roofs as acts of God; others rail bitterly against their landlords; but all cling desperately to their houses lest worst should befall. So long as the housing shortage continues the local authorities cannot do much to make existing houses more livable. They can 'condemn' a house, but they cannot order it to be pulled down till the tenant has another house to go to; and so the condemned houses remain standing and are all the worse for being condemned, because naturally the landlord will not spend more than he can help on a house which is going to be demolished sooner or later. In a town like Wigan, for instance, there are over two thousand houses standing which have been condemned for years, and whole sections of the town would be condemned *en bloc* if there were any hope of other houses being built to replace them. Towns like Leeds and

Sheffield have scores of thousands of 'back to back' houses which are all of a condemned type but will remain standing for decades. . . .

I sometimes think that the price of liberty is not so much eternal vigilance as eternal dirt. There are some Corporation estates in which new tenants are systematically deloused before being allowed into their houses. All their possessions except what they stand up in are taken away from them, fumigated, and sent on to the new house. This procedure has its points, for it *is* a pity that people should take bugs into brand new houses (a bug will follow you about in your luggage if he gets half a chance), but it is the kind of thing that makes you wish that the word 'hygiene' could be dropped out of the dictionary. Bugs are bad, but a state of affairs in which men will allow themselves to be dipped like sheep is worse. Perhaps, however, when it is a case of slum clearance, one must take for granted a certain amount of restrictions and inhumanity. When all is said and done, the most important thing is that people shall live in decent houses and not in pigsties. I have seen too much of slums to go into . . . raptures about them. A place where the children can breathe clean air, and women have a few conveniences to save them from drudgery, and a man has a bit of garden to dig in, *must* be better than the stinking back-streets of Leeds and Sheffield. On balance, the Corporation Estates are better than the slums; but only by a small margin. . . .

 Orwell feared that fascism was on the rise. The solution was to consciously move to a humane form of socialism.

At present the situation is desperate. Even if nothing worse befalls us, there are the conditions which I described in the earlier part of this book and which are not going to improve under our present economic system. Still more urgent is the danger of Fascist domination in Europe. And unless Socialist doctrine, in an effective form, can be diffused widely and very quickly, there is no certainty that Fascism will ever be overthrown. For Socialism is the only real enemy that Fascism has to face. The capitalist-imperialist governments, even though they themselves are about to be plundered, will not fight with any conviction against Fascism as such. Our rulers, those of them who understand the issue, would probably prefer to hand over every square inch of the British Empire to Italy, Germany, and Japan than to see Socialism triumphant. It was easy to laugh at Fascism when we imagined that it was based on hysterical nationalism, because it seemed obvious that the Fascist states, each regarding itself as the chosen people and patriotic *contra mundum*, would clash with one another. But nothing of the kind is happening. Fascism is now an international movement, which means not only that the Fascist nations can combine for purposes of loot, but that they are groping, perhaps only half consciously as yet, towards a world-system. For the vision of the totalitarian state there is being substituted the vision of the totalitarian world. As I pointed out earlier, the advance of machine-technique must lead ultimately to some form of collectivism, but that form need not necessarily be equalitarian; that is, it need not be Socialism. *Pace* the economists, it is quite easy to imagine a world-society, economically collectivist—that is, with the profit principle eliminated—but with all political, military, and educational power in the hands of a small caste of rulers and their bravos. That or something like it is the objective of Fascism. And that, of course, is the slave-state, or rather the slave-world; it would probably be a stable form of society, and the chances are, considering the enormous wealth of the world if scientifically exploited, that the slaves would be well-fed and contented. It is usual to speak of the Fascist objective as the 'beehive state', which does a grave injustice to bees. A world of rabbits ruled by stoats would be nearer the mark. It is against this beastly possibility that we have got to combine.

The only thing *for* which we can combine is the underlying ideal of Socialism; justice and liberty. But it is hardly strong enough to call this ideal 'underlying'. It is almost completely forgotten. It has been buried beneath layer after layer of doctrinaire priggishness, party squabbles, and half-baked 'progressivism' until it is like a diamond hidden under a mountain of dung. The job of the Socialist is to get it out again. Justice and liberty! *Those* are the words that have got to ring like a bugle across the world. For a long time past, certainly for the last ten years, the devil has had all the best tunes. We have reached a stage when the very word 'Socialism' calls up, on the one hand, a picture of aeroplanes, tractors, and huge glittering factories of glass and concrete; on the other, a picture of vegetarians with wilting beards, of Bolshevik commissars (half gangster, half gramophone), of earnest ladies in sandals, shock-headed Marxists chewing polysyllables, escaped Quakers, birthcontrol fanatics, and Labour Party backstairs-crawlers. Socialism, at least in this island, does not smell any longer of revolution and the overthrow of tyrants; it smells of crankishness, machine-worship, and the stupid cult of Russia. Unless you can remove that smell, and very rapidly, Fascism may win.

To sum up: There is no chance of righting the conditions I described in the earlier chapters of this book, or of saving England from Fascism, unless we can bring an effective Socialist party into existence. It will have to be a party with genuinely revolutionary intentions, and it will have to be numerically strong enough to act. We can only get it if we offer an objective which fairly ordinary people will recognize as desirable. Beyond all else, therefore, we need intelligent propaganda. Less about 'class consciousness', 'expropriation of the expropriators', 'bourgeois ideology', and 'proletarian solidarity', not to mention the sacred sisters, thesis, antithesis, and synthesis; and more about justice, liberty, and the plight of the unemployed. And less about mechanical progress, tractors, the Dnieper dam, and the latest salmon-canning factory in Moscow; that kind of thing is not an integral part of Socialist doctrine, and it drives away many people whom the Socialist cause needs, including most of those who can hold a pen. All that is needed is to hammer two facts home into the public consciousness. One, that the interests of all exploited people are the same; the other, that Socialism is compatible with common decency.

As for the terribly difficult issue of class-distinctions, the only possible policy for the moment is to go easy and not frighten more people than can be helped. And above all, no more of those muscular-curate efforts at class-breaking. If you belong to the bourgeoisie, don't be too eager to bound forward and embrace your proletarian brothers; they may not like it, and if they show that they don't like it you will probably find that your class-prejudices are not so dead as you imagined. And if you belong to the proletariat, by birth or in the sight of God, don't sneer too automatically at the Old School Tie; it covers loyalties which can be useful to you if you know how to handle them.

Yet I believe there is some hope that when Socialism is a living issue, a thing that large numbers of Englishmen genuinely care about, the class-difficulty may solve itself more rapidly than now seems thinkable. In the next few years we shall either get that effective Socialist party that we need, or we shall not get it. If we do not get it, then Fascism is coming; probably a slimy Anglicized form of Fascism, with cultured policemen instead of Nazi gorillas and the lion and the unicorn instead of the swastika. But if we do get it there will be a struggle, conceivably a physical one, for our plutocracy will not sit quiet under a genuinely revolutionary government. And when the widely separate classes who, necessarily, would form any real Socialist party have fought side by side, they may feel differently about one another. And then perhaps this misery of class-prejudice will fade away, and we of the sinking middle class—the private schoolmaster, the half-starved free-lance journalist, the colonel's spinster daughter with £75 a year, the jobless Cambridge graduate, the ship's officer without a ship, the clerks, the civil servants, the commercial travellers, and the thrice-bankrupt drapers in the country towns—may sink without further struggles into the working class where we belong, and probably when we get there it will not be so dreadful as we feared, for, after all, we have nothing to lose but our aitches.

1. Write a review in which you compare the effectiveness of Orwell's description of the life and significance of the coal miners in *The Road to Wigan Pier* with the description of lives in Zola's *Germinal*.
2. To what extent do you agree with the suggestion that Orwell was the "Dickens" of his generation?
3. Based upon your reading of Mussolini and Hitler, evaluate Orwell's fears about the dangers of fascism.
4. What solutions did Orwell propose for the West? To what extent do they follow the democratic and liberal traditions?

■ ■ ■

BERTOLT BRECHT

Bertolt Brecht (1898-1956) was among the most influential playwrights of the twentieth century. A German, Brecht came to maturity during the inter-war years after having been horrified by his experiences as a medical orderly in the First World War. He became interested in Marxism and, during the 1930s worked with the Communist Party against the Nazis. All of Brecht's work dealt with the major social and political issues of his time. He is best known for *The Threepenny Opera* (1928), which he wrote with Kurt Weill, and for numerous long plays, including *The Life of Galileo* (1938).

◆A Brecht's *Galileo* is a parable about humanity, using the figure of Galileo as a means of working out the relationship between society, the individual conscience, and truth. Galileo, the great seventeenth century scientist, had insisted that the earth rotated around the sun, and as a result had many difficulties with church authorities. Brecht used the moment to discuss freedom and authority during the fascist period. In the following scene Galileo discusses his discoveries with his friend Sagredo.

SAGREDO *hesitates to approach the telescope*: I have a feeling very like fear, Galileo.

GALILEO: I am now going to show you one of the shining, milk-white clouds of the Galaxy. Tell me what it is composed of.

SAGREDO: Those are stars. Countless stars.

GALILEO: In the constellation of Orion alone there are five hundred fixed stars. Those are the many worlds, the numberless others, the further stars of which Giordano spoke. He did not see them; he predicted them.

SAGREDO: But even if the earth is a star, that's still a long way from the assertions of Copernicus that it revolves round the sun. There is no star in Heaven round which another one revolves. Except that the moon revolves round the earth.

GALILEO: Sagredo, I have been wondering. Since the day before yesterday I have been wondering. There is Jupiter. *He focuses on it*. There are four smaller stars close by it, which you can only see through the telescope. I saw them on Monday, but took no particular notice of their position. Yesterday I looked again. I could have sworn that all four had changed their position. I made a note of it. Now their position is different again. What's this? I saw four. *Excitedly*: Look! Look!

SAGREDO: I see three.

GALILEO: Where is the fourth? Here are the tables. We must calculate what movements they could have made.

They set to work excitedly. It grows dark on the stage, but on the circular horizon Jupiter and its satellites are still visible. When it becomes light again, Galileo and Sagredo are still sitting there, with their winter cloaks on.

GALILEO: It is proved. The fourth can only have gone behind Jupiter, where it cannot be seen. There you have a star round which another revolves.

SAGREDO: But the crystal sphere to which Jupiter is attached?

GALILEO: Yes, where is it now? How can Jupiter be attached to anything when other stars circle round it? There is no framework in Heaven, there is no fixity in the universe. There is another sun!

SAGREDO: Calm yourself. You think too quickly.

GALILEO: Quickly! Rouse yourself, man! What you have seen, no one has seen before.—They were right.

SAGREDO: Who? The Copernicans?

GALILEO: And the others! The whole world was against them, and they were right. This is something for Andrea! *Beside himself with excitement, he runs to the door and shouts*: Signora Sarti! Signora Sarti!

Source: Bertolt Brecht, *The Life of Galileo* (London: Methuen and Co. Ltd., 1963), pp. 39-42, 45-46, 68-72, 116-19.

SAGREDO: Galileo, calm yourself!

GALILEO: Sagredo, excite yourself! Signora Sarti!

SAGREDO *turns the telescope away*: Will you stop roaring around like a lunatic?

GALILEO: And will you stop standing there like a cod-fish—when the truth has been discovered.

SAGREDO: I am not standing like a cod-fish, but I tremble lest it may in fact be the truth.

GALILEO: What?

SAGREDO: Have you entirely lost your senses? Do you really no longer know what you are involved in, if what you see there is true? And you go shouting about for all the world to hear: that the earth is a star and not the centre of the universe.

GALILEO: Yes! And that the whole, vast universe with all its stars does not revolve round our tiny earth—as must be obvious to everyone.

SAGREDO: So that there are only stars there!—And where then is God?

GALILEO: What do you mean?

SAGREDO: God! Where is God?

GALILEO *angrily*: Not there! Any more than he could be found on earth, if there were beings up there and they were to seek him here!

SAGREDO: Then where *is* God?

GALILEO: Am I a theologian? I'm a mathematician.

SAGREDO: First and foremost, you are a man. And I ask you, where is God in your universe?

GALILEO: In us or nowhere.

SAGREDO *shouting*: As the heretic Giordano said?

GALILEO: As the heretic Giordano said.

SAGREDO: That was why he was burnt! Not ten years ago!

GALILEO: Because he could prove nothing. Because he only stated it.—Signora Sarti!

SAGREDO: Galileo, I have always regarded you as a shrewd man. For seventeen years in Padua and for three years in Pisa you patiently instructed hundreds of pupils in the Ptolemaic system which the Church supports and the Scriptures, on which the Church is founded, confirm. You thought it untrue, like Copernicus; but you taught it.

GALILEO: Because I could *prove* nothing.

SAGREDO *incredulously*: And you believe that makes a difference?

GALILEO: All the difference in the world! Look here, Sagredo. I believe in mankind, and that means I believe in its commonsense. Without that belief I should not have the strength to get up from my bed in the morning.

SAGREDO: Then I will tell you something. I do *not* believe in it. Forty years among men has consistently taught me that they are not amenable to commonsense. Show them the red tail of a comet, fill them with black terror, and they will all come running out of their houses and break their legs. But tell them one sensible proposition, and support it with seven reasons, and they will simply laugh in your face.

GALILEO: That is untrue—and a slander. I cannot understand how you, believing such a thing, can yet love science. Only the dead are no longer moved by reason.

SAGREDO: How can you confuse their miserable cunning with reason?

GALILEO: I am not speaking of their cunning. I know they call a donkey a horse when they want to sell, and a horse a donkey when they want to buy. That is their cunning. The old woman who, on the eve of a journey, gives her mule an extra bundle of hay with her horny hand; the mariner who, when laying in stores, thinks of storms and calms ahead; the child who pulls on his cap when it is proved to him that it may rain—they are my hope—they all listen to reason. Yes, I believe in the gentle power of reason, of commonsense, over men. They cannot resist it in the long run. No man can watch for long and see how I—*he lets fall a stone from his hand to the floor*—drop a stone, and then say: 'It does not fall'. No man is capable of that. The temptation offered by such a proof is too great. Most succumb to it, and in the long run—all. Thinking is one of the greatest pleasures of the human race. . . .

SAGREDO: Don't go to Florence, Galileo.

GALILEO: Why not?

SAGREDO: Because the monks are in control there.

GALILEO: At the Florentine court there are scholars of repute.

SAGREDO: Lackeys.

GALILEO: I will seize them by their necks and drag them in front of the telescope. Even monks are human, Sagredo. They succumb to the temptation of proof. Copernicus, don't forget, demanded that they believe his figures; but I only demand that they believe their eyes. If the truth is too weak to defend itself, it must go over to the attack. I will take hold of them and force them to look through that telescope.

SAGREDO: Galileo, I see you setting out on a fearful road. It is a night of disaster when a man sees the truth. And an hour of delusion when he believes in the commonsense of the human race. Of whom does one say 'he's going into it with his eyes open'? Of the man on the path to perdition. How could those in power leave at large a man who knows the truth, even though it be about the most distant stars? Do you think the Pope will hearken to your truth when you say he is in error, and yet not hear that he is in error? Do you think that *he* will simply write in his diary: January the tenth, 1610—Heaven abolished? How can you wish to leave the Republic, with the truth in your pocket, and fall into the snares of monks and princes, telescope in hand? Sceptical as you are in your science, you are as credulous as a child about everything that seems to you to facilitate your tasks. You don't believe in Aristotle, but you believe in the Grand Duke of Florence. A little while ago, when I watched you at your telescope and you saw those new stars, it seemed to me as if I saw you standing amid the blazing faggots, and when you said you believed in proof, I smelt flesh burning. I love science, but I love you more, my friend. Do not go to Florence, Galileo.

GALILEO: If they accept me, I will go. . . .

 Galileo is brought before the church authorities.

Enter Cardinal Ballarmin and Cardinal Barberini. In front of their faces they each hold a mask of a lamb and a dove respectively on the end of a stick.

BARBERINI *pointing his index finger at Galileo*: 'The sun also ariseth, and the sun goeth down, and hasteneth to his place where he arose.' So saith Ecclesiastes, the Preacher. And what says Galileo?

GALILEO: When I was so high, your Eminence—*he indicates with his hand*—I stood on a ship and I cried out: the shore is moving away! Today I know that the shore stood still and the ship moved away.

BARBERINI: Shrewd, shrewd. What one sees, Bellarmin, namely the constellations revolving, need not be true; think of the ship and the shore. But what is true, namely that the earth rotates, cannot be seen! Shrewd. But his moons of Jupiter are hard nuts for our astronomers to crack. Unfortunately, I too read some astronomy at one time, Bellarmin. It sticks to one like a burr.

BELLARMIN: Let us move with the times, Barberini. If star-charts based on a new hypothesis simplify navigation for our sailors, then let them use these charts. We only dislike teachings which contradict the Bible. *He waves in greeting towards the ballroom.*

GALILEO: The Bible.—'He that withholdeth corn, the people shall curse him.' Proverbs.

BARBERINI: 'Wise men lay up knowledge.' Proverbs.

GALILEO: 'Where no oxen are, the crib is clean; but much increase is by the strength of the ox.'

BARBERINI: 'He that ruleth his spirit is better than he that taketh a city.'

GALILEO: 'But a broken spirit drieth the house.' *Pause.* 'Doth not truth cry aloud?'

BARBERINI: 'Can one go upon hot coals and his feet not be burned?' Welcome in Rome, friend Galileo. You know her origin? Two little boys, so runs the legend, received milk and shelter from a she-wolf. From that hour on, all children have had to pay for the she-wolf's milk. But in return the she-wolf provides all sorts of pleasures, heavenly and earthly, ranging from conversations with my learned friend Bellarmin to the company of three or four ladies of international reputation. May I display them to you?

He leads Galileo to the rear, in order to show him the ballroom. Galileo follows reluctantly.

BARBERINI: No? He insists on a serious conversation. All right. Are you sure, friend Galileo, that you astronomers are not simply concerned with making your astronomy more manageable? *He leads him to the front again.* You think in terms of circles and ellipses and equal velocities, simple movements that your mind can grasp. But what if it had pleased God to make his stars move like this? *With his finger moving at varying speeds he describes in the air an extremely complicated track.*

GALILEO: Your Eminence, if God had constructed the universe like that—*he repeats Barberini's track*—then he would also have constructed our brains like that—*he repeats the same track*—so that they would recognise these very tracks as the simplest possible. I believe in reason.

BARBERINI: I hold reason to be inadequate.—He is silent. He is too polite to say now that he holds me to be inadequate. *He laughs and returns to the balustrade at the back.*

BELLARMIN: Reason, my friend, does not reach very far. All around we see nothing but crookedness, crime and weakness. Where is truth?

GALILEO *angrily*: I believe in reason.

BARBERINI *to the clerks*: There is no need to take this down. This is a scientific conversation between friends.

BELLARMIN: Consider for a moment all the trouble and thought it cost the Fathers of the Church, and so many after them, to bring a little sense into this world (is it not a little repellent?). Consider the brutality of the landlords in the Campagna who have their peasants whipped half-naked over their estates, and the stupidity of those poor people who kiss their feet in return.

GALILEO: Horrible! On my journey here I saw . . .

BELLARMIN: We have placed the responsibility for the meaning of such happenings as we cannot comprehend—life consists of them—on a higher Being, and we have explained that such things are the result of certain intentions, that all this happens according to one great plan. Not that this has brought about complete reassurance; but now you have to accuse this supreme Being of not knowing for certain how the stars move, a matter on which *you* are perfectly clear. Is that wise?

GALILEO *preparing to explain*: I am a true son of the Church . . .

BARBERINI: He is incorrigible. In all innocence he tries to prove God a complete fool on the subject of astronomy! Do you mean that God did not study astronomy sufficiently before he indited the Holy Scriptures? My dear friend!

BELLARMIN: Does it not appear probable to you that the Creator knows more about His own handiwork than does the handiwork itself?

GALILEO: But, gentlemen, man can misinterpret not only the movements of the stars, but the Bible too.

BELLARMIN: But the interpretation of the Bible is, after all, the business of the theologians of the Holy Church, eh?

Galileo is silent.

BELLARMIN: You see. You are silent now. *He makes a sign to the clerks.* Signor Galilei, tonight the Holy Office has decided that the teachings of Copernicus, according to which the sun is the centre of the universe and motionless, while the earth is not the centre of the universe and is moving, are futile, foolish and heretical. I have been entrusted with the duty of informing you of this decision. *To the first clerk*: Repeat that.

FIRST CLERK: His Eminence Cardinal Bellarmin to the aforementioned Galileo Galilei: The Holy Office has decided that the teachings of Copernicus, according to which the sun is the centre of the universe and motionless, while the earth is not the centre of the universe and is moving, are futile, foolish and heretical. I have been entrusted with the duty of informing you of this decision.

GALILEO: What does that mean?

From the ballroom can be heard boys' voices singing another verse of the poem:

'I said: the lovely season flieth fast;
So pluck the rose—it still is May.'

Barberini gestures Galileo to be silent while the song lasts. They listen.

GALILEO: But the facts? I understood that the astronomers of the Collegium Romanum had accepted my observations.

BELLARMIN: With the expression of the deepest satisfaction, which does you the greatest honour.

GALILEO: But the satellites of Jupiter, the phases of Venus . . .

BELLARMIN: The Holy Congregation has made its decision without considering these details.

GALILEO: That means that all further scientific research . . .

BELLARMIN: Is well assured, Signor Galilei. And that, in conformity with the Church's view that we cannot know, but we may research. *He again greets a guest in the ballroom.* You are at liberty to expound even this teaching through mathematical hypotheses. Science is the legitimate and dearly beloved daughter of the Church, Signor Galilei. Not one of us seriously believes that you desire to undermine the authority of the Church.

GALILEO *angrily*: Authority grows feeble from being abused.

BARBERINI: Does it? *He claps him on the shoulder, laughing loudly. Then he looks sharply at him and says, not unkindly*: Don't throw out the baby with the bath-water, friend Galileo. We don't do that either. We need you, more than you need us. . . .

 Galileo recants, and he reflects on his actions.

ANDREA: Then why did you recant?

GALILEO: I recanted because I was afraid of physical pain.

ANDREA: No!

GALILEO: I was shown the instruments.

ANDREA: So there was no plan?

GALILEO: There was none.

Pause.

ANDREA *loudly*: Science knows only one commandment: contribute to science.

GALILEO: And that I have done. Welcome to the gutter, brother in science and cousin in treachery! Do you eat fish? I've got fish. What stinks is not fish but me. I sell cheap; you are a buyer. Oh irresistible sight of a book, the sacred goods! Mouths water, and curses drown. The Great Babylonian, the murderous cow, the scarlet woman, opens her thighs and everything is different! Hallowed by our haggling, whitewashing, death-fearing society!

ANDREA: Fear of death is human! Human weaknesses are no concern of science.

GALILEO: No! My dear Sarti, even in my present situation I still feel capable of giving you a few tips about science in general, in which you have involved yourself.

A short pause.

GALILEO *academically, his hands folded over his stomach*: During my free hours, of which I have many, I have gone over my case and have considered how the world of science, in which I no longer count myself, will judge it. Even a wool-merchant, apart from buying cheaply and selling dear, must also be concerned that trade in wool can be carried on unhindered. In this respect the pursuit of science seems to me to require particular courage. It is concerned with knowledge, achieved through doubt. Making knowledge about everything available for everybody, science strives to make sceptics of them all. Now the greater part of the population is kept permanently by their princes, landlords and priests in a nacreous haze of superstition and outmoded words which obscure the machinations of these characters. The misery of the multitude is as old as the hills, and from pulpit and desk is proclaimed as immutable as the hills. Our new device of doubt delighted the great public, which snatched the telescope from our hands and turned it on its tormentors. These selfish and violent men, who greedily exploited the fruits of science to their own use, simultaneously felt the cold eye of science turned on a thousand-year-old, but artificial misery which clearly could be eliminated by eliminating them. They drenched us with their threats and bribes, irresistible to weak souls. But could we deny ourselves to the crowd and still remain scientists? The movements of the stars have become clearer; but to the mass of the people the movements of their masters are still incalculable. The fight over the measurability of the heavens has been won through doubt; but the fight of the Roman housewife for milk is ever and again lost through faith. Science, Sarti, is concerned with both battle-fronts. A humanity which stumbles in this age-old milky mist of superstition and outmoded words, too ignorant to develop fully its own powers, will not be capable of developing the powers of nature which you reveal. What are you working for? I maintain that the only purpose of science is to ease the hardship of human existence. If scientists, intimidated by self-seeking people in power, are content to amass knowledge for the sake of knowledge, then science can become crippled, and your new machines will represent nothing but new means of oppression. With time you may discover all that is to be discovered, and your progress will only be a progression away from mankind. The gulf between you and them can one day become so great that your cry of jubilation over some new achievement may be answered by a universal cry of horror. —I, as a scientist, had a unique opportunity. In my days astronomy reached the market-places. In these quite exceptional circumstances, the steadfastness of one man could have shaken the world. If only I had resisted, if only the natural scientists had been able to evolve something like the Hippocratic oath of the doctors, the vow to devote their knowledge wholly to the benefit of mankind! As things now stand, the best one can hope for is for a race of inventive dwarfs who can be hired for anything. Moreover, I am now convinced, Sarti, that I never was in real danger. For a few years I was as strong as the authorities. And I surrendered my knowledge to those in power, to use, or not to use, or to misuse, just as suited their purposes. *Virginia has entered with a dish and stops still.* I have betrayed my profession. A man who does what I have done cannot be tolerated in the ranks of science.

VIRGINIA: You have been received into the ranks of the faithful.

She walks forward and places the dish upon the table.

GALILEO: Right.—I must eat now.

Andrea holds out his hand. Galileo looks at his hand without taking it.

GALILEO: You yourself are a teacher, now. Can you bring yourself to take a hand such as mine? *He walks over to the table.* Someone passing through sent me geese. I still enjoy my food.

ANDREA: So you are no longer of the opinion that a new age has dawned?

GALILEO: I am. Take care when you go through Germany.—Hide the truth under your coat.

ANDREA *incapable of leaving*: With regard to your estimation of the author we were talking about, I don't know how to answer you. But I cannot believe that your murderous analysis will be the last word.

GALILEO: Many thanks, signor. *He begins to eat.*

VIRGINIA *showing Andrea out*: We do not care for visitors from the past. They excite him.

Andrea leaves. Virginia returns.

GALILEO: Have you any idea who could have sent the geese?

VIRGINIA: Not Andrea.

GALILEO: Perhaps not. What is the night like?

VIRGINIA *at the window*: Clear.

1. Contrast Galileo's belief in proof and reason with the silence and conformity demanded by authority.

2. "If scientists, intimidated by self-seeking people in power, are content to amass knowledge for the sake of knowledge, then science can become crippled, and your new machines will represent nothing but new means of oppression . . . and your progress will only be a progression away from mankind. The gulf between you and them can one day become so great that your cry of jubilation over some new achievement may be answered by a universal cry of horror." Comment on this statement of Galileo's in terms of the development and use of atomic weapons in 1945.

▪ ▪ ▪

JOHN MAYNARD KEYNES

John Maynard Keynes (1883-1946) became the most important economic theorist of capitalism since Adam Smith. Keynes believe that unbridled capitalism contributed to the problems of the Depression and that intervention by the state was necessary in order to prevent some of the problems he witnessed during the 1920s and 1930s. Keynes' *The General Theory of Employment, Interest and Money* (1935) effectively supported the interventionist policies of many democrats who, for social and political as well as economic reasons, wished to put an end to the notion that government ought to stay out of the economy. For Keynes, governments could foster employment and, through wise economic policies, increase wealth while pursuing policies related to ideas of social justice.

A Keynes was a member of the British group that attended the peace conference in Paris which produced the Treaty of Versailles at the end of the First World War. He believed the reparations clauses of the treaty would be harmful and therefore published his critique *The Economic Consequences of the Peace* in 1919.

For one who spent in Paris the greater part of the six months which succeeded the Armistice an occasional visit to London was a strange experience. England still stands outside Europe. Europe's voiceless tremors do not reach her. Europe is apart and England is not of her flesh and body. But Europe is solid with herself. France, Germany, Italy, Austria and Holland, Russia and Roumania and Poland, throb together, and their structure and civilization are essentially one. They flourished together, they have rocked together in a war, which we, in spite of our enormous contributions and sacrifices (like though in a less degree than America), economically stood outside, and they may fall together. In this lies the destructive significance of the Peace of Paris. If the European Civil War is to end with France and Italy abusing their momentary victorious power to destroy Germany and Austria-Hungary now prostrate, they invite their own destruction also, being so deeply and inextricably intertwined with their victims by hidden psychic and economic bonds. At any rate an Englishman who took part in the Conference of Paris and was during those months a member of the Supreme Economic Council of the Allied Powers, was bound to become, for him a new experience, a European in his cares and outlook. . . .

So far as possible, therefore, it was the policy of France to set the clock back and to undo what, since 1870, the progress of Germany had accomplished. By loss of territory and other measures her population was to be curtailed; but chiefly the economic system, upon which she depended for her new strength, the vast fabric built upon iron, coal, and transport must be destroyed. If France could seize, even in part, what Germany was compelled to drop, the inequality of strength between the two rivals for European hegemony might be remedied for many generations.

Hence sprang those cumulative provisions for the destruction of highly organized economic life which we shall examine in the next chapter.

This is the policy of an old man, whose most vivid impressions and most lively imagination are of the past and not of the future. He sees the issue in terms of France and Germany, not of humanity and of European civilization struggling forwards to a new order. The war has bitten into his consciousness somewhat differently from ours, and he neither expects nor hopes that we are at the threshold of a new age.

It happens, however, that it is not only an ideal question that is at issue. My purpose in this book is to show that the Carthaginian Peace is not *practically* right or possible. Although the school of thought from which it springs is aware of the economic factor, it overlooks, nevertheless, the deeper economic

Sources: John Maynard Keynes, *The Economic Consequences of the Peace* (New York: Harcourt, Brace and Howe, 1920), pp. 4-5, 35-37; John Maynard Keynes, *The General Theory of Employment, Interest and Money* (New York: Harcourt, Brace and World, Inc., 1935), pp. 372-73, 374, 377-78, 380-81.

tendencies which are to govern the future. The clock cannot be set back. You cannot restore Central Europe to 1870 without setting up such strains in the European structure and letting loose such human and spiritual forces as, pushing beyond frontiers and races, will overwhelm not only you and your "guarantees," but your institutions, and the existing order of your Society. . . .

B In *The General Theory of Employment, Interest and Money* Keynes reflected on social and governmental policies.

Since the end of the nineteenth century significant progress towards the removal of very great disparities of wealth and income has been achieved through the instrument of direct taxation—income tax and surtax and death duties—especially in Great Britain. Many people would wish to see this process carried much further, but they are deterred by two considerations; partly by the fear of making skilful evasions too much worth while and also of diminishing unduly the motive towards risk-taking, but mainly, I think, by the belief that the growth of capital depends upon the strength of the motive towards individual saving and that for a large proportion of this growth we are dependent on the savings of the rich out of their superfluity. Our argument does not affect the first of these considerations. But it may considerably modify our attitude towards the second. For we have seen that, up to the point where full employment prevails, the growth of capital depends not at all on a low propensity to consume but is, on the contrary, held back by it; and only in conditions of full employment is a low propensity to consume conducive to the growth of capital. Moreover, experience suggests that in existing conditions saving by institutions and through sinking funds is more than adequate, and that measures for the redistribution of incomes in a way likely to raise the propensity to consume may prove positively favourable to the growth of capital.

The existing confusion of the public mind on the matter is well illustrated by the very common belief that the death duties are responsible for a reduction in the capital wealth of the country. Assuming that the State applies the proceeds of these duties to its ordinary outgoings so that taxes on incomes and consumption are correspondingly reduced or avoided, it is, of course, true that a fiscal policy of heavy death duties has the effect of increasing the community's propensity to consume. But inasmuch as an increase in the habitual propensity to consume will in general (*i.e.* except in conditions of full employment) serve to increase at the same time the inducement to invest, the inference commonly drawn is the exact opposite of the truth.

Thus our argument leads towards the conclusion that in contemporary conditions the growth of wealth, so far from being dependent on the abstinence of the rich, as is commonly supposed, is more likely to be impeded by it. One of the chief social justifications of great inequality of wealth is, therefore, removed. . . .

For my own part, I believe that there is social and psychological justification for significant inequalities of incomes and wealth, but not for such large disparities as exist to-day. There are valuable human activities which require the motive of money-making and the environment of private wealth-ownership for their full fruition. Moreover, dangerous human proclivities can be canalised into comparatively harmless channels by the existence of opportunities for money-making and private wealth, which, if they cannot be satisfied in this way, may find their outlet in cruelty, the reckless pursuit of personal power and authority, and other forms of self-aggrandisement. It is better that a man should tyrannise over his bank balance than over his fellow-citizens; and whilst the former is sometimes denounced as being but a means to the latter, sometimes at least it is an alternative. But it is not necessary for the stimulation of these activities and the satisfaction of these proclivities that the game should be played for such high stakes as at present. Much lower stakes will serve the purpose equally well, as soon as the players are accustomed to them. The task of transmuting human nature must not be confused with the task of managing it. Though in the ideal commonwealth men may have been taught or inspired or bred to take no interest in the stakes, it may still be wise and prudent statesmanship to allow the game to be played, subject to rules and limitations, so long as the average man, or even a significant section of the community, is in fact strongly addicted to the money-making passion. . . .

In some other respects the foregoing theory is moderately conservative in its implications. For whilst it indicates the vital importance of establishing certain central controls in matters which are now left in the main to individual initiative, there are wide fields of activity which are unaffected. The State will have to exercise a guiding influence on the propensity to consume partly through its scheme of taxation, partly by fixing the rate of interest, and partly, perhaps, in other ways. Furthermore, it seems unlikely that the influence of banking policy on the rate of interest will be sufficient by itself to determine an optimum rate of investment. I conceive, therefore, that a somewhat comprehensive socialisation of investment will prove the only means of securing an approximation to full employment; though this need not exclude all manner of compromises and of devices by which public authority will co-operate with private initiative. But beyond this no obvious case is made out for a system of State Socialism which would embrace most of the economic life of the community. It is not the ownership of the instruments of production which it is important for the State to assume. If the State is able to determine the aggregate amount of resources devoted to augmenting the instruments and the basic rate of reward to those who own them, it will have accomplished all that is necessary. Moreover, the necessary measures of socialisation can be introduced gradually and without a break in the general traditions of society.

Our criticism of the accepted classical theory of economics has consisted not so much in finding logical flaws in its analysis as in pointing out that its tacit assumptions are seldom or never satisfied, with the result that it cannot solve the economic problems of the actual world. . . .

Whilst, therefore, the enlargement of the functions of government, involved in the task of adjusting to one another the propensity to consume and the inducement to invest, would seem to a nineteenth-century publicist or to a contemporary American financier to be a terrific encroachment on individualism, I defend it, on the contrary, both as the only practicable means of avoiding the destruction of existing economic forms in their entirety and as the condition of the successful functioning of individual initiative.

For if effective demand is deficient, not only is the public scandal of wasted resources intolerable, but the individual enterpriser who seeks to bring these resources into action is operating with the odds loaded against him. The game of hazard which he plays is furnished with many zeros, so that the players *as a whole* will lose if they have the energy and hope to deal all the cards. Hitherto the increment of the world's wealth has fallen short of the aggregate of positive individual savings; and the difference has been made up by the losses of those whose courage and initiative have not been supplemented by exceptional skill or unusual good fortune. But if effective demand is adequate, average skill and average good fortune will be enough.

The authoritarian state systems of to-day seem to solve the problem of unemployment at the expense of efficiency and of freedom. It is certain that the world will not much longer tolerate the unemployment which, apart from brief intervals of excitement, is associated—and, in my opinion, inevitably associated—with present-day capitalistic individualism. But it may be possible by a right analysis of the problem to cure the disease whilst preserving efficiency and freedom.

1. Write a response to Keynes' economic arguments concerning the consequence of World War I, from the point of view of one of the Western "victors."
2. How did Keynes argue that succession duties are beneficial to society in general?
3. What balance did Keynes advocate between individual initiative and the guiding influence of the government?
4. What final criticism did Keynes level at authoritarian states?

▪ ▪ ▪

MARTIN BUBER

Martin Buber (1878-1965), a Jewish religious philosopher was concerned with the relationship between human beings and God. He believed in the importance of personal relationships in defining one's own spirituality. Buber was a professor of religion at Frankfurt in Germany until his dismissal in 1933. He moved to Palestine in 1938, where he supported the establishment of a state in which Arabs and Jews would co-operate. Buber's work, especially his distinction between "I-You" and "I-It," had great influence in Judeo-Christian theology, as he stressed the daily encounter with God and the ethical dimensions of religion.

 In his work *I and Thou* (1923) Buber tried to find the divine in our relations with other human beings.

Basic words are spoken with one's being.

When one says You, the I of the word pair I-You is said, too.

When one says It, the I of the word pair I-It is said, too.

The basic word I-You can only be spoken with one's whole being.

The basic word I-It can never be spoken with one's whole being.

•

There is no I as such but only the I of the basic word I-You and the I of the basic word I-It.

When a man says I, he means one or the other. The I he means is present when he says I. And when he says You or It, the I of one or the other basic word is also present.

Being I and saying I are the same. Saying I and saying one of the two basic words are the same.

Whoever speaks one of the basic words enters into the word and stands in it.

•

The life of a human being does not exist merely in the sphere of goal-directed verbs. It does not consist merely of activities that have something for their object.

I perceive something. I feel something. I imagine something. I want something. I sense something. I think something. The life of a human being does not consist merely of all this and its like.

All this and its like is the basis of the realm of It.

But the realm of You has another basis.

•

Whoever says You does not have something for his object. For wherever there is something there is also another something, every It borders on other Its; It is only by virtue of bordering on others. But where You is said there is no something. You has no borders.

Whoever says You does not have something; he has nothing. But he stands in relation. . . .

•

The world as experience belongs to the basic word I-It.

The basic word I-You establishes the world of relation.

•

Three are the spheres in which the world of relation arises.

The first: life with nature. Here the relation vibrates in the dark and remains below language. The creatures stir across from us, but they are unable to come to us, and the You we say to them sticks to the threshold of language.

The second: life with men. Here the relation is manifest and enters language. We can give and receive the You.

The third: life with spiritual beings. Here the relation is wrapped in a cloud but reveals itself, it lacks but creates language. We hear no You and yet feel

Source: Material for this section is taken from Martin Buber, *I and Thou,* translated by Walter Kaufmann (New York: Charles Scribner's Sons, 1970), pp. 54-55, 56-57, 59-60, 155-57, 164-65.

addressed; we answer—creating, thinking, acting: with our being we speak the basic word, unable to say You with our mouth.

But how can we incorporate into the world of the basic word what lies outside language?

In every sphere, through everything that becomes present to us, we gaze toward the train of the eternal You; in each we perceive a breath of it; in every You we address the eternal You, in every sphere according to its manner. . . .

•

When I confront a human being as my You and speak the basic word I-You to him, then he is no thing among things nor does he consist of things.

He is no longer He or She, limited by other Hes and Shes, a dot in the world grid of space and time, nor a condition that can be experienced and described, a loose bundle of named qualities. Neighborless and seamless, he is You and fills the firmament. Not as if there were nothing but he; but everything else lives in *his* light.

Even as a melody is not composed of tones, nor a verse of words, nor a statue of lines—one must pull and tear to turn a unity into a multiplicity—so it is with the human being to whom I say You. I can abstract from him the color of his hair or the color of his speech or the color of his graciousness; I have to do this again and again; but immediately he is no longer You.

And even as prayer is not in time but time in prayer, the sacrifice not in space but space in the sacrifice—and whoever reverses the relation annuls the reality—I do not find the human being to whom I say You in any Sometime and Somewhere. I can place him there and have to do this again and again, but immediately he becomes a He or a She, an It, and no longer remains my You.

As long as the firmament of the You is spread over me, the tempests of causality cower at my heels, and the whirl of doom congeals.

The human being to whom I say You I do not experience. But I stand in relation to him, in the sacred basic word. Only when I step out of this do I experience him again. Experience is remoteness from You.

The relation can obtain even if the human being to whom I say You does not hear it in his experience. For You is more than It knows. You does more, and more happens to it, than It knows. No deception reaches this far: here is the cradle of actual life. . . .

•

⬦B⟩ Spirituality and action were part of the same experience for Buber. Religion was not a solitary, other-worldly affair.

People speak of the "religious man" as one who can dispense with all relationships to the world and to beings because the social stage that is allegedly determined from outside is supposed to have been transcended here by a force that works entirely from within. But two basically different notions are confused when people use the concept of the social: the community built of relation and the amassing of human units that have no relation to one another—the palpable manifestation of modern man's lack of relation. The bright edifice of community, however, for which one can be liberated even from the dungeon of "sociability," is the work of the same force that is alive in the relation between man and God. But this is not one relation among others; it is the universal relation into which all rivers pour without drying up for that reason. Sea and rivers—who would make bold to separate here and define limits? There is only the one flood from I to You, ever more infinite, the one boundless flood of actual life. One cannot divide one's life between an actual relationship to God and an actual I-It relationship to the world—praying to God in truth and utilizing the world. Whoever knows the world as something to be utilized knows God the same way. His prayers are a way of unburdening himself—and fall into the ears of the void. He—and not the "atheist" who from the night and longing of his garret window addresses the nameless—is godless.

It is said further that the "religious" man steps before God as one who is single, solitary, and detached insofar as he has also transcended the stage of the "ethical" man who still dwells in duty and obligation to the world. The latter is said to be still burdened with responsibility for the actions of agents because he is wholly determined by the tension between is and ought, and into the unbridgeable gap between both he throws, full of grotesquely hopeless sacrificial courage, piece upon piece of his heart. The "religious" man is supposed to have transcended this tension between world and God; the commandment for him is to leave behind the restlessness of responsibility and of making demands on himself; for him there is no longer any room for a will of one's own, he accepts his place in the Plan; any ought is dissolved in unconditional being, and the world, while still persisting, has lost its validity; one still has to do one's share in it but, as it were, without obligation, in the perspective of the nullity of all activity. Thus men fancy that God has created his world to be an illusion and his man to reel. Of course, whoever steps before the countenance has soared way beyond duty and obligation—but not because he has moved away from the world; rather because he has come truly close to it. Duties and obligations one has only toward the stranger: toward one's intimates one is kind and loving. When a man steps before the countenance, the world becomes wholly present to him for the first time in the fullness of the presence, illuminated by eternity, and he can say You in one word to the being of all beings. There is no longer any tension between world and God but only the one actuality. He is not rid of responsibility: for the pains of the finite version that explores effects he has exchanged the momentum of the infinite kind, the power of loving responsibility for the whole unexplorable course of the world, the deep inclusion in the world before the countenance of God. Ethical judgments, to be sure, he has left behind forever: "evil" men are for him merely those commended to him for a deeper responsibility, those more in need of love; but decisions he must continue to make in the depths of spontaneity unto death—calmly deciding ever again in favor of right action. Thus action is not null: it is intended, it is commanded, it is needed, it belongs to the creation; but this action no longer imposes itself upon the world, it grows upon it as if it were non-action. . . .

For Buber, encountering God meant being part of the world.

The encounter with God does not come to man in order that he may henceforth attend to God but in order that he may prove its meaning in action in the world. All revelation is a calling and a mission. But again and again man shuns actualization and bends back toward the revealer: he would rather attend to God than to the world. Now that he has bent back, however, he is no longer confronted by a You; he can do nothing but place a divine It in the realm of things, believe that he knows about God as an It, and talk about him. Even as the egomaniac does not live anything directly, whether it be a perception or an affection, but reflects on his perceiving or affectionate I and thus misses the truth of the process, thus the theomaniac (who, incidentally, can get along very well with the egomaniac in the very same soul) will not let the gift take full effect but reflects instead on that which gives, and misses both.

When you are sent forth, God remains presence for you; whoever walks in his mission always has God before him: the more faithful the fulfillment, the stronger and more constant the nearness. Of course, he cannot attend to God but he can converse with him. Bending back, on the other hand, turns God into an object. It appears to be a turning toward the primal ground, but belongs in truth to the world movement of turning away, even as the apparent turning away of those who fulfill their mission belongs in truth to the world movement of turning toward.

For the two basic metacosmic movements of the world—its expansion into its own being and returning to association [with God]—attain their supreme human form, the true spirit form of their struggle and conciliation, their mixture and separation, in the history of man's relation to God. It is in the return that the word is born on earth; in spreading out it enters the chrysalis of religion; in a new return it is reborn with new wings. . . .

1. How did Buber differentiate between the worlds of experience and relation as characterized by the expressions "I-It" and "I-You"?
2. Explain the movement from "You" to "He/She" in terms of the nature of the worlds of experience and relation.
3. Respond to Buber's statement that the relationship between man and God is "the universal relation into which all rivers pour without drying up for that reason."
4. Applying your understanding of the difference between the "I-You" and the "I-It" relationships, explain Buber's view on the purpose of man's encounter with God.

. . .

SIGMUND FREUD

Sigmund Freud (1856-1939) remained a prolific and creative writer until his death in London, where he lived after leaving Vienna following the Nazi takeover in 1938. Freud continually articulated and restructured his thought in an attempt at clarity and systematization. During this period, among other ideas, Freud worked on a theory of instincts, human sexuality, and his concepts of ego, id, and super-ego.

Freud delivered a series of lectures in Vienna from 1915-1917, which were collected as *A General Introduction to Psycho-Analysis*. In it, he discussed the opposition to his ideas.

> . . . There are two tenets of psycho-analysis which offend the whole world and excite its resentment; the one conflicts with intellectual, the other with moral and æsthetic prejudices. Let us not underestimate these prejudices; they are powerful things, residues of valuable, even necessary, stages in human evolution. They are maintained by emotional forces, and the fight against them is a hard one.
>
> The first of these displeasing propositions of psycho-analysis is this: that mental processes are essentially unconscious, and that those which are conscious are merely isolated acts and parts of the whole psychic entity. Now I must ask you to remember that, on the contrary, we are accustomed to identify the mental with the conscious. Consciousness appears to us as positively the characteristic that defines mental life, and we regard psychology as the study of the content of consciousness. This even appears so evident that any contradiction of it seems obvious nonsense to us, and yet it is impossible for psycho-analysis to avoid this contradiction, or to accept the identity between the conscious and the psychic. The psycho-analytical definition of the mind is that it comprises processes of the nature of feeling, thinking, and wishing, and it maintains that there are such things as unconscious thinking and unconscious wishing. But in doing so psycho-analysis has forfeited at the outset the sympathy of the sober and scientifically minded, and incurred the suspicion of being a fantastic cult occupied with dark and unfathomable mysteries. You yourselves must find it difficult to understand why I should stigmatize an abstract proposition, such as "The psychic is the conscious," as a prejudice; nor can you guess yet what evolutionary process could have led to the denial of the unconscious, if it does indeed exist, nor what advantage could have been achieved by this denial. It seems like an empty wrangle over words to argue whether mental life is to be regarded as coextensive with consciousness or whether it may be said to stretch beyond this limit, and yet I can assure you that the acceptance of unconscious mental processes represents a decisive step towards a new orientation in the world and in science.

Sources: Sigmund Freud, *A General Introduction to Psycho-Analysis* (New York: Liveright Publishing Corporation, 1963), pp. 22-24; Sigmund Freud, *Civilization and Its Discontents* (New York: W.W. Norton and Company, 1961), pp. 42-43, 90, 92.

As little can you suspect how close is the connection between this first bold step on the part of psycho-analysis and the second to which I am now coming. For this next proposition, which we put forward as one of the discoveries of psycho-analysis, consists in the assertion that impulses, which can only be described as sexual in both the narrower and the wider sense, play a peculiarly large part, never before sufficiently appreciated, in the causation of nervous and mental disorders. Nay, more, that these sexual impulses have contributed invaluably to the highest cultural, artistic, and social achievements of the human mind.

In my opinion, it is the aversion from this conclusion of psycho-analytic investigation that is the most significant source of the opposition it has encountered. Are you curious to know how we ourselves account for this? We believe that civilization has been built up, under the pressure of the struggle for existence, by sacrifices in gratification of the primitive impulses, and that it is to a great extent for ever being re-created, as each individual, successively joining the community, repeats the sacrifice of his instinctive pleasures for the common good. The sexual are amongst the most important of the instinctive forces thus utilized: they are in this way sublimated, that is to say, their energy is turned aside from its sexual goal and diverted towards other ends, no longer sexual and socially more valuable. But the structure thus built up is insecure, for the sexual impulses are with difficulty controlled; in each individual who takes up his part in the work of civilization there is a danger that a rebellion of the sexual impulses may occur, against this diversion of their energy. Society can conceive of no more powerful menace to its culture than would arise from the liberation of the sexual impulses and a return of them to their original goal. Therefore society dislikes this sensitive place in its development being touched upon; that the power of the sexual instinct should be recognized, and the significance of the individual's sexual life revealed, is very far from its interests; with a view to discipline it has rather taken the course of diverting attention away from this whole field. For this reason, the revelations of psycho-analysis are not tolerated by it, and it would greatly prefer to brand them as æsthetically offensive, morally reprehensible, or dangerous. But since such objections are not valid arguments against conclusions which claim to represent the objective results of scientific investigation, the opposition must be translated into intellectual terms before it can be expressed. It is a characteristic of human nature to be inclined to regard anything which is disagreeable as untrue, and then without much difficulty to find arguments against it. So society pronounces the unacceptable to be untrue, disputes the results of psycho-analysis with logical and concrete arguments, arising, however, in affective sources, and clings to them with all the strength of prejudice against every attempt at refutation.

But we, on the other hand, claim to have yielded to no tendency in propounding this objectionable theory. Our intention has been solely to give recognition to the facts as we found them in the course of painstaking researches. And we now claim the right to reject unconditionally any such introduction of practical considerations into the field of scientific investigation, even before we have determined whether the apprehension which attempts to force these considerations upon us is justified or not.

These, now, are some of the difficulties which confront you at the outset when you begin to take an interest in psycho-analysis . . . .

B One of Freud's last major works was *Civilization and Its Discontents* (1930). Here he reflected on the nature of civilization and its fragility.

... Perhaps we may begin by explaining that the element of civilization enters on the scene with the first attempt to regulate these social relationships. If the attempt were not made, the relationships would be subject to the arbitrary will of the individual: that is to say, the physically stronger man would decide them in the sense of his own interests and instinctual impulses. Nothing would be changed in this if this stronger man should in his turn meet someone even stronger than he. Human life in common is only made possible when a majority comes together which is stronger than any separate individual and which remains united against all separate individuals. The power of this community is then set up as 'right' in opposition to the power of the individual, which is condemned as 'brute force'. This replacement of the power of the individual by the power of a community constitutes the decisive step of civilization. The essence of it lies in the fact that the members of the community restrict themselves in their possibilities of satisfaction, whereas the individual knew no such restrictions. The first requisite of civilization, therefore, is that of justice—that is, the assurance that a law once made will not be broken in favour of an individual. This implies nothing as to the ethical value of such a law. The further course of cultural development seems to tend towards making the law no longer an expression of the will of a small community—a caste or a stratum of the population or a racial group—which, in its turn, behaves like a violent individual towards other, and perhaps more numerous, collections of people. The final outcome should be a rule of law to which all—except those who are not capable of entering a community—have contributed by a sacrifice of their instincts, and which leaves no one—again with the same exception—at the mercy of brute force.

The liberty of the individual is no gift of civilization. It was greatest before there was any civilization, though then, it is true, it had for the most part no value, since the individual was scarcely in a position to defend it. The development of civilization imposes restrictions on it, and justice demands that no one shall escape those restrictions. What makes itself felt in a human community as a desire for freedom may be their revolt against some existing injustice, and so may prove favourable to a further development of civilization; it may remain compatible with civilization. But it may also spring from the remains of their original personality, which is still untamed by civilization and may thus become the basis in them of hostility to civilization. The urge for freedom, therefore, is directed against particular forms and demands of civilization or against civilization altogether. It does not seem as though any influence could induce a man to change his nature into a termite's. No doubt he will always defend his claim to individual liberty against the will of the group. A good part of the struggles of mankind centre round the single task of finding an expedient accommodation—one, that is, that will bring happiness—between this claim of the individual and the cultural claims of the group; and one of the problems that touches the fate of humanity is whether such an accommodation can be reached by means of some particular form of civilization or whether this conflict is irreconcilable. ...

Civilization was hard-won for Freud, and was itself a source of much anxiety and unhappiness.

> . . . we are very often obliged, for therapeutic purposes, to oppose the super-ego, and we endeavour to lower its demands. Exactly the same objections can be made against the ethical demands of the cultural super-ego. It, too, does not trouble itself enough about the facts of the mental constitution of human beings. It issues a command and does not ask whether it is possible for people to obey it. On the contrary, it assumes that a man's ego is psychologically capable of anything that is required of it, that his ego has unlimited mastery over his id. This is a mistake; and even in what are known as normal people the id cannot be controlled beyond certain limits. If more is demanded of a man, a revolt will be produced in him or a neurosis, or he will be made unhappy. The commandment, 'Love thy neighbour as thyself', is the strongest defence against human aggressiveness and an excellent example of the unpsychological proceedings of the cultural super-ego. The commandment is impossible to fulfil; such an enormous inflation of love can only lower its value, not get rid of the difficulty. Civilization pays no attention to all this; it merely admonishes us that the harder it is to obey the precept the more meritorious it is to do so. But anyone who follows such a precept in present-day civilization only puts himself at a disadvantage *vis-à-vis* the person who disregards it. What a potent obstacle to civilization aggressiveness must be, if the defence against it can cause as much unhappiness as aggressiveness itself! 'Natural' ethics, as it is called, has nothing to offer here except the narcissistic satisfaction of being able to think oneself better than others. At this point the ethics based on religion introduces its promises of a better after-life. But so long as virtue is not rewarded here on earth, ethics will, I fancy, preach in vain. I too think it quite certain that a real change in the relations of human beings to possessions would be of more help in this direction than any ethical commands; but the recognition of this fact among socialists has been obscured and made useless for practical purposes by a fresh idealistic misconception of human nature. . . .

 Freud posed a fundamental dichotomy between instincts and civilization.

> The fateful question for the human species seems to me to be whether and to what extent their cultural development will succeed in mastering the disturbance of their communal life by the human instinct of aggression and self-destruction. It may be that in this respect precisely the present time deserves a special interest. Men have gained control over the forces of nature to such an extent that with their help they would have no difficulty in exterminating one another to the last man. They know this, and hence comes a large part of their current unrest, their unhappiness and their mood of anxiety. . . .

1. Apply Freud's contention that "it is a characteristic of human nature to regard anything which is disagreeable as untrue" to an analysis of the opposition to his theories.

2. Compare Freud's view of humanity in the state of nature with that of Hobbes, Locke, or Rousseau.
3. What impact did humanity's inclination towards aggression have on the organization of civilization?
4. Comment on Freud's view of the role of criticism in contemporary civilization.
5. Respond to Freud's argument that civilization currently demands the impossible of its members when it asks them to "love thy neighbour as thyself."
6. Comment on Freud's concluding paragraph in light of the brutal war fought in the six years following his death.

■ ■ ■

ANNE FRANK

Anne Frank (1929-45) was a young Jewish girl born in Germany. Her family left the country in 1933, after the Nazis came to power, and settled in Amsterdam, Holland. Germany invaded Holland in 1940 and then occupied the country throughout the Second World War. During the occupation the Germans began a systematic persecution of Jews in Holland: first there were anti-Jewish decrees; then in 1942, Jews were being shipped to camps in Germany. The Frank family went into hiding during this time, helped by business associates. Anne and her family were confined for two years to rooms at the top and back of a warehouse until, on August 4, 1944, their hiding place was discovered. During that time Anne, aged thirteen to fifteen, kept a diary which recorded her life, feelings, and growth. It has become a testament to the ability of the human spirit to survive and even flourish in the midst of hatred, persecution, and an enforced solitary life. Anne Frank was sent in 1944 by the Nazis to Auschwitz and then to Bergen-Belsen, where she died in March 1945.

 In 1942 and 1943 Anne recorded what she learned about the fate of fellow Jews.

> . . . I've only got dismal and depressing news for you today. Our many Jewish friends are being taken away by the dozen. These people are treated by the Gestapo without a shred of decency, being loaded into cattle trucks and sent to Westerbork, the big Jewish camp in Drente. Westerbork sounds terrible: only one washing cubicle for a hundred people and not nearly enough lavatories. There is no separate accommodations. Men, women, and children all sleep together. One hears of frightful immorality because of this: and a lot of the women, and even girls, who stay there any length of time are expecting babies.

Source: *Anne Frank: The Diary of a Young Girl*, translated by B.M. Mooyaart-Doubleday (New York: Pocket Books, 1953), pp. 34-35, 57, 71, 200-202, 216, 236-37.

It is impossible to escape; most of the people in the camp are branded as inmates by their shaven heads and many also by their Jewish appearance.

If it is as bad as this in Holland whatever will it be like in the distant and barbarous regions they are sent to? We assume that most of them are murdered. The English radio speaks of their being gassed.

Perhaps that is the quickest way to die. I feel terribly upset. I couldn't tear myself away while Miep told these dreadful stories; and she herself was equally wound up for that matter. Just recently for instance, a poor old crippled Jewess was sitting on her doorstep; she had been told to wait there by the Gestapo, who had gone to fetch a car to take her away. The poor old thing was terrified by the guns that were shooting at English planes overhead, and by the glaring beams of the searchlights. But Miep did not dare take her in; no one would undergo such a risk. The Germans strike without the slightest mercy. Elli too is very quiet: her boy friend has got to go to Germany. She is afraid that the airmen who fly over her home will drop their bombs, often weighing a million kilos, on Dirk's head. Jokes such as "he's not likely to get a million" and "it only takes one bomb" are in rather bad taste. Dirk is certainly not the only one who has to go: trainloads of boys leave daily. If they stop at a small station en route, sometimes some of them manage to get out unnoticed and escape; perhaps a few manage it. This, however, is not the end of my bad news. Have you ever heard of hostages? That's the latest thing in penalties for sabotage. Can you imagine anything so dreadful?

Prominent citizens, innocent people—are thrown into prison to await their fate. . . .

Everything has upset me again this morning, so I wasn't able to finish a single thing properly.

It is terrible outside. Day and night more of those poor miserable people are being dragged off, with nothing but a rucksack and a little money. On the way they are deprived even of these possessions. Families are torn apart, the men, women, and children all being separated. Children coming home from school find that their parents have disappeared. Women return from shopping to find their homes shut up and their families gone.

The Dutch people are anxious too, their sons are being sent to Germany. Everyone is afraid.

And every night hundreds of planes fly over Holland and go to German towns, where the earth is so plowed up by their bombs, and every hour hundreds and thousands of people are killed in Russia and Africa. No one is able to keep out of it, the whole globe is waging war and although it is going better for the Allies, the end is not yet in sight.

And as for us, we are fortunate. Yes, we are luckier than millions of people. It is quiet and safe here, and we are, so to speak, living on capital. We are even so selfish as to talk about "after the war," brighten up at the thought of having new clothes and new shoes, whereas we really ought to save every penny, to help other people, and save what is left from the wreckage after the war. . . .

If I just think of how we live here, I usually come to the conclusion that it is a paradise compared with how other Jews who are not in hiding must be

living. Even so, later on, when everything is normal again, I shall be amazed
to think that we, who were so spick and span at home, should have sunk to
such a low level. . . .

 In May 1944 Anne wrote of her growing sense of self.

> . . . As you can easily imagine we often ask ourselves here despairingly:
> "What, oh, what is the use of the war? Why can't people live peacefully
> together? Why all this destruction?"
>
> The question is very understandable, but no one has found a satisfactory
> answer to it so far. Yes, why do they make still more gigantic planes, still
> heavier bombs and, at the same time, prefabricated houses for reconstruction?
> Why should millions be spent daily on the war and yet there's not a penny
> available for medical services, artists, or for poor people?
>
> Why do some people have to starve, while there are surpluses rotting in
> other parts of the world? Oh, why are people so crazy?
>
> I don't believe that the big men, the politicians and the capitalists alone,
> are guilty of the war. Oh no, the little man is just as guilty, otherwise the
> peoples of the world would have risen in revolt long ago! There's in people
> simply an urge to destroy, an urge to kill, to murder and rage, and until all
> mankind, without exception, undergoes a great change, wars will be waged,
> everything that has been built up, cultivated, and grown will be destroyed
> and disfigured, after which mankind will have to begin all over again.
>
> I have often been downcast, but never in despair; I regard our hiding as a
> dangerous adventure, romantic and interesting at the same time. In my diary
> I treat all the privations as amusing. I have made up my mind now to lead
> a different life from other girls and, later on, different from ordinary house-
> wives. My start has been so very full of interest, and that is the sole reason
> why I have to laugh at the humorous side of the most dangerous moments.
>
> I am young and I possess many buried qualities; I am young and strong
> and am living a great adventure; I am still in the midst of it and can't grumble
> the whole day long. I have been given a lot, a happy nature, a great deal of
> cheerfulness and strength. Every day I feel that I am developing inwardly,
> that the liberation is drawing nearer and how beautiful nature is, how good
> the people are about me, how interesting this adventure is! Why, then, should
> I be in despair? . . .

 Anne was determined to keep her sense of life's worth.

> . . . The world has turned topsy-turvy, respectable people are being sent off
> to concentration camps, prisons, and lonely cells, and the dregs that remain
> govern young and old, rich and poor. One person walks into the trap through
> the black market, a second through helping the Jews or other people who've
> had to go "underground"; . . .
>
> We're going to be hungry, but anything is better than being discovered. . . .
>
> . . . "For in its innermost depths youth is lonelier than old age." I read this
> saying in some book and I've always remembered it, and found it to be true.

Is it true then that grownups have a more difficult time here than we do? No. I know it isn't. Older people have formed their opinions about everything, and don't waver before they act. It's twice as hard for us young ones to hold our ground, and maintain our opinions, in a time when all ideals are being shattered and destroyed, when people are showing their worst side, and do not know whether to believe in truth and right and God.

Anyone who claims that the older ones have a more difficult time here certainly doesn't realize to what extent our problems weigh down on us, problems for which we are probably much too young, but which thrust themselves upon us continually, until, after a long time, we think we've found a solution, but the solution doesn't seem able to resist the facts which reduce it to nothing again. That's the difficulty in these times: ideals, dreams, and cherished hopes rise within us, only to meet the horrible truth and be shattered.

It's really a wonder that I haven't dropped all my ideals, because they seem so absurd and impossible to carry out. Yet I keep them, because in spite of everything I still believe that people are really good at heart. I simply can't build up my hopes on a foundation consisting of confusion, misery, and death. I see the world gradually being turned into a wilderness, I hear the ever approaching thunder, which will destroy us too, I can feel the sufferings of millions and yet, if I look up into the heavens, I think that it will all come right, that this cruelty too will end, and that peace and tranquillity will return again.

In the meantime, I must uphold my ideals, for perhaps the time will come when I shall be able to carry them out.

1. Write a short personal essay on the nature of the human spirit in response to the following statement by Anne Frank: "It's really a wonder that I haven't dropped all my ideals, because they seem so absurd and impossible to carry out."

▪ ◇ ▪

CONTEMPORARY ISSUES & IDEAS: THE WEST SINCE 1945

A fter the Second World War the countries and peoples of Europe and the West had to rebuild much of their ideological base in addition to dealing with their societies and economies. The war ended with two nightmare visions: the freeing of prisoners from Nazi concentration camps—the realization of the calculated genocide of the Holocaust; and the awareness that in nuclear power, humanity now had the capacity to annihilate itself—as indicated when the atomic bombs were dropped on Hiroshima and Nagasaki.

The philosophy of existentialism grew more prominent as the search went on for new ways of defining humanity. Sartre and Camus insisted that human beings recognize that they shape themselves. They supported a quest for values which would be affirmations of life, even in the midst of pessimism and despair. Beckett, placing humanity on a bleak landscape, suggested that the journey of life must be undertaken, however difficult spiritually and psychically. Orwell and others warned about the growth and nature of totalitarian systems which would destroy our freedom to choose. Visual artists, such as Pollock and de Kooning, sought new directions for their works and freer modes of expression.

The Holocaust was acknowledged. Wiesel's work insisted on raising the most fundamental questions about life's meaning and the nature of the relationship between humanity and a deity. He was joined by many people from all faiths and regions. In the 1950s and 1960s, the aged Bertrand Russell became the symbol of attempts to control and eliminate nuclear weapons. He asked that humanity take a grand view of itself, as part of a history and a cosmos. Some politicians, including Kennedy, adopted Russell's themes and contributed to the establishment of treaties on arms control. Still, the nuclear reality continued, and Lipset and others have investigated its effects on society and the human psyche.

Human rights, of all sorts, became a prominent concern and they remain so today. Gandhi led the movement for Indian independence from colonial rule and King the civil rights movement in the United States. Both men practised and preached non-violent resistance to oppression. In the developed West, important issues were raised about Native rights and workers' rights. In the areas of colonialism, a challenge was made to the West to end its racism and the other practices associated with imperialism, while local peoples asserted their own independence. Women's rights were advanced through the feminist movement, and in all areas of the globe there was a questioning of traditional assumptions about the roles of the sexes in economics, society, and politics.

Often, contemporary theology raised issues pertaining to human rights, the philosophy of existentialism, and a consideration of the modern historical experience in the West. Bonhoeffer discussed the need to rethink the structure and fundamental concepts of Christianity, while Tillich investigated human nature in relationship to concepts of the divine. Others insisted that Europe and the West, in recognizing its history, must make a new commitment to help the poor as part of the recovery of an authentic theological framework.

Technology has come to be viewed by many as having a life of its own, an engine which has become the master of the civilization which developed it. Snow asked whether we now have two cultures, a scientific one and a humanistic one, each unable to communicate with or to inform the other. McLuhan investigated the nature of technology itself, in an effort to understand its full impact on our lives.

The issues persist, as humanity continues to grapple, sometimes better, sometimes worse, with the following important questions: Who are we? What are our values? What is true and what is beautiful? How should we organize our society and our government? How can we better understand our relationship to others and to the cosmos? What ought we to do with what we have inherited from the past? What ought we to do in the present? How might we shape the future?

EXISTENTIALISM

Existentialism, a philosophy with roots in the nineteenth century, became prominent after the Second World War. For existentialists, human beings have consciousness and will, but there is no absolute truth to which we can cling for certainty. Rather, we live in a world sometimes described as absurd and full of despair, one in which there is no fixed human nature. We are free to act, however, and through our acts we take responsibility for our ethics and our nature. Humans, existentialists believe, create their own nature, "existence precedes essence," and through choice we decide about our relationship to others and to an objective, uncaring universe. The reflections of existentialists about the human condition touched many who were seeking some philosophical grounding after the events of the first half of the twentieth century.

 In 1946 the French philosopher Jean-Paul Sartre (1905-80) delivered his lecture "Existentialism and Humanism," which helped to clarify the position of the leading existentialist of the time.

> . . . What do we mean by saying that existence precedes essence? We mean that man first of all exists, encounters himself, surges up in the world—and defines himself afterwards. If man as the existentialist sees him is not definable, it is because to begin with he is nothing. He will not be anything until later, and then he will be what he makes of himself. Thus, there is no human nature, because there is no God to have a conception of it. Man simply is. Not that he is simply what he conceives himself to be, but he is what he wills, and as he conceives himself after already existing—as he wills to be after that leap towards existence. Man is nothing else but that which he makes of himself. That is the first principle of existentialism. And this is what people

Sources: Jean-Paul Sartre, *Existentialism and Humanism* (London: Methuen and Co. Ltd., 1948), pp. 28-30, 33-34, 47, 48, 50; Albert Camus, *Resistance, Rebellion, and Death* (New York: The Modern Library, 1963), pp. 20-23; Albert Camus, *The Myth of Sisyphus and Other Essays* (New York: Alfred A. Knopf, 1955), pp. 119-23.

call its "subjectivity," using the word as a reproach against us. But what do we mean to say by this, but that man is of a greater dignity than a stone or a table? For we mean to say that man primarily exists—that man is, before all else, something which propels itself towards a future and is aware that it is doing so. Man is, indeed, a project which possesses a subjective life, instead of being a kind of moss, or a fungus or a cauliflower. Before that projection of the self nothing exists; not even in the heaven of intelligence: man will only attain existence when he is what he purposes to be. Not, however, what he may wish to be. For what we usually understand by wishing or willing is a conscious decision taken—much more often than not—after we have made ourselves what we are. I may wish to join a party, to write a book or to marry—but in such a case what is usually called my will is probably a manifestation of a prior and more spontaneous decision. If, however, it is true that existence is prior to essence, man is responsible for what he is. Thus, the first effect of existentialism is that it puts every man in possession of himself as he is, and places the entire responsibility for his existence squarely upon his own shoulders. And, when we say that man is responsible for himself, we do not mean that he is responsible only for his own individuality, but that he is responsible for all men. The word "subjectivism" is to be understood in two senses, and our adversaries play upon only one of them. Subjectivism means, on the one hand, the freedom of the individual subject and, on the other, that man cannot pass beyond human subjectivity. It is the latter which is the deeper meaning of existentialism. When we say that man chooses himself, we do mean that every one of us must choose himself; but by that we also mean that in choosing for himself he chooses for all men. For in effect, of all the actions a man may take in order to create himself as he wills to be, there is not one which is not creative, at the same time, of an image of man such as he believes he ought to be. To choose between this or that is at the same time to affirm the value of that which is chosen; for we are unable ever to choose the worse. What we choose is always the better; and nothing can be better for us unless it is better for all. If, moreover, existence precedes essence and we will to exist at the same time as we fashion our image, that image is valid for all and for the entire epoch in which we find ourselves. Our responsibility is thus much greater than we had supposed, for it concerns mankind as a whole. If I am a worker, for instance, I may choose to join a Christian rather than a Communist trade union. And if, by that membership, I choose to signify that resignation is, after all, the attitude that best becomes a man, that man's kingdom is not upon this earth, I do not commit myself alone to that view. Resignation is my will for everyone, and my action is, in consequence, a commitment on behalf of all mankind. Or if, to take a more personal case, I decide to marry and to have children, even though this decision proceeds simply from my situation, from my passion or my desire, I am thereby committing not only myself, but humanity as a whole, to the practice of monogamy. I am thus responsible for myself and for all men, and I am creating a certain image of man as I would have him to be. In fashioning myself I fashion man.

This may enable us to understand what is meant by such terms—perhaps a little grandiloquent—as anguish, abandonment and despair. As you will soon see, it is very simple. First, what do we mean by anguish? The existentialist frankly states that man is in anguish. His meaning is as follows—When a man commits himself to anything, fully realising that he is not only choosing what he will be, but is thereby at the same time a legislator deciding for the whole of mankind—in such a moment a man cannot escape from the sense of complete and profound responsibility. There are many, indeed, who show no such anxiety. But we affirm that they are merely disguising their anguish or are in flight from it. . . .

Dostoievsky once wrote "If God did not exist, everything would be permitted"; and that, for existentialism, is the starting point. Everything is indeed permitted if God does not exist, and man is in consequence forlorn, for he cannot find anything to depend upon either within or outside himself. He discovers forthwith, that he is without excuse. For if indeed existence precedes essence, one will never be able to explain one's action by reference to a given and specific human nature; in other words, there is no determinism—man is free, man *is* freedom. Nor, on the other hand, if God does not exist, are we provided with any values or commands that could legitimise our behaviour. Thus we have neither behind us, nor before us in a luminous realm of values, any means of justification or excuse. We are left alone, without excuse. That is what I mean when I say that man is condemned to be free. Condemned, because he did not create himself, yet is nevertheless at liberty, and from the moment that he is thrown into this world he is responsible for everything he does. The existentialist does not believe in the power of passion. He will never regard a grand passion as a destructive torrent upon which a man is swept into certain actions as by fate, and which, therefore, is an excuse for them. He thinks that man is responsible for his passion. Neither will an existentialist think that a man can find help through some sign being vouchsafed upon earth for his orientation: for he thinks that the man himself interprets the sign as he chooses. He thinks that every man, without any support or help whatever, is condemned at every instant to invent man. . . .

What is at the very heart and centre of existentialism, is the absolute character of the free commitment, by which every man realises himself in realising a type of humanity—a commitment always understandable, to no matter whom in no matter what epoch—and its bearing upon the relativity of the cultural pattern which may result from such absolute commitment. . . .

. . . In one sense choice is possible, but what is not possible is not to choose. I can always choose, but I must know that if I do not choose, that is still a choice. This, although it may appear merely formal, is of great importance as a limit to fantasy and caprice. For, when I confront a real situation—for example, that I am a sexual being, able to have relations with a being of the other sex and able to have children—I am obliged to choose my attitude to it, and in every respect I bear the responsibility of the choice which, in committing myself, also commits the whole of humanity. . . .

. . . Man makes himself; he is not found ready-made; he makes himself by the choice of his morality, and he cannot but choose a morality, such is the pressure of circumstances upon him. We define man only in relation to his commitments; it is therefore absurd to reproach us for irresponsibility in our choice. . . .

In the Second World War Albert Camus (1913-60) wrote his "Letters to a German Friend," reflections on why he believed it necessary to fight in the French resistance against the Nazis. He called it "a document emerging from the struggle against violence."

. . . For a long time we both thought that this world had no ultimate meaning and that consequently we were cheated. I still think so in a way. But I came to different conclusions from the ones you used to talk about, which for so many years now, you have been trying to introduce into history. I tell myself now that if I had really followed your reasoning, I ought to approve what you are doing. And this is so serious that I must stop and consider it, during this summer night so full of promises for us and of threats for you.

You never believed in the meaning of this world, and you therefore deduced the idea that everything was equivalent and that good and evil could be defined according to one's wishes. You supposed that in the absence of any human or divine code the only values were those of the animal world—in other words, violence and cunning. Hence you concluded that man was negligible and that his soul could be killed, that in the maddest of histories the only pursuit for the individual was the adventure of power and his only morality, the realism of conquests. And, to tell the truth, I, believing I thought as you did, saw no valid argument to answer you except a fierce love of justice which, after all, seemed to me as unreasonable as the most sudden passion.

Where lay the difference? Simply that you readily accepted despair and I never yielded to it. Simply that you saw the injustice of our condition to the point of being willing to add to it, whereas it seemed to me that man must exalt justice in order to fight against injustice, create happiness in order to protest against the universe of unhappiness. Because you turned your despair into intoxication, because you freed yourself from it by making a principle of it, you were willing to destroy man's works and to fight him in order to add to his basic misery. Meanwhile, refusing to accept that despair and that tortured world, I merely wanted men to rediscover their solidarity in order to wage war against their revolting fate.

As you see, from the same principle we derived quite different codes, because along the way you gave up the lucid view and considered it more convenient (you would have said a matter of indifference) for another to do your thinking for you and for millions of Germans. Because you were tired of fighting heaven, you relaxed in that exhausting adventure in which you had to mutilate souls and destroy the world. In short, you chose injustice and sided with the gods. Your logic was merely apparent.

I, on the contrary, chose justice in order to remain faithful to the world. I continue to believe that this world has no ultimate meaning. But I know that something in it has a meaning and that is man, because he is the only creature to insist on having one. This world has at least the truth of man, and our task is to provide its justifications against fate itself. And it has no justification but man; hence he must be saved if we want to save the idea we have of life. With your scornful smile you will ask me: what do you mean by saving man? And with all my being I shout to you that I mean not mutilating him and yet giving a chance to the justice that man alone can conceive.

This is why we are fighting. This is why we first had to follow you on a path we didn't want and why at the end of that path we met defeat. For your despair constituted your strength. The moment despair is alone, pure, sure of itself, pitiless in its consequences, it has a merciless power. That is what crushed us while we were hesitating with our eyes still fixed on happy images. We thought that happiness was the greatest of conquests, a victory over the fate imposed upon us. Even in defeat this longing did not leave us.

But you did what was necessary, and we went down in history. And for five years it was no longer possible to enjoy the call of birds in the cool of the evening. We were forced to despair. We were cut off from the world because to each moment of the world clung a whole mass of mortal images. For five years the earth has not seen a single morning without death agonies, a single evening without prisons, a single noon without slaughters. Yes, we had to follow you. But our difficult achievement consisted in following you into war without forgetting happiness. And despite the clamors and the violence, we tried to preserve in our hearts the memory of a happy sea, of a remembered hill, the smile of a beloved face. For that matter, this was our best weapon, the one we shall never put away. For as soon as we lost it we should be as dead as you are. But we know now that the weapons of happiness cannot be forged without considerable time and too much blood.

We had to enter into your philosophy and be willing to resemble you somewhat. You chose a vague heroism, because it is the only value left in a world that has lost its meaning. And, having chosen it for yourself, you chose it for everybody else and for us. We were forced to imitate you in order not to die. But we became aware then that our superiority over you consisted in our having a direction. Now that all that is about to end, we can tell you what we have learned—that heroism isn't much and that happiness is more difficult.

At present everything must be obvious to you; you know that we are enemies. You are the man of injustice, and there is nothing in the world that my heart loathes so much. But now I know the reasons for what was once merely a passion. I am fighting you because your logic is as criminal as your heart. And in the horror you have lavished upon us for four years, your reason plays as large a part as your instinct. This is why my condemnation will be sweeping; you are already dead as far as I am concerned. But at the very moment when I am judging your horrible behavior, I shall remember that you and we started out from the same solitude, that you and we, with all Europe, are caught in the same tragedy of the intelligence. And, despite yourselves, I shall still apply to you the name of man. In order to keep faith with ourselves, we are obliged to respect in you what you do not respect in others. . . .

Camus' essay "The Myth of Sisyphus" (1940) was for many a summary of the problems posed by the existentialists. Camus later said: "Although 'The Myth of Sisyphus' poses mortal problems, it sums itself up for me as a lucid invitation to live and to create, in the very midst of the desert."

The gods had condemned Sisyphus to ceaselessly rolling a rock to the top of a mountain, whence the stone would fall back of its own weight. They had thought with some reason that there is no more dreadful punishment than futile and hopeless labor.

If one believes Homer, Sisyphus was the wisest and most prudent of mortals. According to another tradition, however, he was disposed to practice the profession of highwayman. I see no contradiction in this. Opinions differ as to the reasons why he became the futile laborer of the underworld. To begin with, he is accused of a certain levity in regard to the gods. He stole their secrets. Ægina, the daughter of Æsopus, was carried off by Jupiter. The father was shocked by that disappearance and complained to Sisyphus. He, who knew of the abduction, offered to tell about it on condition that Æsopus would give water to the citadel of Corinth. To the celestial thunderbolts he preferred the benediction of water. He was punished for this in the underworld. Homer tells us also that Sisyphus had put Death in chains. Pluto could not endure the sight of his deserted, silent empire. He dispatched the god of war, who liberated Death from the hands of her conqueror.

It is said also that Sisyphus, being near to death, rashly wanted to test his wife's love. He ordered her to cast his unburied body into the middle of the public square. Sisyphus woke up in the underworld. And there, annoyed by an obedience so contrary to human love, he obtained from Pluto permission to return to earth in order to chastise his wife. But when he had seen again the face of this world, enjoyed water and sun, warm stones and the sea, he no longer wanted to go back to the infernal darkness. Recalls, signs of anger, warnings were of no avail. Many years more he lived facing the curve of the gulf, the sparkling sea, and the smiles of earth. A decree of the gods was necessary. Mercury came and seized the impudent man by the collar and, snatching him from his joys, led him forcibly back to the underworld, where his rock was ready for him.

You have already grasped that Sisyphus is the absurd hero. He *is*, as much through his passions as through his torture. His scorn of the gods, his hatred of death, and his passion for life won him that unspeakable penalty in which the whole being is exerted toward accomplishing nothing. This is the price that must be paid for the passions of this earth. Nothing is told us about Sisyphus in the underworld. Myths are made for the imagination to breathe life into them. As for this myth, one sees merely the whole effort of a body straining to raise the huge stone, to roll it and push it up a slope a hundred times over; one sees the face screwed up, the cheek tight against the stone, the shoulder bracing the clay-covered mass, the foot wedging it, the fresh start with arms outstretched, the wholly human security of two earth-clotted hands. At the very end of his long effort measured by skyless space and time without depth, the purpose is achieved. Then Sisyphus watches the stone rush down in a few moments toward that lower world whence he will have to push it up again toward the summit. He goes back down to the plain.

It is during that return, that pause, that Sisyphus interests me. A face that toils so close to stones is already stone itself! I see that man going back down with a heavy yet measured step toward the torment of which he will never know the end. That hour like a breathing-space which returns as surely as his suffering, that is the hour of consciousness. At each of those moments when he leaves the heights and gradually sinks toward the lairs of the gods, he is superior to his fate. He is stronger than his rock.

If this myth is tragic, that is because its hero is conscious. Where would his torture be, indeed, if at every step the hope of succeeding upheld him? The workman of today works every day in his life at the same tasks, and this fate is no less absurd. But it is tragic only at the rare moments when it becomes conscious. Sisyphus, proletarian of the gods, powerless and rebellious, knows the whole extent of his wretched condition: it is what he thinks of during his descent. The lucidity that was to constitute his torture at the same time crowns his victory. There is no fate that cannot be surmounted by scorn.

· · · · ·

If the descent is thus sometimes performed in sorrow, it can also take place in joy. This word is not too much. Again I fancy Sisyphus returning toward his rock, and the sorrow was in the beginning. When the images of earth cling too tightly to memory, when the call of happiness becomes too insistent, it happens that melancholy rises in man's heart: this is the rock's victory, this is the rock itself. The boundless grief is too heavy to bear. These are our nights of Gethsemane. But crushing truths perish from being acknowledged. Thus, Œdipus at the outset obeys fate without knowing it. But from the moment he knows, his tragedy begins. Yet at the same moment, blind and desperate, he realizes that the only bond linking him to the world is the cool hand of a girl. Then a tremendous remark rings out: "Despite so many ordeals, my advanced age and the nobility of my soul make me conclude that all is well." Sophocles' Œdipus, like Dostoevsky's Kirilov, thus gives the recipe for the absurd victory. Ancient wisdom confirms modern heroism.

One does not discover the absurd without being tempted to write a manual of happiness. "What! by such narrow ways—?" There is but one world, however. Happiness and the absurd are two sons of the same earth. They are inseparable. It would be a mistake to say that happiness necessarily springs from the absurd discovery. It happens as well that the feeling of the absurd springs from happiness. "I conclude that all is well," says Œdipus, and that remark is sacred. It echoes in the wild and limited universe of man. It teaches that all is not, has not been, exhausted. It drives out of this world a god who had come into it with dissatisfaction and a preference for futile sufferings. It makes of fate a human matter, which must be settled among men.

All Sisyphus' silent joy is contained therein. His fate belongs to him. His rock is his thing. Likewise, the absurd man, when he contemplates his torment, silences all the idols. In the universe suddenly restored to its silence, the myriad wondering little voices of the earth rise up. Unconscious, secret calls, invitations from all the faces, they are the necessary reverse and price of victory. There is no sun without shadow, and it is essential to know the night. The absurd man says yes and his effort will henceforth be unceasing. If there is a personal fate, there is no higher destiny, or at least there is but one which he concludes is inevitable and despicable. For the rest, he knows himself to be the master of his days. At that subtle moment when man glances backward over his life, Sisyphus returning toward his rock, in that slight pivoting he contemplates that series of unrelated actions which becomes his fate, created by him, combined under his memory's eye and soon sealed by his death. Thus, convinced of the wholly human origin of all that is human, a blind man eager to see who knows that the night has no end, he is still on the go. The rock is still rolling.

I leave Sisyphus at the foot of the mountain! One always finds one's burden again. But Sisyphus teaches the higher fidelity that negates the gods and raises rocks. He too concludes that all is well. This universe henceforth without a master seems to him neither sterile nor futile. Each atom of that stone, each mineral flake of that night-filled mountain, in itself forms a world. The struggle itself toward the heights is enough to fill a man's heart. One must imagine Sisyphus happy.

1. According to Sartre, "man simply is . . . [and] is nothing else but what he makes of himself." Discuss.
2. Create a short concrete analogy illustrating the existentialist belief that what one wills for oneself, one wills for all of humanity.
3. Respond to Sartre's statement that "if God does not exist . . . [then] man is condemned to be free."
4. Expand on Sartre's view of choice and commitment. Compare his viewpoint with that of Wiesel, or Gandhi, or Martin Luther King or Tillich.
5. Stage a dialogue or debate between Camus and his German "friend." Through the words of each participant, dramatize the progression of thought by each individual from a common beginning to such a disparate end.
6. "One must imagine Sisyphus happy." What a statement! Trace the existentialist reasoning that could equate a myth of eternal effort with the quest for happiness.

● ● ●

THE HOLOCAUST

It has been argued that the event which has had the most impact on the West in the twentieth century has been the Holocaust. During the Second World War the Nazis practiced genocide, systematically killing six million Jews, as well as many others, in concentration camps which became the sites of extermination chambers. The Holocaust, a word derived from a Greek term denoting the burning of everything, has become the symbol of humanity's capacity for inhumanity, for a racism and immorality thought to have been left behind by "civilized" society. Much literature has grown up around the Holocaust, which has confronted the meaning of the event in both secular and religious contexts.

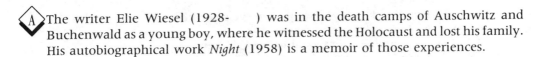

The writer Elie Wiesel (1928-   ) was in the death camps of Auschwitz and Buchenwald as a young boy, where he witnessed the Holocaust and lost his family. His autobiographical work *Night* (1958) is a memoir of those experiences.

The cherished objects we had brought with us thus far were left behind in the train, and with them, at last, our illusions.

Every two yards or so an SS man held his tommy gun trained on us. Hand in hand we followed the crowd.

An SS noncommissioned officer came to meet us, a truncheon in his hand. He gave the order:

"Men to the left! Women to the right!"

Eight words spoken quietly, indifferently, without emotion. Eight short, simple words. Yet that was the moment when I parted from my mother. I had not had time to think, but already I felt the pressure of my father's hand: we were alone. For a part of a second I glimpsed my mother and my sisters moving away to the right. Tzipora held Mother's hand. I saw them disappear into the distance; my mother was stroking my sister's fair hair, as though to protect her, while I walked on with my father and the other men. And I did not know that in that place, at that moment, I was parting from my mother and Tzipora forever. I went on walking. My father held onto my hand.

Behind me, an old man fell to the ground. Near him was an SS man, putting his revolver back in its holster.

My hand shifted on my father's arm. I had one thought—not to lose him. Not to be left alone.

The SS officers gave the order:

"Form fives!"

Commotion. At all costs we must keep together.

"Here, kid, how old are you?"

It was one of the prisoners who asked me this. I could not see his face, but his voice was tense and weary.

"I'm not quite fifteen yet."

"No. Eighteen."

"But I'm not," I said. "Fifteen."

"Fool. Listen to what *I* say."

Then he questioned my father, who replied.

"Fifty."

The other grew more furious than ever.

"No, not fifty. Forty. Do you understand? Eighteen and forty."

He disappeared into the night shadows. A second man came up, spitting oaths at us.

"What have you come here for, you sons of bitches? What are you doing here, eh?"

Someone dared to answer him.

Sources: Elie Wiesel, *Night* (New York: Avon Books, 1969), pp. 39-44, 74-76; *The Poetry of Yevgeny Yevtushenko, 1953 to 1965,* translated by George Reavey (New York: October House, Inc., 1965), pp. 145, 147, 149; Albert H. Friedlander, ed., *Out of the Whirlwind: A Reader of Holocaust Literature* (Garden City, New York: Doubleday and Company, Inc., 1968), pp. 516-17, 518-19.

"What do you think? Do you suppose we've come here for our own pleasure? Do you think we asked to come?"

A little more, and the man would have killed him.

"You shut your trap, you filthy swine, or I'll squash you right now! You'd have done better to have hanged yourselves where you were than to come here. Didn't you know what was in store for you at Auschwitz? Haven't you heard about it? In 1944?"

No, we had not heard. No one had told us. He could not believe his ears. His tone of voice became increasingly brutal.

"Do you see that chimney over there? See it? Do you see those flames? (Yes, we did see the flames.) Over there—that's where you're going to be taken. That's your grave, over there. Haven't you realized it yet? You dumb bastards, don't you understand anything? You're going to be burned. Frizzled away. Turned into ashes."

He was growing hysterical in his fury. We stayed motionless, petrified. Surely it was all a nightmare? An unimaginable nightmare?

I heard murmurs around me.

"We've got to do something. We can't let ourselves be killed. We can't go like beasts to the slaughter. We've got to revolt."

There were a few sturdy young fellows among us. They had knives on them, and they tried to incite the others to throw themselves on the armed guards.

One of the young men cried:

"Let the world learn of the existence of Auschwitz. Let everybody hear about it, while they can still escape. . . . "

But the older ones begged their children not to do anything foolish:

"You must never lose faith, even when the sword hangs over your head. That's the teaching of our sages. . . . "

The wind of revolt died down. We continued our march toward the square. In the middle stood the notorious Dr. Mengele (a typical SS officer: a cruel face, but not devoid of intelligence, and wearing a monocle); a conductor's baton in his hand, he was standing among the other officers. The baton moved unremittingly, sometimes to the right, sometimes to the left.

I was already in front of him:

"How old are you?" he asked, in an attempt at a paternal tone of voice.

"Eighteen." My voice was shaking.

"Are you in good health?"

"Yes."

"What's your occupation?"

Should I say that I was a student?

"Farmer," I heard myself say.

This conversation cannot have lasted more than a few seconds. It had seemed like an eternity to me.

The baton moved to the left. I took half a step forward. I wanted to see first where they were sending my father. If he went to the right, I would go after him.

The baton once again pointed to the left for him too. A weight was lifted from my heart.

We did not yet know which was the better side, right or left; which road led to prison and which to the crematory. But for the moment I was happy; I was near my father. Our procession continued to move slowly forward.

Another prisoner came up to us:

"Satisfied?"

"Yes," someone replied.

"Poor devils, you're going to the crematory."

He seemed to be telling the truth. Not far from us, flames were leaping up from a ditch, gigantic flames. They were burning something. A lorry drew up at the pit and delivered its load—little children. Babies! Yes, I saw it—saw it with my own eyes . . . those children in the flames. (Is it surprising that I could not sleep after that? Sleep had fled from my eyes.)

So this was where we were going. A little farther on was another and larger ditch for adults.

I pinched my face. Was I still alive? Was I awake? I could not believe it. How could it be possible for them to burn people, children, and for the world to keep silent? No, none of this could be true. It was a nightmare. . . . Soon I should wake with a start, my heart pounding, and find myself back in the bedroom of my childhood, among my books. . . .

My father's voice drew me from my thoughts:

"It's a shame . . . a shame that you couldn't have gone with your mother. . . . I saw several boys of your age going with their mothers. . . . "

His voice was terribly sad. I realized that he did not want to see what they were going to do to me. He did not want to see the burning of his only son.

My forehead was bathed in cold sweat. But I told him that I did not believe that they could burn people in our age, that humanity would never tolerate it. . . .

"Humanity? Humanity is not concerned with us. Today anything is allowed. Anything is possible, even these crematories. . . . "

His voice was choking.

"Father," I said, "if that is so, I don't want to wait here. I'm going to run to the electric wire. That would be better than slow agony in the flames."

He did not answer. He was weeping. His body was shaken convulsively. Around us, everyone was weeping. Someone began to recite the Kaddish, the prayer for the dead. I do not know if it has ever happened before, in the long history of the Jews, that people have ever recited the prayer for the dead for themselves.

"*Yitgadal veyitkadach shmé raba*. . . . May His Name be blessed and magnified. . . . " whispered my father.

For the first time, I felt revolt rise up in me. Why should I bless His name? The Eternal, Lord of the Universe, the All-Powerful and Terrible, was silent. What had I to thank Him for?

We continued our march. We were gradually drawing closer to the ditch, from which an infernal heat was rising. Still twenty steps to go. If I wanted to bring about my own death, this was the moment. Our line had now only fifteen paces to cover. I bit my lips so that my father would not hear my teeth chattering. Ten steps still. Eight. Seven. We marched slowly on, as though following a hearse at our own funeral. Four steps more. Three steps. There it was now, right in front of us, the pit and its flames. I gathered all that was left of my strength, so that I could break from the ranks and throw myself upon the barbed wire. In the depths of my heart, I bade farewell to my father, to the whole universe; and, in spite of myself, the words formed themselves and issued in a whisper from my lips: *Yitgadal veyitkadach shmé raba. . . .* May His name be blessed and magnified. . . . My heart was bursting. The moment had come. I was face to face with the Angel of Death. . . .

No. Two steps from the pit we were ordered to turn to the left and made to go into a barracks.

I pressed my father's hand. He said:

"Do you remember Madame Schächter, in the train?"

Never shall I forget that night, the first night in camp, which has turned my life into one long night, seven times cursed and seven times sealed. Never shall I forget that smoke. Never shall I forget the little faces of the children, whose bodies I saw turned into wreaths of smoke beneath a silent blue sky.

Never shall I forget those flames which consumed my faith forever.

Never shall I forget that nocturnal silence which deprived me, for all eternity, of the desire to live. Never shall I forget those moments which murdered my God and my soul and turned my dreams to dust. Never shall I forget these things, even if I am condemned to live as long as God Himself. Never.

The barracks we had been made to go into was very long. In the roof were some blue-tinged skylights. The ante-chamber of Hell must look like this. So many crazed men, so many cries, so much bestial brutality! . . .

The Kapo wanted to bandage the victim's eyes, but he refused.

After a long moment of waiting, the executioner put the rope round his neck. He was on the point of motioning to his assistants to draw the chair away from the prisoner's feet, when the latter cried, in a calm, strong voice:

"Long live liberty! A curse upon Germany! A curse . . . ! A cur—"

The executioners had completed their task.

A command cleft the air like a sword.

"Bare your heads."

Ten thousand prisoners paid their last respects.

"Cover your heads!"

Then the whole camp, block after block, had to march past the hanged man and stare at the dimmed eyes, the lolling tongue of death. The Kapos and heads of each block forced everyone to look him full in the face.

After the march, we were given permission to return to the blocks for our meal.

I remember that I found the soup excellent that evening. . . .

I witnessed other hangings. I never saw a single one of the victims weep. For a long time those dried-up bodies had forgotten the bitter taste of tears.

Except once. The Oberkapo of the fifty-second cable unit was a Dutchman, a giant, well over six feet. Seven hundred prisoners worked under his orders, and they all loved him like a brother. No one had ever received a blow at his hands, nor an insult from his lips.

He had a young boy under him, a *pipel*, as they were called—a child with a refined and beautiful face, unheard of in this camp.

(At Buna, the *pipel* were loathed; they were often crueller than adults. I once saw one of thirteen beating his father because the latter had not made his bed properly. The old man was crying softly while the boy shouted: "If you don't stop crying at once I shan't bring you any more bread. Do you understand?" But the Dutchman's little servant was loved by all. He had the face of a sad angel.)

One day, the electric power station at Buna was blown up. The Gestapo, summoned to the spot, suspected sabotage. They found a trail. It eventually led to the Dutch Oberkapo. And there, after a search, they found an important stock of arms.

The Oberkapo was arrested immediately. He was tortured for a period of weeks, but in vain. He would not give a single name. He was transferred to Auschwitz. We never heard of him again.

But his little servant had been left behind in the camp in prison. Also put to torture, he too would not speak. Then the SS sentenced him to death, with two other prisoners who had been discovered with arms.

One day when we came back from work, we saw three gallows rearing up in the assembly place, three black crows. Roll call. SS all round us, machine guns trained: the traditional ceremony. Three victims in chains—and one of them, the little servant, the sad-eyed angel.

The SS seemed more preoccupied, more disturbed than usual. To hang a young boy in front of thousands of spectators was no light matter. The head of the camp read the verdict. All eyes were on the child. He was lividly pale, almost calm, biting his lips. The gallows threw its shadow over him.

This time the Lagerkapo refused to act as executioner. Three SS replaced him.

The three victims mounted together onto the chairs.

The three necks were placed at the same moment within the nooses.

"Long live liberty!" cried the two adults.

But the child was silent.

"Where is God? Where is He?" someone behind me asked.

At a sign from the head of the camp, the three chairs tipped over.

Total silence throughout the camp. On the horizon, the sun was setting.

"Bare your heads!" yelled the head of the camp. His voice was raucous. We were weeping.

"Cover your heads!"

Then the march past began. The two adults were no longer alive. Their tongues hung swollen, blue-tinged. But the third rope was still moving; being so light, the child was still alive. . . .

For more than half an hour he stayed there, struggling between life and death, dying in slow agony under our eyes. And we had to look him full in the face. He was still alive when I passed in front of him. His tongue was still red, his eyes not yet glazed.

Behind me, I heard the same man asking:

"Where is God now?"

And I heard a voice within me answer him:

"Where is He? Here He is—He is hanging here on this gallows. . . . "

That night the soup tasted of corpses.

B The Russian poet Yevgeny Yevtushenko (1933-   ) wrote his powerful poem "Babii Yar" in 1961. Babii Yar, a ravine on the outskirts of the Russian city of Kiev, was the site in September 1941 of the systematic killing of over 30 000 Jews by the Germans who were then in control of the territory. The event was nearly forgotten until Yevtushenko's reminder, but the poem deals with anti-Semitism as a Western phenomenon, not exclusively tied to the Holocaust.

BABII YAR

No monument stands over Babii Yar.
A drop sheer as a crude gravestone.
I am afraid.
        Today I am as old in years
as all the Jewish people.
Now I seem to be
        a Jew.
Here I plod through ancient Egypt.
Here I perish crucified, on the cross,
and to this day I bear the scars of nails.
I seem to be
        Dreyfus.
The Philistine
        is both informer and judge.
I am behind bars.
        Beset on every side.
Hounded,
      spat on,
        slandered.
Squealing, dainty ladies in flounced Brussels lace
stick their parasols into my face.
I seem to be then
        a young boy in Byelostok.
Blood runs, spilling over the floors.
The bar-room rabble-rousers
give off a stench of vodka and onion.
A boot kicks me aside, helpless.
In vain I plead with these pogrom bullies.
While they jeer and shout,
        "Beat the Yids. Save Russia!"
some grain-marketeer beats up my mother.
O my Russian people!
      I know
        you
are international to the core.
But those with unclean hands
have often made a jingle of your purest name.

I know the goodness of my land.
How vile these antisemites—
                              without a qualm
they pompously called themselves
"The Union of the Russian People"!
I seem to be
              Anne Frank
transparent
              as a branch in April.
And I love.
              And have no need of phrases.
My need
              is that we gaze into each other.
How little we can see
                              or smell!
We are denied the leaves,
                              we are denied the sky.
Yet we can do so much—
                              tenderly
embrace each other in a dark room.
They're coming here?
                              Be not afraid. Those are the booming
sounds of spring:
                              spring is coming here.
Come then to me.
                              Quick, give me your lips.
Are they smashing down the door?
                                        No, it's the ice breaking . . .
The wild grasses rustle over Babii Yar.
The trees look ominous,
                              like judges.
Here all things scream silently,
                              and, baring my head,
slowly I feel myself
                              turning gray.
And I myself
              am one massive, soundless scream
above the thousand thousand buried here.
I am
       each old man
                       here shot dead.
I am
       every child
                       here shot dead.
Nothing in me
              shall ever forget!
The "Internationale", let it
                              thunder

when the last antisemite on earth
is buried forever.
In my blood there is no Jewish blood.
In their callous rage, all antisemites
must hate me now as a Jew.
For that reason
              I am a true Russian!

◀C▷ In 1965, shortly before his death, the Christian theologian Paul Tillich (1886-1965) engaged in conversation with Albert H. Friedlander about the meaning of the Holocaust. Friedlander recorded the conversation:

> "Shoah—a fascinating word," said Dr. Tillich. "I did not realize that there is already a technical vocabulary about what happened in those days: holocaust and Shoah. It is a Biblical word, of course: 'a devastating storm.' But you know, it is only one storm in the whole history of Jewish life. You must teach it as part of the other persecutions: the Inquisition, the Middle Ages—they are all part of the story."
>
> Dr. Tillich was offering me advice on a projected book that would try to teach aspects of the holocaust to Jewish high school students; and he was intensely interested in all phases of the project. We had first met at a civil rights rally in East Hampton; and the proximity of the synagogues to the Tillich place had made further conversations possible.
>
> "But *why* is this all part of the Jewish story?" I asked Dr. Tillich. "When our high school students turn to you as a friend—and as a Christian theologian viewing Jewish history—how will you answer their question: why did it happen to *us*?"
>
> We sat quietly for a while, pondering the question. Then, Tillich broke the silence.
>
> "I've been asked that question before," he said. "One of the judges in the Eichmann trial came to me when it was all over. He spent the whole day with me, asking the question in countless different ways. Week after week, he had been plowing through the material dealing with the destruction of European Jewry. And he felt the need for an answer that was not really mine to give."
>
> "You see," said Paul Tillich, "you cannot just ask: why did it happen to *us*? It happens to all, and it is still taking place. We do have particular questions about the nature of the world in which we live. And philosphy helps us analyze the structures of being which we encounter in every meeting with reality. But you asked an ultimate question. You asked about the meaning of this reality for us; and that is a question for theology. Now, there is the revelation in Judaism that gives you an answer; and there is the revelation in Christianity that helps me in understanding what happened. But we each have to reach our own answers; and while they will agree, your students must discover the answer of Judaism. Nevertheless, there are some answers that I can give, and that I have given before. They deal with the fact that Hitler represented everything to which Judaism was opposed, that Judaism simply had to be the opponent of the false nationalism which we find in National Socialism. . . .

The Jewish people, said Tillich, is uniquely the people of time. It represents the eternal fight between time and space. It stayed alive even when living space was constantly taken from it by the other nations of the world. Seen just as a people in space, it has had a tragic history; but seen as the people of time, it stands beyond tragedy, for it is an eternal people. It will always be persecuted (this applies also to the true Christian in the Church who fights the battle of time over space), because its mere existence challenges those pagan gods found within might, imperialism, injustice, demonic ecstasy—personified by the Nazi and similar groups. There will always be those who hate and fear the One God and those who follow Him. And there will always be the need for Israel to be the witness of the One God.

"Are you then saying," I asked Paul Tillich, "that Jews will always be persecuted? That this is God's will?"

Dr. Tillich shook his head.

"Remember what I said before. it happened to all, and it is still taking place. All Jews and Christians who believe in the One God and in universal justice have to confront this evil in the world. Church and synagogue must be united here in fighting for the realization of God's justice in history. Sometimes I talk about God's providence, by which I understand God's creative activity. And when I talk about God's justice, I mean this in the Hebrew sense: the word *tzedakah* must be understood as creative justice and not in the Aristotelian sense."

For some reason, we started to continue the discussion in German; perhaps, because Tillich was upset by the way in which the term "God" is used in any language.

"So many people," said Paul Tillich, "talk about *'der liebe Gott'* as though he were just a super-human figure who could do everything possible or impossible. There is so much primitive, perverted thinking about God by people who insist on seeing Him in man's image. God is not a kindly father-figure. He is the ground of all being, and His imprint is upon everything. *'Der liebe Gott'* who is all powerful does not exist: man's freedom is a limitation here that must be recognized if man is to assert himself and is to gain his victory over space. We should not ask: why does God permit suffering? Instead, we should recognize that there is that in the depth of our being which will enable us to challenge evil, to overcome suffering, to work for the fulfillment of the ultimate goal which is the goal of history. And part of Jewish suffering, and part of Jewish greatness, is that the Jew has historically aligned himself with universal justice, and has been the great opponent of evil. But have your students read the prophets: let them read Second Isaiah and Jeremiah." . . .

1. Contrast the deep despair expressed by Wiesel with the optimism of Anne Frank.
2. Comment on Wiesel's experience from the point of view of Sartre. How might Sartre have responded to the question, "Where is God now?"
3. What literary devices did Wiesel use to link his experiences with some of the important concepts in the Judaic and Christian tradition?
4. Discuss the ways in which Yevtushenko took the tragedy of Babii Yar and extended it into a universal condemnation of anti-Semitism.

5. Explain Tillich's definition of the difference between a people of time and one of space.
6. How might Tillich have answered Wiesel's question "Where is God now?"

. . .

HUMAN RIGHTS

Human rights remained in the foreground of issues that concerned the West. Many movements in North America and Europe stressed the importance of ending inequalities based upon race, origin, class, sex, or age. These movements often translated into social action, as groups rallied to press governments. Often, the issue of human rights remained the West's major intellectual link with the Enlightenment, as leading thinkers formulated their arguments in terms reminiscent of those used in the eighteenth century by *philosophes* in favour of a system protecting natural and political rights.

The leading figure in the civil rights movement for blacks in the United States was Martin Luther King (1929-68), a clergyman, who used the tactic of non-violent civil disobedience to press for equality. In 1963 King was arrested in Birmingham, Alabama. He wrote his "Letter from Birmingham Jail" as a reply to his critics and as a justification of his actions.

> . . . I cannot sit idly by in Atlanta and not be concerned about what happens in Birmingham. Injustice anywhere is a threat to justice everywhere. We are caught in an inescapable network of mutuality, tied in a single garment of destiny. Whatever affects one directly, affects all indirectly. Never again can we afford to live with the narrow, provincial "outside agitator" idea. Anyone who lives inside the United States can never be considered an outsider anywhere within its bounds.
>
> You deplore the demonstrations taking place in Birmingham. But your statement, I am sorry to say, fails to express a similar concern for the conditions that brought about the demonstrations. I am sure that none of you would want to rest content with the superficial kind of social analysis that deals merely with effects and does not grapple with underlying causes. It is unfortunate that demonstrations are taking place in Birmingham, but it is even more unfortunate that the city's white power structure left the Negro community with no alternative.

Sources: Martin Luther King, Jr. *Why We Can't Wait* (New York: Harper and Row, 1964), pp. 78-87; Thomas R. Berger, *Fragile Freedoms* (Toronto: Clarke Irwin and Company Limited, 1982), pp. 219-20, 251-54; Ajit Jain, ed., *Solidarity* (Baton Rouge, Louisiana: Oracle Press, 1983), pp. 179-81.

In any nonviolent campaign there are four basic steps: collection of the facts to determine whether injustices exist; negotiation; self-purification; and direct action. We have gone through all these steps in Birmingham. There can be no gainsaying the fact that racial injustice engulfs this community. Birmingham is probably the most thoroughly segregated city in the United States. Its ugly record of brutality is widely known. Negroes have experienced grossly unjust treatment in the courts. There have been more unsolved bombings of Negro homes and churches in Birmingham than in any other city in the nation. These are the hard, brutal facts of the case. On the basis of these conditions, Negro leaders sought to negotiate with the city fathers. But the latter consistently refused to engage in good-faith negotiation.

Then, last September, came the opportunity to talk with leaders of Birmingham's economic community. In the course of the negotiations, certain promises were made by the merchants—for example, to remove the stores' humiliating racial signs. On the basis of these promises, the Reverend Fred Shuttlesworth and the leaders of the Alabama Christian Movement for Human Rights agreed to a moratorium on all demonstrations. As the weeks and months went by, we realized that we were the victims of a broken promise. A few signs, briefly removed, returned; the others remained.

As in so many past experiences, our hopes had been blasted, and the shadow of deep disappointment settled upon us. We had no alternative except to prepare for direct action, whereby we would present our very bodies as a means of laying our case before the conscience of the local and the national community. Mindful of the difficulties involved, we decided to undertake a process of self-purification. We began a series of workshops on nonviolence, and we repeatedly asked ourselves: "Are you able to accept blows without retaliating?" "Are you able to endure the ordeal of jail?" We decided to schedule our direct-action program for the Easter season, realizing that except for Christmas, this is the main shopping period of the year. Knowing that a strong economic-withdrawal program would be the by-product of direct action, we felt that this would be the best time to bring pressure to bear on the merchants for the needed change.

Then it occurred to us that Birmingham's mayoral election was coming up in March, and we speedily decided to postpone action until after election day. When we discovered that the Commissioner of Public Safety, Eugene "Bull" Connor, had piled up enough votes to be in the run-off, we decided again to postpone action until the day after the run-off so that the demonstrations could not be used to cloud the issues. Like many others, we waited to see Mr. Connor defeated, and to this end we endured postponement after postponement. Having aided in this community need, we felt that our direct-action program could be delayed no longer.

You may well ask: "Why direct action? Why sit-ins, marches and so forth? Isn't negotiation a better path?" You are quite right in calling for negotiation. Indeed, this is the very purpose of direct action. Nonviolent direct action seeks to create such a crisis and foster such a tension that a community which has constantly refused to negotiate is forced to confront the issue. It seeks so to dramatize the issue that it can no longer be ignored. My citing the creation of tension as part of the work of the nonviolent-resister may sound rather shocking. But I must confess that I am not afraid of the word "tension." I have earnestly opposed violent tension, but there is a type of constructive, non-violent tension which is necessary for growth. Just as Socrates felt that it was necessary to create a tension in the mind so that individuals could rise from the bondage of myths and half-truths to the unfettered realm of creative analysis and objective appraisal, so must we see the need for nonviolent gadflies to create the kind of tension in society that will help men rise from the dark depths of prejudice and racism to the majestic heights of understanding and brotherhood.

The purpose of our direct-action program is to create a situation so crisis-packed that it will inevitably open the door to negotiation. I therefore concur with you in your call for negotiation. Too long has our beloved Southland been bogged down in a tragic effort to live in monologue rather than dialogue .

One of the basic points in your statement is that the action that I and my associates have taken in Birmingham is untimely. Some have asked: ''Why didn't you give the new city administration time to act?'' The only answer that I can give to this query is that the new Birmingham administration must be prodded about as much as the outgoing one, before it will act. We are sadly mistaken if we feel that the election of Albert Boutwell as mayor will bring the millennium to Birmingham. While Mr. Boutwell is a much more gentle person than Mr. Connor, they are both segregationists, dedicated to maintenance of the status quo. I have hope that Mr. Boutwell will be reasonable enough to see the futility of massive resistance to desegregation. But he will not see this without pressure from devotees of civil rights. My friends, I must say to you that we have not made a single gain in civil rights without determined legal and nonviolent pressure. Lamentably, it is an historical fact that privileged groups seldom give up their privileges voluntarily. Individuals may see the moral light and voluntarily give up their unjust posture; but, as Reinhold Niebuhr has reminded us, groups tend to be more immoral than individuals.

We know through painful experience that freedom is never voluntarily given by the oppressor; it must be demanded by the oppressed. Frankly, I have yet to engage in a direct-action campaign that was ''well timed'' in the view of those who have not suffered unduly from the disease of segregation. For years now I have heard the word ''Wait!'' It rings in the ear of every Negro with piercing familiarity. This ''Wait'' has almost always meant ''Never.'' We must come to see, with one of our distinguished jurists, that ''justice too long delayed is justice denied.''

We have waited for more than 340 years for our constitutional and God-given rights. The nations of Asia and Africa are moving with jetlike speed toward gaining political independence, but we still creep at horse-and-buggy pace toward gaining a cup of coffee at a lunch counter. Perhaps it is easy for those who have never felt the stinging darts of segregation to say, ''Wait.'' But when you have seen vicious mobs lynch your mothers and fathers at will and drown your sisters and brothers at whim; when you have seen hate-filled policemen curse, kick and even kill your black brothers and sisters; when you see the vast majority of your twenty million Negro brothers smothering in an airtight cage of poverty in the midst of an affluent society; when you suddenly find your tongue twisted and your speech stammering as you seek to explain to your six-year-old daughter why she can't go to the public amusement park that has just been advertised on television, and see tears welling up in her eyes when she is told that Funtown is closed to colored children, and see ominous clouds of inferiority beginning to form in her little mental sky, and see her beginning to distort her personality by developing an unconscious bitterness toward white people; when you have to concoct an answer for a five-year-old son who is asking: "Daddy, why do white people treat colored people so mean?"; when you take a cross-country drive and find it necessary to sleep night after night in the uncomfortable corners of your automobile because no motel will accept you; when you are humiliated day in and day out by nagging signs reading "white" and "colored"; when your first name becomes "nigger," your middle name becomes "boy" (however old you are) and your last name becomes "John," and your wife and mother are never given the respected title "Mrs."; when you are harried by day and haunted by night by the fact that you are a Negro, living constantly at tiptoe stance, never quite knowing what to expect next, and are plagued with inner fears and outer resentments; when you are forever fighting a degenerating sense of "nobodiness"—then you will understand why we find it difficult to wait. There comes a time when the cup of endurance runs over, and men are no longer willing to be plunged into the abyss of despair. I hope, sirs, you can understand our legitimate and unavoidable impatience.

You express a great deal of anxiety over our willingness to break laws. This is certainly a legitimate concern. Since we so diligently urge people to obey the Supreme Court's decision of 1954 outlawing segregation in the public schools, at first glance it may seem rather paradoxical for us consciously to break laws. One may well ask: "How can you advocate breaking some laws and obeying others?" The answer lies in the fact that there are two types of laws: just and unjust. I would be the first to advocate obeying just laws. One has not only a legal but a moral responsibility to obey just laws. Conversely, one has a moral responsibility to disobey unjust laws. I would agree with St. Augustine that "an unjust law is no law at all."

Now, what is the difference between the two? How does one determine whether a law is just or unjust? A just law is a man-made code that squares with the moral law or the law of God. An unjust law is a code that is out of harmony with the moral law. To put it in terms of St. Thomas Aquinas: An unjust law is a human law that is not rooted in eternal law and natural law. Any law that uplifts human personality is just. Any law that degrades human personality is unjust. All segregation statutes are unjust because segregation distorts the soul and damages the personality. It gives the segregator a false sense of superiority and the segregated a false sense of inferiority. Segregation, to use the terminology of the Jewish philospher Martin Buber, substitutes an "I-it" relationship for an "I-thou" relationship and ends up relegating persons to the status of things. Hence segregation is not only politically, economically and sociologically unsound, it is morally wrong and sinful. Paul Tillich has said that sin is separation. Is not segregation an existential expression of man's tragic separation, his awful estrangement, his terrible sinfulness? Thus it is that I can urge men to obey the 1954 decision of the Supreme Court, for it is morally right; and I can urge them to disobey segregation ordinances, for they are morally wrong.

Let us consider a more concrete example of just and unjust laws. An unjust law is a code that a numerical or power majority group compels a minority group to obey but does not make binding on itself. This is *difference* made legal. By the same token, a just law is a code that a majority compels a minority to follow and that it is willing to follow itself. This is *sameness* made legal.

Let me give another explanation. A law is unjust if it is inflicted on a minority that, as a result of being denied the right to vote, had no part in enacting or devising the law. Who can say that the legislature of Alabama which set up that state's segregation laws was democratically elected? Throughout Alabama all sorts of devious methods are used to prevent Negroes from becoming registered voters, and there are some counties in which, even though Negroes constitute a majority of the population, not a single Negro is registered. Can any law enacted under such circumstances be considered democratically structured?

Sometimes a law is just on its face and unjust in its application. For instance, I have been arrested on a charge of parading without a permit. Now, there is nothing wrong in having an ordinance which requires a permit for a parade. But such an ordinance becomes unjust when it is used to maintain segregation and to deny citizens the First-Amendment privilege of peaceful assembly and protest.

I hope you are able to see the distinction I am trying to point out. In no sense do I advocate evading or defying the law, as would the rabid segregationist. That would lead to anarchy. One who breaks an unjust law must do so openly, lovingly, and with a willingness to accept the penalty. I submit that an individual who breaks a law that conscience tells him is unjust, and who willingly accepts the penalty of imprisonment in order to arouse the conscience of the community over its injustice, is in reality expressing the highest respect for law.

Of course, there is nothing new about this kind of civil disobedience. It was evidenced sublimely in the refusal of Shadrach, Meshach and Abednego to obey the laws of Nebuchadnezzar, on the ground that a higher moral law was at stake. It was practiced superbly by the early Christians, who were willing to face hungry lions and the excruciating pain of chopping blocks rather than submit to certain unjust laws of the Roman Empire. To a degree, academic freedom is a reality today because Socrates practiced civil disobedience. In our own nation, the Boston Tea Party represented a massive act of civil disobedience.

We should never forget that everything Adolf Hitler did in Germany was "legal" and everything the Hungarian freedom fighters did in Hungary was "illegal." It was "illegal" to aid and comfort a Jew in Hitler's Germany. Even so, I am sure that, had I lived in Germany at the time, I would have aided and comforted my Jewish brothers. If today I lived in a Communist country where certain principles dear to the Christian faith are suppressed, I would openly advocate disobeying that country's antireligious laws. . . .

◇B◇ Native rights—the rights of aboriginal peoples in various areas where the West has settled—is an important issue. In Canada, where a Charter of Rights was passed in 1982 as part of its constitution, the debate has been focussed by Thomas Berger (1933-   ). He wrote the following in his book *Fragile Freedoms* (1982).

The issue of aboriginal rights is the oldest question of human rights in Canada.

At the same time it is also the most recent, for it is only in the last decade that it has entered our consciousness and our political bloodstream. It began with the White occupation of a continent already inhabited by another race, a race with its own cultures, its own languages, its own institutions, and its own way of life. Today the members of that race are advancing claims to the lands they once occupied and calling for self-determination and self-government. These claims give rise to fundamental issues, and we have come to understand that these issues are somehow bound up with what happened long ago. And they are: for the claims of the present day are founded on aboriginal rights.

Aboriginal rights are simply the rights to which Native peoples are entitled because they are the original peoples of Canada. Until recently, the idea of aboriginal rights seemed irrelevant to Canadian concerns. But during the 1970s we began to realize that aboriginal rights are the axis upon which our relations with the Native peoples revolve. To recognize aboriginal rights is to understand the truth of our own history, while, for the Native peoples, such recognition is the means by which they may achieve a distinct and contemporary place in Canadian life.

The emergence of Native peoples as a political force in the 1970s occurred because of initiatives that Indians, Inuit and Metis all over Canada have taken themselves. One thing is common to all of these initiatives: the idea of aboriginal rights. The Native peoples own idea of themselves has acquired a sharper focus. At the same time, our own ideas about Native peoples are undergoing a great change: once thought to be peoples on the margins of our history and irrelevant to present-day concerns, they are now seen by a growing number of Canadians as having a moral, indeed, a constitutional right to fashion a future of their own. . . .

In the past, we sought to make the Native peoples over in our own image. These efforts towards assimilation have failed. The Indians, the Inuit and the Metis survive, determined to be themselves. In the past their refusal to assimilate was usually passive, even covert. Today, this refusal is plain and unmistakable, a fact of national life that cannot be ignored. And now there is a constitutional provision which will give the Native peoples the means to enforce their right to a distinct place in Canadian life. . . .

The Native peoples do not want to recreate a world that has vanished. They do, however, want to find a place in the world that we have forced upon them. Indian treaties, Indian reserves, the Indian Act—these are all institutions that we have devised to manage the Native peoples primarily for our own convenience. Now they want to develop institutions of their own fashioning; they are eager to see their cultures grow and change in directions they have chosen for themselves. They do not wish to be objects of sentimentality. They do not want Native culture, Native communities and the Native economy to be preserved in amber for the amusement and edification of others. They do not want to return to live in tents and igloos. Like us, they are residents of the twentieth century. They, too, live in a world in which progress has an industrial and technological definition. However, because the Native peoples use the technology of the dominant society, that fact does not mean that they should study only English or French in school, that they should learn no history except ours, or that they should be governed by our institutions alone.

It will take time for the Native peoples to limn their claims, for their claims are not limited to land and resources. They wish to achieve a measure of self-determination and self-government, and they see their claims as the means by which these things will be achieved. They are already undertaking to define their claims in the fields of education, health and social services—claims as significant to the urban Native as the rural Native. For instance, Native people complain that in school their children are told about the kings and queens of England and about the brave band of settlers who established the colony of New France on the shores of the St. Lawrence River. All that, they say, is your history. What about our history? They want schools in which their children can study Native history, Native languages, Native lore, and Native rights. Of course they also want their children to speak English or French, as the case may be, to understand the history of our European antecedents and their expansion into the New World, and to study mathematics, natural sciences, and everything else a person needs to know to function in the dominant society. But they must have schools in which they can learn about who they are as well as who we are. The Nishga Indians now have their own school district; it is one of the first in Canada to embrace a predominantly Native population. In June, 1979, ten years after the trial of their land claim before the Supreme Court of British Columbia, the first class graduated from the Nishga Secondary School.

If, in working out settlements of Native claims, we try to force Native development into moulds that we have cast, the whole process will end in failure. No tidy, bureaucratic chart will be of any use; and no governmental policy or program can succeed unless it takes into account the Native peoples' determination to remain themselves—Indian, Inuit or Metis. For this reason, the Native peoples must have distinct social, economic and political institutions. At the same time, they must have access to the social, economic and political institutions of the dominant society. When we are devising such arrangements, it is important to understand precisely what we are talking about. We are not talking about apartheid. In South Africa, the Blacks have been confined to *bantustans*; they have no right to live, to vote, or to work in South Africa except on sufferance. What Natives peoples in Canada are asking for is the right to their own institutions, to the extent that they require them to preserve their culture and their sense of collective identity, and access to the institutions of the dominant society. Only if we were to deny them such access could our policy be said to be one of apartheid.

Canada is committed to a fair settlement of Native claims. This has come about because our institutions have offered the means for redress, and our tradition of tolerance has demanded that redress be made. Of course, this is only a beginning. But it offers to Canada an opportunity to make a contribution to human rights for indigenous peoples everywhere. Pierre Trudeau has suggested that,

> Canada could become the envied seat of a form of federalism that belongs to tomorrow's world. . . . Canada could offer an example to all those new Asian and African states who must discover how to govern their polyethnic populations with proper regard for justice and liberty. . . . Canadian federalism is an experiment of major proportions; it could become a brilliant prototype for the moulding of tomorrow's civilization.

It is all very well to say that Canadian institutional arrangements may speak to the emerging nations of Asia and Africa. But why not to our own hemisphere? There are 50 million Native people in North and South America, almost everywhere dispossessed, everywhere poor, everywhere powerless. In the past they refused to die; today they will not be assimilated. They insist that we must address the issues that have pursued us for almost 500 years, since Columbus set foot in the New World. How can we work out a just relationship between the dominant societies established by the white Europeans and the indigenous peoples of North and South America? In Canada this can be achieved through a fair settlement of Native claims. The settlement of these claims may, therefore, be important to men and women in many countries, truly a "prototype for tomorrow's civilization."

◊C◊ In Poland, in 1980, the workers' movement *Solidarity* grew, with strikes and marches. In August of that year the government and the strike committee agreed to "The 21 Demands":

1. The recognition of free trade unions independent of Party and State, as provided for by Convention 87 of the International Labour Organisation, which was ratified by the Polish People's Republic.
2. The right to strike and a guarantee of security for persons engaged in or assisting a strike action.
3. Freedom of speech and the printed word, and the right to publish, all of which are guaranteed by the Constitution of the Polish People's Republic. We demand immunity from arrest and harassment for persons engaged in independent publishing, and access to the mass media for persons of all religious persuasions.
4. The reinstatement of persons dismissed from their work after the strikes of 1970 and 1976 and students expelled from educational establishments. Freedom for all political prisoners including Edmund Zadrozynski and the Kozlowski brothers. We demand an end to repressive actions against citizens for their beliefs.
5. Mass media coverage for the Interfactory Strike Committee and its 21 demands.
6. Public information on the socio-economic state of the country, public discussion on a reform programme and decisive measures to bring the country out of a state of crisis.
7. Strike pay (at the holiday rate) for persons taking part in the present strike action. These payments to be made out of official union funds.
8. An all round wage increase of 2,000 zl per month to compensate price increases.
9. The introduction of a 'sliding scale' of pay increases to compensate for inflation.
10. Adequate supplies of food for the domestic market and the export only of surplus food.
11. The abolition of 'commercial prices' and the 'internal export system'.
12. The introduction of meat rationing until the market regains stability.
13. Official appointments be made on the basis of qualifications and not party membership. We demand the abolition of special privileges for the police and security services, the abolition of special sources of supply and the equalisation of family allowances, etc.
14. The lowering of the retirement age of women to 50 years, and of men to 55 years or to allow retirement on completion of thirty working years by women and thirty-five by men.
15. An increase in pensions and social benefits.
16. An improvement in the Health Service to secure adequate medical care for working people.
17. An improvement in creche and kindergarten facilities.
18. The introduction of 3 years maternity leave for women.

19. Shorter waiting periods for the allocation of housing.
20. Travel allowance increases from 40 zl to 100 zl and the introduction of a bonus for absence from home.
21. Work-free Saturdays and the introduction of additional paid leave or regular days off work for those engaged in the four shift system, in round-the-clock work, or those who have to work on Saturdays.

1. Comment on Martin Luther King's explanation of the purpose of non-violent direct action.
2. Respond to King's distinction between a "just" and an "unjust" law.
3. Account for Berger's claim that an equitable settlement to Native claims may set a global standard for " 'tomorrow's civilization'."
4. Assess the "21 Demands" in terms of its place in the historical development of declarations of rights from the American Revolution to the present.

▪ ▪ ▪

IDENTITY AND SOCIETY

All major reflections on the human condition raised the problem of identity. Who are we? How do we relate to society? In the face of the history of the twentieth century there were a number of warnings and affirmations: a belief we must be on guard against authoritarian and totalitarian structures; a sense that in the void we must affirm life and its meaning, even in the midst of doubt.

A. The novel *1984* by George Orwell (1903-50), published in 1949, was among the most widely read works challenging totalitarianism and asking readers to reflect on the nature of freedom and the human condition. At the end of the book O'Brien, the representative of authority, has defeated the hero, Winston Smith, by psychological means.

> The Chestnut Tree was almost empty. A ray of sunlight slanting through a window fell yellow on dusty tabletops. It was the lonely hour of fifteen. A tinny music trickled from the telescreens.
>
> Winston sat in his usual corner, gazing into an empty glass. Now and again he glanced up at a vast face which eyed him from the opposite wall. BIG BROTHER IS WATCHING YOU, the caption said. Unbidden, a waiter came and filled his glass up with Victory Gin, shaking into it a few drops from another bottle with a quill through the cork. It was saccharine flavored with cloves, the specialty of the café. . . .

Sources: George Orwell, *1984* (New York: New American Library, 1983), pp. 236, 239-41, 244-45; Samuel Beckett, *Waiting for Godot* (New York: Grove Press, Inc., 1954), pp. 51, 57-60.

. . . His thoughts wandered again. Almost unconsciously he traced with his finger in the dust on the table:

$$2 + 2 = 5.$$

"They can't get inside you," she had said. But they could get inside you. "What happens to you here is *forever*," O'Brien had said. That was a true word. There were things, your own acts, from which you could not recover. Something was killed in your breast; burnt out, cauterized out . . . .

He did not attempt to kiss her, nor did they speak. As they walked back across the gate she looked directly at him for the first time. It was only a momentary glance, full of contempt and dislike. He wondered whether it was a dislike that came purely out of the past or whether it was inspired also by his bloated face and the water that the wind kept squeezing from his eyes. They sat down on two iron chairs, side by side but not too close together. He saw that she was about to speak. She moved her clumsy shoe a few centimeters and deliberately crushed a twig. Her feet seemed to have grown broader, he noticed.

"I betrayed you," she said baldly.

"I betrayed you," he said.

She gave him another quick look of dislike.

"Sometimes," she said, "they threaten you with something—something you can't stand up to, can't even think about. And then you say, 'Don't do it to me, do it to somebody else, do it to so-and-so.' And perhaps you might pretend, afterwards, that it was only a trick and that you just said it to make them stop and didn't really mean it. But that isn't true. At the time when it happens you do mean it. You think there's no other way of saving yourself and you're quite ready to save yourself that way. You *want* it to happen to the other person. You don't give a damn what they suffer. All you care about is yourself."

"All you care about is yourself," he echoed.

"And after that, you don't feel the same toward the other person any longer."

"No," he said, "you don't feel the same."

There did not seem to be anything more to say. The wind plastered their thin overalls against their bodies. Almost at once it became embarrassing to sit there in silence; besides, it was too cold to keep still. She said something about catching her Tube and stood up to go.

"We must meet again," he said.

"Yes," she said, "we must meet again."

He followed irresolutely for a little distance, half a pace behind her. They did not speak again. She did not actually try to shake him off, but walked at just such a speed as to prevent his keeping abreast of her. He had made up his mind that he would accompany her as far as the Tube station, but suddenly this process of trailing along in the cold seemed pointless and unbearable. He was overwhelmed by a desire not so much to get away from Julia as to get back to the Chestnut Tree Café, which had never seemed so attractive as at this moment. He had a nostalgic vision of his corner table, with the newspaper and the chessboard and the ever-flowing gin. Above all, it would be warm in there. The next moment, not altogether by accident, he allowed himself to become separated from her by a small knot of people. He made a half-hearted attempt to catch up, then slowed down, turned and made off in the opposite direction. When he had gone fifty meters he looked back. The street was not crowded, but already he could not distinguish her. Any one of a dozen hurrying figures might have been hers. Perhaps her thickened, stiffened body was no longer recognizable from behind.

"At the time when it happens," she had said, "you do mean it." He had meant it. He had not merely said it, he had wished it. He had wished that she and not he should be delivered over to the—

Something changed in the music that trickled from the telescreen. A cracked and jeering note, a yellow note, came into it. And then—perhaps it was not happening, perhaps it was only a memory taking on the semblance of sound—a voice was singing:

"Under the spreading chestnut tree
I sold you and you sold me—"

The tears welled up in his eyes. A passing waiter noticed that his glass was empty and came back with the gin bottle. . . .

A shrill trumpet call had pierced the air. It was the bulletin! Victory! It always meant victory when a trumpet call preceded the news. A sort of electric thrill ran through the café. Even the waiters had started and pricked up their ears.

The trumpet call had let loose an enormous volume of noise. Already an excited voice was gabbling from the telescreen, but even as it started it was almost drowned by a roar of cheering from outside. The news had run round the streets like magic. He could hear just enough of what was issuing from the telescreen to realize that it had all happened as he had foreseen: a vast seaborne armada secretly assembled, a sudden blow in the enemy's rear, the white arrow tearing across the tail of the black. Fragments of triumphant phrases pushed themselves through the din: "Vast strategic maneuver—perfect co-ordination—utter rout—half a million prisoners—complete demoralization—control of the whole of Africa—bring the war within measurable distance of its end—victory—greatest victory in human history—victory, victory, victory!"

Under the table Winston's feet made convulsive movements. He had not stirred from his seat, but in his mind he was running, swiftly running, he was with the crowds outside, cheering himself deaf. He looked up again at the portrait of Big Brother. The colossus that bestrode the world! The rock against which the hordes of Asia dashed themselves in vain! He thought how ten minutes ago—yes, only ten minutes—there had still been equivocation in his heart as he wondered whether the news from the front would be of victory or defeat. Ah, it was more than a Eurasian army that had perished! Much had changed in him since the first day in the Ministry of Love, but the final, indispensable healing change had never happened, until this moment.

The voice from the telescreen was still pouring forth its tale of prisoners and booty and slaughter, but the shouting outside had died down a little. The waiters were turning back to their work. One of them approached with the gin bottle. Winston, sitting in a blissful dream, paid no attention as his glass was filled up. He was not running or cheering any longer. He was back in the Ministry of Love, with everything forgiven, his soul white as snow. He was in the public dock, confessing everything, implicating everybody. He was walking down the white-tiled corridor, with the feeling of walking in sunlight, and an armed guard at his back. The long-hoped-for bullet was entering his brain.

He gazed up at the enormous face. Forty years it had taken him to learn what kind of smile was hidden beneath the dark mustache. O cruel, needless misunderstanding! O stubborn, self-willed exile from the loving breast! Two gin-scented tears trickled down the sides of his nose. But it was all right, everything was all right, the struggle was finished. He had won the victory over himself. He loved Big Brother.

B ▷ The work of Samuel Beckett (1906-   ) has had a profound effect on the West, helping to articulate the sense of loss of purpose after the Second World War. In the play *Waiting for Godot* (1953), Beckett's characters inhabit a bleak landscape, wondering about their purpose in life. Yet there is a strange optimism, somewhat like that of Camus, in Beckett's work.

. . . . .

POZZO: Help!

VLADIMIR: To help him—

ESTRAGON: *We* help *him*?

VLADIMIR: In anticipation of some tangible return.

ESTRAGON: And suppose he—

VLADIMIR: Let us not waste our time in idle discourse! (*Pause. Vehemently.*) Let us do something, while we have the chance! It is not every day that we are needed. Not indeed that we personally are needed. Others would meet the case equally well, if not better. To all mankind they were addressed, those cries for help still ringing in our ears! But at this place, at this moment of time, all mankind is us, whether we like it or not. Let us make the most of it, before it is too late! Let us represent worthily for once the foul brood to which a cruel fate consigned us! What do you say? (*Estragon says nothing.*) It is true that when with folded arms we weigh the pros and cons we are no less a credit to our species. The tiger bounds to the help of his congeners without the least reflexion, or else he slinks away into the depths of the thickets. But that is not the question. What are we doing here, *that* is the question. And we are blessed in this, that we happen to know the answer. Yes, in this immense confusion one thing alone is clear. We are waiting for Godot to come—

ESTRAGON: Ah!

POZZO: Help!

VLADIMIR: Or for night to fall. (*Pause.*) We have kept our appointment and that's an end to that. We are not saints, but we have kept our appointment. How many people can boast as much?

ESTRAGON: Billions.

VLADIMIR: You think so?

ESTRAGON: I don't know.

VLADIMIR: You may be right. . . .

Vladimir goes towards Estragon, contemplates him a moment, then shakes him awake.

ESTRAGON: (*wild gestures, incoherent words. Finally.*) Why will you never let me sleep?

VLADIMIR: I felt lonely.

ESTRAGON: I was dreaming I was happy.

VLADIMIR: That passed the time.

ESTRAGON: I was dreaming that—

VLADIMIR: (*violently*). Don't tell me! (*Silence.*) I wonder is he really blind.

ESTRAGON: Blind? Who?

VLADIMIR: Pozzo.

ESTRAGON: Blind?

VLADIMIR: He told us he was blind.

ESTRAGON: Well what about it?

VLADIMIR: It seemed to me he saw us.

ESTRAGON: You dreamt it. (*Pause.*) Let's go. We can't. Ah! (*Pause.*) Are you sure it wasn't him?

VLADIMIR: Who?

ESTRAGON: Godot.

VLADIMIR: But who?

ESTRAGON: Pozzo.

VLADIMIR: Not at all! (*Less sure.*) Not at all! (*Still less sure.*) Not at all!

ESTRAGON: I suppose I might as well get up. (*He gets up painfully.*) Ow! Didi!

VLADIMIR: I don't know what to think any more.

ESTRAGON: My feet! (*He sits down again and tries to take off his boots.*) Help me!

VLADIMIR: Was I sleeping, while the others suffered? Am I sleeping now? To-morrow, when I wake, or think I do, what shall I say of to-day? That with Estragon my friend, at this place, until the fall of night, I waited for Godot? That Pozzo passed, with his carrier, and that he spoke to us? Probably. But in all that what truth will there be? (*Estragon, having struggled with his boots in vain, is dozing off again. Vladimir looks at him.*) He'll know nothing. He'll tell me about the blows he received and I'll give him a carrot. (*Pause*). Astride of a grave and a difficult birth. Down in the hole, lingeringly, the grave-digger puts on the forceps. We have time to grow old. The air is full of our cries. (*He listens.*) But habit is a great deadener. (*He looks again at Estragon.*) At me too someone is looking, of me too someone is saying, He is sleeping, he knows nothing, let him sleep on. (*Pause.*) I can't go on! (*Pause.*) What have I said?

He goes feverishly to and fro, halts finally at extreme left, broods. Enter Boy right. He halts. Silence.

BOY: Mister . . . (*Vladimir turns.*) Mister Albert . . .

VLADIMIR: Off we go again. (*Pause.*) Do you not recognize me?

BOY: No sir.

VLADIMIR: It wasn't you came yesterday.

BOY: No Sir.

VLADIMIR: This is your first time.

BOY: Yes Sir.

Silence.

VLADIMIR: You have a message from Mr. Godot.

BOY: Yes Sir.

VLADIMIR: He won't come this evening.

BOY: No Sir.

VLADIMIR: But he'll come to-morrow.

BOY: Yes Sir.

VLADIMIR: Without fail.

BOY: Yes Sir.

Silence.

VLADIMIR: Did you meet anyone?

BOY: No Sir.

VLADIMIR: Two other . . . (*he hesitates*) . . . men?

BOY: I didn't see anyone, Sir.

Silence.

VLADIMIR: What does he do, Mr. Godot? (*Silence.*) Do you hear me?

BOY: Yes Sir.

VLADIMIR: Well?

BOY: He does nothing, Sir.

Silence.

VLADIMIR: How is your brother?

BOY: He's sick, Sir.

VLADIMIR: Perhaps it was he came yesterday.

BOY: I don't know, Sir.

Silence.

VLADIMIR: (*softly*). Has he a beard, Mr. Godot?

BOY: Yes Sir.

VLADIMIR: Fair or . . . (*he hesitates*) . . . or black?

BOY: I think it's white, Sir.

Silence.

VLADIMIR: Christ have mercy on us!

Silence.

BOY: What am I to tell Mr. Godot, Sir?

VLADIMIR: Tell him . . . (*he hesitates*) . . . tell him you saw me and that . . . (*he hesitates*) . . . that you saw me. (*Pause, Vladimir advances, the Boy recoils. Vladimir halts, the Boy halts. With sudden violence.*) You're sure you saw me, you won't come and tell me to-morrow that you never saw me!

Silence. Vladimir makes a sudden spring forward, the Boy avoids him and exit running. Silence. The sun sets, the moon rises. As in Act 1. Vladimir stands motionless and bowed. Estragon wakes, takes off his boots, gets up with one in each hand and goes and puts them down center front, then goes towards Vladimir.

ESTRAGON: What's wrong with you?

VLADIMIR: Nothing.

ESTRAGON: I'm going.

VLADIMIR: So am I.

ESTRAGON: Was I long asleep?

VLADIMIR: I don't know.

Silence.

ESTRAGON: Where shall we go?

VLADIMIR: Not far.

ESTRAGON: Oh yes, let's go far away from here.

VLADIMIR: We can't.

ESTRAGON: Why not?

VLADIMIR: We have to come back to-morrow.

ESTRAGON: What for?

VLADIMIR: To wait for Godot.

ESTRAGON: Ah! (*Silence.*) He didn't come?

VLADIMIR: No.

ESTRAGON: And now it's too late.

VLADIMIR: Yes, now it's night.

ESTRAGON: And if we dropped him? (*Pause.*) If we dropped him?

VLADIMIR: He'd punish us. (*Silence. He looks at the tree.*) Everything's dead but the tree.

ESTRAGON: (*looking at the tree*). What is it?

VLADIMIR: It's the tree.

ESTRAGON: Yes, but what kind?

VLADIMIR: I don't know. A willow.

Estragon draws Vladimir towards the tree. They stand motionless before it. Silence.

ESTRAGON: Why don't we hang ourselves?

VLADIMIR: With what?

ESTRAGON: You haven't got a bit of rope?

VLADIMIR: No.

ESTRAGON: Then we can't.

Silence.

VLADIMIR: Let's go.

ESTRAGON: Wait, there's my belt.

VLADIMIR: It's too short.

ESTRAGON: You could hang on to my legs.

VLADIMIR: And who'd hang on to mine?

ESTRAGON: True.

VLADIMIR: Show all the same. (*Estragon loosens the cord that holds up his trousers which, much too big for him, fall about his ankles. They look at the cord.*) It might do at a pinch. But is it strong enough?

ESTRAGON: We'll soon see. Here.

They each take an end of the cord and pull. It breaks. They almost fall.

VLADIMIR: Not worth a curse.

Silence.

ESTRAGON: You say we have to come back to-morrow?

VLADIMIR: Yes.

ESTRAGON: Then we can bring a good bit of rope.

VLADIMIR: Yes.

Silence.

ESTRAGON: Didi.

VLADIMIR: Yes.

ESTRAGON: I can't go on like this.

VLADIMIR: That's what you think.

ESTRAGON: If we parted? That might be better for us.

VLADIMIR: We'll hang ourselves to-morrow. (*Pause.*) Unless Godot comes.

ESTRAGON: And if he comes?

VLADIMIR: We'll be saved.

Vladimir takes of his hat (Lucky's), peers inside it, feels about inside it, shakes it, knocks on the crown, puts it on again.

ESTRAGON: Well? Shall we go?

VLADIMIR: Pull on your trousers.

ESTRAGON: What?

VLADIMIR: Pull on your trousers.

ESTRAGON: You want me to pull off my trousers?

VLADIMIR: Pull ON your trousers.

ESTRAGON: (*realizing his trousers are down*). True.

He pulls up his trousers.

VLADIMIR: Well? Shall we go?

ESTRAGON: Yes, let's go.

They do not move.

Curtain

1. "Winston Smith's victory over himself, is actually the final victory of the state over the individual." Account for this statement with reference to life in a totalitarian state as presented in *1984*.
2. Stage, with a few classmates, this excerpt from *Waiting for Godot*. Discuss as a group the view of existence depicted by Beckett.

• • •

NUCLEAR CATASTROPHE

The advent of nuclear weapons has been a major concern throughout the world since 1945, as humanity has realized it has the capacity to annihilate itself. Peace movements grew after the war, and many studies have been done on the effects of the nuclear reality on the human psyche. The two major nuclear powers, the United States and the Soviet Union, have debated disarmament since the 1950s, sometimes successfully negotiating treaties limiting nuclear weapons. Still, the issue persists, as human beings reflect on the potential of science for destruction as well as its benefits.

The philosopher and mathematician Bertrand Russell (1872-1970) was a leader of peace and disarmament movements until his death. In 1956 Russell posed the problem of a nuclear war.

... Here, then, is the problem which I present to you, stark and dreadful and inescapable: Shall we put an end to the human race; or shall mankind

Sources: *The Basic Writings of Bertrand Russell*, edited by Robert E. Egner and Lester E. Denonn (New York: Simon and Schuster, 1961), pp. 730-32; Gwyn Prins, ed. *Defended to Death*, (Harmondsworth: Penguin Books, 1982), pp. 121-23; Robert Jay Lifton and Richard Falk, *Indefensible Weapons* (New York: Basic Books, 1982), pp. 103-10.

renounce war? People will not face this alternative because it is so difficult to abolish war. The abolition of war will demand distasteful limitations of national sovereignty. But what perhaps impedes understanding of the situation more than anything else is that the term 'mankind' feels vague and abstract. People scarcely realize in imagination that the danger is to themselves and their children and their grandchildren, and not only to a dimly apprehended humanity. And so they hope that perhaps war may be allowed to continue provided modern weapons are prohibited. I am afraid this hope is illusory. Whatever agreements not to use hydrogen bombs had been reached in time of peace, they would no longer be considered binding in time of war, and both sides would set to work to manufacture hydrogen bombs as soon as war broke out, for if one side manufactured the bombs and the other did not, the side that manufactured them would inevitably be victorious.

On both sides of the Iron Curtain there are political obstacles to emphasis on the destructive character of future war. If either side were to announce that it would on no account resort to war, it would be diplomatically at the mercy of the other side. Each side, for the sake of self-preservation, must continue to say that there are provocations that it will not endure. Each side may long for an accommodation, but neither side dare express this longing convincingly. The position is analogous to that of duellists in former times. No doubt it frequently happened that each of the duellists feared death and desired an accommodation, but neither could say so, since, if he did, he would be thought a coward. The only hope in such cases was intervention by friends of both parties suggesting an accommodation to which both could agree at the same moment. This is an exact analogy to the present position of the protagonists on either side of the Iron Curtain. If an agreement making war improbable is to be reached, it will have to be by the friendly offices of neutrals, who can speak of the disastrousness of war without being accused of advocating a policy of 'appeasement'. The neutrals have every right, even from the narrowest consideration of self-interest, to do whatever lies in their power to prevent the outbreak of a world war, for if such a war does break out, it is highly probable that all the inhabitants of neutral countries, along with the rest of mankind, will perish. If I were in control of a neutral government, I should certainly consider it my paramount duty to see to it that my country would continue to have inhabitants, and the only way by which I could make this probable would be to promote some kind of accommodation between the powers on opposite sides of the Iron Curtain.

I, personally, am of course not neutral in my feeling and I should not wish to see the danger of war averted by an abject submission of the West. But, as a human being, I have to remember that, if the issues between East and West are to be decided in any manner that can give any possible satisfaction to anybody, whether Communist or anti-Communist, whether Asian or European or American, whether white or black, then these issues must not be decided by war. I should wish this to be understood on both sides of the Iron Curtain. It is emphatically not enough to have it understood on one side only. I think the neutrals, since they are not caught in our tragic dilemma, can, if they will, bring about this realization on both sides. I should like to see one or more neutral powers appoint a commission of experts, who should all be neutrals, to draw up a report on the destructive effects to be expected in a war with hydrogen bombs, not only among the belligerents but also among neutrals. I should wish this report presented to the Governments of all the Great Powers with an invitation to express their agreement or disagreement with its findings. I think it possible that in this way all the Great Powers could be led to agree that a world war can no longer serve the purposes of any of them, since it is likely to exterminate friend and foe equally and neutrals likewise.

As geological time is reckoned, man has so far existed only for a very short period—1,000,000 years at the most. What he has achieved, especially during the last 6,000 years, is something utterly new in the history of the cosmos, so far at least as we are acquainted with it. For countless ages the sun rose and set, the moon waxed and waned, the stars shone in the night, but it was only with the coming of man that these things were understood. In the great world of astronomy and in the little world of the atom, man has unveiled secrets which might have been thought undiscoverable. In art and literature and religion, some men have shown a sublimity of feeling which makes the species worth preserving. Is all this to end in trivial horror because so few are able to think of man rather than of this or that group of men? Is our race so destitute of wisdom, so incapable of impartial love, so blind even to the simplest dictates of self-preservation, that the last proof of its silly cleverness is to be the extermination of all life on our planet?—for it will be not only men who will perish, but also the animals, whom no one can accuse of Communism or anti-Communism.

I cannot believe that this is to be the end. I would have men forget their quarrels for a moment and reflect that, if they will allow themselves to survive, there is every reason to expect the triumphs of the future to exceed immeasurably the triumphs of the past. There lies before us, if we choose, continual progress in happiness, knowledge, and wisdom. Shall we, instead, choose death, because we cannot forget our quarrels? I appeal as a human being to human beings: remember your humanity, and forget the rest. If you can do so, the way lies open to a new Paradise; if you cannot, nothing lies before you but universal death.

◆B In 1963 John F. Kennedy (1917-63), president of the United States, spoke about the need for peace. The speech helped to create a climate in which treaties banning the testing of nuclear weapons were negotiated.

What kind of peace do I mean? What kind of peace do we seek? Not a Pax Americana enforced in the world by American weapons of war. Not the peace of the grave or the security of the slave. I am talking about genuine peace, the kind of peace that makes life on earth worth living, the kind that enables men and nations to grow and to hope and to build a better life for their children—not merely peace for Americans but peace for all men and women— not merely peace in our time but peace in all time.

I speak of peace because of the new face of war. Total war makes no sense in an age where great powers can maintain large and relatively invulnerable nuclear forces and refuse to surrender without resort to those forces. It makes no sense in an age when a single nuclear weapon contains almost ten times the explosive force delivered by all the Allied air forces in the Second World War. It makes no sense in an age when the deadly poisons produced by a nuclear exchange would be carried by wind and water and soil and seed to the far corners of the globe and to generations yet unborn . . .

I speak of peace, therefore, as the necessary rational end of rational men . . . Some say that it is useless to speak of peace or world law or world disarmament—and that it will be useless until the leaders of the Soviet Union adopt a more enlightened attitude. I hope they do. I believe we can help them do it. But I also believe that we must re-examine our own attitude— as individuals and as a Nation—for our attitude is as essential as theirs. And . . . every thoughtful citizen who despairs of war and wishes to bring peace, should begin by looking inward—by examining his own attitude toward the possibilities of peace, toward the Soviet Union, toward the course of the cold war and toward freedom and peace here at home.

First: Let us examine our attitude toward peace itself. Too many of us think it is impossible. Too many think it is unreal. But that is a dangerous, defeatist belief. It leads to the conclusion that war is inevitable—that mankind is doomed—that we are gripped by forces we cannot control.

We need not accept that view. Our problems are manmade—therefore they can be solved by man . . . No problem of human destiny is beyond human beings. Man's reason and spirit have often solved the seemingly unsolvable— and we believe they can do it again . . .

. . . history teaches us that enmities between nations, as between individuals, do not last forever. However fixed our likes and dislikes may seem, the tide of time and events will often bring surprising changes in the relations between nations and neighbors.

So let us persevere. Peace need not be impracticable, and war need not be inevitable. By defining our goal more clearly, by making it seem more manageable and less remote, we can help all peoples to see it, to draw hope from it, and to move irresistibly toward it.

Second: Let us reexamine our attitude toward the Soviet Union. It is discouraging to think that their leaders may actually believe what their propagandists write. It is discouraging to read a recent authoritative Soviet text on *Military Strategy* and find, on page after page, wholly baseless and incredible claims . . .

. . . it is sad to read these Soviet statements—to realize the extent of the gulf between us. But it is also a warning—a warning to the American people not to fall into the same trap as the Soviets, not to see only a distorted and desperate view of the other side, not to see conflict as inevitable, accommodation as impossible, and communication as nothing more than an exchange of threats.

No government or social system is so evil that its people must be considered as lacking in virtue. As Americans, we find communism profoundly repugnant as a negation of personal freedom and dignity. But we can still hail the Russian people for their many achievements—in science and space, in economic and industrial growth, in culture and in acts of courage.

Among the many traits the peoples of our two countries have in common, none is stronger than our mutual abhorrence of war. Almost unique among the major world powers, we have never been at war with each other. And no nation in the history of battle ever suffered more than the Soviet Union suffered in the course of the Second World War. At least 20 million lost their lives. Countless millions of homes and farms were burned or sacked. A third of the nation's territory, including two thirds of its industrial base, was turned into a wasteland—a loss equivalent to the devastation of this country east of Chicago.

. . . both the United States and its allies, and the Soviet Union and its allies, have a mutually deep interest in a just and genuine peace and in halting the arms race. Agreements to this end are in the interests of the Soviet Union as well as ours—and even the most hostile nations can be relied upon to accept and keep those treaty obligations, and only those treaty delegations, which are in their own interest.

So let us not be blind to our differences—but let us also direct attention to our common interests and the means by which those differences can be resolved. And if we cannot end now our differences, at least we can help make the world safe for diversity. For, in the final analysis, our most basic common link is that we all inhabit this small planet. We all breathe the same air. We all cherish our children's future. And we are all mortal.

C The psychiatrist Robert Jay Lifton (1926-   ) wrote in 1982 about the psychological effects of nuclear weapons.

. . . over decades, there was the psychological process of "learning to live with the bomb," which scientists came to share with political and military leaders along with the rest of us; specific forms of numbing evolved that blocked out what happened at the other end of nuclear weapons and enabled one to get on with things.

What I am calling psychic numbing includes a number of classical psychoanalytic defense mechanisms: repression, suppression, isolation, denial, undoing, reaction formation, and projection, among others. But these defense mechanisms overlap greatly around the issue of feeling and not feeling. With that issue so central to our time, we do well to devote to it a single overall category, which we can observe operating in different ways and under different conditions in virtually any individual mind.

Psychic numbing has to do with exclusion, most specifically exclusion of feeling . . . .

We may thus speak, very generally, of three levels of numbing: the numbing of massive death immersion; the numbing of enhancement; and the numbing of everyday life. The first, the numbing of massive death immersion, is epitomized by Hiroshima and Nagasaki. The "paralysis of the mind" already mentioned involves a radical dissociation of the mind from its own earlier modes of response—from constellations of pain and pleasure, love and loss, and general capacity for fellow feeling built up over a human lifetime. We may, indeed, speak of the mind being severed from its own forms. When that happens, psychic action—mental process in general—more or less shuts down. There are in-between states in which limited forms of planning and action (flight or rescue of family members) can occur, even though feelings are largely blunted.

The numbing of enhancement is of the opposite variety. Here feeling is diminished in some spheres of the mind in order to make possible more accomplished behavior or more intense feeling in other spheres. One can point to the selective professional numbing of the surgeon, who cannot afford to feel the consequences of failure. Or to that of the painter or musician, who block out a great variety of influences in order to enhance and intensify the image or the musical phrase.

Finally, there is the problematic category of the numbing of everyday life. Here we may say that the ordinary brain function of keeping out stimuli becomes strained by the image overload characteristic of our time . . . .

Nuclear numbing arrives, so to speak, on this psychological soil. And when people are deeply uneasy about what and how much to feel, the specific call to feel what happens on the other end of a nuclear weapon is not a very inviting one. A more compelling call to feel may be experienced around the sense of power and allegedly increased security offered in connection with more advanced and sophisticated (both bigger and smaller) nuclear weapons. Further, we *domesticate* these weapons in our language and attitudes. Rather than feel their malignant actuality, we render them benign. In calling them "nukes," for instance, we render them small and "cute," something on the order of a household pet. That tendency was explicit in the naming of the two atomic bombs dropped on Japanese cities—the first "Little Boy" suggesting a newborn baby or small child, the second "Fat Man" after Winston Churchill. (So universal is the bomb-related impulse toward numbing that even Japanese survivors domesticated their bomb by referring to it with the not-unpleasant-sounding term *pikadon*, or "flash-boom.")

Many have commented on the anesthetizing quality of the language of nuclear weapons, sometimes referred to as "nukespeak." What are we to make of terms like "nuclear exchange," "escalation," "nuclear yield," "counterforce," "megatons," or of "window of vulnerability" or (ostensibly much better) "window of opportunity." Quite simply, *these words provide a way of talking about nuclear weapons without really talking about them*. In them we find nothing about billions of human beings incinerated or literally melted, nothing about millions of corpses. Rather, the weapons come to seem ordinary and manageable or even mildly pleasant (a "nuclear exchange" sounds something like mutual gift-giving).

Now, much of this domesticated language is intentionally orchestrated by military or political bomb managers who are concerned that we stay numbed in relation to the weapons. But it is a process in which others collude, so that we may speak of a more or less spontaneous conspiracy of linguistic detoxification that contributes to the comfort of just about everyone. Part of the linguistic conspiracy involves technical distancing—an American Secretary of State, for instance, avoiding painful issues by referring to the existence of "quantitative and qualitative questions" and to "an exceedingly complex process."

This pattern of numbing via technicization has extensive cultural roots. But the "nuclear experts" serve a special function here, something on the order of hired anesthetists. They contribute to the numbing by further technicizing everything, by excluding human victims from their scenarios, and by conveying the sense that nuclear matters are completely under control because they are in the hands of experts. Not only are the rest of us excluded from matters presumably beyond our technical capacities, but we tend to collude in our own exclusion as a way of retreating to the resignation-cynicism-waiting-for-the-bomb-axis.

The truth is that we have found no language, and perhaps there is none, to express the destructiveness, evil, and absurdity of the nuclear devices. The problem existed for Hiroshima and especially for survivors of that first bomb. One wrote: "There exist no words in any human language which can comfort guinea pigs who do not know the cause of their death." Here the writer refers both to the dead and to other survivors who (as nuclear "guinea pigs") fear ambiguous but deadly symptoms of radiation effects or "A-bomb disease." A few survivors emphasized the term "nothingness" as coming closest to what was needed. One suggested that the atomic bomb be commemorated by leaving a completely empty area around the place where the bomb struck Hiroshima, a representation of "nothingness at the hypocenter—because that is what there was" and because "Such a weapon has the power to make everything into nothing." In a similar spirit, a colleague recently suggested to me that we speak no longer of nuclear war but only of the "nuclear end" or "ending." Even when determined to imagine and feel as strongly as possible images of past and potential atrocity, we experience barriers in doing so. There is a real question about how much ultimate atrocity the human mind is capable of taking in and absorbing—to which our tentative answer must be: much less than the full narrative, but considerably more than we have.

We may speak, then, of a historical or even evolutionary paradox: The degree of numbing of everyday life necessary for individual comfort is at odds with the degree of tension, or even anxiety, that must accompany the nuclear awareness necessary for collective survival.

We have many reasons, then, for avoiding a holier-than-thou (or more feeling-than-thou) attitude toward psychic numbing. For one thing, no one, psychologically speaking, can live in the realm of nuclear weapons all the time. Even those who are preoccupied with the problem find themselves slipping in and out of it, and for the most part they are relieved (though sometimes they feel guilty) about that being the case. And however great one's involvement with these matters, there are moments in which one suddenly realizes that one has been blocking out important nuclear truths that others have confronted more directly . . . .

In response to nuclear weapons, numbing is all too easy, widespread, and "natural" for just about everyone. But in saying that, and in depicting these various forms of numbing—indeed, in exploring our mind's dilemmas around nuclear weapons—we are doing something that only human beings can do. We are reflecting on ourselves and our situation in the service of greater awareness. And in that awareness, even just its beginning, lies our hope.

1. It has been many years since Bertrand Russell wrote his statement. Write a critique of his arguments from the perspective of someone living at the present time.
2. Précis Kennedy's speech and compare its contents with current American statements regarding the Soviet Union and its leadership.

3. Survey the local media for a period of a few weeks. Using Lifton's observations as a guide, note references to the nuclear issue and comment on his observations regarding the "anesthetizing quality of the language of nuclear weapons."

• • •

COLONIALISM AND ITS REMNANTS

The era of colonialism ended in the period after 1945, as empires were dismantled and old colonies achieved their independence. Often, this was not without some struggle in Asia and Africa, as colonial peoples demanded autonomy and an end to what they regarded as the oppression of outsiders. New leaders appeared, and a new attempt to understand imperialism and colonialism—from the perspective of the oppressed—came into view.

A Mohandas K. Gandhi (1869-1948) was a major figure in the independence of India and a leading advocate of non-violent resistance. Gandhi's personal saintliness, his philosophy, and his determination to uphold human dignity made him one of the major political figures in modern world history.

> Some friends have told me that truth and non-violence have no place in politics and worldly affairs. I do not agree. I have no use for them as a means of individual salvation. Their introduction and application in everyday life has been my experiment all along.
>
> No man could be actively non-violent and not rise against social injustice no matter where it occurred.
>
> Passive resistance is a method of securing rights by personal suffering; it is the reverse of resistance by arms. When I refuse to do a thing that is repugnant to my conscience, I use soul-force. For instance, the government of the day has passed a law which is applicable to me. I do not like it. If by using violence I force the government to repeal the law, I am employing what may be termed body-force. If I do not obey the law and accept the penalty for its breach, I use soul-force. It involves sacrifice of self.
>
> Moreover, if this kind of force is used in a cause that is unjust, only the person using it suffers. He does not make others suffer for his mistakes. Men have before now done many things which were subsequently found to have been wrong. No man can claim that he is absolutely in the right or that a particular thing is wrong because he thinks so, but it is wrong for him so

Sources: Mohandas Gandhi, *Readings from Gandhi* (Bhavnager, India: Lok-Milsap Trust, 1969), pp. 46, 49, 52-53, 58-59, 71, 75-76; Frantz Fanon, *The Wretched of the Earth* (New York: Grove Press, Inc., 1948), pp. 44-45, 100-103, 314-16, 13-14, 24-25; Steve Biko, I *Write What I Like* (New York: Harper and Row, 1978), pp. 95-98.

long as that is his deliberate judgment. It is therefore meet that he should not do that which he knows to be wrong, and suffer the consequence whatever it may be. This is the key to the use of soul-force.

It is my dream that my country may win its freedom through non-violence. And, I would like to repeat to the world times without number that, I will not purchase my country's freedom at the cost of non-violence. . . .

Non-violence to be a potent force must begin with the mind. Non-violence of the mere body without the co-operation of the mind is non-violence of the weak or the cowardly, and has therefore no potency. If we bear malice and hatred in our bosoms and pretend not to retaliate, it must recoil upon us and lead to our destruction.

I do not believe in short-violent-cuts to success. . . . However much I may sympathise with and admire worthy motives, I am an uncompromising opponent of violent methods even to serve the noblest of causes. There is, therefore, really no meeting-ground between the school of violence and myself. But my creed of non-violence not only does not preclude me but compels me even to associate with anarchists and all those who believe in violence. But that association is always with the sole object of weaning them from what appears to me their error. For experience convinces me that permanent good can never be the outcome of untruth and violence.

I object to violence because when it appears to do good, the good is only temporary; the evil it does is permanent. I do not believe that the killing of even every Englishman can do the slightest good to India. The millions will be just as badly off as they are today, if someone made it possible to kill off every Englishman tomorrow. The responsibility is more ours than that of the English for the present state of things. The English will be powerless to do evil if we will but do good. Hence my incessant emphasis on reform from within.

History teaches one that those who have, no doubt with honest motives, ousted the greedy by using brute force against them, have in their turn become a prey to the disease of the conquered. . . .

My non-violence does not admit of running away from danger and leaving dear ones unprotected. Between violence and cowardly flight, I can only prefer violence to cowardice. Non-violence is the summit of bravery. And in my own experience, I have had no difficulty in demonstrating to men trained in the school of violence the superiority of non-violence. As a coward, which I was for years, I harboured violence. I began to prize non-violence only when I began to shed cowardice.

I am not pleading for India to practise non-violence because it is weak. I want her to practise non-violence being conscious of her strength and power. I want to recognize that she has a soul that cannot perish and that can rise triumphant above every physical weakness and defy the physical combination of a whole world. . . . If India takes up the doctrine of the sword, she may gain momentary victory. Then India will cease to be the pride of my heart.

I must continue to argue till I convert opponents or I own defeat. For my mission is to convert every Indian, even Englishmen and finally the world, to non-violence for regulating mutual relations whether political, economic, social or religious.

If India makes violence her creed, and I have survived, I would not care to live in India. She will cease to evoke any pride in me. My patriotism is subservient to my religion. I cling to India like a child to its mother's breast, because I feel that she gives me the spiritual nourishment I need. She has the environment that responds to my highest aspiration. When that faith is gone, I shall feel like an orphan without hope of ever finding a guardian. . . .

We want freedom for our country, but not at the expense or exploitation of others, not so as to degrade other countries. I do not want the freedom of India if it means the extinction of England or the disappearance of Englishmen. I want the freedom of my country so that other countries may learn something from my free country, so that the resources of my country might be utilised for the benefit of mankind. Just as the cult of patriotism teaches us today that the individual has to die for the family, the family has to die for the village, the village for the district, the district for the province, and the province for the country, even so, a country has to be free in order that it may die, if necessary, for the benefit of the world. My love therefore of nationalism or my idea of nationalism, is that my country may die, so that the human race may live.

We are all members of the vast human family. I decline to draw any distinctions. I cannot claim any superiority for Indians. We have the same virtues and the same vices. Humanity is not divided into watertight compartments. I would not say: 'India should be all in all, let the whole world perish.' That is not my message. India should be all in all, consistently with the well-being of other nations of the world. I can keep India intact and its freedom also intact only if I have goodwill towards the whole of the human family and not merely for the human family which inhabits this little spot of the earth called India. It is big enough compared to other smaller nations, but what is India in the wide world or in the universe? . . .

My notion of democracy is that under it the weakest should have the same opportunity as the strongest. That can never happen except through non-violence.

I have always held that social justice, even unto the least and lowliest, is impossible of attainment by force. I have believed that it is possible by proper training of the lowliest by non-violent means to secure the redress of the wrongs suffered by them. That means is non-violent non-co-operation. Freedom received through the effort of others, however benevolent, cannot be retained when such effort is withdrawn. In other words, such freedom is not real freedom. But the lowliest can feel its glow, as soon as they learn the art of attaining it through non-violent non-co-operation.

The fact that there are so many men still alive in the world shows that it is based not on the force of arms but on the force of truth or love. Therefore, the greatest and most unimpeachable evidence of the success of this force is to be found in the fact that, in spite of the wars of the world, it still lives on.

Thousands, indeed tens of thousands, depend for their existence on a very active working of this force. Little quarrels of millions of families in their daily lives disappear before the exercise of this force. Hundreds of nations live in peace. History does not and cannot take note of this fact. History is really a record of every interruption of the even working of the force of love or of the soul. Soul-force, being natural, is not noted in history. . . .

Complete civil disobedience is rebellion without the element of violence in it. An out-and-out civil resister simply ignores the authority of the State. He becomes an outlaw claiming to disregard every unmoral State law. Thus, for instance, he may refuse to pay taxes, he may refuse to recognise the authority of his daily intercourse. He may refuse to obey the law of trespass and claim to enter military barracks in order to speak to the soldiers, he may refuse to submit to limitations upon the manner of picketing and may picket within the proscribed area. In doing all this he never uses force and never resists force when it is used against him. In fact, he invites imprisonment and other uses of force against himself. This he does because and when he finds the bodily freedom he seemingly enjoys to be an intolerable burden. He argues to himself that a State allows personal freedom only in so far as the citizen submits to its regulations. Submission to the State law is the price a citizen pays for his personal liberty. Submission, therefore, to a State law wholly or largely unjust is an immoral barter for liberty. A citizen who thus realises the evil nature of a State is not satisfied to live on its sufferance.

When a body of men disown the State under which they have hitherto lived, they nearly establish their own government. I say nearly, for they do not go to the point of using force when they are resisted by the State. Their 'business', as of the individual, is to be locked up or shot by the State, unless it recognises their separate existence, in other words bows to their will. Thus three thousand Indians in South Africa after due notice to the Government of the Transvaal crossed the Transvaal border in 1914 in defiance of the Transvaal Immigration Law and compelled the government to arrest them. When it failed to provoke them to violence or to coerce them into submission, it yielded to their demands. A body of civil resisters is, therefore, like an army subject to all the discipline of a soldier, only harder because of want of excitement of an ordinary soldier's life. A civil resistance army requires the fewest number of soldiers. Indeed one *perfect* civil resister is enough to win the battle of Right against Wrong.

My work will be finished, if I succeed in carrying conviction to the human family that every man or woman, however weak in body, is the guardian of his or her self-respect and liberty. This defence avails, though the whole world may be against the individual resister. . . .

B Frantz Fanon (1925-61), a black French psychiatrist and revolutionary, analysed the nature of colonialism in *The Wretched of the Earth* (1961). He bitterly attacked white concepts and white domination in calling for revolutionary action.

. . . For a colonized people the most essential value, because the most concrete, is first and foremost the land: the land which will bring them bread and, above all, dignity. But this dignity has nothing to do with the dignity of the human individual: for that human individual has never heard tell of it. All that the native has seen in his country is that they can freely arrest him, beat him, starve him: and no professor of ethics, no priest has ever come to be beaten in his place, nor to share their bread with him. As far as the native is concerned, morality is very concrete; it is to silence the settler's defiance, to break his flaunting violence—in a word, to put him out of the picture. The well-known principle that all men are equal will be illustrated in the colonies from the moment that the native claims that he is the equal of the settler. One step more, and he is ready to fight to be more than the settler. In fact, he has already decided to eject him and to take his place; as we see it, it is a whole material and moral universe which is breaking up. The intellectual who for his part has followed the colonialist with regard to the universal abstract will fight in order that the settler and the native may live together in peace in a new world. But the thing he does not see, precisely because he is permeated by colonialism and all its ways of thinking, is that the settler, from the moment that the colonial context disappears, has no longer any interest in remaining or in co-existing. . . .

Thus the native discovers that his life, his breath, his beating heart are the same as those of the settler. He finds out that the settler's skin is not of any more value than a native's skin; and it must be said that this discovery shakes the world in a very necessary manner. All the new, revolutionary assurance of the native stems from it. For if, in fact, my life is worth as much as the settler's, his glance no longer shrivels me up nor freezes me, and his voice no longer turns me into stone. I am no longer on tenterhooks in his presence; in fact, I don't give a damn for him. Not only does his presence no longer trouble me, but I am already preparing such efficient ambushes for him that soon there will be no way out but that of flight. . . .

. . . In reality the colonial system was concerned with certain forms of wealth and certain resources only—precisely those which provisioned her own industries. Up to the present no serious effort had been made to estimate the riches of the soil or of mineral resources. Thus the young independent nation sees itself obliged to use the economic channels created by the colonial regime. It can, obviously, export to other countries and other currency areas, but the basis of its exports is not fundamentally modified. The colonial regime has carved out certain channels and they must be maintained or catastrophe will threaten. Perhaps it is necessary to begin everything all over again: to change the nature of the country's exports, and not simply their destination, to re-examine the soil and mineral resources, the rivers, and—why not?—the sun's productivity. Now, in order to do all this other things are needed over and above human output—capital of all kinds, technicians, engineers, skilled mechanics, and so on. Let's be frank: we do not believe that the colossal effort which the underdeveloped peoples are called upon to make by their leaders will give the desired results. If conditions of work are not modified, centuries will be needed to humanize this world which has been forced down to animal level by imperial powers.

The truth is that we ought not to accept these conditions. We should flatly refuse the situation to which the Western countries wish to condemn us. Colonialism and imperialism have not paid their score when they withdraw their flags and their police forces from our territories. For centuries the capitalists have behaved in the underdeveloped world like nothing more than war criminals. Deportations, massacres, forced labor, and slavery have been the main methods used by capitalism to increase its wealth, its gold or diamond reserves, and to establish its power. Not long ago Nazism transformed the whole of Europe into a veritable colony. The governments of the various European nations called for reparations and demanded the restitution in kind and money of the wealth which had been stolen from them: cultural treasures, pictures, sculptures, and stained glass have been given back to their owners. There was only one slogan in the mouths of Europeans on the morrow of the 1945 V-day: "Germany must pay." Herr Adenauer, it must be said, at the opening of the Eichmann trial, and in the name of the German people, asked once more for forgiveness from the Jewish people. Herr Adenauer has renewed the promise of his people to go on paying to the state of Israel the enormous sums which are supposed to be compensation for the crimes of the Nazis.

In the same way we may say that the imperialist states would make a great mistake and commit an unspeakable injustice if they contented themselves with withdrawing from our soil the military cohorts, and the administrative and managerial services whose function it was to discover the wealth of the country, to extract it and to send it off to the mother countries. We are not blinded by the moral reparation of national independence; nor are we fed by it. The wealth of the imperial countries is our wealth too. On the universal plane this affirmation, you may be sure, should on no account be taken to signify that we feel ourselves affected by the creations of Western arts or techniques. For in a very concrete way Europe has stuffed herself inordinately with the gold and raw materials of the colonial countries: Latin America, China, and Africa. From all these continents, under whose eyes Europe today raises up her tower of opulence, there has flowed out for centuries toward that same Europe diamonds and oil, silk and cotton, wood and exotic products. Europe is literally the creation of the Third World. The wealth which smothers her is that which was stolen from the underdeveloped peoples. The ports of Holland, the docks of Bordeaux and Liverpool were specialized in the Negro slave trade, and owe their renown to millions of deported slaves. So when we hear the head of a European state declare with his hand on his heart that he must come to the aid of the poor underdeveloped peoples, we do not tremble with gratitude. Quite the contrary; we say to ourselves: "It's a just reparation which will be paid to us." Nor will we acquiesce in the help for underdeveloped countries being a program of "sisters of charity." This help should be the ratification of a double realization: the realization by the colonized peoples that *it is their due*, and the realization by the capitalist powers that in fact *they must pay*. For if, through lack of intelligence (we won't speak of lack of gratitude) the capitalist countries refuse to pay, then the relentless dialectic of their own system will smother them. It is a fact that young nations do not attract much private capital. There are many reasons which explain and render legitimate this reserve on the part of the monopolies. As soon as the capitalists know—and of course they are the first to know—that their government is getting ready to decolonize, they hasten to withdraw all their capital from the colony in question. The spectacular flight of capital is one of the most constant phenomena of de-colonization. . . .

Come, brothers, we have far too much work to do for us to play the game of rearguard. Europe has done what she set out to do and on the whole she has done it well; let us stop blaming her, but let us say to her firmly that she should not make such a song and dance about it. We have no more to fear; so let us stop envying her.

The Third World today faces Europe like a colossal mass whose aim should be to try to resolve the problems to which Europe has not been able to find the answers.

But let us be clear: what matters is to stop talking about output, and intensification, and the rhythm of work.

No, there is no question of a return to Nature. It is simply a very concrete question of not dragging men toward mutilation, of not imposing upon the brain rhythms which very quickly obliterate it and wreck it. The pretext of catching up must not be used to push man around, to tear him away from himself or from his privacy, to break and kill him.

No, we do not want to catch up with anyone. What we want to do is to go forward all the time, night and day, in the company of Man, in the company of all men. The caravan should not be stretched out, for in that case each line will hardly see those who precede it; and men who no longer recognize each other meet less and less together, and talk to each other less and less.

It is a question of the Third World starting a new history of Man, a history which will have regard to the sometimes prodigious theses which Europe has put forward, but which will also not forget Europe's crimes, of which the most horrible was committed in the heart of man, and consisted of the path-ological tearing apart of his functions and the crumbling away of his unity. And in the framework of the collectivity there were the differentiations, the stratification, and the bloodthirsty tensions fed by classes; and finally, on the immense scale of humanity, there were racial hatreds, slavery, exploitation, and above all the bloodless genocide which consisted in the setting aside of fifteen thousand millions of men.

So, comrades, let us not pay tribute to Europe by creating states, institutions, and societies which draw their inspiration from her.

Humanity is waiting for something from us other than such an imitation, which would be almost an obscene caricature.

If we want to turn Africa into a new Europe, and America into a new Europe, then let us leave the destiny of our countries to Europeans. They will know how to do it better than the most gifted among us.

But if we want humanity to advance a step further, if we want to bring it up to a different level than that which Europe has shown it, then we must invent and we must make discoveries.

If we wish to live up to our peoples' expectations, we must seek the response elsewhere than in Europe.

Moreover, if we wish to reply to the expectations of the people of Europe, it is no good sending them back a reflection, even an ideal reflection, of their society and their thought with which from time to time they feel immeas-urably sickened.

For Europe, for ourselves, and for humanity, comrades, we must turn over a new leaf, we must work out new concepts, and try to set afoot a new man.

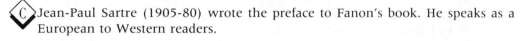 Jean-Paul Sartre (1905-80) wrote the preface to Fanon's book. He speaks as a European to Western readers.

Europeans, you must open this book and enter into it. After a few steps in the darkness you will see strangers gathered around a fire; come close, and listen, for they are talking of the destiny they will mete out to your trading centers and to the hired soldiers who defend them. They will see you, perhaps, but they will go on talking among themselves, without even lowering their voices. This indifference strikes home: their fathers, shadowy creatures, *your* creatures, were but dead souls; you it was who allowed them glimpses of light, to you only did they dare speak, and you did not bother to reply to such zombies. Their sons ignore you; a fire warms them and sheds light around them, and you have not lit it. Now, at a respectful distance, it is you who will feel furtive, nightbound, and perished with cold. Turn and turn about; in these shadows from whence a new dawn will break, it is you who are the zombies.

In this case, you will say, let's throw away this book. Why read it if it is not written for us? For two reasons: the first is that Fanon explains you to his brothers and shows them the mechanism by which we are estranged from ourselves; take advantage of this, and get to know yourselves seen in the light of truth, objectively. Our victims know us by their scars and by their chains, and it is this that makes their evidence irrefutable. It is enough that they show us what we have made of them for us to realize what we have made of ourselves. But is it any use? Yes, for Europe is at death's door. But, you will say, we live in the mother country, and we disapprove of her excesses. It is true, you are not settlers, but you are no better. For the pioneers belonged to you; you sent them overseas, and it was you they enriched. You warned them that if they shed too much blood you would disown them, or say you did, in something of the same way as any state maintains abroad a mob of agitators, *agents provocateurs*, and spies whom it disowns when they are caught. You, who are so liberal and so humane, who have such an exaggerated adoration of culture that it verges on affectation, you pretend to forget that you own colonies and that in them men are massacred in your name. Fanon reveals to his comrades—above all to some of them who are rather too Westernized—the solidarity of the people of the mother country and of their representatives in the colonies. Have the courage to read this book, for in the first place it will make you ashamed, and shame, as Marx said, is a revolutionary sentiment. You see, I, too, am incapable of ridding myself of subjective illusions; I, too, say to you: "All is lost unless . . ." As a European, I steal the enemy's book, and out of it I fashion a remedy for Europe. Make the most of it . . .

. . . [Fanon] has shown the way forward: he is the spokesman of those who are fighting and he has called for union, that is to say the unity of the African continent against all dissensions and all particularisms. He has gained his end. If he had wished to describe in all its details the historical phenomenon of decolonization he would have to have spoken of us; this is not at all his intention. But, when we have closed the book, the argument continues within us, in spite of its author; for we feel the strength of the peoples in revolt and we answer by force. Thus there is a fresh moment of violence; and this time we ourselves are involved, for by its nature this violence is changing us, accordingly as the "half native" is changed. Every one of us must think for himself—always provided that he thinks at all; for in Europe today, stunned as she is by the blows received by France, Belgium, or England, even to allow your mind to be diverted, however slightly, is as good as being the accomplice in crime of colonialism. This book had not the slightest need of a preface, all the less because it is not addressed to us. Yet I have written one, in order to bring the argument to its conclusion; for we in Europe too are being decolonized: that is to say that the settler which is in every one of us is being savagely rooted out. Let us look at ourselves, if we can bear to, and see what is becoming of us. First, we must face that unexpected revelation, the strip tease of our humanism. There you can see it, quite naked, and it's not a pretty sight. It was nothing but an ideology of lies, a perfect justification for pillage; its honeyed words, its affectation of sensibility were only alibis for our aggressions. A fine sight they are too, the believers in non-violence, saying that they are neither executioners nor victims. Very well then; if you're not victims when the government which you've voted for, when the army in which your younger brothers are serving without hesitation or remorse have undertaken race murder, you are, without a shadow of doubt, executioners. And if you choose to be victims and to risk being put in prison for a day or two, you are simply choosing to pull your irons out of the fire. But you will not be able to pull them out; they'll have to stay there till the end. Try to understand this at any rate: if violence began this very evening and if exploitation and oppression had never existed on the earth, perhaps the slogans of non-violence might end the quarrel. But if the whole regime, even your non-violent ideas, are conditioned by a thousand-year-old oppression, your passivity serves only to place you in the ranks of the oppressors.

◇ The South African nationalist leader Steve Biko (1946-77) died while being held in detention by the security police of his country. Biko had led the black consciousness movement in South Africa and had been banned from public life because of his ideas. His death further galvanized the black movement. In 1973 Biko's essay "Black Consciousness and the Quest for a True Humanity" was published in Great Britain.

As one black writer says, colonialism is never satisfied with having the native in its grip but, by some strange logic, it must turn to his past and disfigure and distort it. Hence the history of the black man in this country is most disappointing to read. It is presented merely as a long succession of defeats. The Xhosas were thieves who went to war for stolen property; the Boers never provoked the Xhosas but merely went on "punitive expeditions" to teach the thieves a lesson. Heroes like Makana who were essentially revolutionaries are painted as superstitious trouble-makers who lied to the people about bullets turning into water. Great nation-builders like Shaka are cruel tyrants who frequently attacked smaller tribes for no reason but for some sadistic purpose. Not only is there no objectivity in the history taught us but there is frequently an appalling misrepresentation of facts that sicken even the uninformed student.

Thus a lot of attention has to be paid to our history if we as blacks want to aid each other in our coming into consciousness. We have to rewrite our history and produce in it the heroes that formed the core of our resistance to the white invaders. More has to be revealed, and stress has to be laid on the successful nation-building attempts of men such as Shaka, Moshoeshoe and Hintsa. These areas call for intense research to provide some sorely-needed missing links. We would be too naive to expect our conquerors to write unbiased histories about us but we have to destroy the myth that our history starts in 1652, the year Van Riebeeck landed at the Cape.

Our culture must be defined in concrete terms. We must relate the past to the present and demonstrate a historical evolution of the modern black man. There is a tendency to think of our culture as a static culture that was arrested in 1652 and has never developed since. The "return to the bush" concept suggests that we have nothing to boast of except lions, sex and drink. We accept that when colonisation sets in it devours the indigenous culture and leaves behind a bastard culture that may thrive at the pace allowed it by the dominant culture. But we also have to realise that the basic tenets of our culture have largely succeeded in withstanding the process of bastardisation and that even at this moment we can still demonstrate that we appreciate a man for himself. Ours is a true man-centred society whose sacred tradition is that of sharing. We must reject, as we have been doing, the individualistic cold approach to life that is the cornerstone of the Anglo-Boer culture. We must seek to restore to the black man the great importance we used to give to human relations, the high regard for people and their property and for life in general; to reduce the triumph of technology over man and the materialistic element that is slowly creeping into our society.

These are essential features of our black culture to which we must cling. Black culture above all implies freedom on our part to innovate without recourse to white values. This innovation is part of the natural development of any culture. A culture is essentially the society's composite answer to the varied problems of life. We are experiencing new problems every day and whatever we do adds to the richness of our cultural heritage as long as it has man as its centre. The adoption of black theatre and drama is one such important innovation which we need to encourage and to develop. We know that our love of music and rhythm has relevance even in this day.

Being part of an exploitative society in which we are often the direct objects of exploitation, we need to evolve a strategy towards our economic situation. We are aware that the blacks are still colonised even within the borders of South Africa. Their cheap labour has helped to make South Africa what it is today. Our money from the townships takes a one-way journey to white shops and white banks, and all we do in our lives is pay the white man either with labour or in coin. Capitalistic exploitative tendencies, coupled with the overt arrogance of white racism, have conspired against us. Thus in South Africa now it is very expensive to be poor. It is the poor people who stay furthest from town and therefore have to spend more money on transport to come and work for white people; it is the poor people who use uneconomic and inconvenient fuel like paraffin and coal because of the refusal of the white man to install electricity in black areas; it is the poor people who are governed by many ill-defined restrictive laws and therefore have to spend money on fines for "technical" offences; it is the poor people who have no hospitals and are therefore exposed to exorbitant charges by private doctors; it is the poor people who use untarred roads, have to walk long distances, and therefore experience the greatest wear and tear on commodities like shoes; it is the poor people who have to pay for their children's books while whites get them free. It does not need to be said that it is the black people who are poor.

We therefore need to take another look at how best to use our economic power, little as it may seem to be. We must seriously examine the possibilities of establishing business co-operatives whose interests will be ploughed back into community development programmes. We should think along such lines as the "buy black" campaign once suggested in Johannesburg and establish our own banks for the benefit of the community. Organisational development amongst blacks has only been low because we have allowed it to be. Now that we know we are on our own, it is an absolute duty for us to fulfil these needs.

The last step in Black Consciousness is to broaden the base of our operation. One of the basic tenets of Black Consciousness is totality of involvement. This means that all blacks must sit as one big unit, and no fragmentation and distraction from the mainstream of events be allowed. Hence we must resist the attempts by protagonists of the bantustan theory to fragment our approach. We are oppressed not as individuals, not as Zulus, Xhosas, Vendas or Indians. We are oppressed because we are black. We must use that very concept to unite ourselves and to respond as a cohesive group. We must cling to each other with a tenacity that will shock the perpetrators of evil.

Our preparedness to take upon ourselves the cudgels of the struggle will see us through. We must remove from our vocabulary completely the concept of fear. Truth must ultimately triumph over evil, and the white man has always nourished his greed on this basic fear that shows itself in the black community. Special Branch agents will not turn the lie into truth, and one must ignore them. In a true bid for change we have to take off our coats, be prepared to lose our comfort and security, our jobs and positions of prestige, and our families, for just as it is true that "leadership and security are basically incompatible", a struggle without casualties is no struggle. We must realise that prophetic cry of black students: "Black man, you are on your own!"

Some will charge that we are racist but these people are using exactly the values we reject. We do not have the power to subjugate anyone. We are merely responding to provocation in the most realistic possible way. Racism does not only imply exclusion of one race by another—it always presupposes that the exclusion is for the purposes of subjugation. Blacks have had enough experience as objects of racism not to wish to turn the tables. While it may be relevant now to talk about black in relation to white, we must not make this our preoccupation, for it can be a negative exercise. As we proceed further towards the achievement of our goals let us talk more about ourselves and our struggle and less about whites.

We have set out on a quest for true humanity, and somewhere on the distant horizon we can see the glittering prize. Let us march forth with courage and determination, drawing strength from our common plight and our brotherhood. In time we shall be in a position to bestow upon South Africa the greatest gift possible—a more human face.

1. What influence do you feel Gandhi's philosophy had on Martin Luther King?
2. Contrast Gandhi's statement " we want freedom for our country, but not at the expense or exploitation of others" with the objectives of European imperialism.
3. Outline Gandhi's view of the role of civil disobedience.
4. Write an editorial piece responding to Fanon's view that Europe owes economic reparations to the Third World.
5. Comment on Fanon's reference to the "moral reparation of national independence."
6. Respond to Fanon's call to action from the point of view of a resident of a European colony in the early 1960s.
7. Comment on Sartre's warnings and his contention that Fanon's charges are an attack against western practices based on western values themselves.
8. On the basis of your readings of Steve Biko, give your reaction to the viewpoint: "Many white South Africans contend that the black majority is unable to govern itself."

▪ ▪ ▪

TECHNOLOGY AND CULTURE

The second half of the twentieth century witnessed rapid industrial and technological change, to the point where it became difficult to absorb change and the new information systems arising out of technological innovations. The role of technology itself in the development of culture and society has been a matter of considerable investigation and concern.

A lecture given by C.P. Snow (1905-80) in 1959, "The Two Cultures and the Scientific Revolution," focussed debate about the intellectual life of the West. Snow, not unlike Ortega y Gasset a generation earlier, believed that the West was becoming dangerously divided between a scientific and a humanistic culture, each ignorant of the other.

> . . . There have been plenty of days when I have spent the working hours with scientists and then gone off at night with some literary colleagues. I mean that literally. I have had, of course, intimate friends among both scientists and writers. It was through living among these groups and much more, I think, through moving regularly from one to the other and back again that

Sources: C. P. Snow, *The Two Cultures: and A Second Look* (Cambridge: Cambridge University Press, 1965), pp. 2, 3-4, 5, 10-11, 16; Marshall McLuhan, *Understanding Media* (New York: McGraw-Hill Book Company, 1964), pp. 7-8, 22-23, 24-25, 176-78.

I got occupied with the problem of what, long before I put it on paper, I christened to myself as the 'two cultures'. For constantly I felt I was moving among two groups—comparable in intelligence, identical in race, not grossly different in social origin, earning about the same incomes, who had almost ceased to communicate at all, who in intellectual, moral and psychological climate had so little in common that instead of going from Burlington House or South Kensington to Chelsea, one might have crossed an ocean. . . .

. . . I intend something serious. I believe the intellectual life of the whole of western society is increasingly being split into two polar groups. When I say the intellectual life, I mean to include also a large part of our practical life, because I should be the last person to suggest the two can at the deepest level be distinguished. I shall come back to the practical life a little later. Two polar groups: at one pole we have the literary intellectuals, who incidentally while no one was looking took to referring to themselves as 'intellectuals' as though there were no others. I remember G. H. Hardy once remarking to me in mild puzzlement, some time in the 1930's: 'Have you noticed how the word "intellectual" is used nowadays? There seems to be a new definition which certainly doesn't include Rutherford or Eddington or Dirac or Adrian or me. It does seem rather odd, don't y' know.'

Literary intellectuals at one pole—at the other scientists, and as the most representative, the physical scientists. Between the two a gulf of mutual incomprehension—sometimes (particularly among the young) hostility and dislike, but most of all lack of understanding. They have a curious distorted image of each other. Their attitudes are so different that, even on the level of emotion, they can't find much common ground. . . .

The non-scientists have a rooted impression that the scientists are shallowly optimistic, unaware of man's condition. On the other hand, the scientists believe that the literary intellectuals are totally lacking in foresight, peculiarly unconcerned with their brother men, in a deep sense anti-intellectual, anxious to restrict both art and thought to the existential moment. And so on. Anyone with a mild talent for invective could produce plenty of this kind of subterranean back-chat. On each side there is some of it which is not entirely baseless. It is all destructive. Much of it rests on misinterpretations which are dangerous. . . .

. . . It is obvious that between the two, as one moves through intellectual society from the physicists to the literary intellectuals, there are all kinds of tones of feeling on the way. But I believe the pole of total incomprehension of science radiates its influence on all the rest. That total incomprehension gives, much more pervasively than we realise, living in it, an unscientific flavour to the whole 'traditional' culture, and that unscientific flavour is often, much more than we admit, on the point of turning anti-scientific. The feelings of one pole become the anti-feelings of the other. If the scientists have the future in their bones, then the traditional culture responds by wishing the future did not exist. It is the traditional culture, to an extent remarkably little diminished by the emergence of the scientific one, which manages the western world.

This polarisation is sheer loss to us all. To us as people, and to our society. . . .

There seems then to be no place where the cultures meet. . . .

Understanding Media, by Marshall McLuhan (1911-80), was one of many works in which the Canadian social thinker developed a theory of the relationship of media to social change and civilization.

In a culture like ours, long accustomed to splitting and dividing all things as a means of control, it is sometimes a bit of a shock to be reminded that, in operational and practical fact, the medium is the message. This is merely to say that the personal and social consequences of any medium—that is, of any extension of ourselves—result from the new scale that is introduced into our affairs by each extension of ourselves, or by any new technology. Thus, with automation, for example, the new patterns of human association tend to eliminate jobs, it is true. That is the negative result. Positively, automation creates roles for people, which is to say depth of involvement in their work and human association that our preceding mechanical technology had destroyed. Many people would be disposed to say that it was not the machine, but what one did with the machine, that was its meaning or message. In terms of the ways in which the machine altered our relations to one another and to ourselves, it mattered not in the least whether it turned out cornflakes or Cadillacs. The restructuring of human work and association was shaped by the technique of fragmentation that is the essence of machine technology. The essence of automation technology is the opposite. It is integral and decentralist in depth, just as the machine was fragmentary, centralist, and superficial in its patterning of human relationships.

The instance of the electric light may prove illuminating in this connection. The electric light is pure information. It is a medium without a message, as it were, unless it is used to spell out some verbal ad or name. This fact, characteristic of all media, means that the "content" of any medium is always another medium. The content of writing is speech, just as the written word is the content of print, and print is the content of the telegraph. If it is asked, "What is the content of speech?," it is necessary to say, "It is an actual process of thought, which is in itself nonverbal." An abstract painting represents direct manifestation of creative thought processes as they might appear in computer designs. What we are considering here, however, are the psychic and social consequences of the designs or patterns as they amplify or accelerate existing processes. For the "message" of any medium or technology is the change of scale or pace or pattern that it introduces into human affairs. The railway did not introduce movement or transportation or wheel or road into human society, but it accelerated and enlarged the scale of previous human functions, creating totally new kinds of cities and new kinds of work and leisure. This happened whether the railway functioned in a tropical or a northern environment, and is quite independent of the freight or content of the railway medium. The airplane, on the other hand, by accelerating the rate of transportation, tends to dissolve the railway form of city, politics, and association, quite independently of what the airplane is used for. . . .

. . . There is a basic principle that distinguishes a hot medium like radio from a cool one like the telephone, or a hot medium like the movie from a cool one like TV. A hot medium is one that extends one single sense in "high definition." High definition is the state of being well filled with data. A photograph is, visually, "high definition." A cartoon is "low definition," simply because very little visual information is provided. Telephone is a cool medium, or one of low definition, because the ear is given a meager amount of information. And speech is a cool medium of low definition, because so little is given and so much has to be filled in by the listener. On the other hand, hot media do not leave so much to be filled in or completed by the audience. Hot media are, therefore, low in participation, and cool media are high in participation or completion by the audience. Naturally, therefore, a hot medium like radio has very different effects on the user from a cool medium like the telephone. . . .

An example of the disruptive impact of a hot technology succeeding a cool one is given by Robert Theobald in *The Rich and the Poor*. When Australian natives were given steel axes by the missionaries, their culture, based on the stone axe, collapsed. The stone axe had not only been scarce but had always been a basic status symbol of male importance. The missionaries provided quantities of sharp steel axes and gave them to women and children. The men had even to borrow these from the women, causing a collapse of male dignity. A tribal and feudal hierarchy of traditional kind collapses quickly when it meets any hot medium of the mechanical, uniform, and repetitive kind. The medium of money or wheel or writing, or any other form of specialist speedup of exchange and information, will serve to fragment a tribal structure. Similarly, a very much greater speed-up, such as occurs with electricity, may serve to restore a tribal pattern of intense involvement such as took place with the introduction of radio in Europe, and is now tending to happen as a result of TV in America. Specialist technologies detribalize. The nonspecialist electric technology retribalizes. The process of upset resulting from a new distribution of skills is accompanied by much culture lag in which people feel compelled to look at new situations as if they were old ones, and come up with ideas of "population explosion" in an age of implosion. Newton, in an age of clocks, managed to present the physical universe in the image of a clock. But poets like Blake were far ahead of Newton in their response to the challenge of the clock. Blake spoke of the need to be delivered "from single vision and Newton's sleep," knowing very well that Newton's response to the challenge of the new mechanism was itself merely a mechanical repetition of the challenge. . . .

Of the many unforeseen consequences of typography, the emergence of nationalism is, perhaps, the most familiar. Political unification of populations by means of vernacular and language groupings was unthinkable before printing turned each vernacular into an extensive mass medium. The tribe, an extended form of a family of blood relatives, is exploded by print, and is replaced by an association of men homogeneously trained to be individuals. Nationalism itself came as an intense new visual image of group destiny and status, and depended on a speed of information movement unknown before printing. Today nationalism as an image still depends on the press but has all the electric media against it. In business, as in politics, the effect of even jet-plane speeds is to render the older national groupings of social organization quite unworkable. In the Renaissance it was the speed of print and the ensuing market and commercial developments that made nationalism (which is continuity and competition in homogeneous space) as natural as it was new. By the same token, the heterogeneities and noncompetitive discontinuities of medieval guilds and family organization had become a great nuisance as speed-up of information by print called for more fragmentation and uniformity of function. The Benvenuto Cellinis, the goldsmith-cum-painter-cum-sculptor-cum-writer-cum-condottiere, became obsolete.

Once a new technology comes into a social milieu it cannot cease to permeate that milieu until every institution is saturated. Typography has permeated every phase of the arts and sciences in the past five hundred years. It would be easy to document the processes by which the principles of continuity, uniformity, and repeatability have become the basis of calculus and of marketing, as of industrial production, entertainment, and science. It will be enough to point out that repeatability conferred on the printed book the strangely novel character of a uniformly priced commodity opening the door to price systems. The printed book had in addition the quality of portability and accessibility that had been lacking in the manuscript.

Directly associated with these expansive qualities was the revolution in expression. Under manuscript conditions the role of being an author was a vague and uncertain one, like that of a minstrel. Hence, self-expression was of little interest. Typography, however, created a medium in which it was possible to speak out loud and bold to the world itself, just as it was possible to circumnavigate the world of books previously locked up in a pluralistic world of monastic cells. Boldness of type created boldness of expression.

Uniformity reached also into areas of speech and writing, leading to a single tone and attitude to reader and subject spread throughout an entire composition. The "man of letters" was born. Extended to the spoken word, this literate *equitone* enabled literate people to maintain a single "high tone" in discourse that was quite devastating, and enabled nineteenth-century prose writers to assume moral qualities that few would now care to simulate. Permeation of the colloquial language with literate uniform qualities had flattened out educated speech till it is a very reasonable acoustic facsimile of the uniform and continuous visual effects of typography. From this technological effect follows the further fact that the humor, slang, and dramatic vigor of American-English speech are monopolies of the semi-literate.

These typographical matters for many people are charged with controversial values. Yet in any approach to understanding print it is necessary to stand aside from the form in question if its typical pressure and life are to be observed. Those who panic now about the threat of the newer media and about the revolution we are forging, vaster in scope than that of Gutenberg, are obviously lacking in cool visual detachment and gratitude for that most potent gift bestowed on Western man by literacy and typography: his power to act without reaction or involvement. It is this kind of specialization by dissociation that has created Western power and efficiency. Without this dissociation of action from feeling and emotion people are hampered and hesitant. Print taught men to say, "Damn the torpedoes. Full steam ahead!"

1. Respond to Snow's lament that "This polarization [between the literary and the scientific] is sheer loss to us all. To us as people, and to our society." Do you agree with Snow's analysis? To what extent does it still hold true today?

2. McLuhan's phrase "the medium is the message" has become overused to the point of becoming a cliché. In the process, much of the original meaning has become obscured. Write a short précis of the arguments that he uses to explain his concept.
3. Distinguish, with examples, between hot and cool media.
4. Respond to McLuhan's assertions regarding the impact of print technology.

▪ ▪ ▪

FEMINISM

Feminism has become one of the most important ideas promulgating social change in the West. It not only discussed and fostered women's rights, but also developed new concepts about the role of women in society and culture. All feminists stressed the importance of challenging inherited sexual stereotypes. Feminism became a mass movement in the 1960s as women agitated for political and social reform throughout the world.

A Simone de Beauvoir (1908-86) published her work *The Second Sex* in 1949. The book was an important landmark in documenting the thesis that women have been given a lesser status than men in Western culture, and that they have been made victims of an unjust system.

> . . . In truth, to become a creative artist it is not enough to be cultivated— that is to say, to make exhibitions and bits of information a part of one's life. Culture must be apprehended through the free action of a transcendence; that is, the free spirit with all its riches must project itself toward an empty heaven that it is to populate; but if a thousand persistent bonds hold it to earth, its surge is broken. To be sure, the young girl can today go out alone and idle in the Tuileries; but I have already noted how hostile the street is to her, with eyes and hands lying in wait everywhere; if she wanders carelessly, her mind drifting, if she lights a cigarette in front of a café, if she goes alone to the movies, a disagreeable incident is soon bound to happen. She must inspire respect by her costume and manners. But this preoccupation rivets her to the ground and to herself. "Your wings droop." At eighteen T. E. Lawrence took a long bicycle tour through France by himself; no young girl would be allowed to engage in any such escapade, still less to adventure on foot in a half-desert and dangerous country, as Lawrence did a year later. Yet such experiences are of incalculable influence: through them an individual, in the intoxication of liberty and discovery, learns to regard the entire earth as his territory.
>
> Woman is in any case deprived of the lessons of violence by her nature: I have shown how her muscular weakness disposes her to passivity. When a boy settles a dispute with his fists, he feels that he is capable of taking care

Sources: Simone de Beauvoir, *The Second Sex* (New York: Alfred A. Knopf, 1957), pp. 712-15, 721-22, 728-31; Betty Friedan, *The Feminine Mystique* (New York: Dell Publishing Company, Inc., 1963), pp. 37-38, 326, 360-61, 362-64.

of himself; at the least, the young girl should in compensation be permitted to know how it feels to take the initiative in sport and adventure, to taste the pride of obstacles overcome. But not at all. She may feel herself alone *in the midst* of the world, but she never stands up *before* it, unique and sovereign. Everything influences her to let herself be hemmed in, dominated by existences foreign to her own—and especially in the matter of love she abnegates herself instead of asserting herself. In this connection bad luck or unattractiveness are often blessings in disguise. It was her isolation that enabled Emily Brontë to write a wild and powerful book; in the face of nature, death, and destiny, she had no other backing than her own resources. Rosa Luxemburg was ugly; she was never tempted to wallow in the cult of her own image, to make herself object, prey, trap; from her youth, she was wholly spirit and liberty. Even so, it is very seldom that woman fully assumes the anguished tête-à-tête with the given world. The constraints that surround her and the whole tradition that weighs her down prevent her from feeling responsible for the universe, and that is the deep-seated reason for her mediocrity.

The men that we call great are those who—in one way or another—have taken the weight of the world upon their shoulders; they have done better or worse, they have succeeded in re-creating it or they have gone down; but first they have assumed that enormous burden. This is what no woman has ever done, what none has ever been *able* to do. To regard the universe as one's own, to consider oneself to blame for its faults and to glory in its progress, one must belong to the caste of the privileged; it is for those alone who are in command to justify the universe by changing it, by thinking about it, by revealing it; they alone can recognize themselves in it and endeavor to make their mark upon it. It is in man and not in woman that it has hitherto been possible for Man to be incarnated. For the individuals who seem to us most outstanding, who are honored with the name of genius, are those who have proposed to enact the fate of all humanity in their personal existences, and no woman has believed herself authorized to do this.

How could Van Gogh have been born a woman? A woman would not have been sent on a mission to the Belgian coal mines in Borinage, she would not have felt the misery of the miners as her own crime, she would not have sought a redemption; she would therefore have never painted Van Gogh's sunflowers. Not to mention that the mode of life of the painter—his solitude at Arles, his frequentation of cafés and brothels, all that nourished Van Gogh's art in nourishing his sensitivity—would have been forbidden her. A woman could never have become Kafka: in her doubts and her anxieties she would never have recognized the anguish of Man driven from paradise. There is hardly any woman other than St. Theresa who in total abandonment has herself lived out the situation of humanity: we have seen why. Taking her stand beyond the earthly hierarchies, she felt, like St. John of the Cross, no reassuring ceiling over her head. There were for both the same darkness, the same flashes of light, in the self the same nothingness, in God the same plenitude. When at last it will be possible for every human being thus to set his pride beyond the sexual differentiation, in the laborious glory of free existence, then only will woman be able to identify her personal history, her problems, her doubts, her hopes, with those of humanity; then only will she be able to seek in her life and her works to reveal the whole of reality and not merely her personal self. As long as she still has to struggle to become a human being, she cannot become a creator.

Once again: in order to explain her limitations it is woman's situation that must be invoked and not a mysterious essence; thus the future remains largely open. Writers on the subject have vied with one another in maintaining that women do not have "creative genius"; this is the thesis defended by Mme Marthe Borély, an erstwhile notorious antifeminist; but one would say that she sought to make her books a living proof of feminine illogicality and silliness, so self-contradictory are they. Furthermore, the concept of a creative "instinct" must be discarded, like that of the "eternal feminine," from the old panel of entities. Certain misogynists assert, a little more concretely, that woman, being neurotic, could not create anything worth while; but they are often the same men that pronounce genius a neurosis. In any case, the example of Proust shows clearly enough that psychophysiological disequilibrium signifies neither lack of power nor mediocrity.

As for the argument drawn from history, we have just been considering what to think of that; the historical fact cannot be considered as establishing an eternal truth; it can only indicate a situation that is historical in nature precisely because it is undergoing change. How could women ever have had genius when they were denied all possibilty of accomplishing a work of genius—or just a work? The old Europe formerly poured out its contempt upon the American barbarians who boasted neither artists nor writers. "Let us come into existence before being asked to justify our existence," replied Jefferson, in effect. The Negroes make the same reply to the racists who reproach them for never having produced a Whitman or a Melville. No more can the French proletariat offer any name to compare with those of Racine or Mallarmé.

The free woman is just being born; when she has won possession of herself perhaps Rimbaud's prophecy will be fulfilled: "There shall be poets! When woman's unmeasured bondage shall be broken, when she shall live for and through herself, man—hitherto detestable—having let her go, she, too, will be poet! Woman will find the unknown! Will her ideational worlds be different from ours? She will come upon strange, unfathomable, repellent, delightful things; we shall take them, we shall comprehend them." It is not sure that her "ideational worlds" will be different from those of men, since it will be through attaining the same situation as theirs that she will find emancipation; to say in what degree she will remain different, in what degree these differences will retain their importance—this would be to hazard bold predictions indeed. What is certain is that hitherto woman's possibilities have been suppressed and lost to humanity, and that it is high time she be permitted to take her chances in her own interest and in the interest of all. . . .

It must be admitted that the males find in woman more complicity than the oppressor usually finds in the oppressed. And in bad faith they take authorization from this to declare that she has *desired* the destiny they have imposed on her. We have seen that all the main features of her training combine to bar her from the roads of revolt and adventure. Society in general—beginning with her respected parents—lies to her by praising the lofty values of love, devotion, the gift of herself, and then concealing from her the fact that neither lover nor husband nor yet her children will be inclined to accept the burdensome charge of all that. She cheerfully believes these lies because they invite her to follow the easy slope: in this others commit their worst crime against her; throughout her life from childhood on, they damage and corrupt her by designating as her true vocation this submission, which is the temptation of every existent in the anxiety of liberty. If a child is taught idleness by being amused all day long and never being led to study, or shown its usefulness, it will hardly be said, when he grows up, that he chose to be incapable and ignorant; yet this is how woman is brought up, without ever being impressed with the necessity of taking charge of her own existence. So she readily lets herself come to count on the protection, love, assistance, and supervision of others, she lets herself be fascinated with the hope of self-realization without *doing* anything. She does wrong in yielding to the temptation; but man is in no position to blame her, since he has led her into the temptation. When conflict arises between them, each will hold the other responsible for the situation; she will reproach him with having made her what she is: "No one taught me to reason or to earn my own living"; he will reproach her with having accepted the consequences: "You don't know anything, you are an incompetent," and so on. Each sex thinks it can justify itself by taking the offensive; but the wrongs done by one do not make the other innocent.

The innumerable conflicts that set men and women against one another come from the fact that neither is prepared to assume all the consequences of this situation which the one has offered and the other accepted. The doubtful concept of "equality in inequality," which the one uses to mask his despotism and the other to mask her cowardice, does not stand the test of experience: in their exchanges, woman appeals to the theoretical equality she has been guaranteed, and man the concrete inequality that exists. The result is that in every association an endless debate goes on concerning the ambiguous meaning of the words *give* and *take*: she complains of giving her all, he protests that she takes his all. Woman has to learn that exchanges—it is a fundamental law of political economy—are based on the value the merchandise offered has for the buyer, and not for the seller: she has been deceived in being persuaded that her worth is priceless. The truth is that for man she is an amusement, a pleasure, company, an inessential boon; he is for her the meaning, the justification of her existence. The exchange, therefore, is not of two items of equal value. . . .

◆B De Beauvoir wanted society to adopt a new attitude towards the relationship between the sexes.

I shall be told that all this is utopian fancy, because woman cannot be "made over" unless society has first made her really the equal of man. Conservatives have never failed in such circumstances to refer to that vicious circle; history, however, does not revolve. If a caste is kept in a state of inferiority, no doubt it remains inferior; but liberty can break the circle. Let the Negroes vote and they become worthy of having the vote: let woman be given responsibilities and she is able to assume them. The fact is that oppressors cannot be expected to make a move of gratuitous generosity; but at one time the revolt of the oppressed, at another time even the very evolution of the privileged caste itself, creates new situations; thus men have been led, in their own interest, to give partial emancipation to women: it remains only for women to continue their ascent, and the successes they are obtaining are an encouragement for them to do so. It seems almost certain that sooner or later they will arrive at complete economic and social equality, which will bring about an inner metamorphosis.

However this may be, there will be some to object that if such a world is possible it is not desirable. When woman is "the same" as her male, life will lose its salt and spice. This argument, also, has lost its novelty: those interested in perpetuating present conditions are always in tears about the marvelous past that is about to disappear, without having so much as a smile for the young future. It is quite true that doing away with the slave trade meant death to the great plantations, magnificent with azaleas and camellias, it meant ruin to the whole refined Southern civilization. The attics of time have received its rare old laces along with the clear pure voices of the Sistine *castrati*, and there is a certain "feminine charm" that is also on the way to the same dusty repository. I agree that he would be a barbarian indeed who failed to appreciate exquisite flowers, rare lace, the crystal-clear voice of the eunuch, and feminine charm.

When the "charming woman" shows herself in all her splendor, she is a much more exalting object than the "idiotic paintings, overdoors, scenery, showman's garish signs, popular chromos," that excited Rimbaud; adorned with the most modern artifices, beautified according to the newest techniques, she comes down from the remoteness of the ages, from Thebes, from Crete, from Chichén-Itzá; and she is also the totem set up deep in the African jungle; she is a helicopter and she is a bird; and there is this, the greatest wonder of all: under her tinted hair the forest murmur becomes a thought, and words issue from her breasts. Men stretch forth avid hands toward the marvel, but when they grasp it it is gone; the wife, the mistress, speak like everybody else through their mouths: their words are worth just what they are worth; their breasts also. Does such a fugitive miracle—and one so rare—justify us in perpetuating a situation that is baneful for both sexes? One can appreciate the beauty of flowers, the charm of women, and appreciate them at their true value; if these treasures cost blood or misery, they must be sacrificed.

But in truth this sacrifice seems to men a peculiarly heavy one; few of them really wish in their hearts for woman to succeed in making it; those among them who hold woman in contempt see in the sacrifice nothing for them to gain, those who cherish her see too much that they would lose. And it is true that the evolution now in progress threatens more than feminine charm alone: in beginning to exist for herself, woman will relinquish the function as double and mediator to which she owes her privileged place in the masculine universe; to man, caught between the silence of nature and the demanding presence of other free things, a creature who is at once his like and a passive thing seems a great treasure. The guise in which he conceives his companion may be mythical, but the experiences for which she is the source or the pretext are none the less real: there are hardly any more precious, more intimate, more ardent. There is no denying that feminine dependence, inferiority, woe, give women their special character; assuredly woman's autonomy, if it spares men many troubles, will also deny them many conveniences; assuredly there are certain forms of the sexual adventure which will be lost in the world of tomorrow. But this does not mean that love, happiness, poetry, dream, will be banished from it.

Let us not forget that our lack of imagination always depopulates the future; for us it is only an abstraction; each one of us secretly deplores the absence there of the one who was himself. But the humanity of tomorrow will be living in its flesh and in its conscious liberty; that time will be its present and it will in turn prefer it. New relations of flesh and sentiment of which we have no conception will arise between the sexes; already, indeed, there have appeared between men and women friendships, rivalries, complicities, comradeships—chaste or sensual—which past centuries could not have conceived. To mention one point, nothing could seem to me more debatable than the opinion that dooms the new world to uniformity and hence to boredom. I fail to see that this present world is free from boredom or that liberty ever creates uniformity.

To begin with, there will always be certain differences between man and woman; her eroticism, and therefore her sexual world, have a special form of their own and therefore cannot fail to engender a sensuality, a sensitivity, of a special nature. This means that her relations to her own body, to that of the male, to the child, will never be identical with those the male bears to his own body, to that of the female, and to the child; those who make much of "equality in difference" could not with good grace refuse to grant me the possible existence of differences in equality. Then again, it is institutions that create uniformity. Young and pretty, the slaves of the harem are always the same in the sultan's embrace; Christianity gave eroticism its savor of sin and legend when it endowed the human female with a soul; if society restores her sovereign individuality to woman, it will not thereby destroy the power of love's embrace to move the heart.

It is nonsense to assert that revelry, vice, ecstasy, passion, would become impossible if man and woman were equal in concrete matters; the contradictions that put the flesh in opposition to the spirit, the instant to time, the swoon of immanence to the challenge of transcendence, the absolute of pleasure to the nothingness of forgetting, will never be resolved; in sexuality will always be materialized the tension, the anguish, the joy, the frustration, and the triumph of existence. To emancipate woman is to refuse to confine her to the relations she bears to man, not to deny them to her; let her have her independent existence and she will continue none the less to exist for him *also*: mutually recognizing each other as subject, each will yet remain for the other an *other*. The reciprocity of their relations will not do away with the miracles—desire, possession, love, dream, adventure—worked by the division of human beings into two separate categories; and the words that move us— giving, conquering, uniting—will not lose their meaning. On the contrary, when we abolish the slavery of half of humanity, together with the whole system of hypocrisy that it implies, then the "division" of humanity will reveal its genuine significance and the human couple will find its true form. . . .

Betty Friedan (1921-   ) wrote *The Feminine Mystique* (1963) in order to discuss the American scene and its values. The book called for new attitudes and perceptions about women.

The feminine mystique says that the highest value and the only commitment for women is the fulfillment of their own femininity. It says that the great mistake of Western culture, through most of its history, has been the undervaluation of this femininity. It says this femininity is so mysterious and intuitive and close to the creation and origin of life that man-made science may never be able to understand it. But however special and different, it is in no way inferior to the nature of man; it may even in certain respects be superior. The mistake, says the mystique, the root of women's troubles in the past is that women envied men, women tried to be like men, instead of accepting their own nature, which can find fulfillment only in sexual passivity, male domination, and nurturing maternal love.

But the new image this mystique gives to American women is the old image: "Occupation: housewife." The new mystique makes the housewife-mothers, who never had a chance to be anything else, the model for all women; it presupposes that history has reached a final and glorious end in the here and now, as far as women are concerned. Beneath the sophisticated trappings, it simply makes certain concrete, finite, domestic aspects of feminine existence—as it was lived by women whose lives were confined, by necessity, to cooking, cleaning, washing, bearing children—into a religion, a pattern by which all women must now live or deny their femininity.

Fulfillment as a woman had only one definition for American women after 1949—the housewife-mother. As swiftly as in a dream, the image of the American woman as a changing, growing individual in a changing world was shattered. Her solo flight to find her own identity was forgotten in the rush for the security of togetherness. Her limitless world shrunk to the cozy walls of home. . . .

"Easy enough to say," the woman inside the housewife's trap remarks, "but what can I do, alone in the house, with the children yelling and the laundry to sort and no grandmother to babysit?" It is easier to live through someone else than to become complete yourself. The freedom to lead and plan your own life is frightening if you have never faced it before. It is frightening when a woman finally realizes that there is no answer to the question "who am I" except the voice inside herself. She may spend years on the analyst's couch, working out her "adjustment to the feminine role," her blocks to "fulfillment as a wife and mother." And still the voice inside her may say, "That's not it." Even the best psychoanalyst can only give her the courage to listen to her own voice. When society asks so little of women, every woman has to listen to her own inner voice to find her identity in this changing world. She must create, out of her own needs and abilities, a new life plan, fitting in the love and children and home that have defined femininity in the past with the work toward a greater purpose that shapes the future.

To face the problem is not to solve it. . . . "What do I want to do?" she begins to find her own answers. Once she begins to see through the delusions of the feminine mystique—and realizes that neither her husband nor her children, nor the things in her house, nor sex, nor being like all the other women, can give her a self—she often finds the solution much easier than she anticipated. . . .

It also is time to stop giving lip service to the idea that there are no battles left to be fought for women in America, that women's rights have already been won. It is ridiculous to tell girls to keep quiet when they enter a new field; or an old one, so the men will not notice they are there. In almost every professional field, in business and in the arts and sciences, women are still treated as second-class citizens. It would be a great service to tell girls who plan to work in society to expect this subtle, uncomfortable discrimination—tell them not to be quiet, and hope it will go away, but fight it. A girl should not expect special privileges because of her sex, but neither should she "adjust" to prejudice and discrimination.

She must learn to compete then, not as a woman, but as a human being. Not until a great many women move out of the fringes into the mainstream will society itself provide the arrangements for their new life plan. But every girl who manages to stick it out through law school or medical school, who finishes her M.A. or Ph.D. and goes on to use it, helps others move on. Every woman who fights the remaining barriers to full equality which are masked by the feminine mystique makes it easier for the next woman. . . .

. . . It took, and still takes, extraordinary strength of purpose for women to pursue their own life plans when society does not expect it of them. However, unlike the trapped housewives whose problems multiply with the years, these women solved their problems and moved on. They resisted the mass persuasions and manipulations, and did not give up their own, often painful, values for the comforts of conformity. . . . And they know quite surely now who they are.

They were doing, perhaps without seeing it clearly, what every man and woman must do now to keep up with the increasingly explosive pace of history, and find or keep individual identity in our mass society. The identity crisis in men and women cannot be solved by one generation for the next; in our rapidly changing society, it must be faced continually, solved only to be faced again in the span of a single lifetime. A life plan must be open to change, as new possibilities open, in society and in oneself. No woman in America today who starts her search for identity can be sure where it will take her. No woman starts that search today without struggle, conflict, and taking her courage in her hands. But the women I met, who were moving on that unknown road, did not regret the pains, the efforts, the risks.

In the light of woman's long battle for emancipation, the recent sexual counterrevolution in America has been perhaps a final crisis, a strange breath-holding interval before the larva breaks out of the shell into maturity—a moratorium during which many millions of women put themselves on ice and stopped growing. They say that one day science will be able to make the human body live longer by freezing its growth. American women lately have been living much longer than men—walking through their leftover lives like living dead women. Perhaps men may live longer in America when women carry more of the burden of the battle with the world instead of being a burden themselves. I think their wasted energy will continue to be destructive to their husbands, to their children, and to themselves until it is used in their own battle with the world. But when women as well as men emerge from biological living to realize their human selves, those leftover halves of life may become their years of greatest fulfillment.

Then the split in the image will be healed, and daughters will not face that jumping-off point at twenty-one or forty-one. When their mothers' fulfillment makes girls sure they want to be women, they will not have to "beat themselves down" to be feminine; they can stretch and stretch until their own efforts will tell them who they are. They will not need the regard of boy or man to feel alive. And when women do not need to live through their husbands and children, men will not fear the love and strength of women, nor need another's weakness to prove their own masculinity. They can finally see each other as they are. And this may be the next step in human evolution.

Who knows what women can be when they are finally free to become themselves? Who knows what women's intelligence will contribute when it can be nourished without denying love? Who knows of the possibilities of love when men and women share not only children, home, and garden, not only the fulfillment of their biological roles, but the responsibilities and passions of the work that creates the human future and the full human knowledge of who they are? It has barely begun, the search of women for themselves. But the time is at hand when the voices of the feminine mystique can no longer drown out the inner voice that is driving women on to become complete.

1. Write a response to the viewpoint expressed by Simone de Beauvoir. To what extent are her observations still applicable today?
2. Comment on the historical picture of women as painted by Simone de Beauvoir.
3. Outline Friedan's definition of the "feminine mystique" in terms of the role of the housewife in western society.
4. Respond to the statement that "a girl should not expect special privileges because of her sex, but neither should she 'adjust' to prejudice and discrimination."
5. Explore some of the possibilities, depicted by Friedan, coming from the "emancipation" of women.
6. To what extent do you believe that the goals of de Beauvoir and Friedan have been realized today?

• • •

THEOLOGY

Christian theology in the West underwent a critical self-examination in the last half of the twentieth century, in view of the events experienced from 1914-1945. Without losing touch with their fundamental beliefs, many Christians attempted to cope with war and the Holocaust, to embrace some of the ideas of modern philosophy in a theological context, and to reassert the importance of keeping hold of the mission of the religion to aid the poor and suffering.

Dietrich Bonhoeffer (1906-45) was a German Protestant theologian who opposed the Nazi influence in the life of the churches in Germany. In 1943 Bonhoeffer was arrested by the Gestapo for his anti-Nazi work and associations. He was imprisoned in Berlin for eighteen months, then sent to Buchenwald and then Flossenbürg, where he was killed in April 1945. Bonhoeffer's *Letters and Papers from Prison* (1971) focussed many important religious issues.

> . . . What is bothering me incessantly is the question what Christianity really is, or indeed who Christ really is, for us today. The time when people could be told everything by means of words, whether theological or pious, is over, and so is the time of inwardness and conscience— and that means the time of religion in general. We are moving towards a completely religionless time; people as they are now simply cannot be religious any more. Even those who honestly describe themselves as 'religious' do not in the least act up to it, and so they presumably mean something quite different by 'religious'.
>
> Our whole nineteen-hundred-year-old Christian preaching and theology rest on the 'religious *a priori*' of mankind. 'Christianity' has always been a form—perhaps the true form—of 'religion'. But if one day it becomes clear that this *a priori* does not exist at all, but was a historically conditioned and transient form of human self-expression, and if therefore man becomes radically religionless—and I think that that is already more or less the case (else how is it, for example, that this war, in contrast to all previous ones, is not calling forth any 'religious' reaction?)—what does that mean for 'Christianity'? It means that the foundation is taken away from the whole of what has up to now been our 'Christianity', and that there remain only a few 'last survivors of the age of chivalry', or a few intellectually dishonest people, on whom we can descend as 'religious'. Are they to be the chosen few? Is it on this dubious group of people that we are to pounce in fervour, pique, or indignation, in order to sell them our goods? Are we to fall upon a few unfortunate people in their hour of need and exercise a sort of religious compulsion on them? If we don't want to do all that, if our final judgment must be that the western form of Christianity, too, was only a preliminary stage to a complete absence of religion, what kind of situation emerges for us, for the church? How can Christ become the Lord of the religionless as well? Are there religionless Christians? If religion is only a garment of Christianity—and even this garment has looked very different at different times— then what is a religionless Christianity?
>
> . . . I've come to be doubtful of talking about any human boundaries (is even death, which people now hardly fear, and is sin, which they now hardly understand, still a genuine boundary today?). It always seems to me that we are trying anxiously in this way to reserve some space for God; I should like to speak of God not on the boundaries but at the centre, not in weaknesses but in strength; and therefore not in death and guilt but in man's life and goodness. As to the boundaries, it seems to me better to be silent and leave the insoluble unsolved. Belief in the resurrection is *not* the 'solution' of the problem of death. God's 'beyond' is not the beyond of our cognitive faculties.

Sources: Dietrich Bonhoeffer, *Letters and Papers from Prison* Enlarged Edition (New York: Macmillan Publishing Company, and London: SCM Press Ltd, 1971), pp. 279-80, 282, 382-83; Paul Tillich, *The Courage to Be* (New Haven: Yale University Press, 1952), pp. 139-141; Gustavo Gutierrez, *The Power of the Poor in History* (Maryknoll, New York: Orbis Books, 1983), pp. 7, 8, 20-22.

The transcendence of epistemological theory has nothing to do with the transcendence of God. God is beyond in the midst of our life. The church stands, not at the boundaries where human powers give out, but in the middle of the village. That is how it is in the Old Testament, and in this sense we still read the New Testament far too little in the light of the Old. How this religionless Christianity looks, what form it takes, is something that I'm thinking about a great deal.

. . . The church is the church only when it exists for others. To make a start, it should give away all its property to those in need. The clergy must live solely on the free-will offerings of their congregations, or possibly engage in some secular calling. The church must share in the secular problems of ordinary human life, not dominating, but helping and serving. It must tell men of every calling what it means to live in Christ, to exist for others. In particular, our own church will have to take the field against the vices of *hubris*, power-worship, envy, and humbug, as the roots of all evil. It will have to speak of moderation, purity, trust, loyalty, constancy, patience, discipline, humility, contentment, and modesty. It must not under-estimate the importance of human example (which has its origin in the humanity of Jesus and is so important in Paul's teaching); it is not abstract argument, but example, that gives its word emphasis and power. . . .

◈ B ▸ Paul Tillich (1886-1965) delivered the lectures published as *The Courage to Be* in 1952. Here he discussed the dilemma of human beings in the modern world.

. . . Existentialism as it appeared in the 20th century represents the most vivid and threatening meaning of "existential." In it the whole development comes to a point beyond which it cannot go. It has become a reality in all the countries of the Western world. It is expressed in all the realms of man's spiritual creativity, it penetrates all educated classes. It is not the invention of a Bohemian philosopher or of a neurotic novelist; it is not a sensational exaggeration made for the sake of profit and fame; it is not a morbid play with negativities. Elements of all these have entered it, but it itself is something else. It is the expression of the anxiety of meaninglessness and of the attempt to take this anxiety into the courage to be as oneself.

Recent Existentialism must be considered from these two points of view. It is not simply individualism of the rationalistic or romantic or naturalistic type. In distinction to these three preparatory movements it has experienced the universal breakdown of meaning. Twentieth-century man has lost a meaningful world and a self which lives in meanings out of a spiritual center. The man-created world of objects has drawn into itself him who created it and who now loses his subjectivity in it. He has sacrificed himself to his own productions. But man still is aware of what he has lost or is continuously losing. He is still man enough to experience his dehumanization as despair. He does not know a way out but he tries to save his humanity by expressing the situation as without an "exit." He reacts with the courage of despair, the courage to take his despair upon himself and to resist the radical threat of nonbeing by the courage to be as oneself. Every analyst of present-day Existentialist philosophy, art, and literature can show their ambiguous structure: the meaninglessness which drives to despair, a passionate denunciation of this situation, and the successful or unsuccessful attempt to take the anxiety of meaninglessness into the courage to be as oneself.

It is not astonishing that those who are unshaken in their courage to be as a part, either in its collectivist or in its conformist form, are disturbed by the expressions of the Existentialist courage of despair. They are unable to understand what is happening in our period. They are unable to distinguish the genuine from the neurotic anxiety in Existentialism. They attack as a morbid longing for negativity what in reality is courageous acceptance of the negative. They call decay what is actually the creative expression of decay. They reject as meaningless the meaningful attempt to reveal the meaninglessness of our situation. It is not the ordinary difficulty of understanding those who break new ways in thinking and artistic expression which produces the widespread resistance to recent Existentialism but the desire to protect a self-limiting courage to be as a part. Somehow one feels that this is not a true safety; one has to suppress inclinations to accept the Existentialist visions, one even enjoys them if they appear in the theater or in novels, but one refuses to take them seriously, that is as revelations of one's own existential meaninglessness and hidden despair. The violent reactions against modern art in collectivist (Nazi, Communist) as well as conformist (American democratic) groups show that they feel seriously threatened by it. But one does not feel spiritually threatened by something which is not an element of oneself. And since it is a symptom of the neurotic character to resist nonbeing by reducing being, the Existentialist could reply to the frequent reproach that he is neurotic by showing the neurotic defense mechanisms of the anti-Existentialist desire for traditional safety.

There should be no question of what Christian theology has to do in this situation. It should decide for truth against safety, even if the safety is consecrated and supported by the churches. Certainly there is a Christian conformism, from the beginning of the Church on, and there is a Christian collectivism—or at least semicollectivism, in several periods of Church history. But this should not induce Christian theologians to identify Christian courage with the courage to be as a part. They should realize that the courage to be as oneself is the necessary corrective to the courage to be as a part—even if they rightly assume that neither of these forms of the courage to be gives the final solution.

◇ C A new "liberation theology" has been developed by people working in the Third World. Gustavo Gutierrez (1928-   ) wrote *The Power of the Poor in History* in 1979.

> It is not enough, however, to say that God reveals himself in history, and that therefore the faith of Israel fleshes out a historical framework. One must keep in mind that the God of the Bible is a God who not only governs history, but who orientates it in the direction of establishment of justice and right. He is more than a provident God. He is a God who takes sides with the poor and liberates them from slavery and oppression. . . .
>
> This is the meaning of Yahweh's interventions in history. The purpose of his activity is not to demonstrate his power, but to liberate, and make justice reign:

> Father of orphans, defender of widows,
> such is God in his holy dwelling;
> God gives the lonely a permanent home,
> makes prisoners happy by setting them free,
> ▪ but rebels must live in an arid land [Ps. 68:5-6].

This is Yahweh. His might is at the service of justice. His power is expressed in the defense of the rights of the poor (see Ps. 146:7-9). The real theophany, or revelation of God, is in the liberation of the person who is poor. . . .

Knowledge of God is love of God. In the language of the Bible, "to know" is not something purely intellectual. To know means to love. Sin is the absence of the knowledge of Yahweh, and it is on this that the people will be judged: "Sons of Israel, listen to the word of Yahweh, for Yahweh indicts the inhabitants of the country" (Hos. 4:1).

To know God as liberator *is* to liberate, *is* to do justice. For the Bible, the root of behavior that can be called "just" is in the historical fact that constitutes a resumé of its faith: God delivered us from Egypt: . . .

To deal with a poor man or woman as Yahweh dealt with his people—this is what it is to be just: "He who looks down on his neighbor sins, blessed is he who takes pity on the poor" (Prov. 14:21; cf. Exod. 22:20-23). . . .

Our relationship with God is expressed in our relationship with the poor. . . .

Thus the reciprocal relationship between God and the poor person is the very heart of biblical faith. . . .

The locus of our encounter with the Father of Jesus Christ is the concrete history of men and women. And in Jesus Christ we proclaim to all men and women that Father's love. We have called this history one of conflict. But there is more to it than that. We have also to insist that history—where God reveals himself, and where we proclaim him—must be reread from the viewpoint of the poor, from a point of departure among "the condemned of the earth."

The history of humanity, as someone has said, has been "written with a white hand." History has been written from the viewpoint of the dominating sectors. We have a clear example of this in the history of Latin America and Peru. The perspective of history's vanquished is something else again. But history's winners have sought to wipe out their victims' memory of the struggles, so as to be able to snatch from them one of their sources of energy and will in history: a source of rebellion.

As it has been lived in history, Christianity has largely been, and still is, closely linked with one culture (Western), one ethnic strain (white), and one class (the dominant). Its history, too, has been written from a white, occidental, bourgeois bias.

We must recover the memory of the "scourged Christs of America," as Bartolomé de las Casas called the Indians of our continent. This memory never really died. It lives on in cultural and religious expressions, it lives on in resistance to ecclesiastical apparatus. It is a memory of the Christ who is present in every starving, thirsting, imprisoned, or humiliated human being, in the despised minorities, in the exploited classes (see Matt. 25:31-45). It is the memory of a Christ who not only "freed us, he meant us to remain free" (Gal. 5:1).

But *rereading* history means *remaking* history. It means repairing it from the bottom up. And so it will be a subversive history. History must be turned upside-down from the bottom, not from the top. What is criminal is not to be *sub*versive, struggling against the capitalist system, but to continue being "*super*versive"—bolstering and supporting the prevailing domination. It is in this subversive history that we can have a new faith experience, a new spirituality—a new proclamation of the gospel.

The gospel read from the viewpoint of the poor, the exploited classes, and their militant struggles for liberation, convokes a church of the people. It calls for a church to be gathered from among the poor, the marginalized. It calls for the kind of church that is indicated in Jesus' predilection for those whom the great ones of this world despise and humilate (see Matt. 22:1-10; Luke 14:16-24). In a word, it calls together a church that will be marked by the faithful response of the poor to the call of Jesus Christ. It will spring from the people, this church. And the people will snatch the gospel out of the hands of their dominators, never more to permit it to be utilized for the justification of a situation contrary to the will of the God who liberates. For this God is a God who "reincorporates himself," as Arguedas says—reincorporates himself into a history that bears the mark of the poor, into the popular struggles for liberation, into hope for the exploited.

This reincorporation of God will come about only when the poor of the earth effectuate a "social appropriation of the gospel"—when they dispossess those who consider it their private property. The gospel tells us that the sign of the arrival of the kingdom of God is that the poor have the gospel proclaimed to them. The poor are those who believe and hope in Christ. That is to say the poor are the Christians. Strictly speaking, the Christians are, or should be, the poor who receive the gospel—those in solidarity with the interests, aspirations, and combats of the oppressed and repressed of the world today.

Evangelization, the proclamation of the gospel, will be genuinely liberating when the poor themselves become its messengers. That is when we shall see the preaching of the gospel become a stumbling block and a scandal. For then we shall have a gospel that is no longer "presentable" in society. It will not sound nice and it will not smell good. The Lord who scarcely looks like a human at all (cf. the songs of the Servant of Yahweh in Isaiah) will speak to us then, and only at the sound of his voice will we recognize him as our liberator. That voice will convoke the *ek-klesia*, the assembly of those "called apart," in a new and different way.

Long has the church been built *from within*, in function of Christendom and its extension and preservation in the world—"ecclesiocentrism." A more recent perspective has led some to think of the church *from without*, from the world, from a world that does not believe, a world that often is hostile. . . .

Today we understand even better. We are called to build the church *from below*, from the poor up, from the exploited classes, the marginalized ethnic groups, the despised cultures. This is what we call the project of a popular church, a church that, under the influence of the Spirit, arises from within the masses. . . .

1. How did Bonhoeffer distinguish between religion and Christianity?

2. Comment on Bonhoeffer's depiction of God as "the 'beyond' in the midst of life."
3. Analyse Bonhoeffer's observations as a response to the horrors of Naziism.
4. Assess Tillich's rejection of the "safety" of Christian conformism for the courage to be oneself.
5. To what extent might Tillich be called an existentialist on the basis of this passage?
6. Respond to Gutierrez's call for a "liberation theology" which takes the Church out of the control of its traditional leaders. How does his view compare with those of Martin Luther King and Bonhoeffer?

▪ ▪ ▪

ART AND ARTISTS

The artistic movements that grew after the Second World War stressed abstraction and the desire to have art regarded as autonomous—as a form of expression which did not have to borrow from any other art form. Centered in the 1940s and 1950s in New York, major painters developed new ideas about the nature of art and its relationship to culture and civilization.

◇A◇ The leading Abstract Expressionist painter was Jackson Pollock (1912-56), whose "action paintings" and new methods had great influence on his contemporaries and on subsequent developments in modern art. Pollock discussed his work:

> My painting does not come from the easel. I hardly ever stretch my canvas before painting. I prefer to tack the unstretched canvas to the hard wall or the floor. I need the resistance of a hard surface. On the floor I am more at ease. I feel nearer, more a part of the painting, since this way I can walk around it, work from the four sides and literally be *in* the painting. This is akin to the method of the Indian sand painters of the West.
>
> I continue to get further way from the usual painter's tools such as easel, palette, brushes, etc. I prefer sticks, trowels, knives, and dripping fluid paint or a heavy impasto with sand, broken glass, and other foreign matter added.
>
> When I am *in* my painting, I'm not aware of what I am doing. It is only after a sort of "get acquainted" period that I see what I have been about. I have no fears about making changes, destroying the image, etc., because the painting has a life of its own. I try to let it come through. It is only when I

Sources: Barbara Rose, ed., *Readings in American Art, 1900-1975* (New York: Praeger Publishers, 1975), pp. 123-25; Herschel B. Chipp, ed., *Theories of Modern Art* (Berkeley: University of California Press, 1968), pp. 556-59, 561.

lose contact with the painting that the result is a mess. Otherwise there is pure harmony, an easy give and take, and the painting comes out well.

Modern art . . . is nothing more than the expression of contemporary aims. . . . All cultures have had means and techniques of expressing their immediate aims—the Chinese, the Renaissance, all cultures. The thing that interests me is that today painters do not have to go to a subject matter outside of themselves. Most modern painters work from a different source. They work from within.

. . . new needs need new techniques. And the modern artists have found new ways and new means of making their statements. It seems to me that the modern painter cannot express this age, the airplane, the atom bomb, the radio, in the old forms of the Renaissance or of any other past culture. Each age finds its own technique . . . the strangeness will wear off and I think we will discover the deeper meanings in modern art. . . . [Laymen looking at a Pollock or other modern painting] should not look *for*, but look passively— and try to receive what the painting has to offer and not bring a subject matter or preconceived idea of what they are looking for. . . . The unconscious is a very important side of modern art and I think the unconscious drives do mean a lot in looking at paintings. . . . [Abstract art] should be enjoyed just as music is enjoyed—after a while you may like it or you may not. . . . I like some flowers and others, other flowers I don't like. . . . I think at least give it a chance.

. . . the modern artist is living in a mechanical age and we have . . . mechanical means of representing objects in nature such as the camera and photograph. The modern artist, it seems to me, is working and expressing an inner world—in other words, expressing the energy, the motion, and other inner forces . . . the modern artist is working with space and time, and expressing his feelings rather than illustrating. . . . [Modern art] didn't drop out of the blue; it's part of a long tradition dating back with Cézanne, up through the Cubists, the post-Cubists, to the painting being done today. . . . Well, method is, it seems to me, a natural growth out of a need, and from a need the modern artist has found new ways of expressing the world about him. I happen to find ways that are different from the usual techniques of painting, which seems a little strange at the moment, but I don't think there's anything very different about it. I paint on the floor and this isn't unusual—the Orientals did that. . . .

Most of the paint I use is a liquid, flowing kind of paint. The brushes I use are used more as sticks . . . than [as] brushes—the brush doesn't touch the surface of the canvas, it's just above. . . . I'm able to be more free and to have greater freedom and move about the canvas with greater ease . . . with experience it seems to be possible to control the flow of the paint to a great extent, and I don't use . . . the accident . . . I deny the accident.

[A preconceived image] hasn't been created. . . . Something new—it's quite different from working, say, from a still life where you set up objects and work directly from them. I do have a general notion of what I'm about and what the results will be. . . . I approach painting in the same sense as one approaches drawing—that is, it's direct. I don't work from drawings, I don't make sketches and drawings and color sketches into a final painting.

B ▷ Willem de Kooning (1904-   ) was from the Netherlands, and came to New York in 1925. He, too, was involved in the Abstract Expressionist movement in the United States. In 1951 he discussed "What Abstract Art Means to Me."

The first man who began to speak, whoever he was, must have intended it. For surely it is talking that has put "Art" into painting. Nothing is positive about art except that it is a word. Right from there to here all art became literary. We are not yet living in a world where everything is self-evident. It is very interesting to notice that a lot of people who want to take the talking out of painting, for instance, do nothing else but talk about it. That is no contradiction, however. The art in it is the forever mute part you can talk about forever.

For me, only one point comes into my field of vision. This narrow, biased point gets very clear sometimes. I didn't invent it. It was already here. Everything that passes me I can see only a little of, but I am always looking. And I see an awful lot sometimes.

The word "abstract" comes from the light-tower of the philosophers, and it seems to be one of their spotlights that they have particularly focused on "Art." So the artist is always lighted up by it. As soon as it—I mean the "abstract"—comes into painting, it ceases to be what it is as it is written. It changes into a feeling which could be explained by some other words, probably. But one day, some painter used "Abstraction" as a title for one of his paintings. It was a still life. And it was a very tricky title. And it wasn't really a very good one. From then on the idea of abstraction became something extra. Immediately it gave some people the idea that they could free art from itself. Until then, Art meant everything that was in it—not what you could take out of it. There was only one thing you could take out of it sometime when you were in the right mood—that abstract and indefinable sensation, the aesthetic part—and still leave it where it was. For the painter to come to the "abstract" or the "nothing" he needed many things. Those things were always things in life—a horse, a flower, a milkmaid, the light in a room through a window made of diamond shapes maybe, tables, chairs, and so forth. The painter, it is true, was not always completely free. The things were not always of his own choice, but because of that he often got some new idea. Some painters like to paint things already chosen by others, and after being abstract about them, were called Classicists. Others wanted to select the things themselves and, after being abstract about them, were called Romanticists. Of course, they got mixed up with one another a lot too. Anyhow, at that time, they were not abstract about something which was already abstract. They freed the shapes, the light, the color, the space, by putting them into concrete things in a given situation. They *did* think about the possibility that the things—the horse, the chair, the man—were abstractions, but they let that go, because if they kept thinking about it, they would have been led to give up painting altogether, and would probably have ended up in the philospher's tower. When they got those strange, deep ideas, they got rid of them by painting a particular smile on one of the faces in the picture they were working on.

The aesthetics of painting were always in a state of development parallel to the development of painting itself. They influenced each other and vice versa. But all of a sudden, in that famous turn of the century, a few people thought they could take the bull by the horns and invent an aesthetic beforehand. After immediately disagreeing with each other, they began to form all kinds of groups, each with the idea of freeing art, and each demanding that you should obey them. Most of these theories have finally dwindled away into politics or strange forms of spiritualism. The question, as they saw it, was not so much what you *could* paint but rather what you could *not* paint. You could *not* paint a house or a tree or a mountain. It was then that subject matter came into existence as something you ought *not* to have.

In the old days, when artists were very much wanted, if they got to thinking about their usefulness in the world, it could only lead them to believe that painting was too worldly an occupation and some of them went to church instead or stood in front of it and begged. So what was considered too worldly from a spiritual point of view then, became later—for those who were inventing the new aesthetics—a spiritual smoke-screen and not worldly enough. These latter-day artists were bothered by their apparent uselessness. Nobody really seemed to pay any attention to them. And they did not trust that freedom of indifference. They knew that they were relatively freer than ever before *because* of that indifference, but in spite of all their talking about freeing art, they really didn't mean it that way. Freedom to them meant to be useful in society. And that is really a wonderful idea. To achieve that, they didn't need *things* like tables and chairs or a horse. They needed ideas instead, social ideas, to make their objects with, their constructions—the "pure plastic phenomena"—which were used to illustrate their convictions. Their point was that until they came along with their theories, Man's own form in space—his body—was a private prison; and that it was because of this imprisoning misery—because he was hungry and overworked and went to a horrid place called home late at night in the rain, and his bones ached and his head was heavy—because of this very consciousness of his own body, this sense of pathos, they suggest, he was overcome by the drama of a crucifixion in a painting or the lyricism of a group of people sitting quietly around a table drinking wine. In other words, these aestheticians proposed that people had up to now understood painting in terms of their own private misery. Their own sentiment of form instead was one of comfort. The beauty of comfort. The great curve of a bridge was beautiful because people could go across the river in comfort. To compose with curves like that, and angles, and make works of art with them could only make people happy, they maintained, for the only association was one of comfort. That millions of people have died in war since then, because of that idea of comfort, is something else.

This pure form of comfort became the comfort of "pure form." The "nothing" part in a painting until then—the part that was not painted but that was there because of the things in the picture which were painted—had a lot of descriptive labels attached to it like "beauty," "lyric," "form," "profound," "space," "expression," "classic," "feeling," "epic," "romantic," "pure," "balance," etc. Anyhow that "nothing" which was always recognized as a particular something—and as something particular—they generalized, with their book-keeping minds, into circles and squares. They had the innocent idea that the "something" existed "in spite of" and not "because of" and that this something was the only thing that truly mattered. They had hold of it, they thought, once and for all. But this idea made them go backward in spite of the fact that they wanted to go forward. That "something" which was not measurable, they lost by trying to make it measurable; and thus all the old words which, according to their ideas, ought to be done away with got into art again: pure, supreme, balance, sensitivity, etc. . . .

Personally, I do not need a movement. What was given to me, I take for granted. Of all movements, I like Cubism most. It had that wonderful unsure atmosphere of reflection—a poetic frame where something could be possible, where an artist could practice his intuition. It didn't want to get rid of what went before. Instead it added something to it. The parts that I can appreciate in other movements came out of Cubism. Cubism *became* a movement, it didn't set out to be one. It has force in it, but it was no "force-movement." And then there is that one-man movement; Marcel Duchamp—for me a truly modern movement because it implies that each artist can do what he thinks he ought to—a movement for each person and open for everybody.

If I *do* paint abstract art, that's what abstract art means to me. I frankly do not understand the question. . . .

1. Analyse Pollock's approach with reference to a specific example of his work.
2. Respond to Pollock's opinion that his art is a legitimate reflection of the age.
3. Assess Willem de Kooning's understanding of abstraction and his application of the term to the schools of art which have appeared in its name.

· ◇ ·

INDEX OF AUTHORS